W9-CXL-769

MAGILL'S
LITERARY ANNUAL
2007

MAGILL'S LITERARY ANNUAL 2007

*Essay-Reviews of 200 Outstanding Books
Published in the United States During 2006*

With an Annotated List of Titles

Volume One
A-K

Edited by
JOHN D. WILSON
STEVEN G. KELLMAN

SALEM PRESS
Pasadena, California   Hackensack, New Jersey

LIBRARY OF CONGRESS CATALOG CARD NO. 77-99209
ISBN 978-1-58765-372-8 (set)
ISBN 978-1-58765-373-5 (vol. 1)
ISBN 978-1-58765-374-2 (vol. 2)

FIRST PRINTING

PRINTED IN CANADA

CONTENTS

Publisher's Note ix
Complete Annotated List of Titles xi
Contributing Reviewers xxxvii
Author Photo Credits xl

Absent Minds: Intellectuals in Britain—Stefan Collini. 1
Absurdistan—*Gary Shteyngart* 5
Accidental Genius: How John Cassavetes Invented the American
    Independent Film—*Marshall Fine* 10
After This—*Alice McDermott* 14
Against the Day—*Thomas Pynchon* 18
All Aunt Hagar's Children—*Edward P. Jones* 23
"All Governments Lie!" The Life and Times of Rebel Journalist I. F. Stone—
    Myra MacPherson 27
All Will Be Well—*John McGahern* 31
The Amalgamation Polka—*Stephen Wright* 36
America at the Crossroads: Democracy, Power, and the Neoconservative
    Legacy—*Francis Fukuyama* 40
American Movie Critics: An Anthology from the Silents Until Now—
    Phillip Lopate, editor 45
American Vertigo: Traveling America in the Footsteps of Tocqueville—
    Bernard-Henri Lévy 49
Among the Dead Cities: The History and Moral Legacy of the WWII
    Bombing of Civilians in Germany and Japan—*A. C. Grayling* 54
Anna of All the Russias: A Life of Anna Akhmatova—*Elaine Feinstein* 59
Arthur and George—*Julian Barnes* 64
At Canaan's Edge: America in the King Years, 1965-68—*Taylor Branch* 69
Ava Gardner: "Love Is Nothing"—*Lee Server* 74
Averno—*Louise Glück* 79

Bad Faith: A Forgotten History of Family, Fatherland, and Vichy France—
    Carmen Callil 84
Becoming Abigail—*Chris Abani* 89
Betjeman: A Life—*A. N. Wilson* 93
Betraying Spinoza: The Renegade Jew Who Gave Us Modernity—
    Rebecca Goldstein 97
The Big Oyster: History on the Half Shell—*Mark Kurlansky* 101
Black Swan Green—*David Mitchell* 105

Blind Oracles: Intellectuals and War from Kennan to Kissinger—
  Bruce Kuklick. 110
The Blind Side: Evolution of a Game—*Michael Lewis* 114
Blind Willow, Sleeping Woman—*Haruki Murakami* 119
The Book of Dave—*Will Self.* 124
The Bourgeois Virtues: Ethics for an Age of Commerce—
  Deirdre N. McCloskey 129
Breaking the Spell: Religion as a Natural Phenomenon—
  Daniel C. Dennett 134
The Brooklyn Follies—*Paul Auster* 139

Caesar: Life of a Colossus—*Adrian Goldsworthy* 144
The Cave Painters: Probing the Mysteries of the World's First Artists—
  Gregory Curtis 149
Cell—*Stephen King.* 153
Christopher Marlowe: Poet and Spy—*Park Honan* 157
Clemente: The Passion and Grace of Baseball's Last Hero—
  David Maraniss 162
Consuelo and Alva Vanderbilt: The Story of a Daughter and a Mother
  in the Gilded Age—*Amanda Mackenzie Stuart* 167
Conversation: A History of a Declining Art—*Stephen Miller* 172
Cosmopolitanism: Ethics in a World of Strangers—
  Kwame Anthony Appiah 177
Curry: A Tale of Cooks and Conquerors—*Lizzie Collingham* 182

Dangerous Knowledge: Orientalism and Its Discontents—*Robert Irwin* 187
Dangerous Nation: America's Place in the World from Its Earliest Days to
  the Dawn of the Twentieth Century—*Robert Kagan* 192
Dante: The Poet, the Political Thinker, the Man—*Barbara Reynolds* 197
Dean Acheson: A Life in the Cold War—*Robert L. Beisner.* 201
Dear Ghosts,—*Tess Gallagher* 206
A Death in Belmont—*Sebastian Junger* 210
Death's Door: Modern Dying and the Ways We Grieve—
  Sandra M. Gilbert 215
The Devil's Doctor: Paracelsus and the World of Renaissance Magic
  and Science—*Philip Ball.* 219
Digging to America—*Anne Tyler* 224
The Din in the Head—*Cynthia Ozick* 229
District and Circle—*Seamus Heaney* 233
The Doctor's Daughter—*Hilma Wolitzer* 237
Doing Nothing: A History of Loafers, Loungers, Slackers, and
  Bums in America—*Tom Lutz* 241
The Dream Life of Sukhanov—*Olga Grushin* 245

CONTENTS

The Echo Maker—*Richard Powers* 249
The Echoing Green: The Untold Story of Bobby Thomson, Ralph Branca,
    and the Shot Heard Round the World—*Joshua Prager* 254
Edgar Allan Poe and the Juke-Box: Uncollected Poems, Drafts, and
    Fragments—*Elizabeth Bishop* 258
The Emperor's Children—*Claire Messud* 263
Empires of the Atlantic World: Britain and Spain in America, 1492-1830—
    J. H. Elliott 267
Ether: The Nothing That Connects Everything—*Joe Milutis* 272
Everyman—*Philip Roth* 276
Everything Else in the World—*Stephen Dunn* 281

The Fall of the Roman Empire: A New History of Rome and the
    Barbarians—*Peter Heather* 286
Fear: Anti-Semitism in Poland After Auschwitz, an Essay in Historical
    Interpretation—*Jan T. Gross* 291
Federico Fellini: His Life and Work—*Tullio Kezich* 296
Fiasco: The American Military Adventure in Iraq—*Thomas E. Ricks* 300
Field Notes from a Catastrophe: Man, Nature, and Climate Change—
    Elizabeth Kolbert 304
Fire in the City: Savonarola and the Struggle for the Soul of Renaissance
    Florence—*Lauro Martines* 308
First Lady of the Confederacy: Varina Davis's Civil War—
    Joan E. Cashin 312
Flaubert: A Biography—*Frederick Brown* 316
The Foreign Correspondent—*Alan Furst* 320
Forgetfulness—*Ward Just* 324
Forty Million Dollar Slaves: The Rise, Fall, and Redemption of the Black
    Athlete—*William C. Rhoden* 329
Friendship: An Exposé—*Joseph Epstein* 333

Gallatin Canyon—*Thomas McGuane* 337
Gay L.A.: A History of Sexual Outlaws, Power Politics, and Lipstick
    Lesbians—*Lillian Faderman* and *Stuart Timmons* 341
George Mason: Forgotten Founder—*Jeff Broadwater* 346
A Godly Hero: The Life of William Jennings Bryan—*Michael Kazin* 351
God's Silence—*Franz Wright* 356
God's War: A New History of the Crusades—*Christopher Tyerman* 360
The Good Life—*Jay McInerney* 365
The Great Transformation: The Beginning of Our Religious Traditions—
    Karen Armstrong 370
Grief—*Andrew Holleran* 375
Guests of the Ayatollah: The First Battle in America's War with
    Militant Islam—*Mark Bowden* 379

Half Wild—*Mary Rose O'Reilley* 384
Hershey: Milton S. Hershey's Extraordinary Life of Wealth,
    Empire, and Utopian Dreams—*Michael D'Antonio* 388
Hollow Earth: The Long and Curious History of Imagining Strange Lands,
    Fantastical Creatures, Advanced Civilizations, and Marvelous
    Machines Below the Earth's Surface—*David Standish* 393
Hollywood Station—*Joseph Wambaugh* 397
Horse Latitudes—*Paul Muldoon* 401
House of War: The Pentagon and the Disastrous Rise of American Power—
    James Carroll 406

Imperium: A Novel of Ancient Rome—*Robert Harris* 411
In Search of Nella Larsen: A Biography of the Color Line—
    George Hutchinson 415
In the Middle Distance—*Linda Gregg* 420
Insecure at Last: Losing It in Our Security Obsessed World—
    Eve Ensler 424
Interrogation Palace: New and Selected Poems, 1982-2004—
    David Wojahn 428
Intuition—*Allegra Goodman* 432

James Tiptree, Jr.: The Double Life of Alice B. Sheldon—*Julie Phillips* 437
The Judgment of Paris: The Revolutionary Decade That Gave the World
    Impressionism—*Ross King* 441

Kate: The Woman Who Was Hepburn—*William J. Mann* 446
The Keep—*Jennifer Egan* 451

PUBLISHER'S NOTE

Magill's Literary Annual, 2007, is the fifty-third publication in a series that began in 1954. Critical essays for the first twenty-two years were collected and published in the twelve-volume *Survey of Contemporary Literature* in 1977; since then, yearly sets have been published. Each year, *Magill's Literary Annual* seeks to evaluate critically 200 major examples of serious literature, both fiction and nonfiction, published during the previous calendar year. The philosophy behind our selection process is to cover works that are likely to be of interest to general readers, that reflect publishing trends, that add to the careers of authors being taught and researched in literature programs, and that will stand the test of time. By filtering the thousands of books published every year down to 200 notable titles, the editors have provided the busy librarian with an excellent reader's advisory tool and patrons with fodder for book discussion groups and a guide for choosing worthwhile reading material. The essay-reviews in the *Annual* provide a more academic, "reference" review of a work than is typically found in newspapers and other periodical sources.

The reviews in the two-volume *Magill's Literary Annual, 2007*, are arranged alphabetically by title. At the beginning of both volumes is a complete alphabetical list, by category, of all covered books that provides readers with the title, author, and a brief description of each work. Every essay is approximately four pages in length. Each one begins with a block of reference information in a standard order:

- Full book title, including any subtitle
- *Author:* name, with birth and death years
- *First published:* Original foreign-language title, with year and country, when pertinent
- Original language and translator name, when pertinent
- Introduction, Foreword, etc., with writer's name, when pertinent
- *Publisher:* company name and city, number of pages, retail price
- *Type of work:* chosen from standard categories

Anthropology	Essays	Literary criticism
Archaeology	Ethics	Literary history
Autobiography	Film	Literary theory
Biography	Fine arts	Media
Current affairs	History	Medicine
Diary	History of science	Memoir
Drama	Language	Miscellaneous
Economics	Law	Music
Education	Letters	Natural history
Environment	Literary biography	Nature

Novel	Psychology	Sociology
Novella	Religion	Technology
Philosophy	Science	Travel
Poetry	Short fiction	Women's issues

- *Time:* period represented, when pertinent
- *Locale:* location represented, when pertinent
- Capsule description of the work
- *Principal characters* [for novels, short fiction] or *Principal personages* [for biographies, history]: list of people, with brief descriptions

The text of each essay-review analyzes and presents the focus, intent, and relative success of the author, as well as the makeup and point of view of the work under discussion. To assist the reader further, essays are supplemented by a list of additional "Review Sources" for further study in a bibliographic format. Every essay includes a sidebar offering a brief biography of the author or authors. Thumbnail photographs of the book covers and the authors are included as available.

Four indexes can be found at the end of volume 2:

- Biographical Works by Subject: Arranged by subject, rather than by author or title. Readers can locate easily reviews of biographical works—memoirs, diaries, and letters in addition to biographies and autobiographies—by looking up the name of the person covered.
- Category Index: Groups all titles into subject areas such as current affairs and social issues, ethics and law, history, literary biography, philosophy and religion, psychology, and women's issues.
- Title Index: Lists all works reviewed in alphabetical order, with any relevant cross references.
- Author Index: Lists books covered in the annual by each author's name.

A searchable cumulative index, listing all books reviewed in *Magill's Literary Annual* between 1977 and 2007, as well as in *Magill's History Annual* (1983) and *Magill's Literary Annual, History and Biography* (1984 and 1985), can be found at our Web site, **www.salempress.com**, on the page for *Magill's Literary Annual, 2007*.

Our special thanks go to the editors for their expert and insightful selections: John Wilson is the editor of *Books and Culture* for *Christianity Today*, and Steven G. Kellman is a professor at the University of Texas at San Antonio and a member of the National Book Critics Circle. We also owe our gratitude to the outstanding writers who lend their time and knowledge to this project every year. The names of all contributing reviewers are listed in the front of volume 1, as well as at the end of their individual reviews.

COMPLETE ANNOTATED LIST OF TITLES

VOLUME 1

Absent Minds: Intellectuals in Britain—Stefan Collini 1
An account of the position of intellectuals in twentieth century Britain challenges the idea that there are no real intellectuals in Britain and analyzes the concept of "the intellectual"

Absurdistan—*Gary Shteyngart* 5
Shteyngart spectacularly reaffirms his prominence as a chronicler of the immigrant experience in America with this story of a Russian oligarch's spoiled son who has tasted the inebriating pleasures of America and who now finds himself trapped in a homeland he has learned to despise

Accidental Genius: How John Cassavetes Invented the American
    Independent Film—*Marshall Fine* 10
The first ever authorized biography of forward-looking American actor and independent filmmaker Cassavetes mixes detailed discussions of the making and reception of each of his films with anecdotes from people who worked with him

After This—*Alice McDermott* 14
McDermott chronicles the lives of the Catholic Keane family and Mary Keane's friend Pauline as well as assorted neighborhood and school friends from just after World War II to just after the Vietnam War

Against the Day—*Thomas Pynchon* 18
Pynchon's first novel in nearly a decade, and his longest, offers a fictional counterculture history of the Western world immediately before and after World War I

All Aunt Hagar's Children—*Edward P. Jones* 23
In fourteen elegant stories, the author, a lifelong Washington area resident, tells of the joys, sorrows, and fantastic experiences of the city's African American citizens

"All Governments Lie!" The Life and Times of Rebel Journalist I. F. Stone—
    Myra MacPherson 27
This biography of Stone is intermixed with descriptions of the political climates that he lived through and comparisons of those eras with the current one

All Will Be Well—*John McGahern* 31
  Seventy-one-year-old McGahern reminisces about his childhood in rural west Ireland, recalling his life with a doting mother, insensitive father, and six siblings

The Amalgamation Polka—*Stephen Wright* 36
  In Wright's experimental nonlinear work, young Liberty Fish vows to find his abusive Southern slave-owning grandparents to deepen his understanding of the "slavocracy" that divided his family and drove his abolitionist mother to the north

America at the Crossroads: Democracy, Power, and the Neoconservative
  Legacy—*Francis Fukuyama* 40
  In pursuit of a prudent and effectual approach to U.S. foreign policy, a prominent public intellectual distances himself and his ideas from his former "neoconservative" colleagues and the war in Iraq

American Movie Critics: An Anthology from the Silents Until Now—
  Phillip Lopate, editor 45
  Lopate's anthology is aptly named: It is about "movies," not "film" or "cinema," terms that suggest a rarefied kind of motion picture, and the "critics" are, for the most part, reviewers whose work has appeared in journals and magazines accessible in style and content to the general public

American Vertigo: Traveling America in the Footsteps of Tocqueville—
  Bernard-Henri Lévy 49
  Lévy updates the American journey of Tocqueville and raises some fresh concerns about the viability of the nation's basic values in the face of terrorist threats

Among the Dead Cities: The History and Moral Legacy of the WWII
  Bombing of Civilians in Germany and Japan—*A. C. Grayling* 54
  Grayling presents a critical examination of the morality of the area bombing of German and Japanese cities by British and American forces during World War II

Anna of All the Russias: A Life of Anna Akhmatova—*Elaine Feinstein* 59
  Feinstein traces the life of the great twentieth century Russian poet, placing her within the context of her time and showing how Akhmatova's work, while highly personal, also came to express the feelings and experiences of a nation torn by revolution, terror, and war

Arthur and George—*Julian Barnes* 64
  Looking for meaning beyond his work, a famous novelist tries to prove the innocence of a man falsely imprisoned

At Canaan's Edge: America in the King Years, 1965-68—*Taylor Branch* 69
The final piece of Branch's epic three-volume biography of Martin Luther King, Jr., is at the same time a history of the United States in the critical Vietnam War era and a classic tragedy with two flawed heroes and a host of villains

Ava Gardner: "Love Is Nothing"—*Lee Server* 74
A Hollywood star battles with fame, insecurities, husbands, lovers, and alcohol

Averno—*Louise Glück*. 79
The tenth collection of poems by the former poet laureate of the United States continues Glück's explorations of, in her words, "the virtues of a style which inclines to the suggested over the amplified"

Bad Faith: A Forgotten History of Family, Fatherland, and Vichy France—
   Carmen Callil 84
In writing the life of Louis Darquier, a virulent French anti-Semite, Callil illuminates much of the history of Vichy France and traces the life of Darquier's Tasmanian-born companion and the story of the daughter they abandoned

Becoming Abigail—*Chris Abani* 89
A narrative of a young woman's life in which she creates her own sense of self despite the legacy of her dead mother, the responsibilities of a depressed father, and the terrors endured under her abusive uncle

Betjeman: A Life—*A. N. Wilson*. 93
Sir John Betjeman, born the son of a tradesman, used his talents and charm to become the most popular poet and one of the most loved television celebrities of his time. His personal life was, however, shadowed by melancholy and complicated by his love for two dissimilar women

Betraying Spinoza: The Renegade Jew Who Gave Us Modernity—
   Rebecca Goldstein 97
The author provides a memoir recounting her experiences with the philosophy of Spinoza from her initial exposure as a Jewish schoolgirl to her teaching experience as a professor of philosophy

The Big Oyster: History on the Half Shell—*Mark Kurlansky* 101
Kurlansky uses a study of the oyster harvesting, cooking, and eating habits of the inhabitants of the Hudson River estuary as a way of tracing some of the history of New York City and its environs from the early Dutch explorers to the present

Black Swan Green—*David Mitchell* 105
  *Mitchell's fourth novel chronicles a difficult, yet frequently comic, year in the life
of an adolescent boy in a small English village*

Blind Oracles: Intellectuals and War from Kennan to Kissinger—
  Bruce Kuklick. 110
  *Kuklick explores the influence of a select group of academics on American state-
craft from World War II through the Vietnam War*

The Blind Side: Evolution of a Game—*Michael Lewis* 114
  *Lewis tells how an impoverished, jumbo-sized, barely literate black youngster
evolves into a gridiron wunderkind who becomes a loved member of a privileged
white family in Memphis while coaches of football-mad Southern colleges covet him*

Blind Willow, Sleeping Woman—*Haruki Murakami* 119
  *In this wide-ranging collection of Murakami's short stories, his characters cope
with loneliness, death, and problematical love; occasionally their lives are touched
by the supernatural. By the end of many stories, Murakami's characters have experienced something that can lessen their anguish and bring them new self-knowledge
or joy*

The Book of Dave—*Will Self.* 124
  *Self casts his satirical gaze at religious fundamentalism and global warming in a
tale of two Londons, one contemporary and the other a postapocalyptic, dystopian
fantasy*

The Bourgeois Virtues: Ethics for an Age of Commerce—
  Deirdre N. McCloskey 129
  *This ornate, elegant review of basic virtues—love, faith, hope, courage, temper-
ance, prudence and justice—argues that capitalism can be virtuous and that the virtues, in turn, help to promote economic success for individuals and for society*

Breaking the Spell: Religion as a Natural Phenomenon—
  Daniel C. Dennett 134
  *Because of religion's pivotal importance throughout humankind's history, it war-
rants scientific study, and Dennett uses the methods of the biological and social sciences to explore such questions as how and why religions originated and developed,
and whether they help or hinder the genuine progress of humanity*

The Brooklyn Follies—*Paul Auster* 139
  Nathan Glass comes to Brooklyn to die but instead finds himself and others

Caesar: Life of a Colossus—*Adrian Goldsworthy* 144
  Historian and classics scholar Goldsworthy reviews the public life of the man whose skills as a military leader and politician led to profound changes in the Roman Republic, which he served for nearly four decades

The Cave Painters: Probing the Mysteries of the World's First Artists—
  Gregory Curtis 149
  Curtis presents an engaging and informative study of the magnificent cave paintings found in southern France and northern Spain

Cell—*Stephen King*. 153
  King's apocalyptic vision of the ubiquity of cell phones depicts a society reduced to a primitive state following a mysterious signal that affects everyone using a cell phone at the time, turning them first into violent maniacs and then into zombie-like creatures

Christopher Marlowe: Poet and Spy—*Park Honan* 157
  Using newly discovered sources and focusing closely upon Marlowe's sexuality, apparent atheism, and espionage activities, Honan in this biography provides new insights into the playwright's life and work, though much about Marlowe remains unknown and the subject of conjecture

Clemente: The Passion and Grace of Baseball's Last Hero—
  David Maraniss 162
  An overdue and necessary biography of baseball's first and perhaps greatest Latin American star, who proved his heroism both on and off the field

Consuelo and Alva Vanderbilt: The Story of a Daughter and a Mother
  in the Gilded Age—*Amanda Mackenzie Stuart* 167
  An examination of two privileged, strong-willed people who were social trendsetters as well as suffragists during an age when a successful marriage was the surest path to becoming a woman of consequence

Conversation: A History of a Declining Art—*Stephen Miller* 172
  Miller investigates the history of conversation in the West, from its origins in Athens and Sparta through its flourishing in eighteenth century Britain to what he views as the deplorable state of conversation in twenty-first century America

Cosmopolitanism: Ethics in a World of Strangers—
  Kwame Anthony Appiah 177
  Exploring what it ought to mean for people to be citizens of the world in the twenty-first century, Appiah retrieves and revitalizes the ideal of "cosmopolitanism," which provides reminders of key ethical connections within the diversity of human culture, religion, and politics

Curry: A Tale of Cooks and Conquerors—*Lizzie Collingham* 182
Collingham offers a delightful collection of recipes and vivid history of Indian cuisine, including curry, which has become one of the most popular foods on the planet

Dangerous Knowledge: Orientalism and Its Discontents—*Robert Irwin* 187
Irwin surveys the development of scholarly Western interest in Asia and contrasts his interpretation and approach with that offered by famed theorist Edward Said in the book Orientalism *(1978)*

Dangerous Nation: America's Place in the World from Its Earliest Days to
    the Dawn of the Twentieth Century—*Robert Kagan* 192
A wide-ranging analysis of American foreign policy from the Puritans to the Spanish-American War

Dante: The Poet, the Political Thinker, the Man—*Barbara Reynolds* 197
Reynolds's biography traces the life of Dante Alighieri and provides an accessible introduction to all of his works, particularly his masterpiece, La divina commedia *(c. 1320;* The Divine Comedy, *1802)*

Dean Acheson: A Life in the Cold War—*Robert L. Beisner* 201
Beisner has produced the most comprehensive biography to date of Acheson, the key architect of U.S. foreign policy during the Cold War, whom many scholars consider the greatest American secretary of state

Dear Ghosts,—*Tess Gallagher* 206
In this collection of poems, Gallagher draws upon her belief in an afterlife as a means to survive the painful realities of illness, aging, and destructive political policies

A Death in Belmont—*Sebastian Junger* 210
The author investigates a murder that occurred in his hometown when he was one year old, and which his family discussed many times in later years, speculating on whether the wrong man was convicted and the true murderer was someone who once worked for them

Death's Door: Modern Dying and the Ways We Grieve—
    Sandra M. Gilbert 215
A wave of personal tragedies motivates Gilbert to examine a wide range of cultural, historical, technological, religious, and especially literary responses to death and to grief

The Devil's Doctor: Paracelsus and the World of Renaissance Magic
and Science—*Philip Ball.* 219
*Science writer Ball takes a trip back in time to discover how a daring physician
conceived a configuration of matter and spirit that anticipated modern biochemistry*

Digging to America—*Anne Tyler* 224
*Tyler's novel examines the unexpected connections between an American family
and an Iranian family who both adopt daughters from Korea on the same day*

The Din in the Head—*Cynthia Ozick* 229
*A collection of eighteen essays plus a foreword and afterword showcasing Ozick's
thinking on a variety of subjects, especially on literature and the power of language*

District and Circle—*Seamus Heaney* 233
*Nobel Prize winner Heaney demonstrates once again why he is cherished as one
of the strongest poets writing in English today in this book of poetry, published forty
years after his first book was published*

The Doctor's Daughter—*Hilma Wolitzer* 237
*A story of a middle-aged woman coming to terms with her past, her present, and
her future*

Doing Nothing: A History of Loafers, Loungers, Slackers, and
Bums in America—*Tom Lutz* 241
*A reflective historical examination of writers and artists in America and Europe
who have celebrated the work-free life—prompted by the author's son's apparent
dedication to "slackerdom" as well as his own migrations between the poles of laziness and all-out workaholism*

The Dream Life of Sukhanov—*Olga Grushin* 245
*The story of a Soviet art critic experiencing a series of waking and sleeping
dreams that bring back to him his youthful ideals and ambitions as an artist*

The Echo Maker—*Richard Powers* 249
*Following a near-fatal road accident in Nebraska, a man is diagnosed with
Capgras' syndrome, a rare condition in which he is convinced that those closest to
him are impostors*

The Echoing Green: The Untold Story of Bobby Thomson, Ralph Branca,
and the Shot Heard Round the World—*Joshua Prager* 254
*Prager's work chronicles the lives of pitcher Branca and batter Thomson before
and after one of the most electrifying home runs in baseball history*

Edgar Allan Poe and the Juke-Box: Uncollected Poems, Drafts, and
    Fragments—*Elizabeth Bishop* 258
    Verbal music and striking discoveries turn up in this new posthumous collection,
made even more rewarding by editor Alice Quinn's appendix and copious notes

The Emperor's Children—*Claire Messud* 263
    Messud's novel relates the delayed coming of age of three friends in the months
before September 11, 2001

Empires of the Atlantic World: Britain and Spain in America, 1492-1830—
    J. H. Elliott 267
    A comparison of two great colonial empires, from their origins to their ends

Ether: The Nothing That Connects Everything—*Joe Milutis* 272
    This multidisciplinary historical study explores the many meanings of the ether
from various artistic, literary, philosophical, scientific, and cultural perspectives

Everyman—*Philip Roth* 276
    The life story of an unnamed man recounts his idyllic youth in a loving family, his
three marriages and divorces, his career in advertising, his retirement, his illnesses,
and his death

Everything Else in the World—*Stephen Dunn* 281
    The fourteenth full-length collection of poetry from Pulitzer Prize winner Dunn,
this work artfully explores notions of desire, particularly in relation to marriage, aes-
thetics, love, and social mores

The Fall of the Roman Empire: A New History of Rome and the
    Barbarians—*Peter Heather* 286
    Heather presents a sweeping interpretation of the fall of the Roman Empire that
emphasizes the destructive effects of the barbarian invasions

Fear: Anti-Semitism in Poland After Auschwitz, an Essay in Historical
    Interpretation—*Jan T. Gross* 291
    In a virtual compendium of human savagery and evil, Gross documents the little-
known hate crimes of Poles against Jews especially after the Holocaust, as well as the
causes and results of these devastating actions

Federico Fellini: His Life and Work—*Tullio Kezich* 296
    Kezich has updated his earlier biography of the famed Italian film director

Fiasco: The American Military Adventure in Iraq—*Thomas E. Ricks* 300
  Ricks, assessing the causes and conduct of the U.S. invasion and occupation of Iraq in Operation Iraqi Freedom, stresses that the fiasco of his title derived mainly from the inability of civilian Pentagon leadership and some high level military leaders to understand the real nature of a counterinsurgency

Field Notes from a Catastrophe: Man, Nature, and Climate Change—
  Elizabeth Kolbert 304
  With signs of global warming clearly evident, this book examines how climate changes have affected the earth in the past and how human societies are accelerating similar changes today

Fire in the City: Savonarola and the Struggle for the Soul of Renaissance
  Florence—*Lauro Martines* 308
  Martines focuses on the years from 1494 to 1498 to produce a cultural and social history of the intense conflict that led to Girolamo Savonarola's execution, treating the "factual essentials" of recent scholarship in a style meant to appeal to a popular audience

First Lady of the Confederacy: Varina Davis's Civil War—
  Joan E. Cashin 312
  Married to Jefferson Davis, president of the Confederate states during the American Civil War, Varina Davis exhibited an independence unusual for women of that era

Flaubert: A Biography—*Frederick Brown* 316
  This scholarly biography examines Gustave Flaubert's life and works in the context of the Second and Third Republics and the Second Empire

The Foreign Correspondent—*Alan Furst* 320
  An Italian expatriate in Paris just before World War II, working as a foreign correspondent for Reuters, is brought into the shadow world of espionage

Forgetfulness—*Ward Just* 324
  As the United States begins its War on Terror, an expatriate American painter living in a secluded rural French village suffers the loss of his wife and has to decide whether to exact revenge against her murderer

Forty Million Dollar Slaves: The Rise, Fall, and Redemption of the Black
  Athlete—*William C. Rhoden* 329
  A sportswriter traces the ways in which race has mattered in the history of American sports

Friendship: An Exposé—*Joseph Epstein* 333
An important American essayist, editor, and humorist applies his wit and learning to the contemporary state of friendship

Gallatin Canyon—*Thomas McGuane* 337
McGuane's second collection of fiction, set largely in his adopted state of Montana, examines an assortment of uneasy losers with wry humor and a certain pained compassion

Gay L.A.: A History of Sexual Outlaws, Power Politics, and Lipstick
Lesbians—*Lillian Faderman* and *Stuart Timmons* 341
The authors focus on the development and status of gay culture in Los Angeles from the time the earliest European missionaries tried to convert the indigenous population to Christianity to the beginning of the twenty-first century

George Mason: Forgotten Founder—*Jeff Broadwater* 346
This is the first full biography in thirty years of the man whose 1776 Virginia Declaration of Rights became the model for the constitutional Bill of Rights

A Godly Hero: The Life of William Jennings Bryan—*Michael Kazin* 351
Kazin tries to rehabilitate Bryan's image, arguing that the three-time losing Democratic nominee for president was a populist who helped turn the Democratic Party away from its nineteenth century pro-business stance, preparing the way for the 1930's reform party

God's Silence—*Franz Wright* 356
A biting and brilliant collection of poems that finds the poet having grown more fully into his religious faith

God's War: A New History of the Crusades—*Christopher Tyerman* 360
A reinterpretation of the Crusades, emphasizing a Christian belief system based on aggression, paranoia, and wishful thinking, without condemning it absolutely or absolving Muslims and pagans of responsibility and blame

The Good Life—*Jay McInerney* 365
In the weeks following the September 11, 2001, terrorist attacks on New York City, members of the city's privileged classes reassess their lives, marriages, and values

The Great Transformation: The Beginning of Our Religious Traditions—
  Karen Armstrong 370
  *Armstrong focuses on the period between 900 B.C.E. and 200 B.C.E. when in India,
China, Israel-Judaea, and Greece the great philosophers, including Buddha, Socra-
tes, Confucius, Jeremiah, Ezekiel, Plato, and Aristotle, envisioned the concepts, espe-
cially the ideal of the Golden Rule, which form the bases of many modern religions*

Grief—*Andrew Holleran* 375
  *An elegiac first-person account of an aging single gay man coping with the after-
math of his mother's death and facing the isolating realities of midlife in the era of
AIDS*

Guests of the Ayatollah: The First Battle in America's War with
  Militant Islam—*Mark Bowden* 379
  *Bowden gives a riveting account of the takeover of the American Embassy in Teh-
ran, Iran, in November, 1979, by radical Islamist militants and the subsequent imprisonment of sixty-six American hostages, which lasted 444 days, told from the perspective of the hostages, the hostage takers, and President Jimmy Carter's White
House*

Half Wild—*Mary Rose O'Reilley* 384
  *The poems in O'Reilley's first book of poetry, winner of the 2005 Walt Whitman
Award, explore nature, life, death, and spirit as they wind themselves through land-
scapes of the world and of the soul*

Hershey: Milton S. Hershey's Extraordinary Life of Wealth,
  Empire, and Utopian Dreams—*Michael D'Antonio* 388
  *D'Antonio's comprehensive biography of Milton S. Hershey brings to life the
events of the chocolate mogul's existence, detailing his contributions to his employees, to the orphaned boys for whom he established a boarding school, and to American industry*

Hollow Earth: The Long and Curious History of Imagining Strange Lands,
  Fantastical Creatures, Advanced Civilizations, and Marvelous
  Machines Below the Earth's Surface—*David Standish* 393
  *The book covers the history of scientific theories about another world existing in-
side this planet and how the concept has played out in novels, films, and popular cul-
ture*

Hollywood Station—*Joseph Wambaugh* 397
  *A veteran author returns to his roots, providing a gritty contemporary account of
police work amid the faded glamour of Hollywood*

Horse Latitudes—*Paul Muldoon* 401
    The twelfth collection by this Irish-born American, Pulitzer Prize-winning poet continues and advances his singular features of linguistic invention and dazzling erudition

House of War: The Pentagon and the Disastrous Rise of American Power—
    James Carroll 406
    Carroll presents a historical account of the leaders, policies, and decisions of the Department of Defense, with the thesis that the department has used excessive and unnecessary military force, resulting in great destruction and countless violations of human rights

Imperium: A Novel of Ancient Rome—*Robert Harris* 411
    The long-time confidential secretary of Marcus Tullius Cicero, the famous Roman orator, describes his master's rise to power in a political environment of factionalism, corruption, intrigue, and treachery

In Search of Nella Larsen: A Biography of the Color Line—
    George Hutchinson 415
    This biography of Larsen discloses previously obscure facts about her life and restores her reputation as one of the most significant novelists of the Harlem Renaissance

In the Middle Distance—*Linda Gregg* 420
    Gregg's poetry collection seeks peace and spiritual understanding in the wake of turmoil and loss; it is a meditation on passion from the perspective of middle age

Insecure at Last: Losing It in Our Security Obsessed World—
    Eve Ensler 424
    A playwright and women's rights activist considers her travels around the world and what she learns about security and the various ways this abstract notion is conceived and put into practice in the everyday lives of women and men

Interrogation Palace: New and Selected Poems, 1982-2004—
    David Wojahn 428
    This collection of selected and new poems provides a solid introduction to one of America's most brilliant contemporary poets

Intuition—*Allegra Goodman* 432
    A research biologist's romantic involvement with a colleague dissolves when that colleague goes public with her suspicions that the discovery of a possible cancer-curing virus may be based on falsified data

James Tiptree, Jr.: The Double Life of Alice B. Sheldon—*Julie Phillips* 437
    Phillips presents an account of the life of Alice Bradley Sheldon, artist, psychologist, and writer, who concealed her identity as a writer behind the pseudonym of James Tiptree, Jr., and fooled many people into believing that she was a man

The Judgment of Paris: The Revolutionary Decade That Gave the World
    Impressionism—*Ross King* 441
    A history of some of the Paris art movements in the nineteenth century, set within their political and cultural contexts

Kate: The Woman Who Was Hepburn—*William J. Mann*. 446
    Mann presents the private and public life of Katharine Hepburn, with special emphasis on an in-depth understanding of her personality as formed by her childhood in a family with a fiery father and a free-thinking mother who nevertheless submitted to the dominance of her husband

The Keep—*Jennifer Egan* 451
    Danny accepts his cousin Howard's invitation to the European castle he has purchased although they have not spoken in years. That story takes place inside a story of a writing class held in a prison

VOLUME 2

L'America—*Martha McPhee* 455
    Class and cultural differences accumulate and destroy an international love affair between a wealthy, tradition-soaked Italian boy and an earthy, ambitious American girl

Last Evenings on Earth—*Roberto Bolaño* 459
    With these stories of leftist Chilean expatriates in Europe and Mexico, Bolaño explores the existential absurdity and sudden violence of late twentieth century life

The Last of Her Kind—*Sigrid Nunez*. 464
    Nunez's novel explores the counterculture of the 1960's by juxtaposing the careers of two women who meet as roommates at Barnard College

The Lay of the Land—*Richard Ford*. 469
    In the sequel to the Pulitzer Prize-winning novel Independence Day *(1995), Ford revisits Frank Bascombe as he tries to celebrate Thanksgiving*

The Librettist of Venice: The Remarkable Life of Lorenzo Da Ponte, Mozart's
Poet, Casanova's Friend, and Italian Opera's Impresario in
America—*Rodney Bolt*. 473
Bolt provides a thoughtful and well-researched biography of the fascinating career of the Venetian poet Lorenzo Da Ponte, who not only wrote three librettos for Wolfgang Amadeus Mozart but also became the first professor of Italian at an American university

The Life All Around Me by Ellen Foster—*Kaye Gibbons*. 478
This second volume in a projected series of novels celebrates the undaunted spirit of a notable fictional character now facing her teenage years

The Light of Evening—*Edna O'Brien* 482
A terminally ill woman in a hospital awaits a visit from her daughter and reflects on her life, loves, and estrangement from her children

Lisey's Story—*Stephen King*. 486
Scott was a best-selling and critically acclaimed author who frequently traveled to a parallel world that was both dangerous and healing. Two years after his death, his wife Lisey must travel to that world by herself

Little Money Street: In Search of Gypsies and Their Music in the South
of France—*Fernanda Eberstadt* 490
An American journalist reports on her perplexing and rewarding friendship with a Gypsy family. This book is among the few published accounts of the tragic failure of this "outsider" culture, with its centuries-old codes and mores, to adapt to the demands of postindustrial society

The Looming Tower: Al-Qaeda and the Road to 9/11—
Lawrence Wright. 494
An account of the events and personages, in the United States, the Middle East, and elsewhere, that led to the tragedy of September 11, 2001

The Madonnas of Leningrad—*Debra Dean* 499
An old Russian immigrant for whom dementia and Alzheimer's disease cloud everyday events relives her past as an Hermitage docent during the three-year Nazi siege of Leningrad

The Man Who Could Fly, and Other Stories—*Rudolfo Anaya*. 503
Anaya's stories explore the effects of place, spirit, and human longing on his main characters, who are caught in unusual circumstances

The Man Who Smiled—*Henning Mankell* 507
The fourth volume in the Kurt Wallander detective series in which the murders of two attorneys are investigated and their links to a larger conspiracy probed

The Master Plan: Himmler's Scholars and the Holocaust—
   Heather Pringle 511
Pringle has written the first book-length study of the Ahnenerbe, the research and educational institute that promulgated many of the racial doctrines of the Third Reich

Mayflower: A Story of Courage, Community, and War—
   Nathaniel Philbrick. 515
Looking at the history of the Plymouth settlement from its beginning in 1620 to the devastating King Philip's War in 1675-1676, Philbrick explores the often violent relationship between the colonists and native people, which shaped subsequent U.S. history

Memoirs of a Muse—*Lara Vapnyar* 520
A young Russian decides to emulate the woman she mistakenly believes was Fyodor Dostoevski's great love and continuing inspiration

A Million Nightingales—*Susan Straight.* 524
In the bayous of Louisiana, a mixed-race slave on the brink of adulthood is separated from her mother and sold to another plantation, where she begins to plan her eventual escape

Moral Disorder, and Other Stories—*Margaret Atwood* 528
Atwood's fifth book of stories covers eleven interconnected episodes in the life of a Canadian woman. Emphasizing the act of storytelling, it suggests that the truth of a life may best be captured in narrative

Mortimer of the Maghreb—*Henry Shukman.* 532
Two novellas and four short stories about middle-aged men trying to make up for missed chances and past mistakes

The Most Famous Man in America: The Biography of Henry Ward
   Beecher—*Debby Applegate* 536
This biography of Beecher sensitively portrays the childhood of the famous nineteenth century American preacher, showing how he developed his distinctive approach to the ministry; it then criticizes Beecher's moderate stance on slavery and devotes most of its final pages to the sex scandal that marred Beecher's later years

Murder in Amsterdam: The Death of Theo van Gogh and the Limits of
    Tolerance—*Ian Buruma* 541
    *A Dutch filmmaker is murdered by an angry young Moroccan immigrant, and his
    death prompts a wide reconsideration of the Netherlands's liberal treatment of for-
    eigners*

Mussolini's Italy: Life Under the Fascist Dictatorship, 1915-1945—
    R. J. B. Bosworth 546
    *Bosworth provides a comprehensive study of the lives of Italians during the rise
    and rule of the Fascist state in Italy*

My Father Is a Book: A Memoir of Bernard Malamud—
    Janna Malamud Smith 551
    *This memoir by the novelist's daughter, which attempts to rectify her earlier deci-
    sion not to write about her father's life or to authorize a biographer to do so, is only
    fitfully successful because of the author's ambivalence about what should be included*

My First Seven Years (Plus a Few More)—*Dario Fo* 555
    *Fo provides a hilarious, entertaining memoir of his early youth along the shores
    of Lake Maggiore, his army exploits in World War II, and the beginnings of his life's
    work as storyteller, writer, actor, and social satirist*

Naked in the Marketplace: The Lives of George Sand—*Benita Eisler* 559
    *Eisler's biography concentrates on Sand's many love affairs and on her tumultu-
    ous family life to reveal the woman behind the notorious reputation*

Native American Fiction: A User's Manual—*David Treuer*. 563
    *Treuer asserts that Native American fiction does not exist in the native tradition;
    therefore, its value should be assessed as modern literature, not as a cultural/ethnic
    phenomenon. Native American fiction is doomed if readers, critics, and authors fail
    to ask whether it is good fiction*

Nature Girl—*Carl Hiaasen*. 567
    *Honey Santana, tired of the world's rudeness, lures telemarketer Boyd Shreave
    and his mistress Eugenie into the swamps of the Ten Thousand Islands National Wild-
    life Refuge to teach Shreave some manners, not realizing she is being pursued by her
    crazed former employer, her ex-husband, and her twelve-year-old son*

Nicole Kidman—*David Thomson* 571
    *This biography is a luminous and unique recounting of actor Kidman's life from
    her start in film to her present endeavors*

Not for Specialists: New and Selected Poems—*W. D. Snodgrass* 575
   *This collection surveys the whole of Snodgrass's poetic career, from his early po-
ems of personal experience to the later poems that address, in addition to the poet's
private life, broader subjects and issues, such as the Nazi regime and contemporary
urban life*

Old Filth—*Jane Gardam* 580
   *Eighty-year-old Sir Edward Feathers, nearing the end of his life, finds he must
deal with buried memories of his traumatic early years as a "Raj Orphan," sent back
as a young child from British Malaya to fend for himself in England*

On Late Style: Music and Literature Against the Grain—
   Edward W. Said 584
   *The author investigates musical and literary works with complex and unresolved
elements that reflect the late style of a number of major literary and musical compositions*

Oracle Bones: A Journey Between China's Past and Present—
   Peter Hessler 589
   *Hessler's book profiles Chinese individuals at different levels of society and ex-
amines cultural artifacts of ancient China to illustrate its cultural shifts and economic
reforms as well as China's uneasy relationship with the West*

Osman's Dream: The History of the Ottoman Empire—
   Caroline Finkel 594
   *Finkel recounts the political and military history of the Ottoman Empire from its
beginnings in the thirteenth century through its destruction in the early twentieth century, with an emphasis on its long period of decline and collapse*

A Pentecost of Finches: New and Selected Poems—
   Robert Siegel 599
   The traditions of the bestiary are alive and well in the poetry of Siegel

Persian Fire: The First World Empire and the Battle for the West—
   Tom Holland 603
   *Over the course of a century, the Persian Empire conquered every country in its
westward path until it was finally halted by heroic Greeks determined to remain free*

The Poem That Changed America: "Howl" Fifty Years Later—
   Jason Shinder, editor 607
   *Reflections on the influence and importance of the seminal poem by Allen Gins-
berg, on the eve of its fiftieth anniversary*

Point to Point Navigation: A Memoir, 1964 to 2006—*Gore Vidal* 611
An eminent man of letters reflects on a life lived among politicians, aviation pio-
neers, writers, television talk show hosts, and Hollywood actors, producers, screen-
writers, and directors

The Possibility of an Island—*Michel Houellebecq*. 616
In his latest assault upon modern civilization, the controversial expatriate French
novelist extends the reach of his earlier works several centuries into the future, where
the human race is all but extinct, succeeded by a culture of clones

Purity of Blood—*Arturo Pérez-Reverte* 621
The second of Pérez-Reverte's novels devoted to Captain Diego Alatriste finds the
retired soldier attempting to rescue a virtuous young woman from the depraved friar
of a convent; when his raid fails in an ambush, the captain must save his young
protégé from the clutches of the Inquisition

Queen of the Underworld—*Gail Godwin* 625
A young woman graduates from journalism school in North Carolina and begins a
new job as a reporter for Miami's largest daily newspaper as the city fills with Cuban
exiles fleeing Fidel Castro's government

Radical Innocent: Upton Sinclair—*Anthony Arthur* 630
This well-written biography focuses on Sinclair's personal life and seeks to dem-
onstrate his shift away from socialism and propaganda in the direction of moderation
and literature as art, conjuring up an appealing portrait of Sinclair and of the era in
which he lived

Richard Hofstadter: An Intellectual Biography—*David S. Brown*. 634
The first full biography of a distinguished historian who published ten popular
books and taught at Columbia University for twenty-four years, with an emphasis on
his ideas, historical writings, and political activities

The Right Attitude to Rain—*Alexander McCall Smith* 639
Scottish philosopher Isabel Dalhousie questions the motives of a young woman
engaged to an older, wealthy man as she grapples with her own growing love for a
younger man

The Road—*Cormac McCarthy*. 643
A boy and his father undertake a journey of survival in the aftermath of nuclear
war

Rough Crossings: Britain, the Slaves, and the American Revolution—
Simon Schama 647
An account of the struggle for freedom by thousands of slaves, during and after the Revolutionary War, who believed that their future as free people lay in remaining British rather than becoming American

The Ruins—*Scott Smith* 651
Two young American couples on vacation in Cancun encounter a German tourist who persuades them to help him find his younger brother at a remote Mayan archeological ruin

Salvation Blues: One Hundred Poems, 1985-2005—*Rodney Jones* 655
In this collection drawn from his work of the last twenty years, Jones uses southern subjects—land, language, family—to address the larger issues that have always concerned poets: love, religion, death, and poetry itself

The Secret River—*Kate Grenville* 659
Grenville's timely novel revisits the British settlement of Australia and its consequences for settlers and natives alike

Self-Made Man: One Woman's Journey into Manhood and Back Again—
Norah Vincent 664
While disguised as a man for a year and a half, female author Vincent comes to realize that men are also victims of the patriarchy and that, like women, they are forced into playing roles that stunt their emotional growth

The Shakespeare Wars: Clashing Scholars, Public Fiascoes, Palace Coups—
Ron Rosenbaum 668
Rosenbaum shows that painstaking textual scholarship and close reading as well as thoughtfully directed productions of the plays—not the improvable suppositions of biography—are the most exciting and valuable ways of learning what "Shakespearean" means

The Short Day Dying—*Peter Hobbs* 673
This finely imagined first novel is a first-person account of a year in the life of a young Methodist preacher struggling to find himself, spiritually and otherwise, amid the harsh but beautiful landscape of Cornwall during hard times

Sinners Welcome—*Mary Karr* 678
This fine collection of Karr's poetry includes a cycle of poems retelling the life of Jesus Christ and reflections on the fate of friends, the death of her mother, and the coming of age of her teenage son

Soldier: The Life of Colin Powell—*Karen DeYoung* 682
Based on six in-depth interviews and exhaustive research, this book presents a thorough biography of General Powell, chairman of the Joint Chiefs of Staff, who became George W. Bush's secretary of state and was a possible presidential candidate in the 1996 election

Special Topics in Calamity Physics—*Marisha Pessl* 687
Pessl's debut novel combines a postmodern Nabokovian style with a prep school murder mystery

Spectral Waves—*Madeline DeFrees*. 691
DeFrees' eighth full-length collection of poems covers the gamut from nature poems, particularly focusing on birds, plants, and spiders, through a sonnet sequence for Elvis Presley, to an exploration of the process of aging, especially the development of cataracts in the eye, all explored through extensive use of allusion

A Spot of Bother—*Mark Haddon* 695
In Haddon's second novel for adults, retiree George Hall, suddenly obsessed with dying, tries and mostly fails to deal with his daughter's impending second marriage, his son's homosexuality, and his wife's affair

Spying on the Bomb: American Nuclear Intelligence from Nazi Germany
to Iran and North Korea—*Jeffrey T. Richelson* 699
A detailed and well-documented account of the American intelligence community's efforts to gauge the nuclear weapons programs of other countries, from the beginning of the Manhattan Project to the time of publication

State of Denial—*Bob Woodward*. 704
Woodward's third book about George W. Bush and his administration's military engagement in Iraq presents an indictment of the Bush administration focusing on its denial of the grievous problems these conflicts have generated

Steel Drivin' Man: John Henry, the Untold Story of an American Legend—
Scott Reynolds Nelson 709
Nelson tells the story of the real Henry and the assumed location of his fabled race against a steam-powered drill and takes a look at how the legend of his triumph mushroomed in song and other media of popular culture

Strange Piece of Paradise: A Return to the American West to Investigate My
Attempted Murder and Solve the Riddle of Myself—*Terri Jentz* 713
In 1992, fifteen years after she and a friend were brutally attacked at an improvised campsite in an Oregon state park, the author revisited the scene of the unsolved crime, beginning an eight-year quest that yielded more questions than answers

Stumbling on Happiness—*Daniel Gilbert* 718
Gilbert compiles numerous research studies, primarily from the social sciences, to provide a better understanding of human behavior and how choices that people make affect the future and how they ultimately feel afterward

Suite Française—*Irène Némirovsky* 723
In an unfinished novel published more than sixty years after its author's death in Auschwitz, varied characters experience the German invasion and occupation of France

The Swamp: The Everglades, Florida, and the Politics of Paradise—
   Michael Grunwald 727
This comprehensive history of the damage to the Everglades caused by drainage procedures to make the land usable and, more recently, efforts to repair the ecosystem makes a compelling argument for restoring the Everglades ecosystem

Talk Talk—*T. Coraghessan Boyle* 732
When an identity thief entangles a deaf woman in legal, financial, and employment troubles, she and her boyfriend go after the perpetrator in a determined cross-country chase

The Tango Singer—*Tomás Eloy Martínez* 737
A doctoral candidate writing his dissertation on Jorge Luis Borges's essays on the tango travels to Buenos Aires in search of an elusive and unrecorded tango singer named Julio Martel

A Temple of Texts—*William H. Gass* 741
Gass's collection of essays about great texts and great writing stands as a manifesto of what is wonderful and powerful about the written word and the way it shapes human thought and acts

Terrorist—*John Updike*. 745
A young Arab American, deeply devoted to Islam and repelled by the excesses of American life, becomes a member of a terrorist cell bent on attacking a New York City transportation corridor

Theft: A Love Story—*Peter Carey*. 750
A witty love story-cum-mystery novel about art and its commercialization and about being Australian

There Will Never Be Another You—*Carolyn See* 755
In a poignant and personal, yet unobtrusive style, this novel exposes the external fear, anxiety, and apathy Americans living in a post-September 11 society experience while exploring the internal struggles people undergo throughout various stages of their lives

Things I Didn't Know: A Memoir—*Robert Hughes* 759
This account of the first thirty-two years of Hughes's life traces the influences that led him to become an art critic

Thirst—*Mary Oliver* 763
In this volume, Oliver continues the celebration of nature for which she is well known, but she adds to it an expression of the religious faith that has grown from her experience of grief

Thirteen Moons—*Charles Frazier* 767
A white man adopted by Cherokees reflects on his long life as merchant, lawyer, politician, soldier, poet, and lover

The Three Way Tavern: Selected Poems—*Ko Un* 771
This fine collection of poems that Ko wrote in the 1990's reveals to an English-speaking audience the power of a major Asian poet whose poems focus on a Zen-inspired look at nature, everyday people of Korea, and the author's personal experience

Thunderstruck—*Erik Larson* 776
Larson presents a joint study of the development of long-range wireless communication at the turn of the twentieth century and an infamous murder case the technology helped solve

Timothy Leary: A Biography—*Robert Greenfield* 781
Greenfield has written the first major biography of the man who did most to popularize psychedelic drugs

To Hell with All That: Loving and Loathing Our Inner Housewife—
    Caitlin Flanagan 785
Flanagan characterizes women's interest in white weddings and housekeeping as a form of nostalgia for the ideals of femininity of her mother's generation, rather than as an intention to return to traditional femininity, yet she favors those ideals, especially stay-at-home motherhood

The Tree: A Natural History of What Trees Are, How They Live, and
    Why They Matter—*Colin Tudge*. 789
    *Without plants, there would be no life; without wood, there would be no human
civilization; and human civilization might destroy both unless an understanding of
both spreads. Tudge's book is a loving, lyrical description of trees and their interaction with the entire planet, from prehistory to the present*

Trickster Travels: A Sixteenth-Century Muslim Between Worlds—
    Natalie Zemon Davis. 793
    *A speculative exploration of the life of Leo Africanus, establishing the social, cultural, and religious contexts through which he moved as a Muslim diplomat and poet
before his capture by Christian pirates forced him to make his way through the literary world of papal Rome*

Triumph Forsaken: The Vietnam War, 1954-1965—*Mark Moyar*. 798
    *Moyar presents a well-researched and compellingly written revisionist history of
the origins of the United States' involvement in the Vietnam War, arguing that the
conflict could have been won without the introduction of American combat troops*

Twilight of the Superheroes—*Deborah Eisenberg*. 803
    *These six stories reveal secrets sometimes not recognized by their holders but of
such life-changing impact as to leave scars*

Uncommon Carriers—*John McPhee*. 806
    *In a series of essays, McPhee explains how freight is transported by truck, by ship,
by plane, and by train, traveling along with and telling the stories of the people who
operate them*

Untold Stories—*Alan Bennett* 810
    *Bennett's second collection of autobiographical and journalistic writings offers
further insight into what makes one of England's most accomplished playwrights tick*

Upon the Altar of the Nation: A Moral History of the Civil War—
    Harry S. Stout 814
    *A thoughtful and well-researched study on evolving American religious attitudes
and attempts by members of the clergy in both the Union and the Confederacy to present moral justifications for the Civil War*

The View from Castle Rock—*Alice Munro* 819
    *Munro's most personal book includes five fictionalized family chronicles about
her ancestors and six short stories based on her own life*

Violin Dreams—*Arnold Steinhardt* 823
   This memoir is about the violinist Steinhardt's lifelong passion for making beautiful music playing the violin

Voodoo Heart—*Scott Snyder*. 827
   Snyder's debut collection of seven short stories is located in a romantically deranged America, where, according to the author, the reader will encounter "characters who've been knocked off course in life, either by accidents or bad decisions"

Walt Disney: The Triumph of the American Imagination—*Neal Gabler* 832
   The first comprehensive and fully annotated study of the famous American animator, film producer, and entrepreneur, this generally admiring but candid biography describes the forces behind Disney's drive to build his entertainment empire

War of Nerves: Chemical Warfare from World War I to al-Qaeda—
   Jonathan B. Tucker. 837
   Tracing the history of chemical weaponry in a manner accessible to the general reader, Tucker details the development of supertoxic poisons and argues that in the early twenty-first century we have reached a crossroads that could lead either to renewed proliferation of chemical weapons or to their abolition

The Weather Makers: How Man Is Changing the Climate and What It Means
   for Life on Earth—*Tim Flannery* 841
   Flannery discusses the nature of climate change, its extent, its effects on the ecosystem and civilization, and what can be done about it

Weimar in Exile: Exile in Europe, Exile in America—
   Jean-Michel Palmier. 846
   Palmier delivers a meticulously detailed account of the diverse and far-flung experience of exile for thousands of German political activists, scholars, writers, and artists who were driven out of Germany in the wake of the widespread Nazi repression that accompanied Adolf Hitler's rise to power in 1933

The Whiskey Rebellion: George Washington, Alexander Hamilton, and the
   Frontier Rebels Who Challenged America's Newfound
   Sovereignty—*William Hogeland*. 851
   In response to economic inequities, and triggered by an excise tax on whiskey, western Pennsylvania settlers rebelled against the federal government

The White Man's Burden: Why the West's Efforts to Aid the Rest Have
   Done So Much Ill and So Little Good—*William Easterly*. 856
   The West has spent $2.3 trillion on foreign aid over the past five decades, yet a large proportion of the world's population remains desperately poor; studies indicate aid has contributed nothing, on average, to raise economic growth for poor countries but has often helped to consolidate the power of abusive regimes

William Henry Harrison, and Other Poems—*David R. Slavitt* 861
In his eighty-third book, Slavitt's hand has not lost its cunning; he is a treasure hidden in plain sight

Wizard of the Crow—*Ngugi wa Thiong'o* 865
Primarily a political satire about African governments and society, this lengthy novel additionally takes up social problems, personal relations, philosophy, science, religion, economics, and international politics as major themes within a context of Magical Realism

A Woman in Jerusalem—*Abraham B. Yehoshua* 869
A woman was killed by a bomb, and the human resources manager where she worked is assigned with arranging her funeral; he pieces together her life story and becomes emotionally involved in trying to rescue her from anonymity

The Woman Who Waited—*Andreï Makine* 873
A young folklorist goes to a Russian village and encounters an intriguing middle-aged woman who has waited thirty years for her fiancé, long since reported dead, to return after leaving to fight in World War II

The World to Come—*Dara Horn* 877
After Benjamin Ziskind steals a painting by Marc Chagall during a singles' gathering at a museum, the theft's implications reach back two generations and beyond this life into the world to come

The Worst Hard Time: The Untold Story of Those Who Survived the
    Great American Dust Bowl—*Timothy Egan* 881
Egan describes the lives and trials of some of the people who stayed in the southern high plains during the Dust Bowl years (rather than moving away), the governmental response to their plight, and aspects of the relationship of humans to nature

A Writer's Life—*Gay Talese* 886
A book by a best-selling author about his efforts to write another best-selling book that evolved into this memoir of his life as an author

You Must Set Forth at Dawn—*Wole Soyinka* 890
Nobel laureate Soyinka recounts his relationship with his homeland, Nigeria; his battles with the military dictators, who for long intervals seized power after the nation's independence in 1960; and his exile during the 1990's

CONTRIBUTING REVIEWERS

Michael Adams
*City University of New
York Graduate Center*

Richard Adler
*University of
Michigan-Dearborn*

Emily Alward
*Henderson, Nevada,
District Libraries*

Karen L. Arnold
Columbia, Maryland

Charles Lewis Avinger, Jr.
*Washtenaw Community
College*

Barbara Bair
Duke University

Carl L. Bankston III
Tulane University

Elizabeth H. Battles
*Texas Wesleyan
University*

Milton Berman
University of Rochester

Cynthia A. Bily
Adrian College

Margaret Boe Birns
New York University

Nicholas Birns
*New School University,
Eugene Lang College*

Franz G. Blaha
*University of
Nebraska-Lincoln*

Pegge Bochynski
Salem State College

Steve D. Boilard
*California Legislative
Analysts' Office*

Kevin Boyle
Elon University

Harold Branam
*Savannah State University
(retired)*

Peter Brier
*California State
University, Los
Angeles*

Jeffrey L. Buller
*Florida Atlantic
University*

Edmund J. Campion
University of Tennessee

Sharon Carson
*University of North
Dakota*

Erskine Carter
Black Hawk College

Mary LeDonne Cassidy
*South Carolina State
University*

Dolores L. Christie
*Catholic Theological
Society of America
(CTSA)
John Carroll University*

John J. Conlon
*University of South
Florida, St. Petersburg*

Richard Hauer Costa
Texas A&M University

Frank Day
Clemson University

Paul Dellinger
Wytheville, Virginia

M. Casey Diana
*University of Illinois,
Urbana-Champaign*

Margaret A. Dodson
Boise, Idaho

Robert P. Ellis
*Worcester State College
(retired)*

Thomas L. Erskine
Salisbury University

Thomas R. Feller
Nashville, Tennessee

Rebecca Hendrick
Flannagan
*Francis Marion
University*

Roy C. Flannagan
*South Carolina
Governor's School for
Science and
Mathematics*

Robert J. Forman
*St. John's University, New
York*

Donald R. Franceschetti
*The University of
Memphis*

Jean C. Fulton
Landmark College

Ann D. Garbett
Averett University

Janet E. Gardner
*University of
   Massachusetts,
   Dartmouth*

Leslie E. Gerber
*Appalachian State
   University*

Sheldon Goldfarb
*University of British
   Columbia*

Karen Gould
Austin, Texas

Lewis L. Gould
*University of Texas,
   Austin*

Hans G. Graetzer
*South Dakota State
   University*

Joanne K. Hammond
*Librarian, Chambersburg
   Area School District,
   Pennsylvania*

Diane Andrews
   Henningfeld
Adrian College

Arthur D. Hlavaty
Yonkers, New York

Carl W. Hoagstrom
*Ohio Northern University
   (retired)*

John R. Holmes
*Franciscan University of
   Steubenville*

Joan Hope
*Palm Beach Gardens,
   Florida*

Jeffry Jensen
*Glendale Community
   College*

Fiona Kelleghan
University of Miami

Steven G. Kellman
*University of Texas, San
   Antonio*

Howard A. Kerner
Polk Community College

Grove Koger
*Boise, Idaho, Public
   Library*

James B. Lane
*Indiana University
   Northwest*

Eugene Larson
*Los Angeles Pierce
   College*

William Laskowski
Jamestown College

Leon Lewis
*Appalachian State
   University*

Thomas Tandy Lewis
St. Cloud State University

Bernadette Flynn Low
*Community College of
   Baltimore County*

R. C. Lutz
CII Group

Janet McCann
Texas A&M University

Joanne McCarthy
*Tacoma Community
   College (retired)*

Andrew F. Macdonald
*Loyola University, New
   Orleans*

Gina Macdonald
Nicholls State University

S. Thomas Mack
*University of South
   Carolina-Aiken*

David W. Madden
*California State
   University, Sacramento*

Lois A. Marchino
*University of Texas at El
   Paso*

Patricia Masserman
Microsoft Learning

Mira N. Mataric
*University of Belgrade
   Butler College*

Charles E. May
*California State
   University, Long
   Beach*

Laurence W. Mazzeno
Alvernia College

Seth Michelson
*University of Southern
   California*

Vasa D. Mihailovich
*University of North
   Carolina*

Robert A. Morace
Daemen College

Bernard E. Morris
Modesto, California

Daniel P. Murphy
Hanover College

John Nizalowski
Mesa State College

Robert J. Paradowski
*Rochester Institute of
   Technology*

CONTRIBUTING REVIEWERS

David B. Parsell
Furman University

David Peck
Laguna Beach, California

Marjorie J. Podolsky
*Penn State Erie, The
   Behrend College*

Cliff Prewencki
Delmar, New York

Maureen J. Puffer-
   Rothenberg
Valdosta State University

Edna B. Quinn
Salisbury University

Thomas Rankin
Concord, California

R. Kent Rasmussen
*Thousand Oaks,
   California*

Rosemary M. Canfield
   Reisman
*Charleston Southern
   University*

Mark Rich
Cashton, Wisconsin

Bernard F. Rodgers, Jr.
*Simon's Rock College
   of Bard*

Carl Rollyson
*City University of New
   York, Baruch College*

Joseph Rosenblum
*University of North
   Carolina, Greensboro*

John K. Roth
*Claremont McKenna
   College*

Marc Rothenberg
Smithsonian Institution

J. Edmund Rush
Boise, Idaho

Carroll Dale Short
Birmingham, Alabama

R. Baird Shuman
*University of Illinois,
   Urbana-Champaign*

Thomas J. Sienkewicz
Monmouth College

Charles L. P. Silet
Iowa State University

Carl Singleton
*Fort Hays State
   University*

Amy Sisson
*University of
   Houston-Clear Lake*

Caroline M. Small
Silver Spring, Maryland

Roger Smith
Portland, Oregon

Ira Smolensky
Monmouth College

Jennifer H. Solomon
*University of North
   Carolina-Chapel Hill*

George Soule
Carleton College

Maureen Kincaid Speller
Folkestone, Kent, England

August W. Staub
University of Georgia

Gerald H. Strauss
Bloomsburg University

Paul Stuewe
Green Mountain College

Susan E. Thomas
*Indiana University, South
   Bend*

Paul B. Trescott
*Southern Illinois
   University*

Jack Trotter
Trident College

William L. Urban
Monmouth College

Sara Vidar
Los Angeles, California

Twyla R. Wells
*University of
   Northwestern Ohio*

Donald M. Whaley
Salisbury University

Bob Whipple, Jr.
Creighton University

Thomas Willard
University of Arizona

John Wilson
Editor, Christianity Today

Scott D. Yarbrough
*Charleston Southern
   University*

Author Photo Credits

Rudolfo Anaya: *Michael Mouchette;* Kwame Anthony Appiah: *Greg Martin;* Margaret Atwood: *Courtesy, Vancouver International Writers Festival;* Paul Auster: © *Jerry Bauer;* Julian Barnes: © *Isolde Ohlbaum;* Elizabeth Bishop: *J. L. Castel;* T. C. Boyle: *Courtesy, Allen and Unwin;* Taylor Branch: *J. Brough Schamp/Library of Congress;* Deborah Eisenberg: *Diana Michener;* Joseph Epstein: *Matthew Gilson;* Richard Ford: *James Hamilton ;* Alan Furst: © *Shonna Valeska;* Louise Glück: *James Baker Hall/Library of Congress;* Gail Godwin: © *Jerry Bauer;* Carl Hiaasen: *Elena Siebert;* Sebastian Junger: *Michael Kamber/Courtesy, W. W. Norton & Company;* Mary Karr: © *Marion Ettlinger/Courtesy, HarperCollins;* Stephen King: *Tabitha King;* Mark Kurlansky: *Courtesy, Random House;* Cormac McCarthy: *David Styles;* Alice McDermott: *Eames Armstrong/Library of Congress;* Thomas McGuane: © *Kurt Markus;* Alexander McCall Smith: *Chris Watt/Library of Congress;* Alice Munro: *Courtesy, Vancouver International Writers Festival;* Ngugi wa Thiong'o: *David Mbiyu;* Jay McInerney: *Mary Entrekin/Courtesy, Alfed A. Knopf;* Edna O'Brien: © *Terry O'Neill;* Cynthia Ozick: *Julius Ozick;* Philip Roth: © *Nancy Crampton;* Carolyn See: *Reed Hutchison/UCLA Photo Services;* Wole Soyinka: *The Nobel Foundation;* Gay Talese: *David Shankbone;* Anne Tyler: © *Diana Walker;* John Updike: © *Davis Freeman;* Gore Vidal: © *Jane Bown;* Joseph Wambaugh: *Library of Congress;* Bob Woodward: *Lisa Berg/Courtesy, Simon & Schuster*

MAGILL'S
LITERARY ANNUAL
2007

ABSENT MINDS
Intellectuals in Britain

Author: Stefan Collini (1947-   )
Publisher: Oxford University Press (New York). 526 pp.
  $45.00
Type of work: Literary history
Time: 1896-2006
Locale: The United Kingdom

An account of the position of intellectuals in twentieth century Britain challenges the idea that there are no real intellectuals in Britain and analyzes the concept of "the intellectual"

Principal personages:
   T. S. ELIOT, a poet and critic
   R. G. COLLINGWOOD, a philosopher and historian
   GEORGE ORWELL, a writer
   A. J. P. TAYLOR, a historian
   A. J. AYER, a philosopher

In *Absent Minds* Stefan Collini examines a puzzle that has occupied cultural commentators for more than a century. Why is it that Britain no longer seems to have any intellectuals? In fact, has Britain ever had any intellectuals? If it did, what happened to them? From the outset Collini's intention is to dispel this myth of absence, but, as he points out, to do so is to raise a new set of questions. Why do people so badly want to believe in the nonexistence of British intellectuals, and why has this concern persisted over the years? As Collini observes, there is a "rich tradition of debate about the question of intellectuals," which suggests that the issue has been a regular cause of anxiety.

Collini argues that the denial of the existence of intellectuals, or of a clearly identifiable intellectual community, is a prominent aspect of national self-definition within Britain. Furthermore, those who might be identified as intellectuals are quick to disown the title, suggesting that while it might apply to others, it does not apply to them. Ultimately, the understanding seems to be that intellectuals are a species not native to Britain but instead a foreign import, and thus to be regarded with suspicion. Collini's intention is to demonstrate that this perception is false and to show that Britain does possess its own indigenous intellectuals and always has, no matter how reluctant they might be to embrace the title.

Collini's first task is to define "intellectual," a task that is less straightforward than it might at first seem. It is easy to suppose that by establishing a clear definition one will be able to identify precisely what kind of person is being described, after which it becomes a simple matter of finding such people and labeling them as "intellectuals." In reality, "intellectual" is a word that attracts what Collini calls a "force field" of

∼

Stefan Collini is professor of intellectual history and English literature at Cambridge University. He is a frequent contributor to The Times Literary Supplement, *the* London Review of Books, *and other periodicals. His previous books include* Public Moralists *(1991),* Matthew Arnold: A Critical Portrait *(1994), and* English Pasts *(1999).*

∼

meanings rather than one that is clearly recognizable. The idea of the intellectual, even in the twenty-first century, is still likely to provoke disagreement.

The term emerged in France during the Dreyfus affair (1894-1906). French novelist Émile Zola's open letter "J'Accuse" (1898) prompted more than a thousand writers, scholars, teachers, and other university graduates to put their names to a letter endorsing Zola's charges. The use of titles and educational qualifications as badges of authority prompted the letter's detractors to refer to them as the intellectuals. The term therefore entered common usage in France with a pejorative meaning attached to it. (Given the contrasts often made between pejorative use in Britain and apparently more favorable associations in France, it is worth noting that the term initially carried similarly hostile overtones in France.)

References to the Dreyfus affair brought the term into use in Britain, although there was no obvious term for it to replace and no corresponding situation for it to describe. From the outset British commentators were unclear how and to whom the term should be applied. The Russian term *intelligentsia* also came into English at around the same time although in Russian this did refer to a distinctive social grouping of well-educated people set apart from an otherwise illiterate society. Although committed to being critical of religious and political authority, the intelligentsia were, in Britain, viewed with as much suspicion by those who might be thought to be their natural supporters as by their detractors, reinforcing the sense of unease regarding such continental practices.

Having charted attempts to define the intellectual, Collini turns his attention to finding the missing British intellectuals. As becomes clear almost immediately, intellectuals do exist within British culture and have always existed historically. However, they have gone by many labels, not all of them easily linked to intellectual, and have fallen foul of a practice of denial that began in the nineteenth century. This denial arose from existing assumptions and prejudices, not least the habit of contrasting Britain with nations perceived as being less fortunate. The British prided themselves on being practical, pragmatic, and untheoretical; this distinctive cultural attitude was firmly in place by the time of the Dreyfus affair.

In Britain, scholars were made sober by their involvement in practical matters; continental intellectuals aroused suspicion because of their apparent intellectual specialization, an anxiety that recurs in the history of Britain's intellectuals. The uneasy linking of "highbrow," imported from the United States, with "intellectual" introduced a presumption of antagonistic social groupings and cultural activities being class related, although Britain had a strong tradition of working-class intellectualism, reflected in the popularity of university lectures and the mass publication of popular works on science and the arts.

Collini notes an avowedly self-conscious return after World War II to forms of expression that could be identified as specifically British, a reaction to what he calls the "internationalism of High Modernism." On one hand, the intellectual community is transformed into a cultural aristocracy, with a multigenerational pedigree; on the other, intellectuals are represented as inevitably being at odds with their society but capable of reintegration into mainstream society. It might be more accurate to say that intellectuals were not reintegrated so much as they became a recognized element of the social fabric, participating more conspicuously in daily life through print, radio, and, latterly, television.

If there ever genuinely was a golden age for intellectuals in British society, it was during the 1950's and 1960's, when they were visible and identifiable to people in all areas of society eager for new ideas in a booming postwar culture. Subsequent changes in perceptions of appropriate public roles for intellectuals, along with expansion of the higher education system, and a government-led return to a pragmatic social structure have made intellectuals less visible, although, as Collini is at pains to emphasize, they have not disappeared.

Having noted the firm British belief that they have no intellectuals, Collini carries out comparisons with other European countries and the United States, finding that like the British, other countries view their intellectuals with suspicion or deny their existence. In the case of the United States, commentators specifically note tensions between generalist intellectuals and specialist academics, suggesting that there is no place for the former in an increasingly specialized world. This anxiety is exacerbated by tensions between academics and unaffiliated intellectuals, the academy being regarded as the natural home of the American intellectual. American intellectuals are also haunted by a sense of inferiority when compared with European intellectuals, much as Europeans looked to France.

Given the universal sense that France is the natural home of the intellectual, reinforcing the sense that intellectuals in other countries are somehow exotic, misplaced aliens, it comes as no surprise to discover that France does indeed regard itself as the natural home of intellectuals. The key point Collini wishes to make is not so much that France accords significantly higher standing to its intellectuals as that they have been conspicuously active in France for much longer than elsewhere in Europe.

Having touched on what he calls the "paradoxes of denial," Collini provides case studies of various British intellectuals of the twentieth century and how they represented themselves within society. Twentieth century American poet and literary critic T. S. Eliot believed in the importance of cultural authority and those who exercised it, himself included. He believed in the rigorous exercise of the intellect but was reluctant to use it where this might imply he was anything other than a specialist in criticism. By comparison, R. G. Collingwood, Oxford philosopher and historian, was in later years moved to speak more generally about the crisis he saw threatening society—in other words to speak beyond his specialty. Unlike Eliot, his worldview was more circumscribed as he regarded Oxford literally as the world. His work was published in Oxford journals, remaining unavailable to those he most wished to address.

Author and cultural commentator George Orwell most immediately springs to mind when one considers the twentieth century intellectual. In fact, Orwell attacked intellectuals as a class in what Collini calls a "stylised hostility," presenting himself as rigorously anti-intellectual. His writing therefore embodies a fundamental contradiction, that of an anti-intellectual intellectual attacking his own kind.

A. J. P. Taylor, the quintessential Oxford don, provides an example of someone who stepped too far beyond the role of academic and intellectual to become perhaps the first modern celebrity don in print and on screen. His remarkable fluency endeared him to many, but in the end his seeming ubiquity and distinctive manner would count against him, suggesting that what he actually had to say was worth less than the way he said it. Like Taylor, A. J. Ayer, professor of philosophy at University College, London, and literary journalist, enjoyed a good deal of media attention—most memorably for his radio and television appearances—and became Britain's best-known professional philosopher. Again like Taylor, Ayer enjoyed celebrity, but again the question arose as to how far this fame eroded his serious reputation. Whereas Taylor was promiscuously opinionated, Ayer stuck to a few familiar philosophical positions; gradually, such conservatism came to seem outmoded, while his preference for statements of the demonstrably true or false left him open to accusations of superficiality.

The role of the intellectual in modern British life remains uncertain. Many commentators choose still to claim that they stand apart from society, a notion that Collini dismisses as absurd. It may seem glamorous to be aloof, but as Collini says, the role fulfilled by the intellectual exists within society and cannot easily be ignored. Indeed, he proposes that an intellectual can comfortably exist within society only in places where he or she can engage in dialogue with the culture—in which case, where have the intellectuals gone? Collini cites periodical journalism, television, and radio as their natural modern habitats, alongside university departments. He cautions, however, that with this attachment to the media comes the threat of a slide from authority to celebrity, as intellectuals are often invited to comment publicly on matters remote from their areas of expertise simply because they are familiar faces.

Collini concludes that while the debate about the presence and role of intellectuals continues, perhaps the time has come to no longer regard intellectuals as outsiders but to welcome them as an ordinary part of life.

Maureen Kincaid Speller

Review Sources

The Nation 282, no. 21 (May 29, 2006): 53-57.
New Criterion 25, no. 1 (September, 2006): 52-57.
New Statesman 135, no. 4786 (April 3, 2006): 50-51.
The Spectator 300, no. 9269 (April 1, 2006): 57-58.
The Times Literary Supplement, April 14, 2006, pp. 3-4.

ABSURDISTAN

Author: Gary Shteyngart (1972-   )
Publisher: Random House (New York). 338 pp. $25.00
Type of work: Novel
Time: The post-Soviet era
Locale: Russia and the fictional country of Absurdistan

Shteyngart spectacularly reaffirms his prominence as a chronicler of the immigrant experience in America with this story of a Russian oligarch's spoiled son who has tasted the inebriating pleasures of America and who now finds himself trapped in a homeland he has learned to despise

Principal characters:

MISHA BORISOVICH VAINBERG, protagonist, a Jewish, overweight son of
    a wealthy Russian oligarch
BORIS VAINBERG, Misha's father, whom Misha refers to as Beloved Papa
ROUENNA SALES, Misha's lover from Brooklyn, who goes by the name
    of Desiree in the bar where Misha meets her
ROBERT LIPSHITZ, also known as ALYOSHA-BOB, Accidental College
    buddy of Misha
TIMOFEY, Misha's manservant
JERRY SHTEYNFARB, fictional novelist, based on the novel's author, also
    Accidental College buddy of Misha
LYUBA, Misha's father's twenty-one-year-old wife, then widow, of
    lower-class origins
RAKSA, a "democrat" in Absurdistan
MR. NANABRAGOV, businessman and political figure in Absurdistan
JIMBO BILLINGS, undercover Mossad agent masquerading as a Texas
    oilman
DR. LEVINE, Misha's Park Avenue psychoanalyst

In many ways *Absurdistan* shows Gary Shteyngart to be a remarkably bold writer. Brash in his swipes at the cheapness of American urban culture while happily kicking away the rubble that the defeated, post-Cold War Russian soul has piled around itself, Shteyngart weaves the story of a spoiled young man's crisis of conscience together with that of the imaginary oil-producing nation of the novel's title. While at times Shteyngart delivers his sharp humor at too constant and too strong a pressure, the author's spirited jibes at everything from his character Misha's reluctant Jewishness to America's heavy-handed foreign policy carry the novel along at a fast clip. His thickly written but often powerful evocations of Misha's earnestly felt appetites give heart to what might have otherwise have become bitter and callous global satire.

The story is told by Misha Borisovich Vainberg, age thirty, a self-described "grossly overweight man" who is able to maintain his girth, as well as the "respect" he enjoys receiving from the less fortunate, thanks to the immense wealth of his father, whom he calls Beloved Papa. One of the novel's most colorful characters, Boris Vainberg, the 1,238th richest man in Russia, reached his status via the post-Soviet black market, making his first million off a car dealership that sold anything but cars. Beloved Papa shows his love for his overweight son by sending him, at age eighteen, to America for circumcision, and then to Accidental College in the Midwest for Americanization. Upon Misha's return to St. Petersburg, Beloved Papa promptly murders a visiting Oklahoma businessman and effectively makes it impossible for Misha to leave. Hopes of regaining his now-beloved New York and returning to his Brooklyn lover Rouenna are killed along with the Oklahoman, for the act has left an ineffaceable blot upon Misha's records at the U.S. Immigration and Naturalization Service (INS).

Even when seeing himself in the role of the victim of fate, Misha often has penetrating reactions to his surroundings, as in his introduction to the United States:

> I found myself in a livery cab, roaring through a terrifying Brooklyn neighborhood. In the Soviet Union, we were told that people of African descent—Negroes and Negresses, as we called them—were our brothers and sisters, but to the newly arriving Soviet Jews at the time, they were as frightening as armies of Cossacks billowing across the plains. I, however, fell in love with these colorful people at first blush. There was something blighted, equivocal, and downright Soviet about the sight of underemployed men and women arranged along endless stretches of broken porch-front and unmowed lawn—it seemed that, like my Soviet compatriots, they were making an entire *lifestyle out of their defeat.*

Almost always, however, his insights descend into the sensual. After his first insights while traveling through Brooklyn, he adds that "some of the young girls, already as tall and thick as baobab trees, their breasts perfectly shaped gourds that they regally carried down the street, were the most beautiful creatures I'd seen in my life."

Shteyngart is at his lightest in describing how seriously Misha's weight affects almost every aspect of his life: flab and sweat flap and fly freely across these pages. Misha even reacts to moments of psychic discomfort through the medium of the fleshy "toxic hump" that rides his shoulders. His efforts to find friendship, love, and self-discovery are all affected and shaped by the enormous folds of his physical being. This flesh cannot be easily discarded, however. Even the pleasures of sex, ample as they are, pale beside the raptures of consuming such delicacies as sturgeon kebabs.

The question of weight naturally affects the most important relationship in the book, that between father and son. While Misha feels uncomfortably put upon by Beloved Papa, he dreams of his earlier childhood days, which turn out to be his pre-fat days, when Beloved Papa was physically demonstrative of his love. Misha now spends his father's money freely on pleasures, an indulgence that fails to replace what is lost.

To Misha, Russia is "a nation of busybody peasants thrust into an awkward modernity," and he himself is "an American impounded in a Russian's body." Fortunately, he is not impounded without friends, giving Shteyngart a chance to demonstrate his penchant for colorful and slightly absurd personalities. Accidental College buddy Robert Lipshitz, whom Misha nicknames Alyosha-Bob, has successfully established himself in Russia with the DVD import-export firm aptly named ExcessHollywood. Misha also leans upon the sympathetic ear of Dr. Levine, his New York psychotherapist, via mobilnik. Although oddly invisible for much of the book, manservant Timofey proves an additional constant in Misha's life.

Gary Shteyngart, born in Leningrad, came to the United States at age seven with his family. His first novel, The Russian Debutante's Handbook, *was published in 2002.*

Throughout *Absurdistan* Shteyngart punches the action along with twists of an often violent nature, kicking matters off with explosives that kill Beloved Papa while he is out driving. Although the death changes nothing for Misha at the INS, he soon learns about Absurdistan, where a man of his newly expanded means can obtain a Belgian passport and thus gain entry into the European Union. Less happily, he receives an e-mail from his lover Rouenna stating her involvement with another of Misha's classmates from Accidental College, a novelist with a name close to the author's.

Shteyngart relies upon two mostly offstage characters to effect the action in his novel, one being the nearly faceless INS. The other is this fictional novelist Jerry Shteynfarb, who has become famous for his first novel, "Russian Arriviste's Hand Job," a bit of self-mockery from one who gained fame for first novel *The Russian Debutante's Handbook.* Misha jealously views Shteynfarb as a villain and mourns Rouenna's loss. He then receives an entreaty for company from his dead father's young widow, Lyuba. The two end up in bed, precipitating a new mental crisis that helps propel Misha out of St. Petersburg. "Everything has its limits," he declares.

Established at the Hyatt in Absurdistan, Misha finds a ramshackle city built upon the edge of the Caspian Sea, its shores thick with oil derricks. He learns his father had business dealings here, leaving a favorable impression, and that the Halliburton subsidiary of Kellogg, Brown & Root (KBR) maintains a presence in the region. The country is split between the two factions, the Sevo and the Svanï, who distinguish their members by the crosses around their necks. Near the bottom on the Sevo cross, Christ's small footrest cross-bar tilts to the left; on the Svanï cross, it tilts to the right.

With the assistance of a "democrat" named Raksa, Misha gains the papers he desires, during a meeting behind the Absurdistan McDonald's restaurant. The moment he sets his hands upon the passport, however, events spiral out of his or anyone's control, beginning with Absurdistan's dictator being assassinated. Raksa is killed before Misha's eyes, Alyosha-Bob is taken in by the American Embassy even as it denies Misha entrance, and phone service cuts off, ending recourse to Levine's comfort. War between the Sevo and Svanï begins, culminating with the Western high-rises, including Misha's Hyatt, being destroyed. Cast adrift in a drugged haze among the desperate, homeless, and dying, he finally finds refuge with his manservant and assorted acquaintances in a cheap flophouse, the one hotel remaining. In his new state of misery, he stops eating.

In the midst of the violence, Misha finds hope for a role of importance to play through Mr. Nanabragov, a former business partner of his father and the head of SCROD, the State Committee for the Restoration of Order and Democracy in Absurdistan. After the destruction of the high-rises, and after a period of refusing to eat while dwelling in the squalid hotel, Misha meets an undercover Mossad agent masquerading as a Texas oilman.

From the Mossad agent Misha learns that the political situation in Absurdistan was fabricated to bait the United States into establishing a military presence—a circumstance that would allow private contractors, particularly KBR, to make huge profits. Jimbo Billings also unveils to Misha the lie upon which Absurdistan has built its international image, and upon which Misha had indirectly pinned his own hopes for both being of help and helping himself toward his own goal.

Misha realizes he has been had: "Utterly. Completely. They'd used me. . . . Known right away that they had their man. If 'man' is the right word." While his desire to leave for the West remains undiminished, he learns from Nanabragov what a father will do to keep his child by his side, even if it means imprisoning that child in a country that is becoming unbearable. In learning this, he learns in what way his own father demonstrated his love for his son—far more demonstration than Misha had suspected.

Through this unlikely concatenation of events Shteyngart manages to tell the story of the boy too well insulated against the world. His character is insulated not only by obesity but also by wealth and a privileged attitude and seeks outlets in food, sex, and nearly literal flights of fancy. Misha frequently finds himself in a self-absorbed visionary state in which he is swept up into the air and speeds toward the streets of Manhattan, where he tours the restaurants and other humble attractions now close to his heart. He is able slowly to emerge, to "be a man," as in the dream command that haunts him, but only after serious internal struggles.

While the running jokes and ribaldry offer ample surface entertainment, a knife-blade of political criticism cuts through the underpinnings of this novel. Much of it is suggested rather than stated, as may be gathered from the following elements from Absurdistan. In an early scene, Misha fondly views the Twin Towers of the World Trade Center from his Manhattan apartment. The United States is later described as "a nation known more for its belly than for its brain," words that many of the book's characters might have applied to the narrator. In the prologue, Absurdistan is the country "where the calendar will never pass the second week of September 2001." Then, in the conclusion to the novel, the protagonist is headed "to New York. By any means necessary," on the eve of September 11.

Shteyngart keeps primary focus on a more personal issue, however. The ties between father and son permeate this novel, as do the son's straining efforts to break free. "What I say, you will do. That's what it means to be a man," Beloved Papa tells his son. Later, the son acknowledges that in Russia "a child is just an extension of his parents." In struggling for acceptance by the INS, an agency of the country whose policies end up ruining Absurdistan, Misha is denying the idea that he is no more than that extension, and fighting to establish his own identity.

Misha's narration begins with the declaration "This is a book about love." He adds that it is dedicated to Beloved Papa, the city of New York, his lover Rouenna, and the INS. While the inclusion of the last seems a bit of levity, at first, by the end of the novel it proves to be in earnest. Misha spends troubled moments wondering why he could never feel grief at his father's death, not quite realizing that it is the denied love of his new father, the United States, that has truly shaken his soul.

Absurdistan, flawed at times by obvious artifice and an occasional stab of humor as heartless as it is insightful, emerges in the end as a cohesive and affecting story of a global Everyman teetering at the brink of self-understanding.

Mark Rich

Review Sources

Booklist 102, no. 16 (April 15, 2006): 31.
Elle 21, no. 9 (May, 2006): 126.
Esquire 145, no. 6 (June, 2006): 46.
Kirkus Reviews 74, no. 5 (March 1, 2006): 204.
The Nation 282, no. 22 (June 5, 2006): 28-32.
The New York Review of Books 53, no. 12 (July 13, 2006): 37-39.
The New York Times 155 (April 25, 2006): E8.
The New York Times Book Review 155 (April 30, 2006): 1-10.
Publishers Weekly 253, no. 11 (March 13, 2006): 36.
Time 167, no. 19 (May 8, 2006): 187.
The Wall Street Journal 247, no. 106 (May 6, 2006): P9.
Weekly Standard 11, no. 43 (July 31, 2006): 39.

ACCIDENTAL GENIUS
How John Cassavetes Invented the American Independent Film

Author: Marshall Fine (1950-   )
Publisher: Miramax Books/Hyperion (New York). 482
    pp. $37.95
Type of work: Biography, film, fine arts, and media
Time: The early 1950's through 1989
Locale: New York and Los Angeles

The first ever authorized biography of forward-looking American actor and independent filmmaker Cassavetes mixes detailed discussions of the making and reception of each of his films with anecdotes from people who worked with him

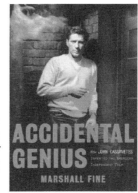

Principal personages:
>   JOHN CASSAVETES, a filmmaker
>   GENA ROWLANDS, his wife
>   KATHERINE CASSAVETES, his mother
>   NICHOLAS CASSAVETES, his father
>   SEYMOUR CASSEL, an actor

The career of actor/director John Cassavetes began in the last days of the Hollywood studio system—when television was just beginning—and continued right up to the end of the 1980's, when American "indie" films and film festivals—most inspired at least in part by Cassavetes' work—captured the wide public imagination. Marshall Fine's absorbing biography *Accidental Genius: How John Cassavetes Invented the American Independent Film* traces this career chronologically, focusing on the aspects of Cassavetes' personality that fed his eccentric yet astoundingly productive work habits.

Fine explores Cassavetes' obsessive, intuitive, aggressive, and highly collaborative creative method and how it generated the raw creative energy that audiences and critics often perceive in his films. The Cassavetes that emerges from Fine's pages was willfully individual, impatient and impulsive, and aggressive both physically and psychologically. Cassavetes was first and always an actor, utterly biased in favor of acting as the heart of theater and film, and he believed that film should showcase human emotion with as little interference as possible. He felt the job of a director was to give the actors something meaningful to do and then either motivate them to do it or get out of their way.

Most important for Fine, Cassavetes encouraged creativity in everyone he knew, asserting an artistic credo in which individual expression mattered most and no obstacle—whether cultural or financial—was insurmountable. Cassavetes' enthusiasm for others' art endeared him tremendously to his colleagues and to young filmmakers. Martin Scorsese credits Cassavetes' enthusiasm after screening *Who's That Knocking at My Door* (1968)—Cassavetes told him it was "better than *Citizen Kane*!"—for giving him a needed boost of confidence as a young director when his technical skills were not quite sufficient to express everything he wanted to say. Legendary African American actress Ruby Dee worked with Cassavetes on *Edge of the City* (1957) and *Virgin Island* (1958) in the late 1950's when the Hollywood system still excluded black actors and relegated them to servant roles. Dee remembers Cassavetes giving her her first movie camera and encouraging her to make her own movies: "He saw a capacity in me that I didn't see in myself."

Film and television critic Marshall Fine regularly reviews visual media for Star *magazine and has been widely syndicated in national magazines, including* Cosmopolitan *and* Entertainment Weekly. *He twice served as the chairman of the New York Film Critics Circle and has published biographies of director Sam Peckinpah and actor Harvey Keitel.*

This inspirational Cassavetes, who valued spontaneity and genuine emotion over technique and was the original DIY (do it yourself) filmmaker, dominates the book. Concerned that this motivating example might fade with time, Fine states that his purpose is to ensure that mainstream audiences and future generations of filmmakers understand Cassavetes' contribution to American film.

Accidental Genius is not an intimate biography, if intimacy is defined as the minute or emotional details of the subject's personal, family, and psychological life. Except for the first few brief chapters, which describe the immigrant origins of Cassavetes' parents, Katherine and Nicholas Cassavetes, his failure at school, and his marriage, Fine barely discusses Cassavetes' personal life at all. Cassavetes did not want a biography, and his wife and children do not discuss him with biographers.

The book is nonetheless strikingly intimate in that its perspective is entirely shaped by people who knew Cassavetes for many years, as a friend as well as a colleague. Although Cassavetes' wife, Gena Rowlands, did not discuss her husband with Fine, she gave her friends permission to talk to him, and this access to the Cassavetes inner circle gives this biography the feel of an "official" record of the memories of Cassavetes' friends and colleagues—about their friend and about what it was like to work with him.

Yet Fine's purpose was not merely to document these memories, and a strong sense of Cassavetes the person emerges from the professional descriptions, as he was clearly a man whose work dominated his personal life. Fine depicts him as having very little interest in and few emotions about anything other than film—one anecdote has Cassavetes so absorbed in work that he does not remember his wife giving birth to their second child. Some of the most personally affecting stories involve his reflections on his work while facing death.

The book devotes three chapters to Cassavetes' major directorial works: one chapter each to the script, the production, and the distribution and reception of each film. In discussing the scripts, Fine does an admirable job of elucidating each film's historical context and relevance to some major sociocultural issue: *Shadows* (1959) and race, *Husbands* (1970) and masculinity, *A Woman Under the Influence* (1974) and the stifling forces of gender expectations and class. In telling the back story of each film, how it was funded and made, Fine weaves into the personal stories of Cassavetes and his favorite actors the history of visual media in the mid-twentieth century: the increasing influence of live television, the significance of the Actors' Studio on the way performers thought about themselves and their craft, the power of market forces over Hollywood films, and the transition of theatrical actors to television and film.

Cassavetes was often accused of making improvised films because he relied so much on the spontaneity and insight of his actors. Fine's meticulous attention to Cassavetes' creative process, however, shows the films to be more intuitive than improvised. Cassavetes was quite controlling in his own way: berating a young actress in *Husbands* until she cried because he wanted her to be crying, recutting both *Shadows* and *Husbands* to make them less audience friendly, physically assaulting a movie agent and ripping his clothes in order to get his attention. Fine connects this intuition to Cassavetes' passion and insistence on following his instincts and creative drive: he mortgaged his house several times to make films and then recut them after test screenings to be less commercial because he believed that cinema should challenge an audience to feel something raw and genuine.

Fine assumes that the reader will be able to draw the connections between Cassavetes' approach and what is now called "independent" film. He does not rigorously follow through on the promise of his subtitle: tracing how Cassavetes is the most significant progenitor of indie cinema. The book briefly defines independent film in the introduction, quoting actor Seymour Cassel saying that "independent film is film that has thought in it," but Cassavetes and his methods come off far more as spontaneous and naturalistic than as deliberative or thoughtful.

Fine is quite explicit about Cassavetes' connections to the economics of contemporary independent film. The indie mantra that commercial funding and artistic integrity have an inverse relationship goes unquestioned as the obvious reason for Cassavetes' pioneering efforts to make commercially and artistically viable films using alternative financing. This is the aspect of independent film that Cassavetes seems to have "invented"—the business model for making a kind of film that inherently has a smaller audience than a blockbuster.

As successful as Fine is at evoking the historical context for Cassavetes' films, he does not situate the films sufficiently in an artistic context. The commonly asserted artistic connection between *Shadows* and the Beat movement is largely ignored. Fine repeatedly points out how Cassavetes' films found more ready acceptance in Europe than in America, but he does not discuss how they compared to contemporaneous European films or what influence they may have had on filmmakers such as François Truffaut and Jean-Luc Godard. He distances Cassavetes from the notion of "art film" but never articulates how the "independent" film of his title differs from it; it is clear that they are not synonyms but the objection to the term "art" seems to be that it turns people off, not that it is an inaccurate designation. Fine's Cassavetes has an identifiably punk spirit: he was fascinated with spontaneity, had contempt for cinematography and was convinced that the technical craft of making a film was inauthentic, and believed that only the actor's honest emotion mattered, even the type of emotion that led to Cassavetes' hard drinking, which eventually caused his death.

Fine presents Cassavetes' films as the product of a singular artistic vision, not a singular consciousness—Cassavetes was too collaborative for that—but a singular energy. Regardless of how many other participants there were in the process, Cassavetes was the engine that drove his films. It was his energy and dedication and sheer will that ensured they were made. For Fine, this is independent. It is also discernibly consistent with the great American cultural metaphors of pioneering spirit and individual achievement through hard work although Fine does not press the connections. For film buffs who notice these gaps, this biography will raise as many questions as it answers.

Fine's biography contains very few criticisms of Cassavetes or his films and thus does not hold up well to academic scrutiny—but it is not intended to. The prose is journalistic and readable, and Fine never descends into gossip or sensationalism. His affection for his subject—and his obvious desire not to violate the trust Gena Rowlands placed in him by giving her approval for the project—occasionally makes him too pro-Cassavetes. He shows little warmth for those who do not understand or appreciate Cassavetes' value, such as *The New Yorker* film critic Pauline Kael, and the narration of anecdotes always favors Cassavetes' point of view. Nonetheless the book does not whitewash Cassavetes' less appealing attributes—particularly his physical aggression and self-absorption; it simply depicts them as part of what made Cassavetes into the artist he was.

Film scholars and aficionados still need a truly academic biography of this significant figure, one that more rigorously situates him historically, with more comparison and outside perspective and one that avoids Fine's "inner circle" approach without being quite as divorced from the personal as self-described Cassavetes expert Ray Carney's work. (Carney argues on his Web site and in interviews that people who knew Cassavetes are too close to him to have accurate opinions on him.) However, Fine's offering does show an altogether human artist—contradictory, passionate, dedicated to the point of obsession—and Fine succeeds in conveying Cassavetes as a proponent of the belief that art is made not by excessive talent or great training or immense skill, but just by getting on with making it, no matter what the obstacle.

Caroline M. Small

Review Sources

Booklist 102, no. 7 (December 1, 2005): 12.
Entertainment Weekly, no. 869 (March 24, 2006): 74.
Film Comment 42, no. 2 (March/April, 2006): 77.
The New York Times Book Review 155 (January 29, 2006): 7.
The Wall Street Journal 247, no. 51 (March 3, 2006): W6.

AFTER THIS

Author: Alice McDermott (1953-   )
Publisher: Farrar, Straus and Giroux (New York). 279
  pp. $24.00
Type of work: Novel
Time: Post-World War II to post-Vietnam War
Locale: Long Island, Manhattan, and Queens in New
  York City; London

McDermott chronicles the lives of the Catholic Keane family and Mary Keane's friend Pauline as well as assorted neighborhood and school friends from just after World War II to just after the Vietnam War

> *Principal characters:*
> MARY ROSE KEANE, first a young working woman, then a wife and
>   mother
> PAULINE, her office friend, who remains a lifelong family friend
> JOHN KEANE, her husband, a businessman without any college training
> JACOB,
> MICHAEL,
> ANNIE, and
> CLARE KEANE, her children

After This continues Alice McDermott's fascination with a Long Island existence dominated by the tenets of Catholic faith and family life that predominated in the Irish family and the neighborhoods she grew up in during the 1950's and 1960's. It begins with Mary's musings about her future as a daughter, sister, and young working woman who has not had much of a social life and sees herself taking care of her father and brother indefinitely unless fate intervenes. Fate takes the form of John Keane, a man she happens to sit next to at a lunch counter in Manhattan who seeks her out again. In their first brief encounter McDermott introduces a theme that runs through the book: desire. After a quick exchange "she turned back to her sandwich. And here, of all things, was desire again. (She could have put the palm of her hand to the front of his white shirt.)"

In later chapters Mary and her daughter Annie stand in line to view the *Pieta* at the world's fair and fall under the spell of desire expressed in great art. Teenage sexuality surfaces in the comments Jacob and Michael make watching girls leave Mass at Saint Gabriel's, references to girls' bodies being pressed into recreation room furniture or mattresses, descriptions of Catholic nuns delivering admonitions about the sin of abortion, and details of Annie accompanying Susan Perischetti to her abortion. Pauline makes comments and thinks about the sexual and marital union of the Keanes throughout the novel, and Annie's taking a British lover in her year of overseas study is one of the novel's primary culminations. The novel is never far from the constricted world of desire, sin, tumult, confession, and longing that permeate the memories of Catholic schoolgirls of McDermott's generation. The veneer of saintly stories and catechism covers the lustful curiosity and naïveté of the Keane girls and their classmates and peppers the conversations of their brothers with references to "good girls," who are fast and "nice girls," who are not. When Michael Keane gets to college, descriptions of how seedy bar owner Ralph sets up his coed conquests replace the story's earlier innuendoes. Despite the fixation on sex and childbearing, the book has few explicit scenes and thrives on suggestion, much the same way teens found titillation in the 1950's and early 1960's before the sexual revolution. Desire in many forms creates tension as the story develops.

Alice McDermott received the prestigious PEN/Faulkner Award for fiction for That Night *(1987) and the National Book Award for* Charming Billy *(1998). She teaches in the writing program at The Johns Hopkins University in Baltimore, Maryland.*

McDermott's title, *After This*, refers to the time "after" the movements away from faith, family, and country that forever altered the world the Keane children inherited and then modified as they grew to adulthood. Like desire, which permeates the book, the title refers to Mary Keane's whole life: her dreams of escaping the single life, her young married state, the baby days of her children, the aging of her husband, her involvement in the church, her old and habitual friendship with Pauline, the death of her son in Vietnam, the loss of a daughter to a foreign man and address. The novel offers a checklist of the assumptions that formed the parameters of Irish Catholic family life and expectations during the postwar and Vietnam eras. What happens to the Keanes happens after they construct a life based on those values. Memory in this book reminds people of what they had wanted, not what happened to them earlier.

McDermott's recounting focuses on the pathos of dreams that do not live up to their possibilities. An edge of nostalgia-tinged disappointment skews everything in the novel toward a melancholy that suggests the waning usefulness of society's faith in patriotism, institutions, and Catholic values in a time of social upheaval. Standing in line at the world's fair, even in the intense heat "Mary Keane was aware of a certain pleasure in being relieved of the burden of a husband." She returns home late, knowing John will not like it, and what is worse her friend Pauline knows his mood swings and demands as well. Mary regrets her confidences about "every moment in their marriage when [she] had not loved her husband, when love itself had seemed a misapprehension, a delusion and marriage . . . simply an awkward pact with a stranger, any stranger."

This ambivalence extends to the church as well. When the Keane family attends Mass in the new Saint Gabriel's, Mary misses the ornate stations of the cross in the old church. John misses the hat clips on the backs of the old pews, which Michael snapped once a Sunday. As with her marriage, however, Mary Keane sticks to the church, watching all four children grow and graduate under the nuns' tutelage. Ultimately, it seems McDermott has her characters embrace their imperfect faith because abandoning it would leave too huge a vacuum.

With a nod toward orthodoxy, Susan Perischetti (the young woman of the abortion episode) meets Michael Keane (a skeptic about his religion) at his college bar. They talk but never feel themselves able to get beyond the kind of surface catching up you do with friends from the old neighborhood after a period of separation. These two characters seem empty. Susan, involved with a man in a "serious relationship," finally extricates herself with the clichéd "It was good to see you, Michael," and he responds in kind. His friends tell him they could see "disappointment, the failure to connect" as she walked away. Below the action of this encounter lurks the hint of a judgment about people who do not honor their religious traditions. They seem adrift.

Guilt is also part of Pauline and Mary's friendship. Pauline's determined and superior spinsterhood gives her an air of disapproval and crankiness that upsets the balance of the Keane household. Out of deference to Clare and Mary and Pauline's long years of friendship, though, Mary and the family tolerate her presence and move her into their home after she takes a bad fall while making her way home from a Sunday dinner at the Keanes'. Cementing Pauline into the family presents another metaphor for the acceptance of the required attitudes toward marriage that define John and Mary Keane's relationship and their orientation toward the church. They seem to continually "move over" to accommodate inconsistencies, doubts, or trials. Their irritations with one another, the necessity of obeying the church's teachings, and their immense grief at the death of their oldest son are to be borne. Pauline is taken in out of a sense of duty, responsibility, and a type of desperate acceptance. She cannot be abandoned any more than the patterns they grew up with can be.

The Keane children struggle to change their legacy. Jacob's life, cut short in Vietnam, makes only a partial turn away. Annie loosens the bond entirely, living in sin in London after a year of study abroad. Smart-mouthed, darling Michael ends up teaching in a Catholic school in Brooklyn, repeating his own youth without enthusiasm. He cannot reinvent himself. Clare, finally, swallows the history whole. Married too early because she gets pregnant, she stays in the house with her new husband, and the future seems to include Pauline living on as a mother-substitute after the Keanes retire and move away. Their struggles with their training and their pasts carry the struggle into the next generation.

For all its tragedies, *After This* is a quiet book. McDermott's archaeological layering of events occurring simultaneously pays everyday life the compliment of intense attention. Readers see and feel each occurrence in a context that protects and suppresses at the same time. Her people are not heroes in any grand sense, but they are steady, dependable people who get up every day and try to meet their responsibilities and experience their joys in a decent, God-fearing way (mostly). They are not the cynical, edgy characters of much contemporary fiction.

They have their bouts of exhaustion with their routines, their irritations with their friends, and their satisfactions at knowing what is expected. What John and Mary do not see coming are the shocks of death and an unwanted pregnancy. Their collapse and resigned return to the rhythm of their life signal the value of a system of faith, however flawed. Reading this novel, one senses McDermott's conviction that keeping the faith has its cost, but the reward is the ability to keep on living, the belief that life and whatever talent one has, as the priest says at book's end, are "a gift."

The Keanes' thoughts about their single lives and their part in the family's dynamic round out a sense of how faith and its practice can create a world where there may be sharp difficulties, but grace offers answers as well as restrictions. It is not a naïve affirmation of faith; it makes its case with a cast of vulnerable people persevering the only way they know how.

Karen L. Arnold

Review Sources

America 195, no. 10 (October 9, 2006): 26-29.
Booklist 102, no. 21 (July 1, 2006): 9.
Kirkus Reviews 74, no. 14 (July 15, 2006): 694.
Ms. 16, no. 4 (Fall, 2006): 74-75.
The New York Times 155 (September 8, 2006): E34.
The New York Times Book Review 155 (September 10, 2006): 15.
The New Yorker 82, no. 28 (September 11, 2006): 83-85.
Publishers Weekly 253, no. 25 (June 19, 2006): 37.
Time 168, no. 13 (September 25, 2006): 82.

AGAINST THE DAY

Author: Thomas Pynchon (1939-   )
Publisher: Penguin Press (New York). 1,085 pp. $35.00
Type of work: Novel
Time: 1893 to the early 1920's
Locale: The United States, Europe, Mexico, Shambhala, and the Center of the Earth

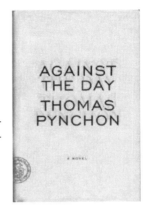

Pynchon's first novel in nearly a decade, and his longest, offers a fictional counterculture history of the Western world immediately before and after World War I

Principal characters:
> LEW BASNIGHT, a "psychical" private detective
> RANDOLPH ST. COSMO, the commander of the sky ship Inconvenience
> YASHMEEN HALFCOURT, a mathematician working with a group of London Pythagoreans
> DEUCE KINDRED, a hired gun who kills Webb Traverse then marries his daughter
> WEBB TRAVERSE, a miner, labor organizer, and "anarchist"
> FRANK TRAVERSE, Webb's son, a mining engineer
> KIT TRAVERSE, Webb's brilliant son, sent to Yale by Scarsdale Vibe
> REEF TRAVERSE, Webb's ne'er-do-well son
> LAKE TRAVERSE, Webb's daughter, marries her father's killer
> SCARSDALE VIBE, a capitalist mine owner who orders the death of Webb Traverse
> NATALIA ESKIMOFF, a medium
> PENNY BLACK, an aviatrix
> DARBY SUCKLING, the Chums of Chance ship's "mascotte"

Everything that Thomas Pynchon's critics have loved about his first five novels is in his sixth, *Against the Day*. Everything that his critics have hated about his novels is there, too. Both lists usually contain the same four or five items. The novels sprawl; at 1,085 pages, *Against the Day* is longer than any of its lengthy predecessors. They contain countless characters, with several hundred in *Against the Day*. They shift from high seriousness to silly songs; there are twenty songs in *Against the Day* (or twenty-one if you count "Very Nice, Indeed," which is simply that phrase sung to the tune of the *William Tell Overture*). They rely on obscure metaphors from mathematics, engineering, and physics; *Against the Day* deals with aetherism, quaternions, double refraction, multidimensional vector-space, and Riemann zeta functions, among other science topics. They are vulgar and obscene. Each of these can be valid complaints against any Pynchon novel—with a quibble over the one about length, which is not true of Pynchon's 1966 novel *The Crying of Lot 49*, and may or may not be true of

1990's *Vineland*—including *Against the Day*. Each complaint, however, can be answered in turn, for *Against the Day* is Pynchon at the top of his game.

The first is sprawl. *Against the Day* certainly does that. The usual assumption of negative critics is that, unlike the similarly sprawling novels of Leo Tolstoy, Pynchon's do not cohere. A Pynchon novel, the mantra goes, is unintegrated fiction for a disintegrated age. Still, there are themes that do promise to hold *Against the Day* together. One theme is that traditional methods of coherence, such as temporal and special sequence, are illusory and, conversely, that things that seem to that same traditional mind totally disparate, such as physics experiments and labor movements, are intimately connected. Exploring such themes takes a vast canvas, and many who reach page 1,085 of *Against the Day* will find even that vast expanse too cramped to portray them adequately.

∼

Thomas Pynchon's Gravity's Rainbow *(1973) received the National Book Award and was nominated for a Pulitzer. His other novels include* V *(1963), which won the William Faulkner Foundation Award;* The Crying of Lot 49 *(1966), which won the Richard and Hilda Rosenthal Foundation Award;* Vineland *(1990); and* Mason and Dixon *(1997).*

∼

Fictionally, the most common method of coherence is plot, and though critics have called Pynchon's works plotless, *Against the Day* does have a discernable thread that runs through the center of the book—though with so many alternate plots, few readers will want to concentrate on it alone. This plot follows the interconnections of two families, that of mining engineer Webb Traverse and billionaire mine owner Scarsdale Vibe. When Traverse becomes a troublesome labor organizer, Vibe hires Deuce Kindred to kill him. What follows takes on the flavor of early twentieth century Western revenge thrillers, but without the moral clarity of that genre. Good guys and bad guys merge as Vibe becomes a foster father to Webb's son Kit, whom he sends to Yale; Webb's daughter Lake marries Kindred; sons Reef and Frank each attempt to deny their implicit duty to avenge their father's murder.

The second complaint is too many characters. There is more truth to this gibe than most. Michiko Kakutani argues in a *New York Times* review that the sheer number of characters leads to shoddy characterization, which leads to poor rapport with the reader: We cannot care about characters dashed in broad strokes. That is true for a majority of the characters in *Against the Day*; however, in a novel with hundreds of characters, what is true for the majority is irrelevant. All most readers ask of any kind of novel is one or two characters they can care about, and *Against the Day* offers several choices, each as deeply characterized as any contemporary reader can expect: Frank Traverse, the avenging son (any member of the Traverse family, in fact); Lew Basnight, the "psychical" detective; Yashmeen Halfcourt, the drop-dead gorgeous mathematician.

The fact that these character types are clichés from the popular adventure fiction of the time period in which the story is set masks Pynchon's real accomplishment in characterization. He has taken cardboard types never intended to be realistically drawn and asked: What would they be like if they were real people in the real world?

What surprises the careful reader of Pynchon is not how facile the virtuous aviator is in fin de siècle adventure fiction but the disturbingly human way Commander Randolph St. Cosmo of the "Chums of Chance" outgrows his dime novel outlines even as we read *Against the Day*. Contributing to this marvelous illusion is Pynchon's adaptation of the dime novel idiom, including hundred-year-old spellings (just as he employed eighteenth century diction and orthography in 1997's *Mason and Dixon*). Darby Suckling, for instance, is not the ship's mascot for the Chums of Chance, but their "mascotte," the spelling indicating how recently the French loan word has attained its modern usage.

The third complaint is silly songs and popular culture. This category is moot in terms of criticism: A reader either likes it or hates it, and no argument is going to sway an individual one way or the other. There is one possible exception—the argument that Pynchon's popular culture references are never gratuitous. They arise naturally out of setting and character. For example, the London scenes occur just at the historical moment that the "googly" (cricket's equivalent of the curve ball in American baseball) revolutionizes the British national pastime. The London chapters are awash in cricketing terms. Often though, the most telling popular culture references are not recognized as popular culture. Character description, for instance, always includes a reference to what type of hat is worn. Porkpies, skimmers, scorcher caps, leghorn straw hats, trilbies, fedoras, slouch hats, beavers—names not even recognized any more—are always just right for the character and the moment, though few readers in the largely hatless twenty-first century would notice. The songs are as accomplished in their Hudibrastic, Tin Pan Alley rhymes as ever. Pynchon's lyrics demonstrate that Broadway need not have relied (as it has) on revivals or British imports to keep the "American Songbook" going. The most stunning tour de force is perhaps a love song addressed to the mathematician Yashmeen, in which she is romantically matched with the names of all the great mathematicians of the age, each brilliantly rhymed: "murmur low/Zermelo," "geniuses/Frobeniouses," "swank array/Poincaré," "though she/Cauchy," "Riemann/dream on," "spots in/Watson," and so on.

The fourth complaint is obscure technical metaphors. This criticism is really a reincarnation of eighteenth century literary figure Samuel Johnson's swipe at metaphysical poets like John Donne. Johnson felt that Donne and poets like him used metaphors for the shock of novelty rather than to convey meaning to the reader. Johnson was wrong, however, about the motives of the metaphysical poets, and critics are mistaken if they think that Pynchon is using analogies to physics and math in *Against the Day* to show off (as, unfortunately, too many of his readers and critics do, urging us to admire them because they can understand Pynchon's most obscure references). He is using them, first, because they occur naturally to him, as he is by training an engineer, but more important, because he is writing in the same humane tradition as Donne, valiantly asserting that developments in science and mathematics are as much a part of our culture as developments in music and architecture. Pynchon came as close as he could to answering the charge of obscurantism in his October 28, 1984, essay in *The New York Times Book Review*, "Is It O.K. to Be a Luddite?" Pynchon's essay marked the twenty-fifth anniversary of scientist cum novelist C. P. Snow's famous Rede lecture on "The Two Cultures" (1959). Snow argued that twentieth century civilization was in danger of fragmenting into two communities—one scientific and one literary—neither able to communicate with the other. Pynchon refused to be pessimistic about the inevitability of that schism, and *Against the Day*—in which political attempts to dominate space and time are cast against mathematics, which treats Newtonian concepts of space and time as irrelevant—is Pynchon's latest contribution to the task of bridging the two worlds.

The fifth complaint is against obscenity and vulgarity. Both are unquestionably present in *Against the Day*. Despite its appearance so late in the year (released November 21, with review copies carefully vetted), *Against the Day* was nominated for the "Bad Sex in Fiction" award for 2006 but lost to *Twenty-Something* by Lain Hollingshead. The dust jacket blurb, said by the publisher to have been written by Pynchon himself, promises "strange and weird sexual practices." The novel delivers. It is not for the squeamish. On the other hand, sexual scenes are brief and infrequent and never gratuitous. Far from titillating, the tone of such tableaux as Lake Traverse giving herself to her father's killer evokes the sadness and emptiness of a "bad girl" trying in vain to find the love she thought she could not get from her father.

Against the Day is not light reading and would not be even at two hundred pages. It is dense with the necessary density of a novel that, like all of Pynchon's fiction, spiritualizes the mathematical and mathematizes the spiritual. Pynchon's conflation of electromagnetic physics and spiritualism in this novel is no random syncretism: It is an accurate portrayal of the interconnection of both disciplines in the years between 1893 and 1922. Casual references in the novel to Sir William Crookes—whose work with cathode rays made the vacuum tube, and therefore radio and television, possible—and to Sir Oliver Lodge—inventor of the spark plug—place them in the seemingly improper context of *Against the Day*'s medium Natalia Eskimoff. Nevertheless, both physicists were prominent spiritualists, and Pynchon's narrative elucidates some of the surprising logic in the connection. Electromagnetic radiation, such as radio waves, suggests communication, connection by invisible means—voices, images, information passing through unseen worlds. The nonscientific world thinks of physicists and mathematicians as hardheaded materialists and realists, but most advances in those fields have been made by speculation that strikes the layperson as mystical, dreamy, or just plain crazy. What if there were more than three spatial dimensions, asked mathematician Herman Minkowski (1864-1909), mentioned in *Against the Day* on pages 324 and 458? What if time as we experience it did not exist, wondered metaphysician J. M. E. McTaggert (1866-1925), mentioned on pages 239 and 412? What if gravitation were simply a geometric function, queried W. K. Clifford (1843-1877), mentioned on pages 249 and 632?

The interplay of religion, physics, and the material world may well be best summed up by Pynchon's choice of title for his sixth novel. *Against the Day* suggests an apocalyptic idiom from the King James Bible, 2 Peter 3:7 but also a photographic term that has implications for modern physics and non-Euclidian geometry. In the technique that early French photographers called *contre-jour*, "against the day," cameras shot into the light source, reducing foregrounded objects to two-dimensional outlines. At the very historical moment that mathematicians, physicists, and science-fiction writers were exploring the implications of multidimensional space, photographers were reminding people how recently the pictorial arts had taught everyone to think in three dimensions. At that same time aeronautics forced map making to become three-dimensional, as aviatrix Penny Black observes on the antepenultimate page of the novel, 1,083. Pynchon knows how long pictorial art has been aware of the geometrical implications of perspective drawing, and he builds into the plot the use of a seventeenth century vogue for anamorphic drawings and paintings that could only be "decoded" by an anamorphoscope, which twists the distorted drawing into a recognizable shape. Pynchon has the Chums of Chance looking for a map that can only be decoded by a paramorphoscope, which reveals more than three spatial dimensions. It is this trans-tertial world that constantly threatens to break into the novel and peeks in at the end as visitors from the future invade the world of the early twentieth century, seeming to promise revelation but leaving their real motives in question.

The only way to sum up *Against the Day* may well be the kind of old vaudeville joke in which Pynchon too often delights. What is the novel about? It's about 1,100 pages.

John R. Holmes

Review Sources

Booklist 103, no. 6 (November 15, 2006): 7.
Library Journal 131, no. 19 (November 15, 2006): 59.
The Nation 283, no. 20 (December 11, 2006): 11-16.
New Statesman 135 (December 4, 2006): 54-55.
The New York Times 156 (November 20, 2006): B1-B8.
The New York Times Book Review 156 (November 26, 2006): 1-26.
The New Yorker 82, no. 39 (November 27, 2006): 170-172.
Publishers Weekly 253, no. 43 (October 30, 2006): 34.
The Spectator 302 (November 25, 2006): 46-47.
Time 168, no. 21 (November 20, 2006): 74-75.
The Times Literary Supplement, December 1, 2006, pp. 21-22.

ALL AUNT HAGAR'S CHILDREN

Author: Edward P. Jones (1950-   )
Publisher: Amistad (New York). 399 pp. $25.95
Type of work: Short fiction
Time: 1900-1999
Locale: Washington, D.C., with some sections of stories
   set elsewhere

*In fourteen elegant stories, the author, a lifelong Wash-
ington area resident, tells of the joys, sorrows, and fantastic experiences of the city's African American citizens*

Even more so than most cities, Washington, D.C., is a
place where different levels of society seem to exist in
wholly different worlds. The Washington that fills the
headlines, the arena of government and power, has drawn its share of perceptive fictional portrayals within the nation's literature. The city's African American inhabitants, however, despite making up the majority of its population, until now have remained almost invisible to American literature.

That lack is now being remedied, due to the work of a hitherto little-known but
gifted writer. Edward P. Jones published an earlier book of fourteen short stories, *Lost
in the City*, in 1992. Like *All Aunt Hagar's Children*, its stories are mostly set in "the
District" as the region's inhabitants say. The connections between its stories and
those in the present volume, although sometimes subtle, go beyond setting. In 2002,
his novel of a black slaveholder in the antebellum South, *The Known World*, appeared. It won many awards, including a Pulitzer Prize. Now, in *All Aunt Hagar's
Children*, Jones returns to twentieth century Washington with another fourteen stories, marked by the careful craftsmanship and the convolution of fate and consequences in the city's residents' lives.

This is a community where—at least in Jones's stories—family members disappear for years at alarming rates, where bizarre deaths are commemorated by becoming nicknames for a place or person, where cause and effect are twisted into nonse-
quential patterns. It is also a place where personal sacrifices are made, in the best
American tradition, for an elderly woman's peace of mind or the chance to make a
child's life better than the lives of her elders. Most of the community's members are
migrants from the rural South, or if not migrants themselves, the second- or third-
generation descendants of those who were migrants. These stories span the twentieth
century. Some of the early migrants were not many years removed from slavery. Even
many years later, the city's reputation as the first way station on the way north, drew
southern migrants. In both cases, their connection to places, memories, and the lore of
the South stayed with the new Washingtonians. No less than the members of Congress with whom they share the city, these African Americans remain inhabitants of
their home districts also.

∼

Edward P. Jones grew up in poverty in Washington, D.C., and still lives in the area. His published oeuvre is small—two short-story collections and a novel—but his books have won many major awards in American literature.

∼

In "In the Blink of God's Eye," Washington, D.C., is a long way from Ruth Patterson's birthplace in Arlington, Virginia. Indeed, to a young couple with no transportation except their feet or a rented wagon, it was a formidable distance. Ruth moves there as a newlywed with her husband Aubrey in 1901. He likes the city; his aunt has made a job and room for them in the hotel-boardinghouse "for coloreds" which she runs on 3d Street NW.

To Ruth, Washington is a strange, cold place, where drunken women stumble and fall in the street and wolves prowl after dark. One night Ruth cannot sleep, so, armed with a knife and pistol, she goes out onto the porch. She notices a bundle hanging on the apple tree in the front yard. Curiosity leads her to poke it with the knife, fortunately not very hard, for inside the bundle is a baby. What could be more natural than to care for it? While Aubrey prowls the streets, inquiring who might have lost a baby, Ruth simply marvels at the craziness of a city where babies grow on trees. Forever after, Aubrey regards the baby's coming into their life as responsible for the loss of Ruth's affection, touchingly unaware that even having their own child—which the couple never does—can change the balance of a marriage.

The title story tells of a Korean War veteran who is prevailed upon to investigate a murder. "You the only thing close to the law we got," his mother pleads, convinced that her son's experience rounding up drunk soldiers as a member of the military police qualifies him as a detective. She tells him that Miss Agatha, the murdered man's mother, cannot find any peace until she knows what happened to him, and the D.C. police do not bother to follow up on what they view as the routine murder of a black man. The veteran reluctantly agrees to look into the matter, putting his own plans for a move to Alaska on hold while he pokes around the victim's neighborhood and apartment. In the end neither he nor the reader has solved the murder, but he gives the mother, poor old Miss Agatha, the most plausible answer. Counterpoint to this main story is an equally interesting backstory—a structural trick that Jones uses frequently. The veteran's mother, aunt, and her friend Agatha came to Washington years ago as young women. They were alone and hardly old enough to cope on their own, but they had little choice. They had just beaten a white man who had tried to rape Agatha, and they had to get away from Alabama before he came to or was found.

Woven through these two tales are fragments of others; the last words, in Yiddish, of a woman struck down in the street by a car; a former girlfriend whom the veteran is sure is stalking him. Holding them all together is only the veteran's puzzlement. The way there is no resolution at the end, and the story closes with what may be a small epiphany or merely a sputter; this is vintage Jones.

"Old Boys, Old Girls" brings Caesar, a young hoodlum from Jones's first collection's story "The Young Lions," into adulthood. Now a genuine thug by the world's measure, Caesar does time in Lorton Penitentiary. He emerges with a near-paralyzed arm and no friends. He is even thinking of chancing another murder rap by raiding the resident moneylender's safe, when he learns that an old girlfriend of his is living in the same rooming house. Both are too worn down by life to share more than cigarettes, but he visits her a few times and brings her food. Then he finds her dead. In one of the few redemptive acts of his life, he cleans her body and room. Then he goes out into the sunlight, making the only plans he can for his future life: to find the money to give her a decent burial.

"Root Worker" features a doctor whose mother nightly becomes the prey of "witches" who temporarily paralyze her. Medicine and psychiatry have not helped, and to the doctor's chagrin, a cure comes from an old Carolina root worker.

Jones breaks most of the rules about conventional story structure. In place of plot, his stories are layered with memories, twists of time, seemingly irrelevant solid objects, and ghostly ones as well. Fantastic things happen matter-of-factly and sometimes change the course of characters' lives. Readers new to his writing are likely to be baffled when the narrative segues to tell of an unrelated event, even within the same paragraph. The usual effect, however, is to compress the whole substance of a novel into a short story's space. It is a dazzling accomplishment when it works well, which it usually does in this author's hands.

If Jones ignores dictums about plot, he brings his characters to life masterfully. The flashbacks, add-on identities, and imaginings that stud his characters' consciousness capture their inner life as no mere description could. Although his characters of all ages, genders, and statuses ring true, Jones's very best portrayals are those of older black men, especially those who have done their best to live a respectable life. He can instantly summon up a whole generation's habits in a deft phrase or two: "He was wearing a suit now, as was often the case with [black] men of a certain age. . . . They wore suits out into the world the way knights had worn armor; they wore suits even to baseball games and to shoeshine jobs."

Horace Perkins's predicament in "A Rich Man"—widowed at age sixty, and then his prized 78-rpm record collection and spotless reputation shattered by the crack-using young women he takes in—is both comic and tragic. Few readers will be able to resist a twinge of sympathy, though, for the old man lured into their company by his late-life lust and loneliness.

Noah Robinson (of "Adam Robinson Acquires Grandparents and a Little Sister") is unforgettable. His grandson Adam is a victim of the crack epidemic, which took away his parents, and of the chaotic foster care system. Long after the boy's parents have vanished, Noah and his wife Maggie have the chance to be reunited with the six-year-old and bring him up, along with his baby sister, who already lives with them. Noah is not a rich or educated man, but what he offers the terrified boy—patience and grandfatherly camaraderie—is priceless. Adam keeps asking when he is going home. Noah, though hurt and puzzled by this, tries to meet the boy on his own level and discover what home he is remembering. It turns out that his many past homes are all jumbled in his mind, and Noah gradually manages to get the idea across that "home" is now here, and forever. There is also an extended imagery of trees threaded through the story. Noah notes that trees, plentiful in his youth, are now dying out in many parts of Washington. In reaction, he cultivates a bonsai tree, and he regularly empties out the trash that collects in the wire frame around the tree in front of their apartment house.

Responsibility for Adam means that Maggie and Noah have to give up their own plans to travel in their retirement, but they do not hesitate. Despite the theme of "dreams denied," in many ways this is the book's most hopeful story.

The title *All Aunt Hagar's Children* is an expression that Jones heard his mother use. It refers to the biblical character Hagar, handmaiden to the patriarch Abraham's wife Sarah. According to legend, after conceiving a child by Abraham, Hagar was forced to flee. She became the ancestral mother of the black race. Jones's vision of a black community, varied as it is but sharing a common heritage and moving to Washington, D.C., with some common dreams, draws on the legend's implications. Washington's African American population has always been a vital part of the capital's life. With Jones's stories, it becomes an essential part of the American literary tradition as well.

Emily Alward

Review Sources

The Atlantic Monthly 298, no. 4 (November, 2006): 125.
Black Issues Book Review 8, no. 5 (September/October, 2006): 44.
Booklist 102, no. 21 (July 1, 2006): 7.
Crisis 113, no. 5 (September/October, 2006): 45.
Essence 37, no. 6 (October, 2006): 102.
Kirkus Reviews 74, no. 13 (July 1, 2006): 650.
The New York Times 155 (August 31, 2006): E1-E4.
The New York Times Book Review 155 (August 27, 2006): 12-13.
Publishers Weekly 253, no. 25 (June 19, 2006): 37.

"ALL GOVERNMENTS LIE!"
The Life and Times of Rebel Journalist I. F. Stone

Author: Myra MacPherson (1935-   )
Publisher: Scribner (New York). Illustrated. 576 pp.
  $35.00
Type of work: Biography and current affairs
Time: 1907-1989
Locale: Haddonfield, New Jersey; Philadelphia; and New
  York

*This biography of Stone is intermixed with descriptions
of the political climates that he lived through and comparisons of those eras with the current one*

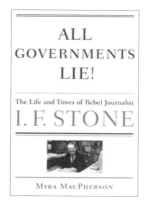

Principal personages:
> ISADOR FEINSTEIN STONE, a famed liberal
>   journalist
> J. DAVID STERN, a newspaper publisher and Stone's long-time boss and
>   friend
> WALTER LIPPMANN, a columnist

Izzy Feinstein grew up admiring the muckrakers of the early twentieth century,
and then he himself became one of the best of them. Quotations from him are often as
applicable now as they were when he uttered them. He is now better known as I. F.
Stone, the name he and his family legally adopted late in 1937 when Izzy was thirty
years old and fascism looked like the face of the future. There was Adolf Hitler's
spread through Europe and the Stalin-Hitler pact, German Bundists in America, and
the Spanish Civil War. Izzy told his brother Lou that opposing fascism was of extreme
importance "and that there was a tendency, when you had a writer by the name of
Feinstein, to discount whatever he wrote because he was Jewish." Although he had
written articles for various magazines and political journals, the public had little reason to notice the name change.

Paying attention to what Stone had to say helped twentieth century readers gain a
greater perspective of how their world was changing. Myra MacPherson, herself a
long-time reporter of the Washington scene, is one such person. Her admiration for
Stone is clear throughout *"All Governments Lie!": The Life and Times of Rebel Journalist I. F. Stone* as is her general agreement with his political leanings.

At thirty, Izzy had already spent nearly half of his life as a chief editorial writer for
major metropolitan newspapers. At the early age of fourteen he had already been a
publisher, with his four-page *The Progress* discussing not high school issues, but
world affairs. Later he told friends, "I started as a publisher and worked my way
down."

When Izzy was sixteen, publisher J. David Stern of the *Philadelphia Record* hired
him as a local correspondent. Soon he was writing editorials for the *Record*. In 1931

Myra MacPherson has also written She Came to Live Out Loud *(1999), about dealing with the universality of grief;* Long Time Passing *(1984), about the Vietnam War; and* The Power Lovers *(1975), about politicians and their marriages. She has written for* The Washington Post, The New York Times, *and numerous magazines.*

he became the youngest chief editorial writer of a major American newspaper. In 1933 when Stern bought *The New York Post*, he brought Izzy along. This was well before the era of newspaper consolidation, and the *Post* was one of sixteen papers in New York City—all with conservative editorial bents. Stern and Feinstein turned the *Post* into the first liberal voice in New York City.

In 1940 another liberal voice emerged when Ralph Ingersoll created the *PM* tabloid, and Stone was welcomed there. More than ten thousand reporters applied to write for *PM*. One of the lucky two hundred hired, Stone exposed the profiteering of United States oil companies selling oil to Hitler's Germany in 1941 and other corporate dealings with the Axis. He railed at Secretary of State Cordell Hull for supporting the Vichy government of Nazi-occupied France. After Stone wrote about the Civil Service Commission "victimizing" suspected liberals in the government, the commission revised its regulations to protect them.

PM did not survive the nation's turn to the right after World War II, and Stone signed on with the new *Daily Compass*, which MacPherson calls "the last fling in New York leftist newspapers." That paper did not last long either. When it folded in 1952, Stone started *I. F. Stone's Weekly*. He produced it for nineteen years, when ill health caused him to shut it down. He continued to write, however, until his death in 1989.

For any investigative journalist, Stone was an inspiration and a model to be learned from. He was, as MacPherson calls him, a "human fact-finding machine." Early in the New Deal of President Franklin D. Roosevelt, he taught himself constitutional law so he could read and understand Supreme Court decisions. Invited to a dinner with three famous legal scholars, he "boned up for that dinner as if I was boning up for an examination" and proceeded to astonish the lawyers with his knowledge. When he was nearly seventy, he learned to read ancient Greek so he could experience Homer, Sappho, and Plato in the original language. He then went on to write a successful book, *The Trial of Socrates* (1988).

Even as a child, he loved reading classic literature. He read André Gide, Honoré de Balzac, and Gustave Flaubert. He devoured Edward Gibbon's six-volume *The History of the Decline and Fall of the Roman Empire* (1776-1788). When imperious department store heiress Jill Lit Stern came into Feinstein's Dry Goods Emporium, young Izzy was entranced by a book instead of tending the store. Miffed at his indifference to serving her, she asked, "*What* are you reading?" His withering reply was "Spinoza." Subsequent conversation made him her protégé and lifelong friend and got him introduced to her publisher husband.

All this scholarship ability paid off not just in knowledge, but in methodology. He could read documents that other journalists had skimmed and find juicy tidbits worthy of exposing to the world. Aside from being a tireless researcher, he had the knack of getting past perceived wisdom to take a fresh look at information sources that others would pass by as old hat or common knowledge.

MacPherson notes that although Stone was an opinion columnist, he insisted on backing everything up with facts. Journalists should not be mere stenographers, he felt; they need to report the news behind official statements. When an official says something important, that is news; if he is lying, that is also news.

He also insisted on remaining aloof from the official sources that some journalists prefer to fawn over. "You cannot get intimate with officials and maintain your independence," he told fellow columnist and Stone biographer Andrew Patner, "They'll use you."

One disappointment in this book is the unprofessional index. It is incomplete and, in places, difficult to use. Some insignificant mentions are indexed, while some important concepts are not; for instance, the American Socialist Party was started just a few years before Stone's birth, and its charismatic leader Eugene Debs was one of young Izzy's heroes. When Izzy was twelve Debs was sentenced to ten years in prison just for making an antiwar speech, and this helped to rouse Izzy's radical spirit. That sentencing is also the focus of MacPherson's discussion of how the United States government acted to stifle free speech and socialist dissent, with complete disregard for the Constitution. The index contains no listing under "Socialist Party" although it does have a string of eight undifferentiated references under "American Socialist Party." This discussion is buried in a string of eighteen undifferentiated references under "free speech." Numerous index entries combine a few subentries with long strings of undifferentiated references; for instance, "Cold War" has twenty-two of the latter and three subentries.

As a sort of subplot, MacPherson frequently contrasts Stone with famed Washington columnist and fellow Jew Walter Lippmann because these two men took such different approaches to journalism. Lippmann prided himself on being friends with presidents and kings. When he visited Paris, his mail was forwarded in care of French military leader and statesman Charles de Gaulle. Although he advised younger colleagues to remain detached, he was "more engaged with more presidents from [Woodrow] Wilson to Lyndon Johnson than *anybody* in the press!" according to *New York Times* journalist James (Scotty) Reston.

Far from being a darling of the governmental elite, Stone was the victim of smear campaigns and was the subject of a huge Federal Bureau of Investigation (FBI) file. He was one of few journalists who dared to ridicule FBI director J. Edgar Hoover at the height of his power, calling him a "glorified Dick Tracy." He knew that Hoover would retaliate, and indeed the FBI bugged his telephone, picked through his garbage, and noted the cigars he bought and the letters he wrote to his hearing-aid company. MacPherson tried for years to obtain the FBI file on Stone, and eventually received about five thousand pages of them. Even then much information was redacted or simply missing from the files.

The National Press Club once blackballed Stone after he invited an African American man to lunch there in 1941, during the Jim Crow era. Only in 1981 did a younger generation of National Press Club members honor him. Lippmann, though, was proudly a member of the Cosmos Club, which refused membership to women and African Americans and had tacit quotas for Jews. Lippmann also supported various right-wing causes, such as the 1938 Southern filibuster against a federal antilynching bill. In 1957, however, he praised President Dwight D. Eisenhower for sending federal troops to desegregate schools during the violent times in 1957 in Little Rock, Arkansas.

Lippmann, regarded by some as the United States' most influential journalist, showed no concern in the early 1930's as Hitler climbed to power. Hitler was "Europe's problem," he wrote. Stone, meanwhile, read Hitler's *Mein Kampf* (1925-1926) and predicted in the *Philadelphia Record* that "the shifty-eyed little Austrian paperhanger" would become chancellor of the Reich. In 1933 Stone predicted that ignoring the Hitler menace would result in war. Not until 1938 did Lippmann take up that problem, recommending a solution to the "overpopulation" problem in Europe: shipping all the Jews to Africa. He called Hitler statesmanlike and civilized.

Later, the *Record* (with Stone as chief editor) carried another insensitive Lippmann column with a disclaimer that referred to him as "one of America's foremost publicists" and one whose ideas "often disagree with" *Record* policies. Even as World War II went on and the death camps became known, Lippmann wrote nothing about them. While Stone frantically urged relaxation of United States immigration policies to admit more Jewish refugees, Lippmann opposed the quota change.

MacPherson says that the two men symbolized a schism among Jews of the time, with Lippmann and Stone coming "from opposite sides of the ghetto." The one wore expensive suits to Harvard and cultivated a "disinterested, elevated, and cool style." The other "was red-hot, passionate, and spoke for the masses." There was never any shortening or nickname for "Walter," but everyone from Einstein to elevator operators called Isador "Izzy."

J. Edmund Rush

Review Sources

Booklist 103, no. 2 (September 15, 2006): 8.
The Boston Globe, October 15, 2006, p. E6.
Columbia Journalism Review 45, no. 3 (September/October, 2006): 59-61.
Kirkus Reviews 74, no. 13 (July 1, 2006): 667.
Library Journal 131, no. 12 (July 1, 2006): 88.
Los Angeles Times, October 18, 2006, p. E1.
Mother Jones 31, no. 5 (September/October, 2006): 100.
The Nation 283, no. 8 (September 18, 2006): 15.
The New York Times Book Review 156 (October 15, 2006): 6, 25.
Publishers Weekly 253, no. 23 (June 5, 2006): 48.

ALL WILL BE WELL

Author: John McGahern (1934-2006)
First published: Memoir, 2005, in Great Britain
Publisher: Alfred A. Knopf (New York). 289 pp. $25.00
Type of work: Memoir
Time: The 1940's and 1950's
Locale: County Leitrim, Ireland

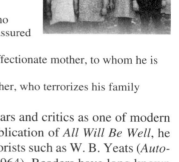

Seventy-one-year-old McGahern reminisces about his childhood in rural west Ireland, recalling his life with a doting mother, insensitive father, and six siblings

Principal personages:
SEAN MCGAHERN, a sensitive boy who matures into an independent, self-assured writer
SUSAN MCGAHERN, Sean's serene, affectionate mother, to whom he is devoted
FRANK MCGAHERN, Sean's brutal father, who terrorizes his family

John McGahern has long been regarded by scholars and critics as one of modern Ireland's most important novelists, and with the publication of *All Will Be Well,* he enters the august company of other major Irish memoirists such as W. B. Yeats (*Autobiography,* 1938) and Seán O'Faoláin (*Vive Moi!,* 1964). Readers have long known that events from McGahern's life—the death of his mother and abusiveness of his father—have provided raw material for his fiction, but this book reveals that the connection between life and fiction is even more profound.

McGahern recounts his growing up in the shadows of the Iron Mountains in rural County Leitrim, a region so poor and backward there are few radios and no indoor plumbing or central heating. Yet to a small boy, in the company of the mother he adores, such an otherwise unprepossessing place becomes wondrous and paradisal, and he recalls especially strolls along the country lanes, "There was a drinking pool for horses along the way, gates to houses, and the banks were covered with all kinds of wild flowers and vetches and wild strawberries. My mother named these flowers for me as we walked, and sometimes we stopped and picked them for the jamjars."

Anything that threatens his pastoral idyll—school, an impatient priest, his obdurate father—is a source of distraction or pain. McGahern describes in detail the dynamics of a profoundly dysfunctional family, with parents living apart, the father residing in the local police barracks and occasionally visiting his growing family, while continually complaining that his wife's relatives disrupt their lives. Through a series of parental letters, the reader sees portraits of a remarkable, unfailingly patient and faithful wife and an insinuating, domineering autocrat. Caught in the middle are McGahern and his sisters and brother.

When his mother contracts breast cancer and moves to Dublin for treatment, the

∽

John McGahern's first novel, The Barracks *(1963), brought him instant attention. He continued to teach primary school until he was fired for writing* The Dark *(1965), which was banned by the Catholic Church. His novel* Amongst Women *(1990) was short-listed for the Booker Prize and filmed as a BBC television drama. In 2002, he published his sixth novel,* By the Lake. *He died in 2006 of colon cancer.*

∽

young McGahern is confused and lost, only to be elated when she returns and resumes her job as a teacher. When she relapses and eventually dies, the boy is devastated. The second half of the memoir reviews his years with his unpredictable father until he wins a scholarship at a teaching college, moves away to Dublin, and forever limits his contact with his father.

The first half of the narrative is nothing less than an affectionate paean to the mother who refuses corporal punishment for her pupils and children and who forever attempts to protect her loved ones from the casual violence of her husband. McGahern praises her practicality, cheerfulness in the face of endless adversity, and unflagging ability to support and encourage others, family, friends and neighbors. The woman also has a vein of iron, rejecting her husband's proposal of marriage for years and insisting on the purchase of a cottage he opposes.

A deeply spiritual woman, her greatest ambition is that her son become a priest and say his first Mass in her presence. The boy positively thrives under her love and attention, and when she asks who he loves most, expecting him to answer God and the Virgin Mary, he always responds, "'You, Mother.'" What the boy knows of eternity comes not through his religious training but from her: "Our heaven was here in Aughawillan. With her our world was without end." She faced death stoically, genuinely believing it is God's will, telling her son she is needed in Heaven, while the young Sean reflects that "the Lord has many servants, and I had but the one beloved."

The portrait of his father, dramatically antithetical to that of the mother, is of a man who insists the world match his mercurial moods and whose religiosity is a showy formalism. The boy is as much repulsed as he is fascinated by Frank McGahern: "I knew him better than any living person, and yet I never felt I understood him, so changeable was he, so violent, so self-absorbed, so many-faced. If it is impossible to know oneself, since we cannot see ourselves as we are seen, then it may be almost as difficult to understand those close to us, whether that closeness be of enmity or love or their fluctuating tides."

The senior McGahern makes his children feel that are burdens, yet repeatedly enlists them in schemes to make money, forcing them to cut peat or knock on neighbors' doors to sell potatoes. He repeatedly beats each of them, to the point that one of the girls is so profoundly traumatized that she is forced to stay in a hospital for two months. When his wife lies dying, he refuses to visit her, only to appear at her cottage and move all of her furniture, except that in the room where she expires, and carts it and the children off to the barracks. After her death he refuses to allow the family to attend the funeral, and then, within a few months, begins a campaign to court her sister as a future bride. He forces his sons to sleep in his bed, where he fondles them each night.

McGahern concludes that his father was happiest while a soldier in the Irish Republican Army during the Anglo-Irish conflict, yet the man refuses to disclose much about his past and is pathologically secretive. The same person who has a will to dominate others and who is proud of his position as a police officer is also a pathetic example of the colonized subaltern who hates his own people and admires Protestants. "He considered them superior in every way to the general run of his fellow Catholics, less devious, morally more correct, more honest, better mannered, and much more abstemious."

The vision of a domineering patriarch is mirrored in McGahern's impressions of the Catholic Church in Ireland. Although he thrives under the tutelage of the Christian Brothers while in high school, McGahern's contact with village priests is less than salutary. When his father and he have one of their few pleasant adventures, they stop in a adjoining parish for Mass, where the priest grabs Sean by the ear and insists he stay the afternoon for catechism; this ends only when his father threatens violence. On another occasion a priest interrupts the church service to chastise the boy for fidgeting. McGahern also describes the visits of a traveling order that inflicts its version of doctrine on the village: "Every few years Redemptorists came to the village like a small band of strolling players and thundered hell and damnation from the pulpit. . . . The Redemptorists were brought in to purify through terror, and were appreciated like horror movies."

When the writer's second novel is banned, he is dismissed from his teaching position because of the Church's overwhelming power to hire and fire teachers. When McGahern protests the unfairness of the job action, he is informed that

> "If it was just the auld book, maybe—maybe—we might have been able to do something for you, but with marrying this foreign woman you have turned yourself into a hopeless case entirely. . . . And what anyhow entered your head to go and marry this foreign woman when there are hundred and hundreds of thousands of Irish girls going around with their tongues out for a husband?"

In essence, McGahern's infractions amount to subverting the authority of an institution more powerful and capricious than his father.

The memoir also provides an occasionally revealing glimpse of Ireland in the middle decades of the twentieth century. On one hand, this is an intensely provincial country struggling to establish a postcolonial identity in an atmosphere that simply replicates colonial repression. When the Irish constitution was written, the Catholic Church was given privileged status as the official church of the state, and McGahern notes the collusion of the Church and state had "brought about an Irish society that was childish, repressive and sectarian." At school, children were punished if they did not advance in their compulsory Irish language classes. Writing a banned book was less offensive than selling the same work, and expressions of true individuality were regarded as threats to the status quo. The lesson, McGahern concludes, was rigid conformity, and everywhere he turned that lesson was reinforced.

On the other hand, his Ireland, an Ireland that had vanished by the end of the twentieth century thanks to increased economic opportunities and greater secularization, was something to be cherished. Here neighbors and extended family members love and aid one another, and ancient customs die hard. For instance, when the local butcher learns that McGahern is a published author, he asks him to intercede in a private quarrel by creating an unflattering portrait of an adversary, as the original Gaelic poets once did. Material privation is seen as a means by which fundamental values remain intact, and after having been separated from his homeland for years, all the author wants is to return and take up residence in his former hometown.

Although this is McGahern's only work of nonfiction, it bears many hallmarks of a well-wrought novel. Some critics have lamented the work's seeming formlessness and lack of clear chapter or division breaks. Such criticisms are simply misguided. The narrative does, in fact, have a definite sense of form, moving chronologically from childhood to maturity. Indeed, far more attention is given to the writer's childhood, the period he clearly sees as the most crucial in shaping the man and artist he would become. His teaching and writing careers are passed over in only a few pages and treated rather cursorily. For example, no mention is made of his own illness with colon cancer, first discovered in 2002, from which he died four years later.

The absence of conventional chapters actually emphasizes the seamless, fluid workings of memory, which is as much McGahern's subject as the lives he so meticulously records. He frequently prefaces or interrupts a memory or observation with phrases of uncertainty, such as "I must have been extraordinarily happy," suggesting that this is not the stuff of research and proof but deep, sometimes elusive feeling. Thus the memoir reads like a reverie, with thoughts and events flowing into one another.

The loose structure can also be seen as the writer's resistance to all forces of conformity, whether intellectual, religious, or literary, and his artistic and experiential credo can be summed up as "the belief that the best of life is lived quietly, where nothing happens but our calm journey through the day, where change is imperceptible and the precious life is everything." The memoir is additionally organized around intricate image patterns of light and dark, with his mother associated with the sun and warm illumination and his father with darkness and inwardness.

The title of the American edition comes from an empty pontification in one of his father's letters, which McGahern ironically turns into a testament that life itself can transcend all that would wound and diminish the individual. The book ends where it begins, with a tribute to the writer's mother. After all the pain and abuse his father inflicted, McGahern nurses no grievances but thinks of his mother, "When I reflect on those rare moments when I stumble without warning into the extraordinary sense of security, that deep peace, I know that consciously and unconsciously she has been with me all my life." *All Will Be Well* is a beautiful epitaph to a life well lived.

David W. Madden

Review Sources

The Boston Globe, April 16, 2006, p. D7.
The Guardian, April 7, 2006, p. 23.

Kirkus Reviews 73, no. 24 (December 15, 2005): 1313.
New Statesman, September 19, 2005, p. 52.
The New York Review of Books 53, no. 5 (March 23, 2006): 32-34.
The New York Times 155 (February 18, 2006): B19.
The New York Times Book Review 155 (February 26, 2006): 21.
Publishers Weekly 252, no. 47 (November 28, 2005): 34.
The Spectator, September 17, 2005, pp. 47-48.
The Times Literary Supplement, October 28, 2005, p. 26.

THE AMALGAMATION POLKA

Author: Stephen Wright (1946-   )
Publisher: Alfred A. Knopf (New York). 323 pp. $24.95
Type of work: Novel
Time: 1844 to the 1860's
Locale: Upstate New York and South Carolina

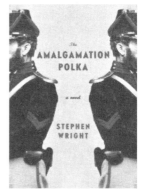

In Wright's experimental nonlinear work, young Liberty Fish vows to find his abusive Southern slave-owning grandparents to deepen his understanding of the "slavocracy" that divided his family and drove his abolitionist mother to the north

Principal characters:
> LIBERTY FISH, a young Northerner of mid-
> nineteenth century America
> THATCHER FISH, his father
> ROXANA MAURY FISH, his mother
> AROLINE FISH, his aunt
> EUCLID, a one-eyed former slave and Liberty's childhood friend and
> teacher
> MA'AM L'ORANGE, Liberty's teacher
> ARTHUR FIFE, Liberty's childhood friend, a pirate and hermit
> CAPTAIN ERASTUS WHELKINTON, captain of *The Croesus*, which
> Thatcher and Liberty ride upstream
> DR. FITZGIBBON, local dentist who performs sideshow tooth extractions
> COLONEL FOGGBOTTOM, tonic salesman
> ASA MAURY, Roxana Fish's father
> IDA MAURY, Liberty's grandmother
> DIETY, the Maury family's abused slave and cook
> PHINEAS FOWLER, Liberty's childhood playmate and fellow soldier
> MRS. SARAH POPPER, Southern woman whose plantation is raided by
> Yankee troops
> ELLSBERRY SIMMS, Southern hermit who claims his Georgian homestead
> as Northern
> CAPTAIN WALLACE, captain of the *Cavalier*, which Asa and Liberty
> board to the Bahamas
> THE FRIPPS, fellow Southerners taking the *Cavalier* to escape the Union
> army

With *The Amalgamation Polka*, Stephen Wright has transformed the historical novel genre into an experimental, postmodern art form. Taking risks throughout the book, Wright creates Liberty Fish's family, who have been torn apart by slavery and the "slavocracy." His mother, Roxana, comes from violent and cruel Southern cotton plantation owners. His father, Thatcher, comes from Northern textile merchants who, while not slave owners themselves, profited from the slave labor of the South. Liberty's parents rebelled against their parents and the way of life that provided them a comfortable existence to ensure that their son know only a life of freedom for all. Yet it is his parents' beliefs about freedom and equality, a divisive ideology he is too young to understand, that cause Liberty to be ridiculed and shunned by his peers and adults.

In a postmodern fashion, Wright jumps from era to era and character to character within Liberty's young life, creating a nonlinear format that grants the author artistic freedom and the reader an enjoyable and cerebral experience. Filled with minor yet memorable cameos, the novel constantly changes location and dialect as new characters introduce diverse settings and colloquialisms. In that regard, Wright has written a novel not simply about the Civil War but also about America and the characters and cultures that make up its madness on the whole.

~

Stephen Wright's other novels are Meditations in Green *(1983),* M31: A Family Romance *(1988), and* Going Native *(1994). He has taught at Princeton, Brown, and the New School in New York City and has received the Maxwell Perkins Prize, the Guggenheim Fellowship, the Whiting Writers' Award, and the Lannan Literary Award.*

~

The first section of the book begins with Liberty's birth in the fall of 1844, where it is established that the Fishes are liberal Northern abolitionists who lecture on the evils of slavery and help runaway slaves make their escape by allowing their house to serve as a stop on the Underground Railroad. As a result, Liberty's childhood is filled with unexplained guests who disappear as quickly and silently as they arrived. The reader experiences Liberty's upbringing through a series of chapters, each a self-contained short story of an adventure and life-changing moment for Liberty. His experiences include being stoned by boys whose parents support slavery, being taught by the eccentric Ma'am L'Orange, and becoming a pirate who roams secret passageways with the hermit Arthur Fife.

Wright continues his carnival of characters and locations as Liberty and his father board Captain Erastus Whelkinton's *The Croesus* for a trip through the Erie Canal toward Niagara Falls. The journey turns into a sort of rite of passage as Liberty experiences such oddities as witnessing Dr. Fitzgibbon's sideshow tooth extractions, which may be viewed for fifty cents, and Colonel Foggbottom peddling his miracle tonic; catching illegal and unwelcome glances at women's undergarments; and, at his father's prodding, pretending to be deaf and mute in front of the proper Thornes. The trip also offers heated and hate- filled conversations by antiabolitionists and some dangerously close calls as he and Thatcher express their opinions against slavery.

It is upon his return home that Liberty is personally struck by the emotional impact of slavery. He spies his mother reading a letter that emotionally debilitates her. His father explains that the letter is a hate-filled message from her plantation home, and he shares Roxana's background with Liberty. Once he realizes where she came from and how upsetting her past is to her, Liberty takes it upon himself to protect his mother and hides every letter that is ever received from Redemption Plantation.

The novel advances to Liberty's late teen years and the raging Civil War. Despite protests from their families, Liberty and his childhood friend Phineas Fowler join the army at age sixteen and go off to war. As Liberty leaves his home, his mother—whom, unbeknownst to him, he is seeing for the last time—begs him not to "play the hero for anyone. There will be more than enough fools scrambling for that position and you will, no doubt, witness what becomes of them." In the grisly yet humorous Antietam battle scene, Liberty is faced with death and human destruction at every turn. He survives only by a series of mistakes, clumsiness, and luck.

Liberty receives a letter while on the battlefield informing him of his mother's death. She had received a letter from her parents blaming her for the war and destruction of the country. The letter so upset her that she took a carriage in a rash state and ran it off the road. Liberty vows to find her Southern family and let them know what their hatred has done. After a graphically and poetically described, particularly physically and mentally grueling battle, resulting in scores of dead, Liberty abandons his division in search of Redemption Plantation.

Liberty arrives at Redemption after meeting a variety of Southerners along his journey, including Mrs. Sarah Popper, who avows, "this horrible, evil war, it's never going to end . . . . Even after it's over it will continue to go on without the flags and the trumpets and the armies." He also meets the Southerner Ellsberry Simms, a self-appointed Yankee who has declared his land property of the North. Upon his arrival at Redemption Plantation, the stories Liberty heard of his relatives come vividly back to him, and he wonders, "Was it possible . . . to be visited for even a mercifully brief instant by a piercing nostalgia for a past one had never personally experienced?" as he realizes nothing could have prepared him for his relatives.

While searching for his grandfather, Liberty encounters two slaves who appear to have had their flesh partially eaten away as if by acid. Liberty asks what has occurred, and they explain that they were part of "the doctor's" experiments. Perplexed and horrified, Liberty continues his search, which leads him to an old shed from which he hears activity. Inside he finds his grandfather, who appears to be a mad eugenics scientist. When Liberty asks if he is Asa Maury, his grandfather replies, "What's in a name?" thus beginning a long semantics battle. Asa quickly shares his life's work with Liberty: changing African Americans into white people, for he believes he "can end the curse of color by eliminating color entirely." He takes Liberty to a makeshift maternity ward where he displays his accomplishments: mulattoes, in whose breeding Asa has personally taken part. Liberty is struck by his grandfather's contradictory lifestyle and states that he feels "obliged to point out the curious irony that you [Asa], an unapologetic, antiabolitionist soul stealer, working alone in secret, have surpassed every other member of this tormented family, including us Northern agitators, in the pursuit of amalgamation. You not only promote intimate relations between the races, you actively practice it," a revelation that is lost on Maury.

The insanity does not end with his grandfather, as Wright craftily adds more comedic relief to what is an extremely disturbing household. Liberty finds his grandmother to be a violent, mean-hearted hypochondriac. Ida Maury would just as soon slice a person's hand with a knife (which she does to her cook Diety for undercooking turnips) as she would shake it.

The Yankee army encroaches on Redemption as Asa is trying to force Liberty to participate in his breeding experiment, and the lunacy of the plantation inhabitants becomes startlingly apparent as they are under siege by the North. Ida insists on staying with the house as Asa pleads with her to flee. Unsuccessful, Asa loads Liberty and two slaves, Monday and Tempie, into a wagon to make their escape. Monday drives them to the harbor, where they talk their way onto the *Cavalier*, a ship headed for the Bahamas. Once aboard, the two meet Captain Wallace and fellow fleeing Southern gentry the Fripps, and Asa manages to offend the lot. His madness reaches new heights when he discovers Tempie, who has known only a life of misery, has hanged herself. Asa begins to lash out at everyone and ultimately attempts to commandeer the *Cavalier*. Liberty manages to trick Asa and rescues the captain and crew but cannot save Asa in his madness from jumping overboard to his watery grave.

Once the ship reaches port, Liberty begins his long journey home to upstate New York. He reaches his childhood home and finds his father overcome with joy upon his return. After a brief reunion with Liberty's aunt Aroline, Thatcher takes Liberty to visit his mother's tombstone. Liberty loses track of time as he sits alone at the grave with a deeper understanding and appreciation of the circumstances of his mother's upbringing that led to her escape from Redemption Plantation and her family. He is awoken from his meditative state by childhood friend, caregiver, and former slave Euclid, who consoles Liberty as he has Liberty's entire life. Liberty realizes that through the trauma of war and the internal strife within his family, "it's America . . . and you, whoever you are, will be all right. It's America, and everything was going to be fine."

The book's final lines sum up the theme of Wright's novel: in America, whatever type of odd character you may be, you will be all right and everything will be fine. *The Amalgamation Polka* serves as a historic melting pot, each chapter introducing diverse and interesting characters who together make up not only Wright's ambitious postmodern novel but also America itself. The eloquent speech that Wright bestows upon each character makes the novel a pleasure to read, and the novel's characters, with their bizarre quirks and adventures, make the book humorous and entertaining from start to finish.

Sara Vidar

Review Sources

America 194, no. 13 (April 10, 2006): 25-26.
Booklist 102, no. 8 (December 15, 2005): 25.
Esquire 145, no. 2 (February, 2006): 44.
Kirkus Reviews 73, no. 22 (November 15, 2005): 1211.
The New York Times 155 (February 14, 2006): E6-E8.
The New York Times Book Review 155 (February 19, 2006): 1-9.
Publishers Weekly 252, no. 46 (November 21, 2005): 26.
Review of Contemporary Fiction 26, no. 2 (Summer, 2006): 91-92.
The Times Literary Supplement, May 26, 2006, p. 22.

AMERICA AT THE CROSSROADS
Democracy, Power, and the Neoconservative Legacy

Author: Francis Fukuyama (1952-   )
Publisher: Yale University Press (New Haven, Conn.).
   226 pp. $25.00
Type of work: Current affairs
Time: The early twenty-first century
Locale: The United States and the world

In pursuit of a prudent and effectual approach to U.S. foreign policy, a prominent public intellectual distances himself and his ideas from his former "neoconservative" colleagues and the war in Iraq

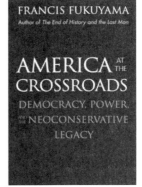

In *America at the Crossroads*, Francis Fukuyama reexamines issues raised in his best-known work, *The End of History and the Last Man* (1992), in light of developments in American foreign policy following the September 11, 2001, attacks on the United States by al-Qaeda. *The End of History and the Last Man* established Fukuyama as a noted "public intellectual," a term used to describe (more or less) scholarly authors who attempt to get their message out to significant portions of the general public as well as influential elites. Public intellectuals vary greatly both in the rigor of their work and in their political orientation. What they have in common is an interest in bringing the knowledge they have accumulated to bear upon crucial decisions made by those in power. In order to do this, public intellectuals must be able to render the findings of scholars, which tend to be esoteric and highly specialized, into accessible form for those who wield power. This, in turn, means melding disparate scholarly findings from a daunting variety of disciplines (and subdisciplines) into a coherent view of the world, one that gives fruitful guidance as public policies are formed and implemented.

In *The End of History and the Last Man*, Fukuyama proved himself to be profound and provocative. He demonstrated great breadth of learning, drawing on a rich array of scholarly works in political science, political theory, economics, sociology, and history. In addition, Fukuyama wrote with great clarity, addressing complex issues and carefully weighing alternative viewpoints without becoming obtuse or simplistically one-sided. Fukuyama's findings, like those of other public intellectuals, were controversial. According to Fukuyama, the end of the "Cold War" signaled the long-term historical triumph of liberal democracy over alternative political visions stemming from "the left" (such as socialism and communism) as well as from "the right" (such as theocratic and other forms of authoritarianism). It follows that the goal of American foreign policy should be to do everything possible to facilitate this development globally, leading to a tolerant, enlightened, and peaceful future. Fukuyama's projection of the future put him squarely into the camp of "neoconservative" thinkers who, seeing no other path to national or global stability, wished to use American power to transform the world. Some of these neoconservatives would ride into power with President George W. Bush in 2000, coming to be seen as prime architects of both the Bush administration's War on Terror and the war in Iraq.

In *America at the Crossroads*, Fukuyama passes judgment on the performance of neoconservative policy makers as well as the overall Bush administration, finding both to be severely wanting. Putting it most bluntly, Fukuyama suggests that neoconservatives not only failed in their goal of uniting wisdom and power but actually set the cause back by launching an ultimately self-defeating war in Iraq, one that he argues is based on a deeply flawed principle of "preventive war." Because neoconservatism now is closely identified with the latter principle (and other related misconceptions), Fukuyama sheds the neoconservative label and proclaims the need for a new and better approach to American foreign policy, which he calls "realistic Wilsonianism."

Francis Fukuyama is professor of international political economy and director of the International Development Program at The Johns Hopkins University. Fukuyama's previous books include The End of History and the Last Man *(1992),* Trust: The Social Virtues and the Creation of Prosperity *(1995),* State-Building: Governance and World Order in the Twenty-first Century *(2004), and* Nation-Building Beyond Afghanistan and Iraq *(2006).*

Derived from a series of lectures Fukuyama delivered at Yale University in April of 2005, *America at the Crossroads* opens with a brief preface in which the author outlines his previous self-identification as a neoconservative and points to the start of the war in Iraq as a juncture at which he and other neoconservatives parted ways. In his opinion, the Bush administration pursued a disastrous policy in Iraq. Fukuyama's goal in this book is to explain where the Bush administration went wrong, why, and what can be done to avoid similar mistakes in the future.

In the first chapter, "Principles and Prudence," Fukuyama begins by summarizing the responses of the Bush administration to September 11, which he breaks down as follows: first, passage of the Patriot Act and establishment of the Department of Homeland Security (in order to be better prepared to ward off such attacks); second, the war in Afghanistan (in order to hit back at the perpetrators of the September 11 attacks); third, articulation of the Bush doctrine defending the use of preventive war (presented as a proactive step to reduce the chances of future attacks); and fourth, implementation of preventive war in Iraq.

Fukuyama believes that the third and fourth responses presented above have been badly misguided. The doctrine of preventive war (as opposed to that of preemptive strikes, where there is hard evidence of imminent attack) seeks to respond to long-term threats that do not easily yield to any precise analysis. As such, preventive war doctrine is both dangerous, as it is no great trick for agile minds to conjure up future threats, and damaging to the global image of the United States, because it makes American use of power appear to be arbitrary and heavy-handed. The war in Iraq is an unfortunate example.

Fukuyama also isolates a number of additional, related errors. He thinks that the

Bush administration erred in assessing the overall threat of global terrorism. On the other hand, it was overly optimistic about the likelihood of world public opinion supporting the war in Iraq and the challenges involved with the reconstruction of Iraq once Saddam Hussein had been removed from power. Fukuyama then moves on to look for an approach to public policy that might help to avoid such mistakes in the future. He outlines four existing approaches. Realism, Jacksonian nationalism, and liberal idealism are presented as flawed relics of the past, with neoconservatism presented as a corrective to all three. Fukuyama makes it clear that a new approach is now needed, one he dubs realistic Wilsonianism.

In the second chapter, "The Neoconservative Legacy," Fukuyama presents a detailed account of the neoconservative movement over the last fifty years, pointing out its intellectual roots, diversity (for example, not all neoconservatives have been Republicans), and four basic principles with regard to foreign policy. These principles are a belief that the nature of foreign political regimes matters and that U.S. foreign policy should reflect liberal-democratic values, a concordant belief that American power has been and should continue to be used as a positive force in the world, distrust of social engineering, and skepticism with regard to the efficacy of international law and institutions in providing global security or justice. It is important to note that these principles remain at the core of Fukuyama's concept of realistic Wilsonianism.

It is, in reality, only the last six years or so of neoconservatism in practice that Fukuyama is abandoning. In analyzing this divergence, Fukuyama accepts an analogy offered by Ken Jowitt, a writer who has likened Fukuyama to Karl Marx, and the neoconservative activists who helped to engineer the war in Iraq to Vladimir Ilich Lenin. While Marx maximized the importance of objective conditions in determining historical progress (thus limiting the need for violence), Lenin championed the revolutionary will, which would rip results from history whether it was ready or not. Fukuyama makes clear his disdain for Leninism, old and new. On the other hand, he does not blame neoconservatives alone for the missteps of the Bush administration, suggesting that Bush came to wear the neoconservative mantle late in the game, after he could no longer claim to have been an insightful realist about weapons of mass destruction and Hussein's alleged connection with al-Qaeda.

In the third chapter, "Threat, Risk, and Preventive War," Fukuyama revisits the problems incumbent with the notion of preventive war in the absence of a clear standard of acceptable and unacceptable risks.

Chapter 4, "American Exceptionalism and International Legitimacy," examines the problem of getting the American people and world public opinion to accept the special role of the United States in spurring global progress. Though most Americans are open to the notion that the United States is a unique and morally superior agent in world affairs, they wish to tend their own gardens rather than looking for foreign adventures. On the other hand, global public opinion is distrustful of American power, particularly when it is exercised unilaterally. This situation calls for diplomatic skills and pliability that the Bush administration was unable or unwilling to muster.

In chapter 5, "Social Engineering and the Problem of Development," Fukuyama points out the failure of Bush administration neoconservatives to heed one of their own cardinal principles, the distrust of social engineering. In blithely taking on the task of reconstructing Iraq, the Bush administration ignored most of what is known about political development: for example, that nation and state building must precede the formation of democratic institutions and that the successful transition to liberal democracy requires a strong internal movement for such change—something that is far from spontaneous or universal. Had these truths been at the forefront, the United States would have been far more sober-minded about taking responsibility for building a new and improved Iraq. On the other hand, Fukuyama does believe that the United States can use its influence to make conditions better for positive change, including the spread of liberal democracy in the long run. These changes cannot be forced from without, however.

In chapter 6, "Rethinking Institutions for World Order," Fukuyama remains skeptical about the United Nations but still sees the necessity of striking a balance between going it alone and working with allies. In addition, Fukuyama is optimistic about the natural growth of international cooperation and institutions below the level of chief executives. In short, he suggests the need for and appropriateness of a more flexible and friendlier view of international institutions. In addition, he argues for the emphasis on "soft" over "hard" applications of U.S. power (that is, voluntary over coercive and peaceful over violent) and, accordingly, for refinement of U.S. "soft" assets and capabilities comparable to the state of military readiness.

Chapter 7, "A New Kind of Foreign Policy," presents a brief conclusion, arguing for realistic Wilsonianism, which, by now, has been revealed to combine the essentials of traditional neoconservatism (minus the mistakes of Bush neoconservatives) with a deeper understanding of the dynamics of regime change, a somewhat more open-minded view toward international law and institutions, and an accent on peaceful methods of making U.S. influence felt.

America at the Crossroads has drawn considerable attention from reviewers and commentators. Critics of the war in Iraq and the Bush administration have lauded the book for what they see as further validation of their positions. Given the decline in popular support for the war at the time of publication, the bulk of responses have tended to accept Fukuyama's premise that the war in Iraq has been a major misstep. There has also been a more hesitant reaction to the particulars of his diagnosis and the remedy he proposes. In particular, Fukuyama's preservation of the husk of neoconservativism in his "realistic-Wilsonianism" has kept some reviewers from fully embracing his analysis. On the other side are those who, like President Bush and his advisers, treat the war in Iraq as an unavoidable work in progress, one that will be positively resolved if Americans stay the course. This perspective has been less visible among reviews of Fukuyama's book. Indeed, the response of the war's avid supporters seems to have been to ignore *America at the Crossroads*.

America at the Crossroads presents a compelling critique of neoconservatives, the Bush administration, and the war in Iraq. It also offers hope for the future. There is a sizable audience for both the bad and the good news Fukuyama has to offer.

Ira Smolensky

Review Sources

The Chronicle of Higher Education 52, no. 32 (April 14, 2006): B15.
The Economist 378 (March 18, 2006): 79-80.
The National Interest, no. 84 (Summer, 2006): 123-130.
National Review 58, no. 7 (April 24, 2006): 54-56.
New Statesman 135 (March 27, 2006): 48-49.
The New York Times Book Review 155 (March 26, 2006): 1-9.
Washington Monthly 38, no. 5 (May, 2006): 44-45.

AMERICAN MOVIE CRITICS
An Anthology from the Silents Until Now

Editor: Phillip Lopate (1943-   )
Publisher: The Library of America (New York). 720 pp.
    $40.00
Type of work: Film
Time: 1915-2005
Locale: Hollywood and New York

Lopate's anthology is aptly named: It is about "movies," not "film" or "cinema," terms that suggest a rarefied kind of motion picture, and the "critics" are, for the most part, reviewers whose work has appeared in journals and magazines accessible in style and content to the general public

In his introduction to *American Movie Critics: An Anthology from the Silents Until Now*, Phillip Lopate praises film criticism as an art and states that he included writers who wrote "elegant, eloquent" prose. With the exception of Hugo Münsterberg's oft-anthologized but turgid social science prose and Bell Hooks's "cool" poststructuralist essay on *Pulp Fiction* (1994), he has succeeded. Lopate has not included essays containing the kind of jargon usually found in film schools and "academic" journals written by the few for the few either. It is an eminently readable collection of reviews and essays.

Lopate attempts "to uncover the narrative trajectory by which the field [film criticism] groped its way from the province of hobbyists and amateurs to become a legitimate profession." The book, which is divided chronologically into four parts, begins with the silent era and the transition to sound, and the reviewers are, for the most part, amateurs whose expertise is in other fields. Poet Carl Sandburg reviewed movies for the *Chicago Daily News* in addition to his other work for the newspaper, and his reviews are little more than plot summaries and gushings about film stars. Vachel Lindsay, also an outstanding poet, offers more content and insight, particularly in his analysis of Douglas Fairbanks. H. D. (Hilda Doolittle), the third poet included, was a regular film reviewer, and her response to Carl Dreyer's *The Passion of Joan of Arc* (1928) is a well-written, sensitive, and subjective account of her experience as she watched the film. Edmund Wilson and H. L. Mencken, famed for their literary and social criticism, are also included—but probably because Lopate is determined to demonstrate just how widespread the interest in film was at this time. William Troy and, particularly, Cecilia Ager, who were primarily film reviewers, are the pleasant surprises in the first section of the book. Ager's reviews, ironic and scathingly mocking, focus on clothes and actresses and address questions about women's roles in films. In a comment that could have been made by Dorothy Parker, she writes, "Oftentimes nice girls are that way because their figures don't give them any choice."

~

After receiving degrees from Columbia University and the Union Graduate School, Phillip Lopate taught in the New York City public schools. He has written novels, poetry, film reviews, and essays. The recipient of a Guggenheim Fellowship, he has the Adams Chair at Hofstra University, where he is a professor of English.

~

"Masters and Moonlighters," the second part, covers the late 1930's and the 1940's and includes two of the five film critics Lopate considers the best in their field, Otis Ferguson and James Agee, both of whom died relatively early in their careers. Lopate gives Ferguson, whom he describes as "the first working film critic who put everything together," thirty of the seventy pages devoted to this period. Ferguson praises Mae West's films and declares that she presents "the most honest and outrageous and lovable vulgarity that ever was seen on the screen" and writes that attempts to censor her are futile unless the censors "lock her in a plaster cast." He also praises Jimmy Cagney and Humphrey Bogart, but he is less enthusiastic about Katharine Hepburn, whom he describes as having never been "more than a couple of mannerisms and a hank of hair to start with." He is equally hard on Orson Welles and his widely acclaimed *Citizen Kane* (1941), often described as one of the best films ever made, in part because of its technical innovations. According to Ferguson, *Citizen Kane* represents "no advance in screen technique at all," and he goes on to state that the film "makes me doubt that Orson Welles really wants to make pictures." (Incidentally, one of the strengths of Lopate's book is the inclusion of negative contemporary responses to films that have since become "classics.")

Unfortunately, James Agee, perhaps the best writer among the film critics, receives only half the space accorded to Ferguson. Himself a novelist (*A Death in the Family*, 1957) and a screenwriter (*The Night of the Hunter*, 1955, and *The African Queen*, 1951), Agee is particularly adept at discussing novel-to-film adaptations and the scripts of films. His reviews of *The Lost Weekend* (1945) and *The Story of G. I. Joe* (1945) are models of insight and clarity. The remainder of part 2 consists of Siegfried Kracauer's remarks on the German psyche and the German film industry, Robert Warshow's seminal work "The Gangster as Tragic Hero," one of the best essays on genre films, and Melvin B. Tolson's remarkable essay on the racism implicit and explicit in *Gone with the Wind* (1939).

Part 3, encompassing the 1950's through the 1970's, is titled "The Golden Age of Movie Criticism" and contains the other three of Lopate's five best film critics: Manny Farber, Pauline Kael, and Andrew Sarris. Farber's essay on "underground films" champions masculine action movies (regarded as "B" movies) and their directors (Howard Hawks, Samuel Fuller, and Robert Aldrich); his reappraisal has stood the test of time. Rather than focus on individual films, Farber devoted himself to film trends and distinctions between what he considered "termite" and "masterpiece" art. This emphasis on non-Establishment films pervades part 3. Parker Tyler writes about Andy Warhol's *Blue Movie* (1969) and also provides a homoerotic reading of *Double Indemnity* (1944), a film usually considered part of the hard-boiled film noir genre.

Sarris's essays also involve reappraisal, in this case of writer/director Billy Wilder, whom he admits he "grossly underrated" when he compiled his list of "pantheon" directors in his *The American Cinema* (1968). Sarris also reevaluates John Wayne, seen by many as a star rather than an actor, who in his later films comes to embody the "displaced loner," especially in *The Searchers* (1956). Kael, the only one of the three "greats" known primarily as a reviewer of individual films, is represented by a longish essay on "Trash, Art, and the Movies," in which she makes the same case for "trash" as Farber makes for "underground" and "termite" movies. In the three reviews included she demonstrates her fondness for Jean-Luc Godard, praises Robert Altman for the "European" quality of his *McCabe and Mrs. Miller* (1971), and lauds the achievement of Barbra Streisand in *Funny Girl* (1968).

A few of the nineteen other critics in part 3 address genre films: Paul Schrader, a writer and director in the film noir tradition, delineates the stylistics and cultural contexts in which film noir flourished in the 1940's; Susan Sontag defines the science-fiction film; Brendan Gill discusses "blue" movies; and Molly Haskell, associated with women's films, focuses on actors Joan Crawford and Katharine Hepburn before concluding her longish essay with an analysis of feminism in *Lost in Translation* (2003). John Simon, perhaps the most caustic and most entertaining if infuriating film reviewer of the period, discusses Peter Bogdanovich's *The Last Picture Show* (1971) in terms of its roots in the work of other directors and finds Bogdanovich wanting as a film critic ("he was never a serious critic, only an auteurist hero-worshiper") and as a director whose derivativeness causes the film to rise only "to the heights of pastiche." On the other hand, he finds Roman Polanski's *Chinatown* (1974) not only a throwback to earlier genre movies but also a skillful updating of those films.

Stanley Kauffmann, another outstanding film reviewer, receives, like Simon, little space, especially in light of the several Vincent Canby reviews Lopate includes. Other film reviewers receiving short shrift are Dwight MacDonald, whose critique of *82* (2000) is a model for the film review; Arlene Croce, whose contrast between the grace of Fred Astaire (and Ginger Rogers) and the athleticism of Gene Kelly is invaluable; and Barbara Deming, who in the course of a review of *Casablanca* (1942) points out that movies reflect "our anxieties rather than our inner strengths" and calls attention to the unique and complex nature of Rick's actions in a love story set in wartime. Two other essays deserve notice: James Baldwin's comments on *Lady Sings the Blues* (1972), which he finds is related to "the black American experience in about the same way, and to the same extent that Princess Grace Kelly is related to the Irish potato famine: by courtesy," and Eugene Archer's discussion of Charlie Chaplin's *A King in New York* (1957) in terms of Chaplin's problems with McCarthyism.

Unlike the first three sections, the last features no more than three reviews per critic, with the result that readers may be frustrated by the lack of coverage of a particular writer. However, the last section contains some of the most interesting reviews and essays. While not a film scholar, Stanley Cavell's discussion of *The Lady Eve* (1941) in relation to William Shakespeare's battle of the sexes comedies provides new insights into that film. David Denby covers Frederic Wiseman's documentaries *Central Park* (1989) and *High School* (1968), and Carrie Rickey provides a fresh perspective on male-bonding films. Two of the best writers represented are David

Thomson, who discusses the work of Cary Grant and Howard Hawks, and Paul Rudnick, who, using the persona of Libby Gelman-Waxner, skewers *Dances with Wolves* (1990) in "A Boy Named Sioux." While some older films (*Imitation of Life*, 1934, and *Trouble in Paradise*, 1932) are rescued from critical obscurity by James Harvey and Roger Ebert, respectively, the trend is toward negative reviews of films, particularly successful Hollywood features. Kenneth Turan bucks popular taste in resinking the *Titanic* (1997), Stuart Klawans pans *Gladiator* (2000), and A. O. Scott describes *Sideways* (2004) as "the most overrated film of the year." While praising Spike Lee's *Do the Right Thing* (1989) as "an antiracist taboo buster," Armond White faults Lee's *Malcolm X* (1992) as a "scandalous sellout" made palatable for white audiences.

In his introduction, which serves as a history of both film and film criticism, Lopate maintains that here is "no hard line" between film reviewing and film criticism. This claim is true if film theory is excluded from film criticism, which is wisely ignored in his book, especially since the criterion for inclusion was the way the essays were written. Moreover, the choices were made on a personal basis, with his agreement or lack thereof a factor in the decision. For the most part, his book contains well-written essays by established film critics whose names are familiar to filmgoers, but he also includes writers such as Barbara Deming and Cecilia Ager, both of whom are relatively unknown. Although Lopate's critics are preponderantly East Coast, he has also reprinted the work of a few minority critics, although some of these selections (James Baldwin and Ralph Ellison) are far more noted for their fiction than their film criticism.

The same holds true for white writers, such as Mencken, Sandberg, and H. D., who were perhaps included because of their stature or because there were relatively few serious, full-time critics in the earliest period. While it is possible to quibble about selections (such as the omission of Rex Reed), Lopate has produced a book of well-written and insightful essays about film. There is nothing like it available in a single volume. The only significant problem with the book is its lack of an index. While Lopate acknowledges that several directors and actors appear in several essays (Chaplin appears a dozen times), there is no convenient way of accessing diverse comments on individual people.

Thomas L. Erskine

Review Sources

The Atlantic Monthly 297, no. 2 (March, 2006): 113-116.
Cineaste 31, no. 4 (Fall, 2006): 89-90.
Film Comment 42, no. 2 (March/April, 2006): 76.
National Review 58, no. 12 (July 3, 2006): 52-53.
The New York Times 155 (June 4, 2006): 36-39.
Variety 403, no. 9 (July 24, 2006): 39.

AMERICAN VERTIGO
Traveling America in the Footsteps of Tocqueville

Author: Bernard-Henri Lévy (1949-   )
Translated from the French by Charlotte Mandell
Publisher: Random House (New York). 309 pp. $24.95
Type of work: Current affairs, sociology, and travel
Time: 2004-2005
Locale: The United States

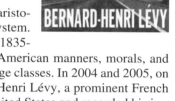

Lévy updates the American journey of Tocqueville and raises some fresh concerns about the viability of the nation's basic values in the face of terrorist threats

In 1831-1832, Alexis de Tocqueville, a French aristocrat, toured the United States to report on its prison system. Out of this sojourn was born *Democracy in America* (1835-1840), Tocqueville's classic two-volume study on American manners, morals, and politics, which is still required reading in many college classes. In 2004 and 2005, on a commission from *The Atlantic Monthly*, Bernard-Henri Lévy, a prominent French culture critic, made a similar journey through the United States and recorded his impressions in *American Vertigo: Traveling America in the Footsteps of Tocqueville*.

Notwithstanding the title, Lévy attempts to discourage readers from comparing his book with Tocqueville's, which he admits he barely knew before his journey to America. It is impossible to avoid the comparison, however, given the subtitle and the assignment to retrace Tocqueville's footsteps. Still, there are marked differences. Tocqueville's book investigates a form of government that was innovative in his time, the American democracy, and the citizens who lived under this system. Lévy engages in episodic meandering and produces a travelogue whose form owes as much to Beat author Jack Kerouac as to Tocqueville, though in the end Lévy does deliver some forceful analysis of what he has observed.

There are marked similarities between the two books as well. Tocqueville's *Democracy in America* offered high praise for the democratic experiment, along with earnest warnings about the tyranny of the majority. In the same vein, Lévy's *American Vertigo* energetically defends the United States against "this sinister and French and largely European passion that is known as anti-Americanism," though he himself deplores those Americans whom he views as obsessed with consumerism and "drugged on patriotism" and despises the country's leader, President George W. Bush—Lévy calls him "something of a child."

Thanks to Lévy's international celebrity status (*Vanity Fair* called him "Superman and prophet") and the prestige of *The Atlantic*, he had entrée to prominent Americans in many fields: luminaries of the Democratic and Republican presidential nominating conventions of 2004; Hollywood figures such as Warren Beatty, Sharon Stone, and Woody Allen; and world-class authors Norman Mailer and James Ellroy. Lévy also

∾

Bernard-Henri Lévy's films include the documentaries Bosna! *(1994) and* Un Jour dans la mort de Sarajevo *(1993; A Day in the Death of Sarajevo). His books include* La Barbarie à visage humain *(1977;* Barbarism with a Human Face, *1979) and* Qui a tué Daniel Pearl? *(2003;* Who Killed Daniel Pearl?, *2003).*

∾

talked with many ordinary people, including sex workers and lap dancers, college students, and Pentecostal Christians. Like Tocqueville, Lévy visited several U.S. prisons and made his own trenchant assessment. Indeed, the commentary on the American penal system is among the strongest points of Lévy's otherwise uneven literary performance.

American Vertigo comprises two parts. The first two-thirds (titled "Le Voyage en Amérique") is devoted to the author's 15,000-mile journey through the Pacific Northwest, the Midwest, the South, and New England. This section, though rich in detail, reads less like a polished narrative than like a set of travel notes. On one hand, it contains not a few overblown descriptions, with some sentences running an entire page long. On the other hand, this section contains many incomplete sentences—"Baffling story. Singular situation. Nothing in common, in fact, with the fundamentalists. . . . Yearning for secession"—giving his delivery a staccato feel. Because of these stylistic traits, something about the sights and sounds he is observing becomes lost in translation.

Similarly, several of the interviews with prominent people can be frustratingly sketchy, although Lévy is seldom shy about disclosing his opinion of his interviewees. Richard Perle, the neoconservative philosopher and former government official, surprises Lévy with a strong critique of the Bush administration's conduct of the war in Iraq. For a while it looks as though Perle and Lévy—who openly detests neoconservatism, Bush, and the Iraq War—might find some common ground. In the end, Lévy remarks to the reader, "I tell myself that this man [Perle] and I surely don't belong to the same family. This is where I stand."

Lévy is an incorrigible name-dropper, flaunting his connections to famous people across the political, ideological, intellectual, and artistic spectra. Reporting on his conversations with Americans, he even works in their probable affinities with long-dead European philosophers: neoconservative William Kristol is a "Platonist bereft of the ideals"; philosopher Francis Fukuyama is "a Hegelian"; Morris Dees has a "nightly Pascalian revelation in an American airport." In his most incongruous and obscure reference of this type, Lévy calls the United States itself "a country where Hollywood has supplanted Hegel."

Another oddity in this section of the book is that, after extremely brief encounters with American citizens, Lévy sometimes boasts implausible flashes of insight. Outside Montgomery, Alabama, for example, he listens to a young man "tell me, as if he were justifying himself, about his attachment to this region," and he describes for the reader his sudden realization that the young man has "all the reflexes of Southern culture" and the "studied nonchalance . . . so characteristic of the region."

At times, Lévy engages in idle speculation that is downright absurd, as when he imagines "a chorus of furies" denouncing a presidential run by Senator Hillary

Rodham Clinton. Referring to the affair between President Bill Clinton and White House intern Monica Lewinsky in the Oval Office, he imagines these "furies" demanding to know if American voters would "want a female president who, instead of having a head for business, would only be obsessed . . . with what happened there— no, here, beneath this desk, on this corner of the carpet?"

Lévy professes a great admiration for the United States while generally deploring what he calls "the thick ignorance of European anti-Americanism," but, paradoxically, as a traveler he often zeroes in on the sordid side of the American lifestyle. As if determined to report on the culture's most sensational aspects, he seeks out strip clubs and bordellos, churches obsessed with marketing their faith, and a Texas gun show where Nazi paraphernalia are sold. One is compelled to ask how the over-representation of the sleazy side in his itinerary validates Lévy's claims of affection for America. The most likely answer is in his perception of the United States as a nation of contradictions—hardly an original assessment among visiting foreign pundits. In fact, if there is anything unique about this appraisal, it lies in Lévy's colorful and ambivalent exposition: "this magnificent, mad country, laboratory of the best and the worst, greedy and modest, . . . puritan and outrageous, facing toward the future and yet obsessed with its memories."

Toward the close of the first section, beginning to sum up his impressions, Lévy forsakes ambivalence to make some very straightforward—and sound—observations, especially about the U.S. prison system. He visited five prisons on the U.S. mainland, expecting them to provide "answers about the nature of the society that has bred" this system. When he comes to a sixth prison, Guantánamo Bay, he perceives that this complex, though isolated from the mainland and reserved for suspected "enemy combatants" who are denied ordinary rights, is nevertheless a microcosm of the entire system: He argues that Guantánamo, "as we'll see, is not unconnected to the other five [prisons]" and that its "most revolting and unacceptable characteristics can be quite directly explained by the general regime of detention that I was able to observe elsewhere and that says much, unfortunately, about contemporary America." Lévy enumerates the direct resemblances between Guantánamo and the other five prisons: its "undertow of violence" as on Rikers Island, its "policy of isolation and banishment" as at Alcatraz, the "absence of perspective and of horizon" as at Angola, and so on. Later, to sum up Guantánamo, he adds, "What you are bound to recognize is that it is a miniature, a condensation, of the entire American prison system."

The book's final one-third, presenting Lévy's ruminations ("Reflections") about where he has been and what he has seen, is more cogent than the first part. It is in this section, too, that Lévy addresses crucial questions about the country that preoccupy him. Acknowledging his debt to Tocqueville ("Was there a better guide to lead me . . . ?"), he adds, "But the questions, for the main part, are my own."

One of his crucial questions is, "What does it mean to be an American?" He elaborates: "Who are we? What remains of the old British Puritan credo that spawned our fine, noble nation?" Lévy points out that Americans, even the poor, "continue to be viewed as an elite people, sure of itself and domineering." He also contends, however, that "no large modern nation today is as uncertain as this one, less sure of what it is becoming, less confident of the very values, that is to say, the myths, that founded it." The "vertigo" of the book's title comes from Tocqueville's contemporary Benjamin Constant, who applied the term to the Reign of Terror following the French Revolution. According to Lévy, Tocqueville expected to uncover and explain the same phenomenon in the United States. Indeed, Lévy believes that he himself has done so.

As Lévy sees it, this "vertigo" is indicated by a wide variety of disparate symptoms, including an obsession with the "crumbling" past and what he calls "A social obesity. An economic, financial, and political obesity." In effect, Lévy is arguing that many American institutions have grown larger than is necessary to deliver their required services.

Nevertheless, in a supremely hopeful mood, he concludes that "in the sheer fact of being American, or at least expressing yourself like one and wanting to be one, there is a gentleness, a lightness, an element of freedom and, in a word, of civilization, that makes this country one of the few countries in the world where, despite everything, you can still breathe freely today."

Another of Lévy's crucial questions concerns "American Ideology and the Question of Terrorism (the Current State of Affairs)." Here, he begins with a roundup of philosophical views about the worldwide terrorist threat. One theory, he reports, contends that terrorism is doomed to be ineffectual because the liberal democracy it seeks to destroy has already prevailed on the world stage. In short, this is an "End of History" although "there will, of course, be other events." A contrasting theory holds that "History is not over" and "These few years devoid of significant wars, which have allowed you to launch your neo-Hegelian gospel, were merely a 'holiday from history.'"

By itself, this abstract theorizing might simply enrage anyone who lost a loved one in the attacks of September 11, 2001, or in the war in Iraq. Lévy's main point here, however, is closer to the mark. He is concerned with whether the effort by neoconservatives in the Bush administration to justify interrogation by torture and other degrading practices in military prisons and the abrogation of privacy and other civil rights due to the current obsession with security will lead to the ultimate destruction of basic American values:

> Of course the American antitotalitarian left is outraged by Guantánamo. . . . I heard . . . the question of pure principle that emerges from the very existence of such a lawless zone. . . . Either we believe that America is at war—in which case these detainees must benefit from prisoner-of-war status and from the protections accorded by the Geneva Convention. Or we subscribe to . . . police treatment—and then all the rights normally granted to prisoners by common law need to be recognized. But . . . this is a scandal . . . and I have not heard it denounced clearly enough. How many people are there in the United States who have spoken out loudly and firmly . . . ?

Lévy cautions against "those jihadists about whom you can't say enough times that they aim to destroy what is best about the United States: freedom of speech and thought, equality, women's rights, democracy." With the word "jihadists," perhaps Lévy is not referring solely to radical Muslims.

Lévy admits, however, that despite misgivings about contemporary America, he continues to admire the nation's ideals and to believe that it is viable. He concludes his book with this buoyant declaration: "the America of Washington, Roosevelt, and Kennedy is indeed finely equipped to deal with the great intellectual and moral reform that will allow it, without renouncing any fraction of its identity, to revive its reasons for believing in itself."

Thomas Rankin

Review Sources

American Spectator 39, no. 3 (April, 2006): 60-62.
Booklist 102, no. 9/10 (January 1, 2006): 48.
Commentary 121, no. 4 (April, 2006): 74-76.
Kirkus Reviews 73, no. 23 (December 1, 2005): 1267.
Library Journal 131, no. 3 (February 15, 2006): 136.
National Review 58, no. 2 (February 13, 2006): 49-50.
The New York Times 155 (February 4, 2006): B17.
The New York Times Book Review 155 (January 29, 2006): 1-9.
Publishers Weekly 252, no. 49 (December 12, 2005): 52.

AMONG THE DEAD CITIES
The History and Moral Legacy of the WWII Bombing
of Civilians in Germany and Japan

Author: A. C. Grayling (1949-   )
Publisher: Walker (New York). 361 pp. $25.95
Type of work: History
Time: 1942-1945
Locale: Germany and Japan

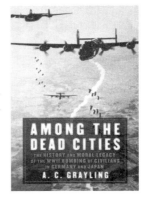

Grayling presents a critical examination of the morality of the area bombing of German and Japanese cities by British and American forces during World War II

Principal personages:
ARTHUR HARRIS, head of Royal Air Force
  (RAF) Bomber Command, 1942-1946
CHARLES PORTAL, head of RAF Bomber
  Command, 1940, and British Chief of
  Air Staff, 1940-1945
WINSTON CHURCHILL, prime minister of the United Kingdom, 1940-
  1945, 1951-1955
VERA BRITTAIN, British author, pacifist, and critic of area bombing dur-
  ing World War II
HENRY MORGENTHAU II, U.S. Secretary of the Treasury, 1934-1945
HENRY STIMSON, U.S. Secretary of War, 1940-1945
CURTIS E. LeMAY, American general in charge of incendiary attacks on
  Japanese cities, 1944-1945
JOSEPH GOEBBELS, German minister for Public Enlightenment and Pro-
  paganda, 1933-1945
ALBERT SPEER, German minister of Armaments and War Production,
  1942-1945

After World War II, the Allies held trials for war crimes and crimes against humanity in both Germany and Japan. The most famous of those were held at Nuremberg and resulted in the death penalty for German leaders such as Herman Göring, General Wilhelm Keitel, and Joachim von Ribbentrop and in lengthy prison terms for others, such as Rudolf Hess and Albert Speer. In Japan in similar trials seven Japanese leaders were sentenced to death and sixteen to life imprisonment. The war crimes included violations of the accepted procedures of war and mistreatment of civilians. Crimes against humanity included, among other offenses, large-scale atrocities. Only the actions of individuals in the defeated nations were subject to trial. As victors, the Allies were the judges, not the judged.

In *Among the Dead Cities: The History and Moral Legacy of the WWII Bombing of Civilians in Germany and Japan*, University of London philosopher A. C. Grayling seeks to judge the actions of the victors by the standards of the war crime trials. Spe-

cifically, he asks whether the bombing of
German and Japanese cities and civilian populations by British and American forces were
war crimes. In doing this, Grayling denies
that he is equating the Allied bombing with
Nazi genocide. He recognizes that the Holocaust was an unparalleled crime but asserts
that an evil cannot be made good by the existence of a still greater evil.

~

*A. C. Grayling is Professor of
Philosophy at Birkbeck, University of
London. Many of his writings are in
philosophy, mainly on the theory of
knowledge, metaphysics, and logic. He
has also written widely on current
events and contributes to the* Financial
Times *and* The Economist.

~

Grayling makes a great deal of the distinc-
tion between area bombing, the targeting of
an entire locality and its inhabitants, and pre-
cision bombing, the targeting of particular military objectives. Although his concern
is with both British and American activities in Germany and Japan, he concentrates
on the British bombing of German cities and focuses specifically on Operation Gomorrah, the attacks on Hamburg in late July and early August, 1943. At the end of the
book, he explains the use of the Hamburg bombing as his principal example. Most of
the cities attacked by Allied bombers were hit in 1944 and 1945, after it was already
clear that the Allies would win the war. Moreover, the bombs that fell on Hamburg
were of the fairly conventional incendiary and high-explosive type, unlike the atomic
variety that devastated Hiroshima and Nagasaki. Thus, according to Grayling, if the
destruction at Hamburg can be judged a crime, the aerial assaults on other cities were
even more clearly criminal.

Grayling begins by telling the story of how the bomber war developed. At the beginning of the war, the British opposed the bombing of civilian populations. However, after the 1940 German Luftwaffe bombing of the Dutch city of Rotterdam, the
British government, under the leadership of Prime Minister Winston Churchill, authorized the bombing of German territory, although official policy continued to be to
avoid unnecessary harm to civilians. Under the leadership of Sir Charles Portal, first
as head of Bomber Command and then as Chief of Air Staff, though, the Royal Air
Force (RAF) began to become less careful about avoiding collateral damage to civilian populations while hitting military targets and then shifted toward targeting the civilians themselves. Portal's successor as head of Bomber Command, Sir Arthur Harris, strongly advocated area bombing of civilian inhabitants of Germany, even when
there were few distinct military targets, in order to spread terror and undermine German morale. With Operation Gomorrah, the strategy of area bombing was embraced
wholeheartedly.

The Americans had supported precision bombing as having greater military value
than area bombing. While they joined the British in bombing Hamburg and other cities, the RAF dropped most of the explosives. In Japan, though, the Americans were
the ones doing the bombing. This did not begin in earnest until late in the war, in 1945,
after American forces had taken the Mariana Islands and the resistance of Japanese
fighters had been reduced sufficiently to allow highly successful aerial attacks on Japanese cities. General Curtis E. LeMay devised the strategy of low-level attacks at

night by planes carrying loads of incendiary bombs that would lay waste to Japan's mainly wooden cities. The massive incendiary bombing gave way to the atomic bombs dropped on Hiroshima and Nagasaki, the last acts of the war.

After describing the general development of the bombing, Grayling turns to the experiences of those who were bombed. In his narration, these events come across as genuine atrocities. Survivors recalled their own sufferings and their horrific memories of people who were burned alive or driven insane. Those who were bombed did not, however, seem to suffer loss of morale, nor were German and Japanese war production apparently diminished by area bombing. Nazi propaganda minister Joseph Goebbels cited Allied bombing as proof that the Allies were aiming at the death and destruction of all Germans and as a reason that Germans should rally behind the Nazi government. Productions minister Albert Speer claimed, in lectures given after the war, that German war production had actually increased under the bombing.

From the experiences of the bombed, Grayling moves to the intentions and thoughts of those who planned area bombing. He details the historical emergence of bombing from the air and the arguments of its early advocates. He explores the possibility that the bombing of Germany may have been part of an effort to institute the plans of U.S. treasury secretary Henry Morgenthau, who advocated the postwar dismemberment and deindustrialization of Germany so that it would never be able to wage war again. Grayling also considers the possibility that atomic bombs were dropped on Japan to display American power to the Soviet Union and relates the high-level debates within the United States about whether atomic bombs should be dropped on cities. U.S. Secretary of War Henry Stimson was a key figure in questions about the fates of both Axis countries since Stimson opposed the Morgenthau Plan, argued against dropping the bombs in Japan, and managed to have the historic Japanese city of Kyoto withdrawn from the list of places to be destroyed. Ultimately, Grayling concludes, the bombing was driven less by explicit plans than by events and, particularly in Germany, by the autonomy of the Bomber Command, which became gradually dedicated to the destruction of Germany.

Grayling asks whether a condemnation of area bombing would be anachronistic because people today might see it as unnecessary while people in Britain and America during the war might have seen it as essential to their survival and victory. To answer this question, he turns to the writings of critics of the bombing policy during the war. The notable writer and pacifist Vera Brittain, in her book *Seed of Chaos* (1944), deplored her own country's policy of burning and exploding civilians.

Having looked at the bombing from these different angles, Grayling proceeds to consider it as a moral case. He argues both prosecution and defense. As prosecutor, he presents the case against area bombing. He uses the principles enunciated at the Nuremberg Trials to see how the Allies would have been judged if they had been the defendants. He concludes that although the Allies were certainly just in waging war, dropping incendiary bombs on civilian dwellings and intentionally causing death and suffering to noncombatants violated every principle of waging the war according to just means. As defense, Grayling looks at the justifications offered for the bombing. He cites the claim of Sir Arthur Harris that the bombing saved lives of Allied soldiers, a justification also commonly used by American defenders of the use of atomic bombs. Grayling responds, drawing on Vera Brittain, that one cannot justify saving soldiers' lives by sacrificing civilians. This would be morally equivalent to placing civilians in front of soldiers as a shield on the battlefield. He also maintains that it was unnecessary to win the war. Ultimately, Grayling is a far better prosecutor than a defense attorney, possibly because he had reached his decision at the first page of the book and the reader knows the outcome long before reaching the formal statement of the moral case.

Finally, Grayling renders his decision. Area bombing in Germany and Japan was not necessary, nor was it proportionate to the challenge faced by the Allies. It was a clear violation of humanitarian principles in law. It violated the moral standards of Western civilization. It was a crime.

Few readers will be taken in by Grayling's efforts at evenhandedness. The book is a condemnation offered in a tone of balanced reasoning, not a genuine weighing of justifications and moral problems of area bombing. It may be undermined somewhat by Grayling's recognition that the bombers were carried along by the unfolding of the war and the logic of events, rather than by their own long-term plans. There are also some issues Grayling does not seem to face entirely. While the Allies were clearly on the winning side by the time they began area bombing, it was still not clear when they would win and both soldiers and civilians would die as long as the war continued. Whether area bombing shortened the war is a much more difficult question to answer than whether it won the war. In addition, war production may have increased under bombing, but it could well have increased even more as Germany and Japan prepared a desperate fight to bring the war to a draw, without destruction across their urban areas. There is, finally, the issue of just what one should do with a moral judgment of historical events. The Nuremberg Trials and the war crimes trials in Japan were not held to decide on ethical problems in the abstract but to pass sentence on individuals widely believed to deserve punishment. Grayling is adamant that he does not mean to condemn the men who risked their lives carrying out the Allied bombing mission. This leaves one wondering how there can be a crime with no criminals. He does suggest that this sad history can be used as a way of guiding actions in the future. As Grayling points out repeatedly, though, the moral principles he uses to condemn the bombing were already recognized when the bombing occurred.

While many readers will struggle with these questions, Grayling has raised some important problems. Being on the side of right does not guarantee that all of one's actions will be right. The Germans and Japanese who suffered and died in horrible conditions were just as human and, more often than not, just as innocent as their British counterparts who died under German bombing. *Among the Dead Cities* is a book that is both important and troubling.

Carl L. Bankston III

Review Sources

America 195 (August 28-September 4, 2006): 27-30.
The Atlantic Monthly 297, no. 5 (June, 2006): 95-100.
Booklist 102, no. 7 (December 1, 2005): 16.
Kirkus Reviews 74, no. 1 (January 1, 2006): 27.
Publishers Weekly 252, no. 43 (October 31, 2005): 40.
School Library Journal 52, no. 7 (July, 2006): 134-135.
The Times Literary Supplement, April 28, 2006, p. 26.
Weekly Standard 11, no. 43 (July 31, 2006): 27-30.

ANNA OF ALL THE RUSSIAS
A Life of Anna Akhmatova

Author: Elaine Feinstein (1930-   )
First published: 2005, in Great Britain
Publisher: Alfred A. Knopf (New York). Illustrated. 331
    pp. $27.50
Type of work: Literary biography
Time: 1889-1966
Locale: Russia

*Feinstein traces the life of the great twentieth century
Russian poet, placing her within the context of her time and
showing how Akhmatova's work, while highly personal,
also came to express the feelings and experiences of a nation torn by revolution, terror, and war*

> *Principal personages:*
> ANNA ANDREEVNA AKHMATOVA, a poet
> NIKOLAY STEPANOVICH GUMILYOV, her first husband, a poet
> LEV NIKOLAEVICH GUMILYOV, her son
> OSIP MANDELSTAM, a poet
> OLGA A. GLEBOVA-SUDEIKINA, an actress
> VLADIMIR SHILEIKO, Anna's second husband, a scholar
> NIKOLAY PUNIN, Anna's long-time lover, an art historian

At the beginning of her great poem *Rekviem* (1963; *Requiem*, 1964), Anna Akhmatova wrote,

> In the terrible years of the Yezhov terror I spent seventeen months waiting in line outside
> the prison in Leningrad. . . . Standing behind was a young woman, with lips blue from
> the cold, who . . . asked me in a whisper (everyone whispered there), "Can you describe
> this?" And I said, "I can." Then something like a smile passed fleetingly over what had
> once been her face.

In *Requiem*, Akhmatova made good her word, becoming, as she said in that work, the
voice of a hundred million Russians enduring Stalin's reign of terror. In another of her
masterpieces, *Poema bez geroya* (1960; *A Poem Without a Hero*, 1973)—over which
she labored for more than twenty years, from 1940 to 1962—she would compose an
elegy for the beauty and the beautiful destroyed by revolution and two world wars.

Born in Bol'shoy Fontan, a small town near Odessa, on June 23, 1889, Anna
Andreevna Gorenko was the third child of naval engineer Andrey Gorenko and his
second wife, Inna. Anna grew up outside St. Petersburg at Tsarskoe Selo, where the
tsars had their summer palace. Her family was not literary: Anna recalled that there
was only one book of poetry in the house. Yet by the age of eleven she had begun to
write poems, and by thirteen she had read the French symbolists, who deeply influ-

~
*A poet and novelist as well as a
biographer, Elaine Feinstein has
written biographies of Alexander
Pushkin, Ted Hughes, and Marina
Tsvetaeva. She also has translated the
poetry of Tsvetaeva, Margarita Aliger,
Yunna Morits, and Bella Akmadulina.*
~

enced her early work. The family spent their summers in a dacha near the Black Sea. Anna told her parents that someday that house would bear a plaque stating that she had lived there. It does.

In her last year at the Fundukleyevskaya gymnasium in Kiev, Anna published her first poem, "On His Hand Are Many Shiny Rings" (1907), in the short-lived periodical *Sirius* edited by the poet Nikolay Stepanovich Gumilyov, who dedicated his second volume of poetry to her and who, after a long and tempestuous courtship that included at least two suicide attempts by him, married Anna on April 25, 1910. Because Anna's father objected to her publishing poetry under the family name, she adopted the nom de plume of a Tatar prince and descendant of Genghis Khan, Akhmat, who, she believed, was related to her through her mother.

Whatever passion Gumilyov and Akhmatova had for each other quickly evaporated. Both soon began to take lovers, and after the birth of Anna's only son, Lev, on October 1, 1912, they agreed to an open marriage, though Gumilyov's affairs depressed Anna. The year 1912 also saw the publication of her first volume of verse, *Vecher* (evening), containing forty-six poems, most of them about the pangs of love. Although she initially admired French and Russian symbolist poets—Alexander Blok and Innokenty Annensky served as early Russian models—she, along with Gumilyov and Osip Mandelstam, soon became a leading exponent of Acmeism. In *Anna of All The Russias*, Elaine Feinstein compares this movement to the contemporary imagism in its quest for clarity and precise imagery about specific experiences.

Her second volume, *Chetki*, meaning "beads" but usually translated as "rosary," appeared in 1914; its poems again largely concern lost love. "The Voice of Memory," for example, written in June, 1913, and subtitled "For O. A. Glebova-Sudeikina," recalls the suicide of Vsevolod Knyazev after he saw his lover coming home with another man. Sudeikina would reappear in *A Poem Without a Hero* as "Confusion Psyche" and "The Columbine of the 1910's." Akhmatova may herself have been in love with Sudeikina, just as later she had a passion for another actress, Faina Ranevskaya. Akhmatova had many lovers throughout her life, and they became subjects of her poems. The artist Boris Anrep, whom she met in early 1915, looms large in her verse of this period and, indeed, throughout her life. When Anrep fled to England, she accused him of deserting not only her but all of Russia. Her third volume of poetry, *Belaya staya* (1917; *The White Flock*, 1978), already reflects this fusion of the personal and the national that would mark so much of her later work.

After divorcing Gumilyov on August 8, 1918, Akhmatova married Vladimir Shileiko, a scholar of the ancient Middle East. The marriage was unhappy: Shileiko was a domestic tyrant who objected to his wife's writing. Depressed, Anna produced little work in 1919 and 1920. In 1921 she left her husband, whom she would divorce in 1926, for the composer Artur Lurye, who was living with Sudeikina. Feinstein carefully traces the complicated love lives of the Russian avant-garde, though the welter of names can at times prove overwhelming.

Anna began writing again, publishing *Anno Domini MCMXXI* in 1922. While some of its contents recall her earlier (and in the twenty-first century still much admired) poems about love, many describe the recent horrors of World War I, the Revolution, and the Civil War. In one of these pieces she describes a mother's grief at the death of her nineteen-year-old son. Another begins, "Everything is looted, spoiled, despoiled,/ Death flickering his black wing."

Like Anrep, Lurye emigrated. Even before he left Russia, Anna had taken a new lover, art historian Nikolay Nikolaevich Punin. Although Punin was married to the physician Anna Ahrens and had several other lovers, as did Anna, Anna sometimes referred to him as her third husband. In 1925 Anna moved into Punin's flat in the Sheremetev palace, where she would live most of her life. Punin slept with her in one room, while his wife slept in another. Later, Punin would move back with his wife, while Anna remained in the flat. Anna's relationship with Punin was tortuous, but he defended her work against a rising tide of hostile criticism from the Soviet regime.

In 1922 Trotsky attacked her poetry as irrelevant to the Revolution. Mikhail Kuzmin, once her friend, called her a relic in 1923. Gumilyov had been shot as an anti-Soviet conspirator in 1921, and after 1925 her poetry was not published in Russia for over a decade. Her son also suffered because of his family connections. Feinstein details the tragic rift that grew between Akhmatova and Lev, whom she deeply loved. He was repeatedly arrested in the 1930's and 1940's, tortured, and twice sent to Siberian labor camps for long periods. He believed that she should have done more to try to secure his release and that she should have written more to him and come to see him. She in turn believed that he was being punished because of her and that distancing herself from him might protect him from further suffering. It was while she was waiting to deliver a package to Lev in the Leningrad prison that the episode occurred that she described at the beginning of *Requiem*.

Her literary fortunes improved as World War II began. She was asked to prepare a selection of her poems for publication, and on January 5, 1940, she became a member of the Leningrad Writers' Union. The Moscow Writers' Union sent her 3,000 rubles, and she was granted a pension of 700 rubles a month. In April the periodical *Leningrad* published some of her poetry; this was the first time since 1925 that her work was officially sanctioned. Although the proposed volume of her poems was never published and the few copies printed were banned, Akhmatova began writing prolifically. On September 3, 1940, she started her "Northern Elegies," which would appear in "Sed'maia kniga" (the seventh book), never published as a separate volume. That fall she began *A Poem Without a Hero*. As she had done before, she memorized her verses, afraid to commit them to paper.

When the German army besieged Leningrad, Akhmatova, along with many other writers and artists, was evacuated to central Asia. On the plane she composed a love poem to her beleaguered city: "The birds of death are flying high./ Who now will rescue Leningrad?" In her Tashkent refuge Akhmatova worked on *A Poem Without a Hero*, and her later work often recalls her time there, as in "Tashkent Pages" (1959).

The siege of Leningrad ended in January, 1944; Akhmatova returned in June. Before the war, she had fallen in love with the physician Vladimir Garshin, who at the time was married. His wife died during the siege, and he asked Anna to marry him. By the time of her return, however, he had fallen in love with another doctor, Kapitolina Grigorievna Volkova, whom he married in 1945. Akhmatova removed his name from the dedication to part of *A Poem Without a Hero* and destroyed their correspondence.

On the night of November 15-16, 1945, Akhmatova received a visit from the Oxford scholar Isaiah Berlin, then attached to the British Embassy in Moscow. She would write various love poems to Berlin, who in turn secured for her an honorary doctorate from Oxford in 1965. She later claimed that this visit began the Cold War. Stalin certainly suspected Berlin of being a spy, and on August 9, 1946, Protokol 172 denounced her work. Not until Khrushchev criticized Stalin in 1956 (then dead three years) was she rehabilitated; when Berlin returned to see her that summer, she was too afraid to meet with him. Yet just hearing his voice on the telephone sparked "Shipovnik tsvetet," published in *Beg vremeni* (1965) and translated as "Sweetbriar in Blossom" in 1990, a cycle of poems that she dedicated to him.

In her final years she enjoyed immense popularity. Four major young Russian poets paid court to her: Joseph Brodsky, Anatoly Nayman, Yevgeny Rein, and Dmitri Bobyshev. All addressed poems to her, and she reciprocated. Her work returned to print; a 1960 edition had a print run of 1.7 million copies. She even was given a small dacha in Komarovo, the village where she would be buried. During these years she received many awards in Russia and abroad. After her death in 1966, UNESCO marked the centenary of her birth by declaring 1989 the Year of Anna Akhmatova.

A scholar of Alexander Pushkin's work, Akhmatova had observed that all the courtiers, ministers, and aristocrats who had persecuted and despised the poet during his life were to become merely names in the indexes to Pushkin's works. A similar fate awaited the Soviet apparatchiks who had denounced her, withdrawn her pension, and persecuted her son. Her small St. Petersburg apartment, now the Akhmatova Museum, is a site of pilgrimage for her many admirers, who memorize her poetry out of love as she had once done out of fear. That other great twentieth century Russian female poet, Marina Tsvetaeva, aptly named her Russia's literary ruler, "Anna of all the Russias." For as Akhmatova wrote in the epigraph to *Requiem*: "Not where the sky's dome enclosed a foreign space,/ Nor where foreign wings sheltered and reassured,/ But among my people I took up my place,/ There, where by an ill fate, my own people were."

Joseph Rosenblum

Review Sources

Booklist 102, no. 12 (February 15, 2006): 36.
Kirkus Reviews 74, no. 1 (January 1, 2006): 27.
London Review of Books, September 1, 2005, p. 13.

The Nation 283, no. 2 (July 10, 2006): 30-34.
The New Republic 234, no. 23 (June 19, 2006): 33-37.
The New York Review of Books 53, no. 11 (June 22, 2006): 40-42.
The New York Times Book Review 155 (March 19, 2006): 20.
Publishers Weekly 253, no. 1 (January 2, 2006): 46-47.
The Spectator 298 (July 2, 2005): 30-32.
The Times Literary Supplement, September 16, 2005, p. 13.

ARTHUR AND GEORGE

Author: Julian Barnes (1946-   )
First published: 2005, in Great Britain
Publisher: Alfred A. Knopf (New York). 388 pp. $25.00
Type of work: Novel
Time: 1859-1930
Locale: England, Scotland, Wales, Austria, Switzerland,
   Egypt, and South Africa

*   Looking for meaning beyond his work, a famous novel-*
ist tries to prove the innocence of a man falsely imprisoned

Principal characters:
        SIR ARTHUR CONAN DOYLE, a physician
          and novelist
        LOUISA "TOUIE" HAWKINS DOYLE, his first wife
        JEAN LECKIE DOYLE, his second wife
        MARY FOLEY DOYLE, his mother
        CHARLES ALTAMONT DOYLE, his father, an artist
        ALFRED WOOD, his secretary
        CONNIE DOYLE HORNUNG, his sister
        ERNEST WILLIAM HORNUNG, Connie's husband, a novelist
        GEORGE EDALJI, a lawyer
        THE REVEREND SHARPURJI EDALJI, George's father, a Church of En-
          gland vicar
        MAUD EDALJI, George's sister
        HORACE EDALJI, George's younger brother
        BRYAN CHARLES WALLER, Mary Doyle's lodger and lover
        CAPTAIN GEORGE AUGUSTUS ANSON, chief constable of Staffordshire
        INSPECTOR CAMPBELL, a Staffordshire police officer

    Best known for such postmodern novels of ideas as *Flaubert's Parrot* (1984), *A History of the World in Ten and One-Half Chapters* (1989), and *England, England* (1999), Julian Barnes makes a major departure with *Arthur and George.* Inspired by real events in Victorian and Edwardian England, the novel has a more linear narrative and more fully developed characters than is typical for Barnes. It does, however, re-semble his earlier works in looking at how individuals cope with the complexities of their times.

    Sharpurji Edalji is a Church of England vicar in Great Wyrley, Staffordshire. The Indian immigrant and his English wife have three children, George, Maud, and Hor-ace. After the Reverend Edalji fires a servant in 1893, the family receives a string of anonymous, threatening letters for two years. In 1903, the hate mail resumes, around the same time as a series of mutilations of farm animals. On the flimsiest of evidence, George, now a Birmingham lawyer and author of a popular book on the rights of railway passengers, is convicted of the crimes and sentenced to seven years in prison. Then, after serving three years, he is suddenly released. Freedom, however, is not enough, as he says: "I want my name back again. . . . To live a quiet, useful life. A normal life." He writes to Sir Arthur Conan Doyle, one of the most famous Englishmen in the world because of the popularity of his Sherlock Holmes stories. The outraged Arthur sets out to prove George's innocence.

In addition to alternating the stories of Arthur and George, Barnes draws sharp portraits of each and contrasts their quite different personalities. Though Arthur is the artist and George the attorney, George is the more contemplative one, living his life inwardly compared to Arthur's rambunctiousness. George, "acute at sensing the expectations of others," tries to accomplish what will please his family and more firmly establish him as an Englishman. Growing up in the vicarage, he models his behavior after his father's teachings. Though George outgrows his father's religion, he remains firmly grounded as a moral

Julian Barnes came to be regarded as an important novelist with Flaubert's Parrot *(1984), which received the Geoffrey Faber Memorial Prize and the Prix Medicis.* Metroland *(1980) won the Somerset Maugham Prize, and* Talking It Over *(1991) won the Prix Femina. Married to literary agent Pat Kavanagh, Barnes has also published crime novels as Dan Kavanagh.*

person who perceives the world as orderly and expects to see correct behavior rewarded and lawbreakers punished.

While George is passive, Arthur, who grows up reading about chivalric ideals, longs to right wrongs himself. Arthur must serve George's cause, less for the man himself than for the principles involved. Just as George fervently tries to believe that the truth will protect him, the adult Arthur sees the world in the clear, black-and-white terms exemplified by the adventure tales of his boyhood favorite, Captain Mayne Reid.

Arthur begins writing not only because of the failure of his medical practice but also to make up for his artist father's failures as a man and a husband. He writes stories to rescue his abandoned mother by describing the fictional rescue of others. Literary success, however, is not enough: "What did a knight errant do when he came home to a wife and two children in South Norwood?"

Arthur's belief in a chivalric code has a counterpoint in George's faith in the law, which gives order to his world. This faith makes the unfairness of his ordeal all the more painful. George's sense of fair play results in his refusal to accept the possibility that racial prejudice contributes to his dilemma. When he is told, as a boy, that he is "not a right sort," he pretends not to know what is meant.

Both characters long to believe in a world in which all "is clear and true and happy, as everything ought to be." Even in prison, George adapts, feeling "a sense of order that was almost edging towards contentment." George finds a similar peace in rules and routine as Arthur does in such rules-driven sports as cricket and golf. The two characters are also alike in having multiple selves. George is both the prisoner reconciled to his fate and the innocent victim longing for freedom, understanding how people go "mad from missing ordinary things." Arthur is a successful writer and loving husband and father who feels a deep incompleteness in his life.

Sexual mores are among the many topics Barnes examines in *Arthur and George*. When Bryan Charles Waller, the Doyle family lodger, inherits an estate in Yorkshire, Arthur's beloved Mam moves in with him, despite the fifteen-year difference in their ages. When Waller marries, the Mam moves to a cottage on his estate but continues their affair. Arthur's sex life ends when his consumptive wife, Touie, becomes an invalid. He falls in love with the young Jean Leckie, but his chivalric code will not allow him to consummate the relationship until almost a decade later, after Touie has died and he and Jean have married.

This repression, however, is partly responsible for his assistance to George. Arthur identifies with George because he feels imprisoned by his fame and by his inability to live openly with Jean. George longs for a normal, married life but never comes close, spending most of his adult life living with his sister. Arthur has experience with women but does not understand them: "Knowing women less, he is able to idolize them more." He is appalled when he ejaculates after kissing Jean for the first time: "What happened in that room must never happen again."

Barnes attacks hypocrisy through E. W. Hornung, Arthur's brother-in-law. Even though Arthur has allowed him to adapt his Sherlock Holmes character into Raffles, his gentleman burglar, Hornung refuses to acknowledge Jean and reprimands Arthur for his compromising behavior. Despite Arthur's love for Touie, Jean, the Mam, and his daughters, he is much more comfortable in the company of men. Barnes presents Arthur as the embodiment of both Victorian virtues and the limitations of his era.

Barnes does not attempt to explain Arthur's consuming interest, despite Jean's initial repugnance, in spiritualism. Medicine, literature, sports, and family life just do not provide enough diversions for the endlessly curious Arthur: "He could not ever quite shake off the feeling that all he had achieved was just a trivial and specious beginning; that he was made for something else." His faith in an afterlife provides solace that life itself is only the beginning.

George's persecution has a much more benign parallel in Arthur's inability to escape the shadow of Sherlock Holmes: "The fellow was rapidly turning into an old man of the sea, clinging round his neck." The great detective gives him fame and fortune, opens doors that would have been closed otherwise. Arthur meets H. G. Wells, dines with Oscar Wilde, and becomes friends with James M. Barrie and Jerome K. Jerome. However, he would rather concentrate on writing historical novels such as *Micah Clarke* (1889) and *The White Company* (1891), "which he had always known were the best of him." Even killing off Holmes is no solution, because reader demand and publisher pressure force Arthur to resuscitate his hero.

Unusual for Barnes, there is not much humor in *Arthur and George*, except for a few humorous moments courtesy of Arthur albatross. When someone suggests using bloodhounds to Inspector Campbell, the officer in charge of the mutilation investigation, he responds, "Mr. Holmes, they were the footprints of a gigantic hound!" There is also irony in Arthur employing Holmes's techniques to help George, enlisting his secretary, Alfred Wood, as his Dr. Watson. When Arthur identifies the real culprit, he is dismayed that the process has not been as dramatic as with Holmes: "It's not meant to happen by following simple steps. It's meant to seem utterly insoluble right up until the end." George is irritated that, in not acting in the orderly fashion the law demands, Arthur has contaminated the evidence against the felon: "Sir Arthur had been too influenced by his own creation." As a result, George finds himself permanently in a limbo where he is neither guilty nor innocent.

While Barnes is far from didactic, *Arthur and George* can be seen to address the historical mistrust of immigrants in Britain. He makes clear that the citizens of Great Wyrley have misgivings about more than just the Edalji family. They are anti-Irish and resent the police for enforcing laws with which they disagree. George is most annoyed by the refusal to recognize his nationality and professional status, especially by the police, one of whom says, "I found myself thinking at one point, if you shut your eyes, you'd think him an Englishman." George cannot even insist upon having his surname pronounced correctly by the authorities. The inherent racism in British society adds to the Kafkaesque nature of George's trial. Mutilations can continue after his arrest, others can confess, forensic and handwriting experts can lie. George finds "his character no longer of his own authorship but delineated by others."

While *Arthur and George* received mostly enthusiastic reviews and was considered a frontrunner for Britain's prestigious Booker Prize, some reviewers complained that the novel is too conventional. Compared with the postmodern brilliance of *Flaubert's Parrot*, it certainly is, yet Barnes, who could easily have repeated himself through using a self-conscious narrator, almost matches his achievement in the earlier novel with his in-depth look at the complexities and contradictions of his characters, even if they are finally not quite as compelling as Gustave Flaubert.

Both novels also have outstanding set pieces: the narrator's reflections on the infidelities of his wife, a modern Emma Bovary, in *Flaubert's Parrot* and George attending a massive séance in honor of the passing of his benefactor. George arrives as a skeptic and is horrified when the medium appears to be calling forth the spirit of his father. He undergoes an intensity of emotion unlike anything else he has experienced. Then his realization that the séance is, in fact, so much hocus-pocus tumbles him back into the ordered reality he can understand. Barnes audaciously portrays the counterbalance between the need for something beyond everyday life and the comfort derived from this very banality. *Arthur and George* looks at the quest for knowledge and justice and the shaky nature of what society considers the truth.

Michael Adams

Review Sources

The Atlantic Monthly 297 (January/February, 2006): 179.
Booklist 102, nos. 9, 10 (January 1, 2006): 22.
The Economist 376 (July 9, 2006): 74.
Entertainment Weekly, no. 858 (January 13, 2006): 80.
Kirkus Reviews 73, no. 19 (October 1, 2005): 1041.
London Review of Books 27, no. 17 (September 1, 2005): 25-26.
Los Angeles Times Book Review, January 15, 2006, p. 8.
The Nation 282, no. 7 (February 20, 2006): 34-36.
The New Leader 88, no. 6 (November/December, 2005): 42-44.
New Statesman 134 (July 11, 2005): 49-50.
The New York Review of Books 53, no. 6 (April 6, 2006): 12-14.
The New York Times 155 (January 10, 2006): E1-E8.
The New York Times Book Review 155 (January 15, 2006): 1-11.
People Weekly 65, no. 3 (January 16, 2006): 45.
Publishers Weekly 252, no. 44 (November 7, 2005): 49.
The Times Literary Supplement, July 8, 2005, p. 19.
The Wall Street Journal 247, no. 11 (January 14, 2006): P10.
The Washington Post Book World, January 15, 2006, p. 15.

AT CANAAN'S EDGE
America in the King Years, 1965-68

Author: Taylor Branch (1947-   )
Publisher: Simon & Schuster (New York). Illustrated.
  1039 pp. $35.00
Type of work: Biography and history
Time: 1965-1968
Locale: Selma, Alabama; Memphis, Tennessee; Atlanta,
  Georgia; New York, Boston, Washington, Chicago,
  Los Angeles, and numerous other locations across the
  United States, as well as Vietnam

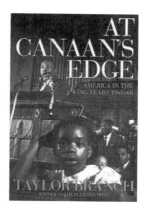

The final piece of Branch's epic three-volume biogra-
phy of Martin Luther King, Jr., is at the same time a history
of the United States in the critical Vietnam War era and a
classic tragedy with two flawed heroes and a host of vil-
lains

Principal personages:
> MARTIN LUTHER KING, JR., Baptist minister and head of the Southern
>   Christian Leadership Conference (SCLC)
> LYNDON B. JOHNSON, thirty-sixth president of the United States (1963-
>   1968), who helped to enact the historic civil rights legislation for
>   which King fought
> J. EDGAR HOOVER, the powerful head of the Federal Bureau of Investiga-
>   tion (FBI) who worked to undermine King's life and programs at
>   every turn
> RALPH ABERNATHY, like King, an SCLC minister, and one of King's
>   closest friends and advisers
> STANLEY LEVINSON, King's most trusted white adviser
> STOKELY CARMICHAEL, the black power advocate and one of the leaders
>   of the Student Nonviolent Coordinating Committee (SNCC)
> ANDREW YOUNG, one of King's most effective lieutenants in the SCLC
> ROBERT F. KENNEDY, former attorney general of the United States, who
>   came to oppose Johnson's Vietnam War policy
> JAMES BEVEL, another young civil rights leader in the SCLC who both
>   supported King and clashed with him

Taylor Branch spent decades researching and writing his massive three-volume biography of Martin Luther King, Jr. *Parting the Waters: America in the King Years,*
1954-1963 (1989) won the Pulitzer Prize in history, and *Pillar of Fire: America in the*
King Years, 1963-1965 (1998) was an equally compelling narrative of the next critical period in the life of the civil rights leader and of the United States. Now, in *At Ca-*
naan's Edge, Branch concludes this trilogy with a detailed account of the last three
years of King's life. Like the earlier volumes, *At Canaan's Edge* is a fascinating, de-

Taylor Branch's other books include the novel The Empire Blues *(1981), but he is best known for his three-volume biography of Martin Luther King, Jr. The first volume won the National Book Critics Circle Award as well as the Pulitzer Prize in history. Branch lives with his wife in Baltimore, Maryland.*

tailed biography at the same time it is a brilliant analysis of the United States in one of its most defining moments. Even more, however, *At Canaan's Edge* has the advantage of knowing what went before, and it builds on the first two volumes to conclude the life of its extraordinary subject, summarize the Civil Rights movement he headed, and describe the nation that struggled to understand and undertake what he asked.

The outline of this biography and history is easy to follow. *At Canaan's Edge* opens in Selma, Alabama, in February of 1965, with the plan to march fifty miles (through Lowndes County, where no black person had voted in the twentieth century) to Montgomery, the state capital, to dramatize nationally the need for voting rights legislation. This first of four books in the volume, titled "Selma: The Last Revolution," is itself book-length at 202 pages and re-creates this remarkable moment in American history when national television broadcast images of American citizens being attacked by state troopers and police for demanding their civil rights. It was perhaps the height of the Civil Rights movement, and of King's career, and helped to propel much of the progress (and some of the violence) that would follow.

At the very same moment, the second major figure in this story, President Lyndon Johnson, who would be so important in getting historic civil rights legislation through Congress, was about to begin an eight-year bombing campaign against North Vietnam and to sink deeper into a war that would divide the nation irreversibly and which would finally force him out of office. As he watched television footage of the brutalities on the Edmund Pettus Bridge out of Selma that night of March 7, 1965, Johnson agonized to friends about Vietnam: "I can't get out. I can't finish it with what I have got. So what the hell can I do?" The two figures of King and Johnson, both surrounded by violence, provide the double focus of this last volume of Branch's biography.

The story of the Civil Rights movement after Selma, Branch shows, is one of increasing tension between King and the Southern Christian Leadership Conference (SCLC), with their philosophy of nonviolence on one hand, and the growing forces on the other side, first of Stokely Carmichael and the Student Nonviolent Coordinating Committee but soon of Elijah Muhammad and the Black Muslims, the Black Panthers, and other advocates of black power. The Civil Rights movement King had led for years created its own momentum after Selma and went off in directions he could neither predict nor stop. Violence begat violence.

King himself, while he continued to work for civil rights progress nonviolently, became increasingly caught up in two other issues: first the question of poverty, which he came to see as a root cause of so many of the nation's ills. (He moved into a slum flat in Chicago with his family in January of 1966 to dramatize urban poverty and began to plan what he called the Poor People's Campaign and a march on Washington.) He also, however, came to see that the other enemy of basic rights for his people was the very war in Vietnam in which Lyndon Johnson felt trapped, that "the greatest purveyor of violence in the world today—[is] my own government." The final campaign before his assassination took King to Memphis, Tennessee, to organize support for the sanitation workers' strike for better pay and working conditions, but the war in Vietnam he increasingly opposed would last another five years after his death.

The volume is long, but it is difficult to see where cuts could be made. Branch includes more than two hundred pages of notes and bibliography, which attest to the detailed account of the history he is rendering. What makes the story so compelling, in fact, is the detail with which it is told, which re-creates the history for readers forty years after its finish. The life of Martin Luther King, Jr., is also the story of America in one of its defining moments, for King was one of the main figures moving the country forward, what Branch here calls lifting "the patriotic spirit of the United States toward our defining national purpose."

At Canaan's Edge captures that double story in all its richness and complexity: the Civil Rights movement moving forward to effect changes in both federal law and human consciousness and the United States sinking deeper into the morass of Vietnam. Branch sketches the background of issues that arise—racial, military, historical—and paints the broad cultural canvas against which this history is moving. Readers can see life as it then occurred, but with the accent marks at different places: The death of two sanitation workers in a gruesome accident draws King to Memphis, for example, but the event people read about in their national papers in February of 1968 is the birth of Lisa Marie Presley in another Memphis hospital. It is the middle of the 1960's, with all the change and confusion that decade embodied, from the Beatles to the New Left, from hippies to teach-ins, from urban riots in American cities to the Six-Day War in the Middle East.

Branch's titles for his three volumes suggest but Old Testament parallels, but also emerging from this account are the outlines of an almost classic Greek tragedy, a powerful drama with not one but two tragic figures. King's weaknesses are clear here—his misjudgments, his depressions, his philandering. Branch captures King's highest moments as well, however: the sermons and speeches that moved the nation. "I've been to the mountaintop," King proclaimed in his last sermon in Memphis on April 3, 1968, "and I have s-e-e-e-e-e-n the promised land." The power of that vision continues to reverberate today.

Johnson was an equally complex leader. On one hand, as Branch shows again and again, Johnson accomplished a great deal in the few years he led the United States, enacting important legislation in immigration, education, and health care (Medicare), as well as the Voting Rights Act of 1965 and other civil rights bills benefiting women and minorities. In many ways, Johnson was a brilliant leader, who could both charm and bully others into doing his will. (He would swing from hugging King in one meeting to avoiding him in the next.) Johnson stood as an Abraham Lincoln-like figure in domestic policy and yet he could not extricate himself from Vietnam. The quicksand almost swallowed him and certainly sunk any further political ambitions he had. Branch takes readers back and forth between these two tragic heroes.

There are more than enough villains in this tragedy as well. The greatest is J. Edgar Hoover, whose illegal surveillance of King went on for years. He paid informants and had agents working tirelessly to uncover damaging stories about the head of the SCLC. (Many of Branch's sources for the facts and quotations in his notes read simply "Wiretap of telephone call," "reports by police surveillance," and so on.) He undercut King's support at every turn; tragically, if some of the many police and FBI agents who were watching King that day in April, 1968, in the Lorraine Motel had turned their gaze outward, they might have stopped James Earl Ray from killing King.

Like the word "terrorist" at the start of the twenty-first century, the word "communist" was all Hoover had to utter in order to get anything he wanted, legal or not. The media fluctuated between casting its news subjects in hero and villain roles. "Don't you find that the American people are getting a little bit tired, truly, of the whole civil rights struggle?" Mike Wallace asked King on CBS in 1966, in a continuing attempt by media to stall the movement. *The New York Times* castigated King for his criticism of war policy and helped to perpetuate the war. On the other hand, it was images of the violence in Selma that helped to mobilize white America in support of civil rights. The popular tide against the Vietnam War turned in part because of reports like Harrison Salisbury's in *The New York Times* in 1967 on the damage to civilian targets that American bombing was inflicting in North Vietnam and observations like Walter Cronkite's in February of 1968, "that we are mired in stalemate seems the only realistic, if unsatisfactory, conclusion."

The themes in this double tragedy are equally clear. One is violence, the way America deals with its enemies, within and without. At the beginning of Branch's account only a handful of Americans had been killed in Vietnam, but by the end the numbers were in the thousands and growing, and the figures for Vietnamese dead are staggering. Likewise in the Civil Rights movement: Branch follows from the start some of the people who will be killed in this crusade, people such as Jimmie Lee Jackson—"a twenty-six-year-old pulpwood worker whose application to register for the vote had been rejected five times"—James Reed, Viola Liuzzo, Jonathan Daniels, James Meredith, and other people who were working to improve life for themselves and for others. Their murderers are at first acquitted, but by the end of this account all-white juries are beginning to find the courage to mete out justice. In fact, the larger theme of this book is the confirmation of the underpinning principles of American democracy, the self-governance and nonviolence which can lead to change.

The America Branch describes in this volume is torn by dissent and violence but emerges in the end stronger and fairer. The tragic heroes have fallen, but others have risen to carry their flags forward, and King's is still waving decades later. As Branch says, Martin Luther King "grasped freedom seen and unseen, rooted in ecumenical faith, sustaining patriotism to brighten the heritage of his country for all people. These treasures abide with lasting promise from America in the King years."

David Peck

Review Sources

American Scholar 75, no. 2 (Spring, 2006): 133-135.
The Economist 378 (February 18, 2006): 79-80.
Kirkus Reviews 73, no. 24 (December 15, 2005): 1306.
The Nation 282, no. 12 (March 27, 2006): 31-34.
The New York Review of Books 53, no. 6 (April 6, 2006): 20-26.
The New York Times 155 (January 13, 2006): E35-E42.
The New York Times Book Review 155 (February 5, 2006): 1-9.
The New Yorker 81, no. 45 (January 23, 2006): 86-91.
Publishers Weekly 252, no. 50 (December 19, 2005): 54.

AVA GARDNER
"Love Is Nothing"

Author: Lee Server
Publisher: St. Martin's Press (New York). 551 pp.
  $29.95
Type of work: Biography
Time: 1922-1990
Locale: North Carolina, Virginia, New York City, Los
  Angeles, Palm Springs, Spain, Paris, Rome, London,
  Mexico, Nevada, Miami, Cuba, Kenya, Tanganyika,
  Uganda, Rio de Janeiro, Pakistan, Australia, Vienna,
  Leningrad

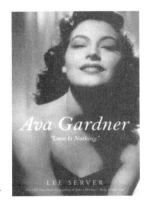

A Hollywood star battles with fame, insecurities, hus-
bands, lovers, and alcohol

> *Principal personages:*
> AVA GARDNER, an American film star
> BEATRICE ELIZABETH "BAPPIE" GARDNER, her eldest sister
> MICKEY ROONEY, her first husband, an actor
> ARTIE SHAW, her second husband, a musician
> FRANK SINATRA, her third husband, an actor and singer
> HOWARD HUGHES, an eccentric billionaire
> LOUIS B. MAYER, founder and president of Metro-Goldwyn-Mayer
> LUIS MIGUEL DOMINGUÍN, a Spanish bullfighter

For two decades, Ava Gardner was one of the most glamorous and popular Hollywood stars. Gardner had great difficulties coping with fame, and her so-called private life, constantly on display in newspapers and magazines, was a mess: three tumultuous marriages to celebrities, numerous affairs, and a serious drinking problem, all overshadowing her work on the screen. Lee Server's *Ava Gardner: "Love Is Nothing"* tries to strike a balance between her film career and her tumultuous off-camera life.

Ava Lavinia Gardner was born December 24, 1922, in Johnston County, North Carolina. After her father, Jonas Gardner's, farm began to fail, her mother, Molly Gardner, became the cook and housekeeper at a series of boardinghouses in North Carolina and Virginia. Following high school, Gardner went to New York to stay with her eldest sister, Beatrice, known as Bappie, then living with photographer Larry Tarr.

In the spring of 1941, a Metro-Goldwyn-Mayer employee saw a photograph of Ava taken by Tarr. Because of her striking looks and despite her thick southern accent, MGM signed Gardner to a seven-year contract, and Bappie accompanied her to Hollywood. Studio portraits revealed Gardner as "enticing, mysterious, and erotic, a dark dream of succulent desirability." Yet MGM already had one sex symbol, Lana Turner, and did not know what to do with another. Server portrays MGM boss Louis B. Mayer as a hypocrite who extolled family values in his studio's films while condoning the rampaging immorality of his underlings.

~

Lee Server has written eight other books, including Screenwriter: Words Become Pictures *(1987),* Danger Is My Business: An Illustrated History of the Fabulous Pulp Magazines *(1993),* Sam Fuller: Film Is a Battleground *(1994),* The Golden Age of Ocean Liners *(1996), and* Asian Pop Cinema: Bombay to Tokyo *(1999).*

~

Gardner married Mickey Rooney, MGM's biggest star, only because Bappie, her mother, and her friends said she should. A virgin at the time of the 1942 wedding, she knew little about men or sex but soon became an expert. While Rooney was fun to be with, he was also a selfish, domineering philanderer, and the couple divorced the following year.

Gardner appeared in four short films and had small, often uncredited, roles in twenty-one features during this early period. She never considered herself as having any talent beyond her looks and "saw acting as an embarrassing ordeal." This insecurity, as well as her failed first marriage, contributed to the drinking problem that would dominate her life for the next forty years.

Gardner met Howard Hughes in 1943, and the eccentric businessman, aviator, and filmmaker continued to pursue her for many years, often asking her to marry him although he was already engaged to someone else. She liked Hughes but thought he was likely to be sexually incompatible with her, was offended by his assuming he could buy her affections, and was disturbed by his spying on her.

Always a big fan of popular music, Gardner was thrilled to meet one of her favorites, Artie Shaw, the jazz clarinetist, bandleader, and composer. In 1945, Shaw made her the fifth of his eight wives. Gardner's friend and sometimes rival Lana Turner was number three. Shaw considered himself an intellectual and forced Gardner to read seriously for the first time. He was also aloof, condescending, and less interested in sex after they were married. Her drinking increased, and they divorced in 1946.

While married to Shaw, Gardner finally got the breaks she had been looking for. MGM loaned her to United Artists for the low-budget melodrama *Whistle Stop* (1945). Although this film had little impact, producer Mark Hellinger saw it and cast Gardner in Universal's *The Killers* (1946) opposite newcomer Burt Lancaster. *The Killers* expanded Ernest Hemingway's short story "The Killers" (1927) into one of the major films noir of the postwar period. Hellinger chose Gardner because he believed she "could convince audiences a man would steal, go to prison, die for her." The role would be the template for the rest of Gardner's career: sexy, seductive temptresses who lead men astray.

Although *The Killers* had made her a star, MGM still did not know what to do with her, assigning her to a supporting role in *The Hucksters* (1947). Only after she had returned to Universal for leads in *Singapore* (1947) and *One Touch of Venus* (1948) did the Mayer factory give her leading roles. Of these films, however, only the minor noir classic *The Bribe* (1948) has much to offer. Like Lauren Bacall, Jane Greer, Lizabeth Scott, and Gene Tierney, Gardner had the makings of an indelible noir star, and her sultry talents would have been better served at Twentieth Century-Fox or Warner Bros. than at the comparatively staid MGM.

Gardner had met Frank Sinatra several times over the years, but they finally hit it off after leaving a party in Palm Springs to shoot out street lights from the singer's convertible. The relationship had many potential pitfalls. While Gardner's career was soaring, Sinatra's was in decline, as he sold fewer records and was offered fewer film roles. From the beginning, they had loud public arguments but always relented hours or days later. Then there was the matter of Sinatra's marriage to the mother of his three children. An outraged press accused Gardner of breaking up the marriage, though Sinatra had long been an adulterer. Even after Gardner divorced him, the couple reunited periodically until Sinatra's fourth and final wife curtailed his contact with her.

Gardner fell in love with Europe when she went to Spain for Albert Lewin's exotically artsy *Pandora and the Flying Dutchman* (1951) and resolved to forsake Hollywood. She returned to MGM only for the studio to replace her singing in *Show Boat* (1951) with the voice of a trained singer. Her earthy, bluesy style was thought to clash with the more polished singers in the cast, though she remained on the soundtrack recording.

As she became a bigger and bigger star, conservative MGM grew increasingly concerned by "her radical social life." The problem was not only the drinking and the numerous sexual affairs but Gardner's open friendships with "Negroes." At a party at William Holden's house, Ronald Reagan stumbled upon a white male artist, a black female model, and Gardner swimming nude in their host's pool. The future president was so startled he almost fell in himself. Gardner, however, did not care what anyone thought of her wild ways. According to her friend Esther Williams, "she had gone from famous to infamous to notorious and was now regarded as something of a menace to polite society." Even costar Robert Mitchum, known for his carousing, retreated from Ava's bad influence.

Server goes into detail about some of her many affairs, especially the one with bullfighter Luis Miguel Dominguín and her messy relationship with the violent-when-drunk George C. Scott. He also describes her nonromantic friendships with Hemingway, writer Robert Graves, and jazz musician Miles Davis. She spent time with Cuban dictator Fidel Castro during the first year of his revolution and lived in a Madrid apartment over that of exiled Argentine dictator Juan Peron, who complained to Francisco Franco, Spain's iron-fisted ruler, about Gardner's noisy behavior.

Server provides interesting behind-the-scenes glimpses of most of Gardner's films. She had difficulty with director John Ford on *Mogambo* (1953) until she told him off. They then became friends, and she delivered her only Academy Award nominated performance. On the way from location shooting in Africa to London, cinematographer Robert Surtees gave Gardner and actress Grace Kelly a tour of Roman whorehouses. She clashed with actor Humphrey Bogart and director Joseph L. Mankiewicz on *The Barefoot Contessa* (1954), establishing a pattern that would continue for many years. She saw being difficult as a means of revenge against MGM. Server provides an excellent account of how MGM grew timid about the interracial love story in *Bhowani Junction* (1956) and butchered director George Cukor's version.

A newspaper account of a clash Gardner and Anthony Franciosa, her costar in *The Naked Maja* (1958), had with photographers in Rome inspired Federico Fellini's *La dolce vita* (1960) and the creation of the term *paparazzi*. Nicholas Ray, director of *55 Days at Peking* (1963), liked her despite her moodiness and tendency to forget her lines, but her unpredictability may have contributed to his heart attack during the filming. On the Mexican set of *The Night of the Iguana* (1964), director John Huston gave Gardner, costars Deborah Kerr and Richard Burton, and Elizabeth Taylor, visiting husband Burton, gold-plated derringers as if to challenge them to shoot each other. Gardner's wildness had moderated somewhat by the time she starred in Roddy McDowell's *Tam Lin* (1970). Costar Joanna Lumley is the source of several charming anecdotes about Ava's final starring role.

In her painful final years, weakened by a stroke and lupus, Gardner began to reflect on her life. Her antagonism toward Hollywood softened, and she took pleasure in watching her films on television, remembering only the good things about each.

As good as this biography is, it is not quite as good as Server's *Robert Mitchum: "Baby, I Don't Care"* (2001). While Gardner and Mitchum are similar, Mitchum had a longer, more varied career and battled even more demons. Server writes passages of the Mitchum biography in a tough guy, noirish style befitting his subject. He tries for a similar effect with the Hemingwayesque opening of *Ava Gardner: "Love Is Nothing"* with the words, "Some who knew their old movies said it was all just like the one of hers with the funeral at the beginning and the end and the blue-gray clouds and the black umbrellas and the mourners in the rain." Given his subject's stature as a love goddess, Server allows his style to become more purple elsewhere: "To see her in the flesh was said to have made the blood race, the hair on the arms stand up. To know her more intimately was to surrender to mad passions, to risk all." He shifts to a hipster style to reflect the feelings of Artie Shaw: "Hey, he loved her too. But when a thing like a marriage started to crumble, man, there was nothing for it but to get on your way, get moving before something fell on your head."

Server is especially good at pinpointing the qualities that separated Gardner from the other female stars of the late 1940's: "Her cynical demeanor and sometimes less than wholesome glamour made her fit company for the new generation of male stars . . . the corps of unsmiling, morally ambiguous men of postwar cinema." Server's best writing comes during a long passage on the behavior of Rome's roving photographers:

> On nights when the stars failed to provide sufficient scandalous behavior, photographers stepped forth and provoked it, taunting and challenging this or that celebrity into a temper tantrum, a grab for the offending camera, an absurd chase through the street, a wrestling match or a punch-out, with luck all of it caught on film by the photographer's nearby partner—and sold the next morning to the highest bidder.

If Gardner had lived a happy, conventional domestic life, Server probably would not have bothered with this biography, at least the fourth about the star. Her marriages, affairs, and frequently outrageous behavior dominate her image because, like contemporaries Glen Ford, Rita Hayworth, Van Johnson, and Richard Widmark, Gardner made only a handful of memorable films, with *The Killers* easily her best. Her unwillingness to take acting seriously and MGM's failure to create worthy projects for her only compounded her sad legacy.

Michael Adams

Review Sources

Booklist 102, no. 13 (March 1, 2006): 54.
Kirkus Reviews 74 (February 1, 2006): 126.
London Review of Books 28, no. 17 (September 7, 2006): 9-10.
Los Angeles Times Book Review, May 14, 2006, p. 2.
The New Republic 234, nos. 21/22 (June 5, 2006): 35-37.
The New York Times 155 (April 17, 2006): E1-E8.
The New York Times Book Review 155 (April 23, 2006): 1-11.
Sight and Sound 16, no. 7 (July, 2006): 94.
The Spectator 300 (April 29, 2006): 47-48.
The Times Literary Supplement, May 19, 2006, p. 20.

AVERNO

Author: Louise Glück (1943-   )
Publisher: Farrar, Straus and Giroux (New York). 79 pp.
 $22.00
Type of work: Poetry

The tenth collection of poems by the former poet laureate of the United States continues Glück's explorations of, in her words, "the virtues of a style which inclines to the suggested over the amplified"

There is an inherent paradox in the concept of a "philosophical poetry." Either the poetic properties dominate to the extent that the philosophical aspects are reduced to a shallow summary that betrays the essence of the proposition, or the weight of the thought is so dense that it detracts from the qualities of language that give poetry its primary appeal. The lyric impulse that is so fundamental to poetic power tends to be antithetical to reasoned discourse, as Plato feared to the degree that he proposed banishment of the poet from his ideal republic. While it may be argued that a poet's way of seeing is philosophical in the most fundamental fashion, Emily Dickinson's contention that she recognized the occurrence of a poetic impulse by the feeling that the top of her head was about to blow off reinforces the disparity between "mind" and "skin."

Nonetheless, there is a tradition of meditative verse, which flourished in the seventeenth century in the work of writers such as Richard Crashaw (c. 1613-1649), Henry Vaughan (1621-1695), John Milton (1608-1674), and, most notably in the latter part of his life, John Donne (1572-1631). It is significant that each of these men was ruled by a religious perspective notably absent from much modern American poetry, which is built on the rhythms, language, and styles of vernacular speech and makes the styles of a philosophical poetics seem outmoded, stodgy, academic, or even irrelevant.

Louise Glück, whose poetry has followed an individual, personal course from her first volumes, has said admiringly of John Berryman's "Street" that it "is a poetry of mind, of mind processing information—not a mind incapable of response but a mind wary of premature response." In no way relying on the doctrinal buttress that the seventeenth century poets assumed, Glück has developed a poetic voice sufficient to disclose the intricate working of an "open mind, a mind resistant to closure" that does not relinquish the "lyric intensity" which she praises in Rainer Maria Rilke's "Archaic Torso of Apollo." Without attempting a reconciliation of the lyric and the philosophical to the detriment and diminution of both, Glück has achieved a kind of coalescence wherein both disciplines remain robust and vigorous. Her poetry is not so much a meditation on the world but a passionate engagement of the self with its own existence.

In previous volumes, Glück has established some of the cornerstones of her method. *Vita Nova* (1999) takes Dante's poem *La vita nuova* (c. 1292) as a basis for

~

Louise Glück, former poet laureate of the United States, has won many awards for her work, including the Pulitzer Prize for The Wild Iris *(1992), the National Book Critics Circle Award, and the Bollingen Prize.*

~

an extensive consideration of "Immortal Love" and "Earthly Love" using some of the most prominent of classical figures (Orpheus and Eurydice, Dido and Aeneas) as the subject and focus of myths that maintain enduring resonance into modern times. *The Seven Ages* (2001) continues this approach, with the mythic as a frame around the life of a woman at middle age recalling past experiences and reconsidering them with respect to her sense of self in the present. Glück has always been keenly conscious of the substance of the natural world, and in *The Seven Ages* she takes summer as a span of time, its floral abundance as a sensory spur and its emblem as a highpoint, a signal of the inevitability of an eventual decline in everything.

These elements are employed again in *Averno*, the title of the volume taken from a small crater lake in southern Italy that was regarded in Roman times as the entrance to the underworld. The seasonal focus here is autumnal tilting toward winter, introduced in "October," the first poem in the book. The personal perspective is that of Persephone, whose entrance in the second poem "Persephone the Wanderer" sets the location in transit between earthly and "other-earthly" realms.

As her publishers point out, all of Glück's books since *Ararat* (1990) proceed as a sequence, although this does not mean a sequential procession as much as an architecture in which the interplay among poems has a particular consequence. "October" launches a journey that is begun literally as a quest, the poem occurring as a series of questions that enable the speaker to orient herself in uncomfortable terrain ("winter again") and winter as a season, a psychic place, and a region of the cosmos. An ethos of uncertainty pervades the poem, as the speaker seems to wonder "is it cold again," citing as evidence:

> didn't Frank just slip on the ice,
> didn't he heal, weren't the spring seeds planted
>
> didn't the night end,
> didn't the melting ice
> flood the narrow gutters
>
> wasn't my body
> rescued, wasn't it safe
>
> didn't the scar form, invisible
> above the injury

The absence of question marks tends to blend queries simultaneously with assertions, suggesting a moment in time, and reflections from beyond that moment. The difficulty for the poet is the fact that while she can no longer "hear your voice" (which is not ascribed to a specific person), she also claims to "no longer care/ what sound it makes," indicating an inclination toward removal from a relationship. Fearing the consequences implicit in this realization, she concludes the questioning with a poignant appeal, "weren't we necessary to the earth." Seeking evidence to support this supposition, she asks "the vines, were they harvested?"—this time placing the question mark as a summary and reaching for a link between the poetic personas and the universe.

This is the first of the six poems in the "October" section. The second one takes the speaker of the first poem, the "I" who sought answers that were unlikely to be available, and begins to limn the outlines of the mind forming the thoughts and experiencing sensory impressions. "I know what I see," the poet declares, providing a base for observation, and then, with conviction, "You hear this voice? This is my mind's voice." It is as direct a declaration of perception as will occur in this book. What remains to be clarified is the "you" who may be listening, as well as the other "you" who resides in the poem itself, the one who is told at the poem's close: "Tell me this is the future,/ I won't believe you./ Tell me I'm living,/ I won't believe you." Apparently, evidence of existence depends on perception rather than external reassurance.

As a means of creating or conveying perception, the relationship between the self and the world is crucial. "*Come to me*, said the world," the poet writes in the third section, explaining "What others found in art,/ I found in nature." The fourth section illustrates this, concentrating on the spirit of the season. "This is the light of autumn, not the light of spring," Glück indicates, with images of wear and drain: "*I strained, I suffered, I was delivered.*" Although the "light of autumn" has "turned on us," she still believes that "Surely it is a privilege to approach the end/ still believing in something." This thought sets up the fifth section, in which the poet moves past discouragement toward a hesitant inclination toward action. In a stirring change in tone, she observes after stating that "there is not enough beauty in the world," that "Neither is there candor, and here I may be of some use."

The turn from uncertainty to capability is enlivening, as the poet confidently assures "I am/ at work, though I am silent," an operating principle of her aesthetic resolution. Even if it might be the "artist's/ duty to create/ hope," there is the perpetual problem "but out of what? what?" and the word "hope" is "itself/ false a device to refute/ perception." Nonetheless, the poem ends on a surge of hope in the final short stanza: "*you are not alone,/ the poem said,/ in the dark tunnel.*"

The final poem in the section contains a muted acceptance of what can assuage the ultimate aloneness of the human. Blending the self with the world, the poet says, "My friend the earth is bitter; I think/ sunlight has failed her." It continues "Between herself and the sun,/ something has ended./ She wants, now, to be left alone;" With a note of deep resignation, Glück concludes "I think we must give up/ turning to her for affirmation," which implies, inevitably, that something else must exist to which one might turn. In this case, it is "my friend the moon," seen as "beautiful tonight." However, nothing is ever simply complete in itself, so it is not surprising when the poet continues "but when is she not beautiful?" This idea opens another avenue of exploration while it concludes "October" with as positive a feeling as Glück allows.

The ambiguity of the linkage of the self to Earth, Sun, and Moon through the perceptual apparatus of the mind, the subject/object connection shifting within the field of the poem, contributes to the philosophical inquiry that informs *Averno*. By using the myth of Persephone as an analogue for the poet's self in and within the world, Glück permits a more direct kind of participation than the distance maintained through the introductory sections of "October." The daunting voyage that Persephone takes into the underworld has been signaled by the closing stanza of section 3, in which the poet adamantly exclaims "death cannot hurt me/ more than you have harmed me/ my beloved life." This is how the poet has chosen to accept the invitation by the world to "*Come to me*," repeated twice in the second section of "October."

The beginning of "Persephone the Wanderer" is a dynamic retelling of the myth, citing scholars, interrogating their assumptions, moving within Persephone's point of view, and incisively reinterpreting and expanding the meaning of the myth. The poem that immediately follows, "Prism," recapitulates some of the material of Glück's earlier volumes, regathering the poet's personal experience of marriage into twenty mostly brief parts, many of them like cryptic anecdotes, such as number 4, which begins:

> When you fall in love, my sister said,
> it's like being struck by lightning.
>
> She was speaking hopefully,
> to draw the attention of the lightning.

It concludes with the poet mentioning that in childhood the effect of love on adults seemed "not of lightning/ but of the electric chair." This poem is like a chronicle of maturity, when (as in number 17) "The self ended and the world began." The poems "Echoes" and "Fugue," which conclude the first part of the book, are metaphysical reflections on how this maturation was marked by realization of the power of the soul, which is introduced to the poet's consciousness by saying "I am your soul, the winsome stranger," and which is epitomized by the last lines of this part: "Then the music began, the lament of the soul/ watching the body vanish."

What might appear to be a level of dejection too deep for return is counterbalanced by the story of Persephone's return to the light of Earth. In "The Evening Star," the first poem of the second part, the poet observes "Tonight, for the first time in many years/ there appeared to me again/ a vision of earth's splendor."

"Landscape" follows, with many manifestations of an earthly vitality, although generally shadowed by an ominous awareness of "The field parched, dry—/ the deadness in place already/ so to speak." In this part of the book, there is a continuing alternation between nearly rapturous response to the sensory appeal of the earth and anticipation of disappointment. In "Blue Rotunda," a poem composed of many brief fragments separated by a point in space, the poet admits "I want/ my heart back/ I want to feel everything again—," which is hedged by "the light saying/ *you can see out/ but you can't go out*," a reminder of the enclosures of the mind.

The title poem, "Averno," which Glück notes was also "Ancient name Avernus," draws on both its linguistic derivation from the Latin "to arrive" and its visual sugges-tion of an avenue or path. The sense of arrival corresponds to understanding that comes with later middle age, and the path that has been followed is akin to the life's journey to this point. The last poems in the book are attempts to understand how de-partures and returns can be assimilated into a larger context. They lead toward another version of "Persephone the Wanderer." More than a retelling or a recapitulation, this concluding poem is a projection of the poet's mind into the reconstituted psyche of Persephone living both as a mythic memory and as an inhabitant of the present, a philosophic contingency that cannot be proved but can be convincingly portrayed if the lyric invention of the poet is well-suited to the task.

Leon Lewis

Review Sources

America 194, no. 12 (April 3, 2006): 34.
Booklist 102, no. 13 (March 1, 2006): 56.
Library Journal 130, no. 20 (December 15, 2005): 134.
The New Republic 235, no. 6 (August 7, 2006): 29-32.
The New York Review of Books 53, no. 11 (June 22, 2006): 16-19.
The New York Times Book Review 155 (March 12, 2006): 16.
Publishers Weekly 252, no. 42 (October 24, 2005): 39.

BAD FAITH
A Forgotten History of Family, Fatherland, and Vichy France

Author: Carmen Callil (1938-   )
*First published: Bad Faith: A Forgotten History of Fam-
    ily and Fatherland*, 2006, in Great Britain
Publisher: Alfred A. Knopf (New York). 607 pp. $30.00
Type of work: Biography and history
Time: 1897-1980
Locale: France, England, and Australia

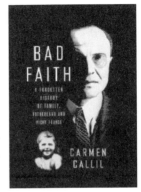

*In writing the life of Louis Darquier, a virulent French
anti-Semite, Callil illuminates much of the history of Vichy
France and traces the life of Darquier's Tasmanian-born
companion and the story of the daughter they abandoned*

Principal personages:
> LOUIS DARQUIER (1897-1980), also known
>   as Louis Darquier de Pellepoix, Vichy commissioner for Jewish
>   affairs, 1942-1944
> MYRTLE JONES (1893-1970), Darquier's longtime companion, probably
>   in a bigamous marriage
> ANNE DARQUIER (1930-1970), Louis and Myrtle's daughter whom they
>   abandoned to the care of an English foster family; also Carmen
>   Callil's psychiatrist
> LOUISE DARQUIER, Louis's mother
> HENRI-PHILIPPE PÉTAIN (1856-1951), a French military hero of World
>   War I and head of the Vichy government
> PIERRE LAVAL (1883-1945), the prime minister of France under the
>   Vichy government; executed after the war
> RENÉ BOUSQUET (1909-1993), the Vichy chief of police responsible for
>   the deportation and deaths of thousands of Jews; protected after the
>   war by close friends such as François Mitterand, president of France,
>   1981-1995

About 1962, when Carmen Callil was a young Australian woman living in Italy,
she attempted suicide and was taken to London, where three days a week, for seven
years, she spent an hour with a young half-Australian psychiatrist named Dr. Anne
Darquier. However, when she arrived for her appointment on September 7, 1970, nobody answered the doorbell and Callil learned later in the day that Darquier was dead,
probably by suicide. Callil was surprised to learn at the funeral that she was to be buried as Anne Darquier de Pellepoix, a name she was not to hear again until a year or so
later when she watched Marcel Ophuls's television documentary *Le Chagrin et la
pitié*, or *The Sorrow and the Pity: The Story of a French Town in the Occupation*
(1971). The town in the title was Cahors, in southwest France, home of the man who
was born Louis Darquier but who added de Pellepoix to his name. Darquier appears in

Ophuls's film shaking hands with Reinhard Heydrich, the brutal head of the Reich Central Security office until he was killed by Czech assassins. It was the sudden reappearance of this name that impelled Callil to undertake the years of research that produced this brilliant book.

    Louis Darquier was born on December 19, 1897, in the small town of Cahors in southwest France. His father, Pierre, was a respected physician, his mother, Louise, a "churchy woman" who entertained a lot. His older brother, René, became a prosperous businessman whom the irresponsible Louis turned to many times for money. Louis's younger brother, Jean, followed Pierre's career as a doctor, whereas Louis's hopes in medicine ended when he failed a crucial chemistry exam. He enlisted early in World War I, in 1915, and served well despite infractions in his conduct. After the war, Louis entered the wheat trade, a business dominated by wealthy Jews, but his financial misdoing forced his resignation in 1926 and precipitated his anti-Semitism. Two malignant figures, Édouard Drumont, a rabidly anti-Semitic Catholic, and Charles Maurras, the intellectual godfather of the right-wing Action Française movement, further infected him with the anti-Semitism so endemic in the Catholic Church of the time. Much of the activity generated by these fascist bigots was financed by perfume magnate François Coty, l'Oréal founder Eugène Schueller, and brandy king Jean Hennessy.

    The woman who was to pass as Madame Myrtle Darquier was born Myrtle Marian Ambrosine Jones in Carrick, Tasmania, in 1893. Pursuing a mediocre career as an actress and singer, Myrtle probably met Louis in France where her first husband was performing for the troops in World War I. In 1928, these two liars and frauds married and after a quick visit to Tasmania presented themselves to London's Mayfair society as Baron and Baroness Louis Darquier de Pellepoix. By 1930, though, they were destitute and forced to give up their new baby, Anne, to Elsie Lightfoot of Oxfordshire, the nanny they had hired. They soon returned to Paris, wheedled money from René over the years, and endured Louise Darquier's contempt for Myrtle.

    Economic conditions in France, complicated by an influx of postwar immigrants, spawned the riots of February 6, 1934, which protested Premier Édouard Daladier's government. Seventeen people died, and among the fifteen hundred injured was Louis Darquier, shot in the thighbone. Capitalizing on his role in these events, in July, 1934, Louis started the first of his many organizations, the Association des Blessés et Victimes du 6 Février, and took a job as deputy editor of a right-wing newspaper, *Le Jour*. A year later he was gone from *Le Jour*, probably for stealing funds, but in May, 1935, he was elected to the Paris city council. After the Socialist leader Léon Blum was beaten up in February, 1936, Blum's adherents sacked the Action Française office in rue Asseline, and Louis was later to date his anti-Semitic career to that affair.

    It was probably the "professional anti-Semite" Henry Coston who introduced Louis

Carmen Callil was born in Melbourne, Australia, and moved to the United Kingdom in 1960. She founded Virago Press and later became managing director of Chatto & Windus. She is the author, with Irish novelist Colm Tóibín, of The Modern Library: The Two Hundred Best Novels in English Since 1950 *(1999).*

to the anti-Semitic hoax *The Protocols of the Elders of Zion* (1903?), and in 1936 he publicly attacked Coston's Popular Front enemies. It was in this period, Callil explains, that Louis began to reject "Catholic and nationalist anti-Semitism in favour of the French version of the Nazi racist variety." In May, 1936, during a Popular Front parade in Paris, the drunken Louis assaulted three Jews in a restaurant, an outburst that earned him an invitation to visit Berlin to meet "friends and politicians." Louis's connections through Coston encouraged him to apply to the German embassy in Paris for money, and in January, 1937, he received his first Nazi check, for 2,500 marks.

In 1937 at a meeting in Geneva, Louis spewed out a diatribe against the French government that got him kicked out of Switzerland but earned him a generous subsidy from Goebbels's propaganda office, money that enabled him to start his first real newspaper, *La France enchaînée* (France in chains). However, when war broke out in September, 1939, "Hitler's Parrot," as Louis had come to be called, was mobilized and served well as a lieutenant until captured and imprisoned in Poland. In March, 1942, Louis's name appeared on two lists of candidates the Germans drew up to head a central agency in Vichy France for the "Aryanization" of Jewish wealth. This new Commissariat Général aux Questions Juives (CGQJ) passed over Louis and appointed someone else head, but Louis was released from prison in July and wangled a temporary appointment with CGQJ that provided a retainer of eight thousand francs.

Marshal Pétain became head of the Vichy state in July, 1940, and the oppression of French Jews began with a struggle between Vichy and Germany for their wealth. Louis's appointment as the head of CGQJ began in March, 1942, and his biggest coup was his discovery of the enormously valuable hidden Jewish art collection—the Schloss Collection. By July, 1943, the CGQJ had grabbed and sold Jewish assets worth 1,289,139,035 francs. Louis, however, pursued his own ends with the CGQJ and "wanted to lead a national Vichy anti-Semitic movement; he wanted a purified Christian France, not a pagan Nazified *patrie*. In this manner he managed to alienate everyone." Xavier Vallat, Louis's predecessor as Commissioner for Jewish Affairs, had run a disciplined if brutal system, but the religious element in Vichy's approach clashed with the German division of people into Aryans and non-Aryans, causing many disputes.

Louis's chronic dishonesty emerged immediately in his new job. Callil says of his laziness and venality, "From his first hour, therefore, Darquier made matters worse for his German masters, and brought relations between Vichy ministries and the German authorities to a new low." When the Allies landed in North Africa in November, 1942, Hitler ordered German troops to take over Vichy France and the problem of Louis was set aside. By appointing the efficient Joseph Antignac, an able civil servant, as his chief of staff in Paris, Louis was able to keep his job until the disgusted Nazis finally sacked him in February, 1944.

In 1942 Pierre Laval came into power as head of the government and appointed René Bousquet his secretary-general for the police. Bousquet was a brilliant manipulator who between April, 1942, and December, 1943, deported 57,908 Jews and arranged the deaths of thousands of communists and others. Bousquet immediately removed Vallat's police force, the Police aux Questions Juives, from Louis's control, beginning their venomous relationship. "After the Liberation, protected by François Mitterand, Bousquet lived happily and richly until 1978," when Louis Darquier exposed his ruthlessness in a sensational interview in Spain, an interview that Callil includes as an appendix.

Louis Darquier's star fell fast in 1943. The Germans shut down all of his institutes and groups by October, Pétain publicly called him *un bourreau*, "a butcher," and in December the order for his dismissal was sent to Vichy. The fanatic anti-Semite Paul Sézille ranted, "As for Darquier de Pellepoix, he thinks only of his stomach, his women and his re-election. We helped him at the beginning, but he has betrayed us. He disgusts us. One day his punishment will come." Nevertheless, even as D day approached in June, 1944, and the Nazis were hurriedly dispatching thousands—many of them children—to the death camps, Louis's luck held out. He did not leave France until September, 1944, when his brother René hid him in the trunk of his car and drove him to meet sympathizers who got him over the Pyrénées into Spain. He carried phony papers identifying him as Jean Estève, and in Madrid he was provided with a full identity. He soon had a young mistress, a Spanish passport, and a low-paying job teaching French. On July 31, 1946, he became the father of another daughter, Teresa. In Paris, on December 10, 1947, "Darquier sans Pellepoix" was sentenced to death in absentia. By 1950 Myrtle had joined Louis in Madrid, while unknown to her he was paying a nearby cleaning lady to raise Teresa. They liked to call themselves Barón y Baronesa Louis d'Arquier de Pellepoix. Myrtle died of a heart attack in Madrid on June 18, 1970, while Louis lingered on until August 29, 1980, when he died in a spa in the Sierra de Málaga with Teresa tending him.

With Jean Darquier's help, the French Ministry of Justice found Myrtle in London and arranged for a meeting between her and Anne. In 1946 Anne traveled to Paris to meet her grandmother Louise, and she returned to England a convert to Catholicism and an admirer of French composers. Sometime in 1948 or 1949 Anne visited in Madrid the man she had long thought to be her aristocrat father, only to learn that he was an impostor with a monocle. Great effort led to Anne's becoming in 1961 Dr. Anne Darquier, B.A., B.M., B.Ch. Oxon, D.P.M. She trained as a Jungian analyst under Robert Hobson, an eccentric character who enjoyed lecturing students on the psychopathology of the foreskin. Callil says of Anne's death: "Although she was courting oblivion, it is unlikely that Anne was courting death. Hers was one of those silent suicides, in which stopping the pain, rather than the ending of life, is the point."

At the conclusion of her long story, Callil makes this remark:

> What caused me anguish as I tracked down Louis Darquier was to live so closely to the helpless terror of the Jews of France, and to see what the Jews of Israel were passing on to the Palestinian people. Like the rest of humanity, the Jews of Israel "forget" the Palestinians. Everyone forgets; every nation forgets.

A consequence of this postscript was a protest against Callil's book leading to the French Embassy's cancellation of a dinner in her honor in New York.

Frank Day

Review Sources

Booklist 102, no. 22 (August 1, 2006): 30.
Library Journal 131, no. 15 (September 15, 2006): 71.
London Review of Books 28, no. 11 (June 8, 2006): 27-28.
New Statesman 135 (October 10, 2006): 51-52.
The New York Times 156 (October 12, 2006): E9.
The New York Times Book Review 155 (September 17, 2006): 22.
Publishers Weekly 253, no. 27 (July 10, 2006): 67.
The Spectator 300, no. 9271 (April 15, 2006): 43-44.

BECOMING ABIGAIL

Author: Chris Abani (1969-   )
Publisher: Akashic Books (New York). 28 pp. $12.00
Type of work: Novella
Time: 2002-2003
Locale: Nigeria and London

A narrative of a young woman's life in which she creates her own sense of self despite the legacy of her dead mother, the responsibilities of a depressed father, and the terrors endured under her abusive uncle

Principal characters:
> ABIGAIL, a Nigerian teenager who is taken
> to London to live with her cousins
> FATHER, Abigail's father, who has never
> recovered from her mother's death in childbirth
> MARY, Abigail's older cousin, who lives in England
> PETER, Mary's husband, who runs a youth prostitution ring from his
> house
> DEREK, social worker assigned to Abigail's case, with whom she falls in
> love
> MOLLY, Derek's wife

From the crackling opening lines to the final, quiet image, *Becoming Abigail* blends language and style to transcend traditional genres of writing. Though the book is a story in novella form, the chapters are a series of prose poems rich with image and cadence from the hand of experienced poet Chris Abani. The narrator moves the reader through Abigail's story, alternating between times delineated by the chapter headings "Now" and "Then." The form of the novella sets up one of the most important dynamics of the story, which is that this is a difficult and painful story to tell. The plot and the content are too expansive for a short story; however, to place the character of Abigail within the vastness of a novel would mean to lose her.

When the novella begins, Abigail is inside the memory of her mother's funeral, which she attended as an infant but she remembers as though she were already an adolescent. She is aware even as she remembers that this memory is partly the fabrication of her imagination influenced by her father's depression. Abigail's story is, to a great extent, the exploration of the contingency of memory. In the "Now" sections, Abigail is standing alone, smoking cigarettes in the cold night air. She remembers all the events that led her to where she currently stands. She relies upon all of her senses, particularly her sense of touch, to evoke in her mind what is written on her body. For Abigail, knowledge is far more than mental; it is the intersection of the body and experience.

Abigail grows up in a rural village in Nigeria with only her father. He constantly

*Chris Abani is originally from Nigeria.
His novel* Graceland *(2004) was the
winner of the 2005 PEN/Hemingway
Award and a finalist for the* Los
Angeles Times *Book Prize. He has also
won a PEN Freedom-to-Write Award
and a Lannan Literary Fellowship. His
other works include the novel* Masters
of the Board *(1984) and the poetry
collections* Kalakuta Republic *(2000),*
Daphne's Lot *(2003), and* Dog Woman
(2004).

reminds her that her mother (whose name was also Abigail) died in childbirth, for which he blames Abigail, and that every day she grows to look more like her mother. In the distant "Then," Abigail is depicted in various mourning rituals for her mother which may also be read as mourning for herself as well. As she becomes an adolescent, Abigail begins to rebel in attempts to turn her father's attention to her and away from her mother. She tries to remind him that there is life present, while he is only concerned with and consumed by death.

Her father decides to send her to London to live with her cousins Mary and Peter. Abigail does not want to leave her father, even though he and Peter promise her a better life in London. In the week before she is supposed to leave with Peter, Abigail comes home to find her father has committed suicide. Though she already had no choice other than to go with Peter, there is now nothing at all to hold her at home. Abigail does not trust Peter because she is already aware of what men can do. In this area of knowledge, she trusts her own memories. At ten Abigail is coerced into sex with a different cousin and then forbidden from telling anyone what they did. When she is twelve, Peter molests her before his wedding to her cousin, though this does not surprise Abigail. She claims that this event did not affect her greatly, but the fact that it remains in her memory proves otherwise.

Although she is not a sophisticated traveler, Abigail is aware of the illegal means by which Peter gets her into England. She arrives with a false passport and visa; thus, once Abigail enters the new country, she finds that she does not exist. The idea of nonexistence is recurrent, beginning with her father's regard; that she is both expected to become her mother Abigail and yet always a disappointment because she can never be that Abigail. Growing up, she ponders whether she even exists, or is she already a ghost? In this new country, Abigail tries to affect a more English accent by practicing along with voices in films. She recalls her father's memory of how her parents were treated on a visit to London in the 1950's, their blackness so strange that it frightened people. When Abigail first comes to England, she is overwhelmed by all the white faces. Abani does not separate race from the other aspects of his characters' identities. For Abigail, being black is inseparable from being an immigrant and being a woman.

In the first few days, Peter further takes hold of her identity by taking her shopping. He pays for her clothes and food and expects her to do as he commands. At the cosmetics counter, Peter asks the woman working there to make Abigail look older and sexier. Back at their house, he brings men around, planning to make a prostitute of Abigail. When she refuses to cooperate, Peter forces her to stay in a dog house in the back yard, where she must eat on her hands and knees. He rapes her and urinates on her, but she is not fully defeated no matter how violently he treats her. When she can no longer live there, she bites off his penis and runs away.

At first the character of Derek is shrouded from the reader; early snapshots of him reveal that he is white and English, but layers of his relationship with Abigail are not illuminated until later. The narrator only reveals that Derek is now absent from Abigail's life, though he remains a fierce presence in her thoughts. As the story progresses, and the time between "Then" and "Now" shrinks ever closer to the present moment, more details begin to surface. Derek is Abigail's social worker, with whom she falls in love. The two know each other for only a few weeks. He seems to fall in love with her as well, talking to her as though she were an adult lover. He risks his own life in order to have a sexual relationship with her in the downstairs rooms of his own home. After his wife finds them together in the kitchen, he loses his job. He then is convicted of statutory rape.

Abigail finds herself now completely alone in the world. There is no going back to Mary and Peter's house and certainly no return to Nigeria. Derek is Abigail's desire. Despite Abigail's belief in the purity of her and Derek's love, the reader may find it difficult to empathize with Derek. He is an intriguing character because he simultaneously represents systems of oppression and protection. As an older male and a white British citizen, he could represent the colonizer falling for the colonized. As the social worker in charge of Abigail's case, he is someone who ought to know better than to become romantically involved with her. Ultimately what Derek was thinking during the time of their brief affair is far less important than the results of their actions. Abigail is left feeling that she is being punished for making her own choices. She pleads to the court, but her testimony only seals his fate. Still the narrator empathizes with the pain of her life, caught between the abuses of men and circumstances she cannot control, and permits the beauty of her own methods of coping to blossom.

Scenes of Abigail ritually burning and cutting her own skin recur throughout the novella, both as action and voyeurism. She chooses to create her own kind of memories, both to capture the events as they occur and to remind herself that she does exist. No matter what has happened to her in her life, no matter who has abandoned her, she is still here. Abani's skill with imagery works well here as he navigates the very private act of self-mutilation. Through the brief pain of the cuts or burns, Abigail feels a momentary sense of control of her body, senses, and memory. When Derek asks her what the dots of scarring are for, she points and tells him, "my hunger, my need, mine, not my mother's . . . here, here, here, me, me, me. Don't you see?" She needs him to see her for who she is, not as her mother or as an object, nor forget her as though she is a ghost.

Becoming Abigail is a coming-of-age story, complete with a journey and self-realization. Abigail seeks to find herself caught between the bedlam of memory and injustice. Critically acclaimed for its compact size and breathtaking language, *Becoming Abigail* is successful in its portrayal of this young woman who is imbued with loss from the moment of her birth. Though readers may not be surprised by the end and may disagree strongly with the choice she makes, it is important to note that this is a decision Abigail comes to on her own. In the final moments of the story, Abigail takes control of her destiny. She refuses further attempts to help her or control her or take advantage of her. In the end, she accepts her life for what it is, and she accepts her memories. Although the decision she faces is far from simple, it is hers alone to make.

Jennifer H. Solomon

Review Sources

Booklist 102, no. 13 (March 1, 2006): 60.
Essence 37, no. 1 (May, 2006): 85.
Library Journal 131, no. 2 (February 1, 2006): 68.
Los Angeles Times, May 14, 2006, p. 10.
The Nation 283, no. 1 (July 3, 2006): 36.
The New York Times 155 (March 19, 2006): 11.
Publishers Weekly 253, no. 2 (January 9, 2006): 30-31.

BETJEMAN
A Life

Author: A. N. Wilson (1950-   )
Publisher: Farrar, Straus and Giroux (New York). 375
   pp. $27.00
Type of work: Literary biography
Time: 1906-1985
Locale: England

*Sir John Betjeman, born the son of a tradesman, used
his talents and charm to become the most popular poet and
one of the most loved television celebrities of his time. His
personal life was, however, shadowed by melancholy and
complicated by his love for two dissimilar women*

Principal personages:
> SIR JOHN BETJEMAN, poet laureate and best-selling poet, architectural
>   critic, television celebrity
> ERNEST EDWARD BETJEMAN, his father, a manufacturer
> LADY PENELOPE (CHETWODE) BETJEMAN, his wife
> LADY ELIZABETH CAVENDISH, sister of the Duke of Devonshire,
>   Betjeman's mistress
> PRINCESS MARGARET, sister of the Queen of England, friend of Elizabeth
>   Cavendish and Betjeman
> SIR MAURICE BOWRA, Oxford don and mentor

A. N. Wilson is one of England's most prolific writers. He has written many novels, the finest of which may be *Incline Our Hearts* (1988). He has written works on religion and cultural history and biographies of the authors John Milton, Leo Tolstoy,
C. S. Lewis, and Hilaire Belloc. At one time he was set to write a biography of novelist Iris Murdoch but then was dismissed. After her death, he published an account of
his memories of her, an account that was seen by many reviewers as spiteful and jealous. His recent novel *My Name Is Legion* (2004), a story focusing on the world of
London newspapers, was even more ferocious and nasty. As a result, readers approaching his biography of John Betjeman, a man whose public persona was one of
charm and benevolence, might wonder what barbs to expect. This biography, however, is not in the least ferocious. It is moderate in tone and, without papering over his
subject's failings, is fair, insightful, and sympathetic.

John Betjeman was born August 28, 1906, on the borders of Highgate, an upper-
middle-class district in north London. He was an only child. The family moved to even
better addresses as John grew up. For holidays, they went to Trebetherick in Cornwall, a
place Betjeman never ceased to love. He attended Highgate School, where one of his
teachers (and later his friend and fellow poet) was T. S. Eliot. He went away to a prep

∾

A. N. Wilson is the author of nineteen novels—including The Sweets of Pimlico *(1977),* The Healing Art *(1980), and* Wise Virgin *(1982)—five biographies, such as* Tolstoy *(1988), and many other works. He is a Fellow of the Royal Society of Literature.*

∾

school in North Oxford and then to the "public" school Marlborough. By that time his tastes were becoming clearly aesthetic, and he became more and more of an eccentric. It is not surprising that he did not get along with his father, Ernest Edward Betjeman, a manufacturer of cabinets.

In 1925 he chose to matriculate to Magdalene College, Oxford, possibly because Lord Alfred Douglas, the close friend of his aesthetic hero, Oscar Wilde, studied there. Betjeman was an inattentive student but enjoyed Oxford's social life, especially the salons of teachers like the legendary Maurice Bowra. There he made lifelong friends: cartoonist Osbert Lancaster, art historian Kenneth Clark, poets A. L. Rowse and W. H. Auden, and journalist Randolph Churchill. Betjeman was forced to leave Oxford without a degree because he failed a minor examination, and his tutor, the eventually famous C. S. Lewis, disliked him and would not stand up for him. He then went to London and worked in various jobs until in 1930 he joined the staff of the magazine *The Architectural Review*. In London, Betjeman roomed with Randolph Churchill in a Mayfair house owned by Edward James, who was rumored to be both the son and grandson of Edward VII. All through these years, Betjeman would spend days traveling about and looking closely at Anglican churches.

In 1931 his first book of poems, *Mount Zion*, was published. About this time he became friendly with the Mitford girls (Diana, Nancy, Pamela, and Unity) and their friends, including the novelist Evelyn Waugh and biographer Lytton Strachey. Soon afterward, he married Penelope Chetwode, the daughter of Field Marshall Sir Philip Chetwode, later Lord Chetwode. He and Penelope moved to a house in Berkshire, near enough for Betjeman to get to London easily. The housekeeping was messy. Wilson prints a hilarious photograph showing Penelope posing with her horse— inside the house. Betjeman became a film critic, supervised a series of travel guides, and published a book on architecture, *Ghastly Good Taste* (1933).

During World War II, he employed his charm as the press officer to the British ambassador in Dublin. He did such a good job that the Irish Republican Army considered assassinating him. After the war, Betjeman's career took off. His poetry became popular; his *Collected Poems* of 1958 sold two million copies. He continued many journalism projects. He became a television celebrity, creating and appearing in programs on architecture, specifically church architecture, and important places, often those associated with an important poet or novelist.

In 1951 he fell in love with Lady Elizabeth Cavendish. Though he never divorced his wife and remained on fairly good terms with her, his liaison with Lady Elizabeth continued to the end of his life. In his later years he went from triumph to triumph, both with his writings and his television appearances. He was knighted in 1969 and made poet laureate in 1972. A few years after that the effects of his Parkinson's disease became more apparent. He treated his depression with alcohol. Toward the end, he suffered strokes and had a heart attack. He died on May 19, 1984, and was buried near his home in Wales.

These are bare facts of Betjeman's life, but exactly when some of them occurred would be hard or even impossible to discover by reading Wilson's biography. Another biography of Betjeman exists—three volumes published between 1988 and 2004 by Bevis Hillier. Wilson does not mention it in *Betjeman*, though in a review Wilson called one of its volumes a "hopeless mishmash." It is almost as if Wilson has set out to write a biography that is unlike Hillier's, unlike conventional biographies. Wilson does not obfuscate, but there are not many dates in this book. He ends his book, not with the death of the biographical subject, but with that of Betjeman's wife.

For most readers that will not be a problem. Wilson has done his own research, which has been prodigious. He has spoken to as many of Betjeman's friends as he could. He has had access to family letters and vividly fleshes out the painful details of Betjeman's marriage to Penelope by quoting her agonized letters, written in such a way as to mimic a Cockney accent. He also details Betjeman's talent for friendship, which may have reached its zenith when he and Lady Elizabeth arranged for a flat on the Isle of Dogs where Princess Margaret could rendezvous with her future husband, Anthony Armstrong-Jones. He is an artist, not just a biographer. He writes well— always the apt word, never an awkward phrase. Reading this book is a pleasure.

One example of Wilson's artistry is his opening section. He does not start by telling about when the Betjeman family came to England from the Netherlands in the eighteenth century. He does get around to these facts, but he begins his story near its end—and begins it dramatically. One is just off King's Road, Chelsea, in London on a Sunday morning sometime in the 1980's. A large black car brings a middle-aged woman to a door from which emerge a tall aristocratic woman and an elderly man in a wheelchair. The two women push him up the road to a church near Sloane Square. By this time most readers will guess that the elderly man must be the subject of the biography, John Betjeman. Wilson springs his surprises, however. The two women who push him are the sister of the duke of Devonshire and Princess Margaret—not bad for a man whose father was in trade.

Wilson's artistry is also apparent in how he intrudes himself easily and effectively into his narrative. Sometimes he simply notes how much he was affected as a young man by Betjeman's television programs. More often the reader finds Wilson exercising admirable judgment. He evokes the complexities of Betjeman's relations with his wife and his mistress (and other women as well). He notes Betjeman's homosexual streak, active as a young man but probably not amounting to more than flirtations as an older adult. He treats the poet's relationship with his son Paul but will not draw a definite conclusion. He evokes Betjeman's personal complexity: He was "a melancholic introvert with an exhibitionistic compulsion." Though racked by doubts and guilt, he could project, in the words of his mistress, a "blinding charm."

Wilson's judgment also shows in his treatment of Betjeman's ideas, which blend his devotion to the Anglican Church and his passion for architecture—increasingly as he grew older to the church architecture of the past. He saw a bad, ugly, ungracious England appearing. At the same time, the monuments of the old order, especially old churches, were being destroyed. He promoted these ideas in his television programs and in his poetry. Wilson thinks that Betjeman became "the best apologist for Anglicanism of his generation, far more persuasive . . . than his old tutor C. S. Lewis."

The biographer is perhaps at his finest when he writes with great nuance and sensitivity about Betjeman's poetry. Betjeman's verse is unlike that of any of the giants of his century, not like William Butler Yeats nor Eliot nor Auden. It is not derivative of other poets' work. It is frankly based on several unusual influences: music hall songs, the Anglican hymnbook, and Oliver Goldsmith's eighteenth century poem *The Deserted Village*. That poem, which his father read to him over and over, was, like many of his own works, an elegy for a departed world. In many ways the poetry's mix of tones resembles the man's. Both mix "larkiness" and "serious emotion"; one poem dramatizes "lust mingled with piety." When telling of Betjeman's appointment as poet laureate, Wilson lists what he thinks are Betjeman's thirty best poems. Most readers would agree with him, especially about his early poems "The Arrest of Oscar Wilde at the Cadogan Hotel" and the "Death of King George V."

The comments on Betjeman's most famous poem, "A Subaltern's Love-song," are particularly revealing. In the poem, the narrator tells of his love for Miss Joan Hunter Dunn, a lithe, sexy, tennis-playing young woman. The day ends with them sitting in a car at a Gold Club and becoming engaged. Readers have long admired this poem as describing the narrator's progress to love in a light-hearted, but moving, way. Wilson remarks that Joan Hunter Dunn "represented not only a picture of the athletic young womanhood he found so erotically alluring, but also a vision of his England" in time of war.

After *Betjeman* was published in England, the London *Sunday Times* revealed that Wilson had been the victim of an elaborate hoax. A passionate and sexy letter supposedly by Betjeman that Wilson quoted in his book was revealed to be a fake. When examined closely, it became clear that the first letters of successive sentences spelled out an obscene statement about Wilson himself. It was later revealed that the hoax was perpetrated by Bevis Hillier, the biographer whom Wilson had criticized. Wilson's English publisher was able to remove the letter from some of but not all the copies that it printed. The American publisher, whose copies had already been printed in England, included an erratum note from Wilson.

George Soule

Review Sources

The Daily Mail, August 14, 2006, pp. 24-25.
Kirkus Reviews 74, no. 18 (September 15, 2006): 944.
The New York Times Book Review 156 (December 3, 2006): 28-29.
Publishers Weekly 253, no. 40 (October 9, 2006): 48-49.
The Spectator 301 (August 19, 2006): 33-34.
The Times Literary Supplement, September 15, 2006, p. 36.

BETRAYING SPINOZA
The Renegade Jew Who Gave Us Modernity

Author: Rebecca Goldstein (1950-   )
Publisher: Schocken Books (New York). 304 pp. $19.95
Type of work: Memoir, history, and philosophy

The author provides a memoir recounting her experiences with the philosophy of Spinoza from her initial exposure as a Jewish schoolgirl to her teaching experience as a professor of philosophy

Principal personages:
> REBECCA GOLDSTEIN, a philosopher
> BARUCH SPINOZA, a seventeenth century
>   philosopher
> ALBERT EINSTEIN, a physicist

Of the major figures in Western philosophy, Baruch Spinoza may well be the most admirable as well as the most remote. Both physicist Albert Einstein and philosopher Bertrand Russell openly admired his thinking and his integrity. While few scientific thinkers would be willing to endorse Spinoza's claim that the universe can be understood by reason alone, his ideas resonate with those of some modern cosmologists. At the same time Spinoza's theories of the emotions and the mind-body relationship have a certain appeal for modern neuroscientists. Though Spinoza could not accept revealed religion in its Jewish or any other form, he championed religious liberty. Later in life, his *Tractatus theologico-politicus* (1670; *A Theologico-Political Treatise*, 1862) would argue that the Pentateuch could not have been the work of the historical Moses but combined the writing of other, later writers—initiating the so-called higher criticism of Scripture now accepted by many scholars and seminary professors.

Spinoza was born in 1632 to a family of Marranos—Portuguese Jews who had nominally converted to Catholicism under duress but continued to practice their religion in secret before migrating to the Netherlands where they could resume their Jewish identity and outward observance. Spinoza received a traditional Jewish education and was soon recognized as an exceptional scholar. In 1656, however, he was placed in *kherem* (excommunicated) by the Jewish community of Amsterdam. Excommunication was not unusual in the Amsterdam Jewish community and was often temporary. Spinoza's excommunication was particularly harsh, however, and permanent. How it came about that a twenty-three-year-old man should be subjected to such a harsh penalty and the effect of the penalty on Spinoza's work are principal themes of *Betraying Spinoza: The Renegade Jew Who Gave Us Modernity*.

Three themes intertwine throughout the memoir. First, there is an introduction to Spinoza's thought. There is also the reflection of a mature scholar on her first exposure to Spinoza as a young orthodox Jewish girl attending a girls-only yeshiva in

~

Rebecca Goldstein is a professor of philosophy and a fellow of the American Academy of Arts and Sciences. She has received many fellowships and awards including a MacArthur Fellowship in 1995. Her novels include The Mind-Body Problem *(1983),* Mazel *(1995), and* Properties of Light *(2000).*

~

Manhattan. Then there is the history of European Jews, their thought and persecution as it certainly influenced the Jewish community in the Netherlands. Shifts from one strand to another, which would be out of place in a history or biography, are appropriate in this memoir and act to keep the reader engaged. The writing is clear and interesting, and some critics have read the book in a single sitting, though it is far from light reading.

Goldstein poses a further question: To what extent did Spinoza maintain a Jewish identity, a Jewishness, despite his expulsion from the community and his rejection of its core doctrines? The book does, after all, appear in a series devoted to Jewish thinkers. Without stating her own opinion, she points out that Spinoza kept relatively quiet about his doubts prior to his father's death, in keeping with the precept of *shalom bayis*, keeping peace in the home even if it means diverting time from laudable religious study. In keeping with ancient rabbinic tradition, the young scholar Spinoza mastered a manual trade, lens grinding, and largely supported himself by it in his later life. Though expelled from the synagogue, he did not take the politically pragmatic step of converting to Christianity, though he had many friends among the Dutch Collegiant movement.

Goldstein devotes a rather long chapter to her first exposure, as a student in a religious school, to Spinoza's thought. Her school presented Spinoza as an atheist, an unredeemable apostate, whose faith in reason supplanted his faith in God and gave appropriate cautionary words about what can happen when reason is unrestrained by faith and tradition. The school also expressed offense at Spinoza's decision to learn and publish in Latin, the language of the persecuting Roman church, and to adopt the Latinized form of his first name, Benedictus. It was here that Goldstein's interest in Spinoza was kindled as well as a desire, ultimately, to understand the personal Spinoza. She is particularly interested in the impact of Jewish thinking and history on Spinoza's thought and position in society. Since Spinoza's prescription for human happiness is to turn the mind away from the personal to contemplate the eternal and impersonal attributes of a God inseparable from nature, Goldstein's project constitutes a betrayal of Spinoza's teaching, hence the title of the book.

Goldstein also explains some aspects of Spinoza's philosophy. This is a valuable service to readers whose acquaintance with the man's thought is limited. Spinoza views God and the natural universe as inseparable. Further, God, or the universe, is as it has to be by logical necessity. Reason is supreme. Every aspect of the natural world can be understood by reason alone. God makes no revelation of himself, chooses no special people, hears no prayers, and grants no petitions. There is no afterlife and no resurrection of the dead. Human happiness is to be found only in contemplating the perfection of that God.

Much of the book is devoted to the history of European Jews and their persecution since the time of the Crusades. The Jews of Amsterdam enjoyed a degree of freedom under the Calvinist rulers of the Netherlands but were well aware of their status as members of a minority religion and had a clear interest in not provoking the majority. They were also aware of the possibility of further persecution or forced conversion.

Goldstein divides the Jewish thought of the time into three main components, each of which had some influence on the developing Spinoza. The first is concerned with the letter of the law or torah, which undoubtedly provided a valuable stimulus to the intellectual development of the young Spinoza. The second is a philosophical trend following from the writings of the great scholar and physician Moses Maimonides, whose *Dalālat al-Hā'irīn* (1190; *The Guide of the Perplexed*, 1881-1885) argued for the consistency of Jewish belief with Aristotelian philosophy. In addition Maimonides listed thirteen articles of faith, some of which Spinoza accepted and others he rejected. The third component is mystical, focused on the *Zohar*, or *Book of Splendor*.

By the seventeenth century, mystical and millenialist trends had entered the consciousness of the community. The *Zohar* was composed in Spain in the decade following 1270. Sabbatai Zevi appears on the scene in 1665 claiming to be the promised Messiah but converts to Islam in 1666. The idea that the Messiah would come only after the Jewish people had been dispersed to all the corners of the world prompted an effort to establish Judaism in Brazil and to persuade England to readmit Jews.

At the yeshiva, modernity meant fitting in with the larger gentile society, abandoning the distinctive aspects of Jewish culture. For the more general reader, modernity might mean secularization in general and a general downplaying of the importance of religious belief or willing participation in a pluralistic society.

Spinoza also anticipates the development of the modern sciences of physics and biology. Most physicists accept the world as being comprehensible by human reason but would reject the assertion that the true nature of reality could be determined by reasoning alone. Nonetheless the very existence of theoretical physics as a respected field within physics confirms that a great deal of the world can be understood by thinking about it. Further, there is in the somewhat controversial anthropic principle advanced by some cosmologists the notion that had the fundamental constants of physics been the slightest bit different, life as we know it would be impossible, so we are living in the only logically possible universe that could have living rational beings in it. In the understanding of nature a great many scientists have found something approaching religious satisfaction. Among the most expressive of these was Albert Einstein. Alarmed by the claim that the celebrated physicist was in fact an atheist, Rabbi Herbert Goldstein of New York sent him a cable asking, "Do you believe in God?" Einstein replied, "I believe in Spinoza's God who reveals himself in the orderly harmony of what exists, not in a God who concerns himself with fates and actions of human beings."

Rebecca Goldstein has labeled her book a memoir, thus making no claim to completeness. As she points out, Spinoza's writing is difficult to follow. Spinoza's magnum opus, *Ethica* (1677; *Ethics*, 1870), presented in the form of a mathematics text with definitions, axioms, and propositions, is not for the casual reader.

Donald R. Franceschetti

Review Sources

Commentary 122, no. 5 (December, 2006): 25-30.
Harper's Magazine 312 (May, 2006): 80.
Library Journal 131, no. 7 (April 15, 2006): 79.
London Review of Books, July 20, 2006, p. 19.
The New York Review of Books 53 (May 25, 2006): 41.
The New York Times Book Review 155 (June 18, 2006): 7.
Publishers Weekly 253, no. 12 (March 20, 2006): 47.
Weekly Standard 11, no. 48 (September 11, 2006): 33-34.

THE BIG OYSTER
History on the Half Shell

Author: Mark Kurlansky (1948-   )
Publisher: Ballantine Books (New York). 307 pp. $24.00
Type of work: History
Time: 1609-2006
Locale: New York City and environs

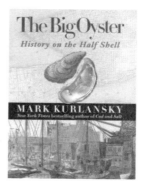

Kurlansky uses a study of the oyster harvesting, cooking, and eating habits of the inhabitants of the Hudson River estuary as a way of tracing some of the history of New York City and its environs from the early Dutch explorers to the present

Principal personages:
JAMES BUCHANAN, also known as "DIAMOND JIM" BRADY, railroad tycoon and legendary gourmand
WILLIAM K. BROOKS, nineteenth century scientist from Maryland who studied oysters
JASPER DANCKAERTS, seventeenth century Dutch traveler
CHARLES DICKENS, nineteenth century British novelist
HENRY HUDSON, seventeenth century British explorer, discoverer of the Hudson River
WASHINGTON IRVING, nineteenth century American author
CHARLES McCAY, nineteenth century Scottish songwriter
PETER STUYVESANT, seventeenth century Dutch soldier and administrator of New Amsterdam
FANNY TROLLOP, nineteenth century British author

Mark Kurlansky is one of the first writers of popular history to successfully capitalize on the intense fascination that the focus of microhistory can generate about its subject. Microhistory is a relatively recent academic approach to the study of the past that concentrates on a single, often small and limited subject, as a lens through which to illuminate a larger, more broadly defined issue. Two of the author's previous books, *Cod: A Biography of the Fish That Changed the World* (1997) and *Salt: A World History* (2003), also use an eatable subject for his microhistorical approach.

In *Cod*, Kurlansky used a study of the codfish to explore the trade routes opened up by the search for the fish and the geopolitical offshoots of that exploration. He also provided a detailed examination of the codfish, its habits, and the habits of those who have eaten it through the ages. With *Salt*, he broadened his search and dealt with salt as a worldwide commodity and traced its gastronomical importance and economic influence through recorded history. In both books the detailed scrutiny of the micro-subject, cod and salt, led him to research larger historical issues, periods, and locales.

The Big Oyster: History on the Half Shell employs the same methodical approach

Mark Kurlansky is author of the best-selling Cod: A Biography of the Fish That Changed the World *(1997) and* Salt: A World History *(2003), as well as* 1968: The Year That Rocked the World *(2003),* The Basque History of the World *(1999), and* A Chosen Few: The Resurrection of European Jewry *(1994). He has also written the novel* Boogaloo on 2nd Avenue: A Novel of Pastry, Guilt, and Music *(2005) and other fiction for both adults and children.*

and again does so through a foodstuff, this time the oyster, but restricts the locale to primarily the Hudson River estuary. The time span is roughly from the time of Henry Hudson's discovery of the river that bears his name, during the first decade of the seventeenth century, until the early twenty-first century. During those four hundred years, both the oysters in the estuary and the marine environment experienced violent degradation. For the most part, the oysters died out when they were overharvested and their breeding grounds destroyed by industrial waste and city garbage. Unfortunately, those that have survived have been rendered so toxic by pollutants that they are no longer eatable. This sad and enlightening story is set against the backdrop of New York City as it rises from a modest trading post at the edge of the far-flung Dutch empire to become one of the world's most vibrant and influential cities.

The book's design is straightforwardly chronological, opening with Hudson's discovery and the arrival of the Dutch and their early settlement of what would become Manhattan and the surrounding boroughs. Kurlansky discusses the loss of the trading center to the British, their loss in turn to the fledgling American nation after the Revolutionary War, and the city's expansion through the nineteenth and twentieth centuries to become the most important urban center in the United States. The narrative is enlivened with the personal stories of not the usual politicians and statesmen but of those most closely associated with the growing, processing, cooking, and eating of oysters. This microhistorical approach gives the reader a new and different understanding of the city and its growth.

Interlarded throughout this narrative is a running discussion of the bivalve, its natural history, gastronomical history, and social history. Readers will learn how it reproduces and grows, matures and ages, where it flourishes and does not, and how it has been harvested over the years. Also included is Kurlansky's discussion of how oysters have been consumed through the ages—raw, boiled, steamed, fried, and so on. Thoughtfully, he has also included some three dozen recipes, most of them historical, which he has conveniently indexed in the back of the book. Oysters also have a literary history and have been covered by such writers as the first century B.C.E. Roman Sergius Orata and the American food writer M. F. K. Fisher, whose *Consider the Oyster* (1941) forms one of the five volumes that make up her famous *The Art of Eating* (1954).

The oyster also has a social history, oddly enough occupying at the same time a place at both the tables of the rich and poor. Kurlansky points out that oysters could be had for pennies from street vendors or could actually be harvested by individuals from the common beds for the evening's meal. On the other hand, since Roman times they have had a place of honor at the tables of the rich. Kurlansky recalls several anecdotes about the railroad magnet Diamond Jim Brady and his frequent companion actress Lillian Russell gorging themselves on meals at Rector's, a New York eatery, and always beginning with a quantity of raw oysters on the half-shell.

The abundance of the oysters discovered by the Europeans who first landed on Manhattan Island was legendary, prompting Kurlansky to remark that before New York was the Big Apple it was the Big Oyster, thus giving this book its title. This book also could have been called "The bivalve (*Crassostrea virginica*) and the city (New York)," because it is the ingenious way Kurlansky weaves the two narratives, one on the rise and fall of the oyster and the other on the rise of the city, that makes this study of particular interest. The indigenous Lenape Indians clearly had been consuming oysters by the millions long before the arrival of the Dutch, as the middens of shells dotted around the coastline and discovered by those early settlers attest. Routinely, the early visitors to these shores write about the fecund oyster beds of the estuary that continued to produce millions of oysters right through the early years of the nineteenth century, when overharvesting required that they be stocked.

Still, by the beginning of the Civil War, New York was the oyster capital of the world—unfortunately, however, in shipping only, as the native beds were by then in decline. Industrial waste and the sheer tonnage of New York's garbage finally did them in by the early years of the twentieth century, when the relaxation of environmental standards during World War II flooded the area with toxic materials still present in the waters. It is the size of the loss as much as anything that highlights the environmental disaster the book chronicles.

This cautionary tale—the first section of the book's title, "The Beds of Eden," and the second half's "The Shells of Sodom" tells it all—is not accompanied by the screed that often accompanies a narrative of environmental despoliation with a condemnation of what takes its place. Kurlansky likes New York City and at times offers up reasons for applauding this particular history of the oyster. Oysters offered employment for African American oystermen and oyster shop owners as well as providing much-needed nourishment for the poor. Oysters and their export helped to publicize New York's prominence. Unfortunately, the destruction of the beds did, in the end, more harm than good, as the disappearance of the oyster beds around the estuary also contributed to the worsening of the pollution of the waters.

Kurlansky mentions one estimate that if the original beds still survived, the oysters in them—natural cleansers of seawater—could clean up the current marine pollution in a matter of weeks. Also with the loss of the oyster, the inhabitants of the city lost something of their connection to the waterways that lie so close to them. For New Yorkers to lose their oysters was for them to lose their taste of the sea. In fact, this very notion of loss is one of the reasons Kurlansky wrote the book. He puts it this way: "How is it that a people living in the world's greatest port, a city with no neighborhood that is far from the waterfront, a city whose location was chosen because of the sea, where great cargo ships and tankers, mighty little tugs, yachts, and harbor patrol boats glide by, has lost all connection with the sea, almost forgotten that the sea is there?"

Is this putting too much emphasis on the little oyster to sustain such a large-scale historical analysis? Such a question might be asked of all microhistorical studies, but Kurlansky is very skillful in working his material—cod, salt, or now oysters—in ways entertaining but also convincing enough to make his case. The oysters here are a reflector of the human attitudes that both destroyed them as well as built the city, and they reflect even larger-scale values that have informed a general American ideology toward nature and the idea of progress. By successfully focusing on an examination of the fate of the humble oyster in this one place over a three-hundred-year span, Kurlansky opens up the possibilities for doing the same kind of study using any number of similar small-scope objects.

From *The Big Oyster*, the reader learns about the fashioning of America's greatest city and also about the natural history of this bivalve and something of how history has regarded oysters and their consumption. Like Eleanor Clark's *The Oysters of Locmariaquer* (1964), for which reprint Kurlansky wrote an introduction and which his book in many ways resembles, *The Big Oyster* engages both the reader's mind and senses. It is elegantly written, witty, and knowing, and at the same time wonderfully entertaining.

Charles L. P. Silet

Review Sources

Booklist 102, no. 3 (October 1, 2005): 4.
Kirkus Reviews 73, no. 20 (October 15, 2005): 1124.
Library Journal 131, no. 2 (February 1, 2006): 92.
The New York Times 155 (March 1, 2006): E1-E6.
The New York Times Book Review 155 (March 5, 2006): 1-7.
Publishers Weekly 252, no. 38 (September 26, 2005): 71.
The Times Literary Supplement, November 10, 2006, p. 32.
The Wall Street Journal 247, no. 57 (March 10, 2006): W4.

BLACK SWAN GREEN

Author: David Mitchell (1969-   )
Publisher: Random House (New York). 294 pp. $24.00
Type of work: Novel
Time: January, 1982-January, 1983
Locale: Worcestershire, England

Mitchell's fourth novel chronicles a difficult, yet frequently comic, year in the life of an adolescent boy in a small English village

Principal characters:
> JASON TAYLOR, a rather breathless thirteen-year-old boy
> MICHAEL TAYLOR, his father, the regional sales director for Greenland supermarket chain
> HELENA TAYLOR, his mother
> JULIA TAYLOR, his sister, a law student
> UNCLE BRIAN LAMB, Helena Taylor's brother-in-law
> HUGO LAMB, Jason's older cousin and his idol
> MRS. DE ROO, his sympathetic speech therapist
> ROSS WILCOX, a bully and Jason's nemesis
> GARY DRAKE, Ross's cousin, also a bully
> DAWN MADDEN, the tough-girl object of Jason's first crush
> MADAME EVA VAN OUTRYVE DE CROMMELYNCK, a Belgian exile
> TOM YEW, a schoolmate's older brother in the Royal Navy
> DEAN MORAN, Jason's schoolmate and best friend

English author David Mitchell never writes the same book twice. After publishing three novels of varied and complicated structure, he returns to a simple linear storyline, producing what is usually a writer's first novel—a semi-autobiographical account of a young person's coming of age. With its precocious teenage narrator and a chronicle filled with British slang and actual events of 1982, *Black Swan Green* has been compared to J. D. Salinger's *The Catcher in the Rye* (1951). The careful structure is still there: thirteen chapters set in consecutive months, the first and last bearing the same title, but done so subtly that a reader might miss it. In each chapter Jason Taylor, the youth in question, learns a new and uncomfortable truth, so that the book could well be subtitled *Jason's Progress*.

Jason, the narrator of *Black Swan Green*, pretends to be more sophisticated than he really is but, in fact, is charmingly innocent. He does not know how to attract a girlfriend and fails to understand most off-color remarks, although he knows enough not to ask questions. Living in the Worcestershire village of Black Swan Green, whose one joke is that there are no swans, Jason is the very picture of a self-conscious, desperate-not-to-be-different adolescent. To his chagrin, his voice is still changing; occa-

David Mitchell wrote his first two novels while teaching English in Hiroshima, Japan. Ghostwritten *(1999) was short-listed for the* Guardian *First Book Award;* Number9Dream *(2001) and* Cloud Atlas *(2004) were finalists for the Man Booker Prize. In 2003, Mitchell was selected as one of* Granta's *Best of Young British Novelists. He lives in West Cork, Ireland.*

sionally he squeaks. Among his endearing qualities are his stammer, his lucky red underpants, and his fondness for his speech therapist's Metro Gnome—so called, he believes, because it is so small.

Jason's family has its own problems. Something is going on between his parents that he does not fully understand. Michael Taylor, his dogmatic and generally absent father, is the short-tempered mid-level executive of a supermarket chain. Jason's mother, Helena, comes to life only after she is invited to manage a friend's successful interior design gallery and shop, which she does very well. His older sister, Julia, refers to him as "Thing." His current hero is his cousin Hugo Lamb, two years older and infinitely cool, who is also an accomplished shoplifter. In the course of a noisy family visit, Jason's father and his Uncle Brian drink too much, argue about traffic routes, and boast about their offspring over a dinner that suggests the disastrous Christmas dinner in James Joyce's *Portrait of the Artist as a Young Man* (1916).

One is aware of an uncomfortable distance between Jason and his father, resulting in an uneasy balancing act. At the same time, it is clear that father and son do love each other. Jason recalls a spoiled vacation (it rained constantly) as one of the best because he and Michael, trapped indoors, played games together every day. In August the two of them visit the coastal resort of Lyme Regis—the father for a business conference, the son for a brief holiday. Their evening date for the film *Chariots of Fire* passes when Michael comes back to the hotel too late and then leaves again with his employer, returning quite drunk in the middle of the night. Nevertheless, in the morning they do fly a kite together on the beach, and in a moment of boyishness his father, who once loved geology, buys Jason a fossil. When by chance they encounter his boss again, Michael Taylor transforms immediately into a fawning subordinate, and the holiday is over. At her gallery, Jason's mother gives him more spending money than his father did (a subtle competition) and takes him to see the movie.

Young Jason frequently holds a dialogue with his inner selves. Maggot is Jason's cowardly self, ever ready to retreat or hide. Unborn Twin is a true alter ego, a critical inner voice that corrects, contradicts, and disapproves of him: "I *should've been born . . . not* you, *you cow.*" Hangman is his treacherous stammer, which he has personified and which always seems worse in winter. Stammering and stuttering are "as different as diarrhea and constipation," and Jason is careful to distinguish between them. While a stutterer will repeat the initial sound, a stammerer cannot articulate the last part of the word: "When a stammerer stammers their eyeballs pop out, they go trembly-red . . . and their mouth guppergupperguppers like a fish in a net." (Mitchell writes from childhood experience.) Jason tries to think ahead to a substitute word, preferably not one beginning with *n, s,* or *g.* Extremely sensitive, he dreads making errors in front of anyone, especially at school or with his father.

Jason has another serious worry besides the stammer, and his name is Ross Wilcox, the toughest boy in school. In the same year as Jason, the bully Ross attracts a horde of hangers-on including Ross's cousin Gary Drake, who is an eager tattletale and almost as cruel. Together they mean trouble, and Jason lives in mortal fear of them while struggling to maintain a low, stammerless profile. He is also suffering from the pangs of a secret crush on Ross Wilcox's tomboyish girlfriend, Dawn Madden, whose "eyes are dark honey" and who seems to revel in her power over boys. In addition, Jason conceals the fact that he writes and publishes poetry in the parish magazine under the pseudonym of Eliot Bolivar.

Responding to an unsigned invitation to discuss his poems, Jason visits the vicarage. However, the person who wishes to talk with him is not the vicar but an elderly lady, Madame Eva van Outryve de Crommelynck, a Belgian exile who, with her husband, is renting the vicarage. Jason longs for but fears her critique because he is so vulnerable. She upbraids him for using too many "beautiful" words ("I answer, 'Go to the hell!'") and challenges him to define "beauty." Jason is stumped: "All this is new. In English at school we . . . don't have to actually think about stuff." Madame Crommelynck encourages him to write only the truth (which in itself is beautiful) but in his own voice, not falsely. She lends him a French novel, ordering him to translate the first chapter by himself, but by the next week she and her husband have disappeared, extradited to Bonn by the West German police in some sort of financial scandal.

From time to time the real world intrudes on Jason. He accidentally sees his classmate's eighteen-year-old brother who is in the Royal Navy, Tom Yew, wake screaming from a nightmare of combat even though he is scheduled to cruise the Mediterranean. Soon afterward, Argentina seizes the Falkland Islands, which Britain claims as its own territory, and the short-lived Falklands War begins. Jason confidently echoes his country's passionate slogans against the Argentineans until Tom's nightmare becomes a reality that affects the whole village.

During a school break, Jason's popularity briefly rises with the cherry knocking escapade. Cherry knocking is tapping at someone's door and fleeing before the door can be opened. When a crotchety neighbor living nearby refuses to give back a football kicked into his yard, Jason temporarily becomes a hero to his schoolmates by daring to tie a string to the man's doorknocker so that the violator can remain hidden. His sudden prestige results in an invitation to join Spooks, a secret club, and there is an initiation. His best (and only) friend, Dean Moran, is also invited. In the evening they are to sneak across people's back gardens undetected, within a specified amount of time. Jason succeeds, but poor Dean falls into the neighbor's greenhouse. Jason wants to rescue him, but the other Spooks want to run. He goes anyway to help his friend, and both are expelled from the club.

Once back in school, Jason still has trouble with the dreaded Hangman. Ross Wilcox has begun to bully him again, and when Jason starts to write a poem, he finds a mouse's head (from biology class) in his pencil case. Jason fails to realize that he is starting to get some help with the bullying; his generally unsympathetic form teacher offers a photocopied sheet of advice, and even the bus driver, no shrinking violet, suggests that slicing Ross Wilcox's tendons would quickly put him out of action.

The Taylor house grows emptier. Julia, who has become rather protective of her brother, has gone off to university in Edinburgh, Jason's mother works in Cheltenham, and his father works in Oxford. When only Jason is home, a Gypsy knife grinder comes to the door, but Jason, who likes him, knows he must ask his mother's permission before hiring him. Another parental argument ensues. Jason's father brings him to a meeting attended by most of the village, formed to protest the creation of a permanent settlement for the Gypsies in their area. Voices are strong and prejudiced until the fire alarm sounds, and the meeting ends in general panic.

Jason visits Dean Moran's house after school to discover that Dean's father, who is part Gypsy, refused to attend the meeting. On his way home, Jason stumbles into some other boys' battle and hides in the woods, staying invisible in order to survive. A large dog seizes the schoolbag containing his homework, and Jason desperately follows it to the quarry and a Gypsy camp. Confronted and accused of spying, he literally falls into the camp, where he is first mistrusted and then welcomed, helped by a kind word from the knife grinder. They talk out their differences, and suddenly Jason realizes he is not stammering.

Later, in the Hall of Mirrors at the local fair, Jason experiences a significant epiphany that turns out to be a restatement of Madame Crommelynck's earlier advice: He must unify his inner and outer selves and not worry about the false outer self of which others are supposed to approve. When he is able to stand up to the bullies, when he can think of his nemesis, Ross Wilcox, as "the poor kid," he is clearly on his way to adulthood.

David Mitchell draws on history to help create a snapshot of Jason's pivotal year, incorporating the use of graphics and newspaper headlines into his text for verisimilitude. The quoted headlines are historical: "GOTCHA" appeared in the London *Sun* after British prime minister Margaret Thatcher ordered the attack that led to the first casualties of the Falkland Islands War. Contemporary popular references include television shows and movies (*The Rockford Files*, *Sesame Street*, *The Great Escape*), athletes, rock stars, bands, even pixie boots. One can feel properly superior when reading such comments as Jason's enthusiastic prediction that "people'll remember everything about the Falklands until the end of the world," or the assertion that Betamax technology will quickly eclipse VHS.

The book is laden with mysteries: a lost tunnel that the Romans built in order to invade Hereford, a crumbling house in the woods, the dark ghost of the butcher's boy who fell through the ice, and a chilling first chapter that leaves a reader eager for more.

Joanne McCarthy

Review Sources

Booklist 102, no. 12 (February 15, 2006): 45.
The Economist 378, no. 8472 (April 8, 2006): 82.

Entertainment Weekly, no. 872 (April 14, 2006): 89.
London Review of Books 28, no. 9 (May 11, 2006): 34-35.
Los Angeles Times, May 15, 2006, p. E9.
The New Republic 235, no. 4 (July 24, 2006): 25-31.
New Statesman 135 (April 24, 2006): 56-57.
New York 39, no. 13 (April 17, 2006): 106.
The New York Times Book Review 155 (April 16, 2006): 19.
The New Yorker 82, no. 9 (April 17, 2006): 82-83.
Poets & Writers 34 (May/June, 2006): 44.
Publishers Weekly 253, no. 15 (January 2, 2006): 33.
Time 167, no. 17 (April 24, 2006): 70.

BLIND ORACLES
Intellectuals and War from Kennan to Kissinger

Author: Bruce Kuklick (1941-   )
Publisher: Princeton University Press (Princeton, N.J.).
   241 pp. $30.00
Type of work: History
Time: 1945-1975
Locale: The United States

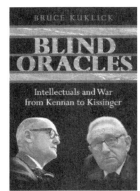

Kuklick explores the influence of a select group of academics on American statecraft from World War II through the Vietnam War

                    Principal personages:
                    GEORGE KENNAN (1904-2005), U.S. State
                        Department official responsible for articulating the United States'
                        post-World War II "containment" policy
                    HENRY KISSINGER (b. 1923), U.S. national security adviser and secretary
                        of state closely associated with America's participation in the Vietnam War
                    WALT ROSTOW (1916-2003), MIT economist who became a foreign policy adviser in the White House and the State Department
                    MCGEORGE BUNDY (1919-1996), President John F. Kennedy's national security adviser in the 1960's
                    ROBERT MCNAMARA (b. 1916), U.S. secretary of defense during several presidential administrations in the 1960's

    For the first century and a half of its existence, the United States tended to avoid global involvement. Focused on settling the American continent and securing its immediate region, the young country generally avoided the international "power politics" that absorbed European and other powers. In the twentieth century, the United States entered World War I, with some reluctance, and then retreated back to isolationism soon after the armistice (despite President Woodrow Wilson's desire to create a global League of Nations). The Japanese attack on Pearl Harbor in 1941 again rousted the United States from its disengagement with the world. This time, the United States emerged from the (second) world war as the preeminent global power for which isolationism seemed an unrealistic option.

    At the time of the Axis powers' defeat, U.S. troops were deployed around the world, and the United States was the only country that possessed atomic weapons. The traditional "great powers" of the world (including Japan, the Soviet Union, Britain, and most of Europe) were militarily and economically exhausted by the war. Popular thought saw the dawning of an "American century," in which the United States would create a new world order based on democracy and, not incidentally, American interests. For a country without a history of global involvement, this was a tall order indeed. How would America move from isolationism to prolonged engagement on the world stage? Would the American economy be affected by peacetime militarizationand a peacetime draft? Would the American public support such an approach?

The author of nine books, Bruce Kuklick is Nichols Professor of History at the University of Pennsylvania. In 2004, he was elected to the American Philosophical Society.

In his book *Blind Oracles*, Bruce Kuklick examines the influence of a select group of well-educated, intelligent academics on American statecraft from World War II through the Vietnam War. These "wise men," as they are sometimes called, applied an analytical, science-based approach to the realm of international politics that was traditionally associated more with personal relationships and dynastic ties.

It is an ambitious project for this relatively short book. The three decades under review were at the height of the Cold War between the Western democracies and the Soviet-led Communist bloc. Kuklick asserts that these men believed in the rightness of their cause—they "knew that . . . America was right and its enemies wrong"—yet their focus was not on ideology but rather on theory. Through such devices as "game theory" and content analysis, they sought to understand how states "acted" in the international environment. The stakes were incredibly high. The period under review was characterized by a bipolar balance of power that had the potential to end civilization with a nuclear world war.

This raises the question of whether it is even possible for scholars to discover objective "laws" of international behavior on which to base their foreign policy prescriptions. This belief, which is implicit in the very field of political "science," has been subject to some criticism. How can state policies, which after all are the product of human decisions, be subject to external laws the way a billiard ball is subject to Newtonian physics? Without directly answering this question, Kuklick seems skeptical about the ability to discover such "laws" with any accuracy.

Kuklick's subject of study contains an important normative question as well: To what extent should the foreign policy of a country, especially in a democracy, be determined by elite "intellectuals" rather than the expressed will of the population? Is rule by these "wise men" desirable, even assuming that they are better informed than the masses?

Kuklick largely ignores these questions. Instead, he focuses almost exclusively on explaining the link between intellectuals' thinking and the policies adopted by the political leadership. Interestingly, he believes that these men had little influence on the actual formulation of policy. Instead, he asserts that "they served to legitimate but not to energize policies." In his view, the world of Washington policy making was one of "Darwinism" where defense intellectuals had to "prune their theories to satisfy the demands of statesmen." If this is the case, one might well ask whether a more fruitful inquiry would have examined those who were instrumental in creating (rather than merely "legitimating") America's postwar foreign policy.

Kuklick focuses on a handful of intellectuals—from the framer of America's "containment" policy, George Kennan, to President Richard Nixon's national security adviser Henry Kissinger—who were especially close to the nation's policymakers. While he does provide some background (of varying depth) on each of these individuals, he does not go so far as to provide biographies or psychological portraits of these men. Instead, he assesses the intellectual contributions of each and how these squared with the foreign policy issues of the day. He also pays attention to some of the academic institutions that groomed them and the think tanks that harnessed them.

Kuklick's narrative is based on extensive primary and secondary source research. Building on his solid understanding of American foreign policies themselves, Kuklick examined the writings and memoirs of "his" intellectuals to develop a clearer picture of their beliefs, theories, and worldviews. He also focused on a selected number of foreign policy events, such as the Cuban Missile Crisis and the (halted) development of the joint U.S.-British Skybolt missile, as case studies. With extensive footnotes and references to other works, the book reads much like a doctoral dissertation.

The book is arranged into chapters that do not quite follow either a chronological order or a thematic progression. The first chapter looks at general theories of "scientific management." The next few chapters examine the first fifteen to twenty years of the post-World War II era from different vantage points: one focused on war theorists, one focused on the contributions of the RAND corporation, several examining particular administrations (President John F. Kennedy's) or regionally defined crises (Cuba and Nassau). Later chapters examine, in turn, Harvard's Kennedy School of Government in the Vietnam War era, the Pentagon Papers, and Henry Kissinger. (Kissinger is the only thinker to merit his own chapter in this book.)

What emerges is a far-ranging, if somewhat disjointed and spotty, examination of the intellectual underpinnings of America's postwar foreign policy doctrine. Its incompleteness as a history text could be excused—perhaps even necessitated—on its own terms as a series of case studies to examine the influence of intellectuals on policy making. Indeed, more than an interesting series of vignettes about America's foreign policy development since World War II, Kuklick's project had the potential to explore the factors that influenced the direction of America's diplomatic influence and military might. It is set up to provide valuable insights into normative questions about the development of foreign policy in a democracy—and especially a democracy that happens to be a superpower.

On these terms, however, the book is less than satisfying. Kuklick seems less interested in these questions than in judging the value of his intellectuals' contributions. On that question, he essentially determines that these were not infallible "oracles" of wisdom but rather imperfect humans who blindly "groped in the dark" while professing special insights. Yes, in retrospect it has become clear that these men tended to overestimate Soviet power and global intentions. It is equally clear that the Soviets (and others) did not always act as the theories of American intellectuals had predicted. Kuklick concludes that "American culture paid a high price for a product of dubious value."

What is this product for which America overpaid? Because Kuklick believes that the intellectuals "legitimized" rather than created policy, one must conclude that it is this "legitimization" that is of "dubious value." This is hardly an indictment of the Vietnam War, Mutual Assured Destruction, or other facets of American foreign policy that, in retrospect, have been subject to some legitimate criticism. Instead, it is an indictment (of whatever merit) of the way the policies were "legitimized." Here again is an opportunity to explore what exactly constitutes "legitimacy" with regard to statecraft in a democracy, but this is beyond the scope of Kuklick's study.

In addition to finding his intellectuals wanting in omniscience and purity, Kuklick finds that perhaps the foreign policy-making system itself was flawed. He speculates that, even if the human intellectual limitations could have been overcome—if researchers' quest for more data and knowledge could have been satisfied—it may not have been of any added benefit to policymakers. The system evidently does not value the intellectuals' craft for what it can do on the front end of the policy process, but only on the back end. Perhaps academics are incapable of thinking outside the confines that are defined by policymakers. Kuklick does not explain what, exactly, the limitations on the process are.

At the same time Kuklick is also concerned with the effect of foreign policy events on defense intellectuals (rather than the reverse). He dedicates his final chapter to exploring how, during the last quarter of the twentieth century, these intellectuals responded to the outcomes of American foreign policy during the Cold War—such as the failure to stem the Communist unification of Vietnam and the (perceived) solidification of Soviet control over the Eastern bloc. Kuklick perceives that these men's intellectual powers were pressed into the service of justifying, rationalizing, or explaining America's foreign policy efforts. If not exactly rewriting history, he sees them as interpreting it in a perhaps self-serving way.

One might hope that at the conclusion of his book, Kuklick would offer some lessons—for policy makers, for intellectuals, or simply for students of foreign policy—that stem from the examination of such a critical time for American statecraft. The reader looking for such lessons, or even for compelling conclusions, will be disappointed. The book seems to fizzle out, with Kuklick's intellectuals dethroned as limited, fallible men who in any event did not have a significant role in the development of American foreign policy. This could be a helpful conclusion if it were used as a springboard to shed more light on who and what did shape foreign policy. Or perhaps Kuklick could have suggested ways that academic rigor could better be brought to bear on the flawed political processes that generate policy. Alternatively, Kuklick could have applied his observations about Cold War policy making to the post-Cold War international environment, speculating about a role for intellectuals and theory in a world without clear allies and enemies—where America's largest threats appear to come not from other states but from terrorists. Kuklick does none of this, leaving one to speculate on the relevance of his case studies.

Steve D. Boilard

Review Sources

The Economist 378 (March 25, 2006): 87-88.
Foreign Affairs 85, no. 5 (September/October, 2006): 164-165.

THE BLIND SIDE
Evolution of a Game

Author: Michael Lewis (1960-   )
Publisher: W. W. Norton (New York). 288 pp. $24.95
Type of work: Current affairs
Time: March, 2004, to the end of college football season
in 2005, with many flashbacks
Locale: Memphis, Tennessee, Oxford, Mississippi, and
several other cities

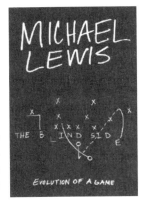

Lewis tells how an impoverished, jumbo-sized, barely literate black youngster evolves into a gridiron wunderkind who becomes a loved member of a privileged white family in Memphis while coaches of football-mad Southern colleges covet him

Principal personages:
> MICHAEL (BIG MIKE) OHER, born MICHAEL JEROME WILLIAMS, a 6-foot
> 5-inch, 330-pound black teenager who miraculously moves from
> squalor to football fame
> SEAN TUOHY, head of an upper-class Memphis family who adopt
> Michael Oher
> LEIGH ANNE TUOHY, Sean's feisty wife who warmly fills the role of
> Mike's mom
> COLLINS TUOHY, teenage daughter of the Tuohys and Michael's play-
> mate
> DENISE (DEE DEE) WILLIAMS, mother of Michael and his many siblings
> TOM LEMMING, a freelance national football scout who is the first to talk
> to Big Mike
> HUGH FREEZE, football coach at Briarcrest

It is likely that few but serious students of baseball and football will go the whole distance with either of Michael Lewis's sports-themed books, *Moneyball: The Art of Winning an Unfair Game* (2003) and *The Blind Side: Evolution of a Game*. *Moneyball* took readers inside the halls of a major-league baseball franchise—that of the Oakland Athletics. This team has combined baseball's lowest payroll with its highest winning percentage through the acuity of general manager Billy Beane, who did it by the numbers—using statistics compiled by a curious battery of "outside insiders" who demonstrated that the traditional yardsticks of success for players and teams may be flawed. Only baseball insiders will grasp Lewis's "new baseball."

While *Moneyball* is replete with baseball anecdotage—intimate and original portraits of big-league ball players and game situations—*The Blind Side* conveys its dedication to football's modern playbook novelistically through one player's poignant—if unlikely—success story. Sometimes, however, Lewis's narrative goes awry. Just as the reader becomes engrossed in that player's drama, the author runs a literary double reverse and starts talking about the evolving game.

The reader does not meet the protagonist of *The Blind Side* until the first page of chapter 2, twenty-five pages into the book. That is because Lewis wants readers to know from the outset the role of his book's antagonist, perhaps professional football history's most violent defensive lineman. In physiology,

∾
Michael Lewis, author of the best sellers Liar's Poker: Rising Through the Wreckage on Wall Street *(1989),* The New New Thing: A Silicon Valley Story *(1999), and* Moneyball: The Art of Winning an Unfair Game *(2003), is a contributing writer for* The New York Times Magazine.
∾

"antagonist" is defined as "a muscle that acts in opposition to other muscles." That is how New York Giants linebacker Lawrence Taylor (L.T.) destroyed opposing quarterbacks throughout the 1980's.

In his zestfully manipulative way, Lewis serves up the menacing presence of L.T. as catalyst for the larger human story that he really wishes to tell. Yet, unless readers accept this subtext for the book's powerful bildungsroman—the rags-to-riches rise of a giant (6 feet 5 inches and 330 pounds) but destitute black teenager—that the primary fact of modern-day football is the position of offensive left tackle, the impact of *The Blind Side* diminishes.

Fifteen years ago this position was the lowest paid in the National Football League (NFL) but is now, after the quarterback, the highest. The offensive left tackle protects the right-handed quarterback's blind side. It is the pass rush the quarterback cannot see coming that results in injuries like the one Lewis describes on page 1: Washington's Joe Theismann's career-ending leg fracture in a 1985 game against L.T. and the New York Giants in a "busted" play that inadvertently caused Taylor to wedge the quarterback beneath another Giants pursuer, with Theismann's leg paying the price.

Injuries to star quarterbacks cause coaches anxiety about their jobs. By the 2004 NFL season the average professional left tackle's salary was $5.5 million a year. In Super Bowl XL, played February 5, 2006, the highest-paid player on the field was Seattle quarterback Matt Hasselbeck, who had just signed a six-year deal worth $8.2 million a year. The second highest was the man who protected Hasselbeck's blind side, left tackle Walter Jones, who earned $7.5 million.

When, in chapter 2, Lewis introduces Michael Oher (pronounced "oar"), he is one of the thirteen children of Denise (Dee Dee) Williams, a crack addict. He does not know his real name, his father, his birthday, or any of the things a child might learn in school—like, say, how to read or write. Moreover, he has no experience playing organized football. When national football scout Tom Lemming, who had received thousands of tapes from football coaches and parents who wanted their kids to make the various high school all-American teams he selected, watched a clip of a Gulliverian express bearing down on a Lilliputian attempting to pass, he knew the boy from Memphis was a special case.

"The tape was grainy and you couldn't see very well," said Lemming, "But when he came off the line, it looked like one whole wall was moving. And it was just one player! You had to look at it twice to believe it: he was that big. And yet he would get out and go chase down, and catch, these fast little linebackers."

After these epiphanies of a man-child playing a boys' game, Lemming tried to reach Michael Oher by phone. However, Big Mike, as he was known to everyone at Memphis's Briarcrest Christian School, seemed incommunicado. He had no home; he did not even have a phone number. School officials, dubious of Lemming's interest, finally arranged to drive Big Mike to the University of Memphis football facility for a face-to-face interview. There is no evidence that Lewis ever met Michael Oher during or after the writing of *The Blind Side*—there are no photos—but this is how Lemming described him:

He looked like a house walking into a bigger house . . . barely fit through the door . . . He was the solid kind. You also see big guys, tall guys who weigh a lot, but they have thin legs. They're fine in high school, but in college they'll get pushed around. He was just massive everywhere.

The British-Irish writer Rebecca West wrote, "There is no conversation. There are intersecting monologues." Between Tom Lemming and Big Mike Oher in the fall of 2004 there were no intersections. The young behemoth refused to speak: "He shook my hand and then didn't say a word."

Something every other high school player in America was dying for Big Mike left on the table: an invitation to play in the U.S. Army All-American Bowl. What never crossed Lemming's mind was that the player he would soon rank the best offensive lineman in the nation did not have the foggiest idea of who Lemming was or why he was asking so many questions. "For that matter," writes Lewis, "he didn't even think of himself as a football player. And he had never played left tackle in his life."

Michael Oher's silent demeanor may have provided the author with a cover and a rationale for presenting a hero who through most of the book comes across as just as indistinct as his tapes. Readers are usually told rather than shown why the chronicle of Big Mike Oher cannot be other than a book-long work in progress.

He had the most intense desire to please, without the ability to do the things that pleased. He had spent his whole life treating his mind as a problem to be covered up. He had grown so accustomed to not sharing a thing about himself, or perhaps never being asked about himself, that he did not even know how to begin.

Squarely at the book's human center are the Tuohys—Sean, Leigh Anne, and their teenage daughter Collins—a wealthy Memphis family who take Mike from the city's slums to their heart and hearth, adopt the giant sixteen-year-old, and reinvent him for football stardom.

"We had a black son before we had a Democrat friend!" jokes the football-loving Sean Tuohy. The author and Tuohy went to elementary school together in New Orleans, and much of *The Blind Side* has an as-told-to sound. What the Tuohys learn about Big Mike would not pass muster in a novel: a grade point average of 0.6, a sixth percentile rating for "ability to learn," an absentee rate of forty-six days in the first term of his first year of first grade. (He took first and second grades twice each.) He slept on an air mattress in a trailer but was so heavy he deflated it. With or without classes, he walked to Briarcrest in winter just to find a place to keep warm.

New York Times book critic Janet Maslin, while commending the author for his sharp dialogue and unerring pull on heartstrings and funny bone, rightly notes that "parts of this book feel like prefabricated movie moments" out of Lewis's preference for "buoyant details" over "the bleak ones that are implicit here."

The book's finest chapter is the sixth (of twelve), "Inventing Michael," which describes a preseason home scrimmage during Oher's senior year, only his second on the Briarcrest team as left tackle—actually a practice game against Munford, a nonconference school, but significantly "the last game of Michael Oher's football career in which the opposing team wouldn't have the first clue who he was."

While coaches saw a future NFL left tackle and everyone at Briarcrest started telling him he was a star, Oher had hardly any interest in football and spent most of his game time in search of someone to fall over. Not even the Tuohys could detect a hint of aggression—until the scrimmage, that is, when a Munford lineman refused to let up on trash talk all directed at Michael ("Hey fat ass, I'm a kill you! . . . I'm a run your fat ass over!"). Only Leigh Anne, his surrogate mother, could tell when something angered Big Mike, but her back was turned when folks in the stands behind her began to laugh. Oher had lifted his tormentor off the ground and was carrying him, 220 pounds and all, well past the end of the field. Later, when asked what had got into Mike, the coach Hugh Freeze blamed the official's slow whistle: "You tell Michael, 'I want you to block until the whistle blows.' Well, he takes that real literal."

In the absence of Michael Oher's voice, a scene like the above brings him to life. So does a later one in the Tuohy home when Mike races down the stairs hell-bent to tackle Collins, the Tuohys's teenage daughter who has swiped her big brother's black pants because she thinks they clash with his blazer.

This brings up what may be a moot point. For all of Lewis's secondhand sightings of Big Mike, why does the publisher deny the reader a single photograph? The nine illustrations in the September 24, 2006, issue of *The New York Times Magazine* (of which Lewis is a staff writer), appearing just prior to the book's publication, would have let readers of the book see why so many coaches pursued him.

If the reader occasionally faults the author for applying lacquer to inner-city horror, Michael Lewis brilliantly affirms the implication that the "blind side" points to a nation's disgrace more than to its games-play. As Lewis told a National Public Radio interviewer, he is chastened by a sense that for every Michael Oher, whose blind path is cleared by a freak dynamic of the football industrial complex, there are a legion of lost kids whose sesames remain closed.

Richard Hauer Costa

Review Sources

Booklist 103, no. 4 (October 15, 2006): 4.
The Economist 380 (September 30, 2006): 95.
The New York Times 156 (October 5, 2006): E9.
The New York Times Book Review 156 (November 12, 2006): 12-13.
People 66, no. 16 (October 16, 2006): 55.
Publishers Weekly 253, no. 39 (October 2, 2006): 29.
The Spectator 302 (November 11, 2006): 59.
Time 168, no. 8 (August 21, 2006): 63.

BLIND WILLOW, SLEEPING WOMAN

Author: Haruki Murakami (1949-   )
Translated from the Japanese by Philip Gabriel and Jay
  Rubin
Introduction by Murakami
Publisher: Alfred A. Knopf (New York). 352 pp. $24.95
Type of work: Short fiction
Time: The 1960's to 2005
Locale: Generally Japan; also Greece, Singapore, and
  Hawaii

In this wide-ranging collection of Murakami's short sto-
ries, his characters cope with loneliness, death, and prob-
lematical love; occasionally their lives are touched by the
supernatural. By the end of many stories, Murakami's characters have experienced
something that can lessen their anguish and bring them new self-knowledge or joy

Principal characters:
> A TEENAGE HOSPITAL PATIENT, who draws a picture of a blind willow
>   and a sleeping woman
> AN UNNAMED WOMAN, who is celebrating her twentieth birthday and
>   whose kindly old employer grants her one wish
> TONY TAKITANI, a lonely technical illustrator who finds and loses a per-
>   fect love
> MIZUKI ANDO, a woman who forgets her name when a talking monkey
>   steals her college name tag
> IZUMI, a young woman who vanishes on a Greek island

As Japanese writer Haruki Murakami enjoys great international fame and popularity and his major literary work has been translated into English, a new collection of his
short stories offers another enjoyable view of his quirky literary universe. What uni-
fies the twenty-five short stories of *Blind Willow, Sleeping Woman* is the encounter
with the extraordinary, if not outright supernatural, by characters who think of themselves as exceedingly normal or mundane. With great literary skill Murakami describes how these characters are shaken out of their apparently tranquil life when the
unforeseen occurs, be it an old lover calling, a tidal wave snatching a life, or a talking
monkey stealing a name tag.

Since the short stories collected in *Blind Willow, Sleeping Woman* cover the first
three decades of Murakami's literary career, a reader can detect that Murakami has remained true to his key themes of contemporary urban alienation and the intrusion of the
extraordinary into ordinary lives as well as to his overweening humanity. Included are
two of his first stories, written in 1981 and 1982, as well as many stories previously
translated into English and published in various magazines. The final five pieces of
Blind Willow, Sleeping Woman were published by Murakami in Japan as *Tokyo*

Haruki Murakami has published novels, short fiction, and nonfiction. He won the Gunzou Literary Prize for his first novel, Kaze no uta o kike *(1979;* Hear the Wind Sing, *1987), and the* Yomiuri Literary Prize for Nejimaki-dori kuronikuru *(1994;* The Wind-Up Bird Chronicle, *1997).*

Kitanshu (2005; *Strange Tales from Tokyo*).

The title story, "Blind Willow, Sleeping Woman," illustrates the special appeal of Murakami's short fiction collected here. The story is told by a young man who has failed at his first attempts to manage adult life. Now he is accompanying his teenage cousin, whom a sports injury has left sonically impaired, to a hospital. Waiting for his cousin in the hospital cafeteria, typical of Murakami's fondness for multilayered narratives jumping across time, the young man remembers another hospital visit in his own teenage years.

Then, eight years ago, he and his friend visited his friend's girlfriend in a hospital where she recuperated from a routine operation. Amazingly, the teenage girl drew a scene from her own poetry on a cafeteria napkin. In her imaginary world, the fictitious plant of a blind willow produces pollen that tiny flies gather. They carry it into the ear of a young woman whom the pollen puts to sleep so the flies can devour her. Attempts to save her come too late.

In just a subordinate sentence, the narrator tells of his friend's death soon after this visit. Leaving the hospital with his cousin, he muses about his past carelessness and experiences a moment where life around him seems to dissipate. Called back to reality by his cousin, he asserts that everything is all right—typical of Murakami's characters, who generally survive encounters with the strange well.

Underlining Murakami's fondness to withhold apparently crucial story details, "Birthday Girl" tells of a young waitress who is granted one wish on her twentieth birthday. This day, fixing the inevitable passing of youth in Japan, appears to pass as a nonevent. However, the kindly old restaurant owner learns of it by accident and promises to grant her one wish. Murakami teases his readers by having the old man commenting on the unusual nature of the young waitress's wish that the author never reveals. This leaves behind a mystery, as do many of Murakami's popular stories and novels.

Sense of loss, untimely death, and all-encompassing loneliness are never far from Murakami's characters. "Tony Takitani," a short story made into a film by Jun Ichikawa in 2003, tells of a quiet technical illustrator. His father is a drifting jazz musician who does not know what to do with his son after his wife dies suddenly three days after giving birth to him.

As so often happens in Murakami's fiction, her death, like other potentially life-shattering events, just happens. An Italian American major in the United States Army that occupied Japan at the end of World War II becomes the baby's godfather and gives him his Western first name. Tony grows up a loner without any emotional bond to his father. Then one day, as mysteriously and as suddenly as his mother died, he falls in love with an unnamed woman. Their marriage is exceedingly happy. The one thing bothering Tony is his wife's addiction to shopping for clothes.

On Tony's suggestion, his wife returns one coat and dress. On her drive home, her car gets hit by a truck, killing her instantly. Tony ends up selling her clothes as well as the jazz records he inherits from his father, ending up "really alone." Murakami refuses to add anything to these last words of his story, making the reader wonder whether Tony's interference in his good fate caused his misery or whether this is just the way of contemporary life.

Two of his first short stories express Murakami's connecting of traditional Japanese ideas and contemporary Western culture. Often this is done through his allusions to Western popular culture; sometimes it is more subtle. In "New York Mining Disaster," just as celebrated French literary critic Roland Barthes was run over by a laundry truck in Paris in 1980 one year before Murakami's short story was published, so is one of the narrator's friends. As the narrator says, "she was flattened in the tragic yet quite ordinary space between a beer-delivery truck and a concrete telephone pole."

In the second early piece, "A 'Poor Aunt' Story," the woman companion of the narrator sums up what could serve as a credo for life in Murakami's literary universe: "We exist here and now, without any particular reason or cause." This Western philosophical notion tracing its roots to German philosopher Ludwig Wittgenstein and later the existentialists is matched with the millennia-old Japanese Buddhist tradition expressed by the narrator when he states, "The whole world is a farce, needless to say." This sentiment has been strongly embraced in traditional Japanese literature from the days of its earliest poems and novels, such as the influential *Heike monogatari* (c. 1371; *The Tale of the Heike*, 1918-1921). As in his popular novels, Murakami is as comfortable with traditional Japanese themes and beliefs as with contemporary Western popular and high culture.

The collision of Western and Japanese culture is taken up by Murakami for his own post-World War II generation. In his "A Folklore for My Generation: A Prehistory of Late-Stage Capitalism," the narrator's friend is confronted with the unyielding will of his high school sweetheart Yoshiko Fujisawa. In spite of her boyfriend's urgings in the late 1960's to discard conventions and plunge into a love marriage, she insists on keeping her virginity and marrying an older man. While the story indicates that Yoshiko is afraid of the harshness of the adult world, there is also a persuading atmosphere of loss and missed chances.

As Murakami states in his introduction, some of his short stories became the basis for novels: "Firefly" turned into *Noruwei no mori* (1987; *Norwegian Wood*, 2000) and "Man-Eating Cats" turned into *Supūtoniku no koibito* (1999; *The Sputnik Sweetheart*, 2001). Readers familiar with the novels will enjoy how "Firefly" ends with a dilemma, the narrator's girlfriend retreating to a sanatorium, which the novel will attempt to resolve. The eerie ending of "Man-Eating Cats," where the narrator's lover Izumi apparently disappears into the air of a Greek island, anticipates the conclusion of the later novel.

"Dabchick," "Nausea 1979," and "Crabs" are humorous tales incorporating a dose of the absurd. The first tells of an imaginary palm-sized alien creature of that name residing in Tokyo's underground, while "Nausea 1979" tells of a philandering jazz aficionado haunted by anonymous prank calls that coincide with a forty-day vomiting bout. The third story tells of the discovery of thousands of maggots in the clams the narrator vomits up in a hotel in Singapore while his girlfriend sleeps happily with the same food in her stomach.

Food and jazz frequently feature in Murakami's stories, and "The Year of Spaghetti" links a solitary cooking obsession to the narrator's loneliness. "The Seventh Man" visits the theme of guilt felt by survivors of a natural catastrophe. As an adult, the narrator tells of having watched in horror as a tsunami swept away his boyhood friend. As Murakami states in his introduction, the idea for the story came to him while surfing, and his character finally overcomes the past.

The last five short stories of *Blind Woman, Sleeping Willow* deal with the mysterious. "Chance Traveler" centers on an uncanny coincidence. The same day the gay protagonist's new woman acquaintance tries to seduce him, which is one day before her second breast cancer examination, the same exam is waiting, he finds out, for his long estranged sister tomorrow. In "Hanalei Bay," a widowed Japanese mother loses her nineteen-year-old son to a shark attack off Hawaii's Kauai Island. Year after year she returns to the island until one day she picks up two Japanese surfers who later tell her they saw the ghost of her son.

"Where I'm Likely to Find It" tells of a sudden disappearance and equally mysterious reappearance. A husband fails to return after he tells his wife he is coming back upstairs from his mother's apartment, two flights below their own. When he is found days later alive hundreds of miles away, he has lost all memory of the intervening time. In the hands of Murakami, the story becomes a perfect allegory of the inexplicable waiting just beneath the surface of routine life.

The last story, "A Shinagawa Monkey," is one of Murakami's finest. Mizuki Ando cannot remember her name anymore. Pragmatically, she creates a bracelet with her name inscribed on it after doctors can find nothing wrong with her brain. She does not tell her husband but visits a woman counselor. Suddenly and with a flourish, Murakami introduces the absurd when it is revealed that a talking monkey made off with her college name tag and has been captured in the Tokyo underground. In masterful fashion Murakami adds serious tragedy to the hilariously absurd when Mizuki learns the monkey also took her college mate's tag. This had been given to Mizuki the night the other woman committed suicide. Mizuki bravely faces the monkey's revelation that she was not loved as a child and does not really love her husband. When she is given back her name tag she remembers her name again. It is implied that this is the first step to making changes in her life.

Haruki Murakami's stories in *Blind Willow, Sleeping Woman* reflect the narrative skill and favorite themes of this successful writer. Darkness lurks everywhere in contemporary life, and loneliness, lack of love, and despair threaten. Once confronted with an uncanny experience, however, most of his protagonists gain a new understanding. Murakami's stories are moving and well crafted and represent a humane, sometimes ironic voice in the postmodern landscape of advanced societies.

R. C. Lutz

Review Sources

Booklist 102, no. 17 (May 1, 2006): 6.
Entertainment Weekly, no. 894 (September 1, 2006): 80.
Kirkus Reviews 74, no. 11 (June 1, 2006): 540.
Library Journal 131, no. 6 (April 1, 2006): 88.
The New Republic 235, no. 17 (October 23, 2006): 34-37.
New Statesman 135 (July 3, 2006): 66.
The New York Times Book Review 155 (September 17, 2006): 14.
People Weekly 66, no. 11 (September 11, 2006): 60.
Publishers Weekly 253, no. 24 (June 12, 2006): 27.
The Times Literary Supplement, June 30, 2006, pp. 21-22.

THE BOOK OF DAVE

Author: Will Self (1961-   )
Publisher: Bloomsbury USA (New York). 496 pp.
  $24.95
Type of work: Novel
Time: 1987-2003 and 510-524 A.D. ("After Dave")
Locale: London

Self casts his satirical gaze at religious fundamentalism and global warming in a tale of two Londons, one contemporary and the other a postapocalyptic, dystopian fantasy

Principal characters:
  DAVE RUDMAN, a cab driver
  MICHELLE BRODIE, his wife
  CARL, their son
  CAL DEVENISH, Michelle's lover
  SYMUN DEVUSH, a Geezer (prophet)
  CARL DEVUSH, his son

Will Self is a satirist and therefore a moralist and therefore a practitioner of a much needed but nearly extinct literary form. It is not hard to understand why. Morality has become the province of religious fundamentalists of all stripes as well as their political allies, joined together even as they oppose one other by a literal-mindedness that leaves no room for self-examination, doubt, or irony. Satire, meanwhile, has been diluted—just another form of comedy in the postmodern consumerscape—rarely practiced and even more rarely heard amid the din of popular humorists whose work is often mistakenly thought to be satirical, for example, the light fare of Dave Barry and David Sedaris and *The New Yorker*'s "Shouts and Murmurs" column. The film *Borat: Cultural Learnings of America for Make Benefit Glorious Nation of Kazakhstan* (2006) is immensely funny, but Sacha Baron Cohen and his fictional persona, clueless Kazakh journalist Borat Sagdiyev, are more like Benny Hill than Lenny Bruce: rudely hilarious much of the time but only sporadically satirical. Interestingly enough, it was around the time that Lenny Bruce's brand of stand-up satire began running afoul of the law that novelist Philip Roth realized just how difficult it would be to write novels any longer, especially satirical ones. As Roth explained in 1960,

> The American writer in the middle of the twentieth century has his hands full in trying to understand, describe, and then make *credible* much of American reality. It stupefies, it sickens, it infuriates, and finally it is even a kind of embarrassment to one's own meager imagination. The actuality is continually outdoing our talents, and the culture tosses up figures almost daily that are the envy of any novelist. Who, for example, could have invented Charles Van Doren? Roy Cohn and David Schine? Sherman Adams and Bernard Goldfine? Dwight David Eisenhower?

～

*Since graduating from Oxford
University, Will Self has published
numerous essays and newspaper
articles in addition to his short fiction
and novels. In 1993, he was included in
Granta magazine's "Best of Young
British Novelists" volume.*

～

At a time when reality was rapidly becoming unwitting self-satire and when Orwellian caricature was already becoming political reality, the satirical novelist could either give up or try as best he or she could to exceed an age whose own excesses have become the everyday fare of a media-saturated society. The Rabelaisian excesses of Robert Coover's *The Public Burning* (1977) are well suited to that novel's postmodern political satire, but more often in the work of Coover and his contemporaries, the satirist's tools—parody, pastiche, farce, burlesque, ridicule—serve either more narrowly literary ends or more broadly philosophical ones. Satire requires a different orientation and a much higher level of dismay and disgust, as in Stanley Kubrick's *Dr. Strangelove* (1964) or Thomas Berger's *Little Big Man* (1964). In Britain, curiously enough, the success of the archly irreverent television show *Monty Python's Flying Circus* (1969-1974) helped make satire a pleasant diversion, lacking the bite of works such as Lindsay Anderson's film *If* (1968).

The reduced role that satire has come to play since the late 1970's makes Will Self's writing (fiction and nonfiction alike) all the more remarkable and welcome. No other writer has practiced the art of excess so persistently, so perfectly, and so perversely as Self, except for the late writer Stanley Elkin, who always treated his characters and their obsessions with a degree of sympathy and respect rarely if ever found in Self's hyperacerbic work, where revulsion rules. Surprisingly for a writer who thrives on excess, as subject and as style, Self (unlike Elkin) is often more successful in short bursts—essays, short stories, and novellas, *The Quantity Theory of Insanity* (1991) and *Cock and Bull* (1992), especially—than over the long haul, as with the disastrous *Great Apes* (1997). *How the Dead Live* (2000) is the chief exception because for it Self devised a central character (based on his mother) whose revulsion exceeds his own. Self's novel *The Book of Dave* is not quite that good, but it comes close in large part because Self hitches his freewheeling satirical imagination not only to an especially timely conceit but also to a carefully defined yet still expansive structure.

The Book of Dave is a tale of two Londons and two times. Eight chapters set in the present (1987-2003) alternate with eight others set in the future (510-524 A.D., that is "After Dave," or more specifically, after the discovery of "The Book of Dave"). The novel moves back and forth not only between the two narratives and therefore the two times (present and future) but between present and past as well within each narrative. Against the tight structure of the two interwoven stories, with the later one reflecting the earlier in funhouse mirror fashion, there is the sprawl not only of years but of intertextual echoes and antecedents. *The Book of Dave* is made in its protagonist's and its author's images, crosscutting its two narratives the way Dave, a cabbie agonistes, cuts back and forth across London and Self cuts back and forth across an array of utopian and apocalyptic texts, including Walter J. Miller, Jr.'s *A Canticle for Leibowitz* (1962), Russell Hoban's *Riddley Walker* (1980), Alisdair Gray's *Lanark* (1981),

H. G. Wells's *The Time Machine* (1894-1895), and Richard Jeffries' little-read *After London* (1885).

Self's main character is doomed, not by planetary catastrophe but by his character, indeed by his very name, for Self dealt with Dave, or rather Daves, before in "Dave Too" (from 1998's *Tough, Tough Toys for Tough, Tough Boys*). That Dave is "so amorphous, so shapeless, so incoherent" as to constitute "a kind of Ur-Dave" a sign of the Daveness, Davidity, and Davitude spreading throughout the land. The new Dave, Dave Rudman, is less amorphous, more grotesque:

> He was a large man with broad shoulders rounded by occupational hunching. He had the standard issue potbelly of the sedentary forty-year-old. . . . His features were handsome enough and taken at a glance they gave an impression of strength and sensuality. . . . Sadly, up close this wavered, then dissolved. His dark eyes were too bulbous and too close set. When he took off his cap he revealed that his hair . . . was gone, leaving behind a lumpy skull, full of depressions and queer mounds. Where his hairline used to be were several rows of little craters. . . . Dave Rudman's face was disorganized by pain, his features driven apart from one another by an antagonism so powerful that it pitted ear against eye, cheek against nose, chin against the world. Five days' stubble gave him a cartoon muzzle.

Dave's pain and seething resentment derive from his failed marriage, which Dave in turn blames on his baldness and the botched hair transplant, with hair harvested from his groin, that left him with a headful of pubic hairs and (compounding the comedy) with paying out "five times as much to get the crinkle-cut hair removed as he'd paid to have it inserted." Dave's crown of pubic thorns is only the most visible sign of his many pratfalls. For the depression caused by his marital woes, Dave is prescribed a drug that causes a long-undiagnosed psychotic reaction that in turn causes Dave to vent his rage against Michelle, the fares he drives, the Public Carriage Office (PCO) that governs London transit (including taxis)—indeed against everything and everyone in the book. Then, influenced by his Jewish aunt's conversion to Mormonism, Dave has the book printed on metal plates that he then clandestinely buries in Michelle's yard for his son Carl to someday find and read. Helped by Dr. Zack Busner (a recurring character in Self's fiction) and a new girlfriend, Dave regains his equilibrium, gives up cabbing, repents his earlier rage, and writes an "Epistle to his Son" in which he renounces the hate-filled Book and advises Carl to love everyone and everything. Then, just before he can commit suicide, Dave is murdered—the last nail in the Chaplinesque Dave's comic coffin.

Dave's personal holocaust is followed (chronologically, not narratively) by a much larger global catastrophe that leaves much of England under water, but not Hampstead, where Dave's book is found and becomes the basis for a new religion. (Here Self, revising Karl Marx, suggests that history occurs twice, the first time as personal history, the second as worldwide farce.) Self's satire of the Davinanity that sweeps the land, or what little of it remains above water, is so devastating because it manages to be only as absurd as it is familiar, with the parallels to actual religions as numerous and identifiable as Self's allusions to utopian and apocalyptic fictions.

Dave is God, the government is a theocracy, the PCO is the established church, "Drivers" are priests, "flyers" are heretics, "fares" are souls, "tariffs" are hours, the sexes are rigorously separated into "dads" and either young "opares" or older "mums," fathers' rights are strictly enforced, sexual abuse of women is permissible, everything bad is "chellish" (after Michelle), and the inhabitants of the now island backwater of Hampstead are Hamsters who speak Mockni (a mix of Cockney and text messaging), not Arpee (RP: Received Pronunciation), the two hilariously juxtaposed in the following catechismal exchange between Driver and Hamsters:

—Thanks, Dave, for picking us up!
—4 pikkin uz up, the dads who remembered the correct response dutifully intoned.
—And for not dropping us off.
—Anfer nó droppinus dahn.

Against the PCO's authority and its Old Testament ethos are Geezers like Symun Devush who, like the later Dave, espouse a gospel of love. For his crime of grievous flying (heresy), Symun is taken to New London, broken on the wheel, and has his tongue cut out. He is then sent back to Ham where he lives alone as the Beastlyman, unrecognized by his London disciple, Antonë Böm, or by his young son, Carl. Accompanied by Böm, Carl travels to New London in search of his lost father, whom he discovers only when he returns to Ham, where he learns that the Beastlyman he had feared, but who is now dead, was his father. When Carl interprets his quest and his role (as the Lost Boy to Symun's Dave) hermeneutically, according to Davinanity, his girlfriend Salli, who had been repeatedly raped while he was away, quickly puts him in his place: "U! U aynt no Loss Boy! . . . Ure a wanka juss lyke enni uvva dad—juss lyke ve dads wot nokked me up."

Mother Nature might feel the same way were Will Self less the city satirist, more the country sentimentalist. Yet, *The Book of Dave* is, for all its characteristically Selfish stylistic pyrotechnics and satirical inventiveness, sadder and less Self-centered than many of its author's earlier works. The inanities Self had mercilessly lampooned before may have been fatal for a husband here (*Cock and Bull*), a tramp there (1993's *My Idea of Fun*). The consequences of global warming, however, seem to have had a sobering effect on Self himself, whose acid satire allows characters, present and future, to be hoisted, and made absurd, by their own petards.

Robert Morace

Review Sources

Booklist 103, no. 1 (September 1, 2006): 59.
Christianity Today 50, no. 11 (November, 2006): 100-101.
Kirkus Reviews 74, no. 15 (August 1, 2006): 749.
London Review of Books 28, no. 13 (July 6, 2006): 31-32.
New Statesman 135 (June 19, 2006): 66.

The New York Times Book Review 156 (November 12, 2006): 52.
Publishers Weekly 253, no. 25 (June 19, 2006): 38.
The Spectator 301 (June 10, 2006): 42-44.
The Sunday Telegraph, May 28, 2006, p. 52.
The Times Literary Supplement, June 9, 2006, p. 25.

THE BOURGEOIS VIRTUES
Ethics for an Age of Commerce

Author: Deirdre N. McCloskey (1942-   )
Publisher: University of Chicago Press (Chicago). 616
  pp. $32.50
Type of work: Economics, history, philosophy

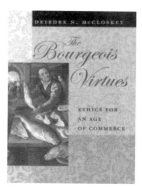

This ornate, elegant review of basic virtues—love, faith,
hope, courage, temperance, prudence and justice—argues
that capitalism can be virtuous and that the virtues, in turn,
help to promote economic success for individuals and for
society

This book is unfair in many ways. For all the serious-
ness of its content, it is written in such a beguiling manner that the reader is seduced
into reading for sheer enjoyment rather than dutifully putting together wisdom and
enlightenment. The author is a brilliant economist, and in the work are economics lectures. The book, however, is no textbook or treatise. Deirdre N. McCloskey is one of
the few living intellectuals who has seen the world from both a masculine and feminine perspective and used this perspective to good effect. It is unfair that this is merely
volume one of a projected four-volume study. No one should know that much.

McCloskey also writes from a Christian perspective from which love, faith, and
hope are characterized as Christian and feminine virtues. Courage and temperance are
pagan and masculine virtues, leaving prudence and justice as androgynous. Several
chapters are devoted to each virtue, taking the reader through an awesome array of literary, philosophical, and historical reference points. Aristotle, Thomas Aquinas, Im-
manuel Kant, and Adam Smith figure prominently.

The word "bourgeois" initially referred to people who lived in towns and cities,
particularly the shopkeepers, professionals, and clerks. Karl Marx appropriated the
term to apply to capitalists (entrepreneurs). The term is often accompanied by a sneer,
most often delivered by "the clerisy"—the intellectuals, readers, and writers, who are
uncritically anticapitalist. "It's the clerisy's job to provide articulations that illuminate our lives. . . For a century and a half a good part of the clerisy has been off duty,
standing in the street outside the factory or office or movie studio hurling insults at the
varied workers there," says McCloskey.

A penetrating section develops the theme "anticapitalism is bad for us," chiefly
through government economic interventions which, at best, generate economic inef-
ficiency and injustice, and at worst, beget mass murder. Now, economic wisdom recognizes that masses of people are moving from poverty to affluence through private
property rights and free markets and not through government ownership and political
foreign-aid programs.

Surely, though, capitalism is about "greed." Not really. Greed has certainly been

Deirdre N. McCloskey (earlier, Donald) is distinguished professor of economics, history, English, and communication at the University of Illinois at Chicago. Earlier books include Crossing: A Memoir *(1999) and* If You're So Smart: The Narrative of Economic Expertise *(1990).*

observed in all types of societies throughout history. It has been condemned in equal degree. Most people learn to moderate or disguise their greed, out of self-interest. It does not win friends or influence people. What capitalism can do is to harness greed to public benefit—provided the greed is constrained by law and by competition. Greed is certainly not a defining feature of the most prominent entrepreneurs. Seeking a high income in order to send children (or grandchildren) to college is not exactly greed.

McCloskey suggests that one understand a bourgeois to be "a city dweller practicing an honored profession or owning a business or functioning at a managerial level in someone else's enterprise, including governmental and non-profit enterprises." So it is not merely a synonym for middle class. The bourgeoisie honor work.

Appropriately for a Christian, the author gives priority of place to the virtue of love, through which one is committed to the true welfare of another. The preoccupation with male-female romantic interactions makes it challenging to deal analytically with love. It need not be a feeling—or not merely a feeling—but a set of actions—basically, what good parents as well as good mates do. McCloskey echoes C. S. Lewis (another intellectual who came late to Christian faith), urging that love needs a transcendent dimension—something beyond the purely secular and pragmatic. Love also needs to be balanced by other virtues, especially justice.

McCloskey aims many darts at the preoccupation of economists with utility maximization, treating prudence as the universal determinant of behavior. The efforts of Nobel Prize-winner Gary Becker to interpret love purely in terms of self-interest will not do. To McCloskey, love extends to solidarity with others, to finding meaning in actions, to commitment and duty. She concludes that "markets and even the much-maligned corporations encourage friendships wider and deeper than the atomism of a full-blown socialist regime or the claustrophobic, murderous atmosphere of a 'traditional' village." With that thought goes a strong attack on the myths of some past social golden age.

Faith combines elements of confidence (that one's actions will somehow turn out all right) and trust. Successful modern market economies rest on high levels of trust in strangers. Hope involves wanting and caring. Christians recognize the importance of both. Both are crucial for entrepreneurs. There may be trade-offs between faith and hope: "The displacing of land by human capital as the main source of wealth sharply devalued faith, the past, the dead hand, the mortgage, the family line, the ancestors. And it upvalued hope, the future, the children, the individual." Modern China exemplifies this transition.

Economists display faith and hope in their conviction that economic wisdom can guide policies to improve people's material life. Echoing Robert Nelson, McCloskey believes that economics has become a modern secular theology, the worship of the practical.

Courage is characterized as masculine and pagan. This is important, because it associates courage with physical violence—the courage of the soldier. This downgrades the courage of the woman who persistently and patiently defends her impaired child before the school authorities. It leads political campaigners to stress they are "fighting" for their constituents, when what is needed are the skills of compromise and negotiation. Business requires courage aplenty, in risky decisions to introduce an innovation, to borrow a lot of money, to sign a long-term contract to deliver, to bargain patiently but firmly with Wal-Mart, with a powerful union, with intrusive or obstructionist officials. Courage unrestrained by other virtues characterizes the modern street gang, the suicide bomber. Temperance is called upon as the moderating influence—but only briefly.

Prudence is a difficult virtue to characterize. In fact, McCloskey uses it to represent self-interest, the choice of appropriate actions to achieve one's goals (and thus the central focus of economics). Well-intentioned efforts to help others, even in a spirit of love or justice, may be vices if not moderated by prudence. Examples include the war in Iraq, or the war on drugs.

Christians can well attend to the observation that "the love or Justice moving us to help others is a vice, not a virtue, when unalloyed with prudence." Unintended consequences are not always benign.

Considering the importance accorded to justice in modern Christian activist literature, it is disappointing that McCloskey never gives it a careful examination. According to the index, the topic appears on only five pages. The nearest one gets to a definition is that justice involves people getting "their due." There is no consideration of the close link between justice and the juridical system of law and its enforcement. The productivity ethics associated with John Bates Clark asserted that the distribution of market incomes in competitive capitalism is just because each person's reward is proportioned to their contribution.

The most powerful complaint against capitalism is that there is poverty and it is unjust. The prevailing remedies in wealthy societies are through government, not market processes.

Periodically, McCloskey urges her reader to view virtues (and other attributes) in terms of exemplars and their stories. Where, though, are the entrepreneurs? If virtue is what virtuous people possess, one needs to meet virtuous entrepreneurs, managers, engineers. One needs more of Paul Mantoux (*The Industrial Revolution*, 1961), Jonathan Hughes (*The Vital Few*, 1986), and Thomas L. Friedman (*The World Is Flat*, 2005). The virtues are attitudes or consequences, but they are not actions. Entrepreneurs are actors, not talkers. McCloskey has a problem classifying William Bennett's claim that "work" is a virtue; it is presented as combining temperance, justice, and courage. McCloskey, like Adam Smith, is not on familiar terms with entrepreneurs. McCloskey appears mainly concerned to conduct a discourse with the clerisy. One is startled when actions suddenly erupt, as when one is asked to imagine a human society without loving parents.

In a stimulating case study, the ethics of scientists (including economists) are evaluated—mostly adversely. Chapter 42 directly addresses the attitudes of religious doctrines toward various aspects of capitalism. The treatment is disappointing. McCloskey accepts the view that the Christian Gospels attack wealth, without looking at the context. In the times and places of the Old Testament, and to a great extent even in Jesus's ministry, "wealth" was overwhelmingly precapitalistic—land, flocks and herds, with social, religious, and political power ascribed and not merely purchased—thus the rich young ruler. One doubts that the rich facing difficulty achieving salvation were the entrepreneurs of burgeoning Mediterranean commerce.

McCloskey is content to observe that many of Jesus's teachings counsel prudence or embody metaphors of economic life. More to the point is that, as often as Jesus denounced various categories of transgressors, merchants and craftspeople do not seem to be among his favorite targets—certainly compared with tax collectors. The parable of the talents is certainly a strong and straightforward endorsement of investment and productivity. McCloskey strongly affirms that Jesus the carpenter lived and worked in a market-oriented society and did not categorically condemn or reject it.

Later the reader receives a useful review of the endorsements of private property by a series of popes, beginning with Rerum Novarum in 1891. The mythology of American "robber barons" is reviewed and refuted, noting (too briefly) that philanthropic support for American universities is a major reason they are the best in the world.

Chapter 43 offers a solid economics lecture, refuting the conventional wisdom that "wasteful" spending (mostly governmental) is warranted because it "creates jobs." Successful capitalism does not require extravagance. It does require—and offer—respect for work, a quality which has been lacking in much of the past and in many low-income societies: "Women and slaves work. Real men smoke."

Will the book be persuasive? The first fifty pages present admirably the case for the defense, brief and to the point, supported by evidence and analysis. From there, rigor and conciseness give way increasingly to fuzziness and digression. The term "prudence" cannot bear the weight put upon it—one associates it more with bureaucratic conservatism than with entrepreneurial élan. The claim that capitalism is unjust is simply not confronted.

In reality, there is capitalism and there is capitalism. Can one expect the current incarnations of capitalism in Russia and China to produce a balanced output of McCloskey's chosen virtues? Most of the book's illustrations reflect the Christian world of Western Europe and the United States. Did virtue propel Europe through the economic outburst of the Renaissance? In 1933, where was the virtue generated by German capitalism? How much virtue is generated by Latin American capitalism? McCloskey might usefully refer to the World Values Survey and the various authors who have based socioeconomic analysis on it.

One may also wonder whether it is capitalism that generates virtues, or simply a free society. Perhaps capitalism can be counted on to arise and flourish spontaneously in a free society. Perhaps human diversity and creativity are sufficient that any free society will generate a pretty good bag of virtues—not because each person manifests them all in proper balance but because each will be represented to excess in a few, with the others acting as counterweights. Some of this perspective is implied in

McCloskey's emphasis on the fact that market economy is humanized by the facts that humans began life as children, have experience with giving and receiving love, and talk to one another.

Paul B. Trescott

Review Sources

Library Journal 131, no. 6 (April 1, 2006): 108.
The New York Review of Books 53, no. 20 (December 21, 2006): 70-73.
The New York Times Book Review 155 (July 30, 2006): 14-15.
Publishers Weekly 253, no. 14 (April 3, 2006): 57.
The Times Literary Supplement, October 20, 2006, pp. 3-4.
The Wall Street Journal 248, no. 18 (July 22, 2006): P10.

BREAKING THE SPELL
Religion as a Natural Phenomenon

Author: Daniel C. Dennett (1942-   )
Publisher: Viking Press (New York). 448 pp. $26.00
Type of work: Science, religion, philosophy, natural history, history of science, psychology, sociology, and ethics
Time: From c. 25,000 B.C.E. to 2006

Because of religion's pivotal importance throughout humankind's history, it warrants scientific study, and Dennett uses the methods of the biological and social sciences to explore such questions as how and why religions originated and developed, and whether they help or hinder the genuine progress of humanity

Principal personages:

CHARLES DARWIN (1809-1882), English naturalist whose theory of natural selection Dennett considers "the single best idea anyone has ever had"

DAVID HUME (1721-1776), British philosopher whose works on religion as a natural phenomenon Dennett sees as precursors to his own

WILLIAM JAMES (1842-1910), American psychologist and philosopher whose book on the "varieties of religious experience" was an influential rational analysis of religion

RICHARD DAWKINS (b. 1941), British biologist whose idea of "memes" as cultural analogues of genes constitutes an important theme in Dennett's book

When Charles Darwin was wrestling with the problem of God's existence, he, like many thinkers throughout history, was troubled by the problem of evil. Unlike his devout wife, who saw ample evidence of divine benevolence in the world, Darwin found an overabundance of needless suffering. For example, he could not understand why a benevolent god would design ichneumon wasps, which laid eggs inside living caterpillars so that their larvae could hatch and devour their hosts, who suffered excruciatingly.

Daniel Dennett, an ardent Darwinian, begins his book *Breaking the Spell* with a similar adaptation that seems more like the product of a Satanic Sadist than a Compassionate Creator. In this instance, parasitic worms take over the brains of certain ants, causing them to climb up blades of grass, where they are eaten by cows, sheep, or goats. The parasite does this because it needs to get into such ruminants to complete its reproductive cycle. This grim example leads Dennett to wonder whether religious ideas in human brains are like this parasite in an ant's brain, compelling humans to behave irrationally, even self-destructively. This example also illustrates how Dennett's

~

Most of Daniel C. Dennett's academic career has centered at Tufts University, and his previous books have included Consciousness Explained *(1991),* Darwin's Dangerous Idea *(1995), and* Freedom Evolves *(2003). He has received two Guggenheim Fellowships and a Fulbright Fellowship, and he was elected to the American Academy of Arts and Sciences in 1987.*

~

negative attitude toward religion often surfaces in the framework and content of his inquiry.

Dennett, a militant atheist who is aware of the adverse connotations of unbelief, has introduced the term "bright" for atheist, hoping that "bright" will accomplish for nonbelievers what "gay" has done for homosexuals. In *Darwin's Dangerous Idea* (1995) he began to show how natural selection helped to explain the structures and functions of all living things, including humans, and he extended his biological approach to language, culture, even ethics. His new book, *Breaking the Spell*, has the goal of making religion part of this naturalistic investigation. The spell that he wishes to break is the taboo against the scientific study of religion. For him, religion is too important to the past, present, and future of humanity to be left solely to theologians and other believers. He fears that theocracies and religious fanatics, if they gain control of modern weapons of mass destruction, will threaten the survival not only of the liberal democracies he favors but also of all human beings on Earth. Therefore the title of his book expresses an urgency that the spell of religion be broken now.

Although Dennett recognizes that atheists constitute a minority in most countries, he sees their numbers growing among the educated, and, in looking back through history, he finds such kindred thinkers as David Hume, John Locke, and William James, whom he calls his "heroes" in his rational study of religious phenomena. However, critics of Dennett's book have pointed out that Hume was not a Dennett-like atheist but a theist who admired the harmonious laws of the universe discovered by Isaac Newton, another theist. Dennett's views of science and religion are also different from those of such modern investigators as Stephen Jay Gould, who believed that science and religion function best when each acts in its own domain. Science's domain comprises observable facts and the theories developed to explain them; religion's domain includes morality and the meaning of life. Dennett views Gould's scheme as implausible and wrongheaded, as Dennett believes that science can and should bridge the gap between science and religion by subjecting religion to scientific scrutiny.

Dennett divides his scientific study of religion into three parts. In part 1, "Opening Pandora's Box," he analyzes how scientific techniques can be used to make sense of religious phenomena. In part 2, "The Evolution of Religion," he describes scientific research on the nature, origin, and development of religions. In part 3, "Religion Today," he describes his views of modern religions and their potential for good and evil. In all three parts he approaches religion from the viewpoint of a philosopher who is convinced of evolutionary biology's explanatory power with regard to both living organisms and human cultures. Just as neo-Darwinians discovered the significance of genes for understanding the fitness of various life-forms, so, too, have such social Darwinians as Dennett and Richard Dawkins emphasized the importance of memes in understanding how religious and other cultural ideas are created, copied, and transmitted. Memes can be ideas, beliefs, words, attitudes, styles, customs, tunes, strategies, and other elements of culture. For both genes and memes, information is passed from generation to generation, but the meme's transmission is nongenetic.

In fact, so many differences exist between genes and memes that critics of Dennett and Dawkins have pointed out that any analogy between genes and memes is bound to be ambiguous, unclear, and unhelpful in explaining the mechanisms of cultural evolution. For example, memes, unlike genes, can be transmitted to nondescendants. Despite these criticisms, Dennett feels that the mimetic approach bolsters his analysis of religion. Indeed, he thinks that religions may be "culturally evolved parasites" whose evil ideas are unknown to their hosts. He sees some religions as malignant features of human culture, best dealt with by isolation, education, or eradication.

In the history of the Earth, religion appeared late in the evolution of Homo sapiens. However, once religion developed, it quickly diversified and spread; Dennett estimates that, over the millennia, more than a million religions have existed. Why were religions so popular? Scholars have suggested several of their uses: to provide comfort in times of suffering and distress, to give meaning to life, to mitigate the fear of death, to explain the inexplicable, and to encourage group solidarity in the face of enemies or threats. Dennett, for his part, believes that humans do not yet know the answer, but he thinks that science can help humankind to discover the answer. For example, the diversification and survival of certain religions might be explained in terms of a Darwinian competition among belief systems in which the "fittest" succeed and those unable to generate and retain followers fail.

Primitive religions were animistic, seeing spiritual agents in stones, storms, and animals. Eventually this animism developed into a belief in gods whose activities were interpreted by shamans. When such early religions (Dennett calls them "folk religions") evolved into organized religions, dogmas that were immune to disconfirmation developed. For Dennett, no organized religion lacks dogmas, and a dogmaless belief system cannot really be a religion.

Market forces played a role in what Dennett calls the domestication of religion, a dynamic process in which leaders adapted religions to changing conditions. One important aspect in the transition from folk to organized religions is the "belief in belief." This sort of belief is only possible in a mature religion, which is able to tolerate those who do not genuinely believe in the divine. (Instead, they believe that they should believe in God.) These believers in belief think that religion is useful for society even if it is not strictly true. Indeed, according to Dennett, many religious people are actually atheists in the sense that Jews are atheist with regard to Baal, Christians are atheist with regard to Apollo, and most believers are atheist with regard to the many gods in which humans have, in the past, believed. Obviously, all religions do not have the same beliefs, but for Dennett the success of religion depends not on uniformity of belief but uniformity in professing beliefs.

Theologians, such as Thomas Aquinas, who have tried to establish God's existence rationally have failed, but what of those who have tried to justify their faith in God by love? For example, Mircea Eliade, the great scholar of religions, insisted that religious phenomena can be grasped only from the inside, not through outside (objective) analysis. Dennett calls this approach "pre-emptive disqualification," and he strongly believes that such scholars are wrong in limiting the investigation of religion to the truly religious.

Recently, some scholars have tried to put certain religious beliefs to objective tests, for example, by experiments in the effectiveness of prayers in healing the sick. So far, these tests have generated mixed results. Dennett has a negative opinion of investigations to determine whether religious people are more moral than atheists because, in his view, any relationship between spirituality and moral goodness is an illusion. The values that he holds sacred are rooted in Enlightenment rationalism and Darwinian natural selection. He wants his readers to accept and spread his Darwinian message, which he believes will help stop the degradation of the environment and mitigate many foibles of human nature. He wants to protect democracy from those with religious agendas, and he proposes as his central policy recommendation the scientific education of all the world's people.

As expected by Dennett and his publisher, *Breaking the Spell* generated controversy. Reviewers in religious journals accused Dennett of misunderstanding the unique nature of religious experience, in which the interpersonal encounter between believer and Revealer plays a pivotal role. Furthermore, Dennett did little to camouflage his hostility to religion, even though he claimed to be engaged in disinterested analysis. It was clear to many religious readers, whom Dennett explicitly targeted, that he believes that a religionless world would be a better place than one under the spell of numerous religions.

What was unexpected by Dennett were the negative reviews in secular and liberal journals. For example, Leon Wieseltier, literary editor of *The New Republic*, reviewed *Breaking the Spell* for *The New York Times Book Review* and accused Dennett of such a crude form of scientism that his book was as superstitious as many of the religions he attacked. Scientism can mean a doctrine holding that scientific methods can and should be applied to all fields of inquiry, but it can also mean making a religion of science. *Breaking the Spell* exhibits both these meanings. Dennett and his disciples responded to what they characterized as a "right-wing attack" on his book by reemphasizing their major contention that science, unlike religion, is a matter of evidence, not belief. Those sympathetic to Wieseltier's views answered that many modern spells remain to be broken, including those generated by atheistic rationalists.

Science and religion are two important ways that humans understand their lives, their societies, and the universe. Both come with powerful emotional underpinnings, as the controversy over *Breaking the Spell* reveals. Throughout history both religious and atheistic ideologies have caused great harm, but it is easy to find examples of both religious believers and atheistic humanists who have done great good. On the other hand, despite the claims of Dennett, questions about the ultimate roles of science and religion in human life are not scientific questions. Both science and religion can and should be understood from both the outside and the inside. Because of the traditional antagonism between science and religion, such an integrated approach to bridging what, to some, seems unbridgeable will be difficult, but the dangers of exacerbating the hostility between these important determinants of human life and meaning could be devastating to human beings, which evolution has shown to be a very fragile species.

Robert J. Paradowski

Review Sources

Booklist 102, nos. 9/10 (January 1, 2006): 27.
Christianity Today 50, no. 5 (May, 2006): 68-69.
Commonweal 133, no. 5 (March 10, 2006): 20-23.
The Economist 378 (February 11, 2006): 78-79.
Kirkus Reviews 74, no. 1 (January 1, 2006): 25.
Library Journal 131, no. 1 (January, 2006): 123.
Nature 439 (February 2, 2006): 535.
New Scientist 189 (March 4, 2006): 48-49.
New Statesman 135 (March 20, 2006): 50-51.
The New York Review of Books 53, no. 11 (June 22, 2006): 4-8.
The New York Times Book Review 155 (February 19, 2006): 11-12.
The New Yorker 82, no. 7 (April 3, 2006): 80-83.
Publishers Weekly 252, no. 47 (November 28, 2005): 47.
Science 311 (January 27, 2006): 471-472.
Scientific American 294, no. 1 (January, 2006): 94-95.

THE BROOKLYN FOLLIES

Author: Paul Auster (1947-   )
Publisher: Henry Holt (New York). 306 pp. $24.00
Type of work: Novel
Time: 2001
Locale: Chiefly Brooklyn

Nathan Glass comes to Brooklyn to die but instead finds himself and others

Principal characters:
> NATHAN GLASS, the story's fifty-nine-year-old narrator
> TOM WOOD, his nephew, a brilliant student now down on his luck
> HARRY BRIGHTMAN, né Harry Dunkel, owner of a secondhand book store
> RACHEL, Nathan's daughter
> AURORA, "Rory," Tom's sister
> LUCY, her daughter
> NANCY MAZZUCCHELLI, the B.P.M. (Beautiful Perfect Mother)
> JOYCE MAZZUCCHELLI, her mother and eventually Nathan's lover
> STANLEY CHOWDER, widower and owner of a New England Inn
> HONEY CHOWDER, Stanley's daughter and eventually Tom's lover
> MARINA GONZALEZ, a waitress

That Paul Auster is one of the most respected and distinctive modern American writers is certain, as is his having been for most of his career better appreciated abroad, especially in France, than in the United States. That has been changing since 1999, with his starting the Story Project for National Public Radio and the publication of four increasingly accessible novels: *Timbuktu* (1999), *The Book of Illusions* (2002), *Oracle Night* (2003), and now *The Brooklyn Follies*. Not that Auster's fiction was ever particularly difficult, only that it has often seemed as European in its sensibility as it is American in its settings and references to mid-nineteenth century writers (such as Edgar Allan Poe, Nathaniel Hawthorne, and Herman Melville).

The big difference between Auster's early and later work, though, may be traced back to his collaboration with director Ang Lee on the film *Smoke* (the 1995 adaptation, or expansive reimagining) of Auster's very short story "Augie Wren's Christmas Story" (1990), with its more fully realized, fleshed out—seemingly real, or at least realistic—characters. The characters of Auster's *The New York Trilogy* (1986) are more or less stick figures, barely, if brilliantly, more than their names and chance encounters in a high-class but bare-bones game of mirror images, labyrinthine twists, and permutational possibilities worthy of Samuel Beckett (an important influence), while those of *The Music of Chance* (1990) are drawn straight from Beckett again and Franz Kafka, with their attenuated humanity and abstract allegorical significances re-

Best known for his novels, such as The Book of Illusions *(2002), Paul Auster is also a respected essayist, translator, poet, and filmmaker. Auster and his wife, the writer Siri Husvedt, are longtime residents of the Park Slope area of Brooklyn.*

tained amazingly well in Philip Haas's 1993 film version. Combining the fairy tale and American tall tale traditions, *Mr. Vertigo* (1994) is more fantastical and richly imagined (in its evocation of early twentieth century America) and less overtly existential but hardly as warmly human as Auster's more recent work in which the existential and metafictional qualities foregrounded in the early work are less obvious even if no less important. As a result, the earlier games-playing (which was never just that) gives way to Auster's and his readers' interest in *The Brooklyn Follies'* "motley bunch of messed up, floundering souls" and "stunning examples of human imperfection."

"I was looking for a quiet place to die," the novel begins. The speaker is fifty-nine-year-old Nathan Glass, soon after his retirement, divorce, and cancer treatment. Bankrolled by the sale of his former home in Westchester, Nathan rents an apartment in Brooklyn, where he was born but has not set foot in the past fifty-six years. "I had no idea who my neighbors were, and I didn't care. They all worked at nine-to-five jobs, none of them had any children, and therefore the building would be relatively silent. More than anything else, that was what I craved. A silent end to my sad and ridiculous life." This would seem a rather unpromising start to a three-hundred-page novel that deals very little with Nathan's past, his "sad and ridiculous life," unless something happens, which, this being an Auster novel, something does.

Nathan begins work on "The Book of Human Folly," "a collection of random jottings, a hodgepodge of unrelated anecdotes" ranging from verbal flubs to "cruel destinies." Then, by chance (which always looms large in Auster's fiction) Nathan runs into his nephew Tom, whom he has not seen in seven years: a once brilliant literature student now overweight and working in a secondhand bookshop owned by a flamboyant homosexual. "So Tom went to work for Harry Brightman," Nathan says, "little realizing that Harry Brightman did not exist."

Nathan's narrative suddenly swerves from Tom, "the long-suffering hero of these Brooklyn follies," to Harry, *né* Harry Dunkel, a man with (as his surname implies) a dark past. In Chicago, the Brooklyn-born Harry marries the youngest daughter of "the Diaper Service King of the Midwest" and opens an art gallery called Dunkel Frères (even though there is no brother, not even a business partner). The gallery thrives thanks to the work of one artist, Alec Smith, whose suicide spells disaster—or would, were it not for another chance arrival, that of Gordon Dyer, whose own work is not very good but who turns out to have a special talent for imitating Smith's style. Dyer, however, is no ordinary forger. He effectively becomes Smith's double (as well as the previously straight Harry's lover), to the point of "taking Smith farther than Smith himself had ever gone."

In this way Dunkel Frères continues to thrive until Smith's widow sees one of the forged works, thanks to the kind of chain of contingent events that Auster's deadpan delivery makes seem not just possible but downright plausible, pure contingency being the postmodern equivalent of Greek fate. Clearly, Nathan's book of human folly (like Harry Dunkel's life) has morphed into something quite different than what he originally planned, and his obsession with his sad, ridiculous life replaced by an interest in other people's lives and stories. Just as his original "hodgepodge of unrelated anecdotes" grew and took on an unanticipated shape and order, so too Nathan's narrative, which at this point is only a little more than a third over.

"Reconnecting with Tom had given me a big boost to my morale," Nathan says, and an even bigger boost to "The Book of Brooklyn Follies," which now swerves to take in Tom's estranged, prodigal sister, Aurora (Rory), who, except for some pictures in a sex magazine, Tom has not seen for years and who therefore exists (so to speak) in Tom's telling (and in Nathan's retelling of Tom's telling, unlike Tom and Harry who exist (again, so to speak) both as physical presences in Nathan's current life and in their stories (Nathan's of Tom, Tom's of himself and of Harry, and Harry's of himself). Over dinner, Tom's dissatisfaction with his current life leads him to discuss his desire to find "a place where you can live life on your own terms," which in turn prompts Harry to tell the others about his own "inner refuge."

Deeply affected by the war photographs he saw in *Life* and *Look*, a young Harry imagined his first Hotel Existence, a place where the children a heroic Harry rounds up all over Europe can find refuge. Then, as Harry says:

> I gave up my dreams of manly courage and noble self-sacrifice. The Hotel Existence shut down, and when it opened again a few years later, it was no longer sitting in a meadow somewhere in the Hungarian countryside, and it no longer looked like a baroque castle plucked from the boulevards of Baden-Baden. The new Hotel Existence was a much smaller and shabbier affair, and if you wanted to find it now, you had to go to one of those big cities where real life began only after dark.

His own morale boosted by Tom's talk and his own recollections, Harry decides to bankroll Tom's dream, as Nathan subsequently learns, by selling a forged manuscript of Nathaniel Hawthorne's *The Scarlet Letter* (1850). The mix of childlike innocence and criminal activity does more than fit the novel's thematic concerns; as anyone familiar with *The Scarlet Letter* knows, Hawthorne's novel is itself a forgery of sorts: a novel which Hawthorne, in "The Custom House Introduction," claims to have found, not himself written.

Then *The Brooklyn Follies* swerves, or tacks, in a different direction (albeit one that sharp-eyed readers will quickly see is connected to Harry's original Hotel Experience). Lucy, Rory's nine-year-old daughter, suddenly appears at Tom's door, her appearance made all the more enigmatic by her muteness. Like Melville's Bartleby the Scrivener, she prefers not to talk. Neither Tom nor Nathan feels he can care for her, and so Tom prevails upon his reluctant stepsister, Pamela, to take her in. Whatever this unwillingness reveals about Tom and Nathan, it allows Auster to move the narrative both ahead and out of Brooklyn.

On route to Pamela's home, Tom and Lucy stop to eat, and Lucy sabotages the car by pouring cans of soda into the gas tank. That necessitates their staying in the small New England town where first they find their "imaginary Eden" in the Chowder Inn. There they learn the story of its owner, Stanley Chowder. Stanley finds reason to hope, and Tom finds not the woman of his dreams (who is in fact the B.P.M.—Beautiful Perfect Mother—he has long observed and silently longed for—from his apartment window) but instead Stanley's daughter, Honey.

Just as Lucy's arrival interrupted the Harry's scheme narrative line, news of Harry's death interrupts the imaginary Eden plot line, thus generating another anecdote or episode in this story project of a novel. No sooner is the tale of Gordon Dyer's treachery told than an incomplete and therefore enigmatic thirty-second message from Rory on Tom's answering machine leads Nathan down to Winston-Salem, North Carolina, where he rescues Rory from an abusive marriage to her former drug-counselor-turned-born-again husband, David Minor.

All's well that ends well, sort of. Harry is dead, but his death gives Tom the means to make a new start, with Honey and with half the proceeds from the sale of Harry's bookstore. (The other half goes to Rufus Sprague, the drag queen—stage name/alter ego Tina Hott—who is so devastated by Harry's death that she wants only to return to Jamaica and have enough money to buy her medications—but not before turning up in full drag at Harry's funeral, where Tina belts out "Can't Help Loving That Man" in a turn that is just as touching as it is funny and that gets to the heart of Auster's human comedy.)

Rory and Lucy get to live rent-free in the B.P.M.'s mother's house, where Rory helps Nancy with her jewelry business after Nancy's husband, James Joyce, leaves her. Much to Joyce's dismay, Nancy and Rory become lovers, as do Joyce and Nathan, who suffers what he believes is a heart attack but later learns is only an inflamed esophagus brought on by eating too much spicy Thai food with Joyce one night. Overhearing so many people's stories during his brief hospital stay gives Nathan the idea for a new writing project, not unlike the National Public Radio's story project and quite different, tonally at least, than Nathan's earlier project, "The Book of Folly." Nathan, with this resolve for a future he never believed in just a few months earlier, steps out of the hospital and walks along the avenue "under that brilliant blue sky . . . as happy as any man who ever lived."

Nathan knows as he writes of his happiness then what he did not know as he walked along the avenue on September 11, 2001: that the first plane used in that day's terrorist attacks on the United States would hit New York's World Trade Center exactly forty-six minutes later. If this is, as many reviewers claim, Auster's happiest novel, it is a novel in which the happiness is willed, a deliberate and self-conscious effort to cheer up the author and his audience amid so much horror: the horror of the attacks and ongoing horror of the George W. Bush administration's response to the attacks. The happiness would ring false, or at least less true, were it not for this self-conscious effort on Auster's part, which extends to the construction of the narrative as something entirely believable and utterly contrived. Indeed, one may well ask how something so obviously contrived can nonetheless appear so natural. The answer, one suspects, has to do with humankind's need for story, not so much plotted story in which the parts are all interdependent and causally related, but story as pure contingency, one thing after another as in the unstoppable *Brooklyn Follies*.

Robert Morace

Review Sources

Booklist 102, no. 3 (October 1, 2005): 5.
The Boston Globe, January 15, 2006, p. K7.
Chicago Tribune, January 22, 2006, p. 4.
The Guardian, November 12, 2005: 11.
The New York Times 155 (January 4, 2006): B2.
The New York Times Book Review 155 (January 8, 2006): 12.
The Observer, November 20, 2006, p. 16.
Publishers Weekly 252, no. 40 (October 10, 2005): 34-35.
Review of Contemporary Fiction 26, no. 1 (Spring, 2006): 146-147.
USA Today, February 16, 2006, p. B12.
The Washington Post, January 15, 2006, p. T7.

CAESAR
Life of a Colossus

Author: Adrian Goldsworthy (1969-   )
Publisher: Yale University Press (New Haven, Conn.).
    608 pp. $35.00
Type of work: Biography
Time: The first century B.C.E.
Locale: Rome, North Africa, and Central Europe

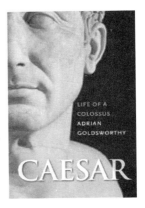

Historian and classics scholar Goldsworthy reviews the public life of the man whose skills as a military leader and politician led to profound changes in the Roman Republic, which he served for nearly four decades

Principal personages:
> GAIUS JULIUS CAESAR, a Roman general
>   and politician
> GNAEUS POMPEIUS (POMPEY), a Roman general and politician
> MARCUS PORTIUS CATO, a Roman senator
> MARCUS TULLIUS CICERO, a Roman senator and orator
> MARCUS LICINIUS CRASSUS, a Roman senator and military leader

While classical scholars may have been arguing since the Renaissance about the true character and accomplishments of the Roman general and politician Gaius Julius Caesar, for the past four hundred years educated people around the world have drawn conclusions about him largely from the portrait created by William Shakespeare. In the English playwright's tragedy *Julius Caesar* (pr. c. 1599-1600), the title character is an aging, imperious, self-absorbed egomaniac, already thinking of himself as a god, unwilling to listen to advice, blind and deaf to warnings that his days are numbered. The constancy of character that he brags of is little more than willful obstinacy. Shakespeare makes it easy to see his faults and understand why men like Brutus could be led easily to join a conspiracy to rid Rome of this dictator and restore republican government. There is a ring of truth to Brutus's explanation to the crowd gathered outside the capitol after the assassination that he struck Caesar down because Caesar was too ambitious, despite Mark Antony's clever rebuttal that eventually incites the populace against the conspirators.

As Adrian Goldsworthy demonstrates admirably in *Caesar: Life of a Colossus*, the real Julius Caesar was a much more complex character, and the Republic he had a hand in bringing down was not as idyllic as Shakespeare's Brutus would have audiences believe. The man who emerges from the pages of Goldsworthy's lengthy yet highly readable biography is a complex figure whose ambition is tempered with a strong dose of political realism and a strain of personal bravery that earned him the admiration of soldiers and fellow statesmen, even among those who begrudged his ascent to power.

Further, the image of Caesar fostered by some historians as the genius destined to rule the Roman Empire is one created with the virtue of hindsight and ignores the truly precarious nature of Roman politics in Caesar's time. Goldsworthy's aim is to present Caesar as a man of his age, examining events of his life in the context of Roman society as it existed when the young nobleman was coming into prominence among his senatorial colleagues. To do so he recreates the story of the Roman Republic during the era now described as the first century before the Christian era. The Romans, however, would not have calculated time that way. In their estimation, they were in the sixth century since the founding of the Eternal City and had been living under a republican form of government for some time. They had developed an elaborate system of checks and balances that virtually prohibited any one senator from gaining too much power or influence over his colleagues. The top officials, known as consuls, served for only a year and then were forced to wait a decade before standing for reelection to this post. However, over the years the Romans had continually extended their domain into the regions along the Mediterranean shores, and retiring consuls were almost guaranteed a provincial governorship. In that post, they were both civil chief and military commander of a region, with an implied if not expressed dictate to enrich the coffers of Rome during their tenure away from the city. If these governors increased their personal wealth at the same time, the rulers of the Republic would politely look the other way.

Adrian Goldsworthy is an Oxford-educated classics scholar who specializes in military history. He is the author of numerous books on ancient Rome, including The Roman Army at War *(1998),* The Punic Wars *(2000), and* The Fall of Carthage *(2003).*

Relying on a variety of extant accounts from the period and on the histories written within two centuries of Caesar's death in 44 B.C.E., Goldsworthy weaves the story of Caesar's rise to power in this republican system. By this time, the high-minded Republic had degenerated into a kind of New York City underworld where senators acted like dons, controlling large groups of thugs that served to enforce their dictates. Offices were bought and sold, laws bent or even ignored so that favorites of powerful senators would be given every opportunity to rise quickly to positions of great power, with the chance for personal profit being a welcome byproduct of political appointment. For a young man to succeed in this world, however, he needed to do something to stand out from the dozens of others seeking professional preferment.

Caesar apparently learned to play the political game from an early age, demonstrating a tendency to set himself apart from his contemporaries in several ways. He was fastidious and iconoclastic in dress and demeanor. He was personally brave and openly ambitious. He was not above bending the law, or even breaking it, when such actions served his advantage. At the same time, he realized that no one who had been successful as a military or political leader had done so without a considerable amount of luck—some of his contemporaries might have called it being under favor of the gods—or without a strong patron. Throughout his career Caesar moved ahead at full steam, so to speak, acting as if every advance might be his last should luck turn against him. To hedge his bets, however, he aligned himself with one or another powerful senator, most particularly Marcus Licinius Crassus, whose vast wealth helped Caesar stave off his many creditors until his own efforts in Gaul made him fabulously wealthy.

The Caesar who emerges from Goldsworthy's biography is a man whose tendency toward clemency and generosity also set him apart from his fellow Romans. Time after time he simply forgave those he defeated in battle or who tried unsuccessfully to curtail his rise to power. Caesar believed that by doing favors for people he could buy their loyalty. He made a career of getting others to be in his debt. At times this behavior paid off for him. Eventually it would cost him his life, however, as one of those with whom he had been especially lenient, Quintus Cassius Longinus, would lead the conspiracy to assassinate him.

As one might expect, the bulk of Goldsworthy's narrative is given over to descriptions of Caesar's military campaigns, in which he was engaged almost continually from 58 to 46 B.C.E., first against rebellious tribes in the provinces and then in a bloody civil war. Military historians have long considered Caesar a brilliant commander, and Goldsworthy does justice to this side of Caesar's life by explaining in detail how he defeated his various enemies. In these encounters Caesar frequently displayed exceptional generosity, opting to allow defeated enemies to retain their lands and even their titles in exchange for acquiescence to Roman rule. On occasion, however, he demonstrated that he could be ruthless, especially when someone he had pardoned took up arms against him for a second time. Usually Caesar made sure that no one got a third chance to oppose him.

Goldsworthy also explains how Caesar used his military prowess and keen understanding of human nature to manipulate his countrymen in political matters as well. With a little coercion and perhaps some bribery, Caesar managed to rise meteorically to the position of consul and then serve two successive five-year terms as provincial governor. Unlike Marcus Portius Cato, the distinguished senator who despised and feared him, Caesar had the knack for aligning himself with the right people and frequently managed to stay out of petty squabbles that cost lesser men their positions. For example, when the time was right, he made public his support for Gnaeus Pompeius, the great general and politician known in history as Pompey. With him and Crassus, Caesar formed what came to be known as the First Triumvirate, a political alliance that allowed all three to secure immense power and wealth and that lasted until Caesar became jealous of the continuing adulation Pompey received from the Roman senate and people.

What makes Caesar's political career even more remarkable is that at the same time he was scheming with so many of Rome's nobility, he was often sleeping with their wives. Like most Romans he married early, and although he seemed to have loved his first wife his own record of divorce and remarriage attests to his recognition that marriage among the nobles was above all a political event. A notorious womanizer, Caesar was constantly shifting his amorous attentions among the spouses of the city's elite or among the concubines of foreign rulers. What may surprise readers of this biography is that the celebrated story of Caesar's affair with the Egyptian queen

Cleopatra is treated as simply another one of those casual liaisons motivated as much by political realities as by personal passion. Only one of his lovers seemed to have engendered a sense of long-term loyalty: Servilia, the wife of Marcus Junius Brutus and mother of a son who bore his father's name. That son, who would eventually become one of Caesar's favorites, and his knife-wielding participation in the dictator's assassination would result in what Shakespeare called "the most unkindest cut of all."

Above all, Goldsworthy notes, Caesar was a great self-promoter. He wrote letters incessantly, keeping in touch with colleagues who could help further his interests, especially when he was away from Rome. Among his frequent correspondents was Marcus Tullius Cicero, the renowned orator whose accounts provide much of the material on which Goldsworthy and other historians rely for insights into the period. Additionally, at the end of every campaigning season while he was engaged in warfare against the Gallic tribes, Caesar composed a *Commentary* outlining his progress in protecting those in his province friendly toward Rome and subjugating those who stood against the Republic. He did the same thing during the years he fought a civil war against the forces of his one-time ally Pompey. While scholars have both noted the exceptional literary quality of these works and applauded Caesar for acknowledging his failures, Goldsworthy points out how these documents paint their author in a most favorable light. If one takes Caesar at his word, it is hard to conclude that there was any other course of action open to him than to take control of the corrupt government by accepting what amounted to dictatorial powers; ironically, if one accepts Caesar's reasoning, the continuance of the Republic depended on his absolute rule.

As Goldsworthy notes, scholars have frequently offered comparisons of Caesar's exploits with those of his historical predecessor Alexander the Great, who in the fourth century B.C.E. had established an empire stretching from the Atlantic to modern-day India. Caesar himself was not prone to such comparison, Goldsworthy suggests; rather, he constantly compared his own career to that of his elder contemporary Pompey, whose exploits had won adulation from the Roman people on numerous occasions. Everything Caesar did seemed in part aimed at besting his self-proclaimed rival. The great civil war he fought against Pompey and his supporters in 49-46 B.C.E. was motivated as much by the sense of injustice Caesar felt in not being appropriately honored for his contributions to Rome as it was by any real threat to the Republic from corrupt politicians.

In the end, Caesar was assassinated by men who thought he had begun to cast too large a shadow over the empire—and its other leaders. It is true that by 44 B.C.E. Caesar had in essence suspended the normal laws of the Republic and had begun to rule under a series of emergency decrees that gave him carte blanche to do what he deemed necessary to preserve Rome's security. In hindsight, the parallels to future despots such as Napoleon Bonaparte and Adolf Hitler are too eerily frightening to overlook. Nevertheless, as Goldsworthy notes, the senators who thrust their knives into the dictator's body had no guarantee that they would be able to restore the Republic when Caesar was in his grave. In fact, subsequent events proved their efforts futile. Within a short time the empire was once again embroiled in civil war, and when the forces of Caesar's adopted son Octavius defeated Mark Antony at the battle of

Actium in 31 B.C.E., the boy whom Antony was sure he could control emerged as the first real emperor of Rome, adding the cognomen Augustus to the family name of Caesar and burying the Roman Republic forever.

Laurence W. Mazzeno

Review Sources

The Atlantic Monthly 298, no. 3 (October, 2006): 126.
Booklist 103, no. 2 (September 15, 2006): 18.
Library Journal 131, no. 15 (September 15, 2006): 67.
Publishers Weekly 253, no. 29 (July 24, 2006): 45-46.
The Spectator 300 (April 29, 2006): 47.
The Wall Street Journal 248, no. 97 (October 24, 2006): D6.
The Washington Times 25, no. 281 (October 8, 2006): B7-B8.

THE CAVE PAINTERS
Probing the Mysteries of the World's First Artists

Author: Gregory Curtis (1944-   )
Publisher: Alfred A. Knopf (New York). Illustrated. 278
    pp. $25.00
Type of work: Fine arts and archaeology
Time: The Paleolithic period to the present
Locale: France and Spain

Curtis presents an engaging and informative study of the magnificent cave paintings found in southern France and northern Spain

Principal personages:
MARCELINO SANZ DE SAUTUOLA, a late
    nineteenth century Spanish lawyer and
    amateur archaeologist who discovered the cave paintings at Altamira
HENRI BREUIL, a twentieth century French priest and leading archaeolo-
    gist
ÉMILE CARTAILHAC, a late nineteenth and twentieth century French
    prehistorian who eventually withdrew his criticism of Sautuola
JEAN CLOTTES, a late twentieth century French archaeologist who has
    done important research at Chauvet cave
ANNETTE LAMING-EMPERAIRE, a twentieth century French anthropolo-
    gist
ANDRÉ LEROI-GOURHAN, a twentieth century French archaeologist who
    is noted for his research on rock art
MAX RAPHAEL, a twentieth century French archaeologist who is famous
    for his study of prehistoric symbol systems

The cave paintings found at Lascaux, France, and Altamira, Spain, have puzzled and fascinated experts and laypersons alike since they were first discovered. In *The Cave Painters: Probing the Mysteries of the World's First Artists*, Gregory Curtis draws the reader into the world of cave art and all of its incredible wonders. The cave site at Altamira was first discovered in the late nineteenth century, and the site at Lascaux was discovered in 1940. Many exemplary studies have been published about them over the years.

The cave paintings of southern France and northern Spain date back to the Paleolithic period, which stretches as far back as 40,000 B.C.E. In 1876, Marcelino Sanz de Sautuola visited the Altamira cave and noticed some paintings on a wall. He returned in 1879 with his daughter, and it was she who came upon a grouping of ceiling paintings of bison. His discovery at Altamira changed Sautuola forever. Curtis suggests that this was "the first time we know of that an artist from the distant Stone Age touched the soul of a modern person." With this discovery, Sautuola attempted to

Gregory Curtis, a respected journalist, served as editor of Texas Monthly *from 1981 to 2000. His first published book was the highly regarded* Disarmed: The Story of the Venus de Milo *(2003). He has written for* The New York Times, The New York Times Magazine, Fortune, Time, *and* Rolling Stone, *among other publications.*

persuade the academic community of the importance of the paintings. He met with ridicule, and experts in the field did not authenticate the Paleolithic art that he had discovered until the early twentieth century. Unfortunately, Sautuola died in 1888 and, therefore, did not live to see his ideas vindicated. Prejudice and preconceived notions of what art is led the academic community in general to recoil at the idea that anyone from the Paleolithic period could have created paintings worthy of respect. It would take time and the bold leap of thought from some remarkable individuals for the cave paintings of southern France and northern Spain to receive their just recognition.

One of the most important French scholars to study cave paintings is Henri Breuil. He was one of the first experts to investigate the site at Lascaux, France. Three boys came upon the cave paintings there, encountering extraordinary depictions of horses, bison, deer, and other colorful animals. Breuil was made aware of this dramatic discovery, and he went to work surveying the area. He found fragments of bones and other items that certainly made it look like humans had occupied the caves. With great flair, Breuil wrote about what he saw and what he thought it all meant to the world of archaeology, anthropology, and art history. He was accused of "romanticizing" the cave paintings and those early humans who had created them. His embellishments made for good reading and helped to popularize the discovery, but he was criticized for some of his dramatizations and inaccurate conclusions. For his time though, Breuil was one of the leading authorities on cave art, and he wrote several important texts on the subject. Because he was a priest, he became known as the "pope of prehistory."

Curtis breathes life into *The Cave Painters* by including fascinating and unusual scholars, such as Breuil, who made it their life's work to understand cave art. In addition to Sautuola and Breuil, some of the towering figures who played pivotal roles in studying cave art are Émile Cartailhac, Jean Clottes, Annette Laming-Emperaire, André Leroi-Gourhan, and Max Raphael. The obsessiveness of some of these characters is the stuff of legend. The academic feuds and the naked ambition of many of these great thinkers add an intriguing texture to Curtis's story.

With his first book, *Disarmed: The Story of the Venus de Milo* (2003), Curtis established himself as an author who knows how to write both informatively and engagingly. He opens *The Cave Painters* with an introduction, "The Naked Cave Men," that explains how the idea of this book took shape. Curtis begins by stating that "This book began in 1995 when my daughter Vivian saw a statue she called 'a naked cave man.'" At the time, the author was traveling in the south of France with his daughter. Curtis became "tremendously excited" by seeing the cave paintings in person. As he realized "Beauty in art or in nature or in a person is always surprising because it is stronger and more affecting than you could have anticipated." In addition to the introduction, the book includes ten chapters, acknowledgments, notes, a bibliography, eight pages of color plates, many black-and-white photographs and illustrations, and an index. Curtis has given each of his chapters informative and amusing titles, such as "The Seductive Axe; The Well-Clothed Arrivals," "The Trident-Shaped Cave; Pairing, Not Coupling," "Three Brothers in a Boat; The Sorcerer," and "Strange, Stylized Women; The World Below the World."

With a few exceptions, "the only people who painted in caves lived in what is now southern France and northern Spain." Despite the many caves that exist in a country such as Germany, there is as yet no evidence that the people who lived there expressed themselves through painting. The cave paintings found in the cave known as Chauvet are considered the oldest. It has been estimated that the paintings at Chauvet, France, are about 32,000 years old. The art at this site is in "full flower," and, strangely, "cave painting remained much the same until it died out about 10,000 years ago." For roughly 22,000 years, the caves of southern France and northern Spain were decorated with amazing skill.

The cave paintings in various parts of France and Spain are some of the most spectacular artistic achievements of Western art. With all the wonder and amazement they have generated, they still remain a puzzle to all concerned. There are seemingly endless questions about the purpose of these paintings, including why only certain animals are the subject of the paintings and why the painters chose to use only a limited number of colors—primarily black and red. These questions and many more have gnawed at archaeologists, art historians, anthropologists, and other scholars alike. No definitive explanation to any of these issues has been found, but with remarkable care, Curtis lays out the history, the debates, and the central figures involved and describes the caves themselves in all of their glory. The cave paintings from this period are not primitive: The tremendous skill it took to complete such cave paintings cannot be underestimated. Curtis makes the crucial point that cave art has "all the refinement, subtlety, and power that great art has had ever since."

Curtis is adept at presenting to the reader the various competing theories that have come to the forefront of the academic world over the years. To this day, debates have not been resolved to the satisfaction of reputable scholars. It seems that each new generation of experts latches onto a new explanation. In the last chapter, Curtis discusses one of the latest theories. The theory primarily states that shamans or religious visionaries may have created the cave art. The author explains that these shamans are believed to be "trying to reproduce the visions they saw while in a magic trance." The idea that those in a "trance" created these marvelous works of "primitive" art has upset several experts. In the end, the mystery may never be solved to the satisfaction of all scholars, but the art remains to fascinate and seduce generations to come.

One of the most intriguing aspects of the author's investigation is his musings on how "the contours of the wall had suggested a head or chest or horns." For Curtis, it was as if the cave already had markings that represented the shape of an animal. As he describes it, "The paintings and engravings—maybe not all of them, but many— weren't adding animals on top of the rock but were a means of pulling out of the stone the animals that were *already there*." One can envisage the rock and a human hand working in concert to create the images. Whether history ultimately unravels the mystery of the cave paintings, it cannot be denied that the ancient cave painters

> took the trouble to create paintings that had graceful lines, subtle color, precise perspective, and a physical sense of volume. The cave painters may or may not have had the idea of art as we understand it, but when they chose to draw an appealing line instead of an awkward one, they were thinking and acting like artists trying to create art in our sense of the word.

In 278 pages, Curtis has written a concise study of the cave paintings and the principal experts who dedicated years to various theories to explain the paintings. Curtis knows the caves intimately as someone who has visited them and not merely as a researcher who has read the books. The sheer spectacle of the paintings has overwhelmed him. The reader vicariously can experience the caves by the guided tour that Curtis leads. From Altamira—which was first discovered in the 1870's—to Chauvet—which was first discovered in 1994—Curtis vividly describes each cave. With *The Cave Painters*, Curtis has written an inviting and vivid exploration of art history, archaeology, anthropology, and metaphysics. It is to the author's credit that he understands well how to keep the reader ever attentive. The book never drags but serves as a stimulating travelogue as it wends its way through the history of cave art and related matters.

Jeffry Jensen

Review Sources

Chicago Tribune, December 3, 2006, p. 8.
The Christian Science Monitor, November 14, 2006, p. 16.
Houston Chronicle, October 29, 2006, p. 3.
Maclean's 119, no. 43 (October 30, 2006): 72.
The New York Review of Books 53, no. 16 (October 19, 2006): 20.
Publishers Weekly 253, no. 29 (July 24, 2006): 49.
The Seattle Times, October 22, 2006, p. M9.
The Washington Post Book World, December 17, 2006, p. 9.

CELL

Author: Stephen King (1947-   )
Publisher: Charles Scribner's Sons (New York). 384 pp.
  $27.00; paperback $10.00
Type of work: Novel
Time: October 1 of the unspecified present
Locale: Boston; rural New Hampshire and Vermont; and
  Kashwak, Maine

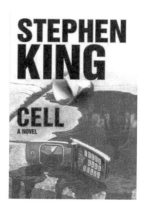

*King's apocalyptic vision of the ubiquity of cell phones
depicts a society reduced to a primitive state following a
mysterious signal that affects everyone using a cell phone
at the time, turning them first into violent maniacs and then
into zombie-like creatures*

Principal characters:
> CLAYTON (CLAY) RIDDELL, young, newly successful graphic novelist,
>   estranged husband of Sharon and father of Johnny Riddell
> TOM MCCOURT, middle-aged gay man who first joins Clay in his fight to
>   escape the madness of Boston
> ALICE MAXWELL, fifteen-year-old who joins Clay and Tom after her
>   family is killed in the initial onslaught of the cell phone violence
> JORDAN, twelve-year-old student at Gaiten Academy, shy, sensitive, and
>   intelligent
> CHARLES ARDAI, (also called The Head), acting headmaster of Gaiten
>   Academy, who has a grandfatherly relationship with Jordan
> DANIEL (DAN) HARTWICK, who, like Clay, has been destroying flocks of
>   mutated humans and who joins Clay on his journey
> DENISE LINK, pregnant traveling companion of Dan
> RAY HUIZENGA, traveling companion of Dan and Denise, the man
>   whose expertise and sacrifice make the novel's climax possible
> THE RAGGEDY MAN (the president of Harvard University), the supernat-
>   ural presence directing the phone-crazed people and tormenting the
>   remaining sane humans

Cell represents a change in direction for Stephen King, preeminent American writer of horror fiction. Throughout his prodigious writing career, King has generally followed the traditional model of beginning his story in a state of normality, giving readers a chance to know the characters before the horror is introduced. For example, while a sense of dread is being developed, the first overt act of violence in *Needful Things* (1991) does not occur until page 274. At the opening of *Cell*, the main character, Clay Riddell, has just signed a deal to publish his first graphic novel; however, before he even has the chance to begin celebrating, or indeed even to tell his estranged wife, Sharon, the news, he is caught up in a sudden, senseless, massive wave of violence spreading throughout Boston. Standing in line at an ice cream vendor's stand,

Clay by chance notices that the people who have become killers, turning upon others with vicious savagery, had been using cell phones at that moment. Those without cell phones, or who were not using them at the time, remain unaffected.

King's use of cell phones as the mechanism to reduce the vast majority of Americans (the characters assume a worst-case worldwide scenario) to mindless zombies offers the opportunity for observation and commentary about the near-ubiquity of cell phones and society's infatuation with and dependence on them. Rather than develop this richly fertile ground for satire, though, King opts for a serious horror novel that pays homage to the two people to whom it is dedicated: Richard Matheson, whose novel *I Am Legend* (1954) depicts one man's struggle against a vampire apocalypse, and George Romero, whose films display in gory yet intelligent detail a gradual takeover of the world by flesh-eating ghouls, horror laced with social satire, from *Night of the Living Dead* (1968) and *Dawn of the Dead* (1979) to *Day of the Dead* (1985) and *Land of the Dead* (2005). Actually, King's novel is closer to Romero's *The Crazies* (1973) in that the infected people act like zombies but are still alive, or Danny Boyle's film *28 Days Later* (2002), wherein a scientifically engineered "rage virus" causes murderously violent behavior in living people on a scale similar to that in King's novel.

One of Clay's first acts as he navigates the hellish Boston streets is to save the life of Tom McCourt, a middle-aged gay man. Small, neat in appearance and keen in intellect, Tom is close enough to society's expectation of his character (even down to his pet cat Rafe) while just skirting stereotypes. He is significant in that he is one of the rare gay men or lesbians ever depicted by King, especially as a main character. If King occasionally seems to be straining too hard to present Tom in a positive light, perhaps he can be forgiven for reacting to accusations of homophobia he discussed in *On Writing* (2000) and which genuinely seemed to hurt him—as he pointed out in that book, it was generally the dialogue of homophobic characters to which readers objected, not his presentation of gay characters. As early in King's career as *The Stand* (1978), lesbian character Dayna Jurgens was presented in a small but very positive, admirable role. The problem is not that King presents gay characters badly but that he rarely depicts them at all, a failing he attempts to remedy—largely successfully—in *Cell*.

The next member of the group gathering around Clay is fifteen-year-old Alice Maxwell, orphaned by the sudden deaths of her parents and very nearly a victim of the initial violence herself. Alice is at first extremely vulnerable (holding onto a miniature sneaker as if it were a talisman); she has a charming quality about her that puts the other characters more at ease, but she is also tough and willing to fight. She says:

> I want to wipe them out. . . . The ones on the soccer field, I want to wipe them out. . . . I don't want to do it for the human race. I want to do it for my mother and my dad, because he's gone, too. I know he is, I feel it. I want to do it for my friends Vickie and Tess. They were good friends, but they had cell phones, they never went anywhere without them, and I know what they're like now and where they're sleeping: someplace just like that . . . soccer field.

As they begin to head north, where Clay hopes against reason to find his son Johnny (and maybe his wife, Sharon, also), they take refuge at Gaiten Academy, a boys' prep school deserted except for head-master Charles Ardai (The Head) and twelve-year-old Jordan, the only remaining student, the two of whom share a bond of mutual re-spect and devotion. The Academy is an old school in the most traditional sense, with its Tudor-style buildings with names like Cheatham Lodge, representing the last ves-tige of a civilization gone to ruin. It also has a soccer field, where Clay's group makes a hor-rifying discovery: more than a thousand zom-bies lying unconscious during the night, packed together and literally filling every available inch of the field (a flock). While Clay and his companions must travel by night, when the creatures are dormant, they must remain hidden inside by day as the be-ings roam, foraging and feasting, an ironic re-versal of the vampire myth. It is this flock that Alice is so furiously intent on destroying.

Stephen King has written more than fifty novels, short-story collections, and works of nonfiction. In 2003, he received the National Book Foundation's Medal for Distinguished Contribution to American Letters and the Horror Writers Association Lifetime Achievement Award.

The aging Ardai ("Of course, I'm an old man and my time is almost over in any case. I'll abide by any decision you make. . . . As long as it's the right one, of course") and the budding computer genius Jordan believe that the cell phone signal stripped human brains down to their lowest level of functioning, wiping them clean as one would a hard drive—and that they are being reprogrammed. No one knows who or what is re-sponsible for the catastrophe, but the group comes to believe that they must destroy the flock at Tonney soccer field, fearing that other flocks are gathering and may even-tually come together if not eliminated. They accomplish this massive destruction but at a terrible cost—a supernatural presence causes The Head to commit suicide by thrusting a fountain pen into his eye, after subjecting the brilliant man to the indignity of being forced to write the word for "insane" in fourteen different languages.

It is at this point that King makes his greatest misstep in an otherwise compelling novel—the introduction of the Raggedy Man, or the president of Harvard University. The novel does not need him, and while it can support him, King's readers have seen this figure too many times before—most pertinently as Randall Flagg in *The Stand*, to which *Cell* inevitably will be compared. In both novels the supernatural antagonist leads a group opposed to the protagonists and sets the protagonists up for execution. In a novel already destined for comparison with its apocalyptic predecessor, inviting unnecessary comparisons by introducing this needlessly familiar parallel element may have been an unwise choice.

That said, King proves his literary powers in the novel's most shocking, horrify-ing, and moving passage: the unexpected, utterly senseless death of one of the major characters. It feels real because it comes as death often does, suddenly and without warning, without the sense of its being a plot device. It evokes pathos because it is a character for whom readers have built great empathy and with whom many identify. It shakes the foundations of both readers and characters because it forcefully brings home the fragility of life: that death is real and can happen to anyone, any time. The terrible vengeance wreaked upon the killers brings cold comfort. This section of the novel demonstrates King writing at the height of his literary abilities.

The survivors move on and meet Dan Hartwick, Denise Link, and Ray Huizenga, traveling companions who have also been eliminating flocks of semi-human creatures along the way. It soon becomes evident that the surviving normal people are being herded like cattle to Kashwak, Maine, an area where there is supposedly no cell phone reception. It is equally evident that the survivors are to have their memories destroyed, while the group of flock-killers is being prepared for a public execution. A combination of ingenuity, self-sacrifice, loyalty, revenge, and luck combine in the novel's suspenseful climax.

While the climax resolves the dramatic tension for most of the principal characters, there is an open-ended coda: It denies closure to one of the final surviving characters, or, rather, it withholds the fate of a character's loved one from the reader. This twist is another difference from King's usual pattern, which is to tie up all loose ends. *Cell* is also shorter and faster-moving than many of King's novels, with very short chapters. The in-depth description for which King is so well known is played down as well. For example, King provides no physical description of the main character, Clay Riddell, at all. He is described as "a young man," and, except for changes in facial expression, that is all. All readers are left to project onto Clay the appearance they envision for him. (King describes other characters in greater detail.) It is difficult to know what to make of this tabula rasa, so drastically different from the minute detail that has become one of King's defining literary qualities.

Finally, *Cell* seems a fusion of King's earlier writing style as seen in works such as *The Stand, 'Salem's Lot* (1975), and *The Shining* (1977), with a new writing style informed by zines, e-books, instant messaging, text messaging, and audio books (a format in which *Cell* is, in fact, available.) *Cell* demonstrates the persistence of theme in the face of changing literary forces.

Charles Lewis Avinger, Jr.

Review Sources

Booklist 102, nos. 9/10 (January 1, 2006): 24.
Library Journal 131, no. 3 (February 15, 2006): 107-108.
Los Angeles Times, January 24, 2006, p. 15L.
Miami Herald, January 25, 2006, p. 2E.
The New York Times 155 (January 23, 2006): E1-E8.
The New York Times Book Review 155 (February 5, 2006): 15.
The Wall Street Journal 247, no. 21 (January 26, 2006): D8.
The Washington Post Book World, February 5, 2006, p. BW03.

CHRISTOPHER MARLOWE
Poet and Spy

Author: Park Honan (1928-   )
Publisher: Oxford University Press (New York). 421 pp.
   $32.50
Type of work: Literary biography
Time: 1564-1593
Locale: Canterbury, Cambridge, and London, England

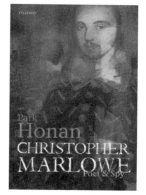

Using newly discovered sources and focusing closely upon Marlowe's sexuality, apparent atheism, and espionage activities, Honan in this biography provides new insights into the playwright's life and work, though much about Marlowe remains unknown and the subject of conjecture

Principal personages:
   CHRISTOPHER MARLOWE, playwright, poet, and erstwhile spy
   THOMAS KYD, fellow dramatist and roommate of Marlowe
   THOMAS WALSINGHAM, patron of Marlowe
   THOMAS WATSON, friend of Marlowe

Christopher Marlowe has been a frequent subject of biographers since Tucker Brooke's landmark 1930 study of the playwright, but there remains as much conjecture as incontrovertible fact about the short life of this first noteworthy English dramatist. Before he was murdered on May 30, 1593, at age twenty-nine, Marlowe had written and seen staged the five plays upon which his reputation stands, an achievement all the more impressive when measured against that of William Shakespeare, his junior by two months, whose output by age twenty-nine consisted of only the minor comedies and histories. Notwithstanding the brevity of Marlowe's career—five or six years at most—he left a legacy of four tragedies that stand with Shakespeare's at the highest rank, a history play that set an early standard for the genre, and an epic love poem (*Hero and Leander*, 1598) on a par with Shakespeare's *Venus and Adonis*, (1593).

It is no wonder then that Park Honan, author of *Shakespeare: A Life* (1998), would choose to write a biography of Marlowe, an acquaintance of Shakespeare and, as some would have it, an erstwhile rival. With the fruits of past scholarship at his disposal and his discovery of new sources, Honan has written the most authoritative study of Marlowe's life and milieu to date. Nevertheless, because so many lacunae remain and much of the documentary evidence is equivocal, many of Honan's conclusions are speculative, qualified, and tentative. In common with previous biographers, he reveals Marlowe through the testimony of others, including the familiar (and perhaps overly stressed) evidence of fellow University Wit Thomas Kyd and that of Marlowe's friend Thomas Watson, whose writings in Latin provide Honan with

～

Park Honan, emeritus professor of
English and American Literature at the
School of English, University of Leeds,
received his Ph.D. from the University
of London. A vice president of the
Marlowe Society, he is the author of
Matthew Arnold: A Life *(1981);* Jane
Austen: Her Life *(1987);* Browning's
Characters: A Study in Poetic
Technique *(1961); and* Shakespeare: A
Life *(1998).*

～

significant new information about Marlowe's life.

Honan utilizes new evidence to strengthen the circumstantial case that a Corpus Christi College portrait of a young man indeed is that of the playwright. Honan's research also has yielded additional facts about Marlowe's comically unsuccessful espionage trip to the Continent, including his arrest and involvement in an abortive counterfeit money scheme. Notwithstanding his gathering of fugitive pieces into a compelling narrative, Honan has not produced the definitive life of Marlowe, who remains a somewhat elusive figure four centuries after his death and likely will remain so.

Honan's title, *Christopher Marlowe: Poet and Spy*, is somewhat misleading because it suggests an equivalence of careers that is not the case. Young Marlowe was first and foremost a playwright and poet, and he dabbled in espionage only occasionally to earn money, cement friendships, and satisfy a desire for adventure. Though he apparently had some assignments as an undercover courier and rendezvoused on the Continent with covert operatives, he accomplished practically nothing in the field of espionage other than fostering a relationship with a patron, who ironically may have betrayed his acolyte and orchestrated his death. On the other hand, the title label of Marlowe as "Poet" accurately reflects Honan's emphasis in the biography, for although he fully credits Marlowe's contributions to the developing tragic drama in Elizabethan England, he deals extensively with the poetry, nondramatic as well as dramatic, suggesting that the Cambridge M.A. was as interested in the language of the theater as in its stagecraft.

Developing his narrative chronologically, Honan begins with Marlowe's childhood and basic education in Canterbury as a shoemaker's son whose intellectual gifts were recognized at an early age. Honan builds upon the scholarship of local historian William Urry and others to provide a comprehensive portrait of the Canterbury milieu in which Marlowe was raised. Honan's approach in these early chapters is the same as later in the book, presenting detailed family histories of Marlowe associates and acquaintances and giving elaborate descriptions of places where he lived. Such information occasionally seems only peripherally relevant to his work, but Marlowe is a product of his environment, and the milieu as well as his formal studies affected his writing. There is, Honan shows, a contemporaneity to Marlowe's subjects and themes, albeit his characters and conflicts are of the past. Honan's treatment of the plays, though in the context of biography, includes close textual analysis as the basis of his interpretations, and he also discusses the plays in relation to the dramas of his contemporaries, notably Shakespeare and his indebtedness to Marlowe.

The portrait of Marlowe the man in the book has two loci: his atheism and his homoerotic tendencies. The former Honan presents through documentary evidence and informed interpretations of events and statements in Marlowe's work. He agrees with earlier biographers that Marlowe probably was gay but adds little to the preexisting equivocal evidence, though marginally bolstering his stance through textual exegesis. He is more convincing in his treatment of Marlowe's atheism, whose stridency may have reflected the young man's braggadocio tendencies more than a deeply held theological position. England at the time was obsessed domestically and internationally with the issue of Catholicism, mainly its political and dynastic ramifications, and Marlowe through friends and patrons was on the fringes of these conflicts.

In fact, throughout his brief life, Marlowe prospered thanks to the largess of others, beginning with an archbishop's scholarship that enabled him to attend Canterbury's King's School; another scholarship to Corpus Christie College, Cambridge; and the continuing patronage of the well-placed Walsinghams, who were interested in him both as a putative playwright and as a potentially useful spy.

More promising as a playwright than as a spy, Marlowe in July of 1587, age twenty-three and with a new Cambridge M.A. in hand, made his way to London, taking up lodgings with Thomas Kyd and becoming part of a coterie that also included Shakespeare and Walter Raleigh. By autumn the first of his two plays about the Tartar warrior and conqueror Tamburlaine was in repertory, and its sequel followed soon after, both presented by the Admiral's Men and with Edward Alleyn, a leading actor of the age, in the title role. (He also would be Faustus and Barabas in Marlowe's next plays.) The two Tamburlaine spectacles introduced to the English stage an epic hero whose exploits are presented through the medium of a sparkling blank verse that raised dramatic poetry to new heights. Further, Honan says, Marlowe eschewed the moralizing of his predecessors, "asking spectators to hear, view, and judge as they please," because the theater is not for "moral example, proof, or beneficial demonstration," but "a place of story and experience."

Remarkably for a novice playwright, young Marlowe "offers a comprehensive view of life, and involves the audience in the Tartar's urgency and purpose." Elizabethans, used to didactic plays, reacted enthusiastically to Marlowe's tragic spectacle and its sequel, and both were revived frequently in London and by touring companies elsewhere. Marlowe's achievement with the Tamburlaine plays is especially remarkable because prior to them he had written only one other play, *Dido, Queen of Carthage*, sometime between 1584 and 1587, which the boy actors of the Chapel Royal presented for the queen. Largely an academic exercise in which the novice playwright gives his own spin to part of the Aeneas story, the play was a collaboration with Thomas Nashe, and the extent of each man's contributions is impossible to determine. What Honan calls "The Tamburlaine Phenomenon" spawned imitations, and the plays of Shakespeare, whose talent did not emerge as quickly as Marlowe's, began to show a Marlovian influence.

Though its first recorded performance was in 1594, Honan thinks *Doctor Faustus* dates from 1589, not long after the second Tamburlaine success, and he calls it "the first great English tragedy with strong mythic and universal qualities." It always has been a scholarly enigma. Not until eleven years after Marlowe's death was the first of nine quarto editions published, including a 1616 text that is longer than its antecedents. Because there are records of others being paid to write additions to the play, positively establishing Marlowe's original text is impossible, though Honan tries, guided by the playwright's sources, attitude toward religion, and evidence of plays whose textual reliability is largely unquestioned. With Alleyn at the height of his craft, and the presence of devils, thunder, and fireworks, *Doctor Faustus* brought an unparalleled excitement to the London stage and made Marlowe a celebrity among his peers, who then tried to emulate him.

While the Tamburlaine plays and *Doctor Faustus* still attracted crowds, Marlowe quickly produced another major success, *The Jew of Malta*. From its first performance (probably late in 1591), this examination of the lust for power and anti-Semitism was a popular favorite. Though it "remains the most thematically elusive of the classic Elizabeth plays," in Honan's judgment, it is "exuberantly theatrical" and a structural "masterpiece, strong in balance and symmetry." This popular success that mixes the genres of comedy, tragedy, farce, and satire and makes the title character both hero and antihero encouraged other playwrights to experiment with the nontraditional and made possible Shakespeare's *The Merchant of Venice* (pr. c. 1596-1597) and lesser plays by others.

Marlowe's name as author appears on another play presented within a few months of *The Jew of Malta. The Massacre of Paris* had ten recorded performances in early 1592 (indicative of its popularity) and was published soon after Marlowe's death. Honan deals minimally with it because merely a fragment of the original survives, and it probably was reconstructed from actors' recollections. However, the subject matter demonstrates the range of Marlowe's interests, including continental history, and his willingness to treat themes whose contemporary relevance that could offend the Revels office.

Honan notes that with his early history plays—about Henry VI— Shakespeare "was opening up English history to realistic and sceptically intelligent treatment." Marlowe's *Edward II* (pr. c. 1592, pb. 1594) clearly follows the Shakespeare model, particularly stylistically: "a full, fairly unadorned manner astonishingly close to the human voice" and with a "cool disinterestedness." Honan also sees Marlowe's chronicle play as the story "of a king undone by a genuine, natural, but blinding infatuation with a male lover," using as his primary sources both historic annals and Raphael Holinshed's *The Chronicles of England, Scotland, and Ireland* (c. 1577).

According to Honan, Marlowe's academic interest in homoerotic desire and his own sexual predilections led him to treat these matters "more realistically than any English playwright had done before," but though *Edward II* "offers the first great depiction of same-sex love for the stage . . . its dramatization of erotic behaviour is subordinated to its focus on power." The play shows, as Honan puts it, "the folly of the impulsive, unheeding will," whose corruption embraces love and politics, causing upheaval to the family as well as the state. *Edward II* is another masterpiece from Marlowe's pen, the like of which London theatergoers had not previously seen. Honan praises its dramatic unity, psychological characterization, new dramaturgy techniques, and contrasting styles of speech. Indebted though he was to Shakespeare, Marlowe "for the moment eclipses him," but within two years or so, when Shakespeare would turn to *Edward II* as the template for his historical tragedy *Richard II*, he would fashion a drama whose powerful ritualistic poetry would cause it to overshadow Marlowe's play. Indeed, during a career that continued for years and into another reign, Shakespeare took precedence over Marlowe as the preeminent English playwright.

Like much of his life, the circumstances of Marlowe's violent death have been difficult for biographers to encompass. Honan uses documentary evidence, including the coroner's report, new information about the conspirators, modern medical opinion, and informed conjecture to develop a credible scenario that serves as an appropriate conclusion to his biography of a brilliant and ambitious young man whose plays ushered in the golden age of English theater and remain vital dramas four centuries later.

Gerald H. Strauss

Review Sources

Booklist 102, no. 8 (December 15, 2005): 14.
Contemporary Review 288 (Summer, 2006): 267.
Library Journal 131, no. 3 (February 15, 2006): 118.
New Criterion 24, no. 9 (May, 2006): 70-73.
The New York Review of Books 53, no. 6 (April 6, 2006): 42-46.
The New York Times 155 (January 18, 2006): E8.
The New York Times Book Review 155 (January 29, 2006): 20.
The Spectator 299 (Ocotber 29, 2005): 44-45.
The Times Literary Supplement, June 2, 2006, p. 27.

CLEMENTE
The Passion and Grace of Baseball's Last Hero

Author: David Maraniss (1949-   )
Publisher: Simon & Shuster (New York). 401 pp. $26.00
Type of work: Biography
Time: 1934-1973
Locale: Puerto Rico and Pittsburgh

An overdue and necessary biography of baseball's first and perhaps greatest Latin American star, who proved his heroism both on and off the field

Principal personages:
    ROBERTO CLEMENTE, 1955-1972, Pittsburgh Pirates right fielder
    VERA ZABALA CLEMENTE, his wife

Baseball players become the proper subjects for a book-length biography when they combine sustained athletic excellence with an aspect of character or personality, such as larger-than-life appetites (Babe Ruth), inner personal demons (Ty Cobb), an Olympian aloofness (Joe Dimaggio), an oracular wackiness in speaking (Yogi Berra, Casey Stengel), a sense of personal worth bordering on hubris (Ted Williams), a heroic struggle against societal opposition (Jackie Robinson), or a career cut off too soon by a failing body (Lou Gehrig, Sandy Koufax). As can be seen from many of these examples, a career spent in or started in a major media center always helps in the spreading of fame, and that is perhaps the only factor that mitigated against the writing of another full-scale biography of the Pittsburgh Pirates' Hall-of-Fame rightfielder Roberto Clemente. Almost every other above-mentioned factor was a part of his complex, often contradictory personality, with the addition to those of another element sadly lacking in all too many athletic careers: the capacity for empathy and altruism that led, in Clemente's case, to a heroic off-the-field action that tragically ended his life.

Now David Maraniss has rectified that omission with his generally excellent biography *Clemente: The Passion and Grace of Baseball's Last Hero*. Even for those who lived during Clemente's career, his accomplishments come as something of a surprise. His cannon of an arm, yes, will never be forgotten, but the statistics are nevertheless extraordinary: two World Series rings, four batting championships (including the highest batting average during the decade of the 1960's, a period known for its fearsome pitching), twelve Golden Gloves for fielding, exactly three thousand hits, and—most impressive of all—a fourteen-game hitting streak during his World Series appearances, a record of postseason clutch hitting that many superstars whose career records dwarf Clemente's can rightly envy. Clemente grew into a hitter who had no weakness. Add to that his movie-star good looks and his popularity with fans, and one can only conclude that the lack of attention paid to Clemente's accomplishments is

due to one factor, one that Clemente complained about throughout his career: that he
was a Spanish-speaking ballplayer from Latin
America.

Even though Jackie Robinson had broken
baseball's color barrier in 1947, baseball
writers in particular remained insensitive to
the problems faced by Latin American ballplayers, problems exacerbated by language,
class, and often race. Clemente, a dark-
skinned native Spanish speaker from Puerto
Rico, was particularly sensitive to any slight
regarding his heritage or home. He insisted
that he had been labeled a "hot dog" in a
newspaper story written during his first
spring training camp with the Pirates, apply-

*David Maraniss is an associate editor
at* The Washington Post, *and he won
the Pulitzer Prize for National
Reporting in 1993. His previous
biographies include* First in His Class
*(1995), about President Bill Clinton,
and* When Pride Still Mattered *(1999),
about football coach Vince Lombardi.*
They Marched into Sunlight *(2003) is
an account of two events of October,
1967: a military operation in Vietnam
and an antiwar protest in the United
States.*

ing a stereotypical charge about Latin ballplayers to him, even though Maraniss cannot find any evidence of this. For years sportswriters wrote their interviews with
Clemente and other Latin ballplayers in a phonetic reproduction of their speech,
which had the effect of depicting the athletes as pidgin-speaking half-wits.

Clemente was often considered withdrawn and aloof (which, at times, he was),
when he was instead sensitive about his fluency in English, which he tried to improve
by watching American Westerns on television (in one of them, *The Lone Ranger*, he
would have seen how demeaning the pidgin English of Tonto was). Maraniss, too, is
sensitive to the problems faced by Clemente in establishing not only his own worth
but also that of other Latin ballplayers. Clemente insisted, for instance, that Dodger
pitcher Sandy Koufax got better press than Giants pitcher Juan Marichal because of
Marichal's ethnicity. Maraniss delves into Spanish-speaking sources, as well as other
less-consulted sources, such as African American newspapers, who more closely followed the careers of Latin ballplayers than larger newspapers did.

As with most sports biographies, Maraniss uses the sports reporting of major
newspapers as an important source, unfortunately falling into their hyperbolic jargon
at times, such as when he says that in the 1960 World Series, Clemente's powerful
throwing arm threatened to turn the base-running Yankee Bill "Moose" Skowron into
"moose meat." Maraniss, as do many biographers, also falls into the trap of over-
identifying with his subject, and as do many sports biographers, roots for his subject.
This is not a complete "warts and all" portrait, as so many modern sports biographies
are. For example, Maraniss delicately hints that Clemente's sexual career was like
that of many ballplayers of the time, as readers have learned exhaustively from other
biographies, but does not go into any details, probably out of respect for Clemente's
wife and family.

For the most part, Maraniss exercises an impartial judgment on those facts he
has uncovered, pointing out Clemente's real frailties, as opposed to those that
sportswriters attributed to him. Most notoriously, Clemente's grousing about his

physical ailments (many of which stemmed from a 1954 auto crash) became magnified into the unspoken feeling that Clemente was a malingerer, a player who "jaked" his responsibilities, in the argot of the times. A major *Sports Illustrated* article about Clemente by Myron Cope in 1966 adopted the nickname of White Sox shortstop Luke Appling, "Old Aches and Pains," for Clemente's condition: "Aches and Pains and Three Batting Titles." The simple fact that refutes these innuendoes and inferences is a record set by Clemente at the end of the 1972 season—his 2,433 games as a Pittsburgh Pirate surpassed the record set by Honus Wagner. Clemente used his physical discomfort much in the way he used his anger as fuel for his accomplishments. He also became interested in how to heal the pain that traditional medical science ignored, and one of his two major post-baseball dreams (the other being to build a sports city for the youth of Puerto Rico) was to build a chiropractic clinic for the poor near his home.

Maraniss does not hide the more unpleasant sides of Clemente's character, such as a mystifying tendency to lash out violently at fans who got too close to him. On the other hand, Clemente developed warm, familial relationships with several young female fans and their families, which, at first, seems at the least unusual but appears to have stemmed from Clemente's need for sister/daughter figures in his life. All accounts tend to agree that while Clemente at times displayed poor impulse control, he could later admit when he was wrong and at heart was a warm, caring individual.

It was this aspect of his personality, combined with his growing ease in a leadership role, that led to his untimely death, a death totally unnecessary, as Maraniss uncovers each step in a tragedy of errors. This story has never been sufficiently reported. Clemente had journeyed to Managua, Nicaragua, in November of 1972 to manage the Puerto Rican national team in the world championships. When the city was devastated by an earthquake in December, he led Puerto Rican relief efforts. He also learned that initial shipments of aid had been impounded by the forces of dictator General Anastasio Somoza, so Clemente felt compelled to accompany the following shipment in order to ensure its delivery to the truly needy, even though he would be apart from his family on New Year's Eve, an important family holiday in Puerto Rico.

A chance encounter at the airport led to Clemente's engaging a totally unairworthy cargo plane, piloted by a tired pilot, owned by a corner-cutting operator, overloaded by more than two tons of cargo that had not been properly stowed aboard the airplane. The plane crashed into the Caribbean Sea shortly after takeoff, and Clemente entered the realm of legend. He became the second ballplayer to have the customary five-year waiting period for entry into the Hall of Fame waived—the first being that other figure of grace chopped down in its prime, Lou Gehrig. Clemente's status in Puerto Rico is almost mythical; not only is a stadium named after him, but he is also depicted as the Good Shepherd in a relief sculpture depicting scenes from his life.

Maraniss's book is not without faults. It could have been more scrupulously edited; one does not make a basket catch by holding one's glove near one's "naval." At one point, Maraniss implies that Don Drysdale, the Dodger pitching ace, threw at Clemente because of Clemente's nationality. (Clemente responded by hitting a home run.) Drysdale was, however, notorious for being an equal-opportunity headhunter;

he would have agreed with Early Wynn, who claimed Drysdale would throw at his own grandmother if she crowded the plate. In Maraniss's otherwise first-rate depiction of Clemente's last days, he makes too much of the fact that Howard Hughes, who was living in Managua at the time of the earthquake, scurried out of the country, while Clemente died trying to save its people. Clemente's glory is not made any brighter by recounting Hughes's neurotic cowardice.

Also, Maraniss does not let readers forget that the Richard Nixon who contributed one thousand dollars to the Roberto Clemente memorial fund and met with Clemente's teammates after his death was at the same time becoming more deeply enmeshed in the scandals that would end his presidency. This becomes relevant when Maraniss points out that it was Nixon's support that enabled Somoza to stay in power, and that Nixon's aides shielded him from the fact that Somoza's military was preventing much of the incoming aid from reaching the earthquake's victims.

In "To an Athlete Dying Young," A. E. Housman declares that the hero's early death ensures that the fate of the aged runner, when "the name died before the man," will not occur for him. Yet, in a sense, that has happened to Roberto Clemente. For instance, Reggie Jackson has been dubbed "Mr. October," but a good argument can be made that Roberto Clemente was an even worthier "Mr. October," not only for his clutch hitting but also for his fielding and base-running, a more complete display of excellence. Maraniss makes a convincing argument that it was Clemente's baserunning in the 1971 World Series that was the turning point in the Pirates' eventual victory. While Gehrig's succumbing to ALS, along with Gary Cooper's portrayal of him in *The Pride of the Yankees* (1942), assured his immortality, Clemente's general fame seems to have disappeared, along with his body, in the ocean. One salient fact points to the cause of this: Gehrig's famous speech on Lou Gehrig Day, with its heartbreakingly ironic declaration that he was "the luckiest man on the face of the earth," was delivered in English, while Clemente's equally moving tribute to his family on Roberto Clemente Day was given in Spanish.

Some critics declare that America's Puritan heritage can be most readily seen in its sexual mores, but it is equally evidenced in the unspoken rules of sportsmanship that lie behind American athletics. The stoic acceptance of pain, whether physical or emotional, the refusal to boast or whine—these mitigate against Americans' acceptance of athletes from other cultures. Clemente's talking about his pains is noted; that he often played through and with them is not. His demand that his excellence be acknowledged is noted; that his excellence was real is not. Maraniss leaves unsaid the comparisons that any baseball fan who reads this story will make: that Clemente performed his deeds in the era just before free agency, so his accomplishments were not disproportionately rewarded as they are today, and also in an era before performance-enhancing drugs were widely available. In these senses, Clemente was "Baseball's Last Hero," but even more important, he was a hero because of the stances he took for the poor and for his country. When Ozzie Guillen, the manager of the 2006 American League All Stars, was being interviewed before the All-Star Game, he unbuttoned his uniform shirt to show the T-shirt he wore underneath. It bore the name of Roberto Clemente. Clemente continues to be a role model for and hero to Latin American ballplayers, who are still misunderstood by American sports culture; David Maraniss's book shows that he should be a hero for everyone.

William Laskowski

Review Sources

Booklist 102, no. 12 (March 1, 2006): 42.
Kirkus Reviews 74, no. 5 (March 1, 2006): 222.
The New York Times 15 (May 18, 2006): E10.
The New York Times Book Review 155 (May 7, 2006): 13.
Progressive 70, no. 7 (July, 2006): 43-44.
Publishers Weekly 253, no. 10 (March 6, 2006): p. 64.
U.S. News & World Report 140, no. 15 (April 24, 2006): 22.
The Wall Street Journal 247, no. 98 (April 27, 2006): D7.

CONSUELO AND ALVA VANDERBILT
The Story of a Daughter and a Mother in the Gilded Age

Author: Amanda Mackenzie Stuart (1954-   )
First published: 2005, in Great Britain
Publisher: HarperCollins (New York). 579 pp. $28.00
Type of work: Biography
Time: The mid-nineteenth to the mid-twentieth century
Locale: The United States, Great Britain, and France

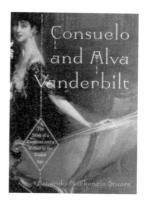

An examination of two privileged, strong-willed people who were social trendsetters as well as suffragists during an age when a successful marriage was the surest path to becoming a woman of consequence

Principal personages:
    ALVA VANDERBILT, wife of William K.
      Vanderbilt
    CONSUELO VANDERBILT, wife of the ninth duke of Marlborough
    OLIVER H. P. BELMONT, Alva's lover and second husband
    JACQUES BALSAN, Consuelo's second husband
    WINSTON CHURCHILL, British prime minister during World War II

It was November 6, 1895, at 12:20 P.M., and the elaborate wedding at New York City's St. Thomas Episcopal Church was on hold.

> The ushers sauntered up to their stations, three on one side of the central aisle and three on the other—then sauntered back to the church porch again. Mr [Walter] Damrosch, who had completed his concert programme, beat time with his baton in silence, his head turned round towards the church door. The Duke of Marlborough began to fidget nervously, and only regained some of his composure when he noted the English sang-froid of his best man. As the delay lengthened, the guests shuffled and whispered. Alva was observed looking uncharacteristically worried. And then decidedly strained. Five minutes passed . . . then ten . . . then twenty . . . and still the bride had not appeared.

The bride-to-be was home weeping uncontrollably at the prospect of entering into matrimony with a loathsome Englishman. Her socially ambitious mother had forced her into the union, however, and there was no way out. Trapped like a bird in a gilded cage, she had been denied contact with the man she loved. Her mother had feigned a heart attack and, when Consuelo remonstrated against the impending nuptials, threatened to shoot the object of her affections (a thirty-three-year-old rake). Attempting to offer comfort by pointing out the advantages to becoming a duchess and at the same time escaping her mother's clutches was Consuelo's father, William Kissam Vanderbilt, whose great wealth made possible a dowry much needed by the financially strapped lord of Blenheim Palace. On to the cathedral they went. An unruly throng of spectators jostled outside to catch a glimpse of the red-eyed eighteen-year-old whose

A writer and producer of independent films, Amanda Mackenzie Stuart has also written historical screenplays. The best-selling Consuelo and Alva Vanderbilt *is her first book.*

vital statistics, including length of hand and foot (eight and a half inches) and shape of nose and chin ("pointed, indicating vivacity") had appeared in the *New York World. Town Topics* described the bridal underwear down to the gold stocking supporters and rosebud-embroidered corset covers.

The mother of the bride, Alva Erskine Smith Vanderbilt, forty-two and recently divorced, hailed from Mobile, Alabama, where her father had been a cotton trader. The family relocated to New York on the eve of the Civil War and to Paris shortly after the cessation of hostilities. Back in the Empire City three years later, the Smiths acquired a villa in fashionable Newport, Rhode Island, and fit in socially with its wealthy summer residents. After financial fortunes took a skid and her parents' health failed, Alva, in the author's words, "took the only option open to her. She put herself on the marriage market for two anxious years" before snagging the handsome grandson of steamship and railroad mogul Cornelius Vanderbilt. The family savior then proceeded to win over the curmudgeonly patriarch. Society dowager Caroline (Mrs. John Jacob) Astor looked down on the Vanderbilts as crude parvenus. Nonetheless, William K. and Alva were part of a younger "smart set" who ultimately found acceptance in the most exclusive circles.

When Cornelius died, a three-million-dollar bequest enabled the couple to purchase nine hundred acres on Long Island for a sporting retreat and watering hole named Idle Hour. Alva worked closely on the specifications with architect Richard Morris Hunt. Alva and Hunt also collaborated on designs for a new Fifth Avenue mansion. Some sixteen hundred invitations went out for the housewarming, and only a handful came back with regrets. Mrs. Astor attended the costume ball in deference to a daughter who otherwise could not have gone (such being etiquette protocol at the time). A star quadrille featured dancers with electric lights in their hair. Fashion arbiter Ward McAllister organized a Mother Goose quadrille, and the costumes for a hobbyhorse quadrille made the participants appear to be on horseback.

Educated at home by Alva, who meted out punishment with a riding whip and employed a steel rod to produce straight posture, Consuelo recalled: "Often as I lay on the bed . . . I reflected that there was in her love of me something of the creative spirit of an artist—that it was her wish to produce me as a finished specimen framed in a perfect setting, and that my person was dedicated to whatever final disposal she had in mind." The demise of William K.'s father, William Henry, in 1885 brought another fifty million dollars into family coffers, making Consuelo at age nine the world's richest heiress. A frustrated architect, Alva supervised construction of Marble House in Newport, whose Gold Room in retrospect symbolizes Gilded Age vacuity. The family took long cruises on a private yacht, perhaps at Alva's behest in a forlorn attempt to curb William's infidelities. His promiscuity wrecked their relationship and embittered her about the possibilities of marital bliss.

After arranging for Consuelo and Charles Richard John Spencer-Churchill, the ninth duke of Marlborough, to meet in England, Alva entertained her prey at Marble House. In what was Newport's summer season highlight, waiters adorned in the style of France's ancien régime served two separate sit-down feasts (supper at midnight and breakfast three hours later). Three orchestras entertained. Next, aboard the Astors' yacht *Nourmahal*, they and their retinue watched Consuelo's father compete in the America's Cup. After losing the first race, *Valkyrie III* was disqualified when its boom struck and broke the topmast stay on Vanderbilt's *Defender*. Protesting to no avail, Lord Dunraven pulled out of the event, and there were no more official Cup challenges for thirty-nine years.

At five feet, two inches, the diminutive duke (dubbed Sunny because he once held the title earl of Sunderland) was six inches shorter than his betrothed. He was ill-tempered, insecure, supercilious, and according to the *New York World*, "hollow-chested" and "very short of stature and some people say of money." Consuelo felt deserted and debased on her wedding night. More accustomed to being with prostitutes than virgins, Sunny was beastly in bed and then seasick throughout the ocean voyage to Europe. Not even "Gay Paree" could revive Consuelo's spirits. After a stop in London, the couple reached Woodstock, to cheering throngs, and proceeded to Blenheim, whose 170 rooms seemed dreary and foreboding to the new duchess. At her service was a palace staff of 40 whose hierarchy mirrored the rigid class system of their "betters." Consuelo hated the stifling protocol of this anachronistic milieu but was considerate to tenants and servants and active in philanthropic work.

Author Amanda Mackenzie Stuart concludes: "Now that Consuelo was finally out of Alva's orbit, the doll-child was giving way to the independent-minded daughter." She was presented at London's royal court and gave birth to two boys ("an heir and a spare") in quick succession. Nonetheless, the Marlboroughs' relationship was in shambles. Sadly, what had started badly only deteriorated. Gloomy, churlish, and frequently absent from Consuelo's side, Sunny had nothing but contempt for things American. After a number of discreet affairs, Consuelo went on a Paris spree with Lord Castlereagh, and the marriage totally unraveled. Winston Churchill, the duke's cousin, mediated a settlement that avoided scandal and allowed both Consuelo and Sunny to share in their sons' upbringing. Still embraced by London's elite, Consuelo was part of a group known as the Souls, who (writes Stuart) favored "intense conversation, tennis, and long walks over gambling and racing and whose relationships were characterized by a complex web of intimacy and extra-marital relationships."

Meanwhile, Alva wed socialite Oliver Belmont and embarked on a lifestyle of "breathtaking" vapidity. With Mrs. Astor a virtual recluse, Alva vied with Mrs. Ogden Mills (née Ruth T. Livingston) for social supremacy. Her relationship with Belmont was apparently loving but stormy, hardly surprisingly when one considers her personality. When upset at Alva, Belmont would sing aloud the following ditty: "Would someone kindly tell me/ For I would like to know,/ Why I got a lemon in the garden of love,/ Where only peaches grow."

After Belmont's death in 1908, Alva embraced feminism. Her role models were the militant Pankhursts, Emmeline and her daughter Christabel, who caused such a storm in their native England. A genius at publicity, especially self-promotion, Alva organized a Political Equality Association (PEA) within the National American Woman Suffrage Association (NAWSA) and enlisted society matrons, striking shirt-waist workers, and African Americans, earning the enmity of NAWSA luminary Carrie Chapman Catt. One Valentine's Day the PEA released heart-shaped balloons with messages urging New Yorkers to extend the franchise to women. When the NAWSA proved overly cautious, Alva helped form the Congressional Union for Woman's Suffrage, which under the leadership of Alice Paul evolved into the National Woman's Party (NWP). Alva was an ardent supporter of those arrested and mistreated for picketing outside the White House in 1917 but avoided direct combat herself. A control freak with a violent temper often unleashed on her staff, she tried to play matchmaker for young protégés and could be vindictive toward adversaries. After her death in 1933, twenty feminist pallbearers escorted the coffin into St. Thomas's. A banner contained Susan B. Anthony's final words: "Failure Is Impossible." It was a fitting summary of Alva's resoluteness.

Though no fan of the Pankhursts, Consuelo supported woman suffrage in Great Britain but was more involved in social betterment. After remarrying in 1921 to lusty Frenchman Jacques Balsan (Sunny also remarried, with disastrous results), she lived in France until forced to flee the Nazis, then divided her later years between New York and Florida. Prime Minister Winston Churchill visited her in January, 1942, between wartime strategy sessions with President Franklin D. Roosevelt and again in 1946 prior to his famous "Iron Curtain" speech in Fulton, Missouri.

Exquisitely mannered, Consuelo nevertheless did not suffer fools. For instance, she once ordered the earl of Carnarvon to leave her premises immediately when he disparaged the French at dinner. To the end, Paris remained her favorite city, but after Germans occupied her residence there she divested herself of it and virtually all its contents. Consuelo's 1951 autobiography, *The Glitter and the Gold*, contrasted the years of her loveless first marriage with her later, more productive life. Consuelo chose to be interred in Oxfordshire near her second son, Ivor, a delicate kindred soul. The tombstone reads: "Mother of the tenth Duke of Marlborough—born 2nd March 1877—died 6th December 1964." Not surprisingly in Consuelo's work, Alva and Sunny emerge as the heavies, although the final text was much softened compared to early drafts. The book reached the best-seller list, surpassed only by the Bible (Revised Standard Edition) and *Tallulah: My Autobiography* (1952).

Those fascinated with the rich and famous will love Amanda Mackensie Stuart's true tale of two headstrong women who challenged the social and political restraints of their time. A *New Yorker* review claimed that "while impeccably researched, [it] lacks psychological acumen," but the reader mercifully is spared didactic behavior analysis. Concerning the protagonists' sex lives, there are hints that Consuelo had a torrid affair with French portraiture artist Paul Helleu and that after Oliver passed away, Alva traveled in lesbian circles, but Stuart avoids unproved assertions.

Presenting the story as a dual biography was clever, as was the frequent insertion of quotations by Edith Wharton, whose novels dissected and skewered the pretensions of New York society and whose last, unfinished work, *The Buccaneers,* has a main character modeled after Consuelo. The final product has historic relevance and is an impressive accomplishment: elegant, compelling, and fair to both daughter and mother, despite the latter's character flaws. As *The New York Times* reviewer Francine Du Plessix Gray notes, the adage "Mother Knows Best" encapsulates the book's ultimate irony. From her own experiences, Alva realized that Consuelo would be more useful and immune to criticism if she were a titled lady.

James B. Lane

Review Sources

Booklist 102, no. 7 (December 1, 2005): 18.
Elle 21, no. 5 (January, 2006): 60.
Kirkus Reviews 73, no. 22 (November 15, 2005): 1226.
The New York Times Book Review 155 (February 19, 2006): 16-17.
The New Yorker 82 (February 13, 2006): 170.
Publishers Weekly 252, no. 44 (November 7, 2005): 67.
USA Today, March 9, 2006, p. D5.
Vogue 195, no. 12 (December, 2005): 265.

CONVERSATION
A History of a Declining Art

Author: Stephen Miller (1941-   )
Publisher: Yale University Press (New Haven, Conn.).
   336 pp. $27.50
Type of work: Literary history, philosophy
Time: From ancient Greece into the twenty-first century
Locale: The Western world

Miller investigates the history of conversation in the West, from its origins in Athens and Sparta through its flourishing in eighteenth century Britain to what he views as the deplorable state of conversation in twenty-first century America

Principal personages:
   MICHEL DE MONTAIGNE, French essayist
   JONATHAN SWIFT, English satirist
   DAVID HUME, Scottish philosopher
   DR. SAMUEL JOHNSON, English author and lexicographer
   JOSEPH ADDISON, English essayist and poet
   JEAN-JACQUES ROUSSEAU, French philosopher and writer

   People may not think much about conversation in general, never mind as an art. They just talk to one another. A common assumption is that anyone can converse. Another is that conversation is ubiquitous and will always be the backdrop of society. Stephen Miller, in *Conversation: A History of a Declining Art*, calls such ideas into question. He is especially concerned about the United States, where he believes "rescuing conversation may be an impossible task in a culture that admires both angry self-expression and nonjudgmental 'supportive' assent."
   Miller begins to define "conversation" in chapter 1, introducing experts from past centuries such as French essayist Michel De Montaigne (who Miller says thought of conversation as an intellectual sporting event that would improve one's mind), French aphorist François La Rochefoucauld (who believed that people were not sensible in conversation because they were thinking about what they wanted to say themselves rather than responding to what was being said to them), and British satirist Jonathan Swift (who felt that conversation suffered from a decline in raillery—"good humored, intelligent wit and banter.") Miller concludes that the meaning of the word "conversation" in eighteenth century Britain is still applicable three centuries later, using what he calls "the age of conversation" as a touchstone throughout this book. Ultimately, the art of conversation—as any art—is hard to pinpoint. The entire book forms an extended definition, relying heavily on belletrist sources, wrapping around and through a variety of places and times, to shed light on the power and importance of what Miller refers to as "real" conversation.

Is there a difference between talk and conversation? Supporting his assertion that they
have generally been used interchangeably,
Miller cites texts as varied as Judith Martin's
*Miss Manners' Guide to Excruciatingly Cor-
rect Behavior* (1983) and Benedetta Craveri's
The Age of Conversation (2005), a study of
conversation in seventeenth and eighteenth
century France. Then Miller turns to Dr. Samuel Johnson, an eighteenth century British
lexicographer and author and one of three
writers who Miller says most influenced his

Stephen Miller, a contributing editor to
The Wilson Quarterly, *is also a
freelance writer. His published essays
focus on major eighteenth century
writers and have appeared in
magazines such as* Sewanee Review,
Partisan Review, *and* The Times
Literary Supplement.

thinking on conversation. Johnson typically did not distinguish between talk and conversation. However, James Boswell (Scottish diarist and renowned biographer of
Johnson) did report one instance where Johnson said that conversation, unlike talk,
demanded an exchange of ideas. Miller, likewise, holds this as a requirement. Another refinement in the unfolding definition centers on the concept of pleasure, which
is rooted in the ideas of David Hume, an eighteenth century Scottish historian and philosopher whom Miller regards as another of his major influences. Hume, Miller reports, believed that good conversationalists were "immediately agreeable" and that
"all the merit a man may derive from his conversation (which, no doubt, may be very
considerable) arises from nothing but the pleasure it conveys to those who are present."

Can conversation, through a pleasurable exchange of ideas, also serve as a means
to an end, such as when trying to gain information from someone or trying to flatter?
Miller quotes twentieth century British political philosopher Michael Oakeshott (the
third major influence on Miller's work) who said that conversation "has no determined course, we do not ask what it is 'for.'" It is "an unrehearsed intellectual adventure" whose "significance lies neither in winning nor in losing, but in wagering."
Oakeshott believed that conversation differentiated human beings from animals and
civilized people from barbarians. It was reading Oakeshott, Miller says, that first
stimulated his own interest in the subject. Then, while writing about eighteenth century British thought a decade later, Miller says he noticed how many writers of that
time considered the quality of a person's conversation to be an important attribute.

Most of the book, as the subtitle suggests, is historical investigation. Although
Miller works through the Renaissance, Enlightenment, Victorian, and modern eras, it
is clear that his heart rests securely in eighteenth century Britain (which, at that time,
included Scotland). Miller explains that the art of conversation was cultivated for its
intellectual and psychological benefits and for the pleasure it afforded. Even then, according to novels, essays, and diaries (such literature serves as Miller's main source
throughout the book), good conversationalists were apparently hard to find. Miller
details the rise of coffeehouses and the varied clubs to which people in polite society
could belong, commenting that "being clubbable, a word coined by Johnson, was a
widely admired trait." Some writers even went so far as to locate conversation at the

source of political stability, arguing that if Britain's upper classes lost the art of conversation, the result would be civil violence.

Miller investigates in detail three major influences on conversation: religion, commerce, and women. Religious enthusiasts—defined by Johnson as those with a "vain belief of private revelation; a vain confidence of divine favour or communication"— were considered poor conversationalists. Johnson and Hume believed that increased commerce and luxury in a society tended to expand "the size of its conversible world." Regarding women, Miller presents the view of men such as Swift, Hume, the oft-cited Dr. Johnson, and Joseph Addison (founder of the first popular magazine, *The Spectator*) that the presence of women improved conversation by encouraging men to behave in a more refined manner. The same observers also believed that women could hold their own in conversation. Miller also includes, however, an extended discussion of Lady Mary Wortley Montagu, at one time a leading figure in England's conversational society who later withdrew to solitude on the Continent, at least in part because she felt most Englishmen did not respect learned women. Elsewhere in the book, Miller also offers conflicting sources without feeling the need to provide resolution.

As a byproduct of his investigations, Miller continues to uncover attributes that promote good conversation, such as a sense of politeness that does not exclude spirited debate; willingness, even desire, to have one's ideas attacked; and the statement that real conversation takes place only among equals. The list of impediments grows to include pretentiousness, anger, and vulgarity. To that list, Swift would add talking about one's own profession, which he called pedantry.

Miller's command of his subject matter is impressive. In his delivery, he tends to stand between the writers he is considering and his readers, using anecdotes for support, drawing general conclusions and paraphrasing rather than quoting directly, and some critics have found this troublesome. One reviewer commented that the book read more like a collection of names than sustained narrative, while another said that "writing a history of conversation without including examples is like writing a history of eating without any recipes. It lacks savour." Readers unfamiliar with the subject matter may find the book slow going, perhaps even disconcerting, in places. However, there is much food for thought here.

Introducing the decline of conversation in later eighteenth century Britain, Miller considers an undercurrent of distrust that had existed even in conversation's heyday, and then he details a growing interest in rural solitude as "requisite for experiencing the sublime pleasures of the imagination." In addition to other influences, Miller investigates the ideas and popularity of Jean-Jacques Rousseau, Swiss-born philosopher and writer, who attacked the conversible world and believed that "sociability prevents the benevolent passions from flourishing." As Romanticism grew, the art of conversation waned.

Ultimately, Miller makes the leap across the Atlantic Ocean to focus on conversation in America. Foreign visitors deplored the state of America's conversation, and Miller says many American writers were unconcerned. These include Henry David Thoreau (who, Miller says, thought conversation was a waste of time), Herman Melville (who equated conversationalists with con men), and poets Walt Whitman and T. S. Eliot. Miller credits novelist Ernest Hemingway with early promotion of the laconic hero—real men do not converse much—who also figures prominently in detective fiction, Hollywood Westerns, and film noir. Then, with the rise of Dale Carnegie's *How to Win Friends and Influence People* (1936), American conversation officially embraced its purposeful role.

Miller blames the 1960's counterculture for leading American conversation even further astray. The focus turned to liberation and subjectivity, he says, and "if all ideas are personal truths, there can be no . . . interchange of ideas." Many viewed rational discourse with distrust and "usually dismissed their critics as repressed souls who suffered from false consciousness," thus undermining the sense of equality necessary for real conversation. In addition, Miller explains that authenticity and total candor came to be prized over politeness. His other enemies of conversation included the use of drugs and listening to music ("especially the music of African-American musicians and their white imitators"). Miller critiques Norman Mailer's ideas in Mailer's influential essay "The White Negro" and extends that discussion to rapper Eminem's lyrics and an explanation of why rapping, in general, is hostile to conversation.

Of special note is Miller's discussion of what he calls anger communities (where "one reads only news and opinion that confirms one's views") and "ersatz conversations" found on television talk shows and talk radio. He also comments on electronic technology, which he calls conversation avoidance devices, with such ferocity that one reviewer suggested that Miller comes off as something of a Luddite. Miller declares that "raillery, the lifeblood of conversation, is not possible in an e-mail or Instant Message," cites the negative influence of IPods and interactive video games as he discusses the nature of sociability, and concludes that America is "moving in the direction of a solipsistic society."

Can conversation be rescued? Miller tosses out the idea of a raillery index to gauge the political stability of a country—"how much its citizens can engage in good-humored disagreement." Raillery is declining in the United States, he says, both because Americans do not value politeness and paradoxically because they are so supportive of diverse views that they do not disagree for fear of giving offense. To rescue conversation, Miller believes, people need to feel that politeness is worth the effort, and he is not hopeful.

Are things really as bad as Miller says? Many people will agree with him wholeheartedly. Others will not. Although Miller introduced his book as an extended essay, an informal attempt to clarify the subject of everyday conversation, some have criticized his liberal use of anecdotal and selective support as well as what they feel are sweeping generalizations. Miller's comments may anger some potential allies more than sway them, for example, the college student reviewing the book who said "Take it easy, geezers." Miller's ideas, however, are important and thought-provoking. The book is a conversation, not a lecture. If the situation is as dire as Miller believes, this work may provide a platform for future action that can make a difference.

Jean C. Fulton

Review Sources

The Christian Science Monitor 98 (March 21, 2006): 13-14.
The Daily Telegraph, April 15, 2006, p. 4.
New Statesman 135 (July 3, 2006): 67.
The New York Review of Books 53, no. 8 (May 11, 2006): 4-6.
The New York Sun, March 1, 2006, p. 16.
The New York Times 155 (March 20, 2006): E1-E7.
The Seattle Times, April 23, 2006, p. K7.
The Spectator 300 (April 1, 2006): 55.
The Times Literary Supplement, July 14, 2006, pp. 3-4.
The Wall Street Journal 247, no. 70 (March 25, 2006): P8.
Washington Monthly 38, no. 6 (June, 2006): 50-52.
Weekly Standard 12, no. 7 (October 30, 2006): 37-38.

COSMOPOLITANISM
Ethics in a World of Strangers

Author: Kwame Anthony Appiah (1954-   )
Publisher: W. W. Norton (New York). 196 pp. $23.95
Type of work: Ethics, philosophy
Time: The twenty-first century

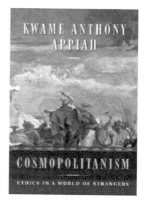

Exploring what it ought to mean for people to be citizens of the world in the twenty-first century, Appiah retrieves and revitalizes the ideal of "cosmopolitanism," which provides reminders of key ethical connections within the diversity of human culture, religion, and politics

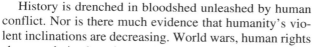

History is drenched in bloodshed unleashed by human conflict. Nor is there much evidence that humanity's violent inclinations are decreasing. World wars, human rights abuses, ethnic cleansing, and genocide characterized much of the twentieth century. There is no assurance that the twenty-first century will be better, but if moral improvement is to take place, the philosopher Kwame Anthony Appiah believes that a revival of an ancient ideal, cosmopolitanism, will be essential in that process.

Appiah's project is to identify and defend an ethical outlook that can work in what the subtitle of *Cosmopolitanism* calls "a world of strangers." The twenty-first century world is both the same and different from the world of the fourth century B.C.E., when ancient philosophers coined the term "cosmopolitan," using it to refer to a "citizen of the cosmos." Then and in contemporary life as well, one has normally been a citizen of a particular place—city, state, or country—not of the universe. Then and in contemporary life as well, the world has been full of strangers, people with whom one has contact but who are not members of one's family or particular community. In the twenty-first century, however, the world's population is approaching nine billion. In space and time, people live closer than ever, but never have there been so many potentially hostile strangers.

Amid these similarities and differences, while immense changes in the world have taken place and indeed partly because of them, a long-standing tradition has grown over the centuries: a person could and should be a citizen of the world. Cosmopolitanism is an idea with links to a variety of significant and long-standing ideals, including the view that all human beings are members of one family, the conviction that there are universal human rights and obligations, and the hope that there can be a cooperating league of nations that advances goals that are beneficial for humankind. On a personal level, cosmopolitanism embodies much needed virtues that include respect for people who are different from ourselves, resistance against discrimination and prejudice, and hospitality toward strangers.

Appealing though these ideals may be, Appiah recognizes that the history of cosmopolitanism has its problems. How, for example, does this outlook fit with the fact

Born in London, raised in Ghana, and educated at Cambridge University in England, Kwame Anthony Appiah is the Laurance S. Rockefeller University Professor of Philosophy at Princeton University. His best-known books include In My Father's House *(1992) and* The Ethics of Identity *(2005).*

that human life is always lived in specific times, places, and cultures, which require loyalties that are particular and local? The cosmopolitan person, it could be argued, will be rootless, which is scarcely a desirable way to live. Such people may profess impartiality or allegiance to "humanity" but care too little for individual persons and communities. Another problem is that cosmopolitanism may not be as universal as it sounds. Values, it seems, are relative to particular times and places. No individuals or groups, not even philosophers, have a privileged access to absolute and objective truth. In fact, cosmopolitanism may be cultural or national imperialism in disguise. Furthermore, the objections continue, cosmopolitanism is simply unrealistic because differences between human groups are too strong. In the twenty-first century a clash of civilizations, reflected especially in terrorism and a war against it, has eclipsed cosmopolitan dreams. Yes, there is talk about "globalization," but that concept is really about international economic competition that may be intensifying differences and inequalities even as it homogenizes the world's products and dominant patterns of communication and consumption. There is talk about "multiculturalism," but it is not clear that its often superficial acknowledgment of cultural and ethnic differences has produced the respect for others that is needed to reform the deeply entrenched social structures in which poverty and injustice dwell.

Appiah recognizes the force of these objections, but far from taking them to be fatal, he thinks that they can lead to a reaffirmation of cosmopolitanism's importance. Rootlessness is no virtue, but that bleak condition is not what Appiah's cosmopolitanism entails. To the contrary, his ethics in a world of strangers underscores that differences between people and particularities about them are crucial for meaningful lives. It follows that life cannot be lived well in conditions where differences and particularities are not respected. Cosmopolitanism affirms the importance of respect for differences and particularities. This respect, however, cannot be practiced by one person or group and ignored by others. The ethical logic of cosmopolitanism insists that the respect must be mutual. Failure to follow this logic consistently results in contradictions that are life threatening and all too often lethal.

Relativism, the view that there are no absolute and universal truths available because human judgment is limited and restricted to culturally and historically conditioned perspectives, exerts considerable influence in human affairs. However, relativism is less convincing and paralyzing than it is sometimes claimed to be. It does not follow that limitations on human judgment preclude recognition of ethical truths that deserve to be universal, that can be defended against the charge that they are only credible in particular times and places, and that can be sustained and even strengthened through critical assessment. As Appiah understands it, much depends on the process of recognition. That process requires active inquiry, not appeals to unquestioned authority. It depends on shared investigation, not on the privileged, exclusive status of one voice or tradition over all others.

What is needed, Appiah contends, is intelligent conversation that emphasizes open give-and-take and includes different and even differing voices. As Appiah uses the idea of conversation, he does not restrict it to literal talk. His sense of conversation refers more broadly to "engagement with the experience and the ideas of others." Conversation does not always lead to agreement, but conversation's importance includes the fact, says Appiah, that "it helps people get used to one another." If the good will of those circumstances prevails, then the chance to locate common ground, which finds room for the variety that enriches human existence, will be vastly improved. One's understanding of that common ground may need to be revised and expanded as history continues to unfold, but human self-correction can keep supporting, without dogmatism, the conviction that there are ethical truths that deserve to be universal. Appiah makes the case that the qualities of cosmopolitanism at its best will be among them.

As for the objection that cosmopolitanism is not a realistic option, Appiah's analysis goes in two fundamental directions. First, his analysis asks whether there is a more realistic alternative. If human beings "stay the course" they seem to be on, the likelihood is that there will be more hostility and conflict, more suffering and injustice, less hospitality for strangers, and less hope for everyone. In such a world, there might be a chance that people would muddle through and not do their worst to one another, but that bet does not appear to be the wisest one to make. Given the circumstances in which human life is taking place in the twenty-first century, Appiah suggests, it is better to strive for a cosmopolitan ethic than to hold back on the problematic grounds that "it won't work."

Second, Appiah strengthens the appeal of his cosmopolitanism by detailing further what its ethics provides and requires. For instance, cosmopolitanism offers joy. It does so by stressing how much there is to learn from other cultures. One can think of how receptiveness to art, literature, food, and music from diverse cultures can enrich personal and communal experience. One does not have to like or accept everything, but openness to variety and to diversity can improve life's quality. Joy of this kind, however, does not have much chance to flourish and last if difference remains a reason for suspicion and conflict. The insight that emerges is an example of one of those truths that deserve to be acknowledged as universal, namely, that differences should be cultivated so that they can be enjoyed and indeed that the differences that deserve to be cultivated the most are those that have the ability to enhance life to the fullest. An important implication of this outlook is that it will be important to pay close attention to the qualities of particularity as individuals and members of communities. In order to enjoy the best that human life in all of its diversity has to offer, individuals have an obligation not only to respect differences but also to be sure to bring to the human table the best in terms of talents, efforts, products, and decisions. At its best, cosmopolitanism is a win-win philosophy, one that replaces zero-sum games with ways that can be better for all.

No philosophy can be convincing if it seems too good to be true. Fortunately, Appiah's outlook does not fall prey to that trap. He acknowledges that differences cannot all be occasions for joy. Often differences put people at odds, and cosmopolitanism will be blind and naive if it fails to take that fact seriously. Perhaps one way out of this dilemma would be to acknowledge that differences are real even to the point of being nonnegotiable and then to follow the adage that one should simply "agree to disagree." That form of cosmopolitanism may work up to a point, but it has its limitations, especially when the stakes are matters of life and death. If a regime is engaged in ethnic cleansing or genocide, for example, a cosmopolitanism based on the idea that one should "agree to disagree" would be morally bankrupt because it would lend support to those who are utterly disrespectful of others.

Appiah's philosophy maximizes appeals for understanding differences and for his conviction that changes in fundamental outlooks come less from winning arguments and more from practical experience. Appiah prizes the latter, which involves give-and-take with others that can dislodge old habits and open one to new ways of thinking. Importantly, this emphasis on inquiry and openness to difference does not put his cosmopolitanism in the agree-to-disagree camp. His version of cosmopolitanism entails that some things—genocide, for instance—are unacceptable. They must be prevented, stopped, and corrected. Appiah's cosmopolitans affirm the truth that "every human being has obligations to every other. Everybody matters: that is our central idea. And it sharply limits the scope of our tolerance." When there are people who think that "some people don't matter at all," writes Appiah, "there is only one thing to do: try to change their minds, and, if you fail, make sure that they can't put their ideas into action."

What if those anticosmopolitan ideas are put into action, as they surely have been in the ethnic cleansings and genocides that have taken place in the twentieth and twenty-first centuries? Appiah's book ends by addressing at least some parts of that question in its final chapter, which is called "Kindness to Strangers." The problem for cosmopolitans, Appiah acknowledges, is how much kindness is owed to strangers and how does a cosmopolitan weigh and prioritize among all the obligations, some of them competing, that he or she may rightly feel. If a reader is looking for a recipe, a principle, a one-size-fits-all resolution to these dilemmas of cosmopolitanism, Appiah's book will close in a frustrating and disappointing way. Nevertheless, Appiah's ending is wise. He concludes that true cosmopolitans are the ones who will not stop thinking about these issues, who will use their intelligence to figure out how to do better in meeting the multifaceted responsibility to show hospitality to strangers and then find the courage to act accordingly.

John K. Roth

Review Sources

Commonweal 133, no. 8 (April 21, 2006): 22-24.
Foreign Affairs 85, no. 3 (May/June, 2006): 151-152.
Library Journal 130, no. 19 (November 15, 2005): 71-72.
Los Angeles Times, January 15, 2006, p. R3.
The Nation 282, no. 4 (January 30, 2006): 25-28.
National Review 58, no. 4 (March 13, 2006): 42-43.
The New York Review of Books 53, no. 11 (June 22, 2006): 46-49.
Publishers Weekly 252, no. 46 (November 21, 2005): 42-43.
Weekly Standard 12, no. 4 (October 9, 2006): 38-39.

CURRY
A Tale of Cooks and Conquerors

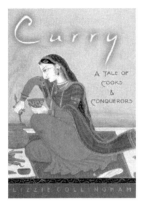

Author: Lizzie Collingham
First published: Curry: A Biography, 2005, in Great Britain
Publisher: Oxford University Press (New York). 315 pp. $28.00
Type of work: History
Time: Before the common era to 2006
Locale: Chiefly India and Britain

Collingham offers a delightful collection of recipes and vivid history of Indian cuisine, including curry, which has become one of the most popular foods on the planet

Lizzie Collingham's small volume *Curry* is a gem of culinary history. Promoted as "the first authoritative history of Indian food," the book is based on exhaustive research and includes numerous maps and photographs, a glossary (translating culinary terms, such as ghee, toddy, and garam masala), and an extensive bibliography. Scholarly footnotes are provided for each chapter. Wonderful anecdotes and local legends are interwoven with the historical narrative, and, at the end of every chapter, there are delicious recipes (for four to eight diners) the reader might like to try. Recipes of historical interest are included in the body of the text, but Collingham does not recommend "roast black rat, " a favorite dish of King Somesvara III, a powerful Hindu king in southern India in the 12th century.

Although *Curry* is well researched and well written, it is not pedantic. It is totally accessible and entertaining to the average reader. Indophiles or anyone who enjoys culinary history or cooking or eating Indian food will love this book. In addition to the obvious merits of the book, its universal enthusiastic acclaim may be due to the fact that the Indian diaspora and the British have spread some variation of Indian food throughout the world. From curry houses in London to "Curry Row" restaurants in New York City to railway stands in Tokyo, there is a large receptive audience for whom the historical study of the origins of Indian food is a welcome and overdue investigation.

Curry contains ten chapters, and Collingham uses menu items for chapter titles. The first chapter, "Chicken Tikka Masala," describes the origin of the internationally popular Indian dish that Robin Cook, the British foreign minister in 2001, hailed as the new British national dish. Contrary to popular belief, chicken tikka masala is not Indian at all. The dish was the creation of an Indian chef in Britain who served tomato soup mixed with spices over meat to cater to British tastes. Its name is a contradiction in terms—"tikka" (oven-roasted meat) is not meant to be eaten with "masala" (gravy) at all.

The next two chapters highlight well-known Indian dishes, biriyani and vindaloo, dealing in historical and geographical con-texts with the influence of the Moguls and Persians, and the Portuguese on Indian cui-sine. "Korma," the next chapter, begins the story of the British influence on Indian cui-sine in India. The following six chapters trace that influence over time—especially the Brit-ish invention of curry and its phenomenal spread throughout Britain and the British Em-pire. "Chai," a great chapter about the intro-duction of tea to India from China, describes how British tea companies, faced with sur-pluses from their China markets, bombarded India in the early 1900's with a campaign that made Indians avid tea drinkers.

Lizzie Collingham, a freelance scholar and writer, taught history at the University of Warwick and was a research fellow at Jesus College, Cambridge, and visiting fellow at the Research School of Social Sciences at the Australian National University, Canberra. Her first book, Imperial Bodies: The Physical Experience of the Raj, c. 1800-1947 *was published in 2001.*

The evolution of Indian cuisine over the last four centuries reflects India's changing civilization. A fascinating interplay of cul-tural, economic, and political influences shaped Indian cuisine as it is known through-out the world, because each successive wave of India's conquerors and settlers adapted their food and cooking preferences to the lo-cal environment. Most well-known Indian dishes are the result of a complex blending of "foreign" foods with native spices, such as black pepper, cardamom, cumin, cori-ander, cinnamon, cloves, ginger, and tumeric. Dishes considered Indian are, there-fore, either the result of assimilation and revision or the invention of creative cooks abroad, as occurred with chicken tikka masala. According to Collingham, there is no such thing as "authentic" Indian cuisine.

Ancient Indian cooking was based on the principles of Ayurvedic (science of life) Hindu medicine, which is still practiced in India and other parts of the world today. According to this belief, foods are categorized as "cold" or "hot" (regardless of tem-perature), and diet is adjusted to keep the body in a balanced state with the climate, season, and one's caste or occupation. (For example, Ayurvedic physicians may pre-scribe cold foods, such as milk, during hot weather, and hot foods, such as peppers, in cooler weather.) For Hindus, eating is a matter of health and religious purity, not just a bodily pleasure, and there are many food taboos. All regional cuisines of India present varying traditions, and within these traditions, many culinary differences, related to caste or class, religion, gender, and marital status, exist.

The consumption of beef was taboo for all Hindus, who regarded the cow as a sa-cred animal. When the Emperor Asoka ruled much of India from 268 to 231 B.C.E., he was influenced by Buddhism to promote vegetarianism. Upper-caste Hindus, espe-cially the Brahmans, became vegetarians. The Jains were strict vegetarians. These di-etary practices were in sharp contrast to those of the Moguls (or Mughals), Muslim invaders from Mongolia, who conquered northern India in the 1600's. The Moguls were big beef and mutton eaters and brought the cooking styles and ingredients of central Asia and Persia to India. Their favorite dishes included nuts and dried fruits in combination with meat, especially minced meat. Akbar, the third Mughal emperor (1555-1605) promoted the synthesis of Persian and central Asian cuisine with Indian cuisine. Persian cooks introduced marinating meat in yogurt to India, and the Mogul court incorporated Indian spices. By the eighteenth century, chilies were included. Many common Mogul dishes relied on rice, lentils, chickpeas, wheat, and seasonings such as saffron and asafetida (instead of the onions and garlic avoided by strict Hindus). These dishes became popular with Hindus. One Persian dish, "rogan josh" (red lamb stew), became much spicier in Kashmir, where it was accepted by the Brahmans, who substituted fennel seeds and asafetida for garlic and onions. Another Persian dish, the delicately flavored "pilau," which was popular throughout the Muslim world, became the spicy "biryani" of India.

The Portuguese influence on Indian cuisine is discussed in the chapter on vindaloo. This traditional Indian food was created when Portuguese spice merchants introduced vinegar marinades to Indian cuisine at the beginning of the fifteenth century. The name "vindaloo" is derived from the mispronunciation of the ingredients of the traditional Portuguese dish, *carne de vinho e alhos* (pork cooked in wine vinegar and garlic). In Goa, Portugal's trading center, local cooks altered the dish to include tamarind and spices, including chilies that the Portuguese had introduced into India from the New World. (Columbus named chilies "pepper of the Indies.") Chilies were readily accepted by the Indians, who used them in many dishes that had previously depended for their hot seasoning on red peppers (long pepper) or black pepper, the hottest spices known in India before the Portuguese came.

British merchants came to India in the seventeenth century and captured the East India trade from the Dutch and Portuguese. The British were enthusiastic meat eaters. They enjoyed the abundance of game in India and employed English, Portuguese, and Indian cooks, who prepared roasts and meat pies served with a repertoire of gravies, sauces, vegetables, and spices. As the cooks exchanged recipes, British cuisine became mixed with that of the Muslim moguls, whose empire dominated northern India at that time. (Southern India developed an imaginative vegetarian cuisine, based in Hindu temples, with a more limited list of ingredients. Temple sweets were a specialty of this region.)

The East India Company overcame the moguls and established British power in great tracts of India. In 1858, the company was abolished, and India was administered by the Crown until gaining independence in 1947. Big dinners were an important focus of Anglo-Indian society. The British introduced their love of roasted meats to India, but Indian cooking shaped the tastes of the British. The Indian chefs working for the British experimented with local recipes, inventing a vast number of new Anglo-Indian dishes. For example, "Khichri," the peasant recipe of boiled rice, lentils, and spices, became "kedgeree" (rice, fish, and hard-boiled eggs), the favorite breakfast of Anglo-Indians. In contrast to the Indians, the British meals were served in courses, beginning with soup. To please the British, Indian cooks in Madras added rice, vegetables, and meat to tamarind broth and served it for a "starter." This became "mulliga-tawny soup" (literally, "pepper water"), another Anglo-Indian favorite.

Curry, the theme of the next chapter, was a British invention. The word "curry" is a generic term the British Raj used for any spicy Indian dish made with gravy or thick sauce. It is a corruption of the Portuguese terms *caril* or *carree*, used to describe the various broths Indians made with butter, ground nuts, spices, and herbs. Although Indians would have referred to each dish by its specific name, the British lumped them all together to describe any Indian stew or ragout. As the British moved from region to region in India, they absorbed the dietary practices and ingredients of one region and took them to the next. Curry became the first pan-Indian cuisine, influencing cooking from Ceylon (now Sri Lanka) to northern India, but it was never a truly national cuisine because it was only eaten by the British in India.

Curry recipes took India to Britain. They were sent home to English housewives from their husbands working for the East India Company, and they were exported to other English colonies, such as Australia. Nostalgic retired East India Company officials ("nabobs") brought their Indian cooks home with them. The Empire of India Exhibition in London in 1895 and other exhibitions featured Indian cafes and restaurants, which increased the interest of upper-class Londoners in Indian food. In the nineteenth century, seamen on oceangoing steamships from the Bangladesh province of Syhlet jumped ship in England. Appalled by the bland English food, they established the first Indian restaurants. From these humble beginnings, Indian food became popular in Britain. Today Britain has numerous Indian restaurants, almost all of them owned by Syhletis.

Indian carryout—frequently curry and chips—has become the favorite food of working-class British. Almost all supermarkets in Britain sell Indian ingredients and have extensive stocks of convenience foods, including chutneys, packets of curries, and frozen Indian meals. The British invented curry powder (ready-mixed spice mixtures), Worcestershire sauce (a sauce created by pharmacists Lea and Perrins of Worcester to imitate a favorite sauce from India), and catsup. Today few associate Worcestershire sauce or catsup, which the British adapted from Chinese soy-based condiments, with India. Indian cooking has suffered "in translation." (For example, the Indians fry spices to release their aromas, but the British throw them into boiling water, which dampens their impact.)

Wherever Indians have gone, they have taken their cuisine with them and developed it in response to new conditions. Indians and curries have traveled the world—from the West Indies to South Africa to the Pacific—and the "mix" of culinary cultures continues to evolve. In the early twentieth century, Punjabi workers in California incorporated local peppers and tortillas in their native dishes. Curry travels well because it embraces change while retaining its identity as Indian. Indian food will continue to be one of the world's greatest cuisines, whatever the influence of foreign ingredients or culinary techniques. Collingham has told the story of its global spread in a most engaging manner.

Edna B. Quinn

Review Sources

Booklist 102, no. 12 (February 15, 2006): 23-24.
Library Journal 131, no. 1 (January 1, 2006): 145.
New Statesman 134 (August 1, 2005): 40.
The New York Times 155 (February 1, 2006): E10.
The New York Times Book Review 155 (February 5, 2006): 18.
Publishers Weekly 252, no. 46 (November 21, 2005): 40-41.
Science News 169, no. 11 (March 18, 2006): 175.
The Times Literary Supplement, November 18, 2005, pp. 11-12.

DANGEROUS KNOWLEDGE
Orientalism and Its Discontents

Author: Robert Irwin (1946-   )
Publisher: Overlook Press (Woodstock, N.Y.). 410 pp. $35.00
Type of work: History, literary criticism, literary history, and literary theory
Time: From ancient times to the present
Locale: Primarily Asia and Europe

Irwin surveys the development of scholarly Western interest in Asia and contrasts his interpretation and approach with that offered by famed theorist Edward Said in the book Orientalism *(1978)*

Principal personages:
IGNAZ GOLDZIHER (1850-1921), a Hungarian Orientalist
ANTOINE ISAAC SILVESTRE DE SACY (1758-1838), a French linguist and Orientalist
GUILLAUME POSTEL (1510-1581), a French linguist and Orientalist
BERNARD LEWIS (1916-   ), an English historian and Orientalist
EDWARD SAID (1935-2003), a Palestinian American literary and cultural theorist

In *Dangerous Knowledge: Orientalism and Its Discontents* (published in Great Britain as *For Lust of Knowing: The Orientalists and Their Enemies*), Robert Irwin consolidates his position as one of Edward Said's most vociferous critics. Although Said's *Orientalism* (1978) was originally published to mixed reviews, it has since attained the status of a classic. Right or wrong, it has challenged the way the West looks at the East and changed the way the East looks at itself in relation to the West. Said defined the term "Orientalism" as a "hegemonic discourse of imperialism" encompassing everything that those in the West might think or say about the East, and especially about the Arab world and the Islamic faith. He argued further that Orientalism has provided an underlying theoretical framework for the forceful Western domination of the Near East and for the establishment of Israel on what had been Arab soil. In *Dangerous Knowledge: Orientalism and Its Discontents*, Irwin calls Said's *Orientalism* a "work of malignant charlatanry in which it is hard to distinguish honest mistakes from willful misrepresentations." According to Irwin, accepting the book's "broad framework as something to work with and then correct would be merely to waste one's time." Hence he restricts most of his disagreements with Said (who died in 2003) to a single penultimate chapter, although many of his comments throughout the book are clearly directed at Said's thesis.

The bulk of *Dangerous Knowledge* is a survey of the Western study of Asia. Irwin acknowledges in his introduction that there have been a number of "Orientalisms."

∽

Robert Irwin teaches medieval history at the University of St. Andrews in Scotland and is the author of The Alhambra *(2004),* The Arabian Nights: A Companion *(1994), and the novels* The Limits of Vision *(1986) and* The Arabian Nightmare *(1983).*

∽

These include an eighteenth century French interest in the eastern shores of the Mediterranean as well as a British decorative style from later in the same century. In the early nineteenth century, Orientalists were those who favored ruling the vast new British territory of India within the framework of existing Muslim and Hindu institutions. Later the term "Orientalist" came to be applied more broadly to anyone studying Asian and/or North African history, languages, and cultures.

Irwin dates the appearance of the first Orientalists in the sixteenth century but sets the stage by outlining East-West contacts in ancient, medieval, and Renaissance times. He touches on Greek historians Herodotus (who wrote about the Greco-Persian wars of the fifth century B.C.E.) and Xenophon (who actually served as a mercenary under Persian prince Cyrus the Younger until the latter's defeat in 401 B.C.E.). Irwin also discusses *The Persians* (472 B.C.E.) by Greek dramatist Aeschylus, finding in it—as well as in the histories—a notable tolerance and open-mindedness about Greece's eastern rivals. That open-mindedness prevailed into Europe's Middle Ages, says Irwin, and was characteristic of both Europeans and Asians. In fact it was actually Arab scholars who discovered and translated the works of Greek scientists, making them available in turn to their European counterparts.

The rise of Islam during the seventh century C.E. at first aroused little concern or even interest in the West, with Catholic scholastics dismissing it for some time as a heresy. According to Irwin, the new religion simply "did not feature largely in medieval European thought." In fact the confessor to Pope Innocent XI viewed Islam as akin to Protestantism. Although the period was characterized by mutual and widespread misunderstanding, Irwin still does not detect a European sense of Eastern backwardness or inferiority. Here again he is at pains to refute Said's arguments about the West's "hegemonic discourse."

This is not to say that Europe was unmindful of Muslim territorial ambitions. Muslim power was at its greatest in the fifteenth and sixteenth centuries and, for a time, seemed to threaten the survival of the Christian West. The city of Constantinople (Istanbul) fell to the Muslims in 1453, to be followed by Belgrade (in the early twenty-first century the capital of Serbia) in 1521. The Muslims besieged the great European city of Vienna in 1529 and again in 1683. However, they were driven completely out of Spain in 1492, and over the next two centuries the threat to Europe abated.

Irwin identifies the first true Orientalist as Guillaume Postel, born in Lower Normandy in 1510. Postel collected manuscripts in Constantinople for the king of France while studying Arabic, Turkish, Greek, Coptic, and Armenian. He not only held the first chair of Arabic in Paris and wrote Europe's first grammar of classical Arabic but also published popular accounts of the Middle East. In addition he was, as Irwin puts it, "quite barmy," having met a woman in Venice whom he identified variously as the

Angelic Pope and the New Eve. After her death, Postel believed that she had returned to possess his body.

"Getting things right," asserts Irwin, "was what the Orientalists did from the sixteenth century onwards." As he is at pains to make clear, however, getting things right involved "academic drudgery and close attention to philological detail." Thus *Dangerous Knowledge* is a story of individuals, many of them pedantic, many of them brilliant, and many of them—like Postel—eccentric to boot. Irwin finds similarities among certain Orientalists and identifies certain overarching trends and developments but admits, "There can be no single chronicle of Orientalism that can be set within clearly defined limits."

Irwin's gallery includes Antoine Isaac Silvestre de Sacy, whom he identifies as the founder of modern Orientalism. De Sacy studied Hebrew out of religious convictions and went on to master Arabic—no mean accomplishment at a time when there were few teachers versed in the subject and virtually no texts to study—and numerous other ancient and modern languages. He became a professor at the École Spéciale des Langues Orientales Vivantes (school of living eastern languages) in Paris, where he was a dry but apparently inspiring teacher, and published a much-needed anthology of Arabic texts, an Arabic grammar, and a study of Persian antiquities. He also helped found a key French association of Orientalists, the Société Asiatique.

Irwin rates Ignaz Goldziher as the greatest Orientalist. A Jew born in Hungary in 1850, Goldziher studied first in Budapest, then went on to Leipzig, Germany, where he took classes under a professor who had been a student of de Sacy. In the mid-1870's he studied with Muslim scholars in Egypt and Syria, finding in the process that he preferred Islam to Judaism and Christianity. Goldziher returned to Hungary soon afterward but found it impossible to secure a suitable academic position in his anti-Semitic homeland until 1905, when he was named Professor of Semitic Philology in Budapest. By then he had written on a variety of subjects: the origins of the Qur'ān, the culture of the Muslim kingdom of Andalusia in Spain, and the body of non-canonical traditions surrounding the Prophet Muhammad.

Among the many other Orientalists Irwin considers are polymath Athanasius Kircher (1602-1680), whose "barminess" may have surpassed even Postel's, and rambunctious explorer and linguist Richard F. Burton (1821-1890), whose salacious translation of *The Arabian Nights* (1884) made him notorious in Victorian Britain. Balancing these more colorful figures are scholars such as Bernard Lewis, whose historical works are notable for their positive portrayal of Islamic culture.

With the acerbically titled chapter "An Enquiry into the Nature of a Certain Twentieth-Century Polemic," Irwin turns specifically to Edward Said and his most famous book. His opening criticism of *Orientalism* is that there are too many things that Said does not get right. The work appears to have been written hurriedly, he says, resulting in a repetitive text and numerous factual inaccuracies.

Among the mistakes that Irwin cites are Said's mischaracterization of the mythology underlying Euripides's play *Bakchai* (405 B.C.E.; *The Bacchae*, 1781), his jumbling of the chronology of Islamic conquests, his conflation of individuals (Jacob Burkhardt and John Lewis Burkhardt) who happen to have shared a surname, and his incorrect dating of British and French control of the eastern Mediterranean. Irwin faults Said for refusing to acknowledge the existence, universally accepted among modern linguists, of an Indo-Aryan family of languages linking Sanskrit, Greek, Latin, and German. He also points out that while some Orientalists were the agents or civil servants of Western powers, a majority were pure scholars, many of whom were and are proponents of Middle Eastern self-determination. Irwin is particularly incensed that although *Orientalism* went through many editions during Said's lifetime, the author pointedly refused to correct any of his errors.

Beyond specific mistakes, Irwin points out that Said seemed unable to decide when the phenomenon he was attacking actually began. At different points, he dated the birth of Orientalism to the establishment of chairs of Hebrew and Arabic by the Council of Vienne in 1312, to the publication of a French encyclopedia of Islam in 1697, and to Napoleon Bonaparte's invasion of Egypt in 1798.

Irwin argues that Said was apparently ignorant of much of the recent scholarship on his subject, assigning currency to critics and historians whose work had been superseded by subsequent research and scholarship. He also charges that Said neglected highly important Orientalist material written in German, presumably because the existence of such a body of work from a country harboring few territorial ambitions in the Middle East would undercut his arguments.

Underlying many of what Irwin sees as Said's problems was his application of the ideas of Michel Foucault and Antonio Gramsci, noted cultural theorists whose basic concepts are actually at odds with each other. Relying on each in turn, Said in effect reasoned in a circle, first that the Orientalists were shaped and their perceptions controlled by the overarching concept of Orientalism (as Foucault might have argued), but then that they had fabricated the controlling concept themselves (as Gramsci might have argued).

Summing up his arguments, Irwin asserts that he cannot believe that *Orientalism* "was written in good faith" and concludes that the picture of the world that the book presents is "richly imagined, but essentially fictional."

Dangerous Knowledge: Orientalism and Its Discontents is essentially two books in one. The first is a history of a little-known discipline by one of its most distinguished contemporary adherents, a potentially dry survey enlivened by Irwin's wit, passion, and learning. The second is a refutation of Edward Said's attack on that discipline, a stinging piece of work likely to damage, although certainly not destroy, Said's reputation. Irwin plans to write at least one more book on the subject, a study of artistic and literary—as opposed to scholarly—depictions of the Orient. Since Said, too, dealt with such depictions, it is clear that the implicit debate between him and his critic is far from over.

Grove Koger

Review Sources

Kirkus Reviews 74, no. 15 (August 1, 2006): 767-768.
Library Journal 131, no. 15 (September 1, 2006): 72.
London Review of Books 28 (June 8, 2006): 14-15.
Publishers Weekly 253, no. 34 (August 28, 2006): 43-44.
Round Table 95 (September, 2006): 627-647.
The Sunday Times, February 5, 2006, p. 54.
The Times Higher Education Supplement, March 10, 2006, pp. 24-25.
The Times Literary Supplement, May 19, 2006, pp. 6-7.
The Wall Street Journal 248, no. 107 (November 4, 2006): P10.
The Washington Post Book World, November 12, 2006, p. 15.

DANGEROUS NATION
America's Place in the World from Its Earliest Days to the Dawn of the Twentieth Century

Author: Robert Kagan (1958-   )
Publisher: Alfred A. Knopf (New York). 527 pp. $30.00
Type of work: History
Time: 1630-1898
Locale: The United States, Great Britain, Mexico, and Cuba

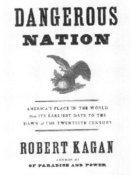

A *wide-ranging analysis of American foreign policy from the Puritans to the Spanish-American War*

Principal personages:
GEORGE WASHINGTON, the leader of the Continental Army during the American Revolution and first president of the United States
JAMES MONROE, the fifth president of the United States and creator of the Monroe Doctrine

One of the most endearing and best-known scenes in early American literature occurs in Washington Irving's short story "Rip Van Winkle" (1819), where the slothful protagonist emerges from a twenty-year slumber to find himself transformed from a British subject into a citizen of an independent America. While most discussions of American foreign policy are far less entertaining, they—like Irving—take as their starting point the American Revolution. As Robert Kagan makes clear in his wonderful book *Dangerous Nation: America's Place in the World from Its Earliest Days to the Dawn of the Twentieth Century*, America's relationships with other countries had their roots in the period long before independence.

Beginning far back in the colonial past, Kagan carefully builds his argument by demonstrating the enormous gap between how Americans regarded themselves and the way they were perceived by the rest of the world. This was evident even as early as the 1630's. Massachusetts Bay Colony governor John Winthrop desired only that he and his followers be allowed to build a "city upon a hill," thus inaugurating a centuries-long tradition of Americans professing their desire for complete isolation. Kagan's response both here and elsewhere is to question such orthodox beliefs. While it is true that Winthrop and his followers proclaimed their need for isolation in order to practice their religion, the truth is that the whole colonial period is marked by what other nations saw as an aggressive expansionism. Puritans undoubtedly felt that their tiny initial settlement in the woods was indeed just as their leader described it; however, the historical record clearly indicates that the budding colony continually encroached upon and eventually displaced the Native American population.

Kagan's revision of this record may at first seem out of place in a discussion of foreign policy, but the author persuasively argues that this territorial expansion had a powerful effect upon British foreign policy. The Native Americans encountered by the colonists did in fact constitute a foreign nation. British authorities took great pains to negotiate treaties with the native tribes in the hope of fostering a peaceful coexistence between two radically different civilizations. The problem was that, while the British government negotiated the agreements with the best of intentions, it was nearly impossible to set any meaningful territorial limits in a seemingly boundless land.

~

Former State Department member Robert Kagan belongs to the German Marshall Fund and the Carnegie Endowment for International Peace. He writes for The Washington Post. *His books include* A Twilight Struggle: American Power and Nicaragua, 1977-1990 *(1996) and* Of Paradise and Power: America and Europe in the New World Order *(2003).*

~

One of Kagan's crucial insights into American history is that it was not New England that proved to be the driving force in the British colonies but rather the Chesapeake Bay area, which was founded earlier and dedicated almost exclusively to commercial ventures. The financial backers of the Chesapeake Bay settlements were far less interested in saving souls than in reaping a windfall from their investment. Kagan is quite right in identifying this aggressive commercialism with its emphasis upon individual gain as the dominant spirit in the British colonies. The desire for greater wealth created the need for ever greater amounts of land, which in turn resulted in encroachment upon Native American territory. Whenever boundaries with Native Americans were fixed by agreement, inevitably some colonists would transgress the barriers, incur tribal wrath, and thus instigate a war that would displace or exterminate the native population. To modern ears, this has the ring of ethnic cleansing, but it was in fact largely motivated by the commercial zeal of the Chesapeake Bay culture.

Kagan identifies a repeated theme in these early years, one seldom noted by other historians. Americans continually abjure imperial aims while engaging in the process of empire building. In the past, territorial expansion for financial reasons led to conflict, and the resulting security issues justified more expansion. This was compounded by the fact that this resulted in a cultural as well as a physical displacement: those natives who chose to live among the colonists were forced to adopt their ways. On the surface, this would seem to be unalloyed hypocrisy, seizing territory from those less powerful while professing the contrary. However, Americans demonstrate a repeated pattern of expansionist behavior while being blind to its consequences.

Kagan traces this territorial rapaciousness to the beginnings of the British Empire. He maintains that the English regarded themselves as a superior people and that they rationalized the subjugation of Ireland and Scotland as a measure justified by the spread of English culture. This is probably the weakest link in Kagan's argument in that while there was some colonization of Ireland, there was hardly any in Scotland, which in the eighteenth century ranked among the poorest nations in Europe, and trade between England and its northern neighbor was virtually nonexistent until the Union of 1707. The really significant aspect of the relationship between England and its weaker neighbors was the cultural hegemony of the crown: the English effectively destroyed the cultures of Ireland and Scotland. It was a pattern that would repeat itself in the New World, where colonials would eventually drive out the French, the Dutch, the Spanish, and the Russians, as well as the Native Americans.

Prior to independence, territorial expansion became a familiar pattern of the colonies leading the mother country. Indeed, one of the original insights of *Dangerous Nation* is the degree to which the American colonies were driving British foreign policy or, as Kagan implies, the degree to which Americans were inadvertently crafting their own foreign policy long before they broke relations with Britain. Never was this truer than in Britain's troubled relationship with the French in America. When a young Colonel George Washington attempted to establish a fort on the Ohio River in 1754, it was at the behest of a land speculator, Virginia governor Robert Dinwiddie. Washington's band of men defeated one small French and Indian force only to be subsequently captured by a larger French military expedition. This in turn prompted the British to attack the French in Canada, thus beginning the bloody conflict known as the French and Indian War. Two years later, the conflict spread to the continent, where it eventually became known as the Seven Years' War.

Somewhat overlooked in Kagan's text is the trenchant irony of Britain's relationship with the colonies. It is astonishing to realize that Great Britain—which in the 1750's was the dominant military power in Europe—was in the unenviable position of having its foreign policy dictated by the actions of a few settlers deep in a wilderness on another continent. This irony is compounded by the fact that it was the financial burden of the French and Indian War that led to the increased taxation that subsequently prompted the colonies to break with Britain. It is a small but significant oversight that Kagan did not include this in his text. Nevertheless, *Dangerous Nation* makes it clear that, to a degree they never realized, Americans have shaped their own destiny. In this same vein, Kagan identifies the Declaration of Independence as the first foreign policy document produced by the new nation. It provided the legal basis for creating alliances with other nations, and it was just such an alliance with France that allowed the young republic to prevail against Britain. Also reflected in the document was the republican ideology of equality that bound the colonies into a nation.

Much of the remainder of *Dangerous Nation* deals with the consequences of slavery, the institution that proved the gravest challenge to that ideology. As other historians have noted, most inhabitants of the newly independent republic recognized that slavery was inconsistent with democracy and that the institution would eventually die out. This was exactly what did occur in northern states in the early decades of the nineteenth century. However, Kagan's claim that in 1804 New Jersey was the last of the northern states to end slavery is quite misleading. While it is true that northern states had passed legislation abolishing the institution, in some instances complete manumission was not immediate. The New York State legislature passed the law ending slavery in 1799, but slavery was actually phased out over a period of years. Slavery did not end completely in New York State until 1827, a scant thirty-four years before the Civil War.

Nonetheless, Kagan is correct in stating that the North and the South diverged both economically and culturally by about 1820. In the North, a paid labor force and increased industrialization created a robust economy; in the South, Britain's increased demand for cotton for its mills and the invention of the cotton gin resulted in a resurgence of slavery, particularly in the Deep South. In contrast to the North's vibrant economy, the South remained largely agrarian, a culture where manual labor was associated with slavery. As Kagan astutely notes, the United States effectively became two separate nations, something that had significant consequences for the nation's foreign policy.

Slavery would have ended sooner had the United States remained within its original borders. Kagan correctly pinpoints the Louisiana Purchase in 1803 as the moment when the nation began to fracture, a fact that was reflected in the foreign policy decisions of the ensuing years. On this point, Kagan's book provides a masterly analysis of the Monroe Doctrine and its consequences. Delivered by James Monroe in December, 1823, when the Federalists were at the height of their power, the doctrine remains one of the key documents in the history of American foreign policy. While its declared intent was that the western hemisphere was to be free of foreign intervention, Kagan argues that the policy more accurately reflected young America in its aggressive expansionist mood. The Federalists' hope was that America's republican ideology would drive Latin American nations toward independence. While most histories view the antebellum period in this decidedly expansionist mode, Kagan's effectively argues that the foreign policy of this period was far more tumultuous.

For a twenty-year period following this Federalist triumph America pulled violently inward, retreating from its professed aim of spreading republican ideals. Kagan correctly associates this reaction with America's antebellum "split personality": Federalist (northern) concern with fostering democracy abroad alternated with (southern) obsession with preventing slave uprisings such as those that rocked Haiti. With the acquisition of more territory came the question of how to admit new states into the union, a process that created bitter debates over whether to admit the new members as free or slave states. In the Missouri Compromise of 1819, for example, slavery was allowed but only below latitude 36 degrees 30 minutes. Appropriately, Kagan suggests that such agreements between two fundamentally different societies came to reflect a de facto foreign policy between different nations, one dedicated to a progressive national government and the other obsessed with states' rights and resistant to change. It is little wonder that the desire to foment democratic reform abroad did not return to American foreign policy until decades after the Civil War.

From the broad sweep of its themes to its pristinely researched details, *Dangerous Nation* is a welcome addition to the canon of works on American history. One could fault Kagan for the absence of maps or even a modest time line, but these are minor shortcomings in a major work. One can only look forward to the planned sequel, which will deal with twentieth century foreign policy.

Cliff Prewencki

Review Sources

Booklist 103, no. 5 (November 1, 2006): 9.
The Economist 381 (October 7, 2006): 90.
Foreign Affairs 85, no. 6 (November/December, 2006): 165.
Library Journal 131, no. 17 (October 15, 2006): 73.
National Review 58, no. 19 (October 23, 2006): 49-53.
The New York Review of Books 53, no. 18 (November 16, 2006): 30-32.
Publishers Weekly 253, no. 32 (August 14, 2006): 192.
The Wall Street Journal 248, no. 91 (October 17, 2006): D8.

DANTE
The Poet, the Political Thinker, the Man

Author: Barbara Reynolds (1914-   )
Publisher: Shoemaker & Hoard (Emeryville, Calif.). Illustrated. 466 pp. $35.00
Type of work: Literary criticism and literary biography
Time: 1265-1373
Locale: Florence, Bologna, and Ravenna Italy

Reynolds's biography traces the life of Dante Alighieri and provides an accessible introduction to all of his works, particularly his masterpiece, La divina commedia *(c. 1320;* The Divine Comedy, *1802)*

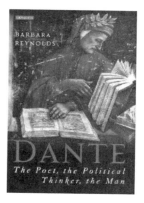

Principal personages:
DANTE ALIGHIERI, a poet
BEATRICE DEI PORTINARI, Dante's muse and his guide through the *Paradiso*
VERGIL, Augustan poet and Dante's guide through the *Inferno* and the *Purgatorio*
BONIFACE VIII, the pope
CAN GRANDE DELLA SCALA, ruler of Verona and Dante's patron
GIOVANNI BOCCACCIO, Dante's first biographer

Dante: The Poet, the Political Thinker, the Man presents Barbara Reynolds's distillation of her lifelong study of Dante. Largely shunning footnotes (other than to Dante's texts) and references to other scholars, she offers personal readings of all of Dante's writings, which she places within the context of his life and his age. While some of her comments will provoke disagreement, her book offers a highly readable introduction to some of the most complex works of the Middle Ages. Although she addresses her book to a general audience, even advanced students of Dante will find it thought provoking and informative.

One recurring theme in Reynolds's account is that of orality. The fourteenth century witnessed a leap in literacy beyond the clerisy. In canto 5 of the *Inferno* (hell), Beatrice explains that she and her lover, Paolo, were first enticed into adultery by reading the story of Lancelot and Guinevere. Indeed, reading pervades *The Divine Comedy*. The Latin Silver Age poet Statius says that reading Vergil's works made him both a poet and a Christian. There are more illustrated manuscripts of Dante's *The Divine Comedy* than of any other secular medieval text. Reynolds pays tribute to the role Giovanni Boccaccio played in popularizing Dante's works by making and distributing copies.

Boccaccio also enhanced Dante's reputation by lecturing on *The Divine Comedy*, for despite the growth of a literate public, most people still could not read. Reynolds argues that Dante's works were always intended to be heard. She suggests that his *De*

A lifelong student of Dante, Barbara
Reynolds completed Dorothy Sayers's
translation of the Paradiso after
Sayers's death. She has also translated
Dante's La vita nuova (c. 1292) and
Ludovico Ariosto's Orlando furioso
(1516, 1521, 1532). Additionally,
Reynolds is the author of a biography
of Sayers and editor of The Cambridge
Italian Dictionary (1981).

vulgari eloquentia (c.1306; English translation, 1890) and *Il convivio* (c.1307; *The Banquet*, 1887) both composed while Dante was living in Bologna, were intended to be presented as series of lectures at the local university, where Dante is known to have taught. These works were left unfinished, perhaps, because Dante failed to find an audience. She thinks that the *Epistola a Cangrande* (1318; *Epistle to Cangrande*), in which Dante explains his purpose in writing his *The Divine Comedy* and his use of allegory in the work, was also designed as a lecture. Similarly, Reynolds notes that poetry in this period was written to be sung; *ballata* were danced as well.

Hence, sounds play an important role in Dante's poetry. Reynolds points out the harsh rhymes Dante uses as he writes about the hoarders and wasters in the fourth circle of hell. Presiding over these sinners is the Greek god of wealth, Plutus, who is enraged by the intrusion of the living Dante. His sputtering speech is reflected in rhymes ending with *-occia*, as his collapse after Vergil's rebuke is heard in the rhyming words ending in *-acca*. Dante employs double rhymes to mimic the hurtling of those condemned to this circle: *viddi, Cariddi, riddi, intoppa, troppa, poppa*. When in canto 27 of the *Paradiso* St. Peter denounces Pope Boniface VIII, the agent of Dante's exile from Florence, Dante uses harsh rhymes (*vaca, cloaca, placa*), and St. Peter repeats three times *il loco mio* (my place) to show his rage at Boniface's usurpation of the Holy See. The pauses in the following line of canto 24 of the *Inferno* capture the breathlessness of Vergil and Dante as they climb over rocks: *chè noi a pena, ei lieve, e io sospinto* (for we barely, he light, I pushing . . .). Sounds also link passages. In canto 26 of the *Inferno*, Ulysses relates how he almost reached Mount Purgatory before his ship sank. The first canto of the *Purgatorio* recalls that ill-fated voyage by using the same rhyme and even two of the three same rhyming words. The third rhyming word varies only slightly: *nacque* (began) in *Inferno* 26.137, *rinacque* (spring up again) in *Purgatorio* 1.135.

Numerology looms large in medieval thought. Reynolds shows how from his very first work Dante consciously played with variations on the number three, which symbolizes the Trinity, and ten, the number of perfection and also unity, since the digits in ten add up to one. *La vita nuova* (c. 1292; *Vita Nuova*, 1861; better known as *The New Life*) contains thirty-one sections built around three canzone. Reynolds describes the poems in *The New Life* as organized into a structure of "1 + 9 + 1 + 9 + 1 + 9 + 1." In *The Divine Comedy* number symbolism appears everywhere. Christ is named nine times in the *Paradiso*. Dante enters the city of Dis in canto 9 of the *Inferno*, and he passes from ante-purgatory into purgatory in canto 9 of that cantiche. Beatrice is named sixty-three times in *The Divine Comedy*, and her name serves as a rhyme word nine times. She appears to Dante in canto 30 of the *Purgatorio*, which is the sixty-fourth canto of the poem (6 + 4 = 10). She identifies herself in the seventy-third line of the canto; again the two numbers add up to ten. The entire *The Divine Comedy* is written in the rhyme scheme of terza rima that Dante created for the poem: aba, bcb, cdc, and so forth. Thus, each stanza consists of three lines, and each rhyme is used three times. The total number of lines in each canto and in the whole poem is divisible evenly by three with one left over, linking unity and trinity.

Reynolds points out other contemporary influences on Dante's masterpiece as well. The mosaics in the cupola of the baptistery in Florence depicted hell, purgatory, and heaven. This design included a Satan with three mouths devouring sinners: Dante would replicate this image in canto 34 of the *Inferno*. The baptismal font of the baptistery served as the model for the cylinders holding the simoniacs in canto 19 of that cantiche. In the cornice of pride in the *Purgatorio* Dante sees carved figures that seem alive. Reynolds notes the new realism in sculpture of the thirteenth century. She singles out Nicola Pisani and his son Giovanni, whose works graced churches in northern Italy, where Dante would have seen them. On a pulpit in Pistoia Giovanni Pisani portrayed Atlas weighted down by a column, as the prideful in the *Purgatorio* bend beneath boulders. Leaving the cornice of pride, Dante observes inlaid scenes that impress him with their realism, excelling, he says, even the skill of Giotto, whose masterful handling of tableaux is recalled here. Dante probably saw Giotto at work in the Scrovegni Chapel in Padua in 1304-1305.

Contemporary concerns pervade Dante's work. Before he became a poet, he had held important political posts in Florence, and he retained an interest in public affairs throughout his life. Among the issues he addresses in his early *The Banquet* is the question of proper government, a subject to which he returned in *De monarchia* (c. 1313; English translation, 1890; better known as *On World Government*, 1957). He wrote as a propagandist for Emperor Henry VII, and Reynolds sees *On World Government* as not merely a detached examination of the ideal form of governance but rather as an attempt to support Dante's patron Can Grande against the assault of Pope John XXII. Dante's involvement in politics ultimately cost him his life, according to Reynolds. In 1321 he went to Venice as part of a delegation seeking to prevent war between that city-state and Ravenna, where Dante was living. Returning from his successful mission, he contracted malaria and died, having just completed the last cantos of *The Divine Comedy*.

That poem is suffused with political commentary. Dante repeatedly denounces the papacy for exercising temporal power. He predicts that the emperor Henry VII will go to heaven, while Boniface VIII is destined for hell. Justinian appears in heaven because he sought to reunite the Roman Empire: Dante longed for the restoration of a unified empire that would prevent city-states from warring against each other and would rein in the political power of the popes. Florence is repeatedly denounced because of its political corruption. Indeed, for Dante political malfeasance is worse than religious abuses. Those who sell church offices are punished in the third ditch of the eighth circle of hell, while Dante places grafters, who corrupt public office, lower down in the fifth ditch.

Much of Reynolds's biographical and critical assessment of Dante follows that of other scholars, but she occasionally offers idiosyncratic views that are thought provoking even if not always convincing. She suggests that throughout his life Dante—and other poets in his circle—took hallucinogenic drugs that caused the visions Dante records in his poems. She posits a homosexual relationship with Dante Forese Donati, whom Dante encounters in the cornice of the gluttons in purgatory. Reynolds supports her case by noting that the description of Forese Donati's departure from Dante echoes that of the sodomite Brunetto Latini in the *Inferno*. Even if Dante was hinting that Donati was homosexual, there is no reason to think that he and Dante had been lovers.

Much ink has been spilled over certain cryptic allusions in *The Divine Comedy*. At the end of the *Purgatorio* Beatrice predicts the coming of *un cinquecento diece e cinque* (a five hundred ten and five) who will end corruption in the church. This enigmatic prophecy tends to be glossed as an anagram. Five hundred in Roman numerals is D, ten is X, and five is V. These letters spell DVX, or ruler. Reynolds posits a different reading: *cinqu'e cento* (five and one hundred). Ten and five written together again make that number. Line 105 of canto 1 of the *Inferno* mentions *feltro*, another word that remains ambiguous. In that passage Dante writes that a savior will emerge *tra feltro e feltro* (between felt and felt). Reynolds understands the term to refer to the felt sheets used in the manufacture of handmade paper. Thus, she interprets the unnamed savior in both cases to be books, perhaps even *The Divine Comedy* itself.

Some of the book's black and white illustrations should have been clearer. The details of the image of the mosaic decoration of the baptistery on page 228, which is important for Reynolds's argument, cannot be seen. The first concern of Reynolds's translations of *The Divine Comedy* is to preserve the poem's rhyme scheme. The result too often is tortured syntax. These are, however, minor flaws. Reynolds has produced a banquet that will delight and inform anyone interested in the greatest poem written since the *Aeneid* (c. 29-19 B.C.E.) and in its creator.

Joseph Rosenblum

Review Sources

Booklist 103, no. 3 (October 1, 2006): 18.
The Economist 381 (December 2, 2006): 84-85.
Library Journal 131, no. 16 (October 1, 2006): 72.
Publishers Weekly 253, no. 31 (August 7, 2006): 42.
The Spectator 301 (July 1, 2006): 47.
The Times Higher Education Supplement, July 21, 2006, p. 24.
The Times Literary Supplement, October 20, 2006, pp. 12-13.

DEAN ACHESON
A Life in the Cold War

Author: Robert L. Beisner (1936-   )
Publisher: Oxford University Press (New York). 800 pp.
    $35.00
Type of work: Biography
Time: 1945-1953
Locale: Washington, D.C.

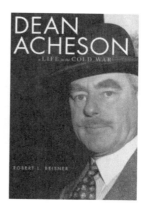

Beisner has produced the most comprehensive biogra-phy to date of Acheson, the key architect of U.S. foreign policy during the Cold War, whom many scholars consider the greatest American secretary of state

Principal personages:
DEAN ACHESON, U.S. secretary of state dur-
    ing the Cold War
HARRY S. TRUMAN, president of the United States
GEORGE KENNAN, a foreign service officer during the Truman adminis-
    tration
ERNEST BEVIN, a British foreign secretary
ANTHONY EDEN, Bevin's successor at the foreign office
ROBERT SCHUMAN, a French foreign secretary
KONRAD ADENAUER, a West German head of state
JOSEPH STALIN, a Soviet head of state

Robert L. Beisner's comprehensive biography focuses on Dean Acheson's years as secretary of state. Acheson's earlier years—his childhood, education, and govern-ment service during President Franklin D. Roosevelt's administration—are treated quickly but effectively. Beisner brings to his account of the man generally regarded as America's greatest secretary of state a full and perceptive understanding of the whole man, demonstrating how Acheson's personality and prejudices informed his world outlook and shaped the policies of President Harry S. Truman.

President Truman's main problem was how to regard the Soviet Union in the years immediately following the end of World War II. Was the Soviet Union under Joseph Stalin's leadership capable of continuing the wartime alliance with the United States that had proved so effective in prosecuting the war against the Axis powers, Germany and Japan? At Yalta, the agreement on postwar conditions that President Roosevelt, British prime minister Winston Churchill, and Stalin had reached was predicated on a spirit of cooperation and a tacit acknowledgement of spheres of influence. With the Red Army occupying half of Germany and much of Eastern Europe, American policymakers tried to safeguard the liberties of countries like Poland, but Soviet pledges to conduct free elections were essentially unenforceable—unless the United States was willing to intervene militarily. This option seemed unthinkable given that

Robert L. Beisner has taught history at the University of Chicago, Colgate University, and the American University. He is former president of the Society for Historians of American Foreign Relations. Other books include From the Old Diplomacy to the New, 1865-1900 *(1975) and the award-winning* Twelve Against Empire: The Anti-Imperialists, 1898-1900 *(1968).*

the United States had just concluded a major war and had already demobilized considerable portions of its military forces.

Nevertheless, many Republicans urged a hostile policy toward the Soviet Union, especially since it soon became clear that in countries like Poland and Czechoslovakia no governments would be permitted to rule that were not subservient to Stalin. In this tense situation, American diplomat George Kennan proposed what came to be known as the "containment" policy. The United States would not go to war against the Soviet Union, but it would resist Soviet infiltration of countries such as Greece and Iran, supplying military and logistical support to countries threatened by communist subversion that sided with the United States.

As secretary of state Acheson early on (by 1947) concluded that most negotiations with the Soviet Union were fruitless. The United States had to bargain from a position of military and economic strength. Largely due to Acheson's efforts and President Truman's wholehearted endorsement, a series of initiatives were introduced to bolster Western Europe and to deflect the Soviet Union from considering any sort of military incursion into nations allied with the United States.

Thus under Acheson the United States promoted the Marshall Plan (economic aid to Western Europe), the North Atlantic Treaty Organization (NATO) military alliance, and a stable pro-Western German government in the part of Germany occupied by U.S., French, and British forces at the end of World War II.

Beisner's biography is especially brilliant on Acheson's support of West Germany. Without Acheson's steadfast belief that West Germany would prove a bulwark against Soviet aggression, the postwar world would have looked quite different.

In retrospect, Acheson's pro-West Germany policy seems inevitable. However Beisner shows how much of a risk Acheson took in working for this new country, which meant Germany would remain divided. The French and the British feared a West German state that might again become militaristic and start yet another war. Acheson also worried that Western Europeans might accept the Soviet plan for a unified but weak neutral Germany that neither side (the West and the Soviets) could dominate. Just the opposite would prove true, Acheson argued: A weak disarmed Germany would simply become a divisive unsteady entity demoralizing its people and making it vulnerable to Soviet subversion.

Acheson was adept at balancing between the British and the French, using one to play off the other when needed. Beisner refutes charges that Acheson was an Anglophile. Some were fooled because Acheson dressed like a British gentleman, Beisner points out. Rather than retreat from an aggressive policy of confronting an aggressive Soviet foreign policy, however, Acheson would stand up even to Winston Churchill when the occasion demanded.

If not an Anglophile, Acheson was Eurocentric, Beisner explains. Acheson knew little about Africa, Asia, and Latin America and interested himself in those continents only when they seemed to impinge on his Cold War European focus. However, as a good administrator he put into important positions Foreign Service officers who did understand those parts of the world and could bring to Acheson's attention events and issues he would otherwise have ignored.

Indeed, Beisner shows that one of Acheson's great strengths was his ability to listen to his staff. He enjoyed morning meetings devoted to airing his staff's concerns. He enjoyed a good argument and fostered it within his department. Beisner cites the testimony of several Acheson subordinates who praised their boss's openness.

The biographer also makes the case that Acheson had a much steadier and consistent command of U.S. foreign policy than his chief rival, George Kennan. Kennan, in fact, is portrayed as a rather wayward personality—inventing the containment policy and then almost immediately backing away from it. At the same time, Acheson knew how to employ Kennan's brilliance and often acknowledged how much he learned from his rather prickly, humorless colleague.

Even the greatest secretary of state, Beisner shows, made significant mistakes. Acheson grossly underestimated the extent of communist subversion within the State Department. Put off by Senator Joe McCarthy's wild charges that the Roosevelt and Truman administrations had been infiltrated by hundreds of Communists, Acheson did little to ascertain what the role of officials like Alger Hiss actually amounted to. Hiss was convicted of conspiracy to commit espionage. Not only did Acheson defend him, but he also said it was inconceivable that a well-educated and dedicated government employee like Hiss could possibly work for a foreign power.

Beisner, relying on recent scholarship, shows conclusively that Hiss was indeed a spy. Even worse, however, according to Acheson's biographer is that in fact Acheson did not know Hiss well. It was Hiss's brother Donald who was Acheson's friend. Donald had been Acheson's law partner, and consequently Donald's probity, in Acheson's view, extended to Alger. Beisner is obviously dismayed at Acheson's willful blindness and suggests that Acheson defended Hiss because the two men shared the same class interests and scorned informers like Whittaker Chambers (Hiss's chief accuser) because he did not fit into their gentlemen's club.

If anything, Beisner might have made more of Acheson's snobbery. It did not help plain-speaking Harry Truman much when Acheson appeared on Capital Hill decked out in his dandyish clothes—a red flag to the bull-like Republicans who resented Acheson's condescension. Beisner insists Acheson actually had good relations with Congress until the McCarthyite mania about Communism usurped Washington's political dialogue. Perhaps so, but it is hard not to see Acheson as a sort of Brahmin who made it all too easy for his midwestern and western Republican opponents to brand the secretary of state as a smug effete liberal who could not see that his own kind (like Hiss) had betrayed him and the country.

On other major conflicts—like the Korean War—Beisner shows that Acheson made many terrible mistakes. He had little understanding of where Stalin actually stood on the war or how the Chinese might react when General Douglas McArthur pushed the invading North Koreans too close to the Chinese border. The resulting U.S. casualties (several thousand in just a seventy-two-hour period) was a debacle the Truman administration never recovered from. Indeed, it had to be a factor in President Truman's decision not to run again in 1952.

Still Beisner does not believe the Korean War could have been prevented or that Acheson's mistakes made that much difference in the long run. Indeed, the U.S. decision to defend South Korea seems, in retrospect, like the decision to establish West Germany, a sound judgment. In Japan as well, Acheson's policies fostered a prosperous democratic country allied to the United States.

The biographer minces no words about Acheson's twenty-year postwar career. It did not amount to much. To be sure, he advised presidents and contributed to important public discussions of U.S. foreign policy; as he aged, though, Acheson became more conservative, more irritable, and so undiplomatic as to render his services to the nation nugatory.

Beisner insists, nevertheless, that the latter-day Acheson should not be confused with the man in his prime. While he was always outspoken, he remained during his years in power an agile tactician, quite willing to amend his views to deal with fast changing events. Truman relied on his judgment, and Acheson developed a rapport with his president that is perhaps unmatched except for that between President Richard Nixon and Henry Kissinger.

If Acheson is the greatest secretary of state, it is because his achievements in Germany, Japan, and Korea were long lasting. Historians with access to Soviet archives and other evidence that Acheson did not have deem his policy decisions to have been wise and even prophetic. At the same time, Beisner does give Acheson's critics a voice in this biography even as he cites other evidence that mitigates their fault finding.

As the study of a man and of his work, it is difficult to see how this biography could be improved. Occasionally, Beisner's care to get the record straight and to confront important issues in separate chapters results in repetition. Still, overall this analytical approach works well, clarifying the man and the issues he confronted honestly and effectively.

Beisner also portrays a colorful cast of characters: the suave French foreign secretary Robert Schuman, the crusty British foreign secretary Ernest Bevin, the elegant British foreign secretary Anthony Eden, the hard-boiled West German head of state Konrad Adenauer, the peevish Kennan, the inscrutable Stalin, and the confident, decisive Truman. What a complex group of individuals to have to deal with, yet Acheson shuttled between them as a shrewd broker, making deals but protecting principles that have stood the test of volatile world affairs.

Carl Rollyson

Review Sources

Booklist 103, no. 2 (September 15, 2006): 17.
The Economist 380 (August 26, 2006): 68.
Library Journal 131, no. 14 (September 1, 2006): 155.
National Review 58, no. 21 (November 20, 2006): 47-48.
The New Republic 235, no. 16 (October 16, 2006): 26-32.
The New York Times 156 (October 4, 2006): E7.
The New York Times Book Review 156 (October 15, 2006): 1-11.
Publishers Weekly 253, no. 29 (July 24, 2006): 47.

DEAR GHOSTS,

Author: Tess Gallagher (1943-   )
Publisher: Graywolf Press (St. Paul, Minn.). 140 pp.
  $20.00
Type of work: Poetry

In this collection of poems, Gallagher draws upon her belief in an afterlife as a means to survive the painful realities of illness, aging, and destructive political policies

In *Dear Ghosts,* Tess Gallagher's elegiac mood and personal conviction create a sense of companionship between the living and the dead, a result of her long-standing fascination with memory and mourning. By refusing to release the valued presences of deceased friends and loved ones—in particular the shade of her husband, short-story writer Raymond Carver—Gallagher enriches her work as a poet and her life as a person.

A notable earlier work, *Moon Crossing Bridge* (1992), is essentially an elegy for Carver in which Gallagher works through her grief over his death without relinquishing his imperishable influence in her life. The success of that volume enhanced Gallagher's prominence as an accomplished poet, a status she had enjoyed since 1976 with the publication of *Instructions to the Double*. The volumes *Portable Kisses: Love Poems* (1992), *Portable Kisses Expanded* (1994), and *My Black Horse: New and Selected Poems* (1995) were well received, but the appearance of *Dear Ghosts,*—made up of new and previously uncollected poems—has been hailed as a triumph.

The comma at the end of Gallagher's title indicates that the work's contents are intended as letters addressed to the deceased as well as the living, reading audience. Gallagher dedicates the work to her cherished ghosts, suggesting that they are both kind and tenacious indwellers of her remarkable life. The term "ghost" naturally refers to the deceased, but at times Gallagher also speaks of spectral qualities within the living. Readers must assume that these figures, often friends of the poet, will at some point survive physical death in a similarly ghostly fashion.

An assortment of ghosts, including those who attain only distant levels of intimacy with the poet, inhabits the unseen world that the poems engage. A variety of circumstances afford opportunities to "see" into these otherworldly dimensions. For example, in "Little Match Box" Gallagher suggests that the existence of a twin moon orbiting beyond the visible one may be intuited by a willing and perceptive person: "Sometimes a glory/ is just that—a guessing-into/ the seen, noticing/ the fringe of presence." Discernment of this rewarding "presence" connects earthly life to distant realms.

New developments in Gallagher's life add richness to this collection. She writes of her struggle with cancer, her experience as the caretaker of her dying mother, and her increased involvement in religious practices of East Asian origin. Other poems draw upon her travels as she returns to the region of her family's roots in Ireland, works as a translator in Romania, and visits friends in Japan. The poet unearths and imparts wisdom from these journeys as well as from events in and around her home in Washington State. An astute observer of nature, Gallagher also explores the physical and spiritual dimensions of a variety of familiar objects such as horses, birds, lilacs, and the moon.

~

A prominent poet, Tess Gallagher is also well known for her work as a fiction writer and translator. Gallagher won a National Endowment for the Arts Award and the Elliston Award in 1976 for Instructions to the Double. *She received the Maxime Cushing Gray Foundation Award in 1990.*

~

The collection opens with a prefatory page containing an adapted segment of the title poem ("black butterflies of the general soul,/ join me to those who are missing") and goes on to describe ghosts as sleeping with their "sweetness intact." The butterflies, black as they may be, lead the speaker to ghosts who retain their desirability even after death. This passage invites readers of the poems that follow to join the poet in her visionary experiences.

The book's fifty-five poems are divided into seven sections, each opening with a quotation identifying connections within the section. Some of the quotations are of Buddhist origin and others, once again, are made up of lines from the title poem, providing a further thread of continuity. Such aids are important, as Gallagher mixes subjects, settings, and styles. A single poem may exhibit lyric intensity, relate narrative content, and call upon the past, present, and future. Readers who have appreciated Gallagher's previous works will probably applaud her continued pairing of opposites such as war and peace, illness and health, life and afterlife. In a similar vein, she complements her frequently conversational phrasing with a generous number of striking expressions and images.

The words of a Buddhist nun, "to be neither separated from words nor/ obstructed by words," introduce the first section of the work. This concept is fully present in the first poem, "My Unopened Life," in which the existence of a parallel life is proposed. This idea remains dominant throughout the poem, even though the words themselves present a series of novel images. The life in question is originally that of the poet, but later in the poem it also belongs to an unknown suicide, "he." As the poem begins, the life that is unopened lies "to the right of my plate/ like a spoon squiring a knife." Although the spoon is round and small in stature, it playfully "escorts" the knife, assuming a dominant role in the poem.

The eating utensils wait patiently for either soup or for the "short destiny/ of dessert at the eternal picnic" that will take place "near the mouth of the sea" on a cloth spread under the "shadowy, gnarled penumbra" of a madrona tree. A penumbra is normally the outer ring of light surrounding a sunspot or the outer and lighter part of the shadow created by an eclipse. From this area of "relative" light the poem moves in the next stanza toward darkness: a cat feeding upon a captive bird, the bird "with its/ belly full of worm," the worm already a denizen of darkness. Yet the worm never questions the overwhelming darkness of its existence.

In the next stanza of "My Unopened Life," the bowl of the spoon collects images from around the room and from the mouth it serves, the mouth a kind of cave from which an unspecified "we" can see the setting of the suicide's house and develop an appreciation for the "delicious/ universe of his intention." The simple act of eating with a spoon has been transformed into a psychic journey.

A sense of the intent of the suicide in stanza 4 prefigures the conclusion of the poem: "So are we each lit briefly by engulfments/ of space," light coming as the "worm in the beak of/ the bird" yields to "sudden corridors/ of light-into-light." Readers will wonder why this light appears where it does and whether such a light will also appear at their deaths.

Two quotations introduce section 4 of the collection. They pair a variation of a line by the Zen master Hakuin, "Listen: a thrush at evening serenading the rain," and the closing thoughts from *Dear Ghosts,* "And I don't know why we are together, dear ghosts,/ or why we have to part. Only that it is precious/ and that I love this run-down subject." The presence of these ghosts is key to "Apparition," which provides an example of the poet's fidelity to familial experiences. The poem narrates a tale Gallagher heard frequently from her uncle. As a young man, he had been visited by the ghost of his brother, the specter appearing when he was carrying water home from a spring. As a youth listening to her uncle's detailed account of the incident, Gallagher could never bring herself to acknowledge the possible truth of the story. She proposes that her silence may have validated their relationship even more effectively than any comment would have and that such silences may also support belief in the spectral dimension.

"Apparition" is followed by a shorter poem, "Unspoken," in which the heart is termed a "leaky bucket," a silent "one that doesn't speak at all." The heart only stands "next to/ speaking." By placing these two poems side by side, Gallagher intensifies the impact of both. Perhaps this placement echoes the position of the thrush's song as it serenades the evening rain in the quotation from Hakuin.

Section 5 of Gallagher's collection also begins with a reference to the role of words, as an editor struggling to find mid-nineteenth century poetry by Buddhist nuns asks, "Could it be that they taught solely through their spiritual/ presence, rather than through words?" A similar concept is embodied in "Moon's Rainbow Body," in which the moon first appears as part of a painting. Through contemplation, the poet suddenly enters the moon, her earthly existence disappears, and she is "so gone the word *gone*/ can't find a mouth/ to say it."

Included in the same section of the book, "Cairo Moon" is a good example of a work inspired by travel. The poem is set in Cairo, Egypt, where Gallagher is escorted by an efficient and personable driver, Ali, who also serves as a guide and bodyguard. He takes the poet to the pyramids, introduces her to his family, and gives her a nickname, "Pasha," a Persian title once used in areas of Turkish rule to designate an important official. The poet is renewed by inhaling the air inside a pyramid, and she wonders whether ancient traces from the workers' hands may have entered into her and given her an eternal role. At the close of the poem, the transformed "Pasha" walks through the city as a reanimation of the sleeping pharaohs.

Although tragedy is central to *Dear Ghosts,* Gallagher uses grief as a means to recovery. Her poems frequently conclude with animated and courageous declarations—endings that are particularly noticeable when pertaining to illness, death, and political oppression. One such poem, "The Violence of Unseen Forms," begins with an epigram from Ranier Maria Rilke expressing his desire "*to feel/ the hand within me that throws larks so high into the sky.*" When Gallagher accepts her role as a haven for the ghost of a dying person, she discovers an interior "deeper hand" that enables her to "learn to throw larks/ for sheer pleasure," an activity that releases her from grief.

In "Weather Report" Gallagher describes the way Romanian writers living under the dictatorial rule of Nicolae Ceaușescu could express themselves honestly but safely. In a society lacking adequate fuel for heating homes, they signified their political position with references to "cold." Gallagher depicts one such writer as wearing gloves while working, an image that causes her to exclaim, "I think I'll take off my gloves./ It's freezing in here./ There's a glacier pressing on my heart." Thus she expresses her outrage at the situation suffered by a fellow writer, proposing to remove her gloves and, if necessary, fight oppression with bare fists.

Long recognized for her sweeping style, Gallagher moves swiftly from subject to subject, connecting personal, national, international, and cosmic circumstances. Although some readers may find such an approach undisciplined, others will enjoy this leveling technique, as it reveals unsuspected relationships among daily events, traumatic memories, and politically induced inequities. In a Buddhist walking meditation, several climbers strung out along a mountain trail appear as one being with many legs. A rush of wind represents an answer to prayer at the gravesite of Raymond Carver. The dementia of a dying parent provides an opportunity for treasuring memories and African violets. A fallen drop of oil becomes a painting, the painter and the poet reveling in an awe-filled appreciation of beauty. In *Dear Ghosts,* Gallagher generously invites readers to share her innermost thoughts on an adventure confirming the value of living an incandescent life.

Margaret A. Dodson

Review Sources

American Poetry Review 35, no. 2 (March/April, 2006): 25.
Booklist 102, nos. 19/20 (June 1-15, 2006): 21.
Library Journal 131, no. 10 (June 1, 2006): 123.
New Criterion 24 (June 4, 2006): 70-77.
Ploughshares 32 (Fall, 2006): 215.
Publishers Weekly 253, no. 14 (April 3, 2006): 40.
The Washington Post, April 30, 2006, p. T12.

A DEATH IN BELMONT

Author: Sebastian Junger (1962-   )
Publisher: W. W. Norton (New York). 320 pp. $24.00
Type of work: Biography and history
Time: 1963
Locale: Belmont, a suburb of Boston, Massachusetts

The author investigates a murder that occurred in his hometown when he was one year old, and which his family discussed many times in later years, speculating on whether the wrong man was convicted and the true murderer was someone who once worked for them

Principal personages:
> ALBERT DESALVO, also known as the Boston Strangler
> BESSIE GOLDBERG, the sixty-three-year-old murder victim
> ISRAEL GOLDBERG, her husband
> ROY SMITH, the convicted murderer of Bessie Goldberg
> ELLEN JUNGER, the author's mother

The "six degrees of separation" theory known to popular culture states that every person in the world is personally connected to every other person via a chain of fewer than six people. The chain between the author and the subjects of this book is considerably shorter than six. When Sebastian Junger was a year old, his family had an addition built onto their house in Belmont, Massachusetts, so that his mother, Ellen Junger, could have her own artist's studio.

Opposite the book's title page is a photograph taken by the contractor on March 12, 1963, which shows the author, his mother, and two of the workers. One of those workers was Albert DeSalvo, who later became infamous as the Boston Strangler. On the previous day, when DeSalvo was working alone at the Junger house, Belmont resident Bessie Goldberg was murdered only 1.2 miles away. (The distance was later determined by police officers.) Roy Smith, a thirty-five-year-old African American former convict, was convicted of the murder. Junger's parents, however, always speculated that DeSalvo was the true murderer. This book is the result of Junger's research into the crime.

There are actually five stories in the book, and Junger skillfully interweaves them. The first is the story of the building of the home addition and Ellen Junger's relationship with DeSalvo. Except for two incidents, it was a cordial businesslike relationship in which the two would occasionally sit down and have lunch together. On his second day on the job, DeSalvo entered the basement from an outside entrance, announced that the washing machine was not working, and tried to entice Ellen to join him there. Fortunately, Ellen had a bad feeling about him and refused. She never mentioned the

incident to anyone until after DeSalvo confessed to the Boston Strangler murders, because she did not want him to get fired.

On another occasion, she caught DeSalvo
fondling one of her art students, a sixteen-
year-old girl. Afterward, she took care that
they were never alone together. When an acquaintance called her to tell her the news of
the Goldberg murder and to lock her doors,
she rushed outside to tell DeSalvo that one of
the strangler murders had occurred nearby.
No one knows if DeSalvo appreciated the
irony.

The second story thread covers the Goldberg murder and Smith's arrest and trial. Mrs.
Goldberg had arranged with an employment
agency to send someone to clean her house.
This person was Roy Smith. Around 2:30
P.M., her husband, Israel Goldberg, telephoned
and spoke to Mrs. Goldberg, who was home
alone with Smith. Smith left the house around
3 P.M., according to witnesses. After stopping
at a store to buy cigarettes, he boarded a bus.
Fifty minutes later, Mr. Goldberg came home

*Sebastian Junger travels around the
world reporting on wars and
interviewing people with dangerous
occupations. He has received a
National Magazine Award and an SAIS
Novartis Prize for journalism. Some of
his magazine articles have been
collected in* Fire *(2001). Another article
led to his writing the acclaimed best
seller* A Perfect Storm *(1997).*

and discovered his wife's dead body. Two minutes later, he came out of the house
screaming for someone to call the police. He could account for his time that day, and
no one believed he could have killed his wife and staged the scene in two minutes, so
he was never seriously considered a suspect. Someone had strangled Mrs. Goldberg
with one of her own stockings and sexually assaulted her, like most of the Boston
Strangler murders. Two off-duty rookie police officers tracked Smith down and arrested him.

The main evidence against Smith was the undeniable fact that he was at the house
on the day of the murder. He claimed that Mrs. Goldberg was still alive when he left,
but fifty minutes is a window of opportunity, albeit small, for someone else to have
entered the house and committed the crime. There were witnesses, however, who tes-
tified that no one entered or left through the house's front door between the time
Smith left and Mr. Goldberg arrived. The argument in favor of Smith's guilt also included the facts that the house was never really cleaned, fifteen dollars were missing,
there was no evidence of a forced entry from the back door or a window, Smith had a
criminal record, and he was an alcoholic.

The argument against Smith's guilt rested on the absence of either a witness or any
physical evidence linking him to the body. This was long before DNA testing. He was
convicted of the murder and sentenced to life in prison. Junger raises the question of
whether DeSalvo's close proximity constitutes reasonable doubt. Smith's trial took

place in 1963, and DeSalvo did not confess to the strangler murders until 1965. An appeals court reviewed the case in 1966 and did not order a retrial.

The third story, and the most interesting one, is a biography of Roy Smith, for which Junger traveled to Mississippi to interview Smith's relatives. The son of a Mississippi preacher living in Oxford, Smith worked in a supermarket and picked cotton before joining the Marines, became a petty criminal after his discharge, served time in Mississippi's maximum security prison, called Parchman Farm, and in New York's in Sing Sing, moved around to different cities, fathered a son, and finally wound up in Boston. His rap sheet included assault with a dangerous weapon, grand larceny, burglary, public drunkenness, and driving under the influence of alcohol. However, it did not include murder or any sex crime.

After his conviction for the Goldberg murder, he became a model prisoner, worked in kitchens, and rose to become the supervisor of one that served 150 meals a day. Because of his good behavior and doubts about his guilt, the state's Advisory Board of Pardons concluded that he would be a good candidate for early release and recommended that his sentence be reduced to time served. A chain smoker, Smith died of lung cancer in 1976, just a few days after Governor Michael Dukakis signed his commutation papers.

Junger discusses the problem of race throughout the book, especially Parchman Farm and life for African Americans in Mississippi and the rest of the United States. It is this aspect that makes the work much more notable than the average "true crime" book. Smith was an African American, and Belmont was a predominantly white community. Because he was a black man walking alone in a white neighborhood, there were several witnesses who not only remembered Smith but also noted the time. The investigating police officers, the prosecutors, the jurors, and the judge were all white males. Even in a liberal state like Massachusetts, the possibility existed that racist views could have biased the jury against Smith.

The book's fourth story is that of the Boston Strangler murders and the investigation. Smith was a suspect for only a few days, because he had the best possible alibi: He was in jail when most of them occurred. There were eleven murders in the Boston area between 1962 and 1964. (Two were added to the list after DeSalvo's confession.) The victims were all unmarried women living in apartments. (Bessie Goldberg did not fit the pattern, because she was married and lived in a house.) Most of the murder victims lived alone. None of the apartments showed evidence of forced entry, so these women must have let someone inside. The intruder then strangled them with a piece of their own clothing and, usually, sexually assaulted them. Then the perpetrator left without leaving physical evidence. There were enough differences among the crimes that investigators believed that there was more than one perpetrator. However, the press asserted that the murders were all connected and named the guilty party the Boston Strangler.

The book's fifth story is a biography of DeSalvo. This part and the one about the strangler murders are the least original parts of the book, because other writers have covered this material. Albert was an abused child who grew up in the Boston area. When he was old enough, he joined the Army and served for eight years. While stationed in Germany, he married a German woman, with whom he had two children. After his discharge, he returned with his family to the Boston area, where DeSalvo made a living working in construction. He was convicted of assault and battery and lewdness in 1961. After his release in 1962, he became the serial rapist known as the Green Man, because he wore green overalls. He would break into a woman's apartment, tie her up at knifepoint, and then either rape her or just leave. He later claimed to have committed three hundred such assaults and was arrested in 1964.

He confessed to the Boston Strangler murders in 1965 but was actually convicted of the Green Man assaults and sentenced to life in prison. He never made any money from various books and films about the Boston Strangler, but he did sell necklaces made by other inmates under the name "Chokers by DeSalvo." He was murdered in 1973. There were several suspects, but no one was convicted. Authorities believed the reason for DeSalvo's murder was that he was dealing in drugs, but some observers believed that he was about to recant his Boston Strangler confession and that the real strangler paid someone to kill DeSalvo. Junger points out that DeSalvo was murdered on the tenth anniversary of Roy Smith's conviction, which would point toward one of Smith's friends.

The reader may ultimately find the book to be unsatisfying because Junger never comes to a firm conclusion. He does believe that DeSalvo is more likely to have been the murderer of Bessie Goldberg than Smith but offers no evidence one way or another and even admits the possibility that a third person could have committed the crime. Two of Junger's sources, *The Boston Stranglers* (1995, 2002) by Susan Kelly and *Search for the Strangler* (2003) by Casey Sherman, confuse the issue by arguing that DeSalvo was not the Boston Strangler. These writers believe he made the confession in order to become rich and famous. (He achieved the latter but not the former.)

Some of their objections to DeSalvo's being the Boston Strangler apply to the Goldberg murder as well. Kelly further confuses the issue by pointing out that Smith lived only a few blocks from one of the strangler victims. Using Junger's logic, Smith's close proximity should have constituted reasonable doubt that DeSalvo committed that particular murder. While it is true that nonfiction is messier than fiction, the authors of the vast majority of "true crime" books have a strong belief about who is or is not guilty. Another flaw is that Junger really needed to write more about Bessie Goldberg. She was the original victim, after all. Finally, the book could really have used a table of contents or an index, especially considering its nonlinear organization. Overall, however, while this book is not on the level of *In Cold Blood* (1965) by Truman Capote, the quality of the writing brings it above the average work of New Journalism.

Thomas R. Feller

Review Sources

Booklist 102, no. 12 (February 15, 2006): 4.
Kirkus Reviews 74, no. 5 (March 1, 2006): 221.

Library Journal 131, no. 6 (April 1, 2006): 110.
New Statesman 135 (June 19, 2006): 67.
The New York Times Book Review 155 (April 16, 2006): 12.
Newsweek 147, no. 15 (April 10, 2006): 58-59.
Publishers Weekly 253, no. 7 (February 13, 2006): 70.
The Spectator 301 (May 20, 2006): 46.
Time 167, no. 15 (April 10, 2006): 75.
The Times Literary Supplement, May 26, 2006, p. 36.
The Wall Street Journal 247, no. 82 (April 8, 2006): P8.

DEATH'S DOOR
Modern Dying and the Ways We Grieve

Author: Sandra M. Gilbert (1936-   )
Publisher: W. W. Norton (New York). 580 pp. $30.00
Type of work: Sociology
Time: 2006

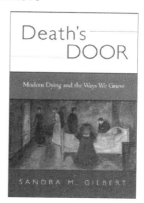

A wave of personal tragedies motivates Gilbert to ex-
amine a wide range of cultural, historical, technological,
religious, and especially literary responses to death and to
grief

Sandra Gilbert draws upon her considerable expertise as
a professor of English and experienced critic and writer of
poetry and fiction in writing *Death's Door*. Nevertheless
the most important influence for this book is a series of unexpected deaths involving close family members. These painful events propel the author in a new direction professionally. She moves away from a concentration in
women's studies, where she had gained considerable success, and toward sustained
work on death and dying. Initially she wrote a memoir about the unexpected death of
her husband, Elliot L. Gilbert (*Wrongful Death*, 1995). Later she professionalized this
acutely personal story with a collection of poems dealing with loss (*Inventions of
Farewell*, 2001). *Death's Door* represents an ambitious reach beyond these books. It
is a complex masterpiece, both painstakingly personal and satisfyingly academic. The
author ventures from her comfort zone of literary criticism into the social sciences
and medicine as she explores the context of the dying. She looks at modern technology and its implications as well as after-death conventions in the work of Jessica
Mitford. The result is best read slowly and reflectively. This is by no means a trivial
work; it contains nuggets worth the reader's trouble to mine.

Part 1 is the most personal section of the book. The author recounts her own journey to the liminal landscape of human passing, not once but a number of times. The
unexpected loss of her husband in 1991, consequent to a hospital admission for a routine surgery, changes the course of her own professional work. This death multiplies
for Gilbert the loss of her three-day-old first child, the wrenching deaths of her father,
her grandparents, and a cherished aunt, all in her view, "before their time." Then
comes the horror and shock of the terrorist attacks of September 11, 2001, events that
raise the experience of personal loss to societal proportions. How does one deal with
the weight of profound and illogical tragedies that shift the sands of personal and cultural security? How does one resist the urge to cross death's threshold and join the departed who have been pulled away without warning? The search for meaning in the
concept of "widow," the struggle to make sense of untimely death in "the after-
midnight blackness" that is more than the sunlessness of nighttime, the work of grieving, of remembering, of sustaining care for the dead: These are the tasks assigned to

∽

*Professor emerita of English at the
University of California, Davis, and
former president of the Modern
Language Association, Sandra M.
Gilbert is the author of several
collections of poetry and criticism and
a memoir, the coauthor with Susan
Gubar of* The Madwoman in the Attic
*(1979), and a finalist for the Pulitzer
Prize and the National Book Critics
Circle Award.*

∽

those who grieve. These are the stuff of Gilbert's explorations.

Human beings who struggle with raw grief resort to various kinds of rituals to remove the pain. Some build alternative imaginary universes of consolation decorated with "Tudor topiary and flashing fountains" (Gilbert quotes Kipling), where their departed loved ones live happily ever after. This construction knits solace from sorrow for some people. Alternately, people compose fantasies to be played out in the world of the living, houses of "what if," where the future still includes those who have died. Some people deal with death by maintaining some form of communication with the deceased. They create snippets of a kind of e-mail that bridges the cyberspace of grief in the hope of retrieving the lost relationship. What Gilbert describes resonates universally with human experience. It is not her journey alone but the well-trod, painful path of human reality. Her account is both candid and captivating. Navel-gazing it is not. The reader is drawn into Gilbert's world as she describes the events following her husband's death, as she speaks of her mother's keening with sorrow when Gilbert's father dies. The descriptions, resonatingly emotional, never become maudlin.

Part 2 of the book moves more aggressively into areas that are new to the author's professional attention. The twentieth century's mode of death differs from that of previous times, even as the constancy of grief remains the same. Modern people do not "expire" as they did in the past—a normal progression of life's experience—but rather enter into a world of "termination." Previous philosophies of death entertained a notion of the passage of the human spirit. They proposed a life beyond this one, a place that provided balm not only for those about to cross through death's door but for those left behind.

Gilbert argues that this notion has undergone a mutation. Modern cultures do not see the event of death in the same way as did their forebears. The massive "death events," especially of the twentieth century's efficient killing technologies of war and of the Holocaust have, she argues, depersonalized the concepts of life and death and have torn away the soothing poultice of hope in an afterlife. Today the dying are "terminated," a practice prefigured by the massive numbers of war casualities as well as by the intentional murders of millions of people in the Holocaust. Face to face with such horror, the comforting notion of a heaven no longer sustains nor consoles the majority of people.

She uses material from poetry, art, and film to make the point. A particularly arresting diptych of photographs pictures a bonneted baby boy ("Gramp Holding Dan") in the arms of his apparently young and vital grandfather. The accompanying picture, taken twenty years later, reverses the order: "Dan Holding Gramp." The elder man is now reduced to a frail and incontinent shell of the vigorous man captured in the earlier frame. Which image is real? Where does one locate one's feelings about the changes in this person, Gramp, and the foreshadow of death that characterize the second photograph? As Gilbert remarks, there are "confusions between life and death with which photography haunts us, complicates grieving, and derides our strategies for denying our own mortality and that of those we love." Who has not looked with nostalgia or grief upon the yellowed photos or home movies of deceased relatives and felt what Gilbert is expressing here?

In a chilling account of the death camps and other twentieth century atrocities, the author sees a parallel to the modern setting of death. Hospitals are the modern place of "termination," places that keep patients in a sort of prison. People now die routinely in sterile, professionalized settings rather than in their own homes. Doctors and nurses help dying people to be terminated, easing the passage of the body from life to death. Gilbert notes her surprise that statistically more people die toward the dinner hour, because that is when the medical staff can come to help the passage. Death often comes as the result of deliberate action rather than, as in the past, as a natural process over which no one had control. One could only stand passively by and watch.

Modern medical advances, if that is what they are, have changed not only the means but the venue and focus of death. Marvels of technology are powerful hands against death's door, holding the final passage at bay until human decision pulls them away. Are the dying, then, prisoners in a bizarre spaceship? The body that tries to die is held captive as a kind of cyborg: only partly human intimately entangled in an embrace of invasive tubes and machines. Only when those in attendance deem the time appropriate are what Gilbert terms "nuanced modes of termination" used to open the door to death. As technology can keep life from slipping through the clutching fingers of tubes and technical interventions, its removal can be timed to fit what is convenient. The patient on life support may feel similar to those prisoners in a concentration camp, waiting to be selected.

In part 3, Gilbert returns to ground more consonant with her academic background. As she notes in the preface, she originally intended *Death's Door* to be a more detached literary excursus that would explore the fate of the elegy in modern culture. Somehow, the immense tragedy of September 11 affected the original intent and caused the author to move beyond her original proposal. This final section probably represents more closely her original intent. Gilbert conducts an extended study of several literary accounts of death and grief, among them the work of poet Sylvia Plath.

A particularly interesting foray in this section of the book looks at the work of the soldier poets of World War I. Readers of Pat Barker's ambitious trilogy *Regeneration* (1991) will appreciate meeting its characters fleshed out, so to speak, in their grim and graphic poetry of war. Much of the poetry that grew from the blood-nourished battlefields of France is discussed at length in this section.

Death's Door represents a thoroughly ambitious task. It expands cultural and religious frames. It looks at technology as well as art and literature. The reader is introduced, without syrup but not without detail, to the ongoing reflection in which the author has engaged since 1991. Gilbert considers the acquired immunodeficiency syndrome (AIDS) crisis, the Vietnam War, the Holocaust, and other seminal historic events that she concludes have shaped how deaths are conceived and processed.

The reader will find the book rigorous and ambitious. He or she is presented with images, both visual and those crafted in words, as well as strong emotion. The book is certainly a fine academic work, including thirty pages of bibliography and extensive footnotes as well as many photographs. Nevertheless, it is accessible to any serious reader. It is powerful, gravid, and sometimes too much to bear. It is tragic but captivating.

For those who lose the people they love through the door of death, that passageway never quite closes, argues the author. Like a persistent foot in the jamb of the entryway, grief never allows total closure. Nevertheless, as Gilbert contends, the struggle to make sense of the irrationality of death, "is in itself a victory." *Death's Door* always remains a bit open to the human need to return to closeted feelings and to process difficult events. This, concludes Gilbert, is good.

Dolores L. Christie

Review Sources

Booklist 102, no. 8 (December 15, 2005): 6.

JAMA: Journal of the American Medical Association 295, no. 17 (May 3, 2006): 2079-2080.

Kirkus Reviews 73, no. 21 (November 1, 2005): 1171.

Library Journal 130, no. 18 (November 1, 2005): 100-101.

The New York Times Book Review 155 (February 26, 2006): 16.

Publishers Weekly 252, no. 41 (October 17, 2005): 53.

THE DEVIL'S DOCTOR
Paracelsus and the World of Renaissance Magic and Science

Author: Philip Ball (1962-   )
First published: 2006, in Great Britain
Publisher: Farrar, Straus and Giroux (New York). Illustrated. 436 pp. $27.00
Type of work: Biography
Time: 1493-1541
Locale: Switzerland and Western Europe

Science writer Ball takes a trip back in time to discover how a daring physician conceived a configuration of matter and spirit that anticipated modern biochemistry

Principal personages:
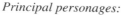
THEOPHRASTUS PHILIPPUS AUREOLUS BOMBASTUS VON HOHENHEIM (1493-1541), Swiss medical reformer known as Paracelsus
WILHELM VON HONENHEIM (1457-1538), his father, a physician
JOHANN FROBEN (1460-1527), Basel publisher and patient of Paracelsus
JOHANNES OPORINUS (1507-1568), sometime assistant to Paracelsus
DESIDERIUS ERASMUS (1466-1536), humanist scholar
MARTIN LUTHER (1483-1546), religious reformer

For an intellectual vagabond who traveled throughout Europe and into Asia and Africa, seldom spending more than a year in any one place, the Swiss physician who called himself Paracelsus left an astonishing body of work. His medical texts alone run to fourteen large volumes in the standard German edition, and his writings on social and theological issues are still being edited. Many of his most important books have been translated into various languages, including modern German: He wrote in Early New High German (*Frühneuhochdeutsch*) with a dash of Swiss German (*Schwyzerdütsch*) and many words of his own coinage. He avoided academic language, as he avoided academics generally, claiming to have learned more from the simple working people he met on his travels—from miners and hangmen and barber-surgeons, from witches and magicians and alchemists.

Paracelsus had a choleric personality and what Philip Ball diagnoses as a persecution complex, but he had such faith in what is now called "holistic medicine" that he could make passionate statements even in a tract on syphilis or gout. In the generous acknowledgments to those who helped him, Ball explains that he never intended to write a biography but was drawn to Paracelsus when he tried to learn about Renaissance alchemy and its appeal to the later scientists. Paracelsus provided a window into the whole world of Renaissance magic and science, as the book's subtitle notes, and indeed Ball is most helpful as a well-informed guide to the intellectual world that produced Paracelsus.

Educated at Oxford and Bristol, Philip Ball is a regular contributor to Nature *and the author of eight books on modern science. The first,* Designing the Molecular World: Chemistry at the Frontier *(1994), won the American Association of Publishers prize for the year's best book on chemistry. The most recent,* Critical Mass: How One Thing Leads to Another *(2004), received the Aventis Foundation Prize for best science book.*

Like this world, Paracelsus was a bundle of contradictions. Ball uses a series of oxymorons to characterize him: "A humble braggart, a puerile sage, an invincible loser, a courageous coward, a pious heretic, an honest charlatan." It is purely coincidental that one of his given names is Bombast. (Ball explains that it originally referred to a form of cotton-wool used in stuffing garments and was afterward attached to inflated language.) It may be coincidental that his self-given name, Paracelsus, implies one who has gone beyond the ancient medical authority Celsus. (Ball suggests it may simply be a classical version of the patronymic Hohenheim, meaning "high place.") At any rate, it was his fortune to be born at a turning point in world history, one year after Columbus set sail for China and in time to witness the traffic that brought both gold and syphilis from the New World.

Paracelsus was close to his physician father, having lost his mother at an early age, and followed his father's steps to study medicine and treat miners suffering from lung ailments. He thus became a forefather of occupational medicine. However, he had wanderlust to an extent unusual for any time. He traveled from one country to another, convinced that each region had its own diseases and its own treatments, as it had its own food and drink. Rejecting the stereotype of the academic physician who would not dirty hands or his fine gown, Paracelsus collected his own chemicals and compounded his own medicines, giving them extraordinary names—for example, Azoth, which combines and first and last letters in the Latin, Greek, and Hebrew alphabets.

Supporters called him the Luther of the physicians (*Lutherus physicorum*) because he placed no trust in old traditions and insisted on the primacy of individual experience. Paracelsus was not flattered. Though he did dedicate a book to the religious reformer, the two never met, and probably would have disagreed on the centrally important topic of God's wish for the age. Paracelsus tended to side with the peasant rebels, while Luther sought support from nobles. Indeed, it is surprising that a man who traveled as widely as Paracelsus met so few of his more famous contemporaries. Perhaps he came closest when tending the Basel publisher Johann Froben, who was host at the time to the great humanist scholar Desiderius Erasmus. They met only once. It was cordial, by all accounts, but the two were as remote from each other as the humanist's classical Latin from the physician's German dialect.

Paracelsus was the stuff of legend—especially the Faust legend, which gets attached to his biography in ways that require a skillful biographer to sort out. Because he is writing about the whole "world" of Paracelsus, Ball devotes a good deal of attention to historical figures like Luther and Erasmus, as well as semi-historical ones like Faust, in order to understand how the medical reforms of Paracelsus fit the larger pattern of reformation in culture and religion.

The chapters follow the course of Paracelsus's career, at the center of which is his tumultuous year as professor of medicine at the University of Basel, beautifully imagined in Georg Wilhelm Papst's classic film *Paracelsus* (1943). Typically, the story moves from Paracelsus to the places he inhabited, many of which Ball has clearly visited, and to Paracelsus's contemporaries. The major writings of Paracelsus are discussed, in the order of their appearance, but usually without much depth. When Paracelsus is quoted, it is usually the memorable aside, often abusive of authorities like those in Basel, where he was lampooned and silenced, and which he was eventually forced to leave under the cover of darkness. He never quite got over the experience. His exhausted amanuensis, Oporonius, never forgave himself for writing down embarrassing information on the doctor's personal hygiene, which was dreadful even for those times.

Of all the topics that Paracelsus wrote about, Ball is most interested in alchemy. Like Paracelsus, he takes this to be the process of purifying substances and making proper use of them. Paracelsus taught that there was an inner alchemist, or Archeus, in every person: an innate intelligence that knows how to absorb the best nutrients and expel the worst toxins. The alchemist in each human was not unlike the God who created the world, in a series of chemical separations and combinations, for the spirit left visible signs wherever it moved. The Paracelsian physician learned to read the marks in the Book of Nature, and thus to help in the work of God by bringing the right cures to an ailing body. It is difficult to separate the theological and the scientific elements in Paracelsus, who called himself a "Doctor of both Medicine and Theology." His abandonment of the traditional four elements (fire, air, earth, water) for a new trinity (mercury, sulfur, salt) may have represented a move from an inorganic to an organic chemistry, as Ball suggests, but also replaced the established natural science of Aristotle with a grouping from the Arabic alchemists, and it placed a Trinity at the center of things.

Ball is also fascinated by the astrology that Paracelsus called a pillar of medicine—not the predictive astrology of newspaper horoscopes but the study of planetary influences. Here, even more than with alchemy, were the prospects of personal and natural "disasters" (literally, "ill starred events"). Here, too, were explanations for the misfortunes blamed on witches, the "wise women" for whom Paracelsus voiced nothing but sympathy. Based on his observations of heavenly bodies and their influences (literally, their "inflowings" into the world), he wrote "prognostications" for whole nations, very much as he gave prognoses for patients. When he died at the relatively early age of forty-seven—whether of poisoning from his laboratory trials, of the drunkenness that his adversaries denounced, or of sheer exhaustion from his travels—he left the strange request that his body be quartered so that it could best absorb the earth's nurture. What was revived, however, was the considerable body of work that he left in manuscript, work championed by a large and appropriately squabbling group of followers known as Paracelsians. The "revivalists" influenced Robert Boyle, Isaac Newton, and a host of modern thinkers.

Ball's intellectual biography has been well received in his native Britain, where it appeared a few months before its American publication. Britain's leading medical journal, *The Lancet*, has praised the author for being both sympathetic and detached, aware of Paracelsus's intellectual appeal but also of his real shortcomings. (The reviewer wonders whether Paracelsus really belongs in the medical pantheon, where a previous generation placed him, and is sure he would choose another physician for his own family.) *The Daily Telegraph* commends Ball for parting from historical practice enough to follow Carl Jung's analysis of Paracelsus's troubled psyche. *The Economist*, however, suggests that the balance of Paracelsus's life and times is somewhat out of whack: that the book might be more helpful if it included more "life" and less "times."

In the United States, *Science News* has praised Ball for his objective account of Paracelsus and of the origins of modern medical chemistry in medieval alchemy and astrology, while *Booklist* has commended the book as a "travelogue" of sixteenth century culture. Lest this seem a strictly mechanical view of healing, Ball points out that it was impossible for Paracelsus or his readers to ignore the theological implications of the "daily bread" on which people fed. "To Paracelsus, the material was spiritual, and the spiritual material." Ball is modern enough to realize that the "spiritual" was often mental, and that some of the illness Paracelsus addressed would now be considered mental.

Ball has one serious handicap: He has no knowledge of German, so is unable to draw upon the large body of specialist scholarship by the Paracelsus Society (*Paracelsusgesellschaft*) and by students of German studies (*Germanistik*). Several excellent studies were published in Switzerland in conjunction with the quincentennial of Paracelsus's birth in 1993, including *Paracelsus: Mediziner, Heiler, Philosoph* (Paracelsus: physician, healer, philosopher) by the folklorist Sergius Golowin and *Paracelsus: Arzt und Prophet* (Paracelsus: doctor and prophet) by the teacher-turned-politician Pirmin Meier.

To be sure, Ball has been able to avoid the rash of Aryan nonsense published about Paracelsus during the Nazi era, including work by the young Will-Erich Peuckert, who would go on to write standard studies of esoterica in Paracelsus's era. Without some knowledge of this pseudo-scholarship, however, it is difficult to assess Jung's wartime writings on Paracelsus, as Martin Haeusler has demonstrated in a recent edition of those texts.

Ball's obvious strengths as a writer and as an observer of twenty-first century science more than compensate for any linguistic shortcomings. He knows enough science to gainsay the often simplistic pronouncements about the theory and practice of an earlier age. The study of Paracelsus will not be his only foray into the science of earlier periods, for he is now writing a study of the intellectual life at Chartres, where he thinks a whole vision of the cosmos was erected alongside the great cathedral. Graced with fifty black-and-white illustrations carefully integrated into the text, *The Devil's Doctor* strikes something of a Faustian bargain with the reader. If you accept the Faustian fumes that hang around the historical figure, Ball seems to say, you will find a key to such secrets as the origin of modern biological medicine.

Thomas Willard

Review Sources

Booklist 102 no. 15 (April 1, 2006): 11.
The Economist 378 (January 21, 2006): 81.
The Lancet 367 (April 29, 2006): 1389-1390.
Library Journal 131, no. 4 (March 1, 2006): 116.
Nature 441 (May 11, 2006): 152-153.
Publishers Weekly 253, no. 1 (January 2, 2006): 43.
Science News 167, no. 19 (May 13, 2006): 303.
The Spectator 300 (February 4, 2006): 41-42.

DIGGING TO AMERICA

Author: Anne Tyler (1941-   )
Publisher: Alfred A. Knopf (New York). 277 pp. $24.95
Type of work: Novel
Time: 1997-2006
Locale: Baltimore, Maryland

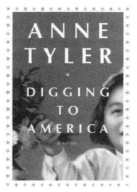

Tyler's novel examines the unexpected connections between an American family and an Iranian family who both adopt daughters from Korea on the same day

Principal characters:
>MARYAM YAZDAN, Iranian-born grandmother of Susan Yazdan
>BITSY DONALDSON, Baltimore suburban housewife, who adopts Jin-Ho
>BRAD DONALDSON, Bitsy's husband
>DAVE, Bitsy's father, who falls in love with Maryam Yazdan after his wife's death
>ZIBA YAZDAN, Maryam's daughter-in-law, who is easily intimidated by white American culture
>SAMI YAZDAN, Maryam's son and husband to Ziba
>SUSAN YAZDAN, Sami and Ziba's adopted daughter from Korea
>JIN-HO DONALDSON, Bitsy and Brad's adopted daughter from Korea

Pulitzer Prize-winning novelist Anne Tyler has had a long and impressive career as a writer whose subtle and nuanced renderings of quirky but likeable characters and their attempts to find their place in their family and community have earned her literary prestige. Indeed, Tyler's focus on family structure and dynamics began in her first novel, *If Morning Ever Comes* (1964), a story about a young man's quest to find out the truth about his father, and has continued in most of her other novels, including *Dinner at the Homesick Restaurant* (1982) and *The Amateur Marriage* (2004). Though Tyler's juxtaposition of two families to provoke comparison and contrast is not unique in her oeuvre, *Digging to America*, her seventeenth novel, does not simply focus on her typical white, suburban, Baltimore community. Rather, Tyler contrasts her customary family with one of Iranian origin.

Though Tyler married Taghi Modarressi, an Iranian-born child psychiatrist in 1963, and the two remained married until his death in 1997, she has never substantially presented Iranian culture in any of her novels. With the exception of an early short story and a set of one-dimensional side characters in her 1991 novel *Saint Maybe*, Tyler has very seldom included characters with differing ethnic backgrounds in her work. *Digging to America* marks a substantial departure for her, with its thematic exploration of foreignness and its effect on those of other ethnic backgrounds living in America.

The novel opens as two groups—the Donaldsons, a typical white, middle-class

Baltimore suburban family composed of Bitsy and Brad Donaldson and their extended relatives, and the Yazdans, Ziba and Sami, a second-generation Iranian American couple and Sami's mother, Maryam—meet at the airport when each group picks up their respective adopted daughters from Korea. After this chance meeting, the families decide to maintain contact in order to provide a sense of cultural heritage for their daughters. Bitsy imagines the two girls growing up together, having sleepovers, and staying in touch with their Korean background.

The two families, however, could not be more different. The Donaldsons arrive with balloons, extended families, video cameras, and a back-slapping demeanor. They seem to fill up the airport. The Yazdans, by contrast, are hardly noticed: "Three people no one had noticed before approached in single file: a youngish couple, foreign-looking, olive-skinned and attractive, followed by a slim older woman with a chignon of sleek black hair knotted low on the nape of her neck." In this opening sequence, Tyler sets up a dichotomy often found in her fiction. Frequently, a loud, often large, boisterous family whose members interact well with others is contrasted with an insular, self-contained family whose members prefer to limit interaction, maintaining an aloofness from others.

Anne Tyler has written seventeen novels, numerous short stories, and Tumble Tower *(1993), a children's book illustrated by her daughter Mitra Modarressi. Tyler's novel* The Accidental Tourist *(1985) won the National Book Critics Circle Award and was made into an award-winning movie in 1988.* Breathing Lessons *won the Pulitzer Prize in 1989.*

One can see this pairing in *The Accidental Tourist* (1985), in which Macon Leary and his siblings are so isolated from others they cannot maintain marriages or friendships, thus becoming reliant on a more engaged person from a more demonstrative family to free them from their insularity. Tyler takes an almost sociological interest in examining different family types to determine which variation is most suitable, and the pairing of the Donaldsons and the Yazdans in *Digging to America* suggests a return to this continuing question in her work.

The novel is filtered through the limited omniscient points of view of several of the main characters, including Sami Yazdan, Ziba Yazdan, Bitsy Donaldson, and even Jin-Ho Donaldson, the Donaldsons' adopted daughter. Though one might expect the novel to focus on the two daughters and how they adapt within their adoptive families, the children become merely the reason the families maintain their connection. Partially because Maryam Yazdan's sections of the novel outnumber those of other characters, and partially because her particular position in the novel is at the nexus of Tyler's preoccupations, the main story line involves her and her developing relationship with Bitsy Donaldson's widowed father, Dave.

Maryam is typical of Anne Tyler's other insular characters, such as Daniel Peck in *Searching for Caleb* (1976) or Macon Leary in *The Accidental Tourist*. She feels comfortable only with her own family or few close friends, often remaining an outsider in most other social situations. A widow who arrived in the United States with her husband when she was nineteen, Maryam has raised her son in an American culture often very foreign to her, producing her own sense of distance from others. As a result of this self-imposed isolation, Maryam develops an emotional self-reliance that limits the necessity of interaction with others. Tyler often characterizes the narrowness of these characters by their limited belongings. Maryam Yazdan is often characterized by her single coffee cup in the sink and her own "sense of stillness and self-containment, standing alone in a crowd."

Though Maryam, Sami, and Ziba resemble other Tyler characters and family types in their limited involvement with others, the Yazdans complicate the typical dynamic by being foreign, a term repeatedly used in the novel to signal both their ethnicity and their outsider status. As Maryam says to Dave at one point early in their courtship: "You start to believe that your life is *defined* by your foreignness. You think that everything would be different if only you belonged." Though Sami and Ziba wish to belong to American culture, Sami is quick to point out American contradictions to other Iranians: how Americans "feel personally outraged by bad luck," claim to be open but then forestall intimacy, and claim to be tolerant but then fail to tell others the rules.

Yet, as the Yazdans spend time with the Donaldsons, they discover many of these generalities to be false. The Donaldsons accept bad events with dignity and reserve. When Dave's wife, Connie, dies from cancer, the family rallies around Dave; he also does not give into self-pity. When Bitsy is diagnosed with cancer, she takes on the chemotherapy with her typical positive attitude. Furthermore, the Donaldsons also allow for intimacy that the Yazdans, particularly Maryam, often refuse.

Tyler suggests that it might be easy to blame feeling left out on being foreign, but in reality, one has to accept personal responsibility for feeling this way. For example, when Ziba becomes upset because she feels Bitsy is undermining her methods of mothering, Sami senses that the argument stems from a cultural misunderstanding, then accuses Bitsy of being pushy and overbearing. Dave tries to talk to him about his anger, but the two end up pushing each other in a kind of mock fight. Ironically, at the end of this episode, Sami begins to feel as if he belongs; he imagines "that to the relatives, the two of them must resemble two characters in some sitcom, two wild and crazy Americans, two regular American guys." Sami seems to realize the fight did not happen because the Yazdans are Iranian. Rather, miscommunication and recovery are part of every family's evolution.

As in other Tyler novels, family get-togethers, parties, and visits serve as arenas for action and confrontation. As soon as the Donaldsons make initial contact with the Yazdans, their connection deepens through frequent phone calls and visits. Eventually, the two families decide to begin annual Arrival Parties to mark the date of the girls' entry into the United States. The Donaldsons host the first party, which includes a video of the girls at the airport, a patriotic cake, and lots of singing. The novel then roughly follows events in the lives of the two families, as revealed at subsequent Arrival Parties. By the first Arrival Party, the friendship between the two women has so-lidified; as Bitsy puts it: "They [the Yazdans] were the first ones she thought of when she was in the mood for company." Eventually, the extended families on both sides—Ziba's parents, the Hakimis, Bitsy's brothers, and their children—all take part in the events. As the Yazdans begin to invite others to their house, the link strengthens. What began as a rather awkward connection between two very dissimilar groups be-comes an extended family, one in which the two groups feel kinship and respect from each other.

Despite the novel's general movement toward acceptance and tolerance, Maryam Yazdan, perhaps because she has lived always on the outside of things, has the great-est difficulty accepting a place at the Donaldsons'. She remains aloof, someone Bitsy calls "superior," and seemingly self-contained. In this, Maryam resembles other Ty-ler characters from insulated families who are self-reliant, unattached, and often lonely. As Tyler shifts viewpoints in the novel, one becomes aware of the limitations of Maryam's behavior. From a distance, she appears extremely put-together, some-one who does not need constant contact or reassurance. She travels frequently. She has dinners with friends in town. She works part-time at a local school. However, by maintaining this constant restraint on her emotions and emotional entanglements, Maryam allows her foreignness to limit her possibilities.

As Dave Donaldson grows fond of her, he recognizes her inability to let anyone get to know her. Her struggle to accept Dave and the clutter of his emotions—both his need for her and the needs he awakens in her—makes up the central struggle of the novel. Eventually Dave proposes, and though Maryam initially agrees, she finds ways to push him away. She complains that he wants to learn too much about Iranian cul-ture, that he takes up too much space, and that he has too many possessions. Even-tually, she rejects his offer, but she is described in the aftermath as someone who "seemed much smaller than usual. In her black blazer and slim black pants, she was a single, narrow figure, straight-backed and slight and entirely alone."

The climax of the novel occurs as Maryam reflects on what she has gained and lost by rejecting both Dave and the conjoined families. Yet, after being cajoled into at-tending yet another Arrival Party, which she accidently sleeps through, she is thrilled when all the Donaldsons arrive at her house to indicate that they want her to attend. As Bitsy says through Maryam's closed door: "'We can't have the party without you. We need you. Let us in, Maryam.'" When Maryam rushes out to join them, she considers the things she loves about Bitsy, her "hopefulness, her wholeheartedness, her manu-factured 'traditions' that seemed brave now rather than silly." By rejecting her soli-tary lifestyle in favor of the larger, American family, Maryam indicates, to some de-gree, her ability to move beyond her self-imposed outsider status.

By focusing on Maryam's character change in *Digging to America*, Tyler com-ments on family dynamics, ethnic identity, and the idea of the outsider in modern cul-ture. While Maryam's final acceptance of the Donaldsons is not a rejection of her own Iranian culture, it does reflect her ability to see the importance of needing others and responding to others' needs, regardless of ethnicity. Furthermore, by using such di-verse families, Tyler also suggests, as she has in other novels such as *Celestial Navi-*

gation (1974), how often family structures that work defy the typical term "family." In *Digging to America*, the Yazdans and the Donaldsons make an unlikely team, but through communication and growth they become a blended family, one that can sustain its members despite their differences.

Rebecca Hendrick Flannagan

Review Sources

Book World 36, no. 17 (April 30, 2006): 1.
Booklist 102, no. 2 (February 15, 2006): 7.
The Christian Science Monitor, May 9, 2006, p. 13.
Kirkus Reviews 74, no. 5 (March 1, 2006): 207.
Library Journal 131, no. 6 (April 1, 2006): 87-88.
The New York Times 155 (May 19, 2006): E25-33.
The New York Times Book Review 155 (May 21, 2006): 14.
Publishers Weekly 253, no. 9 (February 27, 2006): 30.
Southern Living 41, no. 5 (May, 2006): 62.
The Spectator 301 (May 20, 2006): 47.
The Weekly Standard 11, no. 42 (July 24, 2006): 42.

THE DIN IN THE HEAD

Author: Cynthia Ozick (1928-   )
Publisher: Houghton Mifflin (Boston). 243 pp. $24.00
Type of work: Essays

A collection of eighteen essays plus a foreword and afterword showcasing Ozick's thinking on a variety of subjects, especially on literature and the power of language

In *The Din in the Head* Cynthia Ozick delivers a series of literary essays that provokes thought and demonstrates again her exceptional talent as a writer. It is her fifth book of essays, following most recently *Quarrel and Quandry* (2000), winner of the 2001 National Book Critics Circle Award for Criticism, and *Fame and Folly* (1996), which was a finalist for the 1996 Pulitzer Prize. In this collection Ozick addresses a wide variety of issues, but of these the most recurring topic is the novel and its writers and the most consistent theme is the importance of literature.

The title essay, "The Din in the Head," while not the first in the collection, is one that fervently pronounces the literary novel as "the last trustworthy vessel of the inner life," other than one's own consciousness of the world, what she refers to as the "din in the head" of the individual. Much time is spent in crowds; if not literally, then occupied in the crowd mentality that keeps one away from inner contemplation. Films and television belong to the principle of Crowd; technology and electronic devices promote the collective, as do most forms of writing. What used to be called the "personal" essay could be said to promote the inner life, but very few such meditative essays are now published. That leaves the art of the novel. The fictional worlds created by the great writers breathe out the cry of "Life!" and take the solitary reader into the inner life, into self-knowledge.

What the title essay accomplishes—and, indeed, what the other essays similarly accomplish—is to do what is claimed for the personal meditative essay. It is as though the reader is being invited into the writer's mind and thoughtful consciousness, privileged to share and be stimulated by the text to think about things that would otherwise not be considered in the mundane day or busy crowd activities. What makes this especially true of Ozick's essays is her remarkably evocative writing. Her writing is in that way very much like the writing in the art of the novel: It is not susceptible to easy paraphrase or summary. Talking about a great work of fiction never captures the fiction itself; to know what a novel is about, it must be read. The same is true of Ozick's essays.

Given the quality of evocation of emotion and thought that shimmers and shines throughout the essays, it is no coincidence that Ozick herself is also a respected novelist. Her most recent novel, *Heir to the Glimmering World* (2004; published in the United Kingdom as *The Bear Boy*), was a New York Times Notable Book and a Book

Cynthia Ozick's award-winning nonfiction includes her essay collection Fame and Folly *(1996), a finalist for the 1996 Pulitzer Prize, and* Quarrel and Quandry *(2000), winner of the 2001 National Book Critics Circle Award. Her most recent novel,* Heir to the Glimmering World *(2004), was a New York Times Notable Book.*

Sense pick and was chosen by NBC's *Today* Book Club.

That Ozick is a successful novelist contributes to the stylistics of her essays; it also adds authority to her commentaries on other novelists. There are essays on John Updike, Saul Bellow, Leo Tolstoy, and Isaac Babel and more than one on Henry James. An essay on the well-known twentieth century literary critic Lionel Trilling reveals that despite his high reputation for such landmark works as *The Liberal Imagination* (1950), Trilling throughout his life (he died in 1975) bemoaned his role as critic and longed instead to be a novelist, to write fiction that would live long. Ozick also includes a very short essay, "Kipling: A Postcolonial Footnote," in which she notes that Rudyard Kipling was one of the most renowned writers of the early twentieth century, and despite current postcolonial disdain for some of his attitudes, his stories present some of the strongest fiction of the past century. He was a master of narrative, an inventive writer who understood the interiors of his characters.

"What Helen Keller Saw," the first essay in the collection and one of the longest, is a cogent retrospective of the extraordinary woman whose life from the time she was nineteen months old was spent as sightless and nonhearing. There were numerous changes in her public reputation both during her lifetime (1880-1968) and after. Charges were brought against her that she could not possibly have dictated the books attributed to her, that she could not possibly have had the ability to describe things and people or to have any idea about colors or music. Nevertheless, Helen Keller, who learned to read and write Braille and was in fact an avid reader of literature, said of herself: "I observe, I feel, I think, I imagine." As Ozick puts it, "She was an artist. She imagined."

The other long essay in the collection is the final one, "And God Saw Literature, That It Was Good: Robert Alter's Version." The first part of that title, preceding the colon, perhaps best sums up the focus of the entire collection. The specific topic of this essay, however, is Robert Alter's translation of the Pentateuch, *The Five Books of Moses: A Translation with Commentary* (2004). Ozick gives the reader a summary and timetable of the previous translations of the Bible; only three of these have been by a single individual, and of those, only one is a translation into English, the translation by British writer William Tyndale in the sixteenth century. Tyndale was burned at the stake for his effort to make the Bible accessible in the English vernacular, but his work was the major influence on the creation of the King James Version of the Bible, which appeared shortly after, though that long-lasting version was compiled by a group of scholars. No one since Tyndale had attempted a translation of the Bible single-handedly until Robert Alter.

Alter's approach to his translation is to create poetic accuracy and to provide substantial footnotes of explanation. He wants the meaning or meanings of the stories to be as clear as possible and the writing to be as memorable and engaging as possible, to be, in short, good literature. His purpose, Ozick notes, is "to decrease the distance between Scripture and our quotidian lives." She compares his English to the style used by Abraham Lincoln, a plainspoken prose that resonates to Americans with a biblical gravity. In her examination of Robert Alter's translation of the Hebrew Bible, Ozick also discusses the currently popular Bible-as-literature movement. This approach is found mostly in university classes or by those who are not reading for the sake of religious belief. Certainly this is a valid way of reading. The "authority" of the texts can be attributed to the writers themselves, just as a reader would approach a novel and inevitably have a sense of its author.

However, Ozick continues, novels do not deliver commandments. They do not claim to be God's words to humankind. In Alter's translation, Ozick says, the language, the words on their own power draw the reader into a place where God is more than a literary premise; instead, the translation is a text where God is, as Ozick phrases it, "a persuasive certainty—whether or not we are willing to go there."

Ozick is always interested in the history of the Jewish people and the contemporary issues they confront. Of her own fiction, Ozick is undoubtedly best known for her widely anthologized short story "The Shawl" (1980), a powerful and chilling story of a woman who watches her baby being killed in a concentration camp during World War II. In this collection of essays, many of the writers Ozick discusses are Jewish, and she has various comments about Judaism throughout, certainly as indicated in her interest in Robert Atler's translation of books of the Old Testament. She also includes a detailed essay on the place of mysticism, or the lack of its place, in the Jewish faith. This essay is titled "The Heretical Passions of Gershom Scholem."

Gershom Scholem, born Gerhard Scholem, youngest of four sons in a German family in the early twentieth century, was a rebellious thinker and scholar from the time he was a teenager. He became fascinated with the Zionist movement, with the interpretative biblical commentaries of the Talmud, with Hebrew and Yiddish; he changed "Gerhard" to "Gershom," the name of the son of Moses in the Bible. He became especially interested in the largely uncharted topic of Jewish mysticism.

The topic was seldom addressed because it was outside mainstream Judaism. The norm was rationalism; mysticism was not acceptable as a social ideal. Scholem searched out and translated old texts that suggested to him a tradition hidden underneath normative Jewish religious beliefs. While classical Judaism characterized the essence of God as unknowable, various historical texts and documents generally acknowledged as kabalistic, shunned for their connection to magic, indicated to Scholem a Jewish mystical tradition in which the individual could approach God's emanations through a mystical state. Scholem became the first professor of Jewish mysticism at the Hebrew University of Jerusalem, founded in 1925, and published books on the subject. He declared himself not interested in political affairs but was inevitably affected by it all of his life, especially in his Zionism, his desire for a Jewish state. Scholem died in 1982. He is still considered one of the foremost scholars in the study of the Kabbalah, an aspect of Jewish mysticism, and its speculation on the nature of divinity.

Among Ozick's other essays is "Smoke and Fire: Sylvia Plath's Journals," in which she points out that whatever an author might write in a journal or diary, what ultimately is important is the work, in Plath's case particularly her poetry. What the author says or does personally outside the work may be of avid interest to people who knew her or to her readers, but it is the work that counts, that lasts.

In case the readers of Ozick's essays want to know more about Ozick's personality, they can definitely learn that she has a fine sense of humor in addition to a fine mind and an artist's approach to writing. The incontrovertible evidence is the afterword, titled "An (Unfortunate) Interview with Henry James." It is a light-hearted, hilarious fictional interview, in which the female interviewer deliberately and repeatedly asks James about his personal life. It is a perfect ending for the reader who has followed Ozick's intellectual density through all the preceding essays.

Lois A. Marchino

Review Sources

The Baltimore Sun, July 2, 2006, p. 5F.
Booklist 102, no. 17 (May 1, 2006): 64.
The Boston Globe, September 17, 2006, p. D7.
Los Angeles Times, May 28, 2006, p. R3.
The New York Times Book Review 155 (July 2, 2006): 8.
Publishers Weekly 253, no. 17 (April 24, 2006): 48.
St. Louis Post-Dispatch, June 18, 2006, p. F10.
The Times Literary Supplement, November 3, 2006, pp. 19-20.

DISTRICT AND CIRCLE

Author: Seamus Heaney (1939-   )
Publisher: Farrar, Straus and Giroux (New York). 78 pp.
    $20.00
Type of work: Poetry

Nobel Prize winner Heaney demonstrates once again why he is cherished as one of the strongest poets writing in English today in this book of poetry, published forty years after his first book was published

Seamus Heaney's reputation as the greatest Irish poet since William Butler Yeats has been based not only on his beautifully crafted, richly textured language but also on his ability to be true to the difficult times in which he has lived. As a Catholic who grew up in Northern Ireland, he often found himself as the poet with nationalist sensibilities to whom readers turned for a poetic witness to "The Troubles." In *District and Circle*, Heaney pays passing tribute to the world's difficult times, but mainly he pays tribute to poetry's ability to give pleasure simply because of its sentence shape, its metrical complexity, and its evocation of small pleasures and losses rather than bloody, international miseries.

In his poem "Anything Can Happen," based on Horace's *Odes* (23 B.C.E., 13 B.C.E.), Heaney writes about the mythic Roman world in which Jupiter tosses lightning from his galloping thunder cart. He notes also that "the tallest towers" can be "overturned, those in high places daunted,/ Those overlooked regarded." It would be difficult not to recognize why Heaney selected Ode 34 rather than another Horacian ode for his poem base: Clearly reference is being made to the World Trade Center and the start of the war on terror.

Though he recognizes that "anything can happen" in the political realm, in this volume Heaney is more interested in the possibilities afforded by memory, by elegy, and by art than by the struggles of politics. In the first poem in the collection, Heaney resurrects the turnip-snedder, an archaic farm instrument, and describes a violent realm where "turnip-heads were let fall and fed/ to the juiced-up inner blades" of the shredder that "dropped its raw sliced mess,/ bucketful by glistering bucketful." In earlier poems, Heaney might have spoken about human heads meeting blades and the mess of that, but here in *District and Circle*, turnips replace people in the sacrifice.

In "A Clip," another poem of memory, there is nothing more violent than hair being cut. Heaney, however, as is typical, invests the simple scene with the air of surprise: He remarks on "the plain mysteriousness/ Of your sheeted self inside that neck-tied cope—/ Half sleeveless surplice, half hoodless Ku Klux cape." The blood rites of religious and racist practices here are used to help convey the air of the unfamiliar, a child's sense of confused wonder at the one-room, one-chimney house that served as his "first barber shop." The poem ends not with any great revelation or cosmic hap-

Seamus Heaney's first collection of poetry, Death of a Naturalist, *appeared in 1966, and since that time he has published over twenty books of translations, essays, and poetry. He was awarded the Nobel Prize in Literature in 1995 and has taught at Harvard and Oxford Universities.*

pening, but simply the eerie image of "Loose hair in windfalls blown across the floor/ Under the collie's nose. The collie's stare." It is beautiful.

Heaney can use poetry to evoke a scene, but he also can use the scene to express regret, as he does in "Chairing Mary," part 2 of a poem called "Home Help." The home help he refers to here is helping to get the handicapped, "helpless" Mary, who is confined to a chair—not metal but made of "braced timber"—up the stairs every night. The woman is heavy, described as a "hurting bulk," and the two needed to lift her struggle with the chairing choir. However, Heaney does not speak of the miseries of the lifting alone, but rather of the regret he feels now: "I think of her warm brow we might have once/ Bent to and kissed before we kissed it cold." This is a poem that leans toward the sentimental, but any poet unwilling to risk sentimentality will inevitably end up cold and aloof—not Heaney who is warm-blooded, nonironic, a chronicler with a heart.

Heaney is not one to shy away from the mischievous, the seemingly puerile, or the mildly funny. He recollects that nearly universal phenomenon, the first experiment with tobacco, in a light poem called "A Chow." It begins in a comic manner with Heaney, or the speaker, "staring at the freshly scratched initials/ Of Robert Donnelly in the sandstone coping/ Of Anahorish Bridge, with Robert Donnelly/ Beside me. . . ." Though poets often search for ways to avoid repeating words, "Robert Donnelly" is an exception. The bad boy then offers Heaney some chow, or chewing tobacco, after "stripping a dulse-thin film/ Off the unwrapped ounce of Warhorse Plug—/ Bog-bank brown, embossed, forbidden man-fruit." The devilish Donnelly in this garden of Eden/Anahorish offers the poet some pithy advice after the roof of Heaney's mouth, metaphorically, "is thatch set fire to." "'You have to spit,'" says Robert, 'a chow's no good/ Unless you spit like hell.'" Heaney, always described as an earthy poet, a keen advocate for the material world, here blends that interest in bogs, grit, coping stones, and "quid-spurt fulgent" with the comically diabolic.

The strange, strangely defamiliarized world of childhood also seems to be invoked in the poem "The Nod," a sonnet in rhyme and meter. It speaks of the rituals of Saturday evenings when the family would buy beef at the butcher's shop, a rib roast "wrapped up, and bow-tied neat and clean/ But seeping blood." It felt in his hands "Like dead weight in a sling." The small-town feel soon reveals itself as a specific locale when Heaney brings in the realities of the Northern Ireland in which he grew up: The first eight lines of the sonnet describe the buying of the bloody meat, and the last six, after the turn or volta in the sonnet, talk about something more ominous. The blood of the beef becomes tinged with the political world when the B-Men are invoked. The B-Men, or B Specials, were part-time, unpaid members of the Ulster Constabulary used principally to enforce and maintain the political status quo in Northern Ireland. For a member of a Catholic family, like Heaney, the B-Men would be perceived of as a menacing branch of a government that was created, in part, to keep the Catholic, nationalist community at a permanent disadvantage in the nation. In the poem, the B-Men "thronged the town,/ Neighbours with guns, parading up and down." Nothing dramatic happens, but the sinister undertones are evident when the B-Men nod toward Heaney's father "almost past him/ As if deliberately they'd aimed and missed him/ Or couldn't seem to place him, not just then." The implication is that at a later date, the men would certainly place him and perhaps use their "special powers" to put him in his place, and this time guns might be aimed rather than merely nods.

Heaney returns to familiar ground in "The Tollund Man in Springtime." Readers familiar with Heaney's work will recognize a familiar face here—that bog-buried, peat-brown head of the Tollund Man who was dug up in Jutland in the twentieth century after more than one thousand years in the earth, described in 1972, and described again in 1994 in Heaney's poems "The Tollund Man" and "Tollund." Here Heaney allows the Tollund Man to speak for the first time in this sonnet sequence of six persona poems. He is a long way from the bogs of ancient Jutland, here dealing with exhaust fumes and "thickened traffic" and "transatlantic flights stacked in the blue." There is, however, something otherworldly about this being caught in our terror-frightened world of "scans, screens, hidden eyes"; he carries with him "Through every check and scan" some Tollund rushes "bagged in their own bog-damp." The bog-spirit hopes they will keep until he can transplant them, but they soon wither and go to dust. He wonders how to proceed and decides that rather than shake off the dust, he will proceed as "a man would, cutting turf": The Tollund Man "straightened, spat on my hands, felt benefit,/ And spirited myself into the street." This is no longer the Heaney of glum despair, witness of atrocities, and recorder of man's manifold inhumanities; Heaney is now more at ease than ever in the spirit-charged world of feeling benefit from the smallest blessings and moving on.

The reverence Heaney has for nature, his indebtedness to the charged rhythms of the poet Gerard Manley Hopkins, his love for the Germanic quality in the English language for joining words together, and his playful exuberance in choosing words that are both common and recondite are all amply displayed in his small poem called "Planting the Alder." Here there are no allusions to Northern Ireland's troubles or to Heaney's fairly untroubled childhood or to famous poets (various poems in the book pay tribute to Rainer Maria Rilke, Ted Hughes, Pablo Neruda, and W. H. Auden). Instead, Heaney pays tribute to the exuberance of language and revels in the spirit of nature.

> For the bark, dulled argent, roundly wrapped
> And pigeon-collared.
>
> For the splitter-splatter, guttering
> Rain-flirt leaves.

> For the snub and clot of the first green cones,
> Smelted emerald, chlorophyll.
>
> For the scut and scat of cones in winter,
> So rattle-skinned, so fossil-brittle.
>
> For the alder-wood, flame-red when torn
> Branch from branch.
>
> But mostly for the swinging locks
> Of yellow catkins,
>
> Plant it, plant it,
> Streel-head in the rain.

It is Heaney's reverence for the earth, for the machines that smash turnips into animal feed, for quid-spurts, and for a collie's nose, his finding the mysterious and the spiritual in the hard facts or hard woods of this world, and his translation of this reverence into memorable, charged verse that make him a special poet, one of the finest writing today. In his poem "Out of This World," a tribute to the Polish poet and fellow Nobel laureate Czesław Miłosz, Heaney begins with an epigraph that is a question and answer from the Catholic catechism: "*Q. Do you renounce the world?/ A. I do renounce it.*" Heaney then describes "the man/ Who played the saw inside the puddled doorway/ Of a downtown shop" in Belfast; he describes the music as "untranscendent" but also says that Miłosz, and by extension Heaney, "would not have renounced" it, "however paltry." Heaney cannot renounce the world, cannot embrace a philosophy that supports renouncing the world because he is an advocate for the pleasures of the senses, for what language can create and preserve, for the power of poetry to give pleasure through its inventiveness and to preserve through its close, focused attention on the things of this world.

Kevin Boyle

Review Sources

America 195, no. 16 (November 20, 2006): 29-30.
Booklist 102, no. 16 (April 15, 2006): 21.
The Economist 378 (April 15, 2006): 82.
New Statesman 135 (April 17, 2006): 48-49.
The New York Times Book Review 155 (July 16, 2006): 12.
Poetry 188, no. 5 (September, 2006): 457-458.
The Times Literary Supplement, June 2, 2006, p. 8.
Virginia Quarterly Review 82, no. 4 (Fall, 2006): 269-270.

THE DOCTOR'S DAUGHTER

Author: Hilma Wolitzer (1930-   )
Publisher: Ballantine Books (New York). 255 pp. $25.00
Type of work: Novel
Time: 2004-2005
Locale: New York City

A story of a middle-aged woman coming to terms with her past, her present, and her future

> Principal characters:
> ALICE BRILL, a fifty-one-year-old, recently laid off book editor who has begun a new career as a "book doctor" to help aspiring writers
> EVERETT CARROLL, Alice's husband, a frustrated writer working in his family's printing business
> VIOLET STEINHORN, Alice's childhood friend
> MICHAEL DOYLE, a young novelist working on his first manuscript
> SAMUEL BRILL, Alice's father, who is suffering from dementia
> SCOTT CARROLL, Alice and Everett's troubled youngest child
> ANDREA STERN, Alice's therapist

Alice Brill wakes up one morning with the feeling that something is "terribly wrong," and the sensation of dread behind her breastbone remains with her for most of the novel. Alice's journey of self-revelation forces her to reexamine her past, rethink her present, and reenvision her future. While Alice tries to laugh off what she labels a midlife crisis, her friend Violet, always the first to suggest counseling, says "This is the crossroads, kiddo, when you're looking back at all the mistakes you made, and ahead, well, ahead to old age and death." The novel tells Alice's story as she grapples with the sorrow of a crumbling marriage, a father slipping into dementia, a wayward son, a career change, and questions she needs to ask and answer about her childhood and the parents she idolized; she is indeed at a crossroads.

What makes Alice a compelling character is that she is ordinary, and as an ordinary woman, she determines her identity and her view of the world through her relationships. She must look at herself in the various roles she played or plays: daughter, wife, mother, friend, professional. As she examines her relationships with all the people in her life, she comes to learn about herself, yet that knowledge is neither profound nor life-changing. The first-person narrative reminds the reader of Alice's ordinariness by detailing the minutiae of her life, from spring housecleaning to getting a mammogram. The novel avoids becoming mundane by virtue of its wit and descriptions of everyday life that are so recognizable, they are personal. Alice says that what first drew her to write fiction was "so I could get inside someone else's psyche, someone else's experience, even if I had to seek them out in my imagination." The story offers Alice's psyche to the reader.

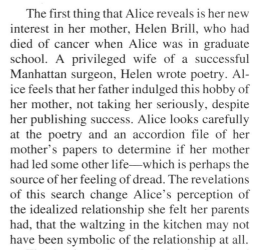

Hilma Wolitzer is the author of the novels Ending *(1974),* In the Flesh *(1977),* Hearts *(1980),* In the Palomar Arms *(1983),* Silver *(1988), and* Tunnel of Love *(1994), as well as the nonfiction book* The Company of Writers *(2001). She has received Guggenheim and National Endowment for the Arts fellowships and an award from the American Academy and Institute of Arts and Letters. Wolitzer has taught writing at the University of Iowa, New York University, and Columbia University.*

The first thing that Alice reveals is her new interest in her mother, Helen Brill, who had died of cancer when Alice was in graduate school. A privileged wife of a successful Manhattan surgeon, Helen wrote poetry. Alice feels that her father indulged this hobby of her mother, not taking her seriously, despite her publishing success. Alice looks carefully at the poetry and an accordion file of her mother's papers to determine if her mother had led some other life—which is perhaps the source of her feeling of dread. The revelations of this search change Alice's perception of the idealized relationship she felt her parents had, that the waltzing in the kitchen may not have been symbolic of the relationship at all.

The dominant dramatic string in the novel is the disintegration of Alice's marriage. The arguments with her husband, Everett (Ev), and their lack of intimacy reach a crisis point over a missing paperweight and their youngest son, Scott. Alice has indulged Scott, who may or may not be involved in drugs but has a history of various troubles. Alice and Everett spar over who is to blame for Scott's situation. In the instance of the paperweight, Alice covers for Scott, who took it one day when he came to get some money from his mother. When the paperweight reappears, Everett discovers Alice's deception, and an argument sends him down the hall, to sleep in the boys' old bedroom. A few weeks of chilly civility end in another argument, and Ev moves out.

This disruption forces Alice to review her relationship with Ev and try to figure out why a once passionate and compatible relationship has languished. As she looks back over their meeting, in a graduate school writing program, to their shared frustrations as writers unable to write, she critiques a relationship that she seems to think may never have been as loving and close as the one she is missing, although what she describes is a strong marriage full of tenderness and strife. Her voice and descriptions are in conflict with the relationship she is describing. This is one of the failings of the story. In the usual unreliability of the first-person narrator, Alice is not convincing. It is never clear that Alice really wants a reconciliation with Ev. She seems petty and intractable and is at her least sympathetic when she is dealing with her marriage.

She seems desperate to be successful, to have a meaningful career, to prove to Ev that she has worth, even though it is never clear that Ev actually demeans her career. She claims that she and Ev had been in competition with each other since graduate school. She says, for example, that she resented his sympathetic treatment after she was fired from her job as "condescending and, at heart, unkind," but because Alice's is the only perception of the relationship, it rings hollow and is self-pitying. Perhaps, however, that is deliberate: the dramatic irony of the narrative. If Alice is really being unfair to Ev, then her pettiness is a symptom of some larger problem.

Alice as professional "book doctor" is another thread in the fabric of her identity. In her role as editor, she feels that she is doing something important by "fixing" people's writing in a similar way that medical doctors like her father fix people's health problems. She discovers Michael Doyle, whose first pages of his debut novel are "exceptionally good." Alice and Michael eventually have a brief but torrid affair, which is perhaps the truest relationship in the book. Alice always sees it as purely physical, as opposite as possible to her relationship with her husband, and she ultimately sees it for what it is, certainly not the answer to her problems. Like the guiltily smoked cigarettes, her affair with Michael is a desperate attempt to be different. Alice recognizes that Michael has the potential as a writer that she never had, and she is able to continue a professional relationship with him even after the affair. She is able to nurture and encourage him, while she cannot, or will not, do the same for Ev.

About midway through the novel, Alice decides to return to her therapist, Andrea Stern, whom she had visited for a few months after she lost her publishing job. In her sessions with Dr. Stern, and in her thinking about them, Alice tries to understand her new obsession with her mother and to uncover a nagging childhood memory that seems to be the cause of her unease. Piecing together a long-obscured memory of what exactly she saw one evening in her father's office when she was ten years old is the driving problem of the novel, but its revelation is more embarrassing and pitiful than liberating.

Looming in the wings of Alice's present problems is her relationship with her father, the once-respected and extremely successful physician whose descent into dementia in the nursing home presses on the consciousness of the narrative even when it is not the subject of the narrative. Alice's helplessness with her father, Samuel, is palpable, and her grief is profound. At this stage in her life, he rarely makes sense, rarely recognizes her, and constantly asks about her mother. Alice cannot get any answers from her father, as his moments of lucidity are fleeting, and it is interesting that his progressive dementia coincides with her feeling of dread and her questions about her mother and her childhood memory. She asks him only when he is unable to answer.

The most clear-eyed view of Alice comes from Violet. A lifelong friend, Violet can see Alice with a frankness that is never cruel but is the most revealing in the novel. While the first-person narrative tries to shape the reader's response to Alice's relationship with Violet, Violet's voice, comments, and insight expose a side of Alice that is vulnerable and flawed, something Alice is unable to admit to herself. Violet's intervention between Everett and Scott show how Violet can react to Alice's blindness in a way that is both honest and affectionate. She refuses to pull any punches with Alice, and that attitude reveals a relationship that is the strongest in the novel.

Much of the action and many of the ideas in the novel are concerned with writers and writing. Alice's frustrations all seem to be tied to her frustrations as a writer, her mother's frustrations as a writer, and her husband's frustrations as a writer. When Michael Doyle and another of Alice's clients, Ruth Casey, are successful with their book projects, Alice finds some measure of redemption, at least vicariously. Alice does come to terms in some ways with her past and her present, and the novel ends with her attempt to reframe her ideas of her future.

The novel is strangely out of time. Alice's conflicts and problems occur in 2003 in New York City, but there is only one mention of time—the word "terrorism" early in the novel. This timelessness is what keeps the novel compelling to the end. Alice is like many Americans, an ordinary person living an ordinary life dealing with ordinary problems, family, aging parents, uncertain career, but the novel is not ordinary at all. Alice herself admits that she reads fiction to get inside someone else's life, because "curiosity and desire and fear made one measly life seem not nearly enough." *The Doctor's Daughter*, rich in description and insight, is a story about human vulnerability, with conflicts that are universal. They are important but not earth shattering, just like ordinary life.

Elizabeth H. Battles

Review Sources

Booklist 102, no. 6 (November 15, 2005): 28.
Kirkus Reviews 73, no. 22 (November 15, 2005): 1210.
Library Journal 130, no. 18 (November 1, 2005): 70.
The New York Times 155 (May 6, 2006): B7-B13.
The New York Times Book Review 155 (March 19, 2006): 19.
Publishers Weekly 252, no. 43 (October 31, 2005): p. 30.

DOING NOTHING
A History of Loafers, Loungers, Slackers, and Bums in America

Author: Tom Lutz (1953-   )
Publisher: Farrar, Straus and Giroux (New York). 363
   pp. $25.00
Type of work: Literary history and sociology

A reflective historical examination of writers and artists in America and Europe who have celebrated the work-free life—prompted by the author's son's apparent dedication to "slackerdom" as well as his own migrations between the poles of laziness and all-out workaholism

Tom Lutz's valuable and readable book swells a tide of recent writing on the meaning and nature of work in the global Information Age. That much low-wage work has become soul-killing, dangerous, or unsustainable is the theme of Barbara Ehrenreich's *Nickel and Dimed*, Eric Schlosser's *Fast Food Nation*, David Shipler's *The Working Poor: Invisible in America*, Mark Robert Rank's *One Nation, Underprivileged: Why American Poverty Affects Us All*, and Beth Schulman's *The Betrayal of Work: How Low-Wage Jobs Fail Thirty Million Americans*. However, even well-paying jobs can be damaging, as Richard Sennett demonstrates in *The Corrosion of Character: The Personal Consequences of Work in the New Capitalism*; here upward mobility is seen as productive of rootlessness, generational strife, compromised family life, and a sense of futility. Allen Wolfe's *Moral Freedom: The Search for Virtue in a World of Choice* powerfully depicts the erosion of the ideals of mutuality and employer-employee loyalty as outsourcing and downsizing come to dominate corporate life.

Is it any wonder, then, that postsecondary, postcollege, and postmodern young people "boomerang" back to their parents, taking up long-term residence on couches and futons? This is where *Doing Nothing* begins, as Lutz's son Cody moves in and commences what seems to be a career of watching television. Recalling his own formative days, Lutz tries to be understanding, but soon enough he is harboring an infuriation whose intensity puzzles him. He cannot suppress the idea that Cody is a major-league slacker—just one more representative of a spoiled and aimless generation. What especially irritates him is that the boy's inactivity seems detached from an interesting purpose. Lutz would have been happy if this work-free lifestyle *protested* something or was a staging event for a move toward, for example, a Buddhist spirituality of detachment. "The couch," he laments, "just seemed like inertia, not the kind of loafing to which one invites one's soul."

So an investigation is launched—into both the origins of the father's feelings about leisure and work and what amounts to a Western literary tradition of celebrating laziness itself. Lutz presents his findings in a loosely chronological way. Thus, his second chapter contrasts Benjamin Franklin, the very architect of the modern work ethic,

*Tom Lutz has served as professor of
English at the University of Iowa and
now lives in Los Angeles. He has also
written* American Nervousness, 1903:
An Anecdotal History *(1991),* Crying:
The Natural and Cultural History of
Tears *(1999), and* Cosmopolitan
Vistas: American Regionalism and
Literary Value *(2004).*

with Samuel Johnson, who "almost single-handedly invent[ed] the slacker." Both men, Lutz notes, confronted a world about to be transformed by the Industrial Revolution, reacting to it differently while nevertheless embracing Enlightenment modes of thought. In the same year that Franklin published *Way to Wealth* (1758), Johnson began his famous *Idler* essays. Here he sardonically rejects famous definitions of humankind in order to establish his own: "Perhaps man may be more properly called the idle animal; for there is no man who is not sometimes idle." The idler is free from envy, rivalry, and strife. He has already "arrived"—at the place that is the natural telos of the species. Unpressured by business, he has time for friends and conversation, for "he who is famed for doing nothing, is glad to meet another as idle as himself."

Chapter 3, "Loungers, Romantics, and Rip Van Winkle," traces the influence of the Scottish magazine *The Lounger*, appreciatively read in the newly created United States. The Lounger differs from the Idler in that he or she (female loungers were singled out) is clearly active of mind, a sort of interdisciplinary gadfly in a time of increased professionalization and compartmentalization. Lutz pays close attention to the Harvard bad-boy Joseph Dennie, "the first truly American slacker," whose trouble with authority makes him a precursor of Marlon Brando's infamous character in *The Wild One* (1953). Editing the passionately Federalist *Gazette of the United States* along with *The Port Folio*, Dennie sided with those who thought too much democracy would bring chaos to the young republic. In the process, claims Lutz, he resisted the approaching regime of industrial efficiency, making useless the work of wordsmiths and connoisseurs, and "men of leisure."

Lutz concludes that self-professed loungers like Dennie "were very much creatures of industrial mercantilism, and their consumerist hedonism . . . was exceedingly modern." The slacker ideal thus contains a contradiction, because it enshrines comfort, abundance, and ease, while denouncing entrepreneurial attitudes that lead to the (mass) production of the furnishings of the good life.

"Loafers, Communists, Drinkers, and Bohemians," Lutz's next chapter, is filled with surprising characters and quotes. Readers learn, for example, that Karl Marx's son-in-law and personal secretary, Paul Lafargue, published a long pamphlet titled *The Right to Be Lazy* shortly after Marx's death in 1883. As Marx had been one of history's purest workaholics, one might suspect a betrayal. In fact, Lafargue remains a true believer, drawing attention to the coming obsolescence of work as mechanized production offers abundant life. Thus, a three-hour workday will soon be sufficient. Uncoerced, joyful participation in intellectual and artistic production is what the working class needs. In a statement worthy of a socialist banner, Lafargue said, "All individual and social misery is born of the passion for work." Consistent with this Epicureanism was his death by suicide in 1911. While still in good health, he and

Laura Marx took poison in their garden so as not to let old age deprive them of "the pleasures and joys" of life. Lutz applauds Lafargue's sense of humor and irony, for here was an against-all-odds slacker, who managed a productive-enough life in the unlikeliest of settings.

Marx's contemporary, Herman Melville (1819-1891), has standing in the slacker pantheon not because of any personal reputation for idleness but for his stunningly absurdist short story, "Bartleby, the Scrivener" (1853). Thoroughly a New York City figure, Melville did not frequent—as did Walt Whitman—Pfaff's tavern in Greenwich Village, "the unofficial center of American Bohemia," according to Lutz. However, by creating Bartleby, Melville provided generations of readers with a prototype of resistance to modern work disciplines.

A Wall Street copyist, Bartleby is at first an agreeable employee. However, he then begins to refuse assignments, stoically and irritatingly saying, "I prefer not to." The employer-narrator, not a harsh man, takes on Bartleby as a kind of philosophical dilemma, offering various scenarios that might motivate this loftily and whimsically indifferent man. These have no effect, and with Bartleby now living at the office, the narrator is the one who finds a different job. Ultimately, Bartleby dies in prison from starvation.

If for nothing else, Lutz's book is valuable as a guide to the evolution of variant models of slackerdom in television, film, and prose fiction. John Hughes's film *Ferris Bueller's Day Off* (1986) and Richard Linklater's *Slacker* (1991) were only the first in a new subgenre. Here, *Wayne's World* (1992), *Clerks* (1994), *Reality Bites* (1994), and *The Big Lebowski* (1998) are representative films. David Gilbert's *The Normals* (2004) "has been called the ultimate slacker novel, since the protagonist is so uninterested in getting ahead that he basically sells his body to science while he is alive, becoming a paid subject in drug trials." Meanwhile, "the avalanche of slacker narratives" is enriched by Elmore Leonard, Carl Hiaasen, and Kinky Friedman, who "focus on low-life loafers."

For all the watching, "down-time," and couch-potato behavior in which Americans engage, they still pay homage to hard work, and they are perceived by other cultures as too dedicated to their jobs. Thus, concludes Lutz, "the figure of the slacker needs to mean different things to different people at different times." The slacker "tradition" that his research has established turns out to be a kind of barometer of the culture's ever-changing appraisal of the role of working and earning in the life cycle. "The history of slackers is the history not just of our distaste for work and our fantasies of escaping it . . . but also a history of complexly distorted perceptions," he writes. Is his son Cody a simple deadbeat or an artist in a period of gestation? He is both, claims Lutz—and neither. As it turned out, Cody soon plunged into the world of Hollywood production, working fourteen-hour days and finding success as a screenwriter.

Doing Nothing is an ambitious and gratifying book, so it is odd to predict that many readers will ask, as they put it down, "Is this really all there is to say?" The explanation for such a response is that while Lutz has engaged a number of important literatures and controversies—sociology, economics, literary history, biography—

some of the most important of these are not addressed. Many young people are happily drowning in "the digital tsunami." Marshall McLuhan, Neil Postman, Todd Gitlin, Neal Gabler, Bill McKinnon, and Mark Crispin Miller powerfully describe the unique allures of an all-entertainment-all-the-time cultural landscape. Cell phones, iPods, DVDs, PlayStations—none of these "converging technologies" are even mentioned by Lutz. A college professor, Lutz does not consider MySpace or Facebook, the latter receiving 250 million hits daily and ranking ninth in Internet popularity. To omit these highly addicting cybernetic activities is inexplicable.

So, too, is Lutz's failure to take up the racial component of "slacker history." (He dismisses this topic in a single paragraph late in the book.) Why would a cultural history avoid America's most popular and damaging image of laziness—the "shiftless" black male? "Coon," "Sambo," "Buckwheat," "Sportin' Life," and "Kingfish" are names that construct a constellation of images and presumed behaviors. In many ways, the American discourse on leisure and work has been centered on the "scandal" of Stepin Fetchit and his precursors. The amount of writing generated on this topic in American history entirely dwarfs the collection of texts with which Lutz works.

Finally, Lutz must also be faulted for fudging the line between scholarship and personal essay. In a largely historical work brimming with quoted material, the decision to not provide notes is inexplicable. Although he provides an extensive bibliography, Lutz deprives his readers of the chance to view the wider context of the quoted material. Here is a kind of "slacking" that is not complex or multifaceted. In this respect, Lutz's work fails because of sheer laziness.

Leslie E. Gerber

Review Sources

Booklist 102, no. 16 (April 15, 2006): 7.
Library Journal 131, no. 8 (May 1, 2006): 108-109.
The New York Times 155 (June 12, 2006): E6.
The New York Times Book Review 155 (June 4, 2006): 11.
Publishers Weekly 253, no. 7 (February 13, 2006): 71-72.

THE DREAM LIFE OF SUKHANOV

Author: Olga Grushin (1971-   )
Publisher: G. P. Putnam's Sons (New York). 354 pp.
    $25.00
Type of work: Novel
Time: Late 1930's-late 1980's
Locale: Moscow, Soviet Union

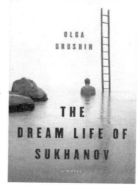

The story of a Soviet art critic experiencing a series of waking and sleeping dreams that bring back to him his youthful ideals and ambitions as an artist

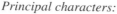

Principal characters:
> ANATOLY PAVLOVICH SUKHANOV, editor in chief of leading Soviet art magazine *Art of the World* and former artist
> NINA PETROVNA SUKHANOVA, Anatoly's wife
> KSENYA SUKHANOVA, rebellious eighteen-year-old daughter of Anatoly and Nina
> VASILY SUKHANOV, selfish, scheming son of Anatoly and Nina
> NADEZHDA SERGEEVNA SUKHANOVA, Anatoly's mother
> FYODOR MIKHAILOVICH DALEVICH, a distant cousin of Anatoly who unexpectedly arrives for a visit
> LEV BORISOVICH BELKIN, artist and estranged friend of Anatoly
> PYOTR ALEKSEEVICH MALININ, father of Nina Sukhanova and a celebrated but untalented Soviet painter
> PAVEL SUKHANOV, Anatoly's father, who died when Anatoly was a boy by jumping from a window

At the opening of Olga Grushin's novel, Anatoly Sukhanov is a content and self-absorbed member of the Soviet bureaucratic ruling class. As editor of the art magazine *Art of the World*, Anatoly primarily oversees the publication of articles routinely condemning Western art and maintains useful social contacts. This comfortable life begins to fall apart after a reception and gallery opening for Anatoly's father-in-law, the celebrated but untalented artist Pyotr Malinin. After a disturbing evening, Anatoly walks out in the rain and meets a friend from his youth, Lev Belkin. Belkin has continued to follow his own efforts at painting, ending up as a shabby figure on the margins of the Soviet art world. The contrast between Anatoly, the successful conformist, and Belkin, the aging bohemian, are stark. After this encounter, though, his own life begins to dissolve and visions from his past intrude increasingly on his awareness.

A growing distance between Anatoly and his beloved wife, Nina, begins to become evident when Nina puts a painting by Belkin on the wall where her father's portrait of her, loaned for display at the opening, had hung. Anatoly begins to be haunted by questions about Nina's relationship with Belkin many years earlier and, insensitive as Anatoly has become, he starts to notice that he and Nina are drifting apart.

*Olga Grushin was born in Moscow and spent her early childhood in Czechoslovakia. She returned to Moscow to study in the 1980's and received a scholarship to study at Emory University in Atlanta from 1989 to 1993. She published short fiction in English in a number of periodicals. The Dream Life of Sukhanov *is her first novel.*

Anatoly's problems begin in earnest, however, when a forgotten relative, Fyodor Mikhailovich Dalevich, shows up at the door of the Sukhanov family's apartment, expecting to stay with them for a week or two. Having arrived in Moscow to research a book on Russian Orthodox icons, Dalevich had been directed to the Sukhanov household by Anatoly's mother. Anatoly himself had inspired Dalevich to begin a career in art while staying with the Dalevich family many years earlier. The protagonist has forgotten this episode in his life, though, as he has forgotten many things left behind him. Still, the contact with the unremembered cousin is the second meeting, after the meeting with Belkin, that send Anatoly into his visions of his past life.

Anatoly relives incidents from a childhood dominated by the longing for a mysteriously absent father. He again sees the crowded apartment where he had lived with his mother and other families and envisions the childhood influence of an aging professor who had first introduced him to art. He is introduced to the dangers of the reflective life when the professor is ridiculed and taunted by the other boys in the household and when the authorities come to arrest the professor, the prerevolutionary owner of the house in which all the families lived.

The beginning of the critic's gradual downfall becomes evident when the staff at his magazine, where he had ruled imperiously, inform him that higher-ups have decided he should take a leave of absence. As Anatoly's professional and family life disintegrate, the dream sequences from his past intrude with increasing frequency. These sequences also move forward through his life, creating a narrative parallel to that of his breakdown. At the same time, it is never completely certain that this is a breakdown. It often seems that Anatoly's dreams are leading him toward an epiphany as much as they are leading him toward a psychological crack-up. It may also be that the epiphany and the crack-up are the same thing, because coming face to face with the truth involves looking into the chaos beneath the apparent order of late Soviet bureaucratic life.

Anatoly becomes aware of the bohemian life of Ksenya, his daughter, who is involved with a popular—and married—musician. This plunges Anatoly back into his own youth in the 1950's, when he and his social circle listened avidly to jazz and studied reproductions of artworks smuggled in from the West. It was at this heady time that Anatoly's friend and fellow artist Lev Belkin introduced him to the beautiful Nina Malinina. Although her father is the mediocre official Soviet artist Pyotr

Malinin, beneficiary of all the perks accompanying Communist Party recognition, Nina shares Anatoly's love of modern art and dreams of helping him achieve his ideals. Over Malinin's opposition, the two of them marry and begin to try to live out the dream of the future that will turn into Anatoly's dream of the past.

Anatoly's ideals shatter when officials stage a show of new trends in art. Soviet leader Nikita Khrushchev's reaction to the new art is so angry that Anatoly and his friends fear they will become permanent outcasts in Soviet society. In fact, Belkin does become something of an outcast, living a bare existence as a member of the Moscow artistic underground. Anatoly considers sticking to his own convictions, but he is dissuaded by his father-in-law. Malinin grudgingly accepts his daughter's husband and offers Anatoly an opportunity to write an article along party lines and thereby become part of the establishment. At first, Anatoly refuses, but Malinin points out that the younger man will only be sacrificing his own family for the sake of paintings that will make no difference to anyone.

Anatoly's success and Belkin's failure seem to bear out Malinin's argument. As Anatoly's life in the present comes apart, he sees in his own family that success can also be hollow. His son, Vasily, seen by Anatoly at the beginning of the novel as an ideal young man, appears in a new character as the dreams from the past wreak their upheaval. Anatoly now sees Vasily as a shallow, self-seeking social climber, interested only in making the right contacts to obtain expensive apartments and elegant clothes.

The most disturbing aspect of Anatoly's dream-driven awareness is his recognition of Nina's distance from him. The domestic comfort he had taken for granted has covered up her disappointment with him and with their life together. The recognition of Nina's disenchantment and the possibility of losing her push Anatoly almost entirely into his dream sequences, and these become almost indistinguishable from the events of his present. This is accompanied, though, by a new understanding of his father's life and death, as he comes to learn facts about his father that his mother had previously kept hidden from him.

Grushin's novel is a multileveled, beautiful piece of work, reminiscent of the fictions of Mikhail Bulgakov and Vladimir Nabokov. She skillfully weaves the dream sequences into the narrative, so that the reader moves back and forth from 1985 to past years with as little warning as Anatoly receives in his psychological time travel. At the same time, the novel effectively retains its forward-moving plot and never completely dissolves into complete subjectivity. Grushin renders Anatoly as a complete human being, a sympathetic figure even in his most arrogant moments, and he becomes more sympathetic as one understands the pressures that have driven him to make his choices.

While the reader may at first be tempted to condemn Anatoly as a sell-out to Soviet bureaucracy, a man who has sacrificed his highest ideals for the easy life, it gradually becomes clear that the good life has come at the cost of real sacrifices. Anatoly has made these sacrifices, at least in the beginning, less for his own advancement than for the well-being of his wife and his children. The novel raises troubling questions about whether the refusal to compromise one's own ideals is necessarily the best choice in many circumstances.

The portrayal of Soviet life is a challenging and useful one for Western readers. Here, a Soviet apparatchik, or bureaucrat, appears as a middle-aged man with local versions of universal problems. His children, young adults, are growing apart from him, and he sees disturbing facets of himself in them. In his daughter, Ksenya, he sees his own youthful rebellious bohemianism and traits that may be admirable but are also potentially self-destructive. In his son, Vasily, he sees the other side of himself, the self-absorbed social climber. Initially proud of Vasily, he grows more appreciative of Ksenya but finds himself deserted by both his children. Having sacrificed his aspirations as an artist for the sake of his wife, he now finds his wife disillusioned with him for deserting those very aspirations. This is not a gray bureaucrat but a human being with problems very much like those of Americans his age.

The Dream Life of Sukhanov can be read as a novelistic rendering of modern Soviet history as well as an exploration of one man's life. As Anatoly's dreams lead him back to his childhood, one sees the drabness and paranoia of the Joseph Stalin era. Anatoly's youthful experimentations coincide with Khrushchev's breaking away from Stalin's suppression and with the brief cultural and intellectual thaw. The crisis that pushes Anatoly into the bureaucratic life is placed at a real event in Soviet history, when Khrushchev angrily repudiated the artistic trends that had emerged from the loosening of the dictatorial grip. Anatoly pursues his placid career throughout the unimaginative but stable Leonid Brezhnev years. His collapse begins at the end of the Soviet era in Russian history, when new social forces rise up to throw the old order into confusion, and Soviet life itself begins to take on a surrealistic character.

Grushin's work would be impressive if it were the product of an experienced author; it is especially admirable as a first novel. She has an elegant style of writing but one that often combines unexpected images and words, perhaps partly a result of the fact that English was not her first language. She brings together complex strands of thought on art, politics, morality, and the experience of being human.

Carl L. Bankston III

Review Sources

Booklist 102, no. 6 (November 15, 2005): 22.
Kirkus Reviews 73, no. 20 (October 15, 2005): 1101.
New Statesman 135 (March 20, 2006): 57.
New York 39 (January 16, 2006): 56-57.
The New York Times 155 (January 5, 2006): E8.
The New York Times Book Review 155 (January 29, 2006): 8.
Publishers Weekly 252, no. 41 (October 17, 2005): 41-42.
The Times Literary Supplement, February 17, 2006, pp. 23-24.
The Washington Post, January 8, 2006, p. BW02.
Weekly Standard 11, no. 38 (June 19, 2006) : 35-36.

THE ECHO MAKER

Author: Richard Powers (1957-   )
Publisher: Farrar, Straus and Giroux (New York). 452
 pp. $25.00
Type of work: Novel
Time: 2002-2003
Locale: Nebraska and Long Island, New York

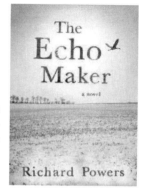

Following a near-fatal road accident in Nebraska, a man is diagnosed with Capgras' syndrome, a rare condition in which he is convinced that those closest to him are impostors

Principal characters:
 MARK SCHLUTER, a twenty-seven-year-old
  slaughterhouse technician who, following a road wreck, is diagnosed
  with Capgras' syndrome
 KARIN SCHLUTER, his thirty-one-year-old sister
 DANIEL RIEGEL, a conservationist, Karin's boyfriend and Mark's child-
  hood friend
 GERALD WEBER, a famous cognitive neuroscientist
 SYLVIE WEBER, his wife
 BARBARA GILLESPIE, an enigmatic nurse's aide
 ROBERT KARSH, a wealthy developer
 TOM RUPP, Mark's workplace buddy
 DUANE CAIN, Mark's workplace buddy

More deftly than any other notable contemporary author not writing science fiction, Richard Powers has managed to inject erudition from a variety of intellectual disciplines, including molecular genetics, theoretical physics, computer science, and musicology into the texture of his fictions. In his ninth book, *The Echo Maker*, Powers appropriates concepts from both ecology and cognitive neuroscience to create an ambitious novel of ideas, one centrally concerned with the very nature of thought and the identity of the thinker.

The story begins late one night on a dark, empty road outside Kearney, Nebraska. The date is February 20, 2002, which rendered numerically as 02/20/02 raises the possibility of some esoteric agency or significance behind the mishap that occurs. A red Dodge Ram truck overturns, pinning its driver and only passenger, Mark Schluter, a twenty-seven-year-old repair technician at a meat-packing plant. After being pulled from the wreckage, Mark remains in a coma for weeks. His sister, Karin, rushes to his side, giving up her job in Sioux City to assist in Mark's recovery. However, when her brother regains consciousness, he insists that although she looks and talks like Karin, the woman hovering over his hospital bed is not in fact his sister but a charlatan pretending to be Karin.

~

A recipient of a MacArthur Fellowship, a Lannan Literary Award, and a James Fenimore Cooper Prize for historical fiction, Richard Powers is writer-in-residence at the University of Illinois at Urbana-Champaign. Among his eight previous novels are The Gold Bug Variations *(1991),* Galatea 2.2 *(1995),* Gain *(1998), and* Plowing the Dark *(2000).*

~

The effect on Karin, who already is distraught over the drift of her life, is devastating. Growing up with a father who was a ne'er-do-well and a mother who was a religious fanatic, she had in effect served as her younger brother's guardian, and his failure now to recognize her compounds her identity crisis. In desperation, she sends a letter to Gerald Weber, a cognitive scientist who seems modeled on neurologist cum author Oliver Sacks and whose best-selling books about bizarre cases of personality disorder have made him into an international celebrity. Intrigued by Mark's symptoms, Weber, a charismatic professor at Stony Brook on Long Island, New York, flies to Nebraska to examine the patient and perhaps add him to the roster of neurological curiosities he has written about in books titled *Wider than the Sky* and *The Three-Pound Infinity*. He diagnoses Mark's conviction that those closest to him are impostors as a manifestation of Capgras' syndrome. "In Capgras," Weber explains to his wife, Sylvie, "the person believes their loved ones have been swapped with lifelike robots, doubles, or aliens. They properly identify everyone else. The loved one's face elicits memory, but no feeling. Lack of emotional ratification overrides the rational assembly of memory." Indeed, as Mark's physical health improves enough for him to go home, the Capgras symptoms spread; Mark comes to believe that his beloved dog Blackie, his buddies Tom Rupp and Duane Cain, and even the entire population of the town in which he lives have all been replaced by counterfeits.

The Echo Maker is a mystery novel in which mysteries planted in the plot point to larger enigmas about the frailty and impermanence of personal identity, the factitiousness of memory, the tenuous bonds between mind and body, and the interconnectedness of all living things. Immediately after the near-fatal accident, when Karin visits her comatose brother in the hospital, she finds an unsigned note beside his bed:

> I am No One
> but Tonight on North Line Road
> GOD led me to you
> so You could Live
> and bring back someone else.

When he regains consciousness and mobility, Mark becomes obsessed with finding out who wrote the note and what exactly it means. He discovers three sets of tire tracks at the desolate scene of his crack-up, and he starts to suspect that someone was trying to kill him the night that his truck swerved off the road—or was he trying to kill himself? If for no other reason, the reader will keep turning the pages of Powers's book in the hope of finding out exactly who or what caused the wreck and why.

An area along the Platte just outside Kearney is the site of an astonishing natural phenomenon that occurs twice a year. For a few weeks, about half a million sand cranes gather there during their annual migration north and south. Each of the five sections of *The Echo Maker* begins with a description of and a meditation on the spectacle of these extraordinary birds, whose habitat is shrinking. The novel even derives its title from a passage recounting ancient myths about a primal language that enabled all species, including cranes and *Homo sapiens*, to communicate. "When animals and people all spoke the same language, crane calls said exactly what they meant," readers are told. "Now we live in unclear echoes." This is a novel composed of and about unclear echoes. Several of the characters struggle to fathom the eerie cry of the cranes, even as the reader attempts to understand what those magnificent, imperiled birds have to do with Mark Schluter's misfortunes.

One connecting thread might be Daniel Riegel, a zealous defender of the sand cranes against human encroachments on their natural environment. He fights to preserve the fragile Buffalo County Crane Refuge, which has been harmed by dams built along the Platte and which could even be destroyed by a commercial consortium's new plan to develop adjacent acreage. Until they had a falling-out fifteen years before, Daniel was Mark's best friend, and he now shares his house and his bed with Karin. Daniel gets Karin a job working with him to save the crane refuge, even as she secretly renews her relationship with Robert Karsh, a wealthy developer who schemes to endanger it. Torn between the developer and the environmentalist, Karin is ever more uncertain of exactly who she is while the reader is teased by conflicting hypotheses that might make sense of the entire novel. Does the fact that Mark's truck wreck occurred beside the sand cranes on a plot of land that Karsh intends to build on help resolve the mystery of what happened on a rural Nebraska road on 02/20/02? Does it help explain the note?

The novel's plot does not so much thicken as dilate through the three trips that Gerald Weber makes from his home on Long Island to the land of the sand cranes. Intent at first with diagnosing not treating the Capgras specimen he finds lying in a hospital bed in Kearney, the famous author begins to doubt both the value and the virtue of what he does. "I'm not an exploiter," Weber tells his wife, "Not an opportunist." However, increasingly mortified by the thought that he has built his brilliant career on the odd maladies of people he studies and then abandons, he doth protest too much: He knows he is a parasite, feeding off the afflictions of others.

One factor that keeps drawing Weber back to Nebraska is his recognition that writing about a man's suffering is not sufficient to fulfill his obligations as a fellow human being: "Responsibility has no limits. The case histories you appropriate are yours." Moreover, when his latest book, *The Country of Surprise*, is universally panned, reviewers attack him personally as a scientific humbug who merely panders to prurient popular fascination with human freaks. Interrogated at a scholarly conference and on television, he feels humiliated, as if the entire basis of his being has come undone.

As he takes increasing interest in Barbara Gillespie, the enigmatic nurse's aide who is extraordinarily attentive toward her patient Mark Schluter, the identity that Weber has painstakingly constructed for himself collapses. He can no longer sustain the illusion of sage scientific luminary. "What did he know about anyone?" he asks himself, convinced that knowledge, especially self-knowledge, is based on self-delusion. Weber, Mark, and Karin, among several of the characters in *The Echo Maker*, experience a disintegration of personality. A student of cerebral structure and function as well as their disorders, Weber is keenly aware of how tenuous the links are connecting different regions of the brain. He marvels at the intricacies of cognition and the complexity of the coordination necessary to produce the coherent pattern that qualifies as consciousness. A decision about whether drugs or behavioral therapy will best help Mark recover raises vexing questions about the ties between mind and body. The self, Weber realizes, is a fiction, the product of an elaborate act of integration that belies its fragmented neurological basis. He broods on the fact that "We were not one, continuous indivisible whole, but instead, hundreds of separate subsystems, with changes in any one sufficient to disperse the provisional confederation into unrecognizable new countries." That dispersion into "unrecognizable new countries" is the mechanism behind the case studies in neurological disorder that have established Weber's reputation. It is also a description of what happens to the star scientist himself.

Moreover, it is also a description of the historical context in which Powers has placed his characters. The terrorist attacks of the year before echo in the background of *The Echo Maker*, a post-9/11 novel that suggests global fragmentation as an analogue to the splintering of personal identity experienced by its principal characters. Conversations occasionally make reference to the buildup to war in Iraq, and Mark's old drinking companion, Tom Rupp, shows up on his doorstep in a National Guard uniform, prepared to be shipped out for combat duty in the Middle East.

Novelists, like other artists, aspire to create *concordia discors*, a unity of disparate, even conflicting, elements. In *The Echo Maker*, Powers assembles such a wide array of materials—Mark Schluter's quest to understand why he found himself in a hospital bed, Gerald Weber's struggle to sustain his identity as a world-renowned scientist, Daniel Riegel's crusade to save the sand cranes, Barbara Gillespie's enigmatic presence in Nebraska—that the work sometimes seems on the verge of splintering into separate novels. "Consciousness works by telling a story, one that is whole, continuous, and stable," Weber contends, "When that story breaks, consciousness rewrites it." With *The Echo Maker*, Powers is not merely telling the story of a man whose identity is shattered when a physical trauma to the head severs the connection between the amygdala and the inferotemporal cortex; the very form of his novel echoes the processes of consciousness in composing and revising the self and the world.

Steven G. Kellman

Review Sources

Artforum 13 (September-November, 2006): 9.
Booklist 102, no. 22 (August 1, 2006): 43.
Entertainment Weekly, no. 900 (October 6, 2006): 77.
Library Journal 131, no. 12 (July 1, 2006): 70-71.
Los Angeles Times, October 1, 2006, p. R12.
The Nation 283, no. 11 (October 9, 2006): 25-28.
The New York Review of Books 53, no. 20 (December 21, 2006): 58-60.
The New York Times Book Review 156 (October 22, 2006): 22-23.
Publishers Weekly 253, no. 27 (July 10, 2006): 48.
The Wall Street Journal 248, no. 83 (October 7, 2006): P13.
The Washington Post Book World, October 8, 2006, p. T06.

THE ECHOING GREEN
The Untold Story of Bobby Thomson, Ralph Branca,
and the Shot Heard Round the World

Author: Joshua Prager (1971-   )
Publisher: Pantheon Books/Random House (New York).
   Illustrated. 498 pp. $26.95
Type of work: Biography and history
Time: Primarily 1951
Locale: The United States, centered in New York

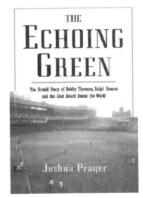

Prager's work chronicles the lives of pitcher Branca and batter Thomson before and after one of the most electrifying home runs in baseball history

> Principal personages:
> BOBBY THOMSON, the New York Giant who hit the home run that won the third game of the 1951 National League playoffs and the pennant for the Giants
> RALPH BRANCA, the Brooklyn Dodger who threw the pitch that Thomson hit, losing the game and the pennant for the Dodgers

Much has been written about the National League pennant race in 1951 and the Bobby Thomson home run that decided it. The Giants trailed the Dodgers by thirteen games late in the season and were assumed by the Dodgers and their manager, Charlie Dressen, to be out of contention. The Giant players and manager, Leo Durocher, were resigned to losing the pennant as well. Everyone assumed the race was over. However, a burst of excellent play by the Giants and miserable play by the Dodgers resulted in a tie at the end of the regular season. A three-game playoff was scheduled with the team that won two of the games winning the pennant. The Giants won the first at Ebbets Field, the Dodgers' home park. The second and third games were played at the Polo Grounds, the Giants' home. The Dodgers won the second game and took a 4-1 lead into the bottom of the ninth in the third. With one out the lead had been cut to 4-2 and runners were on second and third with Thomson scheduled to bat. Branca was called in to pitch to Thomson, who hit the second pitch over the left field wall for a 5-4 Giant win. It became one of the most celebrated home runs in baseball history and made Thomson an immediate hero and Branca an instantaneous goat.

Prager centers his account on the home run and fleshes it out by exploring the two men's lives before and after the hit. However, the focus of the book is on the question of stolen signs and the impact of sign stealing on the home run and on the event's two central figures. The signs at issue are those between pitcher and catcher communicating what pitch is to be thrown. It is much easier for the catcher to catch a pitch if the kind of pitch, fastball, curve, or whatnot, is known. The movement of the ball in flight can then be anticipated. Clearly, the batter would have a much better chance of hitting a known pitch as well, so the pitcher and catcher attempt to share the information with one another while keeping it from the hitter.

The catcher squats behind the batter and with the right hand closed in a fist between the legs opens one or more fingers, pointing them down from the fist, to signal the pitch to be thrown. One finger exposed might mean fastball, two fingers a curve, and so forth. The information in the sign is so important to the batter that elaborate schemes have been concocted by the team on offense to steal the sign and relay (using other cryptic signals) the information to the hitter. In the simplest sign stealing schemes, coaches at third and first base attempt to intercept the sign from a careless catcher. Runners on base, especially second base where the base runner has almost as good a view of the sign as the pitcher, have also been known to steal signs. To counter this, the defensive team uses more complex sign systems. In a simple example, the catcher might give four signs with the fourth one being the one that counts. The sign stealers must know the scheme as well as be able to see the sign. Increasingly more elaborate contests are staged between signers and sign thieves most afternoons and evenings from April through October every year. Prager opines that these contests are part of baseball and this kind of sign stealing is acceptable.

Joshua Prager is a 1994 graduate of Columbia University and a senior special writer for The Wall Street Journal. *His first feature article for the newspaper was nominated for a Pulitzer Prize. In 2001, he wrote an article on the 1951 playoffs, which he expanded into* The Echoing Green.

However, Prager asserts that in July of 1951, the Giants initiated a more devious sign stealing scheme. They stationed a coach in the hidden reaches of their clubhouse in center field. The coach was armed with a telescope through which the opponent's catcher's signs could be clearly seen. After intercepting the sign, the coach relayed the information to the Giants' bullpen by pressing a button that activated a buzzer in the bullpen. The bullpen is where pitchers warm up before entering the game, and the Polo Grounds' bullpen was visible to Giant hitters. The number of buzzes indicated the type of pitch. A member of the bullpen staff responded by moving in such a way as to transfer that information to the batter. Prager reports that this kind of sign stealing, sign stealing aided by devices such as telescopes and buzzers, was considered illegitimate by organized baseball but that there was no actual rule against it.

The early part of the book outlines the logistics and mechanics of the Giants' sign stealing effort and puts it into historical context by tracing the lives of the principal participants and by recalling other historical events of the times. Prager includes a brief section on the history of signaling, including the Stone Age drum, smoke signals, beacon fires, Morse code, and the sign language of the deaf, as well as a more elaborate history of signs and sign stealing in baseball. Prager introduces each chapter with a passage quoted from some literary or journalistic source. The introductory quote for chapter 8, which includes the history of sign stealing and a discussion of other questionable strategies baseball participants use to favor their team, declares baseball players, coaches, and managers to be poor role models for the country's youth. Prager does little more with the idea and he is clearly a fan of the game, so it is interesting that he plants this seed of distrust.

Chapter 12 outlines the lives of Thomson and Branca up to the playoffs. The events are reported by alternating frequently between the two players, giving information on one and then switching to the other. Prager employs this system skillfully; however, readers must pay close attention or they will assign the wrong participant to a given behavior. The times the two players were brought together, as opponents in a game, as barnstorming teammates, and in other ways are included. Thomson is presented as shy and self-effacing, almost implying an inferiority complex, while Branca is described as having a more aggressive and self-confident persona. Both are described as considerate, thoughtful persons with great athletic skills. Early in their careers, each was held to be a potential superstar. Thomson was hailed as the next Joe DiMaggio (one of the greatest hitters of all times), and Branca was declared to be a potential three hundred game winner. Again, Prager links his story with other historical events, recalling each historic event briefly in the appropriate time frame.

In the two chapters that describe the playoff series, Prager again recalls associated contemporary events. The most striking of these is the announcement of the second Soviet atomic bomb test, reported the day of the third playoff game but overshadowed in news reports by Thomson's blast. Another is the development of television. The playoff series was among the first baseball telecasts and the home run may have had a greater impact because of the novelty of television coverage.

The rest of the book traces the effect of the home run on the two men. Neither had the success predicted for him early in his career. Thomson had some respectable years and an especially good year for the Chicago Cubs in 1958. Branca pitched well from time to time for a series of teams including some good outings for the New York Yankees in 1954. It was the only year Branca was with the Yankees, and Prager points out that 1954 was also the only year in a ten-year stretch that the Yankees did not win the American League pennant. Neither could escape the impact of the home run. Branca's role was neither forgiven by Brooklyn fans nor forgotten by baseball fans. Thomson was expected to always produce in similar situations, and though he did so more than once, he could not do so every time and so was a disappointment to some fans and writers. After retiring from baseball each was a successful salesman; Branca sold insurance and Thomson paper products. Again, Prager alternates his reporting between the two and considers the times they were brought together for pictures, old timers' games, autograph signings, and other events—they even sang together at times. As usual, he recalls other contemporary events in appropriate time frames.

Rumors of Giant sign stealing were around before the playoff series, and in time the scheme was exposed. The individual reactions of the two men and the interactions between them in the light of the exposure make for the most intriguing reading of the last chapters. Branca's decision to not bring up the sign stealing, although he learned about it years before it became public knowledge, is one of the most interesting observations; Thomson's humility before and after the exposure is another. Interestingly, the public exposure of stolen signs made no apparent difference in the way people looked at either player's role in the 1951 playoffs.

Prager links the events of his story with other historic events in baseball throughout the book. For example, Thomson was traded to Milwaukee before the 1954 season and broke his leg in spring training. The empty spot on the Braves' roster was filled by Henry Aaron, who was scheduled for another year in the minor leagues before Thomson's injury. As a result, Aaron began his Hall of Fame career a year early. The historic connections outside of sports make the book a bit of a history book as well as a baseball book, and they emphasize the centrality of baseball to life in the United States in the 1950's. For example, when Julius Rosenberg wrote to his wife after the third playoff game, his concern was the Dodgers' loss, not their situation as imprisoned spies, soon to be put to death. Prager takes a few paragraphs to outline the Cold War paranoia of the 1950's. The book is a worthy read for its insights into baseball, 1951, Branca, and Thomson. Prager's mention of other events of the time adds welcome context.

Most reviews of the book mention the exhausting number of chronologically related events that Prager includes, usually considering them overkill. However, the impatient reader can do as some reviewers suggest and skip or skim those digressions. For the patient reader, those numerous asides enhance the feeling of the kind of time it was. A few reviews criticized Prager's elaborate, often clumsy sentences, and there are many. However, if carefully read none obscures the author's intent. Despite these criticisms, reviewers were enthusiastic, praising the work for the depth of the research required and for the scholarship displayed.

The book is quite free of mechanical errors. There is an extensive bibliography, an exhaustive set of notes documenting events described in the text, and a thorough index. Pictures of the people involved in the sign stealing scheme and other aspects of the story add interest. Several pictures of the Polo Grounds clarify the sign stealing mechanics, and two pictures of the field, with players in place and the home run ball in flight, give a feel for the moment. The book's rather mysterious title and the headings for its three parts were taken from a poem with the same title by William Blake.

Carl W. Hoagstrom

Review Sources

Booklist 103, no. 1 (September 1, 2006): 48.
The Boston Globe, October 1, 2006, p. D7.
The Cleveland Plain Dealer, October 15, 2006, p. M5.
Kirkus Reviews 74, no. 14 (July 15, 2006): 716.
The New York Times 156 (October 5, 2006): E8.
The New York Times Book Review 156 (October 8, 2006): 16.
Publishers Weekly 253, no. 23 (June 5, 2006): 50.

EDGAR ALLAN POE AND THE JUKE-BOX
Uncollected Poems, Drafts, and Fragments

Author: Elizabeth Bishop (1911-1979)
Edited and annotated by Alice Quinn
Publisher: Farrar, Straus and Giroux (New York) 367 pp.
  $30.00
Type of work: Poetry

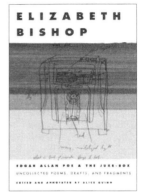

Verbal music and striking discoveries turn up in this new posthumous collection, made even more rewarding by editor Alice Quinn's appendix and copious notes

Elizabeth Bishop was unusual among twentieth century American poets in several ways. She gained a substantial readership, by poetry standards, which is unusual in itself, and she did so by publishing only a handful of books, well spaced over the last three decades of her life. Her poems were spare but not obscure, precise but plainspoken, and concerned with keen observation without neglecting the heart. These were qualities that did much to secure her a favored place among readers, even among those who otherwise rarely dipped into poetry.

Her small published output, mostly contained within four slender volumes, made it almost surprising that when her posthumous *The Complete Poems, 1927-1979*, appeared in 1983, it did not contain a larger and more varied assortment of unpublished work than it did. To readers of poetry, Bishop seemed that rare creature who exerted herself heavily over great spans of time upon a few select verses, honing and refining carefully, without ever engaging in that blizzard of excess most poets go through, and perhaps must go through, in endeavoring to discover their poetic voices. To make Bishop's case more notable, she was undistracted by the demands of an academic life. Although she accepted a position at Harvard in her last decade, Bishop prided herself for many years in leading an existence far from the ivory tower.

For the many readers aware of Bishop's place in American poetry, this new collection, edited by Alice Quinn, must come as a pleasant and long-awaited treat. The poems, fragments, and light verses found in this book are not completely unknown to Bishop readers, since they long have been described, discussed, and sometimes published, in some instances even within the pages of *The New Yorker*, the magazine that first gave the poet a wide audience. The quiet sensibility, the clarity of tone, the concern with close observation of a moment in time, the emotional evenness that was neither effusive nor cold: All the elements that appealed to countless readers of her published works could be found in these works that had not yet reached the eye of the general public. They had remained hidden from general view, either because Bishop herself never reached the point of deeming them fit for print, or because the slow and gradual method Bishop used in composing her poems meant, inevitably, that in the end many would remain unfinished, at least to her eyes. The idea that, to any eyes other than her own, these poems might prove acceptable was strongly suggested in the few manuscripts found and added to the 1983 volume, and it seems firmly established with the publication of this book, *Edgar Allan Poe and the Juke-Box: Uncollected Poems, Drafts, and Fragments.*

Editor Alice Quinn has done what must have been a monumental amount of work in sifting through the many pages of Bishop papers at Vassar College libraries. She has the good luck to have been preceded in her research by Lorrie Goldensohn, who was instrumental in obtaining for Vassar the notebooks of unpublished work placed in the safekeeping of a Brazilian friend of Bishop, Linda Nemer. Quinn is also to be commended for her choice of title, not only for her singling

Elizabeth Bishop won the 1965 Pulitzer Prize in poetry, for Poems: North and South—A Cold Spring, *and the 1970 National Book Award for poetry, for* The Complete Poems. *She died in 1979.*

out of one of the poems of strength and freshness in this large book, which it should be noted is larger than any Bishop published in her lifetime, but also because it points to one of the discoveries represented by this volume.

During her lifetime Bishop was well known to have cited a number of poets as exemplars and inspirations, most frequently George Herbert and Gerard Manley Hopkins but also such closer contemporaries as W. H. Auden and Dylan Thomas. Yet, while the precision and clarity that marked her poetry suggested a kinship with that of America's most original poet of the nineteenth century, Edgar Allan Poe, Bishop's public remarks tended to remain silent on the question. This may have reflected the tendency some feel to downplay early influences; Poe clearly was of large interest to her in the 1930's, to judge from the work in this volume, well before her 1950's arrival as a poet. It may, too, have been the result of the tendency predominant at mid-century to downplay Poe's place in American letters, and to relegate his works to the arena of children's literature. As of this collection's publication, that Poe had major influence on this major poet should go unquestioned.

Lines to be found in the poem "Edgar Allan Poe and the Juke-Box" itself certainly give pointed evidence. "Poe said that poetry was *exact.*/ But pleasures are mechanical/ and know beforehand what they want/ and know exactly what they want." Besides the direct invocation of Poe's critical works, there is the insistent repetition of the third and fourth lines, echoing Poe's methods. The poem describes a darkened room in which the observer feels ill at ease at the nickel juke-box, the drinking, and the sexual tension. The lines that follow seem to state the observer's worries, presumably Bishop's own, about poetry and its exactness and perhaps about its worth and importance. At the end she seems to ask Poe directly whether his "single effect" may be "half as exact as horror here?" As Quinn notes, the poem may have biographic significance in reflecting Bishop's anguish about herself and her poetry, doubts she experienced in advance of the publication of her first book, *North and South*, in 1946, and her move to Brazil in 1951.

Verbal music similar to Poe's appears likewise in other poems, particularly in a group specifically marked with the notation "Bone Key," the planned title of a sequence of Key West poems and a candidate title for her second collection. The poems are "Florida Deserta," describing a Key West town deserted by tourists; "From the shallow night-long graves . . . ," telling of a haunted moment at night near a graveyard; and "The Street by the Cemetery," picturing a street along which the inhabitants sit silently, doing nothing more than gazing out over the town's graves. An appealing musical quality is apparent in all these "Bone Key" poems but especially in "The Street by the Cemetery," with its middle stanza: "They are admiring the long row of white oleanders/ inside the graveyard paling./ The moon goes sailing,/ and hypnotized they sit on the verandahs/ with nothing much to say/ to the neighbors three feet away."

The section containing these "Bone Key" poems is the third one, "1937-1950." Although Quinn indicates Bishop also lived in Washington, D.C., Yaddo, and Nova Scotia during this period, the Key West poems seem to predominate, not only in numbers but also in their freshness and strength. This period proves to have been extremely productive for Bishop.

In the volumes published during her lifetime a few poems of playful fancy appeared that remain as refreshing to read now as they must have been at first publication. Because they hint at an imagination never quite given full play, they seem too few in number, within those collections. A distinct pleasure of *Edgar Allan Poe and the Juke-Box* is the addition to their ranks. Several appear in this "1937-1950" section, with "Dream" being perhaps strongest and of most immediate appeal: "I see a postman everywhere/ Vanishing in thin blue air,/ A mammoth letter in his hand,/ Postmarked from a foreign land." Some readers may prefer Bishop's second version of the same poem, which Quinn fortunately includes in the voluminous notes that occupy the last third of the book, and which has a more sustained and relaxed ending. Another poem, "The walls went on for years & years . . . ," similarly captures a dreamlike vision: "The walls went on for years & years./ The walls went on to meet more walls/ & travelled together night & day./ Sometimes they went fast, sometimes slow;/ sometimes the progress was oblique,/ always they slid away."

Several of the most striking short entries in this volume are love poems. From the "1937-1950" section are two calmly stated but nonetheless warmly evocative works: "Under such heavy clouds of love . . . " and "Valentine." From the fourth section, "1951-1967: Brazil, Seattle, New York," is "Close close all night . . . ," a three-stanza verse with the simplicity of a nursery rhyme that describes lovers asleep together: "close as two pages/ in a book/ that read each other/ in the dark."

One of the most striking discoveries to be found is in this volume's first section, "Poems from Youth." A narrative poem constructed of quatrains of rhymed tetrameter, "Once on a hill I met a man . . . " tells of meeting a man of magical appearance who promises to take the poem's narrator "far away/ To Babylon or Shadow-land." The man delivers on his promise by locking the narrator in a small house set in a place of twilight: "And morning never comes, nor night;/ The shadows never slide away./ Always the four walls are alike—/ Indefinite and gleaming grey." Although someone arrives to speak to the imprisoned soul within the house, the prisoner bids the voice to leave, lest the man return. The poem ends: "And if he came and found me gone/ And his house spoilt, what would he do?" Simple in its presentation, the poem may be placed alongside Bishop's fanciful dream-poems or may instead be taken as allegory.

As Quinn among her copious notes tells of Bishop's turning down a proposal of marriage, and of the loves of her life, who were all women, the poem may be read as the expression of a girl's anxiety at the life her society seems to intend for her: gray imprisonment, even though she may hear a song sung by one outside, whom she glimpses and for whom she "might break down the door."

The structure of this collection has many felicities besides the direct enjoyment offered by the works themselves. Splitting the early works into the three sections of "Poems from Youth," "1929-1936: College, New York, Europe, Florida," and "1937-1950: Key West, Washington, D.C., Yaddo, Nova Scotia," helps the reader gain a clearer sense of the poet's development in the years before and immediately after the success of *North and South*. The following two sections, "1951-1967: Brazil, Seattle, New York" and "1968-1979: San Francisco, Ouro Prêto, Cambridge, Boston," then give pictures of two distinct portions of Bishop's adult life, the former which might be characterized as her Brazil years, and the latter as her Boston years.

The appendix that follows has a number of attractions, including the prose selection "Mrs. Sullivan Downstairs," telling of a time in her childhood while living with her mother's eldest sister near Boston. If it lacks the fine finish of "In the Village," Bishop's short story about Nova Scotia childhood that appeared in her 1965 collection *Questions of Travel*, it is of comparable interest.

Another entry of clear interest is a series of drafts, reproduced in facsimile, of Bishop's villanelle "One Art," one of the highlights of the last collection to appear in her lifetime, *Geography III*, in 1976. This sequence of sixteen facsimiles begins with a first draft that lacks anything remotely stanzaic to its structure and bears the dual possible titles of "How to Lose Things" and "The Gift of Losing Things." The sequence ends with the final, published manuscript, complete with typesetting notes added by the editors at *The New Yorker*, which published the poem in 1975. Exploring the changes is a pleasure—as is reading the raw material of its beginning, which is full of easy, informal wit and humor.

Rarely does it happen that after a book's appendix, one-third of the book still remains. This is the case here, however, and it is a fortunate case, for the information to be discovered in the modestly titled "Notes" is as full of pleasures as are the pages before. *Edgar Allan Poe and the Juke-Box* is almost exhaustively rewarding.

Mark Rich

Review Sources

Antioch Review 64, no. 4 (Fall, 2006): 827-828.
Commentary 121, no. 5 (May, 2006): 82-84.
Lambda Book Report 14, no. 1 (Spring, 2006): 8-9.
Library Journal 130, no. 20 (December 15, 2005): 134.
London Review of Books 28, no. 10 (May 25, 2006): 8-10.
National Review 58, no. 12 (July 3, 2006): 55.
The New Republic 234, no. 12 (April 3, 2006): 33-37.
The New York Review of Books 53, no. 7 (April 27, 2006): 17-19.
The New York Times Book Review 155 (April 2, 2006): 1-11.
Publishers Weekly 252, no. 42 (October 24, 2005): 40.

THE EMPEROR'S CHILDREN

Author: Claire Messud (1966-   )
Publisher: Alfred A. Knopf (New York). 431 pp. $25.00
Type of work: Novel
Time: 2001
Locale: New York City

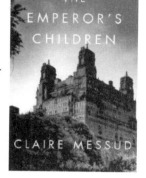

Messud's novel relates the delayed coming of age of three friends in the months before September 11, 2001

Principal characters:
MURRAY THWAITE, a famous cultural critic and journalist
MARINA THWAITE, Murray's daughter and an aspiring writer who has yet to complete her critique of the children's fashion industry
DANIELLE MINKOFF, a documentary producer for a television studio, Marina's college friend
JULIUS CLARKE, a dilettante and freelance writer, a friend of Marina and Danielle
LUDOVIC SEELEY, an Australian magazine editor
FREDERICK "BOOTIE" TUBB, Murray's nephew, a college dropout with aspirations of intellectual sophistication

With only three published books, Claire Messud has established a reputation as one of the more important rising writers in English. Twice a finalist for the PEN/ Faulkner Award and a recipient of a Guggenheim Fellowship, Messud is interested in the life where nothing has proceeded according to plan. In each of her two earlier novels (*When the World Was Steady*, 1994, and *The Last Life*, 1999) as well as the novellas collected in *The Hunters* (2000), Messud tells the stories of characters whose lives are awash in disappointment, who feel keenly their lack of fulfillment. Her novel *The Emperor's Children* deals with a battery of characters whose lives do not seem to reach accord with their ambitions and their pictures of themselves. The novel is in some ways also a narrative about September 11, 2001. Messud is too subtle a writer to make this primarily a story about the national tragedy, however, instead using it as both catalyst and epilogue to the intertwined narratives of her cast of characters.

The novel is loosely focused on three friends, comrades since their college days at Brown, who have collectively crossed the threshold of thirty years of age, the American turning point. First is Marina Thwaite, the daughter of a respected and well-known cultural critic and journalist, Murray Thwaite. Marina signed a book contract years earlier for a cultural critique of children's fashions but has failed to complete (or even write) the book; instead, she keeps pushing her deadline back time after time. The second friend is Danielle Minkoff, a news program and documentary producer for television who keeps missing the opportunity to develop the next big story; she

Claire Messud attended Yale and
Cambridge Universities. Her works
When the World Was Steady *(1994)*
and The Hunters *(2000) were finalists*
for the PEN/Faulkner Award. The Last
Life *(1999) won an Encore Award from*
the London Society of Authors. Messud
was awarded a Guggenheim
Fellowship in 2002.

has never had a serious relationship. The third member of their coterie is their gay friend Julius Clarke, a freelance critic and dilettante who supports himself through "temping" and secretarial work. Each of the three feels that she or he is destined to make a difference or fated to accomplish something special; yet, none of the three has made good on the promise. Marina lives with her parents and fails to work; Julius keeps himself barely afloat with his office jobs and skips from affair to affair; Danielle, the most successful and emancipated of the three, has been unable to produce the program that will make her career. Their senses of themselves seem to be summed up by Marina's declaration to Danielle: "I can't see just taking any dumb thing because it's somehow 'good for me' to have a job. I've got to believe, I mean, I *know* that I'm more serious than that."

The title of Marina's unfinished book is *The Emperor's Children Have No Clothes.* The "emperor" who furnishes the totem at the center of the novel is Marina's father, an aging critic and cultural spokesperson who made his reputation during the heady revolutionary days of the 1960's. Thwaite is a famous intellectual, widely published and successful, an icon of cultural presence whose very eminence seems out of the grasp of the next generation. Like the members of the younger generation, however, Murray is also still filled with the need to be relevant, to accomplish even grander ambitions; he is secretly working on a magnum opus that tries to answer the most human question of them all: how to live.

The circle of the three friends and their revolution around Marina's lofty father, however, are disturbed by the intrusion of three different men. Ludovic Seeley is a magazine editor of a soon-to-launch periodical and a self-styled iconoclast from Australia who is eager to tear down such cultural icons as Murray in order to promote himself. Danielle introduces Seeley to Marina; neither woman realizes that Danielle is attracted to Seeley, but before long the daughter of the icon and the man who would destroy his image are involved and soon engaged to be married.

Also entering the scene is Murray's nephew Frederick "Bootie" Tubb, a college dropout and self-instructing intellectual in training who idolizes Murray and wishes to emulate him. Bootie reads Emerson, considers the kind of thinking he was required to do in college too facile and obvious, and sees in Murray a model for his future self. Perhaps seeing something of his own past in Bootie's hunger for growth, Murray hires his nephew to serve as a kind of secretary. The third (and least important in terms of the novel's themes) interloper is Julius's new lover David Cohen, a young man with a radically different aesthetic than Julius. David also holds to a different notion of fidelity than the licentious Julius.

One of Messud's great strengths as a novelist is revealed in the range and complexity of her characters; the reader finds in her books few paper saints or cardboard villains. Rather, characters are revealed from a variety of perspectives, and even as the reader learns to identify or empathize with a character's point of view, that point of view is suddenly—and subtly—undermined through a shift in perspective to a different character. Ludovic Seeley, for example, in his eagerness to undermine and attack Murray, seems bombastic to Danielle, daring to Marina, and sinister to Bootie. Similarly, Murray is by equal turns sensitive, prideful, arrogant, selfish, brilliant, careless, and caring. Murray clearly perceives himself to be important and quite obviously believes in his own legend. He condescends to his daughter and her friends and has occasionally trampled on his marriage vows. Despite his shortcomings, however, the novel's denouement makes it clear that he is, in many ways, authentic.

In the hands of a lesser writer, either Murray or his unspoken nemesis Ludovic would be the villain of the piece. However, Messud requires more of a reader than a simple assignation or denial of virtue. If Murray, the novel's symbol of the aging baby boomer generation, is the emperor clothed in hubris and self-importance, then what is one to think, the text seems to ask, of these other characters—particularly Marina, Danielle, Ludovic, and Bootie—who define themselves in terms of their relation to him as they orbit around him like planets around a sun?

In a sense, the primary action of the novel reenacts the classic archetype of youth striving mightily to overcome the aged and follows the classic paradigm of the next generation's quest to surpass the previous generation. Marina must prove her worth by leaving her father's house both literally and figuratively. She gains employment (with Seeley), publishes her book, moves out of her parents' spacious Manhattan condominium, and becomes engaged to (and marries) Seeley, the man seeking to supplant her father. Seeley positions himself as the anti-Murray, yet at every opportunity he seeks to follow his example. He tells Danielle that he is coming to the United States from Australia to "foment revolution," just as Murray tells a class of college students about the value of revolutionary activism in the 1960's.

After being spurned by Seeley for Marina (despite the former's ignorance of her interest), Danielle soon finds herself having a romantic affair with Murray. Just as Marina's and Seeley's actions represent their desire to overcome Murray's influence, Danielle's affair with her friend's married father speaks of her own need to live up to Murray's example and expectations. On the other hand, Bootie first wishes to learn from Murray, and then he wishes to become him. Two simultaneous discoveries unsettle Bootie, however, and turn him against his uncle: He finds out about Murray's affair with Danielle and begins reading his uncle's hidden, secret manuscript. His understanding of the book is tainted by his knowledge of Murray's secret life: "He believed now that the Great Man had been an illusion all along, mere window dressing. . . . Bootie felt betrayed, belittled, nullified. He'd pinned his hopes on a hollow man." In response to his newfound animus, Bootie begins writing an expose on Murray for Seeley's soon-to-be-launched new magazine that he thinks will in some indeterminable way diminish Murray—or perhaps teach him a lesson. Bootie's very method—writing an article in a new culture magazine—shows how thoroughly Bootie is in his uncle's shadow.

Julius, on the other hand, confronted with the one serious relationship of his life, finds himself reverting to old habits as he has affairs behind his lover David's back.

Even as he comes to enjoy living in a more fashionable apartment and not having to worry about his financial security, he chafes under the limits of monogamy. The difference between David's view of the world and Julius's is never more obvious than at Marina's wedding to Seeley, and it is not long before Julius's needs drive a final wedge between him and David.

The novel's chronological organization helps to slowly build tension in the story's structure; the novel begins in March, 2001, and each of the major chapter headings is the name of a month; the book progresses inexorably toward September 11, 2001. Marina and Ludovic Seeley's wedding takes place Labor Day weekend, 2001, just before the terrorist hijackings and the destruction of the World Trade Center and the attack on the Pentagon. Even as the various plots of *The Emperor's Children* work toward climax and resolution, the events of September 11 will open new narratives in the lives of the characters.

Wisely, Messud does not overdramatize the events of the day nor does she make any of her characters central players in any acts of heroism or high drama. Largely they are, like almost everyone in New York and the rest of the world on that day, spectators, horrified by the tragedy of the deaths and disturbed by the sequence of events sure to follow in the wake of the terrorists' brutal attacks. Even as Danielle begs—and practically forces—Murray to spend part of the day with her, he leaves to find his wife and to make sure that she and his daughter are uninjured. Seeley is forced to put off the production of his new magazine and takes the attacks almost personally, as if their primary purpose were to thwart his plans.

The three friends are in their thirtieth year in 2001; their childhoods—and presumably their childhood dreams and fantasies—have been laid to bed, just as in some sense the youthful naïveté of the nation has been ended by the events of September 11, 2001. The trio of friends in *The Emperor's Children* will, like those who came before them, have to decide who they are going to be as adults.

Scott D. Yarbrough

Review Sources

Booklist 102, no. 22 (August 1, 2006): 42-43.
Commonweal 133, no. 19 (November 3, 2006): 22-24.
Library Journal 131, no. 10 (June 1, 2006): 108-109.
London Review of Books 28, no. 20 (October 19, 2006): 15-16.
The Nation 283, no. 10 (October 2, 2006): 30.
The New York Review of Books 53, no. 15 (October 5, 2006): 29-31.
The New York Times 155 (August 22, 2006): E1-E8.
The New York Times Book Review 155 (August 27, 2006): 1-10.
Publishers Weekly 243, no. 19 (May 8, 2006): 43.
The Spectator 302 (September 9, 2006): 44-46.
The Washington Post, September 10, 2006, p. BW07.

EMPIRES OF THE ATLANTIC WORLD
Britain and Spain in America, 1492-1830

Author: J. H. Elliott (1930-   )
Publisher: Yale University Press (New Haven, Conn.).
546 pp. $35.00
Type of work: History
Time: 1492-1830
Locale: North and South America

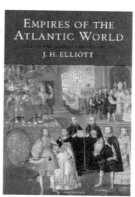

A comparison of two great colonial empires, from their origins to their ends

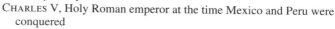

Principal personages:
> ISABELLA OF CASTILE, queen of Spain during the early years of American exploration by Europeans
> CHARLES V, Holy Roman emperor at the time Mexico and Peru were conquered
> HERNÁN CORTÉS, conqueror of Mexico
> JAMES I, king of England during America's early period of British settlement
> CHARLES III, king of Spain during the period of late reforms
> GEORGE WASHINGTON, commander of the Continental army and first president of the United States
> TUPAC AMARU II, leader of the Peruvian native revolt
> PONTIAC, leader of the American Indian effort to drive Europeans out of the Ohio country

In *Empires of the Atlantic World: Britain and Spain in America, 1492-1830*, J. H. Elliott describes how Spanish rulers who found themselves suddenly in possession of vast overseas territories discovered that the strategies for conquest on the Iberian Peninsula had to be modified to suit their new holdings. They had to find ways of conciliating the conquistadores, protecting the natives, assisting the Church, and still make the colonies profitable—and do all this at great distance. Through new institutions such as the Council of the Indies and a centralized administration based on viceroys and governors, and close cooperation with both the secular and regular branches of the Church, they established traditions that would persist to the present day: power exercised from the top, bureaucrats regulating every aspect of economic and social life, strongly differentiated classes, and emphasis on justice, stability, and patronage. At the same time, they made successful efforts to include the diverse peoples in their political and religious systems—not as equals but as represented. Whenever there were complaints, blame could be placed on the governors; credit for redressing grievances was given to the Crown.

It was very different, Elliott shows, in the British colonies. There was no opportunity to exploit conquered peoples or to mine precious metals. Because the British

J. H. Elliott was professor of history at King's College in London from 1968 to 1973, then until 1990 at the Institute for Advanced Studies in Prince, then Regius Professor of Modern History at Oxford until 1997, where he remains as professor emeritus. He received the Prince of Asturias Award in 1996 and the Balzan Prize for History in 1999.

could not incorporate the Indians into their system, they removed them; early efforts to Christianize and "Westernize" them could not be called successful—Indian attacks could be warded off only by excluding them from settled areas, much like the Pale in Ireland. To survive economically, colonists had to find ways by themselves of developing the land's commercial potential.

Land was available in the New World, not so much because there were no inhabitants but because disease cut the native populations so severely and because Spanish injustices in the Caribbean region created a labor problem that lasted well after the importation of slaves began. Sugar and other highly profitable crops required ever-more laborers, workers who, unlike whites, could not quit. There seemed no alternative to the institution of slavery.

Slavery required new codes as well as some difficult choices for the Spanish, as slavery was contrary to natural law, and Spaniards were used to thinking of everything in terms of natural law. Practices in Spain provided slaves with numerous rights. Therefore, once the early tragic decades of Caribbean slavery had passed, Spanish slaves were somewhat better off than British ones.

The British had no experience with slavery, so they adopted policies common in Brazil, practices developed by French, Dutch, and Portuguese colonists of the northeast coastlands. Even in British America, the fate of slaves varied greatly among the island sugar factories, the rice paddies of South Carolina, and the tobacco plantations of Virginia.

Diversity was the principal characteristic of the encounter experience. There were, first of all, the great variety of American Indians, then the various European arrivals—Spanish, Portuguese, French, Dutch, and English. Each group had its different classes, its sometimes unique agriculture (quickly to become modified by local and imported products and animals), and strongly held religious beliefs. In the area of religion, there were not only Protestants and Catholics but also many distinct subdivisions. The Roman Catholics, though seemingly unified, suffered disputes between the secular and regular bodies and among the orders.

Racial mixing provided even greater diversity. The Spanish crown had arranged for those of European ancestry and Indians to have parallel systems of government, but what was the king to do with the colorful mixtures of subjects which were soon produced? According to British policies, people were either white or black, the former associated with freedom, the latter with slavery; yet reality did not quite correspond to that polarity.

In the Spanish world, *Peninsulares* (born in Spain and often sent to America for a few years as administrators, officers, or soldiers) enjoyed the highest status, then Creoles (of Spanish descent but born in the Americas), then American Indians, then blacks. Mestizos (of Spanish and Indian descent) had a difficult choice: If they identified themselves as Indian, they had to pay tribute; if they identified themselves as non-Indian, they were subject to the Spanish Inquisition. Further, all Indians were not equal. The Tlascalans, who had cooperated with Hernán Cortés in overthrowing the oppressive rule of the Aztecs, were given special privileges.

There were competing visions of how to establish a utopia in the New World. Puritans in Massachusetts had their city on a hill, while Jesuits in Paraguay created one of the most interesting directed societies of all time. Elsewhere, Christians sought to make their values effective in daily life and government. The diversity of sects in British America made a state church impossible, while the supposedly uniform state church in Spanish America was riven by disputes among churchmen and church organizations. North American simplicity contrasted with baroque splendor, just as North American economic frenzies dismayed and frightened the settled societies to the south.

Both societies, broadly conceived, were on the move in the 1700's, and an observer who had no sense of the relative rates of change would have said that the Spanish society was superior. That was where the largest cities were found and the greatest yields of silver and major staple crops were produced. Nothing, however, was as it seemed.

If the population of the Spanish empire was growing, it was exploding in British America. This gave British politicians pause. They could see that unless they reigned in their unruly subjects soon, and firmly, they would lose them altogether. Worse, if the colonists were given seats in Parliament equivalent to their numbers, those subjects would eventually become the masters.

If Britain's American colonies had been self-sustaining, as Spain's were, the king's ministers would not have felt the need to require Americans to shoulder a share of the tax burden. If they had been wiser, they would have extended a few seats in Parliament to Americans while keeping real power themselves. Instead, they viewed Americans as a lesser people who had degenerated in both the harsh and soft continental climates. They certainly did not believe that Americans could fight, or would.

British Americans had many advantages when it came to independence. First of all, there was the tradition of self-government, but also there was both a theoretical and practical equality (excepting slaves and Indians) and a widely shared mistrust of parliamentary intentions. Although there were many Tories, they were neither as numerous nor enthusiastic as the Patriots.

Spanish Americans, lacking significant experience at the higher levels of government, tended to be more idealistic. They were certain that they could do as well, if not better, than the administrators sent over by the Bourbon king. They rejected as much of his proposed reforms as they could, as those reforms were all intended to bring more power into the hands of the king and his distant ministers.

Though there were numerous revolts that had limited goals, there was only one serious revolutionary movement contemporaneous with that in British America—the native revival led by Juan Gabriel Condorcanqui. His movement began as a protest against several new practices, most important the requirement that the Indians purchase their goods at the equivalent of a company store. A state monopoly proved terribly grasping, driving prices up and peasants down into debt. Also, although it had not much mattered earlier if Spaniards took native lands, because the population was shrinking, now their numbers were growing. Lastly, a reorganization of government departments had relocated the silver mines in another administration, thereby causing the governor's income to decline, and the recently introduced free trade hurt some local producers.

Condorcanqui, who had been educated by the Jesuits, had been prosecuting a long case in the courts to prove that he was the legitimate heir of the last emperor of the Incas, Tupac Amaru. When he at last lost the hope of becoming a formidable political figure peacefully, he took the name Tupac Amaru II and called on the Incas to rise. He appealed to the Creoles and to churchmen to join him, but they were wary of his emphasis on ancient racial claims and paganism. When those groups remained loyal to Spain, Tupac Amaru's movement collapsed. He was captured and executed in a particularly gruesome manner.

His failure was similar to that of his contemporary, Pontiac, who could not persuade other tribes to put aside ancient quarrels and fight for the common good. Tupac Amaru's Peru was too diverse to work as a unified whole, and so was Pontiac's North America.

It seems that the revolutions in Spanish America would have been long delayed if Napoleon had not overthrown the Spanish monarchy and, after placing his brother on the throne, attempted to institute changes in colonial society similar to those he was making in France. Thus, the first rebels were *Peninsulares* who refused to swear allegiance to the new Bonaparte king. Then the Creoles removed the Spaniards. When the Indians became involved in the revolution in 1812, it quickly became a race war. The cry was originally the same as Tupac Amaru's: Death to the Spaniards. The Creoles in Mexico, too, had correctly understood that their villages would be on the next list.

At length the restored Spanish monarchy twice reimposed royal authority, only to have revolutions at home disrupt the policies intended to pacify the rebels. Many of the revolutionaries were killed. In the end, the new authoritarian governments resembled the old ones.

The contrasts between the Spanish colonies and the British ones were not lost on contemporaries, though few Englishmen were allowed to travel in the Spanish domains. Governmental corruption was obvious—a reminder of the Black Legend, the Spanish misdeeds at the very beginning of the conquests; the backwardness and superstition of the Roman Catholic Church which had been so modified by Enlightenment thought in Europe and which hardly existed in the British colonies; the disinclination to work that stood in such contrast to Yankee hyperactivity; and the seeming stagnation and acceptance of existing conditions when Americans to the north were expanding in terms of population, commerce, and territory under their control.

This was to overstate the reality of the situation. It was not completely in error, but the societies to the south were so complex that even Spanish administrators were unable to balance the particular needs and wants of groups that could be identified by color and class, with some being almost European in tastes and practices, others servile, others essentially savages. What would benefit one group would harm another, and with the state promising to protect everyone's well-being, there was no vital private section to make up for the paralysis at the center.

In British North America, the king's ministers had belatedly tried to create a center, and they had failed. Indians might complain and slaves had to suffer in silence, for there was no effective center to appeal to for protection. The free citizens were busy in furthering their own interests.

William L. Urban

Review Sources

Foreign Affairs 85, no. 5 (September/October, 2006): 171-172.
Library Journal 131, no. 9 (May 15, 2006): 111.
Publishers Weekly 253, no. 11 (March 13, 2006): 53.
The Times Literary Supplement, August 4, 2006, pp. 3-4.
The Virginia Quarterly Review 82, no. 3 (Summer, 2006): 264.
The Wall Street Journal 247, no. 129 (June 3, 2006): P8.

ETHER
The Nothing That Connects Everything

Author: Joe Milutis (1968-   )
Publisher: University of Minnesota Press (Minneapolis).
   208 pp. $29.95
Type of work: History
Time: 1680-present
Locale: Europe, the United States, India, and Japan

This multidisciplinary historical study explores the many meanings of the ether from various artistic, literary, philosophical, scientific, and cultural perspectives

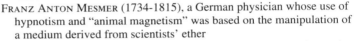

> *Principal personages:*
> HENRI BERGSON (1859-1941), a French philosopher whose idea of the universe as a "metacinema" was "ethereal"
> FRANZ ANTON MESMER (1734-1815), a German physician whose use of hypnotism and "animal magnetism" was based on the manipulation of a medium derived from scientists' ether
> ISAAC NEWTON (1642-1727), an English natural philosopher who used the ether to rationalize gravitational attraction, chemical reactivity, and the behavior of light, electricity, and magnetism
> EDGAR ALLAN POE (1809-1849), an American writer and critic who was "the most energetic transponder of the premodern ether"

The odyssey of the idea of the ether is tortuous, permeated with unexpected developments and populated with fascinating characters: charlatans, geniuses, mystics, and "technopagans." The ether has facilitated such pivotal discoveries as the electromagnetic theory of light (with its subsequent practical applications of the wireless telegraph, radio, and television), but it has also been used by dishonest mediums to prey on the bereaved who seek contact with their loved ones. The ether is an example of a fluid concept because it can be stretched to adapt to a variety of situations. The early history of the ether centered on the cosmological question of the nature of space when it is emptied of all matter. Some scholars see later ideas of the ether as descendants from the ancient Greek philosopher Aristotle's "quintessence," the element composing heavenly bodies but also latent in all things. In the seventeenth century the French philosopher René Descartes treated the universe as a "plenum," completely filled with matter of different sizes, whereas in the cosmos of Isaac Newton ethers filled the heavens and the earth, and they mediated gravitational, chemical, electrical, magnetic, and optical phenomena.

Joe Milutis, whose interests are in art, literature, film, and computer technology, is primarily concerned with the modern, extrascientific history of the ether. Indeed, he does not refer to Sir Edmund Whittaker's monumental work, *A History of the The-*

ories of Aether and Electricity (2 volumes; 1951-1953). Milutis's book is not a systematic treatment of the ether in philosophy, science, or the arts. Rather, it is "a meditation," in roughly chronological order, on some of the many meanings of the ether on both academic and popular levels in both historical and contemporary cultures.

    Ether: The Nothing That Connects Everything has a bipartite structure, with both parts consisting of two chapters. The book also has an introduction, conclusion, and an extensive

∿

Joe Milutis is an assistant professor in media arts at the University of South Carolina. His teaching centers on sound art with an emphasis on experimental media. His research interests are in avant-garde film and video. His writings have appeared in such publications as ArtByte *and* Film Comment.

∿

and helpful set of notes. The introduction, which includes a capsule survey of the ether from the ancient period to the seventeenth century, introduces some of Milutis's principal themes, for example, the ether as a "superflux of sky" and "technology and the ether." The ether is a "superfluid" concept because it overflowed its early cosmological meanings when later scientists, artists, philosophers, and writers extended its significance. Even after theoretical physicist Albert Einstein banished the ether from physics in 1905, it made a triumphal return through new technologies such as radio, which Milutis calls the "ethereal medium par excellence," and the computer, whose systems of networks provide the ether with a seemingly palpable presence, which may create a new "ethereal culture."

    Part 1 of *Ether*, "Radiation and Intellect," deals with how such thinkers and artists as Anton Mesmer, Edgar Allan Poe, and Federico Fellini transmogrified the luminiferous (or "light-bearing") ether of the scientists into something that suited their medical or artistic purposes. Mesmer believed he could manipulate the ether through magnetism and hypnotism to cure human illnesses, but such scientists as Antoine Lavoisier and Benjamin Franklin refuted his claims, accusing him of a retrogressive introduction of occult and magical forces into science. Edgar Allan Poe, who published in both scientific and literary journals, was attracted by the ideas of Mesmer, particularly the ether as massless matter transfusing all things and serving as a vehicle for spiritual forces. Both Poe and Mesmer believed that the ether could be the source of powerful creative and curative energies. In the twentieth century Federico Fellini, in such films as *Le notti di Cabiria* (1957; *Nights of Cabiria*), *8½* (1963), and *Giulietta degli spiriti* (1965; *Juliet of the Spirits*), exhibited his interest in hypnotism and séances, and Milutis sees this filmmaker as open to "the creative energy of the mesmeric continuum."

    Milutis regards the years from 1880 to 1905 as "the era of the disappearing ether" or "ether's crisis period." Experimental physicists failed to discover any evidence for the earth's motion through the ether, and Einstein found that he did not need the ether to probe the universe's deepest mysteries. Nevertheless, playwrights, philosophers, theosophists, yogis, and even cartoon animators discovered an "inner way" to the ether. For example, the theosophist Helena Petrovna Blavatsky believed that the latent spiritual power of humans was almost boundless and that the ether served as a bridge between ancient wisdom and modern science. French philosopher Henri Bergson believed that humans perceive the world through a stream of consciousness. For him, human perception is a form of cinematography or chronophotography in which humans pluck moments from an ethereal whole, just as a filmstrip captures instances of visual experience. In his analysis of August Strindberg's *Ett drömspel* (pb. 1902; *A Dream Play*, 1912), Milutis sees this playwright as striving to create a new theatrical experience between "base matter" and the "mental ocean" of humanity. In the late twentieth century many of the science-inspired stories created by Japanese animators centered on fictional battles fought "not over material resources but over mental energies."

While Milutis draws on twentieth century examples in the first part of *Ether*, part 2, "The Lovely Intangibles," concentrates more fully and extensively on modern ethereal developments. In particular, he is concerned about what he calls the "industrialization of the ether." For example, military and governmental organizations made standardization and allocation of radio frequencies a priority, which Milutis interprets as transforming the ether into property, thereby creating a radiophonic world. Jean Cocteau in his film *Orphée* (1950; *Orpheus*) explored this new ethereal world, and Jack Spicer did something similar in his book *The Heads of the Town up to the Aether* (1962), in which he called poetry "a machine to catch ghosts." Science-fiction writer Arthur C. Clarke explored the evolution of humans into ethereal creatures, and Philip K. Dick in his futurist stories analyzed the interactions of cosmic intelligent ethers with earthly humans. Various artists, both mainstream and countercultural, have been influenced by the ether. Leon Theremin invented an "Aetherophon" (later known by his name) that made the ether audible through the manipulation of radio signals. Other musicians created various other electronic devices to get in touch with the "vibrational universe."

Milutis is also interested in the mainstream media's treatment of ethereal themes. When ordinary people hear the term "ether," they probably think of the anesthetic, which is the common name for diethyl ether, a chemical compound. In the nineteenth century, when this ether's anesthetic properties were discovered, the Russian chemist Dmitri Mendeleev tried to isolate another chemical ether that he believed was an essential component permeating the universe, and he even estimated its weight (nearly one-millionth of a hydrogen atom's mass) and its speed (about 2,250 kilometers per second). In twentieth century media, Milutis has discovered other ethers, for example, a "Communist ether" and the "ether of a United States sky." He even goes so far as to identify capitalism with an ether, because capitalism restructures our experience of the temporal. He uses the television coverage of the first landing of humans on the moon in 1969 to analyze the new world of a collective human consciousness created by this "videospace." He compares this "videosphere" to the "noosphere" of the French Jesuit paleontologist and philosopher Pierre Teilhard de Chardin, who believed a layer of reflective human thought existed around the earth.

Information, particularly computer data, has become the newest ether, according to Milutis. Some see computers as ethereal machines, and others see computer networks as independent republics in ethereal space. This new ether offers the hope of material and spiritual progress, but, like ethers of the past, it has the potential to compromise or destroy human freedom. Because the ethers generated by scientists can be tested and, if falsified, discarded, the extrascientific ethers, which often are beyond the cold grasp of rational analysis, will continue to appeal to people in search of ideas that make sense of how they relate to the universe and to each other. If these new ethers turn out to be illusions, so be it, says Milutis, everyone has "an inalienable right to illusion." These tenuous ethers provide humans with a means of exploring the unanalyzable in human experience, because hidden ethers often determine what is concretely experienced but otherwise mysterious.

Milutis admits that the ultimate meaning of the ether may be that it can never be fully understood. However, certain scientists would respond that particular ethers, for example, the luminiferous ether, can be understood. Milutis claims that this ether was thrown out of science for good at the start of the twentieth century, but this did not mean the end of ethers in science. Einstein himself, in 1915, showed that a massive object could curve space, and curved space (which is not directly perceivable) instructs matter on how to behave (which can be precisely measured). Other modern physical theories, such as quantum electrodynamics, envision empty space as filled with energy fluctuations. This "nothing," that is, empty space, contains potentialities for explaining everything. Indeed, some theoreticians attribute the creation of the universe to an energy fluctuation in empty space. In 2006 a group of Oxford physicists reincarnated the ether in a new form in order to explain the puzzle of dark matter, the mysterious material needed to account for certain galactic data. These new scientific ethers represent yet other nothings that connect everything, and so the quest mentioned in Milutis's subtitle continues not only in the arts but in science as well.

Robert J. Paradowski

Review Sources

Consciousness, Literature, and the Arts 7, no. 2 (August, 2006).
Reference and Research Book News 21, no. 3 (August 1, 2006).

EVERYMAN

Author: Philip Roth (1933-　　)
Publisher: Houghton Mifflin (Boston). 182 pp. $24.00
Type of work: Novella
Time: 1933-2004
Locale: Elizabeth, New Jersey, and the Jersey shore

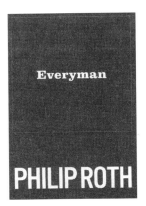

The life story of an unnamed man recounts his idyllic youth in a loving family, his three marriages and divorces, his career in advertising, his retirement, his illnesses, and his death

Principal characters:
UNNAMED NARRATOR
UNNAMED MAIN CHARACTER
HIS MOTHER and FATHER
HOWIE, his older brother
CECILIA,
PHOEBE, and
MERETE, his three wives
RANDY and LONNY, the angry sons of his first marriage
NANCY, the loving daughter of his second marriage
MILLICENT KRAMER, a widow and student in the art class that the main
　　character teaches when he retires to the Jersey shore

Anyone who lives into old age becomes all too familiar with illness and death. It is hardly surprising, then, that older writers find themselves drawn to examining these hard realities. In the past few years, for example, backward glances, dark thoughts, and last things have been prominent parts of works as diverse as Saul Bellow's *Ravelstein* (2000), John Updike's *Villages* (2004), Joan Didion's *The Year of Magical Thinking* (2005), and the late poems of Stanley Kunitz and Czesław Miłosz.

At seventy-three, Philip Roth has had his own share of medical problems and has suffered the personal losses and brushes with mortality that are the lot of someone his age. However, he has been writing about these subjects since the beginning of his fifty-year career. In fact, although he may be best known for treatments of the male body as a source of sex and desire which discomfit or offend many readers, in retrospect it seems that he has written nearly as much about the body as a site of illness and death. His first published story, "The Day It Snowed" (1954), concerns a young boy's first experience of the reality of death and his own death shortly afterward. Roth's first full-length novel, *Letting Go* (1962), begins with a letter from its main character's dead mother. The series of novels about the life and career of his alter-ego Nathan Zuckerman, collected in *Zuckerman Bound* (1985), treats the deaths of both of Zuckerman's parents as well as his own serious illness. *The Counterlife* (1986) imagines the death not only of Zuckerman's brother but of Zuckerman himself.

Since *The Facts: A Novelist's Autobiography* (1988), written after Roth had suffered a serious breakdown and while his father was dying, these subjects have been a central concern of nearly all of his work. *Patrimony: A True Story* (1991) recounts his father's life, illness, and death. *Operation Shylock* (1993) begins with a harrowing description of the suicidal depression its author faced during that 1987 breakdown, which occurred after taking Halcion for an injury. *Sabbath's Theater* (1995) is a long cry of rage against the death of loved ones and the prospect of extinction. Each of the novels in Roth's American trilogy—*American Pastoral* (1997), *I Married a Communist* (1998), and *The Human Stain* (2000)—takes the form of an increasingly isolated and debilitated Nathan Zuckerman recounting and trying to understand the life of a central character who has died. The focus of *The Dying Animal* (2001) is stated in its title. Key moments in Roth's best-selling historical novel *The Plot Against America* (2004) concern the war wounds of young Philip's cousin and the deaths that occur in a Charles Lindbergh-led fascist America.

Philip Roth is recognized as one of America's most distinguished novelists. He has twice won the National Book Award, the PEN/Faulkner Award, the National Book Critics Circle Award, and the W. H. Smith Award for the Best Book of the Year in Britain. He was awarded the Pulitzer Prize for American Pastoral *(1997) and received the National Medal of Arts at the White House in 1998.*

"Can you imagine old age?" the seventy-year-old monologist David Kepesh asks his unidentified listener in *The Dying Animal*. "Of course you can't. I didn't. I couldn't. I had no idea what it was like. Not even a false image—no image. And nobody wants anything else. Nobody wants to face any of this until he has to." Roth has never been an advocate of avoidance; on the contrary, talking about what most people leave undiscussed has been an important part of his stock in trade. So, in this new little book on one of the largest of subjects, "Nobody" becomes "Everyman," and Roth not only imagines what old age is often like, not only creates a seventy-one-year-old man who must face it, but also asks his readers to face it, too—in all its loss, regret, physical decline, and mental confusion but also in its overwhelming memories, nostalgia, and tenderness.

Roth described the book to an interviewer as "very dark," and there is no doubt that it is. It is also masterfully crafted, beautifully written, courageous, and deeply touching—especially for those who have experienced what it describes in their parents or grandparents, their friends, their loved ones, or themselves.

While its title is an allusion to the late fifteenth century medieval morality play of the same name—an allegory in which Everyman meets Death and must review his life and put aside the false values of this world in order to find redemption and salvation—it also refers to the popular meaning of the word in modern times: the idea of a common man whose experiences are representative, if not wholly typical. Roth's unnamed Everyman, like many, has been married and divorced, has injured children as well as former wives by abandoning them to seek happiness with other women, and has had a successful if not deeply satisfying career. He finds his dreams of a pleasant retirement shaken and then shattered by illness, and becomes increasingly isolated and depressed as medical procedures, death, and bad temper cut him off from the people who have mattered most in his life. He spends more and more time remembering the past (especially his parents and his innocent boyhood), vacillates between justifying himself and his life and despairing at the mistakes he has made, makes plans he cannot realize as his constantly failing powers betray him, and confronts all of this without the consolations of religious faith or belief in an afterlife.

The novella contains echoes of William Shakespeare's *King Lear* (c. 1605-1606) and *Hamlet* (c. 1600-1601) as well as Leo Tolstoy's *Smert' Ivana Il'icha* (1886; *The Death of Ivan Ilyich*, 1887), Thomas Mann's *Der Tod in Venedig* (1912; *Death in Venice*, 1925) and *Der Zauberberg* (1924; *The Magic Mountain*, 1927), and Aleksandr Solzhenitsyn's *Rakovy korpus* (1968; *Cancer Ward*, 1968) as well as the medieval morality play. What it echoes most clearly, however, are characters and episodes from Roth's previous fiction and, especially, the two works of nonfiction—*The Facts* and *Patrimony*—in which he has told his readers most about his own boyhood and his family. His Everyman's father is much like the Herman Roth described in the memoirs and also combines qualities of Herman and his younger son, Philip.

Like both fathers, Everyman's philosophy is rooted in hard work and indomitability. Like Herman Roth and his son, the novella's septuagenarian is deeply connected to the past. ("You mustn't forget anything—that's the inscription on his coat of arms," Philip thinks of his father in *Patrimony*.) Like Philip, his Everyman has operations for a hernia at nine and appendicitis at thirty-four and undergoes a quadruple bypass at fifty-six. In addition to having loving and protective parents, they share an admired older brother and memories of a happy boyhood growing up in New Jersey.

The novella's power owes as much to its narrative form as to its subjects. Its first three words are "At the cemetery"; its last three, "from the start." It begins at the end—his funeral—and then goes back to recount his life, concluding on the operating table where he dies, thinking about his beginnings rather than his end, two days before that funeral.

The first fifteen pages of the novella, devoted to that funeral, which introduce all of the book's themes, images, and major characters, are simply extraordinary. The old Jewish cemetery in Elizabeth, New Jersey, where he is being buried next to his parents is described by his daughter, Nancy, in terms that could as easily be applied to the deceased, whose body bears the scars of ten operations, and to many others like him:

> Things have rotted and toppled over, the gates are rusted, the locks are gone, there's been vandalism . . . looking around at the deterioration here breaks my heart—as it probably does yours, and perhaps even makes you wonder why we're assembled on grounds so badly scarred by time.

Then his older brother, Howie, speaks in the pitch-perfect, plainspoken words and cadence of a former Jersey boy that no one has ever captured as well as Philip Roth: "My kid brother. It makes no sense. . . . Let's see if I can do it. Now let's get to this guy. About my brother . . . "

Rhyming with Nancy's reference to time, Howie reminisces about his little brother's youth, telling about how much he loved to spend it with the hundreds of discarded watches in the back room of their father's jewelry store; how he claimed their father's Hamilton watch after his death and wore it until two days before, when he entered an operating room for the last time; and how Nancy has now put a new notch in the band and is wearing it on her wrist. The angry sons then approach the grave. One cannot speak and looks as though he is going to retch. His older brother grabs a clod of dirt, throws it down onto the casket, and says "Sleep easy, Pop," while "any note of tenderness, grief, love, or loss was terrifyingly absent from his voice."

The unidentified narrator, who shares the telling of the story with the thoughts and recollections of its unnamed main character, then closes the section with the observation that.

> Up and down the state that day, there'd been five hundred funerals like his, routine, ordinary, and except for the thirty wayward seconds furnished by the sons—and Howie's resurrecting with such painstaking precision the world as it innocently existed before the invention of death, life perpetual in their father-created Eden, a paradise just fifteen feet wide by forty feet deep disguised as an old-style jewelry store—no more or less interesting than the others.

The next section begins with the main character lying in bed the night before the fatal surgery "remembering as exactly as he could each of the women who had been there waiting for him to rise out of the anesthetic in the recovery room" after each of his operations. The rest of this episodic novella proceeds to review his life in scenes tied to his medical history that blend into memories of the major events in his life. Many of these episodes and memories—especially his thoughts and his conversations with his parents before his hernia operation at nine, his father's funeral, the story of the widow Millicent Kramer, the words his second wife Phoebe says when she learns of his affair with a model which destroys their marriage, his recollections of riding the waves at the Jersey shore as a boy, and the visit he makes to his parents at the same Elizabeth cemetery where he will soon be buried himself—are unforgettable.

"I'm seventy-one. Your boy is seventy-one," he says aloud to his parents at the cemetery in the book's final pages. "Look back and atone for what you can atone for, and make the best of what you have left," his father replies. "Good. You lived," says his mother. "He couldn't go," the episode concludes. "The tenderness was out of control. As was the longing for everyone to be living. And to have it all all over again." In *Everyman*, Philip Roth manages to write a serious book about death and dying that is this full of life and longing.

Bernard F. Rodgers, Jr.

Review Sources

The Atlantic Monthly, May, 2006, p. 120.
Booklist 102, no. 13 (March 1, 2006): 46.
The Nation 282, no. 21 (May 29, 2006): 14-16.
The New Republic 234, no. 19 (May 22, 2006): 28-32.
New Statesman 135 (April 24, 2006): 44-45.
The New York Review of Books 53, no. 10 (June 8, 2006): 8-12.
The New York Times 155 (April 26, 2006): E1-E9.
The New York Times Book Review 155 (May 7, 2006): 1-10.
The New Yorker 82, no. 11 (May 1, 2006): 82-87.
Newsweek 147, no. 18 (May 1, 2006): 63.
Publishers Weekly 253, no. 8 (February 20, 2006): 132.
The Washington Post, May 14, 2006, p. BW07.

EVERYTHING ELSE IN THE WORLD

Author: Stephen Dunn (1939-   )
Publisher: W. W. Norton (New York). 93 pp. $23.95
Type of work: Poetry

The fourteenth full-length collection of poetry from Pulitzer Prize winner Dunn, this work artfully explores notions of desire, particularly in relation to marriage, aesthetics, love, and social mores

Stephen Dunn's *Everything Else in the World* asserts the sensibility of a man as fascinated by the world's ambiguities as those within his heart. To explore those simultaneities, Dunn makes a theme of desire, forcing his readers to rethink its implications in ontology, propriety, art, marriage, love, and more. Throughout the book Dunn works in his trademark voice: avoiding the vatic, attending to idiom, and articulating the subtlest nuances of emotion. Likewise, he thinks in his typical Hegelian fashion: offering an idea, suggesting its counterpoint, and then beginning again from the resultant synthesis. Consequently, the infrastructure for each of this book's thirty-eight poems will read as aesthetically and intellectually familiar to Dunn's long-time readers, who will be both surprised and delighted by the strikingly unprecedented, impassioned, and extended use of love poetry.

Comprising the final section of this polished, tripartite book, the love poetry achieves a newfound intensity and complexity for Dunn. Certainly his previous books include a variety of exquisite, individual love poems, such as "Juarez" in *The Insistence of Beauty* (2004) and "Instead of You" in *A Circus of Needs* (1978). Similarly, his sinuous, supple long poem "Loves," from *Landscape at the End of the Century* (1991), modulates variations on forms of love into a cohesive, extensive catalog of love's myriad manifestations in the speaker's life. In *Everything Else in the World*, though, the thirteen-poem investigation of love combines desire with tenacity to form a sustained, transformative experience for the reader.

This new love poetry forces the reader to engage a novel network of considerations, thereby creating a new landscape of amorous thought and feeling. Strategically, this new landscape begins modestly, with a set of three conventional love poems about a speaker's amorous infatuation with his beloved. The first of those poems, "Infatuation," introduces love as an irrational, irresistible power capable of overwhelming even the wiliest, most experienced connoisseurs of romance. Dunn then inflects that universal, inevitable helplessness with the section's second poem, "The Kiss," which bursts with sensual rhythm and metaphor. In other words "The Kiss" makes physical the emotion of "Infatuation," and the combined effect of the two poems is very moving synesthetically.

However, Dunn revokes that conjured pleasure from the reader by making its ab-

∼

Stephen Dunn's poetry has won many awards, including the 2001 Pulitzer Prize, the 1995 Academy Award in Literature from the American Academy of Arts and Letters, three National Endowment for the Arts fellowships, and grants from the Guggenheim and Rockefeller Foundations. He is the Distinguished Professor of Creative Writing at Richard Stockton College.

∼

sence the subject of the third poem, "Summer Nocturne." A lyrical paean to an absent beloved, the poem is a lamentation on loneliness, with the speaker pitying his isolation before recognizing within it his beloved's indelible presence. That epiphany enlivens him such that he even departs from the poem, which concludes in an abridged final stanza. More precisely, the first three stanzas are each five lines of despair, but the final stanza concludes contentedly after three. Thus, within the section's first three poems Dunn has masterfully titillated his readers by presenting them with an ardent love, concentrating it erotically into a kiss, and then snatching it away—only to return it at the last moment, and then disappear with it again.

Following "Summer Nocturne," the network of love poems takes an abrupt, radical turn with the poem "Bad Plants." An exploration of plant names as metaphors for human behavior, the poem investigates and blurs the divide between socially acceptable and socially objectionable forms of desire. Ultimately the latter prevails, and Dunn concludes with irreverent praise for followers of love's imperatives, however seemingly selfish and destructive the consequences. Thus the poem exhorts its readers to liberate their hearts recklessly from fears of mortality and propriety, and the poem's linguistic play is as pleasurable and potent as it is precise.

Where "Bad Plants" celebrates impulsive behavior, the subsequent poem, "The Slow Surge," honors patience, particularly its potential to extend precious moments of postcoital bliss. Here the rhythm of the poetry slows to a leisurely pace, and the heavily end-stopped lines imbue the poem with stability and strength. Thus Dunn elegantly invites his readers into the private, calm pleasure, though its consequences will prove confoundingly complex.

The complexity of amorous entanglement is exemplified in the subsequent poem, "At His House," which presents a fraternal relationship between two presumably older men who have forfeited intimacy in their respective love lives from a fear of openness with their partners. In relation to the preceding love poems, such a withdrawal is implicitly a form of failure, however understandable or common it may be. More frustratingly, the poem concludes on a perverse note of commiserative pleasure, perpetuating the amorous failures into infinity.

From that pit of self-retardation, Dunn emerges by changing pace with the ardent, effusive passion of "Cardinal Cardinal." Even the title of the poem is intrinsically emphatic due to the verbal and dactylic repetition, and this intensity permeates the poem. Specifically Dunn depicts a male cardinal's compulsion to confront his male challengers, however false their provocation and therefore unnecessary his response. Regardless, the bird overcomes his challengers and locates his mate, whom he delicately regales and seduces at the poem's close. Again, note the arc of the work: Dunn shifts speeds and pitch, working in failure and triumph, celebrating pathos, ecstasy, and confusion. That variation proves remarkably illustrative and affective within the thematic context of desire, and only half of the love poems have been engaged thus far.

After the physical insistence of "Cardinal Cardinal," Dunn drifts off to explore love more obliquely with the symbiotic poems "I Caught Myself Thinking the Horizon" and "Poker Night in Tornado Alley." These poems map the routes of a specific human being through time and space, and along those routes, Dunn poignantly illustrates each human being's intrinsic potential for adventure, danger, joy, loss, and reward.

More specifically, "I Caught Myself Thinking the Horizon" is a subtle, haunting reflection on wasted life and smothered desire. To elucidate this, Dunn presents a speaker short-circuited into inertness by his presumptions of the laboriousness of experience and the tyranny of his imagination. Consequently, he stagnates in his daily life, and the poem concludes with the sky's horizon as a metaphor for unreachable goals in life, which will vanish like the speaker himself.

After that poem's stagnation comes the rowdy "Poker Night in Tornado Alley," which focuses on a lively poker game in rural Minnesota. The poker players need to evacuate town due to an encroaching tornado, but they cannot tear themselves from their game until the final moment. The resultant allegory is clear: Some things are more important than one's physical health, which must at times be risked. Dunn expresses this with zest and bravado, invigorating his readers the way the poker game invigorates its players. Especially compelling are the final four lines, which enact the dizzying self-absorption of a mind frenzied by the need to gamble.

Dunn then shifts pace and tone again with the meditative, becalming poem "Now Wonder." Its ontological concerns continue to be one's need to challenge the arbitrariness of experience, but here the tone is mollifying and carefree. The speaker is outdoors in the Adirondacks with his dog and his beloved, with the humans sipping margaritas while watching the dog at play. Above them, the night sky glitters with stars, and the lovers sit contentedly at ease in the universe.

Then, as if meanly throwing a rock into a lake's pretty surface, Dunn shatters the halcyon splendor of "Now Wonder" with the gritty poem "Cut and Break." Filled with hard, tiring consonance, the poem is an allegorical narrative about masons building a new walkway to the speaker's house. Their labor is continuous, methodical, and exacting, and the poem clearly stands as an ars poetica for Dunn. Particularly, the sweet appeal of the intricate labor becomes apparent, and within the context of the serialized love poems that labor also serves as a metaphor for one's ineluctable drive to create and maintain love in life; syllogistically, the exhausting labor of writing poems then becomes an expression of love.

As the penultimate poem of the third section and, consequently, of the book, "Explanations" seemingly offers comfort and finality with its title. However, one of Dunn's most winning traits is his unreliability; if a poem begins with poise and calm, then it rarely ends that way. Thus, as predictably unpredictable as ever, Dunn quickly dismantles that initial, titular ease by introducing in line three the poem's subject: infanticide.

Specifically Dunn investigates the relationship of desire to infanticide, which he contemplates from a Nietzschean perspective. He posits the ethics of infanticide as a burden upon human parents, who are encumbered by their possession of memory. By contrast, the poem's nonhuman animals (silver foxes) can kill their children because foxes lack the memory and, therefore, the history requisite for human suffering. Thus, by the poem's logic, history would result in unhappiness for an infanticidal parent, though Dunn tweaks the idea of infanticide one final time by concluding the poem with chilling dialogue from serial killer John Wayne Gacy, who endorses a parent's right to infanticide. Thus the comfort of a presumably "explanatory" poem dissolves into a warning about desire's capacity to run amok, even gruesomely, murderously so.

The book's final poem, "From the Tower at the Top of the Winding Stairs," masterfully reasserts a type of control over desire. Working in wide, inviting lines of free verse, Dunn creates a timeless scene of bucolic beauty. Perched in a tower above the countryside, the speaker surveys a mountain range, the sky, and his neighbors, whom he notes planting tomatoes and lettuce in neat fields. Like the Yeatsian allusion in its title, the poem possesses a Yeatsian magic in its music and rhythm, which harmonize into an optimistic, almost heavenly tone halfway through the poem.

Not only is the speaker elevated physically nearer to the heavens than usual, but he also enjoys his distance from the troublesome complexities of the world below. This enhances the poem's sense of placidity and safety, which contrast with the preceding poem's messy, nauseating violence. At the poem's utopian apex, Dunn has politicians shedding their partisan myopia for the betterment of humankind and warring enemies laying down their arms to beg forgiveness from a beneficent universe. Right there, one begins to wonder if this poem's author is really Stephen Dunn, master of emotional complexity and philosophical skepticism.

Immediately thereafter, however, the poem discloses its maker via a swift counterstrike of destruction. The utopian bliss dissolves with the introduction of a house on fire, witnessed by the speaker through a tower window. The blaze provokes philosophical rhapsody on the fragility of life, with the speaker ruing the dependence of living creatures on their environment. He also recollects the calamitous, corrosive effect of daily life, until this dour turn in the poem turns again. The revelation comes through the speaker glimpsing a pinecone and then a leaf, causing him to imagine, however speciously, an order and purpose to life. From that constructed meaning, a subtle joy in life emerges, concluding the poem, the section, and the book.

Without isolating ideal details and articulating them in precise language, tone, and rhythm, Dunn's poems would implode under the weight of their content's intimacy. This is as true of the brutalizing, beauteous cycle of love poems as it is of the various poems in the book's other two sections, though the sustained series of love poems define this book as one of the year's most significant.

Seth Michelson

Review Sources

American Poetry Review 35, no. 4 (July/August, 2006): 8.
The Houston Chronicle, October 29, 2006, Zest, p. 19.
Library Journal 131, no. 14 (September 1, 2006): 150-151.
Publishers Weekly 253, no. 34 (August 28, 2006): 33.

THE FALL OF THE ROMAN EMPIRE
A New History of Rome and the Barbarians

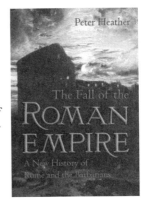

Author: Peter Heather (1960-   )
Publisher: Oxford University Press (New York). Illustrated. 572 pp. $40.00
Type of work: History
Time: The fourth and fifth centuries
Locale: Europe

Heather presents a sweeping interpretation of the fall of the Roman Empire that emphasizes the destructive effects of the barbarian invasions

Principal personages:
VALENS, Roman emperor
ALARIC, Gothic king
AETIUS, Roman general
ATTILA, ruler of the Huns

The British scholar Peter Heather boldly tackles an endlessly disputed question in his simply but aptly titled *The Fall of the Roman Empire: A New History of Rome and the Barbarians.* Since the last Western Roman emperor was deposed in 476 C.E., people have wondered how so powerful and magnificent an edifice as the Roman Empire could collapse before the attacks of barbarian warriors. This debate was given fresh impetus with the publication of the first volume of Edward Gibbon's *The History of the Decline and Fall of the Roman Empire* in 1776. Gibbon's magisterial work is a literary classic, and its intellectual influence persists to this day. Gibbon provided a sophisticated, multifaceted analysis of Roman failure. He followed traditional lines of explanation, however, by emphasizing internal weaknesses that left the Romans vulnerable to invasions by virile barbarian nations. A true son of the eighteenth century Enlightenment, he advanced a famously bold and controversial critique of Christianity, arguing that Christian otherworldliness and pacifism fatally weakened Roman martial resolve.

For the following two centuries, historians worked in Gibbon's shadow. Operating within his conceptual framework, many contented themselves with advancing novel variations on his theme of decline and fall. Lead poisoning from Roman plumbing, overheated public baths, and "race suicide" all at various times were seriously advanced as the root cause of the empire's demise.

In the second half of the twentieth century, a generation of scholars challenged the traditional narrative of Roman decay and collapse. Historians such as Peter Brown emphasized the continuities between the late classical and early Medieval worlds. These scholars argued that the transition from the late empire to the Germanic successor kingdoms was far less traumatic than had been previously thought. Many of the barbarian armies that roamed through Roman provinces in the fifth century had served in or sought to serve in the Roman army. Large numbers of Roman aristocrats and administrators switched their allegiance to German kings who, in turn, allowed their new subjects to continue to live under Roman law. The Roman Catholic Church survived, preserving Rome's diocesan structure and much of the classical world's literary culture. According to this line of interpretation, the date 476 would have been meaningless to

Peter Heather teaches at Worcester College, University of Oxford. He is a leading authority on the late Roman Empire and the barbarians. His previous books include The Goths *(1996) and* Goths and Romans *(1991).*

most contemporaries. Instead of heralding a ghastly descent into the Dark Ages, the fall of the Roman Empire was part of a creative transformation of the European world. These revisionist scholars even coined a new term, late antiquity, to soften the traditional impression that a civilization disappeared with the empire.

Heather robustly rejects this effort to pretty up the fall of the Roman Empire. His account is in many ways a reversion to a more traditional view. Heather returns the barbarian invasions to center stage. His central thesis is that the Roman Empire did not fall of its own weight but was brought down by attacks from outside. He would not disagree with the famous dictum of the French historian Andre Piganiol: "Roman civilization did not die a natural death. It was murdered." Heather has written an absorbing narrative of violent conflict. The Roman state fought back against every barbarian encroachment. The struggle ended only with the empire's powers of resistance. While many Romans came to an accommodation with the barbarians, others carried on local wars against the newcomers, even when all hope of imperial assistance had faded away. The Roman Empire did not go easily.

To buttress his argument, Heather spends the first section of his book making the case that the Roman Empire in the latter half of the fourth century was not on the brink of collapse. Here he takes on the ghosts of Gibbon and many others who assumed that internal weaknesses had to explain the fall of the empire before a comparatively small number of barbarians. An obvious problem for the traditional view, acknowledged by Gibbon himself, is the fact that not all of the empire fell. In the eastern Mediterranean the Roman Empire lived on, prosperous and powerful, centered at its capitol of Constantinople. In the sixth century, Emperor Justinian launched a vigorous campaign to recapture lost territories in the west. The Roman Empire in the east eventually evolved into what historians call the Byzantine Empire, and was not finally extinguished until the Turks captured Constantinople in 1453.

The case has been made that the east benefited from relative geographical isolation. Most of the barbarians struck the long western frontier along the Rhine and Danube Rivers. Those who raided into the Balkans found themselves ultimately frustrated by the formidable defenses of Constantinople. Being saved by an accident of geography will not do for Heather. He is intent on demonstrating that the late Roman Empire did not suffer from any fatal weaknesses, whether economic, military, or moral. To do so he draws upon an impressive knowledge of recent scholarship.

The Roman Empire of the fourth and fifth centuries was very different from the regime established by Caesar Augustus in the last two decades of the first century B.C.E. To avoid the fate of his uncle Julius Caesar, Augustus crafted a political system that softened his autocracy with a partnership with the Senate. Avoiding the deadly title of king, Augustus instead called himself *princeps*, or prince, the first citizen of the state. As a matter of form, the republic lived on. Over time, the principate grew more nakedly authoritarian, but the Senate remained at least symbolically significant, and members of the senatorial class played an important role in administering the empire. This changed during the crisis of the third century. For almost fifty years, from 235 to 284, a series of civil wars and barbarian invasions ravaged the empire. In the east, a resurgent Persian Empire became a dangerous rival. During this period emperors came and went, rarely dying in their beds.

In the end, only the heroic efforts of a succession of soldier-emperors held the Roman Empire together. By the time the last of these, Diocletian, stabilized the situation, the government looked very different than it had during the days of Augustus. The emperor was now an explicitly despotic ruler, addressed as *dominus* or "lord." The empire was administered along military lines, with a growing bureaucracy replacing the Senate. Class rankings grew more elaborate and rigid. The mass of the population labored to pay the taxes necessary to support an enlarged army and state apparatus. Diocletian took the momentous step of dividing the empire with a colleague, in order to meet internal and external threats.

Though a legal whole, the empire would be divided for most of the fourth and fifth centuries. Diocletian's successor Constantine built the great city of Constantinople that became the administrative center of the east and, in terms of splendor, the rival of the city of Rome itself. Constantine also promoted the Christianization of the empire, and churches replaced pagan temples.

Traditionally the dominate created by Diocletian and Constantine has been seen as a necessary but fragile reaction to crisis, too politically and economically rigid to endure the series of shocks that came at the end of the fourth century. Heather disagrees. He sees the late Roman Empire as a success story, painfully adjusting to the strategic challenge posed by the Persians and reasserting control over the frontier. He argues that critics ignore the fact that the empire had always been a cumbersome machine, providing most of its benefits to a small aristocracy. He sifts recent archaeological evidence to demonstrate that most Roman provinces were prospering in the fourth century. Heather believes the empire could have gone on indefinitely had not a tide of barbarian peoples been propelled toward its borders.

What doomed the Roman Empire in the west was a strategic revolution in the barbarian lands caused by the arrival of the Huns in Europe. Originally from central Asia, the Huns were a fierce, nomadic people who began carving out an empire of their own. Thanks to a mixture of archaeological and documentary evidence, Heather is able to track the Huns' progress west. At each stage of their advance, terrified peoples fled ahead of them into the borders of the Roman Empire. The first of these peoples to arrive were the Goths in 376. Initially, the Emperor Valens welcomed them as settlers within the empire. After corrupt Roman officials cheated and exploited them, the Goths went on a rampage in Thrace. In 378 Valens brought up an army to contain them, attacked before reinforcements arrived, and was killed at Hadrianople with more than ten thousand of his troops. After this disastrous defeat, the Romans proved unable to expel the Goths. Emperor Theodosius finally settled them as independent allies on Roman territory. The Goths became a state within the state.

The Gothic army that now acted as a political force in the empire reflected a transformation that had taken place among the barbarians living near the Roman frontier. Exposure to Roman goods and money led to growing social stratification. Older clan organization broke down. Kings emerged, able to attract large followings, making possible the "supergroups" that began to cross into Roman territory as the Huns drove them westward.

The Romans needed strong leadership and a respite to marshal their resources against the new threat. They would not get it. The waves of barbarians kept coming. One of the largest took advantage of an unusual freeze on the Rhine in December, 406, to cross into Roman territory. In the west a series of young and weak emperors led to civil wars that kept the Romans from concentrating their resources against the common foe. Rampaging barbarian armies wreaked economic havoc, depriving the Romans of tax revenues needed to maintain the army. The sack of the city of Rome in 410 by a Gothic army was only an episode in this progress of destruction.

The Western Empire suffered a fatal blow in the 430's, when the Vandals conquered North Africa, the richest province left to the state. By the time Attila and his Huns arrived on the old frontier in the 440's and 450's, the empire in the west was a rump, reduced to little more than Italy. Aetius, the last great Roman commander, was able to maintain the Roman position for a time by playing the Huns and other barbarians against each other. The rapid collapse of the Huns following the death of Attila, however, forced the Roman emperors of the west into the arms of barbarian generals. The failure of an Eastern Roman naval expedition to recapture North Africa in 468 marked the last chance to retrieve the situation in the west. The decision by a German military commander to send the western imperial regalia to Constantinople in 476 was an anticlimactic end to a century of struggle.

Heather is a compelling storyteller. He deliberately writes in an easy, sometimes breezy, style that will appeal to a wide readership. His book will long be the first stop for people looking into the fall of the Roman Empire. His account of the significance of the Huns and the evolution of barbarian society is a significant contribution to modern understanding of the late Roman world. Heather's book will not be the last word on such a profound subject. Supporters of the view that Rome was in decline will not be persuaded by all of his arguments. Questions still remain, such as why the supposedly better-armed and organized Roman army failed to defeat the barbarians decisively after 378. Heather's engaging work will nonetheless introduce many readers to a fascinating historical period that continues to inform any discussion of the rise and fall of great powers.

Daniel P. Murphy

Review Sources

Geographical 77, no. 7 (July, 2005): 88.
History Today 55, no. 8 (August, 2005): 56-57.
Journal of Military History 70 (April, 2006): 489.
The Spectator 298 (August 27, 2005): 30-32.
The Times Higher Education Supplement, January 6, 2006, pp. 26-27.
The Times Literary Supplement, December 23, 2005, pp. 5-6.
Weekly Standard 12, no. 1 (September 18, 2006): 33-34.

FEAR
Anti-Semitism in Poland After Auschwitz,
an Essay in Historical Interpretation

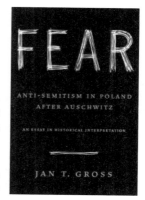

Author: Jan T. Gross (1947-　　)
Publisher: Random House (New York). 303 pp. $25.95
Type of work: History
Time: 1941-2006
Locale: Poland

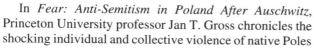

In a virtual compendium of human savagery and evil, Gross documents the little-known hate crimes of Poles against Jews especially after the Holocaust, as well as the causes and results of these devastating actions

In *Fear: Anti-Semitism in Poland After Auschwitz,* Princeton University professor Jan T. Gross chronicles the shocking individual and collective violence of native Poles against Jews after the Holocaust and how the Polish secular and religious authorities were actively complicit in this destruction. Gross organizes his important book into three major subsections. He first deals with Polish postwar anti-Semitism before one of its most horrifying manifestations: the Kielce pogrom. He then examines this dehumanizing pogrom and its ugly results. Finally, he studies Polish anti-Semitism after Kielce, relates it to communism, and confronts readers with his troubling conclusions.

Gross wisely sets his argument in a human context when he cites that more than 90 percent of Polish Jews (three million people) were killed in the Holocaust, as well as "more than half of [Poland's] lawyers . . . two-fifths of its medical doctors and one-third of its university professors and Roman Catholic clergy." After the Nazi murder of about six million European Jews, it is truly incomprehensible that Polish citizens, not Nazis, chased away or destroyed those few Jewish survivors—their own countrymen—who miraculously survived the extermination camps.

The "unwelcoming of Jewish survivors," as Gross terms it, was sometimes subtly but more often overtly violent. Returning Jews were stunned at the animosity that awaited them in the hateful "greeting," "So . . . you are still alive?" Anti-Semitism had metastasized like a cancer. Warnings not to speak loudly in Yiddish became threats to depart Poland quickly, along with beatings, torture, and murder. Many surviving Jews moved to postwar Germany, which was safer for them than their homeland. Right after the war, predatory Poles dug up death camps like Treblinkla and Belzec, hoping to find skulls with gold teeth that the Nazis had missed. Even in death, Jews were regarded by townspeople as fair game for plunder.

The nonchalance of postwar anti-Semitism is shocking. Looking to rent an apartment that was vacated by murdered Jews, a woman was told, "You could have killed 10 Jews and you would have gotten a house." Prosecution of crimes against Jews was

∼

Jan T. Gross serves as Norman B. Tomlinson '16 and '48 Professor of War and Society at Princeton University. His first book was Polish Society Under German Occupation *(1979). He was a finalist for the National Book Award for* Neighbors: The Destruction of the Jewish Community in Jedwabne, Poland *(2001).*

∼

inept and apathetic since witnesses were not deposed and refused to testify against their neighbors. Redolent of those Swiss banks that after the war would not release deposits of people who were gassed and cremated unless the beneficiaries could provide a death certificate, a Polish functionary would not help a Jewish returnee unless she had a non-Jew to vouch for her identity.

Jews were systematically denied food, property, official papers, and employment and were excluded from public schools. Jewish children were selected by Boy Scouts for beatings and torture. In an allusion to longstanding and malignant Church teachings, one young beating victim wrote, "After all, I was a God killer. . . . I was crying because a great and undeserved injury had been done to me. . . . I knew that I had not killed Jesus." Another child's terrifying question encapsulated this entire orgy of hate: "Mommy, was it a human being that was killed or a Jew?"

In Rzeszow in June, 1945, barely a month after the Holocaust ended, a nine-year-old girl was savagely murdered, a Jew was falsely charged, and mass hysteria set in; it was a "ritual murder," said the mob, performed by "Jews who needed blood [transfusions, to fortify themselves] after returning from camps." This modern-day variation on the ancient, baseless superstition that Jews kill Christian children to use their blood to make matzo incited mobs to beat Jews and destroy their property. The falsely imprisoned Jewish suspect was tortured and humiliated with, "Cannibal, murderer of Polish children."

The Kielce pogrom happened July 4, 1946, when an eight-year-old boy disappeared from his family for two days to visit a friend who had a cherry tree. His drunken father told police that the boy had been kidnapped by Jews; when his son returned, healthy and with cherries, the father encouraged the boy to say that he was held by Jews in the basement of the Jewish Committee Building; ironically, the building had no basement.

Undeterred by the truth, rumors swelled and crowds grew. After one innocent Jew was beaten by police, crowds threw rocks at any suspected Jews they could find. Police and military yanked innocent Jews from the building and handed them over to the enraged mob that dragged, kicked, stoned, and killed them. Jewish girls were thrown from third story windows, then "finished off" by the mob. Another wave of hysterical townspeople arrived with iron tools and other weapons; some forty-two Jews were murdered, many more injured. Marauding mobs searched all over town for Jews to murder, even pulling down men's pants to see if they were circumcised. Suspected Jews were dragged off trains, stoned, beaten, and murdered by angry mobs at every station. A few drunken Poles murdered a woman and her newborn child and then went out for dinner, proving that there was clearly no legal penalty for killing Jews.

After the pogrom, the burgeoning Communist Party dismissed the violence as the work of reactionaries; they cancelled a motion to compensate Jews who were victimized by the pogrom since such violence was still occurring. Who, asks Gross, could be terrified and intimidated by the return of traumatized, starving, exhausted Jews? Polish intellectuals could not conceive of such heightened anti-Semitism in a country that had experienced unspeakable barbarism and blood lust under Nazi occupation. "Moral misery and spiritual death" was the price Poles paid for their irrational, malignant hate, one Polish writer warned.

Furthermore, most of the Catholic clergy, embodied by Cardinal August Hlond, published no condemnation of virulent anti-Semitism. In fact, a church commission that falsely indicted Jews for bringing Communism to Poland reported that Jews were getting the hate and violence they deserved because Jews were Communists and Zionists: "They support the regime and run away from it at the same time." This absurd belief equates anti-Semitism with anti-Communism. Only Bishop Kubina of Czestochowa publicly rebuked murderers of Jews, yet his "reward" for his rationality and humanity was censure by the Church for ruining its unanimous public stance against Jews.

Gross concludes his study by disabusing readers of the myth that Jews were mostly Communists, therefore to be hated and feared; this "anti-Semitic slur" was called Judeo-Communism, *Żydokomuna*. Actually only one-fifth of 1 percent of Polish Jews were Communist Party members before the war; moreover, most Communists were not Jews and Jews were not given special privilege in the Communist Party.

Like drinking Christian children's blood, *Żydokomuna* simply presented another bogus pretext to hate Jews. By 1946, Polish Communists were nervous about having Jewish members and most of those few remaining Jews were demoted or replaced. Because of Polish anti-Semitism's extreme toxicity, most survivors of the Holocaust did not become involved in politics, and many tried to flee Poland.

Moreover, the postwar Polish government made crystal clear its view of Jews. In January, 1947, the State Security Service mounted a "theatrical revue" that musically and comically ridiculed Jews. The venue for this show was the little Polish town of Oswiecim, better known as Auschwitz. Afterward, the Communists "encouraged" two additional "waves of Jewish emigration . . . in 1956-57 and in 1968-69." Hitler's dream of a Poland that was *Judenrein* (Jew free) had virtually occurred. So deep and irrational, however, is Polish hatred of Jews that a 2004 nationwide newspaper poll found that 40 percent of those who responded felt that Poland was still "governed by Jews."

Critical reviews of *Fear: Anti-Semitism in Poland After Auschwitz* have uniformly acknowledged the book's stunning impact and importance. Nobel laureate Elie Wiesel, an Auschwitz survivor, expressed rage at Polish hate and apathy about which Gross has written so powerfully. While expressing legitimate shock and revulsion at Gross's findings, all critics praised his meticulous and profound research that commands intellectual assent and stirs emotional horror. Some critics supported Gross's findings by updating evidence of virulent Polish anti-Semitism to May, 2006, when, the day before Pope Benedict XVI visited Auschwitz, Warsaw's preeminent rabbi was attacked in the street by a man yelling, "Poland to the Poles!"—a wartime expression that meant, "Jews, leave Poland!"

Gross's ultimate conclusions paint a black and bleak portrait of the minds, hearts, and souls of many Poles. An example of this unalloyed evil is the July 10, 1941, massacre in Jedwabne in which Christian townspeople—with no orders from Nazi occupiers—locked almost all the town's sixteen hundred Jews in a barn and incinerated them. The chilling title of Gross's book on the massacre is *Neighbors* (2001). The assumption that all Jews are marked for death anyway resulted in an economic boon for many greedy, opportunistic Poles. "If you don't give me all your possessions," many Poles said to Jews, "the Germans will just take them anyway." Most tragic of all is that the few Poles who tried to help and shelter Jews during and after the war often became pariahs in their own town, branded with the most feared of all epithets, "Jew Lover."

Clearly, Poland must face its past and present; the headnote to Gross's book *Neighbors* quotes U.S. president Abraham Lincoln who addressed Congress with, "Fellow citizens, we cannot escape history." Gross sees Polish postwar anti-Semitism as not simply following Hitler's perfidious lead but as something systemic and endemic to Poland. He quotes Roman historian Tacitus who wrote, "It is, indeed, human nature to hate the man whom you have injured." To the Poles, "Jews were so frightening and dangerous," Gross asserts, "not because of what they had done or could do to the Poles, but because of what Poles had done to the Jews." Clearly, since many Poles had looted valuable possessions and property from Jews when their neighbors were deported to death camps, the same Poles reacted with fear (manifested as violence) to see some of the Jews return, perhaps to reclaim what was rightfully theirs.

A "dual sense of shame and contempt," Gross insists, exploded into pogroms and other hate crimes, fueled by over a thousand years of anti-Semitic Christian teaching, the apathy of bystanders, and the absence of governmental and canonical moral authority and responsibility at all levels. Gross's profoundly intelligent and necessary book makes some sense of this abomination, this most ignoble, repulsive, and ungodly of all attitudes and actions, but he cannot explain it fully. No one can. Why did this happen?

In Auschwitz, survivor Primo Levi, deprived of water for four days, reached for an icicle, only to have it yanked away by a Nazi guard. "*Warum?*" (Why?), asked Levi. The guard replied, *Hier ist kein warum* (Here there is no why). Not just Auschwitz, but all of Poland must be called a land of *kein warum* (no why) as Gross proves in his excoriating, unforgettable indictment of savage, human inhumanity. From a small child overheard in the gas chamber at Belzec come the last, haunting words on *kein warum*: "But Mommy, I was a good boy, it's dark, it's dark . . . "

Howard A. Kerner

Review Sources

The Baltimore Sun, July 2, 2006, p. 4F.
Booklist 102, nos. 19/20 (June 1-15, 2006): 10.

The Boston Globe, July 2, 2006, p. K4.
Kirkus Reviews 74, no. 9 (May 1, 2006): 448.
Los Angeles Times, June 25, 2006, p. 5.
The New Republic 235, no. 14 (October 2, 2006): 36-41.
The New York Times Book Review 155 (July 23, 2006): 1-11.
Publishers Weekly 253, no. 22 (May 29, 2006): 48.
The Spectator 302 (September 2, 2006): 36-37.
The Times Literary Supplement, October 6, 2006, p. 27.
The Washington Post, June 25, 2006, p. BW1.

FEDERICO FELLINI
His Life and Work

Author: Tullio Kezich (1928-   )
First published: Federico, 2002, in Italy
Translated from the Italian by Minna Proctor with
    Viviana Mazza
Publisher: Faber & Faber (New York). 444 pp. $35.00
Type of work: Biography, film
Time: 1920-1993
Locale: primarily Rome

*Kezich has updated his earlier biography of the famed
Italian film director*

Principal personages:
>FEDERICO FELLINI, Italian film director
>GIULIA ANNA "GIULIETTA" MASINA, actress and Fellini's wife
>MARCELLO MASTROIANNI, actor and Fellini's "alter ego"
>TULLIO PINELLI, Fellini's screenwriting collaborator
>NINO ROTA, Fellini's music arranger
>AGOSTINO "DINO" DE LAURENTIIS, Italian producer of several Fellini
>   films
>ENNIO FLAIANO, an early collaborator with Fellini
>PIER PAOLO PASOLINI, Italian film director
>ALDO FABRIZI, early screenwriting collaborator with Fellini
>ROBERTO ROSSELLINI, Italian film director

Tullio Kezich's *Federico Fellini: His Life and Work* is an updated revision of his earlier *Fellini*, which was published in 1987 and approved by Fellini himself. After an introduction that describes his first meeting with Fellini in 1952 and which characterizes his subject as an apolitical filmmaker preoccupied with fable, myth, and dreams, Kezich discusses the details of Fellini's birth. He uses the fictional account, that Fellini was born on a moving train, as an example of the way that Fellini's stories often are not true or are only partially accurate. Fellini's portrait of himself as a rebellious hellion is also exaggerated: Fellini was actually an introspective and solitary boy who exhibited a knack for drawing. His account of his "escape" from Rimini, his hometown, also does not jibe with the accounts of his childhood friends, but the "escape" motif does play an important part in Fellini's career, first as a cartoonist, then a screenwriter, and finally as a film director. Fellini's first escape was, perhaps, a flight to join the circus; his second was a train ride with Bianca Soriani, his first love, another embellishment of the truth. These escapes, like many events in his life, reappear with some poetic license later in his films.

Before he went to Rome, he had published some cartoons in *420*, a journal specializing in political satire, and when he and his brother Riccardo arrived in Rome, Fellini began working for *Marc'Aurelio*, a Roman newspaper. In the early 1940's he also wrote for radio and later began his screenwriting career. He also met and married actress Giulietta Masina, his wife for the next fifty years. During the 1940's he was busy avoiding the draft and writing screenplays, primarily for Cesar Zavattini, the noted neorealist film director. He then teamed up with Aldo Fabrizi, another screenwriter, for several films. When the team split, Fellini met Roberto Rossellini

Tullio Kezich, a longtime friend and confidant of Federico Fellini, is the film critic for Corriere della Sera *and the author of several books of film criticism. He has worked in film and television as an actor, screenwriter, and producer and is also an accomplished playwright.*

and worked on his *Rome, Open City* (1945), which was nominated for an Academy Award for Best Foreign Film. In their next collaboration, *Paisan* (1946), Fellini took the lead role and acted as a temporary director in Rossellini's absence. According to Kezich, Rossellini was responsible for awakening Fellini's cinematic vocation. When the duo broke up after *Paisan*, Fellini teamed with Tullio Pinelli and soon got his first directing assignment in *Variety Lights* (1950). When he directed a scene from *The White Sheik* (1952), Fellini, according to Kezich, "became" Fellini, but again Fellini's version of the story does not square with those of other people on the set. Nino Rota did the score for the film and for many of the following Fellini films.

For Kezich, the 1950's were full of good-byes, for Fellini and for Italian culture. *The Young and the Passionate* (1953), for example, signals the end of "small-town Italy, provincial patriotism, variety shows, comic strips, Gypsies, grifters, and prostitutes"—all key ingredients of early Fellini films. The first Fellini film to be distributed internationally, it won many awards and, according to Kezich, influenced such later films as Martin Scorsese's *Mean Streets* (1973), George Lucas's *American Graffiti* (1974), and Joel Schumacher's *St. Elmo's Fire* (1985). *La Strada* (1954), starring Anthony Quinn and Giulietta Masina, was Fellini's next big hit, winning an Oscar for best foreign film and establishing Masina as an international star. Like many Fellini films, *La Strada* can be read as a fable, but the interpretations vary widely. One is that the relationship between the strong man and the submissive woman parallels that of Fellini and his wife, but Masina's view was that Fellini can be found in both her character and in Quinn's. For Kezich, the film is "the most painful and also enigmatic fairy tale of Fellini's life."

Fellini's next major film was *The Nights of Cabiria* (1957), again featuring his wife. During the filming Fellini met Pier Paolo Pasolini, who became a confidant. Although the Roman Catholic Church attempted to censor *The Nights of Cabiria* for its story line about a prostitute, the film garnered an Oscar for best foreign film and a best actress award at Cannes for Masina, who preferred her role to the one she had played in *La Strada*. Perhaps the most beloved of Fellini's films, it was later adapted by Neil Simon as *Sweet Charity* for the stage and then by Bob Fosse for the screen. Fellini's next hit was *La Dolce Vita* (1960), starring Anita Ekberg and Marcello Mastroianni, who was to become Fellini's alter ego, his mirror image, as Kezich describes him. During the filming there were again censorship problems with the Church and a conflict between Fellini and Dino De Laurentiis, the producer, over funding. Fellini got his own chance to be a producer when he and Angelo Rizzoli formed Federiz, a production company, but he was not successful as a producer. When he would not produce Pasolini's "Il posto," the pair's relationship soured.

After his hits in the 1950's, Fellini met Dr. Ernest Bernhard, a psychoanalyst who became a kind of surrogate father to him and who met with him three times a week for the following four years. Bernhard sparked in Fellini an interest in dreams, and Fellini began his *Dream Book* on November 30, 1960. According to Kezich, "From this point on we can say that for Fellini, life is but a dream." In *8½* (1963), which appeared shortly after he began his sessions with Bernhard, Fellini made a movie about filmmaking, and he chose Mastroianni to play the director, or himself. For Kezich, Fellini was looking for a "human mirror, to reflect his own image," and the film is certainly autobiographical. *8½* won several awards, including another Oscar for best foreign film. *Juliet of the Spirits* (1965), *starring Masina, followed on the heels of 8½* but was not successful critically or commercially. Fellini had become increasingly interested in the supernatural and had also experimented with LSD, and the film was saturated with psychoanalytic messages, as was the later *Toby Dammit* (1968), a very personal adaptation of a short story by Edgar Allan Poe.

Fellini began to experience health problems and started to receive what he considered to be coded warnings about making "G. Mastorna's Journey," which he subsequently abandoned even after elaborate preparations had been made for the film. Like the earlier "A Journey for Love," "G. Mastorna's Journey" was not completed, but parts of both films were later incorporated into later works. Nothing was wasted. After the disappointing *Fellini's Roma* (1972), Fellini returned to form with *Amarcord* (1973), another autobiographical film about not only Fellini but also Italian mainstream culture, which he regarded as being depressingly provincial and intent on hiding "the moral and cultural misery of the years of consent." The film about memory earned Fellini his fourth Oscar for best foreign film.

Fellini's *Casanova* (1976), starring Donald Sutherland in the title role, continued the autobiographical strain as Fellini's bickering with Sutherland is seen by Kezich as indicative of Fellini's quarreling with himself, as Fellini saw himself in Casanova the womanizer. With *Orchestra Rehearsal* (1978) the autobiographical elements continue as the conductor and film director's roles are parallel. The orchestra itself, with its amusing, touching, and horrible characters, is an analogy for the world in which Fellini operates. Kezich sees the film as being very political. Not content with political controversy, Fellini next made *City of Women* (1980), which was attacked by feminists, some of whom had not seen the film. Kezich does not regard Fellini as a sexist, despite the roles women have played in his films: "The gist of *La cittá delle donne* [*City of Women*] is pro-woman." Elsewhere in the book, Kezich picks up the escape motif when discussing Fellini's relationships with women. Although he was married to Masina for fifty years and never considered leaving her, he did have many affairs. His "dream" woman, who served as an escape, was ideally a curvaceous beauty (very much like Anita Ekberg) who saw only him. Anna Giovannini was one of those women. Fellini makes his last cinematic comment on the relationship between the sexes in *Ginger e Fred* (1986), starring standbys Masina and Mastroianni as Ginger Rogers and Fred Astaire. Kezich sees the leads as the embodiment of key elements of Fellini's personality. The film is part homage and part critique of commercial television's practice of disrupting films with commercials and of the entire culture's degeneracy.

Fellini's penultimate full-length film, made while his health was declining, was *Intervista* (1987), a film in which Fellini plays himself and the film crew become actors; it is, like *8½*, a film about making a film (in this case an adaptation of Franz Kafka's 1927 work *Amerika*), but in *Intervista*, reality and fantasy merge. Kezich speculates, "Perhaps Fellini has become such an actor in his waking life (as people sometimes insinuate) that he can effortlessly continue his role." Although the film was not presented for competition at Cannes, he did receive a special prize, one created for him, the Fortieth Anniversary Prize. This was just one of the awards that he received near the end of his career. When he turned seventy, the Japanese awarded him the Praemium Imperiale, which brought him one hundred million lira. Three years later, just before his death in 1993, the Hollywood Academy presented him with the Lifetime Achievement Award. Masina died the following year.

The subtitle of Kezich's book, *His Life and Work*, aptly describes the author's narrative strategy, his organization, and his belief that his subject's life and films were intricately merged. Fellini, in effect, escaped into film, and once he switched from screenwriting to directing, his life became film. Kezich sees Fellini's narratives as being autobiographical. In some of the films he is represented by one or more actors, even by himself, and the events in his past are repackaged for cinematic use. Kezich devotes a single chapter to each of Fellini's twenty-four feature films and also covers some of the short films and the unrealized films. In each chapter readers learn about the backgrounds of Fellini's colleagues, production details (financing, set changes, casting), Fellini's health at the time, and the cultural context. The text is supplemented by an eighteen-page time line and an exhaustive index. Kezich's interpretation of the films tends to be psychoanalytic, and despite the complexity of some of the arguments, the writing is neither pedantic nor jargon-ridden. On the contrary, the tone is a bit flippant in spots and there are several amusing anecdotes. It is a thoroughly readable book.

Thomas L. Erskine

Review Sources

Booklist 102, nos. 9/10 (January 1, 2006): 43.
Kirkus Reviews 73, no. 24 (December 15, 2005): 1311.
Library Journal 130, no. 20 (December 15, 2005): 132.
The Nation 282, no. 11 (March 20, 2006): 32-36.
Publishers Weekly 252, no. 45 (November 14, 2005): 53.
Weekly Standard 11, no. 37 (June 12, 2006): 29-31.

FIASCO
The American Military Adventure in Iraq

Author: Thomas E. Ricks (1955-   )
Publisher: Penguin Press (New York). 482 pp. $27.95
Type of work: Current affairs and history
Time: 2000 to the present
Locale: Iraq and Washington, D.C.

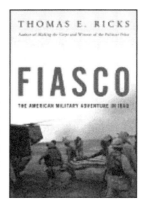

Ricks, assessing the causes and conduct of the U.S. invasion and occupation of Iraq in Operation Iraqi Freedom, stresses that the fiasco of his title derived mainly from the inability of civilian Pentagon leadership and some high level military leaders to understand the real nature of a counterinsurgency

Principal personages:

L. PAUL BREMER III, the chief civilian administrator in Iraq (Director of Reconstruction and Humanitarian Assistance for postwar Iraq); head of Coalition Provisional Authority

GEORGE W. BUSH, the forty-third president of the United States

TOMMY FRANKS, the commander in chief of the United States armed forces from July 6, 2000, until his retirement on July 7, 2003

SADDAM HUSSEIN, the dictator and president of Iraq from July 16, 1979, until deposed by the United States on April 9, 2003

DAVID PETRAEUS, a United States general who fought in Iraq, charged with rebuilding the new Iraqi army

COLIN POWELL, a former chairman of the Joint Chiefs of Staff and Bush's secretary of state, the creator of the Powell Doctrine

DONALD H. RUMSFELD, the longest serving secretary of defense

RICARDO SANCHEZ, a United States Army lieutenant general; head ground commander in Iraq 2003-2004

PAUL W. WOLFOWITZ, Rumsfeld's deputy defense minister under Bush and most aggressive neoconservative advocate of the invasion

ANTHONY C. ZINNI, Middle East expert and military veteran, commander in chief of the United States armed forces until July 6, 2000

The title *Fiasco* encapsulates Thomas E. Ricks's assessment of American military involvement in Iraq, a judgment based on twenty-five years of reporting on the U.S. military and on hundreds of interviews and more than 37,000 pages of documents. While Ricks has a clear point of view about what caused the fiasco and who should be held accountable, he is scrupulously evenhanded, for example, allowing some generals whose performance is judged scathingly by their peers and subordinates to respond in paraphrase and direct quotes.

Ricks points out an advantage of modern technology, sending a short description of a military action taken in Anbar Province to one of the participants querying whether the report is accurate and receiving an answer from seven thousand miles away in the next thirty minutes. He is harsh about Bush, Rumsfeld, and Wolfowitz for falling for Saddam Hussein's bluff that he possessed formidable weapons of mass destruction—a bluff that intimidated his enemies and neighbors. He describes how their optimism about the Iraqi reception of American troops and their relentless optimism about progress in Iraq combined with a lack of engagement allowed the neoconservative war hawks in the Bush administration to run roughshod over all cautions about the dangers of invasion and to grossly underestimate the number of troops required.

∼

Thomas E. Ricks was The Wall Street Journal's *senior Pentagon correspondent for seventeen years and began serving in that capacity for* The Washington Post *in 2000. He has covered U.S. military activities in several countries and has been a member of two Pulitzer Prize-winning teams of national reporters. Ricks also wrote* Making the Corps *(1997) and* A Soldier's Duty *(2001).*

∼

Ricks finds Rumsfeld, in particular, a polarizing figure who saw his real task as reform of the military and whose consequent, relentless paring down of the number of troops set up the conditions of the insurgency. He reports how Rumsfeld's policies came under increasing fire from within the military, especially after his comment that we go to war with the army we have, not the army we would like to have. Ricks is also harsh about Air Force general Richard Myers, chairman of the Joint Chiefs of Staff, and about General Tommy Franks, who led the attack on the Taliban in Afghanistan and the successful invasion of Iraq but who never understood the need for long-term strategic planning as opposed to short-term tactics. These critical evaluations are backed up by testimony and quotes from documents.

Ricks's recurrent theme is that wishful thinking and a shocking lack of cultural understanding led the Pentagon and the upper levels of the U.S. Army to invade Iraq with an inadequate number of troops. He acknowledges that the actual invasion worked very well, though perhaps against an enemy far less capable than originally thought. However, like the dog that caught the car he was chasing, the military was completely unprepared for what to do with Iraq once it had been taken. Bush and his advisors consistently ignored warnings, like those of former commander in chief of the U.S. armed forces, General Anthony C. Zinni, who Cassandra-like repeatedly criticized the proposal to invade Iraq as ill advised and the actions of the Bush presidency in general as problematic.

Bush and Rumsfeld also rejected the advice of Colin Powell, a tragic figure in *Fiasco*, an honorable soldier who wasted his credibility by assuring the United Nations that Saddam Hussein was known to have weapons of mass destruction. The Colin Powell Doctrine, formulated after the debacle of Vietnam as a means of avoiding such quagmires, asserted that no war should be engaged in without overwhelming force capable of rolling over the enemy and a clear goal or exit strategy for the far end. This doctrine was not simply ignored but was actually negated by Bush and Rumsfeld's limits on the troop force and lack of long-term strategy; the lessons of counterinsurgency, so painfully learned in Southeast Asia were also forgotten.

Again and again Ricks quotes experts in the Coalition Provisional Authority responsible for the occupation and reconstruction of the country and Special Forces officers who had been highly successful in Afghanistan to show that no plans were made for Phase IV, the rebuilding. When resistance materialized, the army went to war against the population, calling in air strikes, artillery bombardments, and massive force, destroying houses and even the occasional cow while creating new insurgents willy-nilly. Ricks's repeated motif is that in counterinsurgency, the people are the prize, for without their support the insurgents can disappear into the population with impunity. This obvious truth was simply ignored during the first years of the war.

Key decisions that may have laid the foundation for the insurgency were made by L. Paul Bremer, head of the coalition's rebuilding program. A consul in the Roman sense with enormous powers, Bremer blundered by excluding all former Baath party members from positions of power and authority in the new Iraq, even though tens of thousands of capable doctors, professors, and administrators would be put out of work and left resentful. Bremer also disbanded the Iraqi army and national police, destroying with one pen stroke the only secular institution through which all Iraqis could share a common national identity, and putting up to half a million people out of work. Ricks argues persuasively that the insurgency became the alternative, especially in a society in which personal and family honor trumped all other values: Disrespected and feeling impotent, many of these unemployed Baathists and soldiers would deploy improvised explosive devices, or IEDs, for the hundred dollars offered by the hardcore insurgents.

As American casualties mounted, so did pressure for intelligence about the insurgency, which to this day remains shrouded in mystery (there has never been a credible spokesperson, an office in another country, or any other identifiable face put on the movement). The response under various generals, but especially Ricardo Sanchez, commander of ground troops, was to round up ordinary Iraqis by the thousands for interrogation, sometimes taking family members as hostages if they were not at home. These unfortunates, 90 percent of them completely innocent, were taken from their homes in the night by soldiers who spoke no Arabic and sent to Abu Ghraib prison, where they might languish for three months because translators were in short supply. Sanchez's apparent lack of concern for conditions at Abu Ghraib prison may have exacerbated the prisoner abuse when thousands of detainees were simply dumped on the inadequate holding facilities. In the view of many military commentators, these actions solidified the insurgency by multiplying its supporters and fellow travelers.

By 2005 some more effective measures had been put in place to try to capture hearts and minds, in the old Vietnam phrase, with leaders like Army Major General David Petraeus and Marine Major General James Mattis employing innovative and culturally informed approaches. Ricks, however, shows that by this time, the insurgency had reached a critical mass and had been given time to organize, raise money, and refine its strategy. Despite his successes after contractors had failed miserably to train the new Iraqi army, Petraeus was shunted off to relatively minor jobs once he left the theater of operations—another indication of military misjudgment.

Ricks sees no way that the United States can withdraw from Iraq without leaving behind disaster, an oil-rich rogue state ripe for plucking by the foreign fighters who were drawn to Iraq to do battle in places like Fallujah and Ramadi and who are still there. As he points out, any precipitous withdrawal could lead to a third U.S. invasion to reinstall an acceptable government, just as Israel has had to repeatedly reinvade Lebanon. He imagines four possible scenarios, ranging from the best case, a gradual control of the insurgency such as happened in the Philippines, 1899-1946; a "middling" scenario, such as France in Algeria or the ongoing case of Israel in Lebanon; a "worse" scenario, with civil war, partition, and regional war as various neighbors try to make off with pieces of Iraq; and the worst case or "nightmare" scenario of a new Saladin, a strong ruler who like the twelfth century Salah ed-Din combines personal austerity with a vision of a pan-Arab caliphate, and possibly a war against the West with real, not imaginary, weapons of mass destruction.

Whatever happens, Ricks expects the United States to be in Iraq for a long time. (He praises the prescience of *The Atlantic Monthly*'s reporting on the early days of the invasion; their cover story banner read "Iraq: the Fifty-First State.") He quotes T. X. Hammes, a Marine counterinsurgency expert, who says that we have "lit multiple fuses" in the area and can "expect multiple explosions," perhaps with our grandchildren dealing with them. *Fiasco* is both inspiring about the real heroism of ordinary troops and many mid-level military leaders but depressing about the multiple failures of leadership, both civilian and military, in the top ranks.

Andrew F. Macdonald

Review Sources

The Atlantic Monthly 298, no. 2 (September, 2006): 124-125.
The Christian Science Monitor, October 17, 2006, p. 16.
The Economist 380 (August 19, 2006): 71.
Los Angeles Times, July 28, 2006, p. E17.
The New York Times 155 (July 25, 2006): E1-E6.
The New York Times Book Review 155 (August 13, 2006): 26.
Publishers Weekly 253, no. 32 (August 14, 2006): 28.
Washington Monthly 38, no. 10 (October, 2006): 60-63.

FIELD NOTES FROM A CATASTROPHE
Man, Nature, and Climate Change

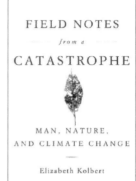

Author: Elizabeth Kolbert (1961-   )
Publisher: Bloomsbury (New York). 210 pp. $23.00
Type of work: Science and the environment
Time: From the 1990's to 2006
Locale: Earth

With signs of global warming clearly evident, this book examines how climate changes have affected the earth in the past and how human societies are accelerating similar changes today

Global warming has grown from a stir of concern over the last few decades to a threat manifesting itself in many parts of the world today. Elizabeth Kolbert has traveled around the world, visiting trouble spots where the evidence is apparent and seeking the advice of experts on location and others researching the phenomenon. The book is divided into two sections—"Part I: Nature" and "Part II: Man." These sections are followed by a chronology that begins with the invention by James Watt of the steam engine in 1769 and ends with global warming events noted in 2005. The book contains a selected bibliography and notes as well as an index.

Kolbert's prose is clear and easy to read, and she effortlessly intertwines anecdotal stories of the effects being observed with hard scientific facts and figures. The melting of arctic ice is clearly not a future concern for the Inupiat people of the Alaskan village of Shishmaref, located on the island of Sarichef, only twenty-two miles above sea level. Kolbert visits the village and reports not only how the melting ice has caused annual subsistence hunting to become more dangerous but also a more serious result: The pack ice that used to serve as a buffer to shelter the village from storms no longer exists, and the village's inhabitants have voted to be relocated, at a possible cost of $180 million dollars to the U.S. government. They may have to give up their traditional way of life.

Following this story of the real effects on people's lives, Kolbert describes how the first major study on global warming was conducted by the National Academy of Sciences in 1979. At that time, only a few scientific groups had begun considering the effects of adding carbon dioxide to the atmosphere; climate modeling was still new. During a five-day meeting at Woods Hole, Massachusetts, the Ad Hoc Study Group on Carbon Dioxide and Climate concluded that climate change would result from rising levels of carbon dioxide. In the twenty-five years since this study was conducted, global warming has progressed according to the models.

Kolbert flies to Fairbanks, Alaska, to meet with geophysicist and permafrost expert Vladimir Romanovsky. They discuss the thawing of permafrost, and he shows her houses that have been abandoned because their foundations are sinking into holes where the permafrost used to support them. He also shows her trees that lean crazily for the same reason—their underlying support has melted away, leaving holes in the earth.

In chapter 2, "A Warmer Sky," Kolbert points out that although the concern for "global warming could be said to be a 1970's idea; as pure science . . . it is much older than that." As long ago as the 1850's, John Tyndall, an Irish physicist studying the absorptive properties of gases in the atmosphere, uncovered what is now known as the greenhouse effect of carbon dioxide.

Next Kolbert visits the Greenland ice sheet, where Konrad Steffen, a professor of geography at the University of Colorado, shares his findings with her. He has noted the appearance of liquid water from melting where none has existed for hundreds or thousands of years. Kolbert also travels to nearby Iceland to discuss glacier melt with experts there.

In chapter 4, "The Butterfly and the Toad," Kolbert examines two species whose existence is being affected by climate change. One, the Comma butterfly of Europe, is appearing farther north of its previous range—acquiring an astonishing fifty miles per decade of migration. On the other side of the range is the golden toad of north-central Costa Rica. This animal appears only at the top of mountain ranges within a very few miles. The breeding habits and early life of this amphibian made it extremely sensitive to any changes in rainfall, and the population was decimated by one unusually warm and dry spring in 1987. A few years later, no more were seen, and the animal is widely believed to be extinct now. Kolbert also discusses mosquitoes and how changing conditions are allowing the spread of these parasites as well as the diseases some species carry.

In part 2, Kolbert looks for past evidence of drastic climate change and finds it in ancient historical records. Scientists studying ancient civilizations have found compellingly similar evidence that climate change has cast down empires. The world's first empire, Akkad, founded in ancient Babylonia in the Middle East, suffered through a drought so severe that the civilization fell. Tell Leilan, a town in what is now Syria, near the Iraqi border, shows evidence of abandonment during the same time period. The drought was so severe that "even the city's earthworms had died out." The Mayan civilization also seems to have collapsed from climate change, as sediment cores taken from Lake Chichancanab in the mid-1990's showed.

These ancient shifts in climate occurred, in some cases, thousands of years before industrialization, the author points out. This indicates that sudden shifts in climate are

Elizabeth Kolbert is a staff writer at The New Yorker. *Before 1999, she was a reporter for* The New York Times. Field Notes for a Catastrophe *grew out of a series of articles written for* The New Yorker, *for which she received the* American Association for the Advancement of Science magazine *writing award. Her other published book is* The Prophet of Love *(2004).*

a natural phenomenon experienced in the past. The increased activities of modern civilization, however, seem to be accelerating this process or perhaps even forcing the process at a time when it might not have happened naturally.

The Goddard Institute for Space Studies (GISS) climate model is explained. A graphical representation of how the world is divided up in the model helps to understand how it works. Kolbert includes a piece of the FORTRAN code for the modeling program, which might be of interest to software enthusiasts. The GISS model shows that doubling carbon dioxide levels will cause a severe drought through most of the continental United States. At least one water resource manager in California, when shown these drought indices, said, "Well, if that happens, forget it."

Paleoclimatologist Peter deMenocal discusses with Kolbert his expertise on ocean cores and on the climate of the Pliocene. When the earth cooled down around two and a half million years ago, it entered the Pleistocene and an age of recurring glaciations. DeMenocal believes that this period was crucial to human development, coinciding as it did with the rise of two branches of hominids, one of which gave rise to homo sapiens. Examining core samples for what lived or did not live during a particular time period, deMenocal discovered that periods of cooler water temperatures occurred every fifteen hundred years or so. He also noted that the switch was abrupt, not gradual, as variations in the earth's orbit would produce. This is an example of a feedback mechanism that increases—"the less rain the continent [of Africa] got, the less vegetation there was to retain water, and so on until, finally, the system just flipped."

DeMenocal also examined sediment layers from the Gulf of Oman for evidence of dolomite dust in order to prove or disprove the theory of massive drought in Tell Leilan. What he found corresponded exactly to the time period of the city's abandonment.

The relative climatic calm of the Holocene, the modern period, has made it possible for civilization to develop. The twin products of agriculture and writing could only develop in a relatively stable environment, in which some variation was tolerable and could be prepared for using the knowledge of previous generations. Kolbert goes on to name several other civilizations that fell after major declines in rainfall patterns.

These changes in climate, and the predictions that have proved to be true, have not gone unnoticed by every modern nation. Twenty-five percent of the Netherlands lies below sea level. The Dutch have already begun a program of adjustment for the coming conditions. A series of television ads in 2003 cautioned citizens about rising water, not as a possibility but as a fact. The Dutch are already preparing to give back some of their land to the sea. On the banks of the River Meuse, one of the Netherlands' largest construction firms is building a development of amphibious houses that can rise and fall with the water level.

Kolbert describes the Vostok core, an 11,775-foot-long ice core drilled in Antarctica. This core allows researchers to see back as far as four full glacial cycles and examine climate changes. A graph illustrates how the Vostok core shows the planet is warmer now than it ever has been during that time period.

Kolbert devotes a chapter to examining worldwide emission levels of greenhouse gases. Titled "Business as Usual," chapter 7 explains why development and industry cannot go on as it has been. There are currently no real consequences to the emission of greenhouse gases, but she and others suggest that there needs to be. Near the end of the chapter, Marty Hoffert, a professor of physics at New York University, mentions the possibility that Western civilization will fail in its transition "from hunter-gatherers to high technology."

The most troubling chapter is "The Day After Kyoto," in which Kolbert examines the George W. Bush administration's position on global warming. She met with Paula Dobriansky, undersecretary of state for democracy and global affairs, whose job it is to explain this position. Dobriansky assured Kolbert that the Bush administration took climate change seriously, but her reassurances ring hollow and noncommittal. At the conference for which this chapter was named, the United States, "having failed to defeat Kyoto," seemed bent on destroying the chances for world agreement on how to proceed to implement the Kyoto Protocol.

The author tries to end the book on a positive note. She points out that humans have been clever and adaptable throughout their geologically short tenure on the earth. She also notes that it will take a global response to meet the challenges of global warming and wonders if humankind will meet those challenges.

This book fills in important details and gives more extensive coverage of subjects on which the Oscar-winning film *An Inconvenient Truth* (2006) can only touch. It may not have the clever graphics that the film's book version has, but it shows more of the real-world effects that are already occurring.

Patricia Masserman

Review Sources

The Christian Century 123, no. 23 (November 14, 2006): 46-49.
Entertainment Weekly, no. 868 (March 17, 2006): 123.
Los Angeles Times, March 19, 2006, p. R4.
Natural History 115, no. 4 (May, 2006): 58.
The New York Times 155 (March 16, 2006): E1-E9.
Publishers Weekly 252, no. 48 (December 5, 2005): 39.
Science News 169, no. 13 (April 1, 2006): 207.
Scientific American 294, no. 5 (May, 2006): 90-93.
The Times Literary Supplement, August 11, 2006, pp. 28-29.

FIRE IN THE CITY
Savonarola and the Struggle for the Soul of Renaissance Florence

Author: Lauro Martines (1927-   )
First published: Scourge and Fire: Savonarola and Renaissance Florence, 2006, in Great Britain
Publisher: Oxford University Press (New York). 336 pp.
  $26.00
Type of work: History and biography
Time: 1472-1498
Locale: Florence

Martines focuses on the years from 1494 to 1498 to produce a cultural and social history of the intense conflict that led to Girolamo Savonarola's execution, treating the "factual essentials" of recent scholarship in a style meant to appeal to a popular audience

Principal personages:
> GIROLAMO SAVONAROLA, a Dominican friar and Prior of San Marco convent in Florence
> POPE ALEXANDER VI, Savonarola's enemy
> KING CHARLES VIII OF FRANCE, a threat to Florence as he marched to Naples

In *Fire in the City*, Lauro Martines describes the life of friar Girolamo Savonarola. He was born into a distinguished family in Ferrara and was the special pride of his grandfather Michele Savonarola, court physician and author of medical studies. The physician tutored the precocious grandson in Latin, preparing him for his great love of the Church fathers, including Jerome and Augustine and Thomas Aquinas. Savonarola studied art at the University of Ferrara and, for reasons not clear, turned against a world that he perceived as corrupt and authored a poem on the destruction of the world that attacked sodomy among the cardinals and bishops. Three years later, in 1475, he wrote "On the Ruin of the Church" and entered the convent of San Domenico in Bologna. In 1479 he was transferred to a convent in Ferrara and in 1482 to the convent of San Marco in Florence, where he taught theology and Scripture for five years before being moved around to various postings. Finally, in 1490 he returned to San Marco, where he was soon elected prior and stayed until his death.

The move back to Florence was arranged by Lorenzo de' Medici (the Magnificent), urged on by Savonarola's admirer Count Pico della Mirandola. Savonarola's Advent sermons of 1490 earned him much attention but annoyed Lorenzo and others who resented his attack on corrupt clergy and the grasping rich. His prophecies of scourges, death, and renewal were especially offensive, as they entangled social questions with religion. When Lorenzo died in 1492, his older son, the irresponsible Piero, became head of the powerful Medici family and supported Savonarola's plan for more asceticism. This reform movement entailed splitting away from the Dominican convents in the north and creating a new alignment with the Dominican convents of Pisa and Fiesole, and it incurred the anger of the lord of Milan, Ludovico Sforza, who at this time was encouraging Charles VIII, king of France, to sweep through Italy and take the kingdom of Naples.

Lauro Martines is professor emeritus of European history at the University of California, Los Angeles. He is the author of April Blood: Florence and the Plot Against the Medici *(2003), as well as* Loredana *(2004), a prize-winning novel of Renaissance Italy.*

Florence suffered a crisis in 1494 with the approach of King Charles's army. Piero responded by proposing an agreement with Charles, but the city rulers rejected this plan angrily, and Piero was forced to flee to Bologna before Charles marched into Florence on November 17. The collapse of the hated Medici family provoked attacks on their collaborators' houses, and to guarantee order in government the city fathers invited back some of the illustrious families who had been exiled by the Medici. Charles argued in vain for the return of Piero, but the Florentines resisted his pleas. At this point, the Signory (a sort of city council) chose Savonarola to head a delegation to negotiate with Charles. Savonarola flattered the king by calling him a servant of God, and on November 28 the king departed for Naples with his army.

With the Medicis overthrown and King Charles gone to Naples, Florence had to decide on a form of government. Only the old Medici collaborators had any governing experience, and class tensions soon surfaced. With Savonarola's support, a Great Council of more than thirty-five hundred citizens, sitting for life, was agreed upon, a body that lasted until 1512, when the Medicis reclaimed power in an armed coup d'état. Savonarola repeatedly preached for peace and unity, rejecting revenge against the Medici and thereby inducing the elite to accuse him of encouraging mob rule. He also played a large role in achieving a right of appeal in prison sentences and in abolishing an ancient tradition of public assemblies designed to manipulate the citizens.

Savonarola's passionate religious feelings emerged in his sermons against the corruption he perceived in the Church, a spiritual rot that infected Florentine politics. His attacks were powerful and effective, making him such a marked man that by 1495 he was protected in the streets by an armed guard. He railed against the "tepid," those whose faith was lukewarm and who focused only on the material externalities of religion, such as clothing, coats of arms, and church ornamentation. Despite his instincts for reform, Savonarola accepted the class system and expected people to stay in their inherited social stations. His leanings toward mysticism verged on a dualism of Good and Evil, and he saw the fall of the Medici as a triumph engineered by God. The new republic was a necessary step in Savonarola's plan to reform Florence.

Savonarola enjoyed the support of groups of boys (*fanciulli*) from well-to-do families who patrolled the streets, watching for objects of pleasure to be confiscated for the great bonfire of the vanities to be lighted on Carnival day (February 16). On that day in 1496, perhaps as many as six thousand thronged the streets of Florence. The omnipresence of these angel-faced young boys elicited charges of sodomy against Savonarola and his friars, and their activities gradually subsided.

With the march of King Charles VIII into southern Italy, Pope Alexander VI was forced to think about the activities of Savonarola and of his claim that Charles was sent to scourge Rome in a cleansing of all Italy. The Holy League, a grouping of Italian states ratified in March, 1495, sought the expulsion of the French, and Sforza requested through intermediaries that the pope chastise Savonarola for his support of Charles. Alexander duly sent the friar a friendly letter, which Savonarola answered bluntly, refusing—probably out of fear for his life—to meet the pope in Rome. The tensions between the pope and the friar continued through 1496, with Savonarola unrelenting in his desire for King Charles to complete his "scourging."

Martines describes the period from November, 1494, through June, 1497, as "The Savonarolan Moment," when the friar's stature and influence were unrivaled in the city. Mainly because of him, San Marco had achieved broad eminence, with many of its friars coming from illustrious families. Political problems, however, plagued Florence. The seaport of Pisa rebelled and fell under the control of Milan and Venice, whose rulers resented Florence's allegiance to King Charles VIII. Savonarola responded to the economic and political upheaval by urging more spirituality and support for the Great Council. San Marco's enemies accused the convent of harboring an "intelligence," a secret party of so-called *Frateschi*, as the Savonarolans were called. Savonarola's enemies (he named them the *Arrabbiati*, or "the Rabid") lacked enough unity to be effective, but a new coalition, the *Compagnacci* ("Ugly Companions"), rose up in early 1498 and aligned themselves effectively with the pope against the friar. Attacks on Savonarola came both from within the Church and from without, including charges that his followers had been lackeys of Piero de' Medici. Piero was even whispered to have delayed the dispatch to Florence of the pope's brief of Excommunication signed on May 13, 1497, but not read out in Florence's churches until June 18. Martines believes that Savonarola was correct in declaring that the campaign against him was really about "the Great Council, the new republic, and in effect the *popolo*."

In March, 1497, Piero de' Medici was mustering troops and planning an attack on Florence, and by April 28 he was outside the city walls. Piero's reinforcements failed to arrive, however, and he retreated. When one of Piero's supporters, Lamberto dell'Antella, was tortured by repeated strappados, he named Bernardo Cambi and Giannozzo Pucci as conspirators, and they quickly identified three more socially prominent Florentines—Bernardo del Nero, Lorenzo Tornabuoni, and Niccolò Ridolfi. All five were found guilty of treason and condemned to death, and their request for an appeal to the Great Council won only an enormous controversy on the night of August 21. When the uproar settled down in the Signoria chambers, the five were immediately led out and decapitated. Martines scoffs at all claims that Savonarola was remiss in not pleading for mercy for the traitors.

The determined Savonarola began preaching again in January, 1498, and his sermons infuriated the pope, who threatened to impose an interdict on Florence. On February 26 the pope ordered the priors to send Savonarola to Rome, but the priors sent a conciliatory response and Savonarola kept on preaching. Domenico Bonsi, a lawyer and the friar's defender in Rome, worked fruitlessly on his behalf, but the curia demanded action. Matters came to a head on March 14, when all the city officials met and after great contention decided two days later that Savonarola should quit preaching.

The next development in the struggle came on March 25, when a Franciscan friar proposed to walk through fire with any one of Savonarola's champions. Elaborate preparations fizzled when the Franciscan failed to meet his Dominican volunteer for the fiery walk, but the crowd's disappointment turned against Savonarola and led to an angry attack on San Marco on Palm Sunday, April 8. The signory made no effort to relieve the siege on the convent, and Savonarola's enemies reigned unchecked, with a dozen men killed in the bitter fighting. By one in the morning the friars had surrendered, and Savonarola was led to the signory by armed guards.

The first trial began on April 9, and the third and last, which was conducted by two Vatican appointees, ended on May 22. Martines prefaces his account with the warning that the record of the three trials is "a treacherous sequence of texts." He thinks the transcripts were "doctored" and notes that all the original trial records disappeared. The questioning focused mainly on political matters and only glanced at religious issues. Savonarola suffered several strappados—his hands were tied behind him, and then he was yanked into the air by his arms and dropped, but not all the way to the floor—before confessing to all the contrived charges.

The execution site in the government square was prepared immediately, and on the morning of May 23 Savonarola and two friars, Domenico da Pescia and Silvestro Maruffi, were executed by hanging after two hours of a humiliating ceremony of degradation—a rite stripping them of their ordination—and then burned to ashes. The finale came as boys from the Florence slums fired stones at the crumbling corpses. Martines describes the last act this way:

> As soon as workers could get safely at the embers and ashes, they swept everything up, heaped it all into carts, and rolled the lot to the Ponte Vecchio, to be dumped into the Arno River. The carts were flanked by the Signoria's mace-bearers, signaling the government's watchfulness and determination to be rid of every remaining bit of the friars, ashes as well. There were to be no relics, nor even the pretext of one.

Frank Day

Review Sources

Library Journal 131, no. 7 (April 15, 2006): 90.
Publishers Weekly 253, no. 8 (February 20, 2006): 149-150.
The Times Literary Supplement, June 23, 2006, p. 7.
The Wall Street Journal 247, no. 117 (May 19, 2006): W6.

FIRST LADY OF THE CONFEDERACY
Varina Davis's Civil War

Author: Joan E. Cashin (1956-)
Publisher: Belknap Press of Harvard University Press
(Cambridge, Mass.). 403 pp. $29.95
Type of work: Biography and history
Time: 1826-1905
Locale: The United States, east of the Mississippi River

*Married to Jefferson Davis, president of the Confederate
states during the American Civil War, Varina Davis exhibited an independence unusual for women of that era*

Principal personages:
VARINA HOWELL DAVIS (1826-1905), wife
of the Confederate president
JEFFERSON DAVIS (1808-1889), her hus-
band, president of the Confederacy
VARINA ANNE (WINNIE) DAVIS (1864-1898), her daughter

In *First Lady of the Confederacy: Varina Davis's Civil War*, Joan E. Cashin depicts Varina Davis as a complex woman. Varina, who balanced a large and extended
family, was sometimes torn between doing her duty to her husband and being true to
her opinions. She was by no means a feminist in the modern sense; no evidence exists,
for example, that she supported the woman suffrage movement in her later years. At
the same time, she was not averse to expressing her own opinions among those she
could trust of her husband's contemporaries and colleagues.

Varina was well read and educated, and she enjoyed conversations about current
events as well as the plots and implications of contemporary books. Both during her
marriage and in the years after Jefferson Davis's death, Varina's books were published in a time when it was considered almost scandalous for a woman of means to
work; her daughter Winnie also became a writer.

The most significant example of Varina Howell Davis's independent thinking, as
presented by Cashin, was a lukewarm acceptance of the secession movement and creation of the Confederate States of America. She maintained friendships in the North
even during the war and was not averse to befriending others who were staunch
Unionists. Her final years were spent in New York City, and in the end she conceded
that it had been best that the Unionists were successful in the war.

Born May 7, 1826, at The Briars, the family plantation in Natchez, Mississippi,
Varina Howell was the second child and first daughter of William and Margaret
Howell. Both sides of the family had been prominently involved with America's
wars. Her grandfather, Major Richard Howell, was a veteran of the revolution who
fought at Brandywine and Germantown and endured the famous winter at Valley
Forge. Richard Howell's brother died in the war, while his cousin, George Read of

Delaware, was among the signers of the Declaration of Independence. Following the victory over the British, Richard Howell entered New Jersey politics, becoming a member of the Federalist Party, and in 1793 was elected to the first of four terms as governor of the state. Indeed Varina Howell had a large extended family, many of whom settled in the North, including most of her thirty-four cousins.

Joan E. Cashin is Associate Professor of History at Ohio State University. Previous books include Our Common Affairs: Texts from Women in the Old South *(1996) and* A Family Venture: Men and Women on the Southern Frontier *(1991), which was named a* Choice Outstanding Academic Book.

Varina's father, William, had been commended for bravery during the War of 1812. Following the war, he eventually settled in Natchez, where he met a local landowner and lawyer, Joseph Davis. It was through Davis that Howell met Margaret Kempe, the woman he would marry. Joseph Davis also had a brother, Jefferson, who would play a significant role in Margaret's life.

Margaret's father, James, likewise had a distinguished military career. During the revolution, he had enlisted as a teenager. During the War of 1812, he again served his country, by participating in the Battle of New Orleans under General Andrew Jackson. Like Howell, he became a wealthy landowner. Both James and his wife, also named Margaret, died in the years after the war. Their daughter, Margaret, inherited enough of her father's estate to be considered a wealthy young woman.

The Howell family into which the younger Margaret Kempe married in 1823 fit well into the Southern stereotype of wealthy, slaveholding landowners. Following a fire in their first home, the Howells moved to The Briars, where they remained until 1850. Varina Howell had an idyllic childhood, inheriting a love of books from her mother and maintaining a close relationship with a woman who would be both adviser and confidant until Margaret Howell's death in 1867. As a child of wealth, Varina had the benefit of a private tutor, as well as education in Madame Grelaud's academy, a school for privileged girls in Philadelphia, Pennsylvania.

The Howell's family fortune did not last. A series of poor financial decisions on the part of William Howell left him increasingly in debt, a state in which even use of Margaret Howell's inheritance did not change. Eventually he went bankrupt and was forced to borrow from friends and relatives. Even Varina's Philadelphia school tuition had to be paid by her godfather.

The Varina Davis depicted by the author was rarely comfortable with the concept of sectionalism. Schooled in the North, well read, including the newspapers of the time, and with numerous Northern relatives, Varina was certainly aware of the growing conflict between the North and South. While she later provided lip service to the Southern cause, often to support her husband, Varina never developed the bitterness toward Northern society as did many later contemporaries.

Born in 1808 and named for President Thomas Jefferson, Jefferson Davis likewise came from a proud military tradition. His father Samuel had fought in the revolution. Three brothers participated in the War of 1812. Educated at Transylvania College in Lexington, Kentucky, Davis later entered West Point in 1824. Following graduation he was posted in the West (Wisconsin), where he met his first wife, Sarah Knox Taylor, daughter of the general and future president.

Davis and Taylor married in 1835. The marriage was short, however, as the bride died three months later from malaria. The tragedy had a lasting impact on Davis, and as pointed out by Cashin, her memory would remain prominent in his mind throughout his marriage with Varina Howell.

Howell and Davis met in December, 1843, in a manner arranged by Jefferson's older brother Joseph. Davis's appearance, six feet tall and exceedingly handsome, immediately made an impact on Varina Howell. As she wrote her mother that evening, she considered him "a remarkable kind of man, ... of uncertain temper, and . . . . a way of taking for granted that everybody agrees with him . . . . which offends me." She was correct in her assessment. Cashin provides numerous examples throughout their marriage in which disagreements between the couple were settled the same way—Varina acceded to his wishes.

The marriage took place on February 26, 1845; Jefferson was eighteen years older than she. Soon afterward, Davis entered politics and was elected to Congress as a member of the Democratic Party. The family moved to Washington, where Varina became an active participant in the city's society. Cashin points out how she blended well with the political factions of the times, and her parties during the mid-1840's included many of the most prominent politicians in the city. While her opinions on the individuals varied, Varina Davis could discuss current issues with the likes of Daniel Webster; Charles Ingersoll, chairman of the Committee on Foreign Affairs, with whom she discussed Lord Byron, among others; John C. Calhoun; and future president James Buchanan. Relatively enlightened with respect to their willingness to listen to a woman, these men each learned to respect Varina Davis as both an excellent hostess and a person with strong opinions independent of those of her husband's. During her time in Washington, Varina would also write and sell a story to a New York magazine.

Jefferson Davis enlisted during the Mexican War, leaving Varina to run the Mississippi plantation, Brierfield, in his absence. It was during this period that the couple had their first major marital difficulty. For some time, Varina had had increasingly strained relations with her in-laws in general and Jefferson's brother Joseph in particular. It was her understanding that Brierfield was owned by her husband. However, Joseph Davis had never turned over the title of ownership, and the plantation was legally his. Varina had expectations that in this dispute, her husband would support her view. However, when Jefferson was home for a visit from the army in 1846, he sided with his brother. Feeling betrayed, she argued with Jefferson as he left to return to the army. It was not helpful that in a letter, he made reference to "female acquaintances" he visited on the way. Davis was well known for his interest in the "ladies," and this would not be the only time she would have suspicions of infidelity. The situation was not helped when she was informed by Joseph that their widowed sister and seven children would shortly be moving to Brierfield. It was clear to Varina that Joseph Davis was the dominant force in the family and that her husband would side with him in any dispute.

That the marriage was in difficulty became clear when Davis returned from the army. In August, 1847, he was appointed to the Senate; Varina did not accompany her husband when he left for Washington. In turn, he wrote to her that "he would not return to Mississippi until she changed for the better." Divorce was not an option, given the social mores of the time and the scandal that would result. In the end, she accepted her husband's wishes and reluctantly acceded to his being her "nobler self."

With the outbreak of the Civil War, Davis was elected president of the Confederacy, moving first to Montgomery, Alabama, and then to Richmond, Virginia. Varina Davis settled into a role as first lady. Her opinions on the war, the North, and secession in general appear torn. She clearly supported her husband. At the same time, however, she secretly maintained frequent contact through letters with both relatives and former friends in the North. She was known to have helped nurse injured Northern prisoners at Confederate hospitals. More significantly, she was also known to make reference to the idea of secession as being doomed to fail.

Certainly Varina Davis had no lack of courage. Using newly uncovered writings and sources, Cashin writes how in the confidence of her mother and, after her death, among her trusted friends, Varina expressed doubts in her husband's abilities as president. Further, she was often not averse to disagreeing equally with politicians or society matrons. Cashin also describes how when Jefferson Davis was captured some months after Robert E. Lee's surrender, Varina placed herself between her husband and the guns aimed at him by Northern soldiers.

Varina dealt with frequent tragedy. In addition to her husband's death in 1889, she suffered the loss of four sons and a daughter, Varina Anne (Winnie), a budding writer and close friend as well as being one of her children. In her last years, Varina moved to New York, creating additional controversy among those in the South who still considered her a symbol of the "Cause." Perhaps symbolizing her independence, she made the decision, responding to her critics with justification and "severe language."

Richard Adler

Review Sources

Booklist 102, no. 21 (July 1, 2006): 23.
Library Journal 131, no. 12 (July 1, 2006): 87.
Publishers Weekly 253, no. 21 (May 22, 2006): 40.

FLAUBERT
A Biography

Author: Frederick Brown (1934-   )
Publisher: Little, Brown (New York). 629 pp. $35.00
Type of work: Literary biography
Time: 1821-1880
Locales: Rouen, France, and its environs; Paris; Egypt
and the Holy Land; Greece

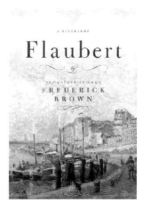

This scholarly biography examines Gustave Flaubert's life and works in the context of the Second and Third Republics and the Second Empire

Principal personages:
GUSTAVE FLAUBERT, novelist
ACHILLE-CLÉOPHAS FLAUBERT, surgeon,
   the novelist's father
CAROLINE FLEURIOT FLAUBERT, the novelist's mother
CAROLINE FLAUBERT HAMARD, the novelist's younger sister
ACHILLE FLAUBERT, surgeon, the novelist's older brother
MAXIME DU CAMP, writer, journalist, photographer, and founding editor
   of *La Revue de Paris*; famous for his travel narrative on the Holy
   Land
LOUIS BOUILHET, Flaubert's literary adviser, to whom he dedicated
   Madame Bovary
ERNEST CHEVALIER, attorney, later attorney general of Angers, France;
   Flaubert's friend
LOUISE RÉVOIL COLET, writer, Flaubert's mistress; inspiration for the
   character of Emma Bovary
GEORGE SAND, née AMANDINE-LUCILE-AURORE DUPIN, French novelist
   linked romantically with Flaubert's friend Alfred de Musset and com-
   posers Franz Liszt and Frédéric Chopin

Gustave Flaubert created immortal literary personalities filled with contradictions. His Emma Bovary desires beauty in her life and escape from ugly provincialism yet succumbs to materialism. She destroys her own happiness and that of her husband in her pursuit. Flaubert's Saint Antoine is an aged anchorite who keenly feels the loss of his physical powers. This holds true in both the first and second versions of *La Tentation de Saint Antoine* (1874; *The Temptation of Saint Anthony*, 1895), a novel Flaubert worked on for nearly thirty years beginning in 1849.

Flaubert understood such contradictory personalities so well because he was one. He shared the provincial background of his Madame Bovary, though he also had, from birth, the enormous advantages of upper-middle-class prosperity. In early nineteenth century France, this was a small class, indeed.

Achille-Cléophas Flaubert, Flaubert's father, was the chief surgeon of Rouen's hospital, known as the Hôtel-Dieu. The Flaubert family lived a mere partition apart from the hospital's ward, so that the realities of life, death, and pain were inescapable. Though being a surgeon did not confer the same prestige as being a physician, the elder Flaubert invested wisely in properties surrounding Rouen and established a comfortable life for himself and his family. The eldest son, Achille, would also become a surgeon who would succeed his father. Two other Flaubert children, Émile-Cléophas and Caroline, would die in infancy, while another Caroline (named after both her sister and mother) would die after the birth of her child. Flaubert's father would die of septicemia, ironically following surgery his son Achille performed.

Frederick Brown has twice received fellowships from the Guggenheim Foundation and the National Endowment for the Humanities. He has written biographies of Jean Cocteau and Émile Zola and variously on French culture and aesthetics.

It would be oversimplification to see Achille in the incompetent Charles Bovary, just as it would be to see Flaubert himself through characters such as Frédéric Moreau, Saint Anthony, or Emma Bovary. Even so, Frederick Brown's study reveals a young man with far too much easy money, no clear early professional direction, and parents far too indulgent. They supported their son's antimonarchist views, somewhat extreme for Rouen, and appeared relatively untroubled by the political protests that nearly resulted in Gustave's failure to graduate from his lycée. After all, they themselves shared his views.

Flaubert's initial interest was in writing for the theater. As a child, he devised plays with his friend Ernest Chevalier. They even created a stock antihero often called *Le Garçon* ("The Kid"), a caricature of their own mischief. Flaubert and his circle carried this into their behavior at school, and his role in an antimonarchist publication nearly prevented his graduation. This, too, shows his iconoclasm, as neither the monarchy nor the empire tolerated polemic well. With some desperation, Flaubert began to read law in 1842, and though he qualified at the first level, he did not complete his degree. His family, in effect, underwrote his apparent indolence and lack of ambition. Though Flaubert watched as his school friends qualified as lawyers, even as his brother Achille succeeded his father, he remained indifferent to achievement and even to publication.

This does not mean that Flaubert had not worked during and after his two years studying law. He had substantially written the first version of *L'Éducation sentimentale* (1869; *A Sentimental Education*, 1898) by 1843 and would continue to revise it for the following two decades. Even so, the general indifference of friends like Ernest Chevalier and Maxime Du Camp to his early work drove Flaubert inward artistically. Flaubert's first epileptic seizure occurred at this time, in the midst not only of his failure at the law but amid the death of his father and the death in childbirth of his beloved sister Caroline.

If one adds these tragedies to Flaubert's seeming lack of success in his chosen profession, the extraordinary two-year trip Flaubert undertook to the East with his friend Du Camp makes some sense, if only because it was a means of escape. Madame Flaubert bore the expense of this adventure, to the cost of more than $100,000 in modern spending power.

Flaubert and Du Camp's trip took them to Egypt, the Holy Land, and Greece and was followed by a reunion with Madame Flaubert in Italy. Flaubert was at his sybaritic worst during these years, as was Du Camp, but each learned much: Flaubert about the impersonal possibilities possible in description, Du Camp about photography and travel writing. Indeed, Du Camp published his travel journals as *Un voyageur en Égypte vers 1850*, to great acclaim following their return. Du Camp notably omits Flaubert entirely from the narrative, making himself the single traveler.

One continuing fear Flaubert had, especially in his early adult life, was that he was subject to grand mal seizures as well as periods of profound depression. The unexpected deaths of his father and the second sister Caroline following childbirth likely made these episodes more acute than they would otherwise have been. This, combined with his failure at law, made him retreat to a stoically private world; it also helped create the aesthetics of detachment he consistently privileges in his fiction. This appears in the moral neutrality he maintains with all of his characters. One does not sense judgment or even authorial presence concerning either Emma Bovary or St. Anthony—or indeed any of the other characters.

This stoic privacy also disinclined Flaubert to publish. The income from his father's estate could easily support him, his mother, and his sister's child, a third Caroline. He claimed to prefer his study in the family's estate, Croisset, to public acclaim and residence in Paris, though he, his mother, and niece would live there for periods starting in the late 1850's. One wonders whether this disinclination to publish resulted from lack of confidence or a realistic assessment of the literary trends of the period. The mid-nineteenth century was a time of turmoil for nearly all of Europe, especially so for France as it swayed from Napoleonic rule back to monarchy back to the Napoleons, then to republic. This instability produced great writing and great art, which was political in its context. Émile Zola's novels, like Jean-Auguste-Dominique Ingres's paintings, were controversial, as they clearly took moral positions.

One can imagine the reaction to Flaubert's provincial housewife in *Madame Bovary* (1857) who not only flouts convention but mixes in social circles far above her own. It was with this unconventional heroine that Flaubert made his public literary debut. This occurred thanks to the work's serialization in *La Revue de Paris*, a periodical supported by several of Flaubert's close friends. When *Madame Bovary* appeared in book form within a year of its serialization, it produced instant notoriety for Flaubert as well as charges of obscenity. Indeed, a trial followed that ultimately cleared the way for the novel's distribution.

True to form, Flaubert seemed disengaged even as he appeared at the trial. He had previously sold publication rights for a mere eight hundred francs (about thirty-two hundred dollars) and serial rights for two thousand francs (about eight thousand dollars). Neither of these transactions was particularly shrewd, but they removed him from the front line of battle. He would have to fight to regain control of publication rights in 1873; though successful, he did not reprint.

Here, then, is the paradox that surrounds Flaubert: a middle-class provincial who lived as an aristocrat on family wealth; a failed lawyer whose public recognition would have been at least delayed had *Madame Bovary* not appeared in general distribution; the ultimate sensualist in his personal life who refrained from sensitivity in his art. He was fond of repeating that an artist should appear no more in his work than God does in nature.

Flaubert's contradictions would have seemed far greater in the nineteenth century than in the twentieth, primarily because so many writers adopted Flaubert's aesthetics to their own works. One sees Flaubertian detachment in the works of Stephen Crane, William Dean Howells, and innumerable later authors. It appears in the paintings of American artist Edward Hopper, whose early inspiration was French impressionism. Even so, Flaubert was capable of great tenderness to his mother and to his niece, the younger Caroline. Caroline would live until 1931, and the epilogue of Brown's study offers the description of a fascinating 1930 meeting between her and the American novelist Willa Cather in Paris. Rather appropriately, they talked about *L'Éducation sentimentale*.

Probably wisely, Brown's impressive study avoids speculation of all kinds. Its strength comes from the author's access to Flaubert's massive correspondence, and it is as much a survey of nineteenth century French history and culture as it is of its subject's life. The absence of speculation and gratuitous psychological probing allows each reader to draw individual conclusions without authorial influences. It is the kind of writing Flaubert himself would have loved: detailed in its descriptions, willing to move far beyond its immediate subject, and most of all, detached.

Robert J. Forman

Review Sources

America 195, no. 8 (September 25, 2006): 33-34.
Booklist 102, no. 12 (February 15, 2006): 32.
New Criterion 24, no. 9 (May, 2006): 66-70.
The New Republic 234, no. 19 (May 22, 2006): 37-41.
The New York Times 155 (April 12, 2006): E1-E10.
The New York Times Book Review 155 (April 16, 2006): 1-11.
Publishers Weekly 253, no. 11 (March 13, 2006): 51.
Sunday Telegraph, June 11, 2006, p. 1.
The Times Literary Supplement, September 1, 2006, p. 5.
The Wall Street Journal 247, no. 88 (April 15, 2006): P8.

THE FOREIGN CORRESPONDENT

Author: Alan Furst (1941-   )
Publisher: Random House (New York). 273 pp. $25.00
Type of work: Novel
Time: 1938
Locale: Western Europe

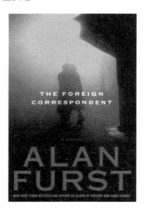

An Italian expatriate in Paris just before World War II, working as a foreign correspondent for Reuters, is brought into the shadow world of espionage

Principal characters:
>CARLO WEISZ, an Italian expatriate living in Paris, foreign correspondent for the Reuters news agency
>COLONEL FERRARA, an Italian military commander who fights against Benito Mussolini's forces in Spain
>S. KOLB, an English spy
>MR. BROWN, Kolb's superior
>ARTURO SALAMONE, leader of the Italian expatriates who resist Mussolini's fascists
>CHRISTA VON SCHIRREN, Weisz's lover, a member of the resistance movement in Berlin

The Foreign Correspondent is the ninth of Alan Furst's World War II-era spy novels. His books have often been compared to those by such suspense novelists as Eric Ambler, John le Carré, and Alistair MacLean. In the poetic diction of Furst's prose, the realism of his plots, and his focus on characters rather than missions, however, Furst belongs in the same class as British writer Graham Greene. Each of the nine novels is set between the late 1930's and the end of World War II, and, with one exception, Furst's main characters are always Europeans. Rather than populating his stories with British or American "saviors" against the fascists, he instead uses people whose worlds have been destroyed by fascism or communism. The characters are never "superspies" who are fighting against mad scientists bent on world domination (as one sees in the James Bond films) but are regular men and women—journalists, ship captains, soldiers, film directors—called upon to perform services that in ordinary times would be mundane but in the context of their war-torn world are extraordinary and dangerous.

Many of Furst's novels are fascinated with the game of détente played between fascism—as instituted by Adolf Hitler in Germany, Benito Mussolini in Italy, and Francisco Franco in Spain—and communism as practiced by Joseph Stalin. As Furst reveals over the course of his novels, the entire history of wartime Europe hinges upon the eventual falling out between Stalin and Hitler and the hesitation shown by the United Kingdom and the United States in getting involved in the budding world war. *The Foreign Correspondent* depicts the growing monster of fascism and the slow march to world war, and it also relates the mounting frustration of those isolated, few people committed to combating its advance.

The thorny complexities of the novel are partly spelled out by the curious heritage of the protagonist, Italian émigré Carlo Weisz. He is a native of Trieste, which was part of the Austrian-Hungarian Empire until 1919; like the city, he "was half-Italian, on his mother's side, and half Slovenian—long ago Austrian, thus the name—on his father's." A product of the best university in Italy, Weisz was able to perfect his English during graduate study at Oxford. After suffering as a journalist under Mussolini's rule until 1935, he finally has made his way to Paris, where he has worked for the past few years as a foreign correspondent for the British news agency, Reuters. In many ways, life is not much simpler for Weisz in France than it was in Italy. In Paris,

Alan Furst found his literary niche with his fifth novel, Night Soldiers *(1988), which focuses on espionage during the World War II era. He has published seven subsequent novels, each set in Europe between 1938 and 1942. Furst has been nominated for the Edgar Award and the* Los Angeles Times *Book Award and has received the Dashiell Hammett Award.*

he is a part of a small underground group working against Mussolini's fascism by publishing the clandestine propaganda newspaper, *Liberazion* (or *Liberty*), one of hundreds of small resistance papers produced by Italian intellectuals who have fled their country. The danger of this enterprise is spelled out from the beginning of the novel, however: The writers and editors of *Liberazione* have been targeted by Mussolini's secret police, active even in Paris, and the novel opens with their assassination of the editor Bottini and his lover Madame LaCroix, the wife of an antifascist French politician. With the execution of Bottini, framed to look like a suicide, the fascists manage to kill a dissenter, defame him and his cause, and cast doubts on the veracity of the politician.

Furst is often interested in the kind of people who capitulate when faced with occupation and oppression, and he is even more interested in those characters who—almost unwillingly—find that they are unable to surrender. Like most Furst characters, Weisz wants to help the cause and work against the forces of totalitarianism, but also like most Furst characters, he is not a two-dimensional heroic figure of the sort one encounters in espionage films. Like many of his predecessors, he is reluctant to commit too fully to his cause, at first because of a reasonable concern for his own safety. Also reminiscent of earlier protagonists, chance, human connections, and the very makeup of his personality conspire to pull him in further than he would have believed, despite the very real dangers. Finally, like those prior characters, his reason for political commitment is often, at root, a personal one.

His first advance in commitment to his cause comes when he takes over as editor of

Liberazione at the behest of his friend Arturo Salamone, the leader of this small resistance cell. He becomes further entangled because of his work as a foreign correspondent: Reuters sends him to cover international units in the Spanish Civil War, and he manages an interview with a famous Italian military commander and refugee, known only as Colonel Ferrara, who has come to Spain to fight a losing battle against the fascists. Before long, British intelligence has decided that Ferrara would make a useful tool in their own handling of fascists, and they send their agent Kolb to secure his release from a French refugee camp. For their plan to succeed, the British must convince Weisz to work with Ferrara to ghostwrite a memoir, a propagandistic work about the evils of fascism titled *Soldier of Freedom.*

Ferrara, in his willingness to sacrifice everything to his cause and to die fighting for freedom and liberty, serves as a symbol in the novel for the indomitable will of the people. He has fought the fascists in Ethiopia, in Spain, and—by helping Weisz create the memoir—in Paris. Furst seems to be pointing out that as long as dictators such as Mussolini and Hitler rise to power, there will be others waiting in the shadows to fight them, no matter how terrible the odds.

Furst creates a somber mood throughout the novel. The opening lines evoke funereal shades of black and gray and foretell an ominous storm: "In Paris, the last days of autumn; a gray, troubled sky at daybreak, the fall of twilight at noon, followed, at seven-thirty, by slanting rains and black umbrellas as the people of the city hurried home past the bare trees." He continues to paint the dark mood richly, so that the ripples of paranoia and fear that surround Weisz and threaten to overwhelm him are palpable. Within a few pages of the opening paragraph, Weisz's predecessor Bottini is assassinated. When Weisz and his compatriot Salamone meet to deliver *Liberazione* to the train conductor who will smuggle it into Italy, they are almost unnerved by passing cars. As the novel continues, the members of the resistance cell are harassed and even beaten by the Italian agents. Their lives are even more compromised than they know, as one of their members is also a spy for the Italian secret police.

The lines that bind Weisz are not only political and professional but also romantic; not long after reuniting with his former lover, Christa, now the wife of a Prussian aristocrat, he finds that she is a member of a resistance organization working to subvert Hitler's Third Reich. She coerces Weisz into smuggling out of Berlin a list of German agents working in Europe. Weisz not only publishes information from the list in *Liberazione* but makes sure that the French authorities who would not be happy with Italian operations within their country receive copies as well. However, it is not long before Weisz realizes that Berlin is about to become a closed city and that his chances of helping Christa escape are diminishing by the day. He sees his opportunity when Mr. Brown and British intelligence ask the correspondent if he would be willing, at the expense of the British government, to greatly increase the size and circulation of *Liberazione*, and actually carry out its production on Italian soil. Weisz knows how problematical the venture will be, for any such procedure would surely bring about the scrutiny of the Italian government, but he agrees to pursue the plan so long as the British agents agree to rescue Christa from Berlin and the tightening grip of the Nazi Party and the Gestapo.

Despite Weisz's precautions and natural savvy, his fears are soon realized. He is sent to Genoa, where he begins procuring paper and a space for his printing press and makes contacts for printing and distribution. Furst's themes of self-loving capitulation versus sacrificial resistance are played out again and again, and before long Weisz is almost arrested, escaping by the slimmest of margins. In a way, this climatic, and almost anticlimatic, episode serves to reveal Furst's entire realistic method. Weisz's motivations are not only patriotic but also personal: He gets to help Christa through pursuing the plan. Second, the plan, which seems to him to be foolhardy, actually is foolhardy, and it results in failure. Third, Weisz's acts as a spy in the novel consist of editing a newspaper that is delivered to a train conductor, ghostwriting a memoir, receiving a sensitive document, and trying to establish a printing press. His escape from harm's way is similarly realistic.

The plots of Furst's novels sometimes can be frustrating to readers raised on espionage fiction of the more escapist variety; perhaps this is one reason Furst is often referred to as a "historical" novelist rather than a spy novelist. Nevertheless, each of his books, as stated earlier, does deal with espionage during the World War II era. Unlike many of his counterparts, however, Furst is unwilling to sacrifice historical fact and realism to his plots. Any informed reader knows that Mussolini will actually stay in power until he is overthrown in 1943, five years after the time of the novel. Furthermore, the German army, with its Nazis and Gestapo that Christa has worked so hard to escape, will invade Paris only two years after the novel's events conclude, on June 14, 1940. Weisz's acts do not avert the invasion any more than they serve to remove Mussolini from power.

This seems to be a large part of Furst's point, however. Realistically, Weisz and his five or six friends can not reasonably expect to make significant changes or to unseat Mussolini, any more than Christa can topple Hitler. Yet they continue to fight, to push on, despite the dangers and the quite real possibility that they may pay with their lives. The closing words of the novel are spoken by Weisz's concierge in response to his wishing her a good night; however, they serve to remind the reader who people like Weisz and his friends are fighting for: "For us all, monsieur. For all of us."

Scott Yarbrough

Review Sources

The Atlantic Monthly 297, no. 5 (June, 2006): 110-113.
Booklist 102, no. 17 (May 1, 2006): 30.
Kirkus Reviews 74, no. 9 (May 1, 2006): 426.
Library Journal 131, no. 9 (May 15, 2006): 88.
The New York Times 155 (June 1, 2006): E1-E7.
The New York Times Book Review 155 (June 18, 2006): 26.
Publishers Weekly 253, no. 15 (April 10, 2006): 44-45.
The Virginia Quarterly Review 82, no. 4 (Fall, 2006): 269.
The Wall Street Journal 247, no. 129 (June 3, 2006): P8.

FORGETFULNESS

Author: Ward Just (1935-   )
Publisher: Houghton Mifflin (Boston). 258 pp. $25.00
Type of work: Novel
Time: November-September, a year or two after September 11, 2001
Locale: France and Maine

As the United States begins its War on Terror, an expatriate American painter living in a secluded rural French village suffers the loss of his wife and has to decide whether to exact revenge against her murderer

Principal characters:
> THOMAS RAILLES, a sixty-five-year-old successful painter and former "odd-jobber" for the CIA who lives in the south of France
> FLORETTE DUFOUR, his French wife
> BERNHARD SINDELAR, Railles's lifelong friend
> RUSS CONLON, Railles's lifelong friend
> CAPTAIN ST. JOHN GRANGER, Railles's reclusive 106-year-old English neighbor
> VICTORIA GRANGER, Granger's Pennsylvania niece
> ANTOINE, a French policeman noted for his expertise in interrogation

In the thirty-six years since he left a distinguished career as a journalist to become a full-time writer of fiction, Ward Just has published fifteen novels, three collections of stories and novellas, and a small volume containing a play and two more stories. The best of these books—including *Forgetfulness*—deserve to be read by anyone who cares about fine writing or the power of the novel to help readers understand themselves and their time.

Readers who recognize Just's name probably think of him as our premier fictional chronicler of Washington, D.C. While he is most certainly that, he is much more. Taken as a whole, his fiction presents a multigenerational portrait of well-to-do and well-connected Americans during the period between the New Deal and the present (although his portrait actually spans "the American Century" back as far as the 1890's and always finds its touchstone in the 1960's). In his pages readers see how individuals, the country, and its government have been shaped by our engagement in World War II, Korea, Cuba, Berlin, Africa, Latin America, Vietnam, and the Middle East. They find an America sharply defined by historical events such as the Cold War, Camelot and the Kennedy assassination, the Vietnam debacle, Watergate, the fall of the Soviet Empire, and, in *Forgetfulness*, 9/11 and the War on Terror. This is an America undergoing profound changes in its social and political fabric, from the rise of the suburbs and the consequent crisis of small-town main streets and urban centers

to the heyday and decline of city and county
political machines, from the emergence of
lawyers as power brokers and fixers to the
evolution of Washington, from a small company town to an international magnet for
money, power, and international intrigue. It is
an America in which both private and public
life are marked by struggles between order
and chaos, stability and change, memory and
amnesia.

*Ward Just—whose father and
grandfather published the* Waukegan
News-Sun *in Illinois—was a foreign
correspondent for* Newsweek *and* The
Washington Post *before devoting
himself to fiction. His short stories have
earned him numerous honors,
including the National Book Award,
Pulitzer Prize nominations, and the
Chicago Tribune's Heartland Award.*

Vietnam inspired Just's first two novels, *A
Soldier of the Revolution* (1970) and *Stringer*
(1974). Written in a prose that evoked com-
parisons to writer Ernest Hemingway, both of these novels also recall novelists Joseph Conrad's and Graham Greene's portraits of burnt-out cases forced to make
moral choices in foreign lands. Like novelists Henry Adams, Gore Vidal, and Allen
Drury before him, Just recognized that Washington could be more than the scene for
potboilers and espionage capers. In early stories such as "The Congressman Who
Loved Flaubert" (1972) and his third novel, *Nicholson at Large* (1975), he began to
stake his claim as poet laureate of the insider's Washington. In *Nicholson at Large* he
also presents his first portrait of an artist. Then, in *A Family Trust* (1978) and stories
such as "Honor, Power, Riches, Fame, and the Love of Women" (1979), he took the
Midwest satirized by Sinclair Lewis in *Main Street* (1920) and *Babbitt* (1922) and
turned its offices, living rooms, and clubs into scenes as ripe for subtle and sophisticated social analysis as American writers Edith Wharton's New York drawing rooms,
F. Scott Fitzgerald's East and West Egg, John O'Hara's Pottsville, John Cheever's
Shady Hill, or John Updike's Tarbox.

By the end of his first decade as a novelist, then, Just had found all but one of the
major subjects and main locations that he would return to throughout his career.
Memories of Vietnam and its implications for American foreign policy would be cen-
tral to *In the City of Fear* (1982), *The American Blues* (1984), and *A Dangerous
Friend* (1999). His Washington—located in Georgetown, Northern Virginia, and
Maryland's Eastern Shore, as well as the Capitol, the White House, the agencies, and
the law firms that advise rather than litigate—would reappear and be refined in *In the
City of Fear*, *The American Ambassador* (1987), *Jack Gance* (1989), the National
Book Award finalist *Echo House* (1997), and a late story such as "Born in His Time"
(2001). He would develop portraits of other writers and artists in the story "Honor,
Power, Riches, Fame, and the Love of Women" and in *The American Blues*, *The
American Ambassador*, *The Translator* (1991), *Ambition and Love* (1994), and *The
Weather in Berlin* (2002). He would again capture moments in the social history of his
Midwest—which includes Chicago, its North Shore suburbs, the downstate Illinois
town he calls Dement—in another of his most memorable stories, "The North Shore,
1958" (1985), as well as in *Jack Gance, Ambition and Love* and the Pulitzer Prize fi-
nalist *An Unfinished Season* (2004).

His fifth subject and location did not emerge until *The American Ambassador*. This was the story of Americans abroad in Europe—especially France and Germany—rather than the Third World. A variation on the Jamesian theme of the complications and misunderstandings created when the New World meets the Old, Just's version is updated to include the particular resentments that the international dominance of American power and culture have caused in Europe since World War II, as well as the effects that America's and Europe's different experiences of the war and, more recently, of terrorism have had on their national characters. A minor theme in *Jack Gance*, *Echo House*, and *A Dangerous Friend*, it plays a crucial role in *The American Ambassador*, *The Translator*, *Ambition and Love*, and *The Weather in Berlin*.

In his first books, Just not only defined his subjects and locations, however, he also began to develop a form that has served him well throughout his career. His main characters are usually educated men and women of the world, as familiar with opera and classical music, history and literature, art and interior decoration, cocktails and clothes, debutantes and duck blinds as they are with politics and power. When readers meet them they are faced with crucial choices or crises. Each of the novels has a plot—there are secret military operations, electoral machinations, deals to be made, careers to be advanced, terrorists to be confronted, intentional or unintentional acts of betrayal, midlife crises, deaths, and more. Plot and straightforward narrative chronology are usually not Just's priorities. Rather, his fiction, like that of Milan Kundera, is full of both brilliant set pieces and fascinating digressions. The set pieces—in *Forgetfulness*, they include the opening chapter describing Florette DuFour's accident and death in the Pyrenees, the description of the first days of Thomas's grief, and his observation and participation in the interrogation of a suspected murderer and terrorist later in the novel—are often unforgettable.

The texture of his work is created, above all, by its unique combination of dialogue and digressions into memory. Just's novels are full of conversations; some continue—with interruptions for memories that fill in past events—for a hundred pages or more. His ear for nuances and idioms is superb, and he understands the power of what is not said, as well as the cadences of how his people actually talk. Rather than plot, what drives Just's novels is the remembrance of things past. His characters are always "remembering," "recalling," "wondering," "reminiscing," or "thinking" of the past, so that the movement of the novels is a constant stream of consciousness from the present into the past and back again. In fact, the past is always present, and his characters are always struggling with the "torrent of memory." For Just, it seems, the novel is as much a means to preserve and understand our common memories as to define how individual character is shaped by personal memory. Without the former, a culture is rootless; without the latter, a character is lost.

Considering Just's style and preoccupations, it is surprising, to put it mildly, to find that he has titled a novel *Forgetfulness*—and no surprise at all to find that the book turns out to be about its impossibility for Thomas Railles. At one point, Thomas thinks that "Amnesia was the curse of the modern world, or its redemption, depending on whether you held to the Old Testament or the New. Forgiveness was the consequence of amnesia." At another, he suggests that "Forgetfulness is the old man's friend." In the end, though, finding redemption without forgetting, struggling to live with his grief without turning to this "old man's friend," foregoing revenge without forgiving become Thomas's challenges.

In this portrait of an internationally recognized expatriate American painter who has withdrawn from the wider world to a remote French village at the foot of the Pyrenees, Just shapes one of his most powerful and thought-provoking tales.

Attempting to flee from the guilt Railles feels when his occasional role as an "odd-jobber" for his friends at the Central Intelligence Agency (CIA) plays some part in the betrayal and murder of an elderly Spanish communist he came to admire, Railles tries to make a new life for himself. He meets, falls in love with, and marries Florette DuFour, a local woman, and together they make a life for themselves that is a kind of idyll. Since withdrawing from the world is no more possible in a Just novel than forgetting, however—for him, the personal is always political, the private life always bound up with the public—the world beyond the valley soon comes calling. Men and women in suits occasionally turn up to talk privately with Thomas about his secret past; a tourist from New York City who was blinded and scarred by the attacks of 9/11 brings the anger and thirst for revenge that followed those events in America into their local village bar. Then, on the autumn afternoon of St. John Granger's funeral, Florette leaves their house to take a walk near the mountains while Thomas is talking with his friends Bernhard and Russ, slips and hurts her leg, and is found dead the next morning with her throat cut.

While America grieves, debates the causes of the 9/11 attacks, and begins to seek revenge, Thomas Railles grieves for Florette, wonders if his activities with the CIA may not be somehow responsible for her death, and then finds himself with the opportunity to join in interrogating—and torturing—the man who killed her, who has been captured by the French police and identified as a Moroccan terrorist. The novel opens with Florette's final hours and closes with Thomas leaving the village, returning to the America he left after the Kennedy assassination, and settling on an island off the coast of Maine.

In between, readers will find all of Just's strengths on display. Florette's and Thomas's memories, the depth of Thomas's first days of mourning, the midwestern town where he grew up, the New York City and America of the Camelot years where he came of age, the shadow world of the American intelligence agencies, the French village where Florette made her life and she and Thomas have made their home, the story of St. John Granger's experience in World War I and just after, the nondescript street and warehouse in Le Havre where the expert French interrogator Antoine practices his trade, the Maine island to which Thomas ultimately retreats—all are brought to vivid life by the power of Just's description, the focus of his vision, and the accuracy of his ear. In the end, *Forgetfulness* seems a parable for our times in which the forces and moral choices that are swirling around all of us are cast in sharp and painful relief.

Bernard F. Rodgers, Jr.

Review Sources

The Atlantic Monthly, October, 2006, p. 127.
Booklist 102, no. 21 (July 1, 2006): 9.
Kirkus Reviews 74, no. 14 (July 15, 2006): 691.
Library Journal 131, no. 15 (September 15, 2006): 49.
The New York Times Book Review 156 (September 24, 2006): 13.
The New Yorker, September 18, 2006, p. 86.
Publishers Weekly 253, no. 29 (July 24, 2006): 32-33.
The Wall Street Journal 248, no. 59 (September 9, 2006): P8.
The Washington Post, September 3, 2006, p. BW5.

FORTY MILLION DOLLAR SLAVES
The Rise, Fall, and Redemption of the Black Athlete

Author: William C. Rhoden (1951-   )
Publisher: Crown (New York). 286 pp. $24.00
Type of work: History, current affairs
Time: From the late nineteenth century to 2006
Locale: The United States

A sportswriter traces the ways in which race has mattered in the history of American sports

FORTY MILLION DOLLAR SLAVES

The Rise, Fall, and Redemption of the Black Athlete

WILLIAM C. RHODEN

Principal personages:
ISAAC MURPHY, famous nineteenth century African American jockey
MOSES FLEETWOOD WALKER, baseball player who briefly integrated the major leagues in the nineteenth century
ANDREW "RUBE" FOSTER, founder of the Negro National League
JACKIE ROBINSON, baseball player who integrated the major leagues in 1947
KELLEN WINSLOW, tight end for the San Diego Chargers in the 1980's whose son also became a successful football player
JOHN THOMPSON, coach of Georgetown University's basketball team, 1972-1999

Many books have been written on the history of the African American athlete, chief among them the tennis star Arthur Ashe's scholarly *The Hard Road to Glory* (1987). In *Forty Million Dollar Slaves*, William C. Rhoden takes a different approach, filled with poetic brio and passionate argument. Rhoden's book has received endorsements from such well-known academics as Cornel West and Arnold Rampersad, and the book alludes to music, literature, and religion as well as history and politics. Its intent is as much prophetic as analytical. Creative figures within its pages range from novelist Ralph Ellison to trumpet player Miles Davis.

In the chapter on athletic style, Rhoden contends it was through the development of a distinct and unmistakable style that African American athletes leveraged their status within the sports industry. The book is also deeply autobiographical. Rhoden himself was an athlete—he played football at a historically black college, Morgan State University in Baltimore, in the late 1960's. He uses his own life experience as a prism through which to interpret events. In one of the most engaging moments of the book, he relates how an elderly resident of the largely African American neighborhood of Harlem, where Rhoden lives, told Rhoden that Babe Ruth, the great white baseball star of the 1920's, lived at 409 Edgecombe Avenue, where Rhoden now lives, walking on the viaduct over the Harlem River to go to Yankee Stadium, where he played. *Forty Million Dollar Slaves* is a personal meditation as well as a social tract.

William C. Rhoden has been a sportswriter for The New York Times *since 1983. He also serves as a consultant for ESPN's* SportsCentury *series and occasionally appears as a guest on the show* The Sports Reporters. *In 1996, Rhoden won a Peabody Award for broadcasting as a writer of the HBO documentary* Journey of the African American Athlete.

Rhoden argues that while black athletes are among the most famous and highest remunerated salaried individuals working today, this fact does not mean that they are in control of their own destinies. Rhoden is aware that his title, which suggests that even an athlete earning forty million dollars can still be a slave, is provocative. Indeed, he gives space to individuals such as black entrepreneur and Charlotte Bobcats owner Robert Johnson, who are unwilling to accept fully Rhoden's analogy. Rhoden's larger point— and it is a point about race in America, not just race in sports—is that the journey to full emancipation for African Americans is not yet complete. Using the analogy of the biblical Exodus frequently used by African Americans to describe their own quest for freedom, Rhoden sees the black athlete as still wandering in the desert, still finding a way in the wilderness nowhere near the promised land of autonomy and equality.

Rhoden traces African American athletic activity back to speculative roots in African culture and verges on suggesting that the intensity of sporting culture in the United States may hinge on this African American influence, although by using comparable situations in Australia and Canada one might argue otherwise. Rhoden gives a somber conspectus on how sports were used on slave plantations to give African American men an outlet for aggressive impulses that might otherwise have been turned against their oppressive masters. Even though sports, especially boxing, became a major avenue for black male empowerment, Rhoden argues that the roots of these athletic practices in the context of slavery should lead historians to think twice about whether athletics are automatically empowering and liberating for black Americans.

Rhoden makes another point relating to the history of race in America, noting that the path to racial equality has not been one of seamless progress; even after the Civil War there have been times when racism and white social control increased rather than decreased. (The political scientist Ira Katznelson made a similar statement in his 2005 book *When Affirmative Action Was White.* For instance, in the late nineteenth century, most horse jockeys were African American; particularly prominent was Isaac Murphy, the most famous jockey of his day, who died at thirty-five. In Murphy's day, black jockeys were the norm, and had been for decades. Apparently, slaves had excelled as jockeys. White anxiety led to the promotion of a new wave of white jockeys as a rejoinder to the threat of African American achievement. Black jockeys went from a being a staple of the horse racing industry to being virtually excluded by the 1920's.

Rhoden also subverts progressive, overly optimistic accounts of baseball history. He reminds the reader that it was Moses Fleetwood Walker, not Jackie Robinson, who was the first black to play in the major leagues of baseball. Rhoden illustrates that baseball, after the turn of the twentieth century, regressed in racial terms. This led first to teams of African American barnstormers who toured the United States thanks to a more stable Negro National League, founded by Andrew "Rube" Foster. Foster, for Rhoden, is emblematic of the largely African American entrepreneur who ran the Negro Leagues during their heyday from the 1920's to the early 1950's. Jackie Robinson's entry into major-league baseball in 1947 is usually considered to mark a great improvement in the history of race in American sports. Rhoden points out, however, that the black entrepreneurs who had owned the Negro League teams were forced out of business by integration and that the newly enfranchised black athletes then played for white owners who, until the arbitration ruling against the reserve clause in 1975, were bound to their teams for life.

Similarly, the integration of college sports led to the decline of historically black colleges such as Grambling and Rhoden's alma mater, Morgan State, which had formerly been athletic titans. Rhoden discusses how white coaches such as Alabama's legendary Paul "Bear" Bryant became open to integration: not because of any profound reorientation of their personal convictions but because they saw African American athletes helping other teams win and did not want their programs to be left behind.

Because of this, African American athletes left programs like Grambling, where they had a support system within the community, and went to universities like Alabama, where they were the most visible representatives of their community on campus. In this environment, argues Rhoden, black athletes were at once enormously privileged and fundamentally disempowered, given amounts of money inconceivable to most people but not truly able to manage their own destinies.

Rhoden shows how some athletes have learned to maneuver within the system. Former football star Kellen Winslow saw that his son, also named Kellen, had potential to play in the National Football League at the same position, tight end, as his father did. The senior Winslow insisted that any college his son attended have a black coach or take the role of African Americans in sports seriously.

Winslow, as a father, was attempting to intervene in the process of what Rhoden terms the Conveyor Belt—the orderly system that transmits athletes from high school to college to the professional leagues and which abides by informal yet rigid hierarchies, of which college is more prestigious than high school and has the better sports program. The Conveyer Belt gives players an assured sense of their career trajectory but fails to put them in control of their careers in a self-determining way. It also, Rhodes argues, gives them a sense of unearned rewards that insulates them from challenging circumstances in which they will be totally free to set their own agenda.

Recruitment of high school players to college is, for Rhoden, the key stage on the Conveyor Belt. On one level, this process is a prodigious feat of redistributing wealth, as athletes from poor families receive access to an educational institution normally reserved for the privileged as well as eligibility to receive all the perks naturally accorded to star athletes in major college programs. The habits of dependency the Conveyer Belt can propagate among athletes is, for Rhoden, a warning sign that all is not right with this process.

Rhoden pays some attention to the parallel history of the African American woman athlete, discussing the tennis player Althea Gibson and the little-known basketball player Luisa Harris. Most of the closing part of the book, however, has to do with the way in which, for all of basketball's current reputation as an African American sport, blacks have so little power within the game.

Rhoden is critical of powerful African Americans in basketball. Michael Jordan is castigated for, in 1990, not supporting Democratic senatorial candidate Harvey Gantt against his conservative opponent, Jesse Helms. John Thompson, the legendary basketball coach for many years at Georgetown University, is criticized for steering players to a white agent. Rhoden may be too hard on Thompson when he characterizes his presence at the McDonald All-America Game in 1983 as a shopping expedition where Thompson was enticing the bored Reggie Williams to play for his team and put it over the top for a championship. Georgetown had the dominant big man of his era in Patrick Ewing, and it had been eliminated the previous two seasons on mishaps that can happen to even the greatest teams in single-elimination playoffs. Williams certainly helped the team, but Thompson had a strong enough hand that he did not need to bid desperately for Williams like an item in the marketplace.

Rhoden cites a remark Chris Webber made in the early 1990's about attending the University of Michigan rather than a historically black college as though Webber was simply lured by the greater exposure of Michigan. Webber, in fact, who had attended a prestigious private school on an academic scholarship, was showing unusual historical perspective in an era when most black players attended largely white universities and did not give it a thought. Webber and Thompson have worked for the same goals that Rhoden so clearly espouses, and certain passages in *Forty Million Dollar Slaves* are too critical of them, especially as Rhoden seems to admire the contentiousness of the 1990's New York Knicks power forward Larry Johnson, who, similarly, had pronounced opinions about the workings of sport in modern-day America.

Such is the risk any book as opinionated as this one inevitably takes. *Forty Million Dollar Slaves* is one of the best books on sports and society to have appeared in this decade.

Nicholas Birns

Review Sources

Black Issues Book Review 8, no. 5 (September/October, 2006): 11.
Booklist 102, no. 18 (May 15, 2006): 15.
Crisis 113, no. 4 (July/August, 2006): 45.
Library Journal 131, no. 9 (May 15, 2006): 106.
The New York Times Book Review 155 (July 23, 2006): 8.
Publishers Weekly 243, no. 19 (May 8, 2006): 60.
Sports Illustrated 104, no. 26 (June 26, 2006): 25.
The Washington Post, August 13, 2006, p. BW08.

FRIENDSHIP
An Exposé

Author: Joseph Epstein (1937-   )
Publisher: Houghton Mifflin (Boston). 270 pp. $24.00
Type of work: Essay
Time: The twentieth century
Locale: Chicago and the East Coast

An important American essayist, editor, and humorist applies his wit and learning to the contemporary state of friendship

Joseph Epstein is a personal essayist, perhaps one of the best practitioners of the form alive today. The personal essay is also called the familiar essay, and it is important to keep both terms in mind because the form is most successful when shadings of each are at play. In his introduction to *The Norton Book of Personal Essays*, which he edited in 1997, Epstein says that "the personal essayist writes, I think, for himself and people—even though he has never met them—he assumes are potentially his friends."

As editor of *American Scholar*, a position he held for more than twenty years, Epstein maintained that when he first took the job he decided that his main criteria for choosing articles and essays would be his own interests and taste. This was not vanity but rather the simple assumption that what appealed to a modest but wide-ranging intellect such as his own would also appeal to the common reader. What served him as an editor also fed his talent as a writer—the "personal" touch, a knack for persuading his readers that he and they were on similar tracks of feeling and thought. Once this is established, Epstein finds just the right tone to seal the pact of familiarity, to make the personal essay "familiar." In *Friendship: An Exposé*, for example, he gets his reader to agree that even though friends are usually drawn from one's one age group, senior adults are not always happy with their peers: "A man or woman who was a creep at forty is unlikely to improve at eighty-five." The colloquial "creep" startles one into jovial compliance. Epstein's familiarity scores a hit.

After writing short and book-length personal essays for almost twenty-five years on such a variety of subjects as ambition, divorce, envy, and snobbery—not to mention dozens of literary and cultural topics—Epstein has finally decided to address the relationship between human beings that is, at bottom, what makes possible the literary form he has made his own. If his readers have been all along "potentially his friends," they can now find themselves addressed, at least in theory, in his latest volume. They must take note, however, that this book on friendship is also, as its subtitle warns, an exposé; it will not fall into sentimentality or hypocrisy but instead peel off the protective layers in which the subject is too often smothered. Epstein is aware that this kind of objectivity involves risks. He worries about the reactions of his personal friends who "will recognize themselves in these pages (though they are for the most part not mentioned by name), some to their pleasure, some to their chagrin, and a few to their strong distaste. . . . I don't claim this is a courageous book, but it is, I fear, rather a reckless one." What about offending his readers, who may not find themselves, at all times, to be the friends that his wit and engaging style are determined to win over?

The answer to this question has everything to do with how effectively Epstein can persuade readers that friendship itself is in need of the kind of dusting and overall scrutiny he insists it deserves. He begins by distinguishing friends from acquaintances. With an acquaintance there is "no obligation on either side, nothing owed but recognition and civility." A friend, on the other hand, is "preferential: one chooses one person over another to draw closer to."

The deeper one gets into this book, the clearer it becomes that Epstein is actually treading a very fine line between the distance of acquaintanceship and the closeness of friendship. His exposé focuses on the truth that friendship falls short of its own idealization. No friendship is perfect, says Epstein, and to stress this insight he maintains that even his deep friendship with Edward Shils, the social philosopher, fell short of the claims that Montaigne (1533-1592) made for the "sublime best friendship" he enjoyed with political philosopher Etienne de La Boetie (1530-1563). In other words, the classical Damon-Pythias myth of perfect friendship is an illusion. Friendship suffers from being held to expectations that are beyond its possibilities in the real world. Nevertheless, Epstein recognizes that it is an experience one cannot live without.

To fall back on this "cooler" sense of friendship, he finds it appropriate to deflate exaggerated notions of intimacy as a norm for judging the value of friendship. "Confessional-intimacy" makes Epstein very nervous. "I do intimacy well only with my wife, but even before I married I shied away from deep intimacy with friends." He refutes Francis Bacon (1561-1626), who in his essay "Of Friendship" praised the value of having a good friend to whom one could "impart . . . whatsoever lieth upon the heart to oppress." "If I strongly felt the need for regular confession," says Epstein, "I would consider psychoanalysis or the Catholic Church." All of Epstein's discomfort with sloppy feeling and undisciplined self-pity as contaminators of the easy, pleasurable, and comfortable sharing of ideas and laughter that he keeps insisting are the best things that friendship has to offer are summed up in the following:

> But how to define "intimacy"? Today most people would define it as something more than just the breakdown of formality into casual, easy relations, marked by reasonable candor; they would instead define intimacy as being permitted to be unashamedly, confessionally yourself, which would include spilling all the beans of your personal life, vast quantities of them, when the need to go on an emotional spree arises.

Epstein feels that he has carte blanche to reexamine the false pieties and illusions of friendship: first, because there are no penetrating and definitive books on the subject (despite the contributions of philosopher and writer Aristotle, essayist Michel Eyquem de Montaigne, and philosopher and essayist Francis Bacon, to name only a few); and second, because the varieties of friendship, the many different forms that it can take, have not been sufficiently taken into account by those who have written about the topic.

Women, says Epstein, are more forgiving of failure and more likely to cross social lines in their friendships. They also find it easier than men do to confide in one another, to share intimacies. Women are better listeners than men. Epstein finishes his comparison of the gender experience of friendship with a somber admonition:

> the more that women become like men in their outlook and ambitions, and the more that hedonism and rivalrousness and *amour-propre* play a central role in their consciousness, the more worn become the cables that hold up the bridge of society, and one of the main such cables is, of course, friendship.

Joseph Epstein is a prominent journalist, essayist, and short-story writer and has published numerous books, including the best-selling Snobbery *(2002). He edited the Phi Beta Kappa Society's magazine* American Scholar *for more than twenty years.*

This is one of those moments, and there are several, when Epstein concedes that friendship thrives on stronger stuff than the pleasant breezes of sociability. There is a touching tribute to a woman friend who, after her death, leaves him with the feeling that "We shared something unspoken, but what?"

Friendships do thrive on commonalities of experience. "Cliques, clans, and communities" determine many of the friendships in anyone's life. Today the influence of technologies like inexpensive long-distance telephoning and e-mail have created new dimensions for friendships that would never have come into being without them. Marriage has become a rival to friendship; family obligations, mainly the time devoted to children, have made inroads on the opportunities for developing friendships.

Friends, despite a widely held misconception, are not always equal in background, temperament, or intellect. Opposites do attract, and perhaps that is why closeness or intimacy is not always in the cards for a successful friendship. Epstein keeps coming back to the idea that, especially as people get older, what they want most from friendship is "talk," pleasant conversation, camaraderie. Adolescence is the time of passionate friendship; indeed Epstein "confesses" that in his school days he was almost too good at making friends. He was a "good guy" who had at his "command a small gift for implying an intimacy that often wasn't really there. I have it still, and it sometimes gets me into difficulties, making people think I have a stronger feeling for them than in fact I do."

With this confession Epstein, perhaps somewhat unwittingly, puts his finger on precisely that quality of attenuated intimacy that has made him so successful at his craft. Friendliness is less than friendship, but if you are genuinely friendly (and charming to boot) then wit, even at times a mildly barbed wit like Epstein's, can move at a friendly pace and eventually make friends on a grand scale.

In his chapter "Broken Friendships," readers gain a sense of the loss and pain as well as the relief and deliverance that well up when meaningful or trying relationships are terminated. His book, however, does nothing to impair the subtle contract that Epstein has drafted through the years with his many readers. They will now have more insight into the style, in every sense of the word, of Epstein's persona as the friendly personal-familiar essayist who knows how to cultivate and keep his many friends, coolly but firmly, authentically but with infinite tact. Readers will also know a bit more about the actual Joseph Epstein, his personal triumphs and tragedies, but not more than is tactfully necessary. He will not let his readers brand him as impersonal, but neither will he discard the mask of his art.

Peter Brier

Review Sources

Booklist 102, nos. 19/20 (June 1-15, 2006): 10.
Elle 21, no. 11 (July, 2006): 64.
Library Journal 131, no. 8 (May 1, 2006): 106.
New Criterion 25, no. 1 (September, 2006): 127-129.
New York 39, no. 29 (August 21, 2006): 78-80.
The New York Times 155 (July 26, 2006): E6.
The New York Times Book Review 155 (July 16, 2006): 8.
Publishers Weekly 253, no. 12 (March 20, 2006): 45.
The Wall Street Journal 248, no. 3 (July 5, 2006): D10.

GALLATIN CANYON

Author: Thomas McGuane (1939-   )
Publisher: Alfred A. Knopf (New York). 220 pp. $24.00
Type of work: Short fiction
Time: The middle and late twentieth century
Locale: The United States, British Columbia, and the
Gulf of Mexico

McGuane's second collection of fiction, set largely in his adopted state of Montana, examines an assortment of uneasy losers with wry humor and a certain pained compassion

Thomas McGuane has had several lives—as a hard-living maverick, a Hollywood screenwriter, and a chronicler of life in the American West, where most of the ten stories in *Gallatin Canyon* take place. His work, characterized by dead-on dialogue and tongue-in-cheek humor, has become increasingly accomplished to the point where he has been favorably compared to literary giants Ernest Hemingway and William Faulkner.

In the title story, the narrator, formerly a dubious peddler of satellite dishes, now presents himself as a respectable trader who is selling his car dealership in Rigby, Idaho. He drives south from Montana through the narrow but heavily traveled Gallatin Canyon with his companion Louise, an attractive lawyer whom he thinks of marrying. The narrator meets his potential buyer and attempts to force him to withdraw his bid so that a later, better offer can be accepted, but his plans do not work out. On their late return via the same treacherous road, a car persists in tailgating them, blinding him with its headlights in the rearview mirror, and the narrator takes matters into his own hands, losing Louise and perhaps his soul in the process.

"Vicious Circle" begins at the local farmers' market amid the Hutterites and the Flathead Lake cherries, where John Briggs encounters a wide-eyed, shy young woman named Olivia, who reluctantly agrees to meet him later for a drink. A self-critical loner, Briggs is tense and awkward; he orders draft beer, she, double whiskeys. While he buys a newspaper for her, she orders a second round. After the bar manager, who obviously knows her, approaches their table to offer a free round, Briggs realizes that Olivia has downed six shots of whiskey in comparison with his three beers. As her defenses slip, she becomes more voluble, then nearly incoherent.

Because Olivia cannot find her own car, Briggs carefully drives her home in his. Her father, a doctor, settles her upstairs, feeds Briggs a tasty supper, and then proposes a demented cure for Olivia's alcoholism: membership in Toastmasters International. Angered, Briggs leaves, but he continues to dream of Olivia. When a rattlesnake bite sends him to the hospital, Olivia, a nurse, mysteriously sedates him.

Later that fall, Briggs is invited to Olivia's wedding to a man who appears to be wearing eyeliner. Finding himself alone in the kitchen with the groom, who orders

In addition to his short stories, Thomas McGuane wrote the screenplays for The Missouri Breaks *(1976) and* Tom Horn *(1980) and has published nine novels and three volumes of essays. He raises cutting horses on his ranch and in 2006 was accepted into the Cutting Horse Hall of Fame.*

him to leave Olivia alone (he already has), Briggs lies to make her look good. In return, she offers a well-enunciated toast, and he finds himself in a state of confusion.

The hapless Briggs appears in another story, "Old Friends," where he receives a sudden and unwelcome visit to his summer home by Erik Faucher, a man he has known ever since they roomed together in boarding school. Briggs appears to be quite competent professionally—he has traveled all over the world—but his personal relationships leave something to be desired. These men are friends by proximity only, by virtue of being in the same place at certain times, as well as by the loyalty they have both been taught to accept. In reality, they do not like each other. Erik, an investment advisor at a Boston bank, has embezzled money and is a fugitive; he telephones Briggs to announce that he will be coming west to join him. He has decided to become a cowboy.

The visit is complicated by Erik's temporary lady friend Marjorie, who is usually intoxicated but who teaches remedial geometry when she is sober. The frustrated Briggs tries to make the best of a bad bargain with these two, but his silent resentment grows. Even though he refuses to betray his so-called friend to the authorities, he certainly wants to, and he is blamed for Erik's arrest. If this were a Bernard Malamud story, Briggs would be the schlemiel.

McGuane's prose is generally laconic, with a tight focus and few explanations, but he incorporates lyric landscapes into his writing, even in a comic tale. For instance, as Briggs and the reluctant Erik view a small homestead cemetery, they see "needle and thread, buffalo, and orchard grass spread like a billowing counterpane around the small headstones, but shining through in the grass were shooting stars, pasqueflowers, prairie smoke, arrowleaf balsam, wild roses . . . "

In "North Coast," the author evokes a very different, wet, green landscape, the coastal rain forest of British Columbia. Amid the dripping moss and ferns and the harsh squawk of ravens, two drug addicts, a guide and a ski instructor, search for an ancient totem pole, a prime example of north coast native art. Their contact in Vancouver is a Sikh antiquities dealer who maintains a lucrative sideline in premium narcotics. Both searchers look forward to generous payment in heroin for their services after they reach Vancouver. There is no real plot here but more of a character study of two people on a downhill slope, well on their way to self-destruction.

The delightful "Cowboy," which appears in *The Best American Short Stories 2006*, is distinguished by the narrator's Northern Plains dialect. Here an itinerant cowhand, fresh out of jail, finds a job with a Montana rancher, whom he refers to as "the old feller," "the old sumbitch," or—only once—a "honyocker" (a cattleman's contemptuous term for a farmer). His employer raises horned Hereford cattle, and the sister (a formerly beautiful, now enormously fat older woman who once belonged to a motorcycle gang—"Used to she was sweet as pudding," says her brother) takes an interest in the young cowboy. She generously supplies him with homemade pie until she realizes that the attraction is not mutual and sends him back to the mobile home out by the barn. Eventually she dies, the cowboy enters into partnership with the old feller until the state installs him at last in a nursing home, and the neighbors begin to plot. The cowboy rides off into the sunset, which in this case would be Idaho. It is a melancholy story but also funny.

McGuane presents a clear view of the backbreaking labor involved in this kind of life: building and mending fences, breaking and shoeing horses, breeding, calving, feeding, and salting the herd (maintaining the salt licks). The joy comes in the character's language and his perceptions.

The real surprise of this collection is the novella, "The Refugee," in which a rapidly deteriorating career alcoholic, Errol Healy, finds himself at the end of his tether. Set in Florida and the Gulf of Mexico, it is a major departure from the other stories. Errol has just lost a toe while mowing a lawn in the middle of the night to impress some woman. At the orange groves where he oversees a Spanish-speaking crew, his employer has issued a final ultimatum: straighten up or be institutionalized.

Errol has asked for and received time off to visit an elderly woman in Key West, Florence Ewing, whom he reveres as a healer and seer. She was the giver of wise advice in earlier years, and Errol hopes she can tell him what to do now, although he is not certain if she is even alive. He plans to sail from the mainland to Key West on his little yawl, a passage that allows McGuane to demonstrate that he clearly knows his way around a sailboat.

Fortifying himself aboard the yawl, Errol makes himself a drink. By the next morning he has drained the bottle and acquired a hangover and, by evening, the shakes. When he reaches Key West, he stops first at a bar where the bartender remembers him and Florence. Still believing that she alone can save him, Errol searches for her house, finds her mute in her bed in the dim living room, and begins to unburden himself.

Years ago, Errol and his best friend Raymond routinely smuggled Cuban refugees into the United States. On their last trip together from Key West to Cuba, Raymond was swept off the deck in a gale and drowned, and Errol still blames himself. The details of Raymond's death are slowly revealed as Errol confesses to the bedridden woman. Unfortunately, Florence does not understand anything he has said, and her caretaker assures him that she will not. Despairing, Errol leaves for the house where he, Raymond, and their friend Caroline used to live, rents a room, and attempts suicide. He survives.

Errol phones his boss to assure him that he is on the way home, but he stops again at a saloon before returning to the dock, blacks out, and remembers nothing until he wakes up aboard the boat the next morning. He is already well into the Gulf Stream, headed toward Cuba or the Bahamas—he cannot tell. Again he endures tremors and hallucinations, then sleeps. By the time he emerges from alcohol withdrawal, a storm is developing into a full-blown hurricane. Praying desperately to the small Cuban statuette of the Virgin Mary in the cabin, Errol recognizes that "*he was guilty of everything.*" Ultimately he finds himself on an unknown island, facing a new world, one entirely without alcohol.

"The Zombie" is a mildly bawdy little story featuring Dulcie Jones, an optometrist's assistant, rodeo barrel racer, "escort girl and sometime police informant." Her unwitting client is Neville Smithwick, Junior; she has been hired by his father, a respectable bank president and believer in fornication, to rid his son of his virginity. There are also two stories of youth recollected: the confusion of an extended Irish Catholic family in Massachusetts coping with the death of its matriarch and a Michigan boy's test of courage as he skates across frozen Lake Erie at night and finds himself in danger far from shore.

"Aliens" follows a retired Boston attorney, widower Homer Newland, who returns to his native Montana to buy a small place in the valley. The paradox is that by returning home at last, Homer has become an outlander, viewed by the inhabitants with suspicion and mistrust. At loose ends after a couple of years, he urges a former lover, Madeleine, to visit. As she alights from the plane, he notices with alarm that her mouth pulls to one side—the once golden girl has had a slight stroke. Theirs is no geriatric idyll. Madeleine wants to change things, like watering the plants, and Homer's choleric daughter dislikes her immediately. Homer is another hapless soul who tries to be helpful but only makes matters worse, while Madeleine hastily flees east, leaving him even more isolated.

McGuane's tone is usually ironic, with an undercurrent of wry humor. A favorite device is understatement, which he uses almost as much as Hemingway does, giving signals that are easily overlooked like the faded photograph on Errol Healy's boat. All of McGuane's people—and this collection is always about people—are in some way aliens, usually trying to do the right thing in a world that should be familiar but never quite connecting their desires with reality.

Joanne McCarthy

Review Sources

Booklist 102, no. 17 (May 1, 2006): 72.
Kirkus Reviews 74, no. 11 (June 1, 2006): 539.
Library Journal 131, no. 7 (April 15, 2006): 69.
Los Angeles Times, July 16, 2006, p. R3.
The New York Times 155 (July 20, 2006): E8.
The New York Times Book Review 155 (September 3, 2006): 1-8.
Outside 31, no. 7 (July, 2006): 30.
Publishers Weekly 253, no. 15 (April 10, 2006): 41-42.
The Seattle Times, July 30, 2006, p. J10.

GAY L.A.
A History of Sexual Outlaws, Power Politics, and Lipstick Lesbians

Authors: Lillian Faderman (1940-   ) and Stuart
   Timmons (1957-   )
Publisher: Basic Books (New York). Illustrated. 464 pp.
   $29.95
Type of work: Current affairs, history, and sociology
Time: From the sixteenth century to the early twenty-first
   century
Locale: Los Angeles

The authors focus on the development and status of gay
culture in Los Angeles from the time the earliest European
missionaries tried to convert the indigenous population to
Christianity to the beginning of the twenty-first century

Principal personages:
   KATHARINE HEPBURN, an American film star
   CARY GRANT, an American film star
   RUDOLPH VALENTINO, a 1920's film idol
   ROCK HUDSON, an American film idol
   GEORGE CUKOR, an influential gay film director
   RICHARD MITCH, a cofounder of *The Advocate*
   RONALD REAGAN, the fortieth president of the United States

Given its prominence as one of America's leading gay meccas, it is surprising that no comprehensive historical account of gay Los Angeles has appeared before this one. Other such studies of gay culture in cities like New York, Philadelphia, Chicago, and Memphis have been published, among the best known of which is George Chauncey's *Gay New York: Gender, Urban Culture, and the Makings of the Gay Male World, 1890-1940* (1994). Chauncey's book, although excellent, is not nearly as encompassing as *Gay L.A.: A History of Sexual Outlaws, Power Politics, and Lipstick Lesbians*, which focuses on gay activity among both males and females, includes people of color, and covers a five-hundred-year time frame.

Lillian Faderman and Stuart Timmons's chapters alternate between lesbianism and male homosexuality. The authors also explore such topics as homosexuality among the Native American tribes that inhabited the coastal regions of what is now California before the arrival in the sixteenth century and later of Europeans with religious agendas that proscribed homosexuality and considered it an abomination.

Overt homosexual activity was condoned and marriage between two members of the same sex was sanctioned by the Native Americans whom the early European explorers encountered along the Pacific coast. Homosexuals, cross-dressers, and transgendered members held honored and respected positions in their tribes, many becoming shamans because they were thought to be imbued with greater spirituality

~

Lillian Faderman, best known for Odd Girls and Twilight Lovers *(1991) and* Naked in the Promised Land *(2003), has published books that focus on ethnic writing and collaborated with Brigitte Eriksson on* Lesbians in Germany *(1990). Stuart Timmons, a freelance journalist, is the author of* The Trouble with Harry Hay: Founder of the Modern Gay Movement *(1990).*

~

than their heterosexual counterparts. Initially these Native Americans were completely comfortable in revealing their sexuality to the missionaries who sought to impose Christianity upon them.

They soon learned, however, that candor about their sexual preferences led to trouble and humiliation for them as the padres forcibly separated same-sex couples and cast in a shameful light something that the natives had long considered natural, even desirable. The authors cite one instance in which "the friars encountered a Santa Clara male Indian who wore women's clothes" and ordered him "to sweep the plaza in the nude for three days, to his intense shame." The humiliated cross-dresser, having done this imposed penance, fled in order to live as he wished in a way that was natural for him.

In Faderman and Timmons's accounts of the early encounters of Native Americans with the proselytizing Christian missionaries is the underlying implication that duplicity was necessary when natives dealt with the white invaders. This duplicity carried over into the gay culture that grew up in most Western societies—certainly among Hollywood film people in the 1920's and beyond.

The studios insisted that their leading men and women project unsullied public images and have an overt appeal to members of the opposite sex. When anything disturbed such images, promising film careers would often come to an abrupt and permanent end. The studios often arranged heterosexual marriages for gay film stars to studio-selected mates, so-called marriages of convenience.

Nevertheless, what went on behind the gates and thick hedges of Hollywood mansions was strictly off-limits to the public. Often a sedate cocktail party would turn into a gay orgy beside the swimming pool soon after the straight guests had gone home. George Cukor, one of Hollywood's most powerful film directors, could easily make or break an actor's career. He relished having handsome young actors attend his pool parties, but if they ever revealed what went on at these parties, they would make Cukor's black list and probably would never find work in Hollywood again.

Actor William Haines and his lover, Jimmy Shields, spent their summers in the seaside resort of El Porto near Laguna Beach, where they entertained much of Hollywood's gay community, including Cukor. When a rumor circulated that Shields had molested a minor, enraged townspeople attacked Haines and his guests, Cukor among them. Haines was tarred and feathered on the adjoining beach. To protect his own reputation, Cukor, who clandestinely fled the unhappy scene, cut off all subsequent contact with Haines, thereby effectively ending the actor's career.

Faderman and Timmons write with insight about how Hollywood was forced to appeal to Middle America, which necessitated the studios' playing a game of deception with the public when they cast gays in starring roles. Large sums of money were at stake. If the public became seriously disenchanted with stars like Rudolph

Valentino, Katharine Hepburn, or Cary Grant, the studios stood to lose large sums of money.

As early as 1921, contracts between the studios and their actors routinely included a morality clause stipulating that the actors do nothing in either their professional or personal lives to offend or outrage public morality. Deviations from such promises constituted breaches of contract, the very threat of which could derail a promising film career.

The authors also point out that tastes changed. Whereas such stars as Katharine Hepburn, Greta Garbo, and Marlene Dietrich could afford to dress quite masculinely during the 1930's, two or three decades later the public was more drawn to distinctly feminine types like Marilyn Monroe and Jayne Mansfield.

Among male stars, the Valentino type had been replaced by stars like Rock Hudson, whose very name was strongly masculine and whose bearing was, quite calculatedly, that of what the authors call a "heterosexual wolf." The studio married Hudson off to the secretary of his agent, but this marriage in no way interfered with Hudson's gay life, which was extremely active, just as Grant's five marriages to women did little to disrupt his long-term homosexual relationship with actor Randolph Scott.

A turning point for gay activists occurred in the Stonewall Rebellion of 1969 when gays turned on a contingent of police officers who came to the Stonewall Bar, a gay hangout in New York City, to arrest patrons on trumped up charges. Stonewall is generally pointed to as the first such uprising by gay people in modern times, but Faderman and Timmons note that similar resistance to the vice squad's raid on the Black Cat, a gay bar in Los Angeles, predated Stonewall by two years. Even before that, police were assaulted by gays who gathered at the Cooper Donut Shop in Los Angeles when the police tried to arrest them for disorderly conduct, which in many cases could amount to little more than such physical contact as holding hands.

Even as gay activism was growing in Los Angeles, the vice squad of the Los Angeles Police Department was actively, often brutally, engaged in persecuting gays, frequently trying to entrap them by planting evidence against them or invading their privacy, as they did with Marvin Edwards. Edwards met a man at the Crown Jewel in downtown Los Angeles, a sedate gay bar with a coat-and-tie dress code. He took this man back to his rented cottage, where the two spent the night.

Edwards did not know that the police were observing him. Although they did not take direct action or arrest him on a morals charge, they took it upon themselves to inform his landlady of what they considered his nefarious activity. The landlady, acting on the information the police had provided gratuitously, immediately evicted Edwards. Clearly his rights of privacy were infringed on, but during this period in Los Angeles' history, little recourse from such outrages existed. Even if they became court cases, the juries hearing them, composed often of people with little understanding of homosexuality, nearly always supported the police.

Until 1967 the gay community had no forceful news outlet, although a mimeographed newsletter aimed at gays had begun. In 1966 Richard Mitch, a member of Personal Rights in Defense and Education (PRIDE), and his lover Bill Rau, who worked in a print shop, set about publishing the first issue of what has become the nation's leading gay news magazine, *The Advocate*. As it achieved nationwide, indeed worldwide, distribution, it put gay issues squarely before vast numbers of readers from every state and from many foreign countries.

The most poignant parts of *Gay L.A.* are the chapters that focus on acquired immunodeficiency syndrome (AIDS), which devastated gay communities throughout the nation during the last two decades of the twentieth century. The authors' apt description of this scourge recounts that "It hit like the bomb that kills people but lets buildings stand—except this bomb killed selectively, and the victims were mostly gay." Both Faderman and Timmons lived through this period and were much involved in the gay community at the time. Both lived in California, one of the states most devastated by AIDS.

As AIDS spread among gay communities, the entire fabric of gay life changed. Gay baths and sex clubs, if they continued to exist, had much reduced clienteles and came under close scrutiny by public health officials. The promiscuity that had long characterized gay life was now shunned by much of the gay community in favor of monogamy. Many intolerant people were convinced that AIDS was God's vengeance on homosexuals.

The federal government was slow to act. President Ronald Reagan paid little public attention to AIDS, so federally funded research that might lead to controlling and even curing the disease was virtually nonexistent. Nevertheless, support began to come from various other sources. Members of the film community worked fervently to raise money that would offer some relief to victims of AIDS and would help to fund needed research. A great deal needed to be done to educate people about AIDS and its transmission.

The American blood supply began to dry up because it was known that AIDS could be transmitted through transfusions of tainted blood. It was determined that transmission could take place among drug addicts who shared needles. Because much of the blood supply was sold to blood banks by drug addicts trying to raise money for a quick fix, the integrity of that supply was severely compromised.

Faderman and Timmons have presented a solidly documented, very readable account of gay life in Southern California. The burgeoning film industry brought to Los Angeles and its environs thousands of attractive young people, many of them gay or bisexual, who aspired to become film stars. Most of them did not succeed, but many realized quite early that sex was a commodity in which they could trade, particularly if they were fortunate enough to catch the eye of someone well placed within the studios.

The authors' coverage is exhaustive and impeccable, ranging from court documents to newspapers and magazines to scrap books and other materials provided by some of the more than three hundred people the authors interviewed in preparing their book. Many of those interviewed were elderly and would likely not have been available for interviews had Faderman and Timmons not approached them when they did.

R. Baird Shuman

Review Sources

The Advocate, no. 972 (October 10, 2006): 74.
Booklist 103, no. 2 (September 15, 2006): 9.
Kirkus Reviews 74 (August 1, 2006): 766.
Library Journal 131, no. 14 (September 1, 2006): 166.
Los Angeles Magazine 51, no. 11 (November, 2006): 204.
Publishers Weekly 254, no. 29 (July 24, 2006): 45.

GEORGE MASON
Forgotten Founder

Author: Jeff Broadwater (1955-   )
Publisher: University of North Carolina Press (Chapel
    Hill). 329 pp. $34.95
Type of work: Biography and history
Time: Late eighteenth century
Locale: Virginia, Maryland, and Philadelphia

*This is the first full biography in thirty years of the man
whose 1776 Virginia Declaration of Rights became the
model for the constitutional Bill of Rights*

Principal personages:
    GEORGE MASON (1725-1792), the author of
        the 1776 Virginia Declaration of Rights
    GEORGE WASHINGTON (1732-1799), a revolutionary leader, first presi-
        dent of the United States
    THOMAS JEFFERSON (1743-1826), the author of the Declaration of Inde-
        pendence, third president of the United States
    PATRICK HENRY (1736-1799), a Virginian orator, Antifederalist leader
    JAMES MADISON (1751-1836), a Virginian leader, fourth president of the
        United States

Jeff Broadwater desires to revive the reputation of George Mason, whose talents
and contributions to American political ideas and practice were widely acknowledged
during his lifetime but since then have been largely overlooked by all except specialists in early American history. It is not a negative comment to note that the fifty-one
pages of endnotes to this gracefully written scholarly biography almost exclusively
cite printed sources. The past forty years have seen an outpouring of elaborate documentary collections dealing with colonial and revolutionary history and subtle and informative monographs analyzing eighteenth century political thought and action.
Broadwater makes effective use of these works in the first full-scale biography of Mason since Helen Hill Miller's excellent 1975 volume.

Mason's life and accomplishments deserve careful study for what one can learn
about both the achievements of the revolutionary generation and the unresolved contradictions in their ideas, especially in regard to slavery.

Mason's father died when he was ten; he was reared by a mother who prudently
managed the family holdings and a lawyer uncle who gave his nephew free access to a
fifteen hundred volume library, one of the largest in the colonies. Along with literary
classics and major contributions to British political thought, one-third of the collection
dealt with law. Studying these books was the most important part of Mason's education.
During his lifetime Mason's legal opinions were respectfully acknowledged by his
neighbors even though he never practiced as a lawyer. When he reached his majority

Mason took control of an estate consisting of five thousand acres in Fairfax County, Virginia. Ninety slaves, working four separate tracts of four hundred to five hundred acres each, kept the plantation largely self-sufficient while growing tobacco to pay for imported luxuries. Like most wealthy Virginians Mason served on the parish vestry, governing local affairs, and as a justice of the county court, deciding both criminal cases and civil lawsuits.

Jeff Broadwater, associate professor of history at Barton College in North Carolina, earned a law degree from the University of Arkansas and a doctorate in American history from Vanderbilt. He published Eisenhower and the Anti-Communist Crusade *(1992) and* Adlai Stevenson and American Politics: The Odyssey of a Cold War Liberal *(1994).*

When Mason's friend and neighbor George Washington wanted a method of legally ignoring the 1765 Stamp Act, he turned to Mason for a plan—which was never implemented because Britain quickly abandoned the tax. Following British adoption of the Townshend Duties in 1769, Mason drafted a nonimportation agreement designed to disrupt trade between Britain and the colonies and lead British merchants to support the American cause. Washington brought the plan to a meeting of the former House of Burgesses in Williamsburg, which approved and forwarded it to the rest of the colonies.

In July, 1774, reacting to the closing of the port of Boston and other Coercive Acts by Britain, Mason composed a series of resolutions challenging Parliament's authority over the colonies that were adopted by the freeholders of Fairfax County. Carried by Washington, they were largely endorsed by the Virginia Convention and in part by the Continental Congress. Other counties passed similar resolves, but Broadwater claims that Mason's Fairfax Resolves were the most detailed, the most radical, and therefore the most influential.

Mason's finest hour and greatest contribution to American political thought and government was his work at the May, 1776, Virginia Conventions. When he arrived, nearly two weeks late, the delegates had already unanimously declared Virginia independent and Mason was immediately put on the committee to prepare a constitution for the new republic. Mason wrote the initial drafts of both the constitution and the declaration of rights with which he prefaced it. The constitution embodied generally accepted eighteenth century American political ideas, providing separation of executive, judicial, and legislative branches of government and creating a powerful lower house of legislature dominant over a weak governor. Creating a list of civil rights as a separate and privileged part of a constitution was a new concept.

Mason's original draft of the declaration began

> That all Men are born equally free and independent, and have certain inherent natural Rights, of which they can not by any Compact, deprive or divest their Posterity; among which are the Enjoyment of Life and Liberty, with the Means of acquiring and possessing Property, and pursuing and obtaining Happiness and Safety.

Thomas Jefferson condensed Mason's draft into the opening of the Declaration of Independence. However, Mason's powerful proclamation of human freedom was too strong for slaveholding Virginians, who diluted the universal assertion by stating that men are "by nature," rather than "born" free, and have "inherent rights"—deleting the word "natural"—which they exercise "when they enter into a state of society," something slaves could not do. The committee added freedom of the press, rights of criminal defendants, and bans on general warrants to Mason's first draft. James Madison proposed, and the convention agreed, to replace Mason's plea for toleration of religious differences with the absolute: "All men are equally entitled to the free exercise of religion."

Broadwater stresses how proud Mason was of the declaration of rights, which proved to be one of the most widely imitated political innovations of the revolutionary years. This first constitutional bill of rights influenced the United States Declaration of Independence, the French declaration of the rights of man and citizen, the first eight amendments to the 1787 federal Constitution, and many state and national constitutions. One of the strongest aspects of the biography is Broadwater's analysis of how Mason's innovation reflected the evolution of British political concepts in America.

Mason served in the Virginia General Assembly during the Revolution but refused to accept appointments representing the state in the Continental Congress, using the excuse of ill health—he suffered throughout his adult life from gout and a painful skin disease—and the need to care for his children. His first wife died in March, 1773, after a difficult pregnancy, leaving him responsible for nine children aged three to twenty. Not until 1787 did he accept a national assignment, after his children were mature and he had remarried. The trip to Philadelphia for the 1787 Constitutional Convention was the first time in his life Mason ventured outside the Chesapeake Bay region.

Although Mason would later become one of the best-known critics of the Constitutional Convention and an active opponent of ratification by Virginia, Broadwater stresses how active and constructive Mason was during nearly all sessions of the meeting. He was one of the most vocal of the delegates, speaking up often and effectively in support of the nationalizing tendency of Madison's Virginia Plan, which became the agenda of the convention. Mason approved the large state-small state compromise that solved an early deadlock by providing that all states would have equal representation in the upper house of the national legislature, while large states might dominate a lower house based on population. Not until a conference committee reported an agreement permitting importation of slaves for twenty more years and granting Congress the right to regulate commerce by majority vote did Mason express strong reservations.

Mason was one of only three delegates who refused to sign the Constitution. Because his list of objections to the proposed Constitution, widely reprinted in Antifederalist newspapers, begins with the statement that there is no bill of rights, many historians assert this was Mason's main reason for rejecting the document. Broadwater agrees it was a significant complaint but is skeptical it was Mason's most important motive for opposing ratification of the Constitution. Mason had a lengthy list of objections to a structure of government he pessimistically predicted would certainly degenerate either into a monarchy or a corrupt aristocracy. He wanted an executive council, not as a cabinet carrying out presidential wishes but as an independent check preventing presidential abuse of power. He thought the Senate too powerful; with their long term in office senators might corruptly dominate the new government. Broadwater notes, however, that in conversations with Jefferson and Madison, Mason objected most strongly to two economic aspects of the document embodying the compromise in which delegates from the Deep South accepted passage of commerce regulations by a simple majority in return for extending the external slave trade.

Mason felt that the convention had rejected a provision he thought essential to the economic security of Virginia while accepting one he considered morally objectionable. Requiring a two-thirds majority to pass commerce legislation, he believed, would give Southern representatives an effective veto and prevent a Northern merchant-oriented majority from enacting legislation deleterious to Southern agriculture interests. Broadwater rejects the idea that Mason's objection to the slave trade simply advanced the interests of Virginia planters who had a surplus of slaves whose value would be lowered by competition with imports. Mason had been attacking the slave trade for decades and had inserted an unrelated denunciation of the trade in the document on the 1765 Stamp Act he prepared for Washington. Madison's notes on the Philadelphia convention include Mason's powerful attack on slavery, stressing its immorality and citing the iniquitous effect it had on both owners and slaves, a statement strong enough for some recent historians to label him an abolitionist. Broadwater argues that label is incorrect, that while Mason deserves credit for realizing the iniquity of a system from which he profited, he could see no way to end it other than the vague hope that stopping importation of new slaves would lead to the eventual extinction of the abhorrent institution. Unlike some Virginian critics of slavery, he took no steps to liberate any of his own slaves. Jefferson freed favorite house servants, Washington emancipated all of his slaves in his will, but Mason willed all of his slaves to his children, along with land and other property.

Mason's list of objections to the Constitution circulated widely and led to many personal attacks that left him embittered. Mason and Patrick Henry tried valiantly but failed in their effort to prevent the 1788 Virginia Convention from ratifying the Constitution before a series of amendments, including a bill of rights, had been added to the document. The convention did agree to send Congress a twenty-article bill of rights and many other desired amendments. Madison promised to push their passage and did secure enactment of the first ten amendments of the Constitution, which clearly echo Mason's 1776 declaration of rights.

The bitterness of the ratification struggle strained previous friendships. Mason reconciled with Madison when they both opposed Alexander Hamilton's program in the first Congress. However, Mason never reestablished his once harmonious partnership with Washington, who never fully forgave him for his vigorous criticism during the 1788 Virginia Convention.

Broadwater records how successfully Mason managed his affairs. Before his death in 1792, Mason had paid off all of his debts and left his children an enhanced estate consisting of fifteen thousand acres on the Potomac, sixty thousand acres in Kentucky, $30,000 in debts owed him, personal property worth $50,000, and three hundred slaves.

His true legacy to the American people, Broadwater believes, was

in his contribution to America's founding documents: the Declaration of Independence through the Virginia Declaration of Rights, the Constitution through his role at the Philadelphia Convention, and the Bill of Rights through his dogged opposition to a Constitution without one.

It is a legacy well worth revisiting in a new century when the American people debate the balance between civil liberty and national security. Broadwater's careful exploration of Mason's career and ideas deserves a wide audience.

Milton Berman

Review Sources

Publishers Weekly 253, no. 28 (July 17, 2006): 146.
The Wall Street Journal 248, no. 62 (September 13, 2006): D10.
The Washington Post Book World, November 5, 2006, p. T02.
Weekly Standard 12, no. 12 (December 4, 2006): 37-39.

A GODLY HERO
The Life of William Jennings Bryan

Author: Michael Kazin (1948-   )
Publisher: Alfred A. Knopf (New York). 374 pp. $30.00
Type of work: Biography
Time: 1860-1925
Locale: The United States

Kazin tries to rehabilitate Bryan's image, arguing that the three-time losing Democratic nominee for president was a populist who helped turn the Democratic Party away from its nineteenth century pro-business stance, preparing the way for the 1930's reform party

A GODLY HERO
THE LIFE OF WILLIAM JENNINGS BRYAN
MICHAEL KAZIN

Principal personages:
WILLIAM JENNINGS BRYAN (1860-1925), Democratic presidential candidate in 1896, 1900, and 1908 and secretary of state from 1913 to 1915
MARY BAIRD BRYAN (1867-1930), his wife and political aide
WILLIAM MCKINLEY (1843-1901), president of the United States, 1897-1901
MARCUS ALONZO HANNA (1837-1904), industrialist, McKinley's campaign manager in 1896
WOODROW WILSON (1856-1924), president of the United States, 1913-1921

Michael Kazin wants to rescue William Jennings Bryan's popular image. Historians have long been aware of the progressive reforms Bryan supported during his years on the national political scene. However, few rate his achievements as favorably as Kazin, whose narrative of Bryan's positive contributions to American political life is a valuable corrective to most Americans' image of Bryan—if they remember him at all—as the bigoted fundamentalist portrayed in Jerome Lawrence's frequently revived play *Inherit the Wind* (1955).

Bryan grew up in southern Illinois, where his father, a small-town lawyer and judge, inculcated Christian religion and ethics in his son. Kazin stresses throughout his biography that Bryan's reform ideas stemmed from his religious beliefs, not from secular sources. In 1881 he graduated from Illinois College in Jacksonville, where studying geology and biology briefly shook his belief in biblical inerrancy; in 1883 he graduated from Union College of Law in Chicago. In 1884 Bryan married Mary Baird; they had three children. Unlike most women of the time, Mary continued her education after marriage, studying law and being admitted to the Nebraska bar in 1888, after the family moved there. She was a significant partner and helpmate to Bryan throughout his political career.

In 1890 Bryan won election as a representative in a year when Democrats took con-

Michael Kazin is a professor of history at Georgetown University. The Guggenheim Foundation, the National Endowment for the Humanities, the Woodrow Wilson Center, and the Fulbright Scholar Program have awarded him fellowships. He has published The Barons of Labor (1987), The Populist Persuasion (1995), and coauthored America Divided: The Civil War of the 1960's (1999).

trol of the House. Half of the Representatives were freshmen, and Bryan received an appointment to the powerful Ways and Means Committee, where he studied economic issues and earned national attention through speeches on the tariff and currency. Bryan was already a practiced orator with a gift for stating complex matters in simple terms which, Kazin notes, even opposition newspapers reported. His lively denunciation of the tariff as an unjustified subsidy of wealthy manufacturers that should be replaced by a graduated income tax, drew congressmen and reporters back into the chamber to listen.

Bryan's speeches on the silver question received even more attention. The years between the Civil War and the 1890's were one of the few deflationary periods in American history, when prices of goods dropped steadily, increasing the value of the gold-backed currency. Both proponents and opponents of using silver equally with gold to back currency were passionately convinced that this would cause significant inflation, which would benefit agriculture but be detrimental to the well-being of manufacturers and urban consumers. The severe depression of the 1890's intensified pressure on farmers, magnified their complaints, and increased their interest in those who, like Bryan, claimed to have a solution for their distress.

Bryan won reelection to the House in 1892 but in 1894 decided to run for the Senate, winning a nonbinding popular vote but failing in the Republican-dominated legislature that still elected senators. Kazin records that Bryan abandoned his law practice after discovering he could make more money lecturing and then toured the West, denouncing the gold standard.

The majority of delegates to the 1896 Democratic National Convention were intent on disavowing Democratic president Grover Cleveland for his insistence on maintaining the gold standard. Few considered Bryan, attending as a delegate from Nebraska, a possible candidate for president. A member of the Platform Committee, he helped write the plank denouncing Cleveland and calling for the monetization of silver and delivered the closing argument in its favor. Bryan had a mellifluous voice and, even more important, the lung power and clear enunciation to be audible in the farthest reaches of huge auditoriums at a time when rivals could not yet benefit from electric amplification. He was probably the only speaker who could be understood by everyone in the convention hall.

His address recapitulated arguments and repeated language Bryan had been honing during his lecture tours. Kazin describes the histrionics with which Bryan delivered his famous peroration. He raised his fingers to his temples as he spoke the words: "You shall not press down upon the brow of labor this crown of thorns, you shall not crucify mankind upon a cross of gold." Bryan then extended his arms straight out from his body and held the Christlike pose for several seconds. The stunned audience exploded in a wild demonstration that projected Bryan into the presidential nomination the next day.

The Republican nominee, William McKinley, observed the long tradition that one did not seek the presidency; the people offered it to a deserving leader. He ran a "front porch campaign," remaining home in Canton, Ohio, as delegations from across the country arrived to pledge support. McKinley's campaign manager, Marcus Alonzo Hanna, meanwhile marshaled the enormous financial resources of the Republicans, flooding the United States with endless speakers, tons of buttons and gewgaws, and more than 120 million pamphlets denouncing Bryan and silver.

Bryan countered by flouting precedent and actively campaigning. Taking his cause directly to the people, he crisscrossed the country by rail, traveling some eighteen thousand miles, delivering more than six hundred speeches. Even newspapers strongly opposed to Bryan felt compelled to cover his innovative campaign, allowing him to reach millions of citizens beyond what his monetary resources permitted. The election aroused enormous interest: Over 79 percent of eligible voters participated, a record not since equaled. McKinley received 7.1 million votes to Bryan's 6.5 million, carrying states with 271 electoral votes to Bryan's 176.

Biographers of Bryan face a severe structural dilemma. The year 1896 is the dramatic highpoint of Bryan's life—the following twenty-nine years were all downhill, as Bryan suffered two more electoral defeats, served an unsatisfactory term as secretary of state, and concluded with the farce of the Scopes trial. Kazin's chapter on 1896 ends on page 79; he conscientiously continues on for nine more chapters and 227 pages of text that necessarily lack the drama and interest of the preceding three chapters.

The issues involved justify Kazin's detailed narrative, even if his evaluation of Bryan is not always convincing. The 1900 election, which Bryan lost to McKinley by an even larger margin, debated American imperialism and whether the United States should undertake to rule an empire in Asia. Kazin, clearly aware of present-day concerns, presents Bryan as a principled anti-imperialist. However, Bryan supported declaring war on Spain, accepted a commission as colonel of a Nebraska volunteer regiment, and railed against the War Department for stranding his regiment in disease-ridden Florida. Kazin unconvincingly tries to absolve Bryan of any responsibility for retention of the Philippines, even though he urged Democratic senators to ratify the annexation treaty, which passed by only two votes.

In 1908 Bryan received the Democratic nomination for president a third time and ran on a platform proposing many progressive ideas that Kazin correctly notes exceeded the reforms Woodrow Wilson later enacted and anticipated some New Deal approaches. Bryan advocated regulation of corporations, tariff reform, a federal income tax, insurance of bank deposits, national control of the money supply, direct election of senators, and he fully supported the program of the American Federation of Labor, which for the first time endorsed a candidate for president. However, Bryan lost once again.

When Wilson asked him to become secretary of state in 1912, Bryan insisted on two conditions. He would not serve alcohol at official functions—a practice ridiculed by the Washington diplomatic corps. He would concentrate on negotiating treaties in which nations agreed that in the event of an international dispute they would avoid war by observing a "cooling off" period during which they would discuss compromise. Thirty nations solemnly signed the treaties in 1913, but when a serious dispute erupted in 1914, no one paid attention to Bryan's "cooling-off" period. Despite his anti-imperialist rhetoric, Bryan supported Wilson's armed intervention in Mexico and the Caribbean region.

Bryan wished to maintain strict American neutrality during World War I and objected to the pro-British bias of Wilson and his cabinet. The differences came to a head over how to respond to the deaths of American citizens when a German submarine sank the *Lusitania*, a British passenger liner. Bryan desired a calm response and resigned over the issue. Kazin concedes, however, that he blurred the impact of his action by signing Wilson's first stern protest note before refusing to consent to a follow-up complaint, but then sent Wilson a cordial letter of resignation. He campaigned for Wilson's reelection in 1916. When Congress declared war, Bryan supported the decision and again tried to enlist.

Out of office, Bryan returned to the lecture circuit, focusing more and more on religious themes. His reform advocacy now centered on prohibition—Bryan's personal intervention with the Nebraska legislature in 1920 is credited with securing that state's ratification of the Eighteenth Amendment. At the urging of his wife, he supported women's right to vote. In the 1920's Bryan became the chief spokesman for those who wanted to ban teaching of Darwinian evolution in publicly supported institutions.

Because Bryan used appeals to the Bible and to Christianity to support his demands for economic reform, Kazin equates his ideas with those of ministers who joined the Social Gospel movement. However, most Social Gospel ministers embraced a postmillennial theology, arguing their reform efforts would hasten the second coming of Christ. In contrast, the growing Fundamentalist movement embraced a premillennial approach, preaching that only the actual return of Christ could bring about significant change. Bryan showed no interest in theological debates; if anything, he had more in common with Fundamentalists who agreed with his denunciation of Darwin than liberal ministers willing to consider reconciling their religious beliefs with evolution.

Kazin praises those who argue that Bryan's basic objection was not to evolution per se but rather to Social Darwinist theories that justified endless wars of conquest and supported eugenicists who would bar the poor and feebleminded from having babies. However, Kazin's own evidence does not sustain this interpretation. Bryan does not cite Social Darwinism or eugenics as a reason to oppose evolution in the extensive testimony and speeches he gave at the Scopes trial. Teaching evolution was objectionable, Bryan argued, because it shook the faith of children and youth in the literal truth of the Bible and Christianity; therefore the state had the right and the duty to protect its young by prohibiting teaching Darwinism.

Kazin consistently condemns Bryan for supporting denial of equal rights to African Americans. Growing up in the racist environment of southern Illinois in the nineteenth century may have as much to do with Bryan's views as the political usefulness for Democratic candidates of conciliating rabidly segregationist southerners. Bryan's defense of the Ku Klux Klan on the floor of the 1924 Democratic convention went well beyond simple political advantage.

The basic thrust of Kazin's book is that Bryan deserves study and sympathy for demonstrating how to support progressive secular reforms from a religious perspective, thus justifying the book title, "A Godly Hero." However, to a greater degree than Kazin is willing to admit, Bryan's behavior at the 1924 convention and the 1925 trial—not just attacks by liberal intellectuals—demonstrated his intellectual aridity and limited social sympathies, tarnishing the memory of his many earlier contributions to progressive reform.

Milton Berman

Review Sources

Booklist 102, no. 11 (February 1, 2006): 18.
Christianity Today 50, no. 6 (June, 2006): 64-65.
Kirkus Reviews 74, no. 1 (January 1, 2006): 29-30.
Library Journal 131, no. 1 (January 1, 2006): 130.
Los Angeles Times, February 5, 2006, p. R12.
National Review 58, no. 12 (July 3, 2006): 51-52.
The New Republic 234, no. 13 (April 10, 2006): 21-28.
The New York Review of Books 53, no. 11 (June 22, 2006): 32-39.
The New York Times Book Review 155 (March 5, 2006): 10.
Publishers Weekly 252, no. 49 (December 12, 2005): 51-52.
The Washington Post Book World, February 5, 2006, p. 6.

GOD'S SILENCE

Author: Franz Wright (1953-   )
Publisher: Alfred A. Knopf (New York). 144 pp. $24.00
Type of work: Poetry

A biting and brilliant collection of poems that finds the poet having grown more fully into his religious faith

Franz Wright comes to the world of poetry as the son of the highly acclaimed American poet James Wright, who won the Pulitzer Prize in poetry in 1972. Franz won the same prize in 2004 for his wonderful collection *Walking to Martha's Vineyard* (2003); they are the only father and son to have both won the award. When he was a child, many influential American poets came by to visit his father, including Anne Sexton, Theodore Roethke, and John Berryman. Young Franz came to believe that all of the luminaries were "nuts." He found them all to be "big drinkers." It took him many years to realize that one could be an artist and still lead a "normal life." As a teenager, he wrote his first poems. It has been reported that his famous father said, "I'll be damned. You're a poet. Welcome to hell." The young Wright learned over time that having a "love for the art itself" is what is crucial.

In 1953, Franz Wright was born in Vienna, Austria. He grew up to appreciate the literary life, but it did not necessarily bring happiness. In fact, Wright became a tortured soul who did not feel comfortable in his own skin. His first poetry collection, *Tapping the White Cane of Solitude*, was published in 1976. Four years later, his famous father died. During most of Franz Wright's adult life, he has struggled with substance abuse and mental illness. At one point in time, he even attempted suicide. The creative fire alone could not sustain him. He became a lost soul who shut down and lost all purpose for living. While as a teenager he had learned the "power in poetry," he now found himself struggling to communicate on even the most rudimentary level. During the 1990's, Wright suffered a complete mental breakdown. It was necessary for him to spend two years in a mental institution. The years of drug and alcohol abuse had taken a heavy toll on his psyche and his physical well-being. In the late 1990's, he converted to Catholicism. This conversion had a dramatic impact on his life: His spiritual awakening helped him to write poetry again; he discovered that he could use poetry as a "healing force."

For Wright, a successful poem seems to have a life of its own. The despair and hopelessness that surrounded him for years was lifted through what he considered a "spiritual intervention." As the author of more than ten volumes of poetry, Wright has come to realize that poetry is his way of communicating to the world. Through poetry, he attempts to get at the heart of the matter. The acclaimed poet Charles Simic has stated that Wright is a miniaturist and has the "secret ambition" to "write an epic on the inside of a matchbook cover." Out of his life experiences, Wright has come to re-

alize that living can be extremely difficult but
that the alternative to living is no alternative
at all. He has come to understand that "life is .
. . suffering."

In addition to his Catholic faith, he has
studied the spiritual teachings of the Buddha.
Out of his personal spiritual journey, Wright
has found a way to carry on, to make the most
of his many talents, to live to the best of his
ability. For more than twenty-five years, he

*Franz Wright is the author of several
highly acclaimed volumes of poetry,
including* Ill Lit: Selected and New
Poems *(1998),* The Beforelife *(2001),
and* Walking to Martha's Vineyard
(2003). Walking to Martha's Vineyard
won the 2004 Pulitzer Prize in poetry.

floundered and led a very self-destructive life. Turning to faith helped to make it possible for him to communicate again, to fully live again. Faith does not come easily
though, and Wright recognizes how difficult it can be to live in the world. For him
there are no easy answers—only the journey, the search for true meaning. Wright sees
poetry as a "solitary pursuit" that has "never been a popular art form in the United
States." With this realization, the poet must find his own voice and be true to it. As
Wright sees it, "the best art" is created by those "who really don't give a damn what
people think of their work."

At ninety-two poems in 144 pages, *God's Silence* is a substantial volume of poetry.
With this new collection, Wright continues to mine many of the same topics that he so
brilliantly delineated in his 2003 collection *Walking to Martha's Vineyard.* The personal journey of discovery of self and the world around him continues to be of prime
importance. While life is a serious endeavor, Wright realizes that he should never take
himself too seriously. Humor (dark or otherwise) is supposed to be a part of human
expression.

God's Silence is divided into four sections. The first section of the collection contains the long poem "East Boston, 1996." In the stanza "Night Walk," he ponders the
idea that "There must be thousands of people/ in this city who are dying/ to welcome
you into their small bolted rooms,/ to sit you down and tell you/ what has happened to
their lives." People want to make connections with others. It may be a difficult process for many, but it is a necessary one nevertheless. At another point in the poem,
Wright speaks to the idea of silences with "The long silences need to be loved, per-
haps/ more than the words/ which arrive/ to describe them/ in time." Patience is something the poet must learn to value. In this age of instant gratification, this is not always
easy.

This is one of the crucial elements of Wright's spiritual journey. He has come to
believe that forgiveness is possible and that a damaged heart can be healed. Each day
brings new challenges, but this is a positive situation. Wright has no desire to venture
into self-destructive territory once again. He recognizes his many shortcomings, his
many vulnerabilities, but he does not let any of his human frailties stop him from
moving forward. His newfound faith in God has taught him that although perfection
may be beyond reach, redemption is possible.

Section II opens with the poem "Beginning Again." This is what the poet must do,
what all living creatures must do to survive. The idea of "patience" comes into play

again as the poem ends with "So we sit there/ together/ the mountain/ and me, Li Po/ said, until only the mountain/ remains." Wright is more than willing to admit his shortcomings, to expose his failings as a human. In the poem "Progress," he readily admits that "Nobody has called for some time./ (I was always the death of the party.)" At times, Wright may appear to be the "tortured soul" who is struggling with his faith, with how best to live a "life worth living." These are issues with which many people wrestle. Wright is not alone, and that makes these poems all the more poignant.

These are not esoteric concerns. In the third section, the poem "A Happy Thought" provides the reader with Wright's concerns about his own death. He compares death to birth with "What frightened me, apparently, and hurt/ was being born. But I got over that/ with no hard feelings. Dying, I imagine,// it will be the same deal, lonesomer maybe,/ but surely no more shocking or prolonged—It's dark as I recall, then bright, so bright." With great care, the poet reveals the spiritual without a heavy hand. Although spiritual lessons can be learned, the poems are not sermons. Wright seems to embrace the paradoxes of life. Both the metaphysical and the personal fill his poetry. The careful reader will relish the surprises that can be found in Wright's poetry. The poet believes that ever since he overcame his mental illness he writes "in the voice of the person I'd like to become, a person not so involved in his own problems but more concerned with others." The individual artist who has this view will grow, will expand his horizons.

The respected American poet Donald Justice sees in Wright a poet who can be "so dark-minded and at the same time so almost playful, so childlike about it all." It is evident in the best poems of *God's Silence* that there is a radiance that shines through. Out of the darkness, out of the gloom, there can be forgiveness and hope for a better future. Wright's spirituality is grounded in daily life. He writes accessible poems, and in so doing his poems speak to the "everyman" in all of us who struggles to make sense of existence. Wright believes in thanking God for a successful poem. He is keenly aware, though, that there is no true "formula" that will always lead to a successful poem. Every time the poet believes that he has found the shortcut to writing a perfectly formed poem, he is doomed to failure. Wright finds himself starting over each time he begins a new poem. As he sees it, "Every poem is an attempt to write The Poem, and is a failure." Even with this knowledge though, he does not give up writing, plugging away at his craft. There is a close link between writing and spirituality. Wright believes that he becomes "a channel or something that is much more intelligent, happier, and more powerful" than he could ever be. He definitely has a "hunger for the energy that comes from above."

The poem "Wake" appears in the fourth section of *God's Silence*. In this touching poem, Wright makes the observation that "I saw my friend the other day/ we were all attending his wake/ and he was the only one there/ who looked like he was well/ Somehow he'd gotten well/ He looked like he was doing fine There/ Everyone else in the room looked just awful." Later in the poem, he hears "God's silence like the sun/ and longed to/ change." In "Scribbled Testament," Wright admits that "I stand before you/ here, some hairy/ primate's fall from grace—/ one of the patients of God,/ one of the orphans of light." The last poem of *God's Silence*, "I Am Listening," ends with

"Proved faithless, still I wait." If the flawed poet wishes to find clarity of purpose and some semblance of peace of mind then he must be willing to wait, to be ever vigilant, to open his heart to the spiritual realm. For the reader of poetry who likes to savor images that pierce the soul, *God's Silence* is one of those rare creations that challenges and enlightens.

Jeffry Jensen

Review Sources

Booklist 102, no. 15 (April 1, 2006): 14.
Library Journal 131 (April 1, 2006): 98.
Los Angeles Times, May 26, 2006, p. E15.
The New York Times Book Review 155 (May 14, 2006): 38.
Publishers Weekly 252 (December 19, 2005): 43.

GOD'S WAR
A New History of the Crusades

Author: Christopher Tyerman (1953-   )
Publisher: Harvard University Press (Cambridge, Mass.).
   1040 pp. $35.00
Type of work: History
Time: 1096-1500
Locale: The Holy Land, Spain, the Baltic, and the Balkans

A reinterpretation of the Crusades, emphasizing a Christian belief system based on aggression, paranoia, and wishful thinking, without condemning it absolutely or absolving Muslims and pagans of responsibility and blame

Principal personages:

URBAN II, pope who called the First Crusade
PETER THE HERMIT, priest who led a poorly organized army to Constantinople
SALADIN, Kurdish sultan who took Jerusalem from the crusaders
RICHARD THE LIONHEART, English king who became a legend in the Third Crusade
INNOCENT III, pope who spread the Crusades into Spain, the Baltic and southern France
FREDERICK II, Holy Roman emperor who recovered Jerusalem briefly
LOUIS IX, French king whose saintliness was insufficient for victory

Medieval societies were violent, both in Christian and Muslim lands. It was impossible for any state that did not defend itself to survive, and with aggressive neighbors on all sides, Christians, Muslims and pagans alike honored and rewarded their warriors. Though rulers agreed that peace and justice were desirable goals, they understood that violence was sometimes necessary against evildoers and that while wars of expansion might be of questionable morality, in the contemporary political world those who remained passive went under.

According to Christopher Tyerman in his book *God's War: A New History of the Crusades*, nothing illustrates this better than the fate of the Carolingian state. Vikings, Magyars, and Muslims rampaged through Germany, France, Britain, and parts of Italy. Only a drastic decentralization of authority and the creation of a new military class (knights) allowed a reorganization of those regions as feudal states. However, just when the Holy Roman emperor seemed on the verge of pulling the many independent regions into a more unified state, one that could extend Roman Christianity northward and eastward, a quarrel with the popes crippled his authority. This contest, known today as the Investiture Controversy, was over control of the church lands in Germany and Italy, and a belief that, once the reformed papacy made itself supreme over secular rulers, it could make Christian principles dominant throughout society.

With popes calling upon nobles, bishops, abbots, and knights to take up arms in defense of the Church, the spiritual climate was made ready for the Crusades. If defending the pope was good, much better was rescuing the Orthodox Church and recovering the holy places in Jerusalem (even though there had been no significant new obstacles to pilgrims worshiping there).

Earlier, such ambitions would have been impossible. By the end of the eleventh century, however, the West was becoming more

Among Christopher Tyerman's numerous books are England and the Crusades, 1095-1588 *(1988),* The Invention of the Crusades *(1998), and* Fighting for Christendom: Holy War and the Crusades *(2004) He was a commentator in the 1995 BBC production of* The Crusades, *starring Terry Jones. He is a lecturer on modern history at Hertford College in Oxford.*

powerful. This was partly because of demographic and cultural changes but was also because the Byzantine and Arab states had been hard hit by the arrival of the Turks in the Middle East. The West's sense of power was increased by the success of Western arms in contests with Byzantines and Muslims in Italy and Sicily—it seemed as though a comparatively small number of knights could defeat any number of enemies, and many knights already had experience in Byzantine service. Knights believed in loyalty, money, and respect for their leaders; Pope Urban II's call for a crusade provided a fourth motivation for holy war—a noble cause.

The concept of a just war was developed in the late Roman Empire. It was, in fact, the only way that any Christian ruler could justify not giving up his lands and retiring into a monastery. The eleventh century concept of holy war combined the Peace of God, the reform of the papacy, the Investiture Controversy, the pilgrimage, and, ultimately, Urban II's creative response to the Byzantine cry for help. In contrast, holy war was nothing new to Muslims. The jihad (often referred to as the "little jihad" in contrast to the "greater jihad," a struggle for personal purity) was widely considered the sixth pillar of Islam. However, with most Arab conflicts being among themselves, there was little aggression against Christian neighbors until the arrival of the Turks in the late eleventh century. The Turkish onslaught brought with it as much death and destruction as the Crusades, if not more. This lent credence to atrocity stories spread by the Byzantines and Western visitors.

There was a rough balance of religions in the Holy Land, perhaps even a slight Christian majority. Pragmatically, Muslim rulers had long allowed Christians and Jews to worship as they pleased, as long as they accepted their subordinate status and paid taxes, but it was not the equality dreamed of by modern apologists. First the Turks, then the crusaders would upset this practical arrangement.

Urban II's dramatic appeal is less accurately understood than is commonly believed, being more legend than history. Urban's intent, however, seems clear—a claim to political leadership over all Europe. There was to be a general peace, religious reform, and an increase in papal authority. His plan was not, as is often asserted, an armed pilgrimage or the rescue of Constantinople.

Peter the Hermit, a priest, was the first to amass a large contingent of crusaders, but his army lacked prominent nobles who could enforce discipline; the armies which came later were better organized. The cost of taking the cross was considerable—conquest and enrichment were minor interests compared to religious enthusiasm, but without money there could be no expedition. Shortages of money partially explained the pogroms of Peter's army in the Rhineland and attacks on peasants in Hungary. When his hordes reached Anatolia, they spread out to seek food and fodder. The hurried push forward led to disaster.

The leaders of the expeditions that arrived shortly afterward were not as rude and ignorant as usually portrayed, especially by the Greeks; nor were the Greeks as fearful and uncooperative as Westerners chose to remember. They all understood the divisions among the Turkish emirs, realized how shaky the foundations of the new Muslim states were, and adopted strategies to take advantage of those weaknesses. The hard-fought victory north of Dorylaeum opened the difficult roads to Antioch, where the decisive contest took place—a siege that lasted from October of 1097 to June of 1098. This almost became the crusaders' grave, but reinforcements and a growing cohesion of the army—and God's help, as in the discovery of the Holy Lance—combined with the treason of a commander entrusted with a vital stretch of walls to deliver the city to the crusaders.

At this point the crusading army divided, with only fourteen thousand proceeding on to Jerusalem. The assault on the holy city was bloody, with perhaps a fifth or a quarter of the crusaders falling in battle, and the victors took due vengeance. A secondary slaughter, conducted in cold blood, came the following day. The numbers of dead were not as great as Muslim propagandists later claimed, but they were horrible enough. Some crusader accounts were taken word for word from the Old Testament and reflected a triumphalist celebration: an army composed of pious men, adventurers, thugs, tourists, and zealots could not have performed such feats without God's help.

The follow-up expeditions of 1101 were failures, modifying both the Muslim fears of the newcomers and the Christians' ambitions for further expansion. After taking the coastal cities, the Franks (as they became known, the French having provided the bulk of the occupying forces) became part of a fractured political landscape of feuding princelings where religious allegiances were less important than political interests. Still, the Latin states, though thoroughly feudal in organization and spirit, recognized that they were responsible for protecting the holy places for all of Christendom.

Tyerman overthrows many of the myths of Frankish boorishness and stupidity but notes that Christian rule was too brief to make a permanent impact on local society. Pilgrims swarmed to Jerusalem, and knights thrilled by the heroic deeds of the First Crusade took the cross themselves. However, the numbers of warriors was too small, a fact that led directly to the creation of military orders—a concept unimaginable earlier but one that combined the popular alternatives of knighthood and a cloistered life. Surprisingly, the church moved slowly to create the protections and immunities that later encouraged taking the cross. Crusaders were few, and expeditions were rare until

1147, when Muslims in a more unified Syria managed to stage a jihad that seemed likely to threaten Christian control of the Holy Land.

The Second Crusade was successful only in Portugal and the Baltic. The failure of the crusader armies at Damascus in 1148 was a warning of what was to come: The defeat at Hattin in 1187 was followed by the loss of Jerusalem and most of the coastal cities to Saladin. The Christian response was the Third Crusade.

The expeditions of 1189 were the best-organized of all the Crusades—the rulers of Germany, France, and England raised large, well-equipped forces; the Italians provided large fleets; and all converged on the strategic port of Acre. However, accident, disease, and personal disputes prevented the crusaders from achieving much. Richard the Lionheart of England came away with immortal renown and with a plan to recover Jerusalem by taking Cairo.

Attacking Egypt was the strategy for the Fourth, Fifth, and Sixth Crusades. The first was famously diverted to Constantinople, a result of muddled rather than malign intentions and of Greek intrigues. Unlike Runciman, the greatest historian of the Crusades, who deplored the sack of the great city as a fatal blow to the Byzantine barrier to the Turks, Tyerman does not see the eastern empire as possessing more than the dullest luster of its former glory.

Crusading energies were diverted to new fields, most important the destruction of the Albigensian heresy in southern France. The crusaders succeeded, at great cost, but the most significant result was to bring this region under the control of the king of France. The Children's Crusade in 1212 illustrates how bizarre popular enthusiasm had become.

Ancillary military expansion in Spain and the Baltic would probably have occurred even if there had been no crusading movement. Politics and cash drove the Spanish Reconquest, not religion. As in the Holy Land, there was the sense of retaking lands lost to invaders, and there was the similar breakdown of organized resistance—the Moors' internecine wars making them vulnerable, and the Almoravids' religious fanaticism reminding Christians that any Muslim foothold on the peninsula was dangerous.

The Crusades in the Baltic were more complex, with military orders and merchants being more involved and with Western chivalry coming to the aid of the Teutonic Knights in Prussia. Some aspects of the enterprise were, however, the same: great violence, and an extension of Western civilization which was so successful that its influence has lasted to the present day.

The end of the crusader presence in the Holy Land in 1291 was followed by further losses, ultimately by the fall of Constantinople itself. The last Crusades were little more than efforts to drive the Turks out of Europe, and they were failures.

In the sixteenth century, the theology behind the Crusades lost its force; not only did indulgences lose their attraction, but mass enthusiasm was no longer easily rallied. Popes had lost their standing, and knights had become officers and gentlemen. The secular state was replacing both empire and papacy; morality was enforced by the state, not the Church. In short, the value system that had energized the crusaders had vanished. Historians cannot render a final judgment on this long episode in

Christian and Muslim history—the Crusades' numerous contradictions and complications cannot be easily explained, much less either justified or condemned unconditionally.

William L. Urban

Review Sources

The Atlantic Monthly 298, no. 4 (November, 2006): 124.
The Christian Century 123, no. 21 (October 17, 2006): 23-24.
The Daily Telegraph, September 10, 2006, p. 44.
Library Journal 131, no. 15 (September 15, 2006): 74.
The Nation 283, no. 20 (December 11, 2006): 44-49.
The New York Review of Books 53, no. 16 (October 19, 2006): 41-45.
Publishers Weekly 253, no. 29 (July 24, 2006): 46.
The Spectator 301 (August 26, 2006): 35-36.
Sunday Times, August 27, 2006, p. 45.
The Times Literary Supplement, September 8, 2006, pp. 4-5.

THE GOOD LIFE

Author: Jay McInerney (1955-   )
Publisher: Alfred A. Knopf (New York). 353 pp. $25.00
Type of work: Novel
Time: September to December, 2001
Locale: New York City

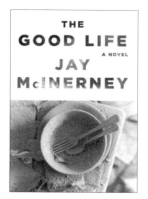

In the weeks following the September 11, 2001, terrorist attacks on New York City, members of the city's privileged classes reassess their lives, marriages, and values

> *Principal characters:*
> CORRINE CALLOWAY, an upper-middle-class New Yorker in her early forties
> LUKE McGAVOCK, a New York banker in his forties, on sabbatical from his job
> RUSSELL CALLOWAY, Corrine's husband, an editor at a distinguished publishing firm
> SASHA McGAVOCK, Luke's wife, a beautiful socialite
> ASHLEY, the McGavocks' teenage daughter
> HILARY, Corrine's wild younger sister
> JERRY, organizer of a downtown New York soup kitchen for rescue and salvage workers

In the weeks and months following the September 11, 2001, terrorist attacks on New York City, many writers and artists who lived in that area found themselves paralyzed by a sense of futility, a pervasive feeling that their familiar tools of art were insufficient for the task of representing a world in which everything seemed to have changed. As months and finally years began to pass, though, serious artists and writers did begin to rise to the task of creating art depicting the new city and new world in which they lived. Jay McInerney, who for more than twenty years had been closely associated with Manhattan thanks to his novels *Bright Lights, Big City* (1984), *Story of My Life* (1988), and *Brightness Falls* (1992), responded to the tragedy with *The Good Life*, a novel set in the days immediately before and after the events of September 11, 2001.

The book is a sequel to *Brightness Falls*, the story of Russell and Corrine Calloway, a New York couple in their early 30's whose working lives and marriage are brought to the brink of destruction by the corporate greed and drug culture of 1980's. *The Good Life* picks up the story of Russell and Corrine on the evening of September 10, 2001, as they host a dinner party for several friends (one of whom will be killed in the collapsing towers of the World Trade Center the following day). The Calloways are now in their forties and are the parents of twins conceived through a convoluted fertility process involving harvesting eggs from Corrine's younger sister Hilary. Though their marriage and family life look perfect to many of their friends, it

Jay McInerney achieved sudden success in 1984, with his critically and popularly acclaimed first novel, Bright Lights, Big City. *He has continued to write books exploring complex human motivations, generally set in New York City. His other novels include* Ransom *(1985),* Story of My Life *(1988),* Brightness Falls *(1992), and* Model Behavior *(1998).*

has become sexually and emotionally stifling for the two of them.

Parallel to the Calloways' story line, readers are introduced to the family of Luke McGavock, a wealthy investment banker who, much to the distress of his socialite wife and teenage daughter, has taken a sabbatical from his powerful and lucrative job in order to write a book about samurai films while he reassess what he wants to do with his life. While the Calloways prepare for their dinner party, the McGavocks attend a charity benefit at the Central Park Zoo, during which Luke becomes increasingly distressed in realizing that his wife may be having an affair with a wealthy mob figure and that his fourteen-year-old daughter has already become adept at drinking and flirting with older men.

The early chapters of the book linger in the evening hours of September 10, setting the stage and introducing readers to the lives and concerns of these characters, particularly Corrine Calloway and Luke McGavock, who will develop into the principal characters during the remainder of the novel. Though the two move in different circles, both are caught up in a society that puts more stock in such things as dressing in the "right" designer's clothes and drinking the "right" champagne than in a person's actual character or behavior.

The author puts on full display the emotional and intellectual shallowness of such obsessions with status, as well as the drug and alcohol problems he presents as an almost inevitable result of this attitude. In the marriages of the central characters, McInerney tells readers that "the pathways of intimacy were clogged from disuse," and the characters feel unspecified longings for something more "real." The interior unhappiness and unattractiveness of these apparently glossy characters makes it nearly impossible for readers to entirely like or relate very well to any of them. At the same time, though, it is difficult not to sympathize with the quiet desperation of people who feel caught in lifestyles that do not reflect who they really are or what they want as they settle into the kind of middle age that they had never imagined.

In a masterful stroke, McInerney's narrative entirely skips the day of September 11. So much has been written about that day, and about the reaction of those who witnessed the terrorist attacks firsthand, that it would be difficult for a novelist to add anything new to the discussion. The story picks up again on the morning of the twelfth, with the meeting of Luke McGavock and Corrine Calloway. Luke, having found himself near the collapsed World Trade Center, spent the previous day digging through the rubble with others in the hope of finding survivors. As he staggers uptown toward his home the next day, he meets Corrine on the street. She offers him bottled water, and he feels compelled to tell her his story. The bulk of the novel from this point on follows these two characters as they try to work through their sense of futility and survivor's guilt by volunteering in a hastily established soup kitchen near the wreckage, and their new friendship becomes increasingly eroticized.

In the emotionally charged atmosphere of post-September 11 Manhattan, this romantic attraction almost inevitably grows into a full-fledged affair. Intermingled with this tenuous romance are musings about spouses, children, parents, and friends as well as half-formed reflections on the fate of New York's people and American culture in general. Perhaps the strongest feature of the novel is the way in which the author captures the striking details of life in this particular time and place, where people once again take up long-discarded smoking and drinking habits and where a prescription for the anthrax-fighting drug Cipro can be considered a "sweet" dinner party favor.

As in other McInerney novels, New York City must itself be considered a character in *The Good Life*. The novel is as much about how New York will recover from the terrorist attacks as it is about the various ethical and personal choices of individual characters. References to vacation homes in Long Island's Hamptons and well-known Manhattan restaurants and nightspots abound. Famous people hover about the periphery of the novel, as when readers learn that writer Salman Rushdie was meant to be a guest at the Calloways' dinner party, though he declined at the last minute. Some critics are annoyed by McInerney's relentless name-dropping, which extends to brand names, street addresses, and hip cultural references. Indeed, those who do not share McInerney's obsession with the minutiae of New York society might not always find it easy to spot when such allusions are being made, let alone what exactly they imply about the characters. The author also seems to delight in pointing out how even longtime New Yorkers can be ignorant of the history and culture of their city.

The Good Life raises a number of ethical dilemmas that swirl around Luke and Corrine's doomed affair. The two characters discover (perhaps a bit too conveniently, as it at least partially mitigates the blame for their own infidelities) that each of their spouses had been having affairs well before September 11. Both also encounter serious problems involving their children: Luke's daughter Ashley turns out to have a drug addiction, while Corrine fears that her sister Hilary has come to take her twin son and daughter away (as Hilary is, in fact, their biological mother). Both Luke and Corrine also worry that their work in the soup kitchen is somehow less genuine, and therefore less valuable, because their motives for doing it combine a charitable impulse with a desire to spend time with each other. Each of these complications seems to ask, but not answer, another difficult question: What does one owe a dishonest spouse? What is best for the children, and how much of their own happiness should parents be ready to sacrifice in order to secure the happiness of their kids? What are charity and altruism, and are motives as important as actions? Perhaps the largest unanswered question involves the extent to which the old rules apply in a world where everything seems to have been changed by one day's senseless violence.

Critical reaction to *The Good Life* was mixed. While McInerney's name assured that the book would be seriously considered, some critics felt that the author's earlier works had already sufficiently covered the terrain of angst-ridden relationships among New York's more glamorous denizens. Indeed, the love story between Corrine and Luke is fairly conventional novelistic fare, spiced with fairly conventional anxieties about middle age and marriage. The prose, while generally vivid and descriptively rich, does occasionally lapse into the clichéd and stilted, especially in some of the longer passages of dialogue. A number of critics noted, as they did with McInerney's previous works, that it can be hard to sympathize with his self-absorbed, privileged characters.

Still, some readers found the book a balm after the tragic events that shook not only the city of New York but also the entire United States and the world. The novel has been acknowledged as a worthy attempt to come to grips with what is left after September 11, 2001, and how New Yorkers, and by analogy the rest of the world's residents, might try to live better lives afterward. Luke and Corrine try to separate their illicit relationship from their everyday lives by maintaining "the illusion that . . . beyond the barricades was a world apart." Part of the novel's point, however, is that no such separation is possible. What happens in one part of one's life must inevitably affect the other parts, just as an isolated terrorist attack will change the political shape of the world.

The title phrase, "the good life," is repeated several times during the course of the novel, always in reference to fairly conventional notions of money and a life of personal ease. In each mention, though, this is a distancing device, a chance for the characters to consider whether or not the existence described in these materialistic terms is really "the good life." Unsurprisingly perhaps, in each case the implied answer is a resounding no. The mass of less successful men and women who lack the opportunities of the Calloways or McGavocks might not be so quick to dismiss these conventional markers of happiness or to feel deeply sorry for those who have but do not appreciate them. For McInerney and his characters, it is clear that a truly good life would be built on something other than money and social status; it would rest on such intangibles as honesty, work of lasting value, and solid human relationships.

Janet E. Gardner

Review Sources

Booklist 102, no. 7 (December 1, 2005): 6.
Kirkus Reviews 73, no. 19 (October 1, 2005): 1049.
Library Journal 130, no. 18 (November 1, 2006): 66.
New Statesman 135 (March 27, 2006): 52-53.
New York 39, no. 4 (February 6, 2006): 72.
The New York Review of Books 53, no. 6 (April 6, 2006): 33-36.
The New York Times 155 (January 31, 2006): E1-E6.

The New York Times Book Review 155 (February 19, 2006): 14.
The New Yorker 81, no. 46 (February 6, 2006): 90-91.
Publishers Weekly 252, no. 47 (November 28, 2005): 21.
The Spectator 300 (March 25, 2006): 38.
Time 167, no. 7 (February 13, 2006): 73.
The Times Literary Supplement, March 10, 2006, pp. 19-20.

THE GREAT TRANSFORMATION
The Beginning of Our Religious Traditions

Author: Karen Armstrong (1946-   )
Publisher: Alfred A. Knopf (New York). 469 pp. $30.00
Type of work: History, philosophy
Time: 1600 B.C.E. to 220 B.C.E.
Locale: India, China, Israel-Judaea, and Greece

*Armstrong focuses on the period between 900 B.C.E. and
200 B.C.E. when in India, China, Israel-Judaea, and Greece
the great philosophers, including Buddha, Socrates, Confucius, Jeremiah, Ezekiel, Plato, and Aristotle, envisioned
the concepts, especially the ideal of the Golden Rule, which
form the bases of many modern religions*

Principal personages:
    AESCHYLUS, Greek dramatist
    ARISTOTLE, Greek philosopher
    BUDDHA, "the enlightened one," teacher who founded Buddhism
    CONFUCIUS, first thinker to state clearly the Golden Rule
    EZEKIEL, Jewish prophet
    EURIPIDES, Greek dramatist
    JEREMIAH, Jewish prophet
    JESUS, Jewish prophet
    MUHAMMAD, Muslim prophet, writer of the Qur'ān
    PAUL, Apostle and first Christian thinker
    PLATO, Greek philosopher
    SOCRATES, Greek philosopher
    SOLON, Athenian arbitrator who stressed the equality of all beings
    SOPHOCLES, Greek dramatist
    ZOROASTER, first major Axial philosopher-theologian

In *The Great Transformation*, Karen Armstrong, who has written several significant works on the history and function of human religions, considers a period identified by the German philosopher Karl Jaspers as the Axial Age. It was at this time,
from the ninth to the fifth century B.C.E., that philosophers, theologians, and mystics
throughout the civilized world promulgated the concepts that would become the
bases for today's major religious traditions: Islam, Judaism, Christianity, Buddhism-
Hinduism, and Confucianism-Daoism. It was a time, argues Armstrong, of a very
great transformation, in which modern religious traditions commenced. Armstrong
points out that there is an urgent need to understand the Axial Age and the transforma-
tions it produced because humankind is currently in a new Axial Age of scientific and
technological achievement that threatens to obscure the religious and philosophic
achievements of the Great Transformation, achievements which, in a dangerous and
complicated world, people desperately need to retain.

Armstrong commences her study with those people she identifies as the earliest Axial thinkers, the Aryans or Indo-Europeans, living on the steppes of southern Russia around 1600 B.C.E. These people called their gods *daevas*, the shining ones. *Daevas* were not immortal. They were subject, as was all matter, to the laws of the universe, and they shared with all other living creatures a spirit. It was thus a serious matter to take the life of any animate thing, for it had, as did humans, a transcendent inner life. It was therefore especially serious to take the life of another human. This belief did not stop the increasing intertribal warfare of the Indo-Europeans. Against this background of violence, the first major Axial philosopher-theologian appears: Zoroaster (c. 1200 B.C.E.). His people were highly conflicted between a desire for peace and a need to destroy their enemies. Zoroaster saw this situation as a conflict between the gods of goodness and those of evilness. He advocated a continuous conflict, but he also introduced the novel idea that when good people triumphed over evil ones, they need not act toward their enemies as their enemies had acted toward them. In their triumph the good must show restraint. With this radical idea, Zoroaster created a preview of the Axial Age's interest in what would ultimately become the human concept of compassion. This compassion could not be legislated but, to be effective and enduring, must come from within the individual who had emptied him or herself of the constraints of the ego. It would be some time before peoples of the Axial Age would understand and embrace such a concept. In India the idea would be enforced by the *rishis*, holy men who developed techniques of concentration that allowed them to break into the unconscious mind. The *rishis* also told the story of the first man, Purusha, who, like Christ, allowed himself to be sacrificed to bring divine order to the cosmos. These priests introduced introspection and self-sacrifice, the fundamental ideals of the Axial Age.

Elsewhere, the great transformation was slower in getting started. China was embroiled in tribal wars for centuries, and the normal practice throughout the region was to try to reach the holy gods through ritual that featured sacrifice of animals and other matter. However, in the ninth century B.C.E. the powerful Zhou dynasty of Chinese kings began to advocate the practice of compassion to go along with the sacrificial rituals. Like the Aryans and Chinese, the Greeks were overwhelmed with wars between the various city-states, as well as outside invaders, culminating in the vast violence and destruction of the Trojan War. This history of violence is reflected in the tales of the Greek gods and of the creation of the cosmos as a duel between Gia, Mother Earth, and Chaos, ruler of heaven. Israel also had a prehistory of turbulence and warfare, so that violence is part of the early history and theology of the Hebrew peoples as well. In an attempt to reach out in some effective manner to spirits beyond themselves and to deal with the culture of violence in which they existed, the early Axial peoples all turned to religious ritual in the eighth century B.C.E.

Karen Armstrong became a Catholic nun when she was seventeen but left her order in 1969. She then took bachelor's and master's degrees in English literature at Oxford University. A former teacher at London University and a radio and television commentator, she has written numerous books on the history and theory of religion.

To make the religious rituals even more complicated was the problem that throughout China, India, Greece, and even Israel—where Bal, in addition to Yahweh, continued to be worshipped—there was no concept of a single God, so that many deities had to be appealed to in multiple ways to reach any effective state of spirituality. Perhaps the most significant contribution of this century was not the rituals themselves but what the Greeks would call katharsis, cleansing of the soul through ritual. Ultimately this state would be achieved by the audience at the performances of the great Greek tragedies of the fifth century B.C.E. Late in the eighth century the Brahman priests of India also urged their congregations to employ rituals, not to reach an external god but to turn their thoughts inward. With practices such as these, the Axial Age had commenced.

The eighth century B.C.E. is analyzed by Armstrong in her most significant and enlightening chapter, titled "Kenosis," which is the Greek term for "emptying out." Kenosis is first presented to Israel in the initial five books of the Hebrew Bible, which had been first written down in the eighth century. In the Bible, Amos and Hosea urge believers to abandon ritual and turn in on one's self to find Yahweh, who is the only god to be reached in this manner—the act of dissolution of the self. Thus Abraham acts with selflessness and compassion in the presence of Yahweh. Abraham's follower Isaiah also has a vision of Yahweh as the only real god, and this new monotheism is confirmed by the salvation of Jerusalem from the hordes of invading Assyrians.

Unlike the Jews, the Greeks became ever-more committed polytheists, and this religious ideal led to a life of contests (agon) among the gods in heaven and also among men on earth. The most famous earthly agon was the Olympic Games, but in Athens it was ultimately the dramatic contests of the Dionysian festival that would lead to a spiritual exercise by the audience. The great poet Homer would set the ultimate ideal even for polytheists by describing how the hero Achilles had achieved sufficient kenosis and compassion by taking pity on Priam, the man who had killed the father of his friend. Like Greece, China continued to hold to rituals, but some Lu ritualists were beginning to entertain the idea of salvation through self-surrender.

India was seeing the emergence of a new class of holy men, the "renouncers," who gave up all of their worldly goods and went into the forest to live on what they could beg and gather. They believed that their lifestyle would unite them with the core of God's being. The most significant of these was the great teacher Buddha, "the enlightened one." It was the renouncers who would inspire the scriptures known as the Upanishads, which urge the believer to seek holiness in the essence of his or her being. Except for the Greeks, the new hero of the Axial Age was thus the inward-looking renouncer, not the warrior, though even the Greeks asked compassion of their warrior-heroes.

Having discovered kenosis, all the people of the Axial Age underwent a period of extreme political or physical dislocation, which caused them to value even more intensely the need for compassion. This period, between 600 and 530 B.C.E., Armstrong considers in a chapter titled "Suffering." The people of Israel were defeated and led into captivity in Babylon, but their prophet Jeremiah urged them to accept things as they were and understand that if they could come through this period of trial they would have their interior spirituality strengthened. Ezekiel accepted the argument of Jeremiah and spread the concept throughout his followers. It was in this spirit that the Bible's Book of Job was written. Ultimately, Jewish ideology would stress respect for the sacred otherness and holiness of all life.

The Athenian Greeks were not forced into exile, as were the Jews, but a civil war seemed imminent. Solon was appointed as an arbitrator between the commoners and the nobles in an attempt to bring peace. It was Solon who stressed equality of all beings and established laws that applied equally to all classes. Soon Athens was to have a major religious festival, the City Dionysia, dedicated to the sufferings of the god Dionysus, in whose honor the great tragedies were performed. In these dramas, the hero always suffered great disasters caused by his unholy pride, hubris, and the audience shared in this spiritual agony. Even as the Greeks were learning to think logically and analytically, they were also learning to surrender themselves to the universality of irrational pain.

The suffering of daily life in India led to a new philosophic tradition called *Samkhya*, which taught that all life was suffering but that turning to one's interior world would bring a spiritual relief. Thus was invented yoga, the technique of entering one's interior spirituality. Meanwhile, life in China was tormented by continuous civil wars, but a great spiritual thinker would arise to lead his people out of misery and war: Confucius. It is with Confucius (c. 530-450 B.C.E.) that Armstrong begins her insightful chapter called "Empathy."

The first clearly to state the Golden Rule, Confucius argued that one enlarges oneself by trying to enlarge others. Another special event of the fifth century B.C.E. was the Persian defeat of Babylon, which allowed the Jews to return to Jerusalem, where they committed themselves to a single god, Yahweh, and rebuilt for him the famous Jerusalem Temple. It was the first unequivocal statement of monotheism in Jewish history. The Greeks were bringing the Axial Age to culmination in another manner with their heavy commitment to philosophic logic. Even as their poets were filling the theaters with heroic sufferings, such as the powerful works of Aeschylus, Sophocles, and Euripides, the Athenian philosophers Socrates, his student Plato, and Plato's student Aristotle, were using not emotion but logic to argue the existence of a supreme being and the need to use one's intellectual processes to discover such a phenomenon.

The latter chapters of Armstrong's powerful and highly detailed study are devoted to bringing the reader up to the modern period, with a consideration of the contributions of Jesus, whom she describes as a devout Jew, Paul, whom she posits as the first Christian and the first to use the term *Christos*, "the Anointed one," those who completed the Hebrew Bible, the writers of the Christian Bible, and Muhammad, writer of the Qur'ān. Each of these religions—Judaism, Christianity, and Islam, as well as Buddha-Hinduism and Confucianism-Daoism—are committed to the belief in compassion for others obtained through the surrender of self-conceit. Indeed, as Armstrong points out the word *islam* means "surrender." Despite the great transformation of the Axial Age and the achievements of the various spiritual thinkers, Armstrong worries that the new Axial Age now in progress is paying too little attention to its predecessor and that the sufferings of the world will never be remedied until the first Axial Age is reembraced in practice as well as in theory.

August W. Staub

Review Sources

Booklist 102, nos. 9/10 (January 1-15, 2006): 21.
Library Journal 131, no. 6 (April 1, 2006): 99.
The New York Times 155 (April 21, 2006): E34.
The New York Times Book Review 155 (April 30, 2006): 21.
Publishers Weekly 253, no. 3 (January 16, 2006): 58.
The Spectator 300 (March 25, 2006): 42-43.
The Times Literary Supplement, June 30, 2006, p. 28.
The Wilson Quarterly 30, no. 2 (Spring, 2006): 106-107.

GRIEF

Author: Andrew Holleran (1943-   )
Publisher: Hyperion (New York). 150 pp. $19.95
Type of work: Novella
Time: January to April, 1999
Locale: Washington, D.C.

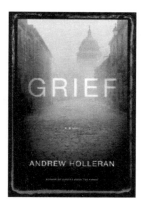

*An elegiac first-person account of an aging single gay
man coping with the aftermath of his mother's death and
facing the isolating realities of midlife in the era of AIDS*

Principal characters:
> UNNAMED NARRATOR, a gay man in his
> mid-fifties, a visiting professor of litera-
> ture
> UNNAMED LANDLORD, a gay fifty-five-year-old civil servant and
> antiques dealer who rents the narrator a room in his row house
> FRANK, a mutual friend, a long-time member of the Dupont Circle gay
> community, who has secured the temporary job and living space for
> the narrator
> BISCUIT, the landlord's female dog, in part alter ego of the narrator
> MARY TODD LINCOLN (1818-1882), widow of U.S. president Abraham
> Lincoln, with whom the narrator identifies
> HENRY ADAMS (1838-1918), American writer-historian, a longtime resi-
> dent of Washington, D.C.

Andrew Holleran's breakthrough first novel, *Dancer from the Dance* (1978), has
since its publication retained its status as a mainstay of gay literature. It pays tribute to
the heyday of gay life in Manhattan in the 1970's. In *Grief*, his fourth novel, Holleran
turns from the lively whirl of parties, baths, and late-night discos of *Dancer from the
Dance* to a more somber and isolated reality of the late 1990's. In *Grief* Holleran's
anonymous, semiautobiographical yet fictional protagonist stands in as a representative of an entire generation of gay men who have survived the devastations of AIDS.
The first-person narrator of *Grief* has reached a late middle age where both spirit and
looks are failing him, and the personal Rolodex is peopled with the dead.

Grief can be read as a third part of a triptych in which Holleran's *Dancer from the
Dance* and *Nights in Aruba* (1983) are earlier installments. In this book as in his others, Holleran is a master of a seemingly plotless, character-driven narrative, the pieces
of which are made from small, and often redundant, details of personal and everyday
life. In *Grief* he repeats or reexamines certain motifs and themes that appeared in his
earlier fiction. These include the search for companionship in a world where connections are elusive and the problems of balancing parts of the self, particularly what can
be the Janus faces of adult gay identity and allegiance to one's family of origin.

Grief begins and ends with a plane ride. The narrative opens as Holleran's protagonist arrives in Washington, D.C., to take on a brief stint as a sabbatical replacement in

~

Andrew Holleran is the pseudonym of a writer whose publications include the novels Dancer from the Dance *(1978),* Nights in Aruba *(1983), and* The Beauty of Men *(1996); the book of essays* Ground Zero *(1988); and the collection of short stories* In September, the Light Changes *(1999).*

~

a literature department of a major university. It ends as he departs to return to the parental home in Florida that he occupies alone after the death of his mother. This travel through the heavens is literally and figuratively transit between two lives. In going to Washington, the narrator shifts away from his identity as the loyal son and primary caretaker for his demanding but beloved mother and moves toward his gay identity and into the homosexual community of Washington's Dupont Circle and the city at large. In each emotional setting—the one he has come into and the one he left behind—the protagonist struggles between poles of alienation and symbiosis. In Washington he struggles most poignantly with loss and grief.

In coming to Washington, the narrator enters a kind of limbo. The house on N Street where he has taken a room is unoccupied upon his arrival and features a marble sculpture that could double as an ornament on a Victorian tomb. In a scenario that repeats at various points throughout his sojourn, he appears reflected eerily back to himself from one of the household's mirrors like a haunt or ghost. In the city where he wanders on long walks in the night, the major buildings loom like mausoleums. The National Gallery, where he attends concerts in Sunday evening off-hours, has a half-lit, underworld-like glow, its exhibits cordoned off from access. The weather, in this in-between place, is neither warm nor cold.

As a boarder, he never succeeds in truly penetrating into the real flesh-and-blood life of his landlord, a middle-aged gay man much like himself, who, though outwardly polite and sociable, rarely relaxes the stringent boundaries that keep the narrator defined in a businesslike way as one of a string of serial tenants, neither lover nor friend. The temporary and replaceable nature of the narrator's domestic existence is underscored by pieces of mail that arrive for former tenants like him, now long gone. They pour through the mail slot and are discarded, forwarding addresses unknown.

While landlord and tenant circle each other like satellites in separate orbits in adjoining space, the narrator turns for sustenance to other quarters. There is his old friend, Frank, who lives up to his name. In a series of frank conversations, this long-time resident of Washington serves as a seriocomic truth teller and soothsayer for the protagonist. Frank, riddled by cancer and having witnessed the vast attrition of gay men to AIDS, is a witty realist. He exclaims that he got a suntan one summer just standing outside during the graveside funerals of friends. He explains that the gay community of Washington in the 1980's seemed like a dinner party where some of the guests "were taken out and shot while the rest of us were expected to go on eating." He nevertheless urges the narrator away from despair, toward life.

There is also the landlord's dog, Biscuit, who is sequestered in a windowless study by day while her master goes away to work. The abandoned, resigned, and closely quartered dog and the lonesome tenant bond in the landlord's absences, yet only to a degree. The dog, like the narrator, maintains a circumscribed order that denies real attachment or intimacy. Frank, ever the armchair psychologist, also reminds the narrator that his relationship with the dog replicates the familiar one of caretaking for his mother.

The protagonist's best companion, oddly, is not a living character, but Mary Todd Lincoln, the widow—or survivor—of the assassinated president of the United States. An edition of her letters graces the bookshelf in the narrator's room, and from the first to the last nights in the house, his reading of her words provides pinpoints of identification for his time in D.C. Henry Adams also looms large, as the narrator passes the historian's former home near the White House on his nighttime ramblings. Lincoln and Adams, who lost his wife Clover to suicide, lived for years in guilt and grief. Their experiences, like the narrator's own, raise questions of the power of the past in the present, the metaphysical nature of death, and the differing ways individuals either recover, or do not recover, from the loss of those they love.

It is only when the narrator confesses to Frank the nature of his own guilt—his failure to reveal his homosexuality to his mother, even though, like the mother in *Nights in Aruba*, she directly asked him about it—that a turning point is reached. Spring comes. Blossoms bloom. The landlord runs naked across the common landing. A kind of exuberance fills the formerly dead air. The semester ends, and the narrator returns as planned to Florida. He flies once more a silent stranger among strangers and falls grateful and penitent to his knees between the beds of his parents.

In its worse sense, *Grief* can be condemned as a shallow narrative of a man about whom little is revealed except the set of facts upon which he privately obsesses. In the first-person access we are given to him as a character, he appears chronically—if understandably due to his social circumstances, his loneliness, and his depression—self-absorbed. Like Mary Todd Lincoln, who descended into a maelstrom of unhappiness and remorse given the repeated blows to her psyche that came with the series of deaths of loved ones in her life, there is both something horrid and genuine and something self-imposed and stunted in the narrator's grief. This can be said to be a strength of Holleran's writing—his unwillingness to create overly idealized characters, or "heroes." His protagonists tend instead to be fragile, smart, funny, and not entirely likable people who squirm quite unheroically and yet carry on in life. In *Grief*, Holleran, a "gay writer," achieves an added level of universality in his appeal, and in the neo-Freudian philosophical matters with which his main character grapples. Though a gay man dealing with expressly gay dilemmas, Holleran's sojourner, a seeker of meaning and connection, is on a journey of love, death, regret, and yearning that is common in some form to all.

Holleran's novel is also strangely uplifting, given its overall theme of depression. In its course, as the narrator visits Ford's Theater and other distinctly Washingtonian settings, he is reminded, through those he meets and sees, that loss cuts across sexual orientation and age—that it is, indeed, a matter of the human condition. Sorrow and abandonment are harbored by almost everyone who touches him tangentially—a fellow tourist is a recent widow, Frank's elderly cat is on death's door, the perpetually cheery but unfailingly remote landlord had his heart broken by a beautiful but habitually unfaithful partner, a seemingly troublesome student confesses he has lost a brother to AIDS. Odd and harmed people frequent the street, and a scam artist rings the doorbell. Meanwhile there is a twinge of inspiration and hope, emergent like the cherry blossoms, in the narrator's dogged effort, in spite of things, to reinvent himself, and in the ongoing lives of the characters, however flawed and compromised they may be.

The narrator suffers a long peripatetic night of the soul in the course of this novel. However, as he moves up and down the stairs of his landlord's house and along the avenues of the nation's capital or appreciates the art in the city's museums, there is something generated within him that is similar to the phoenix rising.

Barbara Bair

Review Sources

The Advocate, July 4, 2006, pp. 57-59.
Booklist 102, no. 18 (May 15, 2006): 23.
Gay and Lesbian Review 13 (September/October, 2006): 39-40.
Kirkus Reviews 74, no. 7 (April 1, 2006): 314.
Lambda Book Report 14, no. 2 (Summer, 2006): 13.
The New York Times Book Review 155 (July 30, 2006): 17.
Publishers Weekly 253, no. 14 (April 3, 2006): 36.
The Washington Post Book World, July 2, 2006, p. 7.

GUESTS OF THE AYATOLLAH
The First Battle in America's War with Militant Islam

Author: Mark Bowden (1951-   )
Publisher: Atlantic Monthly Press (New York). 680 pp.
  $26.00; paperback $15.00
Type of work: History
Time: November, 1979, to January, 1981
Locale: Tehran, Iran, and Washington, D.C.

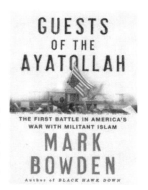

Bowden gives a riveting account of the takeover of the American Embassy in Tehran, Iran, in November, 1979, by radical Islamist militants and the subsequent imprisonment of sixty-six American hostages, which lasted 444 days, told from the perspective of the hostages, the hostage takers, and President Jimmy Carter's White House

Principal personages:

BRUCE LAINGEN, acting ambassador, chargé d'affaires, and hostage
MICHAEL METRINKO, a foreign service political officer and hostage
JOSEPH SUBIC, an army sergeant and hostage
NILUFAR EBTEKAR, also known as "Mary," spokesperson for the hostage
  takers
JIMMY CARTER, president of the United States
HAMILTON JORDAN, Carter's chief of staff
ZBIGNIEW BRZEZINSKI, U.S. national security adviser
CHARLIE BECKWITH, commander of Delta Force
MOHAMMED REZA PAHLAVI, the shah of Iran
IMAM RUHOLLAH KHOMEINI, an Islamic religious leader

Mark Bowden, best known for his 1999 best seller *Black Hawk Down*, a chronicle of an ill-fated encounter between American soldiers and Muslim militants in Somalia, turns his attention to the 1979 Iran hostage crisis in *Guests of the Ayatollah: The First Battle in America's War with Militant Islam*. A journalist with many years' experience, Bowden worked for over five years to gather an impressive number of interviews with those closely involved in the crisis. He also spent a significant amount of time in Iran doing research and interviews. The resulting book is thus comprehensive in its reporting of the events leading up to the embassy takeover and keenly insightful in its analysis of the long-ranging implications of the crisis.

Bowden opens his story on November 4, 1979, in Tehran. It was a turbulent time in the city; the shah of Iran, Mohammed Reza Pahlavi, long associated with the United States, had fled Iran some six months earlier in the wake of a religious revolution against his repressive regime. The return from exile of Ayatollah Imam Ruhollah Khomeini further fanned the revolutionary zeal of his followers. There had been demonstrations and some violence in front of the U.S. embassy for weeks. However, none of the Americans stationed at the embassy nor their political counterparts at home in Washington viewed the situation as particularly volatile. The political situation was nevertheless far more complicated and fraught with peril than the Americans realized. Various factions within Iranian society were vying for control, including the provisional government put into place on the shah's departure and the forces aligning themselves behind religious leaders like Khomeini.

When the U.S. government, under the leadership of President Jimmy Carter, gave permission for the shah to enter the United States for treatment of cancer, the situation in Tehran deteriorated rapidly. Still, on the morning of November 4, the embassy staff and its support personnel regarded the crowd gathering outside the walls as nothing more than protestors, a sight to which they had all grown accustomed. Bowden, by alternating scenes from the perspective of the embassy staff with those from the "student" militants, allows readers to see for themselves how quickly the demonstrations shifted from a desire for a sit-in to a full-scale hostage event.

With a light rain falling, the young militants, calling themselves "students following the imam's line," pushed through the barriers and took control of the embassy. What they expected to be a three-day demonstration, however, turned into a 444-day ordeal—for the hostages, the hostage takers, Carter's administration, and the American public.

At its best, *Guests of the Ayatollah* allows readers to enter the world of the hostages as they are kept isolated and separated through the early dark days of their imprisonment. Bowden captures both the fear and boredom that permeated their daily lives. One of the most poignant stories is that of twenty-eight-year-old Vice Consul Richard Queen, who began to lose the feeling in his left arm shortly after his capture. Throughout the story, his mysterious illness grew worse, until he was unable to hold a cup of tea in his hand or stand without vomiting. Queen was finally released and sent home when his illness became too difficult for the hostage takers to manage, and he was later diagnosed with multiple sclerosis.

The life of chargé d'affaires Bruce Laingen also provides a surreal vignette. At the time of the embassy takeover, he and two of his coworkers were at the Iranian foreign ministry. Although they were not technically hostages, they found themselves stranded in the ministry. Bowden describes them as

> vagabond emissaries to a government that did not exist. . . . They had not been directly forbidden to leave for a friendly embassy, but even if they were not stopped on their way out, the practical problems were considerable. Any embassy that accepted them would itself become a target for these fanatics.

Thus, Laingen and his colleagues "slept on sofas in the ministry's long and narrow formal dining room and spent most of their time during the day in the reception area's central salon," trying to make themselves presentable to visitors from other embassies.

Michael Metrinko's response to being taken hostage demonstrates both the courage and the anger that the Americans displayed over their ordeal. Metrinko, a political officer, was particularly well educated about the Middle East and had fully immersed

himself in Iranian culture. He also had a firm
sense of his own propriety as a representative
of the U.S. government, and he was scrupu-
lous about protecting information that had
been entrusted to him. Nonetheless, he did
not withhold his disdain and hatred for his
captors and continually heaped verbal abuse
upon them. At one point, he was handcuffed
for two weeks as a punishment for his behavior, and he was frequently beaten. Metrinko
seemed to take pride in this: "Metrinko was at
peace with his own behavior. He had fought

~

*Mark Bowden teaches creative writing
and journalism at Loyola College in
Maryland. He reported for* The
Philadelphia Inquirer *for twenty years
and was a national correspondent for*
The Atlantic Monthly. *He is the author
of seven books, including* Black Hawk
Down *(1999), which was nominated for
a National Book Award.*

~

his captors and insulted them every day, right up to the ride to the airport" (the day of
the hostages' release), and "he had fresh scrapes and bruises to show for it."

In marked contrast to Metrinko, a particularly troubling situation surrounded Joe
Subic, a young army sergeant. Subic, for unknown reasons, took it upon himself to
provide significant information about the embassy personnel to the hostage takers.
Although many of the personnel had attempted to keep the knowledge of their positions and their function in the embassy from their captors, Subic "helpfully" supplied
all the details the militants wanted. He revealed a great deal of damaging information,
including who in the group spoke Farsi, a detail that could have been useful for the
hostages in gleaning information about their situation. As Bowden writes, "Subic was
a well-meaning busybody, who seemed compelled to be at the center of attention, and
now he was doing it here, with all of his colleagues tied to chairs." Bowden does not
go so far as to call Subic a collaborator, but later when he describes Subic's role in
planning a Christmas party, there is little doubt that Subic was working with the
enemy:

> Subic said that he was putting together, at the guards' behest, a Christmas party. He was
> their "consultant" for the party. . . . Subic's room also had a desk and a telephone that he
> said he had used on occasion to call out to other embassies in Tehran.

In addition to the stories of the hostages, Bowden weaves in the stories of the men
of Delta Force, an elite group of soldiers training for special operations under the
command of Charlie Beckwith. Although it seemed unthinkable that there would be a
military response to the hostage crisis given the grave danger it would place the hostages in, as the weeks and months dragged on without a diplomatic solution, President
Carter finally gave the go-ahead for a rescue attempt. The story is a tragic one: Not
only were the hostages not freed by the aborted rescue attempt, but eight U.S. service-
men also lost their lives in an accident during the maneuver.

Bowden also draws compelling portraits of the Iranian hostage takers. Generally
known by nicknames such as "Gap-tooth" or "Hamid the Liar," the militants argued
with the hostages daily about the religious and moral rightness of their actions. The
hostages, however, took special exception to the woman known as "Mary," whose
real name was Nilufar Ebtekar. She spoke fluent, American-accented English, and

this fact alone seemed to infuriate the hostages. Currently, Ebtekar serves as the vice president of Iran in the ministry of the environment. Bowden, generally very even-handed when he describes his subjects, found that even twenty-five years after the events recounted in his book, Ebtekar still had a "smarmy, self-certain manner that anyone would find annoying." In addition, he reports that in his interview with her, she revealed "she has not moderated her views of the United States one bit."

Guests of the Ayatollah additionally provides an insider's view of the Carter White House. Bowden acknowledges that the Iran hostage crisis in all likelihood cost Carter the presidency. Although he seems frustrated by the president's actions, he also goes to some lengths to explain the very difficult situation in which Carter found himself. Most interesting of all, he provides excellent pictures of the differing views of National Security Adviser Zbigniew Brzezinski, Secretary of State Cyrus Vance, and White House Chief of Staff Hamilton Jordan. Bowden also discredits reports that Ronald Reagan's staff negotiated secretly with the hostage takers to prevent the release of the hostages until Reagan's inauguration day. Bowden argues that the hostage takers hated Carter so much that they would have waited until he was out of office on their own initiative.

The reportage in *Guests of the Ayatollah* is remarkable. Bowden accumulated hundreds of hours of interviews, many describing the same events from multiple perspectives. With skill and tenacity, Bowden manages to weave these accounts into a coherent narration. This is no small feat; readers trying to sort through the names and experiences of sixty-six hostages, President Carter's staff, the Iranian hostage takers, and the leaders of the Iranian provisional and religious governments will find it difficult at times not to be overwhelmed with the sheer volume of material Bowden presents. Nevertheless, the thread of the story and the individual experiences of the hostages keep the narration on track and ultimately propel the reader to the conclusion: the freeing of the hostages on President Ronald Reagan's inaugural day.

Bowden also provides the kind of insight available only through hindsight. As his subtitle suggests, he sees the takeover of the U.S. embassy and the subsequent hostage crisis as a crucial moment in U.S. history, the moment when Americans first confronted Islamist fundamentalism. He argues that the crisis itself undermined the moderate men in the Iranian provisional government and strengthened the hard-line fundamentalism that set the course for Iranian politics for the next quarter century. In all, *Guests of the Ayatollah* is a remarkable book, one that anyone attempting to understand current-day Iran must read. This work will, in all likelihood, be the benchmark against which all other accounts of the Iran hostage crisis will be measured.

Diane Andrews Henningfeld

Review Sources

Booklist 102, no. 13 (March 1, 2006): 42.
The Economist 379 (May 13, 2006): 93-94.

Kirkus Reviews 74, no. 6 (March 15, 2006): 270-271.
Library Journal 131, no. 7 (April 15, 2006): 89.
National Review 58, no. 14 (August 7, 2006): 45-47.
The New York Times Book Review 155 (May 14, 2006): 30.
Newsday, June 11, 2006, p. C27.
Publishers Weekly 253, no. 16 (April 17, 2006): 174.
Time 167, no. 22 (May 29, 2006): 68-69.
The Wall Street Journal 247, no. 100 (April 29, 2006): P10.
The Washington Times, May 28, 2006, p. B8.

HALF WILD

Author: Mary Rose O'Reilley (1935-   )
Publisher: Louisiana State University Press (Baton
    Rouge). 62 pp. $17.00
Type of work: Poetry

The poems in O'Reilley's first book of poetry, winner of the 2005 Walt Whitman Award, explore nature, life, death, and spirit as they wind themselves through landscapes of the world and of the soul

Mary Rose O'Reilley, well loved by teachers of writing for books such as *The Peaceable Classroom* (1993) and *Radical Presence: Teaching as Contemplative Practice* (1998), published her memoir *The Love of Impermanent Things* simultaneously with her first book of poetry, *Half Wild*. Together, the books offer a testament to a life spent nonviolently in an often violent world and insight into one of the most gifted voices in American poetry today. *Half Wild* was the 2005 winner of the Walt Whitman Award, sponsored by the Academy of American Poets and given to the winner of an open competition of American poets who have not yet published a book of poems.

Poet Mary Oliver served as judge for the 2005 competition and wrote in her citation that O'Reilley's is "a style that celebrates life and dignifies sorrow; that includes the drifter; the Japanese print; deer in the woods; herons in the wetland grass; a lost child recovered but, it could be, forever half wild; and especially, for it is a continuing presence in this book, that mystery we call the soul." Oliver's praise is well earned; the poems of *Half Wild* take the reader on a journey to places where the soul resides, to dark corners where violence intrudes, and to bright spaces where there is a glimpse of grace.

Half Wild is a book of doubles: The first poem is called "Twin," and there are several paired poems such as "The Lost Child" and *L'Enfant Sauvage*. The narrator of "Twin" is an adult who recalls the experience of being born a twin but a twin whose sibling dies shortly after birth. The poem digs deeply into the shared sense of life, the sharing of one womb, unique to twins. Their common beginning, sometimes in one egg, means that twins not only share the womb, they share the same genetic structure, the same composition of flesh. "You were the part of me," O'Reilley writes, "that gave itself to death." In the death of the twin, the narrator also loses a part of herself. In her dreams, she sees her unborn sister's eyes, "sealed with a membrane/ of unknowing." From her dreams, she awakens "with an infant's shriek." In this poem, then, the promise and violence of birth are also the promise and violence of death.

"Twins" seems also connected to the poem "Ritual," a poem about "the one who knocked at the window" but who "has flown away." Taken as a metaphor for birth, and death, the poem speaks of a child just born, who only utters one cry before returning to "the nest of spirits." Indeed, several poems turn to the subject of the child not born or who does not survive. In "Autobiography," for example, the narrator speaks of "warm souls," including "children who pulled back before birth." Likewise, in "Miscarried," a present-tense poem, the narrator is reminded of a daughter, now gone, named Rain: " Sometimes I see her/ in corners/ running/ faster/ than I."

Many of the poems deal with women: their relationships with men, their relationships with one another, and, most poignantly, their relationships with their mothers and daughters. "Persephone," for example, offers the point of view of a missing daughter. In the myth of Demeter and Persephone, Hades steals young Persephone from her mother's side. In her grief, Demeter throws the Earth into coldness and refuses to allow plants to grow. She wins a reprieve for her daughter over death but only on the condition that her daughter has not eaten anything. Persephone,

Mary Rose O'Reilley is a professor of English and environmental studies at the University of St. Thomas. She is a Quaker who has also taken Buddhist precepts. Her previous work includes five books of essays, notably The Barn at the End of the World: The Apprenticeship of a Buddhist Quaker Shepherd *(2001) and* The Love of Impermanent Things: A Threshold Ecology *(2006).*

however, has eaten six pomegranate seeds and so is forced to return to darkness and Hades for six months a year.

In O'Reilley's hands, however, Persephone seems first to be one of the lost babies; "I could still taste her milk/ on my tongue as I entered/ the village of hell." The sensual connection between mother and daughter here is striking; it is the mother's milk that has nurtured the child. Further, the story seems more about choice than abduction. Persephone calls her dalliance with Hades a "droll affair"; she also reports that although her mother wept on her grave, Persephone "loved terrible places, as girls will." The poem turns with a "but" in line 12 as Persephone "skips" home, only to find her mother and garden gone. In a chilling conclusion, O'Reilley writes, "Ashes blow on the hearth./ The child, Panic, clings to my hair."

In a poem with a more modern setting, "The Visit," O'Reilley writes of a daughter visiting her elderly mother. The tenor of their relationship is hinted at in the first line: "Things don't work well in this house." The mother lives in the squalor of the aged, but she tries to hide this from her daughter, not out of love but out of fear that her daughter will "put her away/ on a clean shelf" just as "she put her mother." In contrasting stanzas, O'Reilley first tells readers that "What we fear/ are the things we ourselves have done/ and believe it is right to do." She next tells readers that "what we love are the words/ mothers say in books" rather than the mother who is the subject of the visit. The poem is intensely sad in its acknowledgment that mothers and daughters do great damage to each other, all the while trying to do what is right.

A few poems deal with relationships between men and women. In "Bluebeard's Wife," O'Reilley tells the old story of a woman forbidden by her husband to go into a particular room. The wife has had "so much practice/ not-smelling the dead" that she is able to block from her mind the evidence of her senses, evidence of the cruel deeds her husband has committed against other women. The poem takes an interesting shift, marked by the change from the present tense, describing the wife's current existence, and the future that the narrator imagines for her when she takes the key to the room and opens it. The shift signals a longing for a world of women and wives who will no longer dutifully ignore the violence heaped upon women by men.

Finally, like Mary Oliver, O'Reilley is intensely interested in the natural world. Her images and ideas often take root in the trees, animals, and rocks of Minnesota. Her poems reveal Lake Superior and the North Shore woods as places where she grows to understand that oneness of all life. Thus, while many of O'Reilley's poems are about the inevitability and surety of death, they are also about the rebirth of all living things, the molecules of tree, snake, and bone, the same molecules, miraculously built, destroyed, and rebuilt by the processes of nature.

O'Reilley's theology is idiosyncratic but lovely. The Buddhist influence on her work seems clear in its continual departure and return; birth, death, and rebirth are at the heart of O'Reilley's work. However, the return O'Reilley seems to envision is not just that of the soul making its way to final and blissful nonbeing. Rather, O'Reilley seems to suggest actual physical reincarnation at the most elemental level, in the sense that the component pieces of all animate and inanimate beings will, after being born or composed, ultimately die and decompose and go back into the earth. These component pieces, then, recombine to form new life and new compositions. In "Memory," O'Reilley writes: "I have been trees/ and will be again/ green cells/ in the hearts of grass/ or the snake's quick slide."

While O'Reilley's poems do not seem to argue for the continuation of consciousness through the endless cycle of birth and rebirth, she does seem to argue for the continuation of the mysterious something that can only be described as soul.

The last poem of the book, "Shin Ohashe Bridge," serves as fitting finale to this fine collection. In it, O'Reilley describes a Japanese etching in detail, blurring the lines between the scene composed and the method of composition. Thus, the line "Black crosshatching etches a sudden shower" describes both the scene and the way the scene is created. O'Reilley writes of the figures in the etching, figures unaware that they are held in place by the stroke of a pen. The bridge upon which they walk, seemingly solid to them, is ephemeral and leads to nowhere, and "none of these people,/ for all their hurry, will get home." The poem become allegory: Like the people in Hiroshige's print, readers, too, are caught in the illusion that what they see before them is real. Hiroshige's people "do not know what black scratches/ pin them forever to his page." O'Reilley's verse, literally "black scratches" on the page, extends the illusion outward. She, too, has pinned these characters in the pages of *Half Wild*, just as she has pinned Persephone, Rain, and the half-wild child.

The poems of *Half Wild* linger in the mind and in the body long after the reading is over. Part nature poetry, part theology, part road map, these poems remind readers that they are part of a much larger cycle, something that is at once familiar and mysterious. These poems speak to the heart and to the soul.

Diane Andrews Henningfeld

Review Sources

Library Journal 131, no. 13 (August 1, 2006): 92.
Minneapolis Star Tribune, June 4, 2006, p. F15.

HERSHEY
Milton S. Hershey's Extraordinary Life of Wealth, Empire, and Utopian Dreams

Author: Michael D'Antonio (1955-   )
Publisher: McGraw-Hill (New York). Illustrated. 305 pp. $25.00
Type of work: Biography
Time: 1857-2002
Locale: New York City; Leadville and Denver, Colorado; Lancaster, Titusville, Philadelphia, and Hershey, Pennsylvania; various European venues; Egypt

D'Antonio's comprehensive biography of Milton S. Hershey brings to life the events of the chocolate mogul's existence, detailing his contributions to his employees, to the orphaned boys for whom he established a boarding school, and to American industry

Principal personages:
> MILTON SNAVELY "M. S." HERSHEY, founder of the Hershey Chocolate Company
> HENRY HERSHEY, Milton Hershey's father
> VICTORIA "FANNY" SNAVELY HERSHEY, Milton's mother
> CATHERINE "KITTY" SWEENEY HERSHEY, Milton's wife
> MARTHA "MATTIE" SNAVELY, Milton's aunt, Victoria's sister
> WILLIAM H. "HARRY" LEBKICHER, Milton's accountant and business associate
> WILLIAM F. R. MURRIE, Milton's business associate and confidant

Among the iconic monuments that dot the landscape of industrial achievement in the United States, the five-cent Hershey chocolate bar ranks high. Along with the Ford motor car, Coca Cola, Quaker Oats, and Campbell soups, the Hershey bar has a long history and reflects a great deal about the changing history of the country. Michael D'Antonio is particularly effective in discussing the social and industrial climate in which the Hershey Company originated and prospered. His understanding of the Gilded Age of the latter half of the nineteenth century, of the Panic of 1893, and of other socioeconomic currents that affected the course of both the company and the nation is impressive.

The early life story of Milton Snavely Hershey is one of frustration and failure. The son of Henry Hershey and Victoria "Fanny" Snavely Hershey, Milton was one of two children. Milton's younger sister, Sarena, born in 1862, contracted scarlet fever in 1867 and succumbed to complications accompanying that disease.

Henry Hershey was a dandy who enjoyed dressing in silk clothing. He constantly hatched get-rich-quick schemes that were doomed to failure from the start. He courted Martha Snavely, nicknamed Mattie, the daughter of a prominent and quite wealthy family in Lancaster, Pennsylvania, a Mennonite stronghold some fifty miles west of Philadelphia. In time, his interest shifted to Mattie's sister, Fanny, whom D'Antonio describes as short and round-shouldered.

Something of a free-thinking renegade from the Reformed Mennonite Church, in which her father preached, Fanny married Henry Hershey in 1856. He was attired for the ceremony in a frock coat, striped trousers, a stylish waistcoat, and a high silk hat. Although the pair remained married to each other for the rest of their lives, Henry lived apart from his wife for much of their marriage.

Lancaster was a prosperous city with a brick road reaching clear to Philadelphia. The home of the Conestoga wagon, the precursor of today's eighteen-wheelers, Lancaster had a

A seasoned writer, Michael D'Antonio shared a Pulitzer Prize for The State Boys Rebellion *in 2004. Among his earlier books are* Fall from Grace *(1989),* Atomic Harvest *(1993), and* Mosquito *(2001). His writing has appeared in* The New York Times, *the* Los Angeles Times, Esquire, Time, *and a number of other major publications.*

brisk trade with Philadelphia, transporting its produce to the city from which it purchased manufactured goods and bundles of cash. The Panic of 1857, however, made serious inroads on Lancaster's prosperity.

In 1860, when oil was discovered in the village of Titusville, some 250 miles northwest of Lancaster, an oil rush developed reminiscent of the California Gold rush of 1848. Henry quickly moved his family to what became Oil City, where he invested his meager funds in what turned out to be quite unprofitable speculations. Henry, through the years, went from one unproductive scheme to another, so that Fanny eventually distanced herself from him and centered her life on their son, Milton.

Milton, generally called M. S., was in many ways a dreamer like his father, but he also had a substantial dose of his mother's practicality. His early ventures steered him toward the successful career he eventually established as a candy maker, but the first decade of his candy-making endeavors did not meet with rousing success. They were preceded by an unsuccessful stint in a print shop, embarked upon when he ended his formal education at age twelve.

The first job Milton really liked was making ice cream at the Joseph C. Royer Ice Cream Parlor and Garden. He took great satisfaction in producing something that pleased hordes of enthusiastic customers. Fanny, however, intervened and asked Joseph Royer to engage her son in making hard candy, also produced and sold by Royer's company, because it has a long shelf life, whereas ice cream had to be consumed almost as soon as it was made.

Hershey's first independent venture into the candy business occurred when Philadelphia staged the Centennial Exposition of 1876. Despite an national economic downturn, the exposition attracted more than ten million visitors during its six-month run. With financing from his Aunt Mattie, Hershey opened a candy store on Spring Garden Street in a location that those attending the Exposition had to pass as they went from the exposition to Independence Hall and the center of town.

Milton installed a pipe in his shop's coal chute that infused the air outside the building with the aroma of candy, the scent of which attracted customers in droves. Once the exposition ended, Milton's candy shop, in which his Aunt Mattie and his mother worked long hours wrapping and packaging candy, began to founder and finally, after being buoyed up temporarily by loans from his mother's family, had to close.

Milton had several more misadventures, including two in Colorado and one in New York City, before he developed the art of making a caramel candy that would not stick to the teeth. He learned trade secrets from other candy makers by working for them.

By increasing the fat content of his confections, he produced a unique caramel that sold well. He founded the Lancaster Caramel Company that in the early 1890's occupied 450,000 square feet of factory space in Lancaster and employed 1,400 people in its three factories. Hershey applied some of the assembly line production techniques that Henry Ford developed in the automotive industry to candy making.

As the nation's taste switched from caramels to chocolate in the 1890's, Hershey was able to sell Lancaster Caramel at a decent profit, which he used in part to buy extraordinary equipment displayed at the Columbian Exposition of 1893 and to launch a highly productive process for making chocolate. D'Antonio is at his best when he writes about chocolate, a substance for which he has a considerable enthusiasm, as is evident from his description of the confection:

> the experience of chocolate is not just about taste. It is also about feel. First there's the soft snap as it yields to the teeth. Then the solid pieces dissolve into a satisfying syrup. The thick liquid clings gently to the tongue, melting over the taste buds to deliver intense and then fading shades of flavor.

By 1896, the total focus of the Hershey Company was on chocolate. Hershey experimented for years looking for the best way to produce milk chocolate and finally developed a method, using oil and water, that made him, in essence, the inventor of that product. By 1903, he had the wherewithal to buy acreage near Lancaster, where he built the world's largest chocolate factory. He also had a singular ability to employ competent executives, like William Murrie and Harry Lebkicher, and to delegate considerable responsibility to them.

Hershey was much influenced by the Cadbury family, famed chocolatiers, in Great Britain. D'Antonio relates how that Quaker family entered the business of making candy because for over a century in Great Britain, "Quakers were barred from attending university and thus prevented from becoming lawyers, doctors, or clergy. However, they could start up a business based on a new product like eating chocolate." The Cadbury family was extremely helpful to Milton Hershey as he became their American counterpart.

D'Antonio addresses the moral dimensions of the chocolate industry. Religious people supported this industry because consuming chocolate was presumed to provide a substitute for liquor among those who had drinking problems. As highly moral and ethical people, members of the Cadbury family looked after their workers well. They built a model community, Bournville, where their employees could live inexpensively but had to adhere to the strict moral codes set down by the Quaker owners of the community.

Earlier, Hershey, who visited Bournville, visited a similar model community set up by George Pullman for his employees in Illinois. Here, too, an ideal form of existence was available to those willing to allow Pullman to direct virtually every aspect of their lives.

Surely Milton Hershey had these two model communities in mind when he created the Pennsylvania town he called Hershey, an ideal community over every aspect of which he presided. The street names in this town reflect the chocolate industry: Cocoa and Chocolate Avenues, for example. The street lights are shaped like Hershey's candy kisses.

As in the other communities of this sort to which Hershey had been exposed, there was in Hershey, Pennsylvania, no opportunity for the citizens to elect town officials. Milton Hershey was the town official, ruling over his community like a great philanthropic autocrat. Those who toed the line lived comfortably in Hershey, but any deviations from the set moral code were punished by expulsion.

Hershey himself lived modestly. Indeed, during his last years, he occupied two rooms in the old family house that he gave to the Hershey Country Club as a clubhouse. Although Hershey married Catherine Sweeney in 1898 and remained married to her until her death in 1915, the couple had no children.

In 1910, Milton established in Hershey a model school for orphan boys, the Hershey Industrial School, later renamed the Milton Hershey School. It is supported wholly by the foundation its founder established. This foundation has more than five billion dollars in resources and currently spends $100,000 annually for the education of each one of the eleven hundred students—now girls as well as boys—attending it.

In 1924, Hershey established a school like the one in Pennsylvania as an orphanage and school for Cuban children. The Hershey Chocolate Company owned sugar plantations in Cuba, and this was Hershey's means of expressing his gratitude to the Cubans who worked on the plantations.

The Hershey endowment is eight times larger than that of the United States' next-richest private school, Phillips Exeter Academy. Only six university endowments are larger. Stock in the Hershey Chocolate Company has provided the largesse that not only keeps the school afloat but that has also provided money to establish a medical school and medical center in Hershey.

There has been some thought of divesting the endowment of some of its Hershey stock for greater diversification, but such proposals have been met with strenuous opposition by those who fear that company control could eventually revert to outsiders. Were this to happen, changes that might threaten the jobs of Hershey employees could very well occur.

Milton Hershey, bent on maintaining control of his community even posthumously, gave away most of his money prior to his death, but he created an air-tight trust modeled on the trust Stephen Girard, the founder of Philadelphia's Girard College, established in 1831. Hershey's trust, like Girard's, has thus far weathered attempts to alter it and has grown steadily.

Critics, including *Fortune* magazine, have bemoaned the establishment of trusts bound by immutable provisions. D'Antonio writes that such trusts "inevitably run into problems . . . as times and circumstances change. For this reason, most philanthropic funds grant flexibility to future trustees." The Hershey trust denies the people who run it this flexibility.

R. Baird Shuman

Review Sources

Book World 36 (January 15, 2005): 2.
Booklist 102, no. 7 (December 1, 2005): 11.
Business Week, January 23, 2006, p. 92.
Kirkus Reviews 73, no. 22 (November 15, 2005): 1219.
Library Journal 130, no. 20 (December 1, 2005): 140-142.
The New York Times Book Review 155 (January 15, 2006): 11.
Publishers Weekly 252, no. 46 (November 21, 2005): 43.
The Wall Street Journal 247, no. 13 (January 17, 2006): D8.
Weekly Standard 11, no. 47 (September 4, 2006): 35-37.

HOLLOW EARTH
The Long and Curious History of Imagining Strange Lands, Fantastical Creatures, Advanced Civilizations, and Marvelous Machines Below the Earth's Surface

Author: David Standish
Publisher: Da Capo Press (Cambridge, Mass.). Illustrated. 304 pp. $24.95
Type of work: History and science
Time: 1691-2006

The book covers the history of scientific theories about another world existing inside this planet and how the concept has played out in novels, films, and popular culture

Principal personages:
> L. FRANK BAUM (1856-1919), a fiction writer who wrote an "Oz" book including a journey into an interior earth
> EDGAR RICE BURROUGHS (1875-1950), the Tarzan creator who also wrote a series set in "earth's core"
> SIR EDMOND HALLEY (1656-1742), a comet scientist who also offered an early hollow-earth theory
> RAY PALMER (1910-1977), a science-fiction magazine editor who popularized the hollow-earth concept
> EDGAR ALLAN POE (1809-1849), a writer who popularized the hollow-earth theory in his only novel
> J. N. REYNOLDS (1799-1858), an explorer who tried to generate a South Pole expedition to find an access to the interior of the earth
> RICHARD SHAVER (1907-1975), a writer of stories about a hollow earth he claimed was real
> JOHN CLEVES SYMMES (1780-1829), an author who envisioned a hollow earth with openings at both poles
> CYRUS TEED (1839-1908), the founder of a religion based on his hollow-earth ideas
> JULES VERNE (1828-1905), a French science-fiction writer who wrote a well-known novel about a journey to Earth's center

David Standish demonstrates the whimsical approach he uses throughout *Hollow Earth: The Long and Curious History of Imagining Strange Lands, Fantastical Creatures, Advanced Civilizations, and Marvelous Machines Below the Earth's Surface* in the opening part of his introduction:

> What do Sir Edmond Halley, Cotton Mather, Edgar Allan Poe, Jules Verne, L. Frank Baum, Edgar Rice Burroughs, Adolph Hitler, Admiral Byrd, flying saucers, Superman, Mount Shasta, and Pat Boone all have in common?

~

David Standish teaches magazine writing at Northwestern University's School of Journalism. He has written magazine articles and a previous book, The Art of Money *(2000).*

~

The answer is that each has had some connection to the idea of a hollow Earth, either seriously or peripherally. Mather (1663-1728), best known as the arch-Puritan involved in the Salem witch trials of 1692, mentioned the concept in his *The Christian Philosopher* (1721) where it may have caught the eye of a more prominent hollow-earth popularizer. Hitler (1889-1945) is said to have been interested enough in the idea to send a small expedition to a Baltic island to test out the theory, although Standish admits this is based on the slimmest of data and probably falls more into the folklore category. Admiral Richard E. Byrd (1888-1957) explored both the North and South Poles without finding any of the fabled openings to the earth's interior, but hollow-earth enthusiasts with a conspiracy theory mindset used a few of his innocently made comments to claim that he just might believe there was more at those poles than he actually saw. A writer named Raymond W. Bernard, about whom little is known except that he died in 1965, even published a book purporting to tell of Byrd's hollow-earth adventures: *The Hollow Earth: The Greatest Geographical Discovery in History Made by Admiral Richard E. Byrd in the Mysterious Land Beyond the Poles—the True Origin of the Flying Saucers* (1964). Mount Shasta, in California, has been cited as one of the alleged entries into the inner world. Pat Boone costarred in the Twentieth Century-Fox film *Journey to the Center of the Earth* (1959), which is loosely based on Jules Verne's *A Journey to the Center of the Earth* (1864). These are just the fringe characters or places involved in Standish's hollow-earth history.

Just as practically every civilization has placed its own stamp or series of constellations on the heavens, many also have their own hollow-earth beliefs, not the least of which is the early Christian belief in hell. The scientific history, though, begins with Sir Edmond Halley, best known for his successful tracking of the comet named for him. It seems that Halley also theorized a hollow earth to explain some magnetic discrepancies in the shifting of the North Pole. In fact, he presented papers on the idea three times in 1691 to the London Royal Society, theorizing three concentric spheres beneath Earth's surface rotating independently—and perhaps even supporting life of some sort. Here was the concept that would be adapted by future science-fiction and fantasy writers.

In 1818, a veteran of the War of 1812, Captain John Cleves Symmes began distributing circulars he had written that declared Earth's interior was hollow and habitable and contained solid concentric spheres one within another, with entrances at both poles. He proposed exploring the poles for those entrances if he could get financing. Standish speculates that Symmes may have gotten the concept from a mention in the earlier writings of Cotton Mather. In any case, these theoretical openings were to become known in hollow-earth parlance as "Symmes holes." Nobody ever found one, and Symmes never had his opportunity for a polar expedition. Instead he wrote a novel under the name Captain Adam Seaborn titled *Symzonia: Voyage of Discovery* (1820) about a utopian underground civilization.

One of Symmes's converts was J. N. Reynolds, who also pushed for a South Pole exploratory voyage to uncover a Symmes hole. He finally got one in 1829 for Antarctica, but it did not remain long and concluded that whatever Symmes hole existed must be covered by ice. It is Reynolds who is believed to have interested writer Edgar Allan Poe in the concept. He used it in his short story "Ms. Found in a Bottle" (1833), which he entered in a literary contest sponsored by the *Baltimore Sunday Visitor* and for which he won the $50 first prize. Poe used it again in his only novel-length story, *The Narrative of Arthur Gordon Pym* (1837), first published as a magazine serial.

However it was Verne, the French writer who specialized in extraordinary voyages ranging from starting off in a balloon to circle the world in eighty days to a cannonball trip to the Moon. Verne picked up the hollow-earth idea for *A Journey to the Center of the Earth,* not the first novel to use this idea but certainly the best known. In Verne's story, the Symmes hole entrance is found in Iceland. The small group of explorers finds a prehistoric world existing in Earth's interior, another concept that would be picked up by future hollow-earth writers. Among the many illustrations in Standish's book are some pages from the 1957 Classics Illustrated comic book adaptation of Verne's novel.

While fiction writers were staying busy with the concept, a man named Cyrus Teed was busy launching a religion. Whether he believed what he wrote in *The Illumination of Koresh* (1869) or not, he claimed that God had approached him in the form of a beautiful woman and told him that the heavens and the earth are all illusion, that humankind is actually living on the inner concave surface of the earth. This was but one part of his theology, but he did attract some followers and carve his own niche into the hollow-earth history.

Standish does not limit his research to the hollow-earth connections alone of the personages through whom he outlines the history of the concept. He devotes chapters to the entire lives of Halley, Symmes, Poe, Verne, and Teed, among others, making for some interesting reading beyond the scope of his title. After that, his history becomes more general, covering many of the key hollow-earth stories that followed in the wake of Verne's novel. In doing so, Standish makes a point of showing how the hollow-earth idea is adapted by each generation to its own uses—from the need for "civilized" nations to overcome and colonize more primitive ones to burrowing into the hollow earth as a bomb shelter during the nuclear war scares of the 1950's.

Among the books covered in the later parts of the book is L. Frank Baum's, *Dorothy and the Wizard of Oz* (1908). It was published as a sequel to *The Wonderful Wizard of Oz* (1900) and came out a year after the San Francisco earthquake, a version of which it used as a launching point to hurl Dorothy and the wizard (both back home from Oz as this one begins) into Earth's interior, where they encounter a number of Oz-like fanciful forms of life as they make their way back to the surface.

Edgar Rice Burroughs had already earned a solid reputation as a storyteller, particularly with his Tarzan and John Carter series of novels. Tarzan started as an orphan baby raised by African jungle apes who becomes a kind of king of the jungle. John Carter was a Civil War veteran who finds himself miraculously transported to the planet Mars, where he has a series of adventures among its varied inhabitants. Now

Burroughs launched his Pellucidar series, about scientists inventing a machine that could bore into Earth's surface and carry them below it. Once there, Burroughs's heroes find a prehistoric world and undergo a series of adventures, in several novels, in which the hero from the surface wins the love of the beautiful cave girl from below. For the first time Burroughs wrote a cross-over novel combining a character from one series with another, *Tarzan at the Earth's Core* (1930). Burroughs writes of an expedition aboard a dirigible that flies into one of the Symmes hole entrances on a mission to rescue the regular series hero from captivity.

Standish concludes his hollow-earth history with an account of how a young Ray Palmer, who had become editor of the vintage science-fiction magazine *Amazing Stories* in the 1940's, pulled a letter from a man named Richard Shaver from the wastebasket. It claimed to have details of an "ancient alphabet." Palmer published it, embellishing it as evidence of the existence of ancient Atlantis. Readers proved enthusiastic, and Shaver (perhaps with a lot of rewriting by Palmer) followed up with a manuscript titled "I Remember Lemuria" (1945), the first of a series of tales about a hollow earth with one set of good and one of evil inhabitants who were responsible for the good and the evil that happened to the world's human surface residents. It was Palmer who also popularized the idea of "flying saucers" being alien ships, and soon he linked the two elements of unidentified flying objects and hollow earth, claiming the saucers were ships from the interior civilization. Standish details all this as yet another example of how the hollow-earth idea mutated with the times.

Finally, Standish signs off with examples of the hollow earth in films—*Unknown World* (1951), in which a Burroughs-like boring machine takes passengers seeking refuge from nuclear war; *Superman and the Mole Men* (1951), the motion picture that led to the *Superman* television series with George Reeves (1914-1959), depicting child-size mole creatures popping up through the shaft of the world's deepest oil well and being set upon by frightened humans, and *The Mole People* (1956), in which explorers find a Symmes hole in mountainous Asia and an underground civilization; its introduction includes references to Halley and Symmes, bringing the history full circle.

Standish's light-hearted look at the hollow-earth history, which has drawn favorable reviews, approaches the subject in both a novel and entertaining fashion. His research into the people involved gives the book a resonance that goes well beyond its subject.

Paul Dellinger

Review Sources

The New Yorker 82, no. 28 (September 11, 2006): 80.
Popular Science 269, no. 2 (August, 2006): 87.
Publishers Weekly 253, no. 20 (May 15, 2006): 61.
Science News 170, no. 7 (August 12, 2006): 111.
The Village Voice 51, no. 27 (July 5, 2006): c42.
The Wall Street Journal 248, no. 24 (July 29, 2006): P8.

HOLLYWOOD STATION

Author: Joseph Wambaugh (1937-   )
Publisher: Little, Brown (New York). 340 pp. $24.99
Type of work: Novel
Time: The first few years of the twenty-first century
Locale: Hollywood and Los Angeles

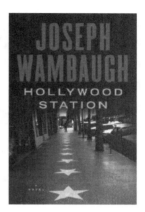

A veteran author returns to his roots, providing a gritty contemporary account of police work amid the faded glamour of Hollywood

Principal characters:
> THE ORACLE, a wizened veteran police sergeant and the shift commander for the Hollywood station
> BUDGIE POLK, a young patrolwoman, new mother, and single parent
> FAUSTO GAMBOA, a grizzled beat cop, Budgie's partner
> MAG TAKARA, a valiant beat cop
> "HOLLYWOOD NATE" WEISS, an experienced beat cop and matinee idol wannabe
> WESLEY DRUBB, a rich kid, rookie cop with a yen for action
> FLOTSAM and JETSAM, a matched set of free-spirited surfers who moonlight as Hollywood station beat cops
> ANDI MCCREA, a Hollywood station detective with career ambitions and a son serving in Iraq with the U.S. Marine Corps
> VIKTOR CHERNENKO, a Ukrainian-born detective fluent in Russian and other Eastern European languages
> FARLEY RAMSDALE, a cynical crystal methamphetamine addict and petty criminal
> "OLIVE OYL," Farley's girlfriend and confederate
> TROMBONE TEDDY, a Hollywood street person, a former jazz musician down on his luck
> UNTOUCHABLE AL, a Hollywood street person with a uniquely effective defense mechanism
> COSMO BETROSSIAN, an up and coming hoodlum formerly of Soviet Armenia
> ILYA ROSKOVA, Cosmo's girlfriend and partner in crime

In *Hollywood Station*, Joseph Wambaugh returns to the stomping grounds he staked out thirty-five years ago with his first novel, *The New Centurions* (1971). In that book and later ones such as *The Blue Knight* (1972) and *The Onion Field* (1973), Wambaugh portrayed the Los Angeles Police Department (LAPD) and the city it serves in a fresh and exciting way. A member of the LAPD from 1960 through 1974, Wambaugh brought unprecedented authenticity to his work. Whether writing fiction, as in *The New Centurions* and *The Blue Knight*, or nonfiction, as in *The Onion Field*,

Former Los Angeles Police Department detective Joseph Wambaugh's other works include The New Centurions *(1971),* The Blue Knight *(1972),* The Choirboys *(1975),* Floaters *(1996), and the nonfiction* The Onion Field *(1973),* The Blooding *(1989), and* Fire Lover *(2002). Wambaugh received the Mystery Writers of America's 2004 Grand Master Award.*

Wambaugh was able to translate his personal experience and that of his confidants into compelling and convincing stories about police work and street life in the unique urban environment that is Los Angeles. In addition to their stark realism, Wambaugh's books displayed considerable literary merit. Though eminently readable, they were stylistically sophisticated and thematically rich, neither idealizing nor vilifying the LAPD. Wambaugh clearly had affection and sympathy for his fellow law enforcement officers. Rather than whitewash the LAPD, however, he included lazy, inefficient, and even dishonest cops in his account of police performance. Apparently, Wambaugh thought that he could better respect and honor his mates by telling the truth as he saw it. Likewise, Wambaugh's lawbreakers were not the super-sadistic villains of action movies. Rather, they reflected the full range of humanity. Some were just struggling to get by. Others were predatory and dangerous. None were one-dimensional or morally simple. Wambaugh also seemed to have a clear understanding that books about police work are actually books about the state of our society. He did a good job of putting crime into the context of society at large, understanding that law enforcers and lawbreakers are part of the greater social structure. Finally, humor played a prominent role in Wambaugh's work, especially his fictional LAPD. This included the author's grimly ironic observations on the human condition as well as the bawdy blue-collar wit of the cops themselves.

Though it has been many years since he wrote about the LAPD, Wambaugh repeats this formula with considerable success in *Hollywood Station*. Times have changed and the LAPD is under federal supervision following the 1991 Rodney King beating and subsequent scandals. Understaffed and under the proverbial microscope, the police of the Hollywood station struggle to do their job in what they see as a perversely hostile environment. Trying to hold everything together is The Oracle, a sage sergeant and shift commander who, after decades of service, has the complete loyalty of the rank and file officers in his charge. These include a colorful cast of characters such as Fausto Gamboa, a grizzled patrolman grappling with changes in the LAPD's culture (and being forced to partner up with a young female officer); Budgie Polk, a new mother, divorced, bucking the female-wary ethos of her fellow officers; Mag Takara, a fearless little dynamo of a female cop; Flotsam and Jetsam, free-spirited surfer cops; "Hollywood Nate" Weiss, an experienced patrolman very much caught up in the glitter of old Hollywood, seeking a career in the movies; and Wesley Drubb, a rookie cop from a rich family, looking for more action than is routinely afforded a

Hollywood patrolman. Also portrayed as part of the Hollywood station crew are several detectives, including Andi McCrea, a single mom whose grown son is fighting in
the Iraq War, and Viktor Chernenko, an immigrant from Ukraine who is assigned the
armed robbery case that provides the focal point of the book's plot.

These police officers function in the environment of early twenty-first century
Hollywood, where eccentric, worn out, or larcenous street folk have replaced the celebrated film stars of the 1930's through the 1960's. Neighborhoods (and their inhabitants) are aging and fading. Drug and alcohol abuse are found in abundance while elements of community solidarity are badly broken. In short, the officers of Hollywood
station police a seamy and depressing locale long past its prime. Among the personalities operating in this shabby environment are Trombone Teddy, a former jazzman
down on his luck; Untouchable Al, a street person who knows how to keep the cops
and most other folks at arm's length (at least); Farley Ramsdale, a misanthropic meth-
head with a variety of illegal schemes; and "Olive Oyl," Farley's much-abused companion.

As with Wambaugh's other LAPD novels, *Hollywood Station* consists of numerous incidents of police work ranging from tragic to comic and including many combinations thereof, swirling around a central plotline. In this case, the plot involves a
rather creative jewel robbery pulled off by Cosmo Betrossian, an Armenian immigrant aspiring to the criminal big time and cultivating a taste for violence, and Ilya
Roskova, Cosmo's Russian immigrant girlfriend. Because the perpetrators are tabbed
as Eastern Europeans, the case is investigated by Detective Chernenko, who pursues
the clues to a wryly effective conclusion in which a number of the above-named characters play crucial roles.

The result is a suspenseful page-turner that will draw readers in and keep them en-
thralled right up to the final page. Wambaugh's characters come alive immediately,
bringing readers into their lives, which for most will be fundamentally alien to their
own. Wambaugh also makes readers care. They laugh, cry, get angry, and experience
fellowship with the characters in *Hollywood Station*. When an officer is brutally assaulted, they feel vengeful. When the meekest character inherits the fruits of crime,
they exult. When the life of a devoted officer ends suddenly, they mourn. In short,
readers are both entertained and emotionally engaged by the book.

Hollywood Station is also thematically rich. Wambaugh's long-term goal of helping the public to better understand police work is on full display here. Wambaugh portrays his police neither as superheroes nor as dull-witted slobs. Instead, they are
flawed working stiffs capable of everything from extreme heroism to supreme laziness. Though they are generally bright and exhibit an impressive amount of know-
how based on experience, they do not instantly grasp the importance of every clue;
nor do they continually spew forth brilliant Sherlock Holmesian deductions. Indeed,
they may not even get the case 100 percent solved. However, neither are Wambaugh's
police officers complete bumblers or, worse yet, authoritarian villains on a power trip.
Throughout the human comedy that is *Hollywood Station*, one discerns an overriding
sense of duty and decency as police deal with the ugly side of human nature.

Wambaugh seems to be somewhat less optimistic, however, about the motives and performance of upper echelon police officials, politicians, and society at large. The perverse working conditions described in *Hollywood Station* indicate a situation in which Americans—including key leaders and the general public—cannot find a healthy balance between dysfunctional, or at best semifunctional, extremes. Wambaugh does not deny the racist (and class-biased) legacy of American society. Of necessity, this also applies to law enforcement, for how could we expect police work not to be in some significant part a reflection of existing social injustices. The answer, Wambaugh suggests, is not to take the Bill of Rights to ridiculous extremes or to hypersensitize people to the "race card," both of which make it difficult for police to do their job, one that remains a vital part of our society. There are still bad guys out there and actual or potential victims in need of protection. As such, we need to give police enough resources and freedom to do their jobs. This is not to advocate a police state or a return to the good old days of rubber hoses and running suspicious ne'er-do-wells out of town without even a passing reference to the niceties of due process. Instead, Wambaugh suggests that there is an elusive middle ground, based on some equally elusive "common sense," in which the police could actually solve problems rather than continually overreact to political fads and, therefore, oscillate between destructive excesses of one kind or another.

Lest the wrong idea be conveyed, neither of these themes gets in the way of *Hollywood Station*'s plot. While it might not be quite accurate to say that Wambaugh totally eschews preaching, he certainly keeps it to an unobtrusive minimum. Instead, the book's characters and their stories are always allowed to occupy center stage, producing a highly engrossing, deeply resonant novel.

Ira Smolensky

Review Sources

Booklist 103, no. 1 (September 1, 2006): 8.
Kirkus Reviews 74, no. 17 (September 1, 2006): 874.
Library Journal 131, no. 16 (October 1, 2006): 63.
The New York Times Book Review 156 (December 10, 2006): 31.
Publishers Weekly 253, no. 38 (September 25, 2006): 43.
The Wall Street Journal 248, no. 130 (December 2, 2006): P9.

HORSE LATITUDES

Author: Paul Muldoon (1956-   )
Publisher: Farrar, Straus and Giroux (New York). 107
    pp. $22.00
Type of work: Poetry

The twelfth collection by this Irish-born American, Pulitzer Prize-winning poet continues and advances his singular features of linguistic invention and dazzling erudition

The title of one of Paul Muldoon's earlier collections *The Prince of the Quotidian* (1994) aptly describes the poetic personae that he wished to present at the stage of his writing life when he had published seven volumes of poetry. In spite of the implications of the title, Muldoon had already distinguished his work by his inventive, even extravagant employment of an allusive technique that carried the often-specific circumstances of the poems toward an imaginative realm constructed from a frame of linguistic possibility.

In *Horse Latitudes*, Muldoon might be seen as claiming to be the Lord of the Land of Allusion, so energetically and enthusiastically has he pushed the styles of allusive exploration toward the outward reaches of a poem's language field. As he told an interviewer in 1996 with respect to innovation, he had already advanced along "a road down which I can't really go any further. The next step is *Finnegan's Wake*," James Joyce's 1939 novel, where he would be "always a kind of fourth-rate Joyce." "On the other hand," he mused, "I don't like the idea that there are limits." This aspect of Muldoon's poetry, however, is just one of several particularly prominent elements that he has introduced and refined in previous volumes.

The jacket cover of *Horse Latitudes* explains that the title is meant to convey a feeling of stagnation, referring to the region "where sailing ships tend to stand becalmed in mid-ocean," where sailors on Spanish vessels transporting horses "would throw their live cargoes overboard to lighten the load." For Muldoon, according to his publisher, this represents "fields of debate in which we often seem to have come to a standstill," but that might be subject to a renewal of motion due to language "restruck and made current."

Although Muldoon's zest for exuberant linguistic invention is one of the defining features of his poetry, perhaps just as important is the implication of a voyage across waters, a recurring consideration in Muldoon's work, and one that has its origins in Muldoon's traverse of the Atlantic from Ireland to America. In *Hay* (1998) Muldoon directly addressed provincial Irish critics who felt that he was turning away from a cultural heritage. His poetry, to the contrary, has been guided by a desire to link what might appear to be disparate entities and by juxtaposing them, offer new ways of seeing and understanding each one. Discussing his work in 2006, Muldoon insisted that there was no "need to get hung up on whether I'm an Irish or American poet. None of that matters."

The prevalence of aquatic imagery in myriad forms is one of the central elements in *Horse Latitudes*, and the circumstances of its occurrences is one of the ways the different subjects and styles in the volume are linked. Muldoon's use of allusion is a technique that has been an identifying signature of his poetry from its inception, developed and refined in following volumes, but has reached the stage in *Horse Latitudes* that it seems to be the singular attribute that commands and controls almost all others.

Poet Gary Snyder's environmental vision of a universe that is "interconnected, interpenetrating, mutually reflecting, and mutually embracing" aptly describes the linguistic fields of many of Muldoon's poems. It is not surprising to learn that Muldoon composes a poem, as Dylan Thomas did, line by completed line. "I can't be bothered writing a draft or something and then throwing it all away or rewriting it" he has observed, and how a word leads to another word is at the core of his method of composition.

The title section of *Horse Latitudes* consists of a nineteen-poem sequence, each title beginning with the letter *B*, each one the name of a place, often a famous battle, like "Bannockburn," or "Bosworth Field," or "Blenheim," "Bunker Hill," or "Bull Run." The apparent subject of the poems is a kind of tryst between the speaker and a woman named Carlotta. The first section of the title poem, "Beijing," introduces the situation and demonstrates the method that Muldoon employs:

> I could still hear the musicians
> cajoling those thousands of clay
> horses and horsemen through the squeeze
> when I woke beside Carlotta.
> Life-size, also. Also terra-cotta.
> The sky was still a terra-cotta frieze
> over which her grandfather still held sway
> with the set square, fretsaw, stencil,
> plumb line, and carpenter's pencil
> *his* grandfather brought from Roma.
> Proud-fleshed Carlotta. Hypersarcoma.
> For now our highest ambition
> was simply to bear the light of the day
> we had once been planning to seize.

Muldoon does not make everything clear, a distinct impediment for some critics, but the obscurity of some of the images is more an inducement to continue on in the sequence than a detriment to understanding. What remains compelling and enticing is the relationship between the two people and the audacity of Muldoon's dexterity with the sonnet, a form generally assumed to belong to another era, generally ill suited to contemporary poetic expression. Muldoon's construction of the linear arrangement uses end-rhyme judiciously, varying to a small degree, but fundamentally linking lines four and five, then three and six, then two and seven, then eight and nine, then

ten and eleven, then one with twelve, then
thirteen with two and seven, and then fourteen—the close of the octet, with six, the last
word (though not the close, necessarily), of
the sestet.

The rhymes rarely seem forced, the form
not twisted or tortured to maintain the scheme.
Once the reader becomes familiar with the
pattern, an anticipation of its appearance—
especially when the poem is spoken, an es-

~

*Paul Muldoon is the author of twelve
books of poetry, including the Pulitzer
Prize-winning* Moy Sand and Gravel
(2002) as well as The End of the Poem
*(2006), the lectures he delivered at
Oxford while professor of poetry there
from 1999 to 2004.*

~

sential act for a poet who is so concerned with sound—contributes to its effectiveness.
Muldoon's variations of the traditional sonnet shape, an adjusted reversal of the octet/
sestet order, is given an additional contextual perspective by his work with the more
conventional shape in the sequence "The Old Country," a poem in thirteen parts that
uses the standard sonnet ambitiously. He has the ability to sustain the dense, rhyme-
locked lines throughout the sequence, as in the start of section VI:

> Every slope was a slippery slope
> where every shave was a very close shave
> and money was money for old rope
> where every grave was a watery grave

It is a dazzling demonstration of a characteristic capacity for syntactic complexity that
has delighted some commentators and irritated others, notably Helen Vendler, who in
a discerning discussion of Muldoon's poetry, accuses him in poems like these of
"showing off as usual" and of being "enamored of the absolutely arbitrary." While
Vendler, in her detailed study, finds many positive attributes in Muldoon's poems,
her critique epitomizes the complaint of critics who would prefer more restraint.
Muldoon, on the other hand, told a British Broadcasting Corporation interviewer in
2004 that one of his goals was "to go to the point where one will really be knocked off
one's feet," and this ambition necessitates the kind of wordplay (or wordwork) that
gives Muldoon's poems their individual signature.

Throughout *Horse Latitudes*, suggested by the title and evident in many poems, is
a preoccupation with water, arguably the fundamental element in Muldoon's cosmos.
In earlier volumes, the titles themselves have indicated something of Muldoon's interest. *New Weather* (1973) arrives or departs with rain; *Why Brownlee Left* (1980)
depends on Ireland as island; *Meeting the British* (1987) requires passage; *The Annals
of Chile* (1994) a voyage; *Moy Sand and Gravel* (2002) pivots from the shoreline of a
home county.

From the start, there is an inclination to move out from Ireland while maintaining
and exploring a basic Irish heritage, somewhat akin to Joyce's establishment of an unavoidable archetype. The island nation, surrounded by water, green with liquid life
("like the river goddesses Banna and Boann" whom Muldoon cites in section VIII of
"The Old Country") is there at the origin, and the pervasive appearance of water as a

multiple metaphor in the poems of *Horse Latitudes* gives the volume a kind of consistency or focus that the range of form and voice resists.

In the opening sequence "Horse Latitudes," Carlotta appears in a "close-knit wet suit" (the section "Baginbun") of which the poet "needs must again make mention" ("Berwick-upon-Tweed") since "Carlotta would climb/ from the hotel pool in Nashville" ("Blaye"). Nautical items abound, as their physical interaction is likened to "a pack mule kicking from a yardarm" ("Boyne") and the demands of a ship under sail: "The way to relieve the tension/ on a line to a windjammer/ is to lubricate the bollard" ("Basra") parallel the couple's actions.

Recollections of a darkened past are often presented with respect to their watery associations. Carlotta is recalled in "Alba" where a local pool is compared to "the Sargasso," and the poet's mother is remembered "Shipping out for good" in "It Is What It Is." In a canal in Belfast, during sectarian strife, the poet speculates that turtles might have "been enlisted by some police forces/ to help them recover corpses" ("Turtles"), and in "Riddle" the poet contemplates identities, declaring that it is "by the buccaneers from whom I still take my cue."

The idea of a journey of discovery toward identity is continued by "The Mountain Is Holding Out," as that opening line becomes a query answered by "for news from the sea," that has not arrived, nor does "the lake confess" and the river is "not coming clean," leading to an instance of waiting where an ambiguous "you and I" have "faced off across a ditch" that is not as wide as the sea but is still a watery course of separation.

The carefully placed last poem in *Horse Latitudes*, "Sillyhow Stride," a heart-felt elegy/tribute to Muldoon's friend, singer Warren Zevon, a sharer of many attributes, deftly inserts subtle references that carry the poet's near-obsessive water consciousness through a bitter lament for loss. The image of Zevon's "little black Corvette (part barge/ part-hermaphrodite brig)" is typical, as is the vision of Rolling Stones member Brian Jones's drowned, possibly drugged ghost, the Everly Brothers (Don and Phil, but known here as Frank and Jesse in reference to Zevon's song "Frank and Jesse James") "crying in the rain," and in a very poignant expression of personal loss, the poet's sister Maureen—previously mourned in "Turkey Buzzards"—joined with Zevon as "her oxygen mask, its vinyl caul/ unlikely now to save Maureen from drowning in her own spit."

The close interlinkage of meaning that is prominent in Muldoon's work is shown by the way that "sillyhow"—an archaic word meaning "caul"—is picked up, but while that provides additional pleasure for the reader who knows this, or is curious enough to look it up, the poem does not depend on that knowledge.

Muldoon's interest in song, apparent from his earliest poems, was exemplified by the "Sleeve Notes" section of *Hay* and has emerged full-blown in his work with the rock band Rackett, for whom he is a lyricist and guitar player. Whatever effect they have on the page, it is obvious that their appeal to the ear, their full sensory structure is paramount. Appropriately, his "Bob Dylan at Princeton, November 2000" combines the daunting erudition that Muldoon wears lightly with a sort of folk-blues rendition that evokes Dylan's modes: "We cluster at one end, one end of Dillon Gym./ 'You

know what, honey? We call that a homonym.'" Muldoon sings, the couplets portraying and commenting on Dylan's postures and performance: "His last time in Princeton, he wouldn't wear a hood./ Now he's dressed up as some sort of cowboy dude."
There are perhaps a few too many syllables in the second line, but bent to music this is
probably permissible.

The blend of immediate experience and a wild mind replete with learning, bursting
with energy, and ready to proclaim a poetics of almost incalculable inclusion makes
Muldoon's poetry fascinating and fulfilling way beyond any quibbles about obscure
content. *Horse Latitudes* is not about a poet becalmed, but one at mid-passage, taking
stock, ready to sail on toward whatever the ocean may offer.

Leon Lewis

Review Sources

Library Journal 131, no. 14 (September 1, 2006): 151.
The New Republic 235, no. 19 (November 6, 2006): 26-33.
The New York Review of Books 53, no. 20 (December 21, 2006): 78-80.
Publishers Weekly 253, no. 30 (July 31, 2006): 53-54.
The Times Literary Supplement, November 24, 2006, pp. 6-8.

HOUSE OF WAR
The Pentagon and the Disastrous Rise of American Power

Author: James Carroll (1943-   )
Publisher: Houghton Mifflin (Boston). 658 pp. $30.00
Type of work: History and current affairs
Time: 1943-2005
Locale: Washington, D.C. and the many places of U.S. military intervention

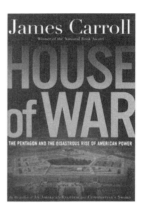

Carroll presents a historical account of the leaders, policies, and decisions of the Department of Defense, with the thesis that the department has used excessive and unnecessary military force, resulting in great destruction and countless violations of human rights

Principal personages:
> JAMES FORRESTAL (1897-1949), secretary of the navy and first secretary of defense
> ROBERT S. McNAMARA (b. 1916), secretary of defense, 1961-1968
> CURTIS LeMAY (1906-1990), chief of staff of the Air Force, 1961-1965
> LESLIE GROVES (1896-1970), directed the Pentagon's construction and headed the Manhattan Project
> JOSEPH F. CARROLL (1910-1991), founding director of the Defense Intelligence Agency
> PHILIP BERRIGAN (1923-2002), Catholic priest who spent eleven years in prison for civil disobedience
> FRANKLIN D. ROOSEVELT (1882-1945), thirty-second president of the United States, 1933-1945
> HARRY S. TRUMAN (1884-1972), thirty-third president of the United States, 1945-1953
> JOHN F. KENNEDY (1917-1963), thirty-fifth president of the United States, 1961-1963
> RONALD REAGAN (1911-2004), fortieth president of the United States, 1981-1989
> GEORGE H. W. BUSH (b. 1924), forty-first president of the United States, 1989-1993
> BILL CLINTON (b. 1946), forty-second president of the United States, 1993-2001
> GEORGE W. BUSH (b. 1946), forty-third president of the United States, 2001-

The son of an Air Force general who served as the first head of the national defense agency, James Carroll grew up in the shadow of the Department of Defense, often roaming the corridors of the Pentagon and personally observing the military elite of the early Cold War years. Like many "military brats" during this patriotic era, he had an idealistic vision of the United States' role in the world, and he daydreamed about following in his father's footsteps. Becoming disillusioned with the Vietnam War, however, to the dismay of his father, he joined the peace movement and became a vociferous critic of the U.S. military-industrial complex. Following his ordination as a Catholic priest, he increasingly identified with the liberal and pacifistic currents within the Church, eventually joining the militant protests of Catholic priests cum peace activists Philip and Daniel Berrigan.

Before becoming a professional writer, James Carroll was a Catholic priest who served as chaplain at Boston University. He has published ten novels and several nonfiction books, including the award-winning Constantine's Sword: The Church and the Jews *(2001).*

In *House of War: The Pentagon and the Disastrous Rise of American Power*, Carroll actually tells two overlapping stories: first, the phenomenal growth of U.S. military power since the Pentagon's construction during World War II, and second, his own personal experiences and reactions to the dramatic events of this history. Some readers will probably find that the highly personal aspect of the book adds to its charm and human qualities. Other readers, however, will think that such an emphasis on his own experiences detracts from the seriousness and objectivity of the book.

The history of the Cold War, or the conflict between communist and capitalist powers from about 1946 to 1991, is commonly interpreted from two alternative schools of thought. Proponents of the so-called orthodox school usually defend U.S. policy as a defensive reaction to communist aggression, whereas "revisionism" almost always blames the United States as the aggressor. *House of War* unquestionably belongs to the second category. Although Carroll concedes the authoritarian nature of the Marxist-Leninist political system, he argues that U.S. policymakers' concern for Soviet objectives were "overblown" and that the Soviet Union was never a real threat to U.S. security. Happy to assume the peaceful intentions of Soviet leaders, he insists that the Cold War and the U.S. expenditure of $14 trillion in military spending were unnecessary—resulting from false perceptions, capitalistic greed, and Pentagon officials' quest for personal and institutional power.

Even Carroll's critics will have to concede that he has done an admirable amount of research for the book, which has almost a hundred pages of endnotes and twenty pages of bibliographic sources. The book is based on a large number of published works, including scholarly secondary accounts as well as memoirs and published documents. Carroll also conducted personal interviews with several of the important participants. Some historians, no doubt, will criticize the book for its lack of archival research, but given the numerous researchers and gigantic literature that has been published during the last half century, it is doubtful that more use of archival materials would have added much to the book.

With his assumption that history is shaped by human beings, Carroll emphasizes the policies, character, and decisions of individual leaders. As one might expect from a former priest, Carroll's strong moralistic temperament predisposes him to look upon history as a battle between the forces of good and evil. When discussing the peace movement, he is willing to justify rather extreme measures. For instance, he writes favorably of the actions of Philip Berrigan and five other activists of the Plow-shares Movement who slipped aboard the USS *The Sullivans* in 1997 to use hammers on the destroyer's weaponry and pour blood into the control system. He approvingly quotes Berrigan's statement at trial: "Our government has intervened in the affairs of fifty nations and has violated the laws of God and humanity by designing, deploying, using, and threatening to use atomic weapons."

Carroll begins *House of War* with the Casablanca Conference in January, 1943, when President Franklin D. Roosevelt, contrary to the wishes of British Prime Minister Winston Churchill, announced that the Axis powers would be required to surrender unconditionally. Because this demand eliminated the possibility of a negotiated peace, it logically implied a threat of total destruction. Before this time, Roosevelt had expressed moral repugnance at the British practice of bombing civilian targets of military significance. At Casablanca, nevertheless, the U.S. and British governments agreed to cooperate in bombing operations, with the two objectives of progressively destroying Germany industry and undermining the morale of the German people. The linkage of these two objectives, Carroll convincingly argues, provided a justification for the large-scale killing of civilians as collateral damage, which is the basis for his declaration that the Pentagon was "born in Original Sin."

Carroll presents an especially detailed account of the incendiary bombing of Tokyo on March 10, 1945, which killed between 80,000 and 100,000 Japanese civilians and rendering a million of them homeless. The napalm, whose use was carefully planned, generated heat so intense that it melted cement, boiled rivers, and turned shelters into ovens. Using this attack as a model, General Curtis LeMay ordered similar destruction on sixty-six other cities, killing almost a million civilians. To highlight the effect of the campaign, Carroll notes that for every word in his six-hundred-page book, more than four Japanese perished in LeMay's incendiary bombings, which ended only when U.S. depots ran out of napalm. In an interview Secretary of Defense Robert McNamara, who had been one of LeMay's assistants, observed that LeMay "had only one thought in mind, which was how to achieve his combat objectives." Although McNamara said that he had not realized the magnitude of the Tokyo bombing at the time, he observed that "It was one of two war crimes with which I can be charged."

In interpreting the decision to use atomic weapons at Hiroshima and Nagasaki, Carroll recognizes that the administration of President Harry S. Truman hoped to hasten the surrender of Japan, but he nevertheless agrees with the revisionist thesis that the president's primary objective was to intimidate the Soviet Union with the United States' willingness to use its awesome power. Carroll also explains the decisions in terms of psychoanalytic reductionism, writing that U.S. policymakers wanted "to exact a fitting revenge for the deep psychological wound Americans, certainly including Truman, had suffered at Pearl Harbor." In his detailed analysis of the decision, Carroll emphasizes that President Truman was influenced by two men: General Leslie Groves, who supervised both the building of the Pentagon and the Manhattan Project, and James Brynes, who was secretary of state at the time.

Like most revisionist historians, Carroll contends that Japan was on the verge of surrender, which if true meant that the use of nuclear weapons was unnecessary. Although he presents some evidence for this view, he ignores the counterevidence. Japan still had about six million reserves as well as five thousand kamikaze aircraft, and in a program called *ketsu-go* Japanese civilians were preparing personal weapons to be used in a fight to the finish. Japanese officials had recently constructed more than a hundred plants for the continued manufacture of airplanes. Even after the bombing of Nagasaki, moreover, the Japanese government remained hesitant to surrender. Without nuclear weapons, despite what Carroll writes, it is quite possible that the war would have continued for some time, and U.S. forces would have suffered hundreds of thousand of casualties if they had invaded the major Japanese islands.

In analyzing the beginning of the Cold War, Carroll argues that the Truman administration's anti-Soviet policies resulted from illusions, misperceptions, and personal ambitions as well as the institutional forces of the military-industrial complex. He asserts that Truman was motivated by a "deep insecurity" and an "inability to take in complexity." Secretary of Defense James Forrestal is characterized as "paranoia's impresario." The Truman Doctrine and the Marshall Plan are described as products of a "paranoid mindset." George F. Kennan's advocacy of containing Soviet expansionism was based on a fundamental misunderstanding of history, and "by portraying Stalin and his system as warmongering monsters, Kennan and his sponsors helped push the Kremlin in that direction." In contrast, when discussing Henry A. Wallace, one of the major critics of Truman's policies, Carroll describes him as a "scientifically sophisticated man," who had more knowledge and understanding than other politicians of the time.

Unlike some revisionist historians, Carroll never denies or minimizes the crimes of Joseph Stalin. He observes, for instance, that the Stalinist terror and resulting famine in Ukraine resulted in the murder of three times as many children as in the Nazi holocaust, and he estimates that twenty million persons were murdered by the state during Stalin's reign. Carroll, however, does not see any evidence that the Soviet leaders after World War II had consciously set out to make satellites of the nations of Eastern Europe. Between 1945 and 1947 the Soviet Union reduced its military forces from eleven million troops to less than three million, which suggests that Moscow was not "the rapacious bear Americans imagined."

Although highly critical of the foreign and military policies of all U.S. presidents, including those of John F. Kennedy, Carroll writes favorably of Kennedy's refusal to listen to LeMay during the Cuban Missile Crisis, followed by his negotiation of the partial test ban treaty of 1963. Carroll is particularly unhappy with Ronald Reagan's anticommunist rhetoric and his increase in military expenditures. In contrast, he praises Soviet President Mikhail Gorbachev for his willingness to negotiate a reduction in nuclear weapons, and he denies that the Soviet leader's moderation was motivated by Reagan's military buildup or the Star Wars program. Rather, Gorbachev was responding to the monumental problems of the Soviet economic system and to the changes in public opinion throughout the world. While acknowledging Reagan's realism in publicly stating that the Soviet Union, under Gorbachev's leadership, was no longer an "Evil Empire," Carroll writes: "Alas, Reagan did not seem to know, even now, that in that other time, he and all others like him had been simply wrong."

In the post-Cold War period, Carroll finds that the Pentagon has continued to be the cause of much death, desolation, and instability. Under President George H. W. Bush's leadership, the war for Kuwait's sovereignty "made a joke of Arab sovereignty." The resulting Gulf War was unnecessary and responsible for the creation of a "new world *dis*order." In interpreting the Balkan wars during the presidency of Bill Clinton, Carroll finds that officials at the Pentagon were actually exercising control of military policy, using human rights as an excuse for massive bombardments that killed thousand of civilians. While critical of the bombing campaigns ordered by Clinton, he expresses even more hostility toward President George W. Bush's War on Terror and the concomitant invasions of Afghanistan and Iraq. Given the large arsenal of U.S. weapons, Carroll writes that it was absurd for U.S. leaders to worry about Saddam Hussein's weapons of mass destruction. The main reason for the invasion of Iraq was that the "unconscious and unaddressed need for revenge had not been satisfied in Afghanistan." One of the unintended consequences of the invasion, moreover, was to encourage Iranian and North Korean leaders to seek nuclear weapons to discourage any similar invasion of their countries.

Historians who are well acquainted with the history of U.S. foreign and military affairs since the end of World War II will not find that *House of War* contains many new facts or innovative interpretations. The book, however, is passionately written, with a great deal of interesting information and many delightful anecdotes. Unfortunately, the book's organization is sometimes confusing and the narrative tends to be somewhat rambling. While some of Carroll's revisionist interpretations are quite reasonable, others are rather extreme and should be approached with caution. Ironically, while denouncing U.S. policymakers for demonizing Communist leaders and militant Islamists, Carroll himself does not hesitate to demonize those responsible for the use of U.S. military power. Readers of the book should compare his interpretations with those of the numerous historians who perceive that the United States was responding, at least in part, to real threats and to antidemocratic forces in the world.

Thomas Tandy Lewis

Review Sources

Booklist 102, no. 11 (February 1, 2006): 4.
The Economist 379 (May 27, 2006): 81-82.
Kirkus Reviews 74, no. 4 (March 1, 2006): 218.
Library Journal 131, no. 5 (March 15, 2006): 85.
The New York Times 155 (June 7, 2006), E1-E10.
The New York Times Book Review 155 (July 2, 2006): 17.
Publishers Weekly 253, no. 15 (April 10, 2006): 63.
The Virginia Quarterly Review 82, no. 4 (Fall, 2006): 259-263.

IMPERIUM
A Novel of Ancient Rome

Author: Robert Harris (1957-   )
Publisher: Simon & Schuster (New York). 307 pp.
$26.00
Type of work: Novel
Time: 79-64 B.C.E.
Locale: Rome

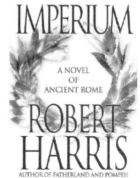

The long-time confidential secretary of Marcus Tullius Cicero, the famous Roman orator, describes his master's rise to power in a political environment of factionalism, corruption, intrigue, and treachery

Principal characters:

> MARCUS TULLIUS CICERO, a lawyer, an orator, a Roman senator, and a consul
> MARCUS TULLIUS TIRO, a household slave, Cicero's confidential secretary, the narrator of the novel
> TERENTIA, Cicero's wife
> QUINTUS, Cicero's younger brother and his campaign manager
> LUCIUS, Cicero's cousin, an idealist
> POMPEY, a Roman general
> JULIUS CAESAR, a young, ambitious politician
> MARCUS LICINIUS CRASSUS, a wealthy Roman
> TITUS POMPONIUS ATTICUS, Cicero's oldest and closest friend, a wealthy Epicurean
> HORTENSIUS, Cicero's rival, a lawyer and orator

Marcus Tullius Tiro is known to history as the inventor of shorthand and the author of a number of books, including a biography of the great orator Marcus Tullius Cicero, whom Tiro served for thirty-six years. Unfortunately, this biography disappeared during the Middle Ages. In his novel, Robert Harris attempts to re-create the lost work, which would probably have been written during Tiro's retirement while he was living on his farm near Puteoli. At the beginning of *Imperium: A Novel of Ancient Rome*, Tiro says that though he has often been questioned about Cicero during the decades that have passed since the great man's death, it is only now, as he is nearing his hundredth year and his own inevitable end, that he is willing to risk writing a book that might prove offensive to someone in power. Tiro takes additional precautions by writing in the shorthand that he invented on rolls of paper he has saved for the purpose. As a result the book is not written in the form of chapters but instead consists of eighteen numbered rolls.

On his deathbed, Cicero had made one request of Tiro: that he tell the truth. Tiro admits that if he is to fulfill that promise, he must show the shady deals that Cicero

⁓

After producing several well-received nonfiction works, Robert Harris began writing best-selling novels, including Fatherland *(1992) and* Enigma *(1995), set during World War II, and* Pompeii *(2003), which takes place in 79 C.E.* Fatherland *was made into a television movie, and* Enigma *was adapted as a film in 2001.*

⁓

made, the deceptions he practiced, and the promises he broke on his way to power. However, as Tiro points out, one has to admire the only man who rose to eminence in republican Rome without the aid of a powerful family, great wealth, or a mighty army to back him.

Unlike most biographies *Imperium* does not begin with the subject's birth. Instead it is made up of two sections, each of which details the events in a brief but crucial period in Cicero's life. The first section, "Senator," begins in 79 B.C.E., when Cicero is a young lawyer of twenty-seven preparing to complete his studies and to perfect his oratorical style with teachers located in Greece and on the island of Rhodes. Cicero has asked to borrow Tiro, who for all of his twenty-four years has lived on the family estate. As it turns out, Cicero finds that he cannot get along without Tiro, and the loan becomes a gift.

After completing his studies, Cicero learns the realities of political life and attains his ambition of becoming a senator. The first part of the book ends with Cicero successfully prosecuting a cruel, corrupt governor of Sicily and then, as an ancient custom permits him to do, assuming the guilty man's praetorian rank. Between Part I, which ends in 70 B.C.E., and Part II, there is a lapse of two years. "Praetorian" begins in 68 B.C.E. and ends in 64 B.C.E., when Cicero is elected consul, thus attaining the "imperium," or supreme power, the goal toward which all of his efforts have been directed.

From the beginning Cicero treats Tiro more like a paid companion than a slave. In Athens Cicero insists on Tiro's remaining with him in the lecture hall, explaining that he needs someone with him who can discuss philosophy. Tiro becomes a member of a small inner circle that includes Cicero's younger brother Quintus, his idealistic cousin Lucius, and the wealthy Titus Pomponius Atticus, who comes to Molon's academy on Rhodes not for the instruction, since he has no intention of becoming involved in public life, but to be in his friend's company. Cicero knows that he can trust any of these four with his life.

Eventually one more person becomes a member of Cicero's inner circle, his wife Terentia. Cicero marries Terentia only because he needs money. One must have assets of one million sesterces to run for senator, and though Terentia has neither beauty nor charm, she is rich. Cicero soon learns that though Terentia's violent temper can make her an unpleasant person to have around, she is extremely intelligent and often more clear-sighted than any of Cicero's other intimates. Tiro points out a number of occasions when Terentia's advice proves to be of immeasurable benefit to her husband. Although this marriage of convenience never turns into a romance, it becomes something more permanent, a lifelong friendship between two people who respect each other and are unflinchingly loyal toward each other.

After managing to get himself elected senator, Cicero spends a year outside of

Rome, as he is expected to do. However when he returns from Sicily, rather impressed with himself, he is treated like a nonentity. He now realizes that to the aristocrats in power he is a "new man," someone without either wealth or connections who has not the slightest chance of becoming important. This experience hardens Cicero's resolve: He decides that he will work longer hours than anyone else, take and win more cases, and make himself a man that even the aristocrats will have to recognize.

In time, Cicero finds out what every lawyer knows: that a seemingly unimportant case may prove to be the turning point of one's career. When a leading citizen of Thermae, Sicily, called Sthenius turns up at Cicero's home, though Cicero vaguely recalls him as the owner of some fine bronzes, at first he only half listens to the Sicilian's story. However, when he learns that Gaius Verres, the governor of Sicily, has stolen Sthenius's art collection and Sthenius has subsequently been accused of forgery and then of the capital offense of spying, Cicero agrees to take the case. Not only are the actions of Verres unconscionable, but Cicero has learned from Sthenius that Verres will be represented by Quintus Hortensius Hortalus, who is considered the first lawyer in Rome. As the case progresses, Cicero finds that politics does indeed make strange bedfellows. After Sthenius is sentenced to crucifixion and has to go into hiding, Cicero has no choice but to obtain the support of Pompey the Great, even though he knows that he will eventually have to pay back the general in one way or another. Since only the tribunes have the power to protect Sthenius, Cicero enters into an alliance with them; again, he has to face the fact that every connection he makes, whether with an individual or with a group, limits his own freedom. Although Cicero finally gets Verres convicted, he has to let Pompey conduct the negotiations for a financial settlement, and for his own reasons Pompey has accepted a much smaller settlement than Cicero wanted and much less than Sthenius and his fellow Sicilians deserved.

In the second part of the novel, Tiro shows Cicero making more moral compromises. Pompey asks Cicero to defend one of his friends, a man who has been as corrupt as Verres, though not as cruel. Lucius begs Cicero not to take the man as a client since he is clearly guilty. However, because he knows that he may need Pompey's help in the future, Cicero takes the case and wins it. Heartbroken by what he sees as Cicero's betrayal of his principles, Lucius kills himself. Cicero is profoundly grieved; moreover, he is increasingly aware that Pompey now considers him no more than a man who has been bought and paid for. Cicero now has to do Pompey's bidding. He is even expected to compliment Pompey on the brilliance of speeches that Cicero has written for him.

Though Pompey fails to become the supreme ruler of Rome, as he had planned to do, Cicero now sees a new threat both to the Republic and to his own goals: The wealthy, unscrupulous Crassus is in the process of buying the upcoming election. In fact having subverted the democratic process, Crassus and his coconspirator, Julius Caesar, intend to seize the government as Caesar will do a decade and a half later when he becomes the military dictator of Rome. However, thanks to Cicero's ambition, and perhaps in part to his principles, the Republic will last a few years longer. With the help of a young nobleman who has been persuaded to aid Cicero, Tiro slips into Crassus's house, makes his way to the room where Crassus always holds his meetings, and conceals himself in a niche behind a wall hanging with a hole in it, a place that Crassus had prepared for the use of his own spies. Though Tiro knows that if he is discovered he will be killed, he is too loyal to Cicero to question the mission. Once installed in the niche, he overcomes his nervousness by focusing on his wax tablets where he is recording in shorthand every word that the conspirators speak. What Tiro hears shocks him, for in addition to buying votes, Crassus and Caesar mean to get popular support by breaking up large estates and distributing small holdings to as many people as possible. After slipping back to Cicero's house later that night, Tiro reads his transcription to Cicero and then makes a suggestion: that Cicero contact the aristocrats, who would be horrified at the idea of land reform. Though they do not like Cicero any more than he likes them, for the moment their interests coincide. They defeat Caesar and Crassus, and Cicero becomes a consul.

Robert Harris's first three novels, *Fatherland* (1992), *Enigma* (1995), and *Archangel* (1998) were all popular successes, and critics praised them as well-written, imaginative, and suspenseful works that were convincing because they had a real basis in history even when their plots took an unhistorical direction. In *Pompeii* (2003), however, Harris did not alter historical events but merely introduced fictional characters. With *Imperium*, he goes one step further. The book is a fictional biography whose narrator almost certainly wrote a book much like Harris's and whose central character played an important part in the history of republican Rome. As a result although *Imperium* is just as suspenseful as Harris's earlier works, it is far more profound. Not only does it afford a glimpse into Roman life and politics, but it provides readers with startling insight into the present. Tiro's descriptions of Cicero charming his constituents—carefully recalling just the right detail, tailoring his talks to local needs, even his way of clasping a voter's hand between his two hands, thus suggesting a special affection—all remind the reader that where politics is concerned, little has changed. Finally, and most important, *Imperium* is a brilliant character sketch. As Tiro says, Cicero succeeded in politics by treating it as a business. Sometimes he could take the high road and probably he would prefer to do so, but often being right simply cost too much.

Rosemary M. Canfield Reisman

Review Sources

Booklist 103, no. 2 (September 15, 2006): 27.
Library Journal 131, no. 14 (September 1, 2006): 137.
The New York Times Book Review 156 (October 22, 2006): 24.
Publishers Weekly 253, no. 29 (July 24, 2006): 35.
The Times Literary Supplement, September 1, 2006, p. 22.
USA Today, September 28, 2006, p. D4.
The Wall Street Journal 248, no. 112 (November 10, 2006): W4.

IN SEARCH OF NELLA LARSEN
A Biography of the Color Line

Author: George Hutchinson (1953-   )
Publisher: The Belknap Press of Harvard University
  Press (Cambridge, Mass.). Illustrated. 611 pp. $39.95
Type of work: Literary biography
Time: 1891-1964
Locale: Chicago, Illinois; Copenhagen, Denmark; New
  York City; and Nashville, Tennessee

*This biography of Larsen discloses previously obscure
facts about her life and restores her reputation as one of
the most significant novelists of the Harlem Renaissance*

Principal personages:
  NELLA LARSEN, a novelist of the Harlem
    Renaissance
  ANNA LARSEN GARDNER, her estranged white half sister
  DR. ELMER S. IMES, her husband, a physicist and teacher at Fisk Univer-
    sity
  CARL VAN VECHTEN, a white author and photographer, a celebrity of the
    Harlem Renaissance

George Hutchinson, author of *The Harlem Renaissance in Black and White*
(1996), brings his considerable knowledge of African American life in the 1920's to
this definitive biography of Nella Larsen. Larsen wrote two novels acclaimed by contemporary critics and readers then disappeared from the Harlem social and literary
scene where she had played a prominent role. Hutchinson's detective work uncovers
previously overlooked evidence from public records and private letters and diaries to
dispute the conjectures of Larsen's two previous biographers. In his reconstruction of
her life and work, the "mystery woman" emerges as one of the most significant writers of the Harlem Renaissance, that exuberant flowering of African American arts and
literature of the 1920's. *In Search of Nella Larsen: A Biography of the Color Line* restores Larsen's work to its position as a prescient feminist portrait of the fragile lives
of black women whose roles were defined by the rules of race and gender in a racist
American society.

With painstaking detective work, Hutchinson uses such documents as a ship's passenger list, records of the New York Public Library system, and public health nursing
records to prove the truth of events previously considered inventions of Larsen's
imagination. Most significantly, he combs the diaries and letters of Carl Van Vechten,
Larsen's close friend, to chart her activities during her Harlem years.

Nellie Walker was born in Chicago on April 14, 1891, the daughter of Mary
Hansen, a Danish immigrant, and Peter Walker, a West Indian of mixed race. Her father disappeared shortly after her birth, and her mother married Peter Larsen, a white

George Hutchinson is Booth Tarkington Chair of Literary Studies at Indiana University, Bloomington. He received National Endowment for the Humanities Fellowships in 1988 and 1989-1990 and the Darwin Turner Prize of the Modern Language Association in 1995 for his work in African American literature.

man. She gave birth to a second daughter, Anna Elizabeth, in 1892. The unwritten rules of Jim Crow at that time decreed a total separation of the races. Nella Larsen, as she began to call herself as an adolescent, was a mulatto, with dark, honey-colored skin. Because of her skin color, she would live in the hidden spaces between the black and white races, belonging to neither.

Larsen's early childhood Chicago neighborhood was the site of saloons, a high crime rate, and interracial prostitution. The circumstances of her birth were a source of shame throughout her life. Hutchinson believes that her seemingly inexplicable choices in life originated from Larsen's fear that her lower-class origins would be discovered and her anxiety that she would be rejected by those whom she loved.

In 1895 Mary Larsen and her two daughters traveled to Denmark, where they lived for three years. They returned to Chicago in 1898, and Nella later enrolled in English literature and creative writing classes at Wendell Phillips High School, training that would support her in her future writing. When the Larsen family moved to a middle-class neighborhood, Nella, the dark child in a white family, felt alienated. Mary Larsen, understanding this, enrolled sixteen-year-old Nella as a boarding student at Fisk Normal School in Tennessee to prepare for a teaching career. However, Nella was expelled at the end of the school year. Since her grades were acceptable, Hutchinson speculates that she had rebelled against the strict social conventions of the school's conservative black community.

Larsen returned to Denmark to live with her mother's relatives from 1908 to 1912. She later claimed educational credentials, probably inflated, for her informal schooling there. She left Denmark at the age of twenty-one, having discovered a different kind of discrimination in a society that regarded her as strange and exotic—again an outsider.

In New York City Larsen trained as a nurse at Lincoln Hospital, receiving a progressive education in liberal arts as well as medical studies. In 1915, a skilled professional, she moved to Tuskegee Institute in Alabama as a teacher and nursing supervisor. A year later she resigned this position, apparently rebelling against the stifling atmosphere of this conservative black institution that exploited its nurses and repressed her individuality.

She returned to New York to teach at Lincoln Hospital. Her course in the history of women in nursing would be reflected in the feminist vision that would distinguish her fiction. In 1919 she married Dr. Elmer Imes, a successful black physicist, and moved to Harlem. Her first published writing, in 1920, was a series of children's games and poems recalled from her early years in Denmark. These pieces appeared in *The Crisis*, the publication of the NAACP.

Deciding to change her career, Larsen broke precedent as the first black woman to earn her certification in the New York Public Library system. Her experience as a librarian undoubtedly encouraged her to write. In 1924 Larsen was appointed head of the Children's Room at the 135th Street Library, a center for African American culture, where she made an important contribution to developing the resources of the children's collection.

That year also marked the beginning of the Harlem Renaissance, the vigorous outpouring of literature, art, and music created by African Americans that would continue throughout the 1920's. In the central chapters of the book Hutchinson examines Larsen's writing career and her participation in the high-living social life of Harlem during the Jazz Age, with its drinking, night clubbing, and constant party going. For the first time, black and white artists and intellectuals socialized freely together. As the wife of a respected scientist, Larsen was accepted into the black professional class. Carl Van Vechten, an influential supporter of the black writers in Harlem and an important voice in the movement, mentioned her frequently in his diaries. This information, previously overlooked by other biographers, enables Hutchinson to trace Larsen's activities in those years.

Larsen was a conspicuous figure, dressing in fashionable clothing and smoking cigarettes, and was noted for her wit and sarcasm. The early photographs in the book show a striking woman with a strong sense of style. However, even as she participated in the Harlem high life, her ideas differed sharply from those who found group identity in their blackness. The child of a white family, Larsen had little experience of black culture, nor could she pass as white. This racial ambiguity continued to haunt her and reinforce her sense of alienation. Standing apart as an observer, she was developing the insights that would inform her two novels, which would constitute, Hutchinson says, "one of the most incisive protests against the inhumanity of the color line and its psychic cost ever penned in American literature."

Larsen's first published adult short stories appeared in 1926 in popular pulp magazines under the pseudonym "Allen Semi," a reversal of the letters of her married name Nella Imes. Larsen decided to leave her library position to write full time. Her first novel, *Quicksand*, was published in 1928 by Knopf, a prominent mainstream publishing house. It was an immediate success, winning the 1929 Harmon Award bronze medal, a prestigious prize for black writers.

Helga Crane, the light-skinned protagonist of *Quicksand*, is a thinly disguised portrait of Larsen herself in the early part of the narrative. Hutchinson sees the central metaphor as a mythical labyrinth, with Naxos as a piercing satire of the Tuskegee Institute where Larsen had served unhappily as a nurse and teacher. Naxos institutionalizes black racial hypocrisy with the same class consciousness of which white society was guilty. Helga Crane, unable to identify with black culture, travels to Denmark. Early passages include recognizable scenes of Copenhagen, evidence that she had indeed lived there. Treated as an exotic outsider, Helga, like Larsen, experiences racism in a different, but no less destructive, form in Europe.

Helga returns to New York where she suffers an emotional breakdown, undergoes an unlikely religious conversion, and marries a black evangelical minister who takes her south. Here she is suffocated by her life as a wife and mother, constantly pregnant, hopeless, and drowning in a metaphorical quicksand. Readers and critics, while praising the eloquence of the writing, found this denouement unrealistic. Hutchinson dissents, interpreting the conclusion as Larsen's keen insight into the catastrophe of a gifted woman forced into a traditional role that will destroy her. Contemporary reviewers praised the novel as a breakthrough in exploring black women's sexuality but missed Larsen's exposition of the hypocrisy of racial and gender stereotyping.

Larsen's second novel, *Passing*, was published in 1929. The title refers to light-skinned African Americans who abandon their heritage and "pass" into white society undetected. The ambiguous relationship between Irene Redfield, a black woman, and Clare Kendry, also black but passing as white, is central to the narrative. Larsen's insights into passing, with its potentially disastrous consequences of discovery, engendered rumors that Larsen herself had passed, a notion Hutchinson dismisses as unlikely. In the novel's conclusion, Clare Kendry either falls or is pushed through an open window to her death. Hutchinson interprets this event as murder, with Irene's jealousy her motive for killing Clare. Clare passes, not to become white, but to acquire material wealth like that of her black acquaintances. Hutchinson notes the author's sympathy with Clare, saying, Clare's "brazen border-crossings threaten the boundaries on which Irene's secure life has been carefully built." He cites Larsen's own insecurities and her ambivalence toward race as prevailing themes in this novel.

Larsen, by this time a celebrated figure in the Harlem Renaissance, gave extensive interviews described as charming and self-mocking but frequently dishonest and revealing an unattractive side of her character. A short story, "Sanctuary," was suspected to have been plagiarized. Although Larsen was exonerated, Hutchinson finds merit in the charge, an irrational choice that might have destroyed her career. Despite this controversy, Larsen won a Guggenheim Fellowship and spent two years in Europe working on her next project. This manuscript, *Mirage*, was rejected by her publisher, as was a later rewrite titled *Fall Fever*.

Larsen's marriage had long been in trouble. Dr. Imes was involved with a white woman, an administrator at Fisk University. After returning to New York in 1933, Larsen suffered a mental breakdown. She attempted a reconciliation with Imes, returning to Fisk for a brief time, but it was clear that the marriage was over. She divorced Imes in 1933 on grounds of cruelty and was awarded alimony, money that supported her until the death of Imes.

Although no manuscripts remain, Hutchinson believes that Larsen continued to write, without success. In 1938 she inexplicably broke off all connections with her friends in New York, suffering a period of instability marked by depression and probable alcohol and drug abuse. She disappeared from public notice for several years. Hutchinson believes that when Dr. Imes died in 1942, Larsen forced herself out of her depression and returned to work out of necessity. She rapidly advanced to the position of chief nurse at Gouverneur Hospital in New York City and later earned a top salary as a head nurse at Metropolitan Hospital. Hutchinson learned that her colleagues respected her highly as a professional.

Nella Larsen died in late March, 1964, still officially employed as a nurse although she had not worked in several months. She was buried in an unmarked grave in Cypress Hills Cemetery in Brooklyn. She had apparently tried to reconcile with her half sister Anna Larsen Gardner but was turned away. In a final irony, Larsen named Anna, who had claimed untruthfully that she did not know of Larsen's existence, as her heir.

Historians debate the causes of the end of the Harlem Renaissance but agree that with the onset of the Great Depression, public interest in African American writers waned. Hutchinson attributes much of this decline to novelist Richard Wright, who accused the writers of the 1920's of selling out to the white world. In the 1960's the Black Arts and Black Power movements dismissed the Harlem Renaissance writers as irrelevant. Nella Larsen's fiction, because it did not address "black" social issues, was overlooked.

African American and feminist critics and teachers have since restored Larsen's fiction to prominence, acknowledging her sophisticated insights into the secret lives of biracial women, neither black not white, unacknowledged by either world.

In this critically acclaimed biography, Hutchinson dispels much of the mystery of Larsen's life by revealing the fears and insecurities that drove many of her unfortunate choices. Although constrained by the racial politics of her time, she was neither a tragic victim nor a black woman ingratiating herself into white society, as some have claimed. Despite the barriers she faced, she was a successful nurse, librarian, and novelist. The author views Nella Larsen as one of the most important writers of her time, who, living and writing at the margins of society, observed with ironic precision the absurdities of the "color line."

Marjorie J. Podolsky

Review Sources

Black Issues Book Review 8, no. 5 (September/October, 2006): 40.
Booklist 102, no. 18 (May 15, 1006): 16.
London Review of Books 28, no. 19 (October 5, 2006): 21-22.
The Nation 283, no. 3 (July 17, 2006): 26-30.
The New York Times Book Review 155 (August 27, 2006): 20.
The Times Literary Supplement, October 6, 2006, p. 26.
The Washington Post, May 21, 2006, p. BW14.

IN THE MIDDLE DISTANCE

Author: Linda Gregg (1942-   )
Publisher: Graywolf Press (St. Paul, Minn.). 66 pp.
  $14.00
Type of work: Poetry
Locale: Texas, Greece, Massachusetts, New York

Gregg's poetry collection seeks peace and spiritual understanding in the wake of turmoil and loss; it is a meditation on passion from the perspective of middle age

In the Middle Distance, which received the 2006 PEN/ Voelker Award in poetry, is about the relationship between love and pain—love in this case meaning all kinds of attachment, any attraction that draws the mind out from itself. The appropriately chosen cover art displays a sixteenth century painting by Lucas Cranach the Elder, known for his moralist art, of Venus and Cupid stealing honey. Both subjects are naked. Their bower is full of angry bees, and Cupid winces with pain as he holds the hive. Venus seems distant, almost disinterested in his pain. The fable was that Cupid, having stolen honey, complained how much pain the tiny bees produced, and Venus, his mother, told him that he was small, too, and that his arrows caused hurt more intense than that of the bees. The quatrain giving the Latin moral of the fable is part of the painting and translates to something like: "When Cupid stole the honey from the hive/ A bee stung the thief on the finger./ And if we also seek pleasures brief and dangerous/ Sadness will mix in with them and bring us pain." There is an interesting contrast between the painting—the nude mother and son, the beehive in his hands, the mother's apparent lack of concern with the son's pain—and the moral, which makes of the scene a lesson. There is something of this combination in the poems—pain, wisdom, a learned detachment that provides another way of seeing.

The poems are about love and solitude, and about what each costs. The connection between pleasure and pain, and how they depend upon each other, is explored in a number of scenes of memory and longing. What comes through most strongly in this collection is a sense of achieved solitude—being alone is a state desired by the speaker for contemplation and inspiration, yet the heightened sense of awareness that comes with solitude brings pain also. Past passions are looked at from a distance; the present is a lucent time of meditation.

Gregg's poems have always gracefully expressed loss and sorrow; this collection marks a kind of reconciliation with loss and a resignation to its inevitability. The title may suggest middle-aged reflections, and the work has a midlife mixture of elegy and promise. What does pain teach? the poems sometimes ask, in many ways, and they provide a variety of answers which all add up to the conclusion that pain teaches wisdom. The persona is generally a woman in her middle life, taking stock. There is sadness and pleasure related to the past. The question of romance, always present in Gregg's work—what is romance, what does it take and give?—is found here, too, but more through memory, more quietly suggested. Romance becomes largely a matter of the mind. Eros is present but veiled. The poems have a dignity of carriage. They invite the reader to accompany the speaker through the late summer garden.

Gregg writes in free verse. The poems in *In the Middle Distance* are mostly short; they are in traditional left-justified free verse style, with no postmodernist typographical play. The poems have true density. Every word counts, and the premise or observation that underlies each work is developed seriously, indirectly, and without evasion. Strongly present in the book is the idea of guilt and punishment, delight and the aftermath of its opposite, that is represented on the book's cover.

Linda Gregg has received National Endowment for the Arts, Lannan Literary Foundation, and Guggenheim Foundation fellowships. She has taught at many universities, including Napa State, Iowa University, and Princeton. Her poetry has appeared in The New Yorker, The Paris Review, The Kenyon Review, *and* The Atlantic Monthly.

Appropriate to the verse is the lack of gimmickry: The poems are not in any edgy format or arrangement, they are not heavy with epigraphs, and there are no notes to them. There is no grand narrative that controls them, except for that of the individual sentience in the indifferent universe and the tales one tells oneself to keep alive. Nevertheless, some of the work leans toward transcendence. The final desire is for a metaphysical, not a physical—or not only a physical—companion. The desire in some of these poems diffuses into such a longing. W. S. Merwin comments, "They are inseparable from the surprising, unrolling, eventful, pure current of their language, and they convey at once the pain of individual loss, a steady and utterly personal radiance." The radiance seems to be both inside and outside the subject. The subject, theme, tone, and language are of one fabric.

What is intriguing about Gregg's work is its deceptive simplicity. The reader may be confronted by a poem of twenty lines or so, perhaps based on an incident, with an apparently straightforward narrative approach. The narratives, however, are interrupted, or they begin in the middle or they stop abruptly and yield to reflections or even to other narratives. Moreover, the hidden centers of these poems compel revisits and concentrated thought. "The Intercontinental Hotel," for instance, begins with the speaker stopping alone at "the elegant bar" for a rest after walking, hearing a "faint singing" and letting it carry her back to a distant past. She asks, "Did I catch the ball when it was thrown? /Have the soul and its ghost given up/ and gone back to sleep?" Then she looks at flowers on the table no one else is looking at, and this tempts her back into the place, the present, and the realization that perhaps life is an accretion of images and emotions, and transactions with the world are beyond words. It is one of the happier poems in the collection and communicates a sense of awareness of peaceful solitude that enhances awareness of place, which lifts and inspires the soul.

The scenes are almost under the surface, but they are there—scenes of Greece, of New York, of Massachusetts. Marfa, Texas, appears as a real and symbolic landscape, a desert point from which to look at populated spaces. The speaker is in Marfa for some of these poems, but her spirit is in other places. Sometimes the location crystallizes to a single line of particulars amid an otherwise meditative poem. On the other hand, sometimes the particulars take over and themselves bear the poem's message. Often the poem seems to be traveling a worn road, only to take off suddenly in a different direction, reinterpreting what has been assumed and accepted, leaving the original setting behind.

Ripening and ripeness are subjects in this work; middle-aged human life is ripeness, and all the implications of ripeness are suggested in the poems. Ripeness is the point of greatest sweetness but also the time to be consumed or else to diminish and spoil. The ripe fruits, the search for ripeness, the attempt to define what it is to be ripe are ideas and images that dominate some of the work. In "Trying to Ripen," the speaker begins by claiming a misapprehension: "I thought if I lived alone/ in stillness, God would be closer." Although she looks at the autumn scene with longing, she says, "There is ripe fruit on the ground./ It is time for migration,/ but I am still not transformed." The rest of the poem describes a vision of nature that includes "a covey of quail/ strong enough now to fly over/ the fence." The sight becomes insight: "I saw distance." The physical seems to contain the metaphysical, and the reader may be reminded of the woman in Wallace Stevens's "Sunday Morning" who is told to substitute a knowledge of rapport with the earth for otherworldly imaginings. Just as the metaphysics that Stevens kicks out of his poem sneak back in through another door, so do they here. Ripening is a melancholy but necessary part of the natural order, as the end of William Shakespeare's *King Lear* (pr. c. 1605-1606) reminds the reader:

> What, in ill thoughts again? Men must endure
> Their going hence, even as their coming hither;
> Ripeness is all.

The other major influence in the ripening process, the sun, appears throughout Gregg's volume, functioning as a multilevel symbol, suggesting both the recurrent and the eternal, light of reality, and epiphany—making one think of Stevens again. Often the sun carries the natural metaphysic of these poems. Walking in sunlight, the speaker sees, responds to, a coming end of the day. The sun sometimes seems to have sentience—to be knowing, or forgiving, which is metaphorical but not completely so. Other poems have the sun as a kind of measurement, a point of view which includes the feel of time passing. In "Purity" the speaker takes a walk along a rural road and notices the maneuvers of police cars, which do not concern or involve her but represent another life. Finally she is left "with animals, insects and birds./ And the silence. I walk toward the sun/ which is always going down." There is a peace tinged with wistfulness in her conclusion.

The quiet way the poet brings up big questions lures the reader into Gregg's speculation. The intensity of her observation and the small and large epiphanies she finds in what she looks at sharpens the reader's observation, too. Each poem is complete in itself.

According to poet Louis McKee, "These poems prove that the pain of loss and disorientation, along with the resilience that can be derived from hope, allows for a moment's serenity. We can hardly ask more. Gregg is one of the more impressive, generous, and wise of today's front-line poets." This is in a sense wisdom poetry—it is experience both distilled and analyzed. The poems of *In the Middle Distance* require a slow and thoughtful reading, not a study of external references. They yield their meaning without the reader having to wrestle with them. Yet the work is highly sophisticated and subtle and can be read on various levels. Gregg will be considered part of the philosophical and sensual stream of poetry that is a strong presence at the beginning of the twenty-first century. Her highly individual style does not play upon persona—there seems sometimes to be a cool, rational, disembodied being talking about passion. This is an intriguing and original kind of poetry.

Janet McCann

Review Sources

Library Journal 131, no. 5 (March 15, 2006): 75.
Poetry 188, no. 5 (September, 2006): 452.
Publishers Weekly 253, no. 11 (March 13, 2006): 43.
The Virginia Quarterly Review 82, no. 3 (Summer, 2006): 272.

INSECURE AT LAST
Losing It in Our Security Obsessed World

Author: Eve Ensler (1953-   )
Publisher: Villard (New York). 200 pp. $21.95
Type of work: Memoir, current affairs, and women's issues
Time: The 1950's to 2006
Locale: New York City; Zagreb, Croatia; Afghanistan; Ciudad Juárez, Mexico; and Sri Lanka

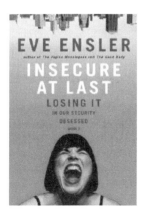

A playwright and women's rights activist considers her travels around the world and what she learns about security and the various ways this abstract notion is conceived and put into practice in the everyday lives of women and men

Though Eve Ensler had been writing, publishing, and performing in plays since the 1970's, it was in 1996, with the startling success of *The Vagina Monologues*, that her name and work began to be well known. *The Vagina Monologues* is a series of lyrical, thought-provoking monologues, all performed by Ensler in the original production, based on the playwright's interviews with a wide variety of women about their bodies in general and their genitalia in particular. The premise behind the play was that by openly naming and discussing matters usually kept private—in this case female anatomy and the wide range of women's sexuality—we can reduce the shame and misunderstandings associated with these matters. Ensler's 2004 play, *The Good Body*, similarly presents a mingling of voices and viewpoints, though this time the emphasis is a little more on Ensler's own experience. The focus of this play is on women's dissatisfaction with their bodies, especially their obsessive attempts to lose weight or otherwise reshape themselves in a desperate effort to achieve some unrealistic ideal of a good body.

Insecure at Last: Losing It in Our Security Obsessed World is Ensler's first published work intended solely for the printed page rather than for performance. In it, the author once again addresses a single difficult and abstract concept—in this case security—from a variety of perspectives in an attempt to arrive at, if not understanding, at least a place closer to understanding than where she and the reader begin. Perhaps the clearest way to categorize the book is as a somewhat rambling memoir that mingles the author's political observations with her personal experience, ranging from her childhood to her professional acting life (including how she came to write and perform her best-known works) and her feminist activism. Though such a description might not entirely satisfy readers who select books based on genre, the truth is that Ensler has never been much concerned with having her works fit into particular categories. The style of the book is, in fact, closely related to that of her best-known plays, which weave together material from interviews with personal experiences and veer dramatically back and forth between laughter, fear, hope, and anger. In the range and purpose of the book, at least, Ensler's many admirers will not be disappointed.

Though not a chronological autobiography, *Insecure at Last* touches on a number of key points from different moments in Ensler's life, showing how each of these contributed to her growing understanding of what security really means. She writes about the physical and emotional abuse her family suffered at the hands of her alcoholic father and about the way he provided the family with surface security in the form of a comfortable middle-class lifestyle while producing terror and anxiety in young Eve, who never knew when he might once again vent his irrational rages on her. She tells of her imaginary childhood friend, Mr. Alligator, whom she fantasized would come to take her away from her frightening family life. Elsewhere, she remarks in passing about the period as a young adult when she tried to lose herself in sexual promiscuity and drug experimentation. She also details bits and pieces of information about her travels, including a near-miss plane crash that made her realize how little control individuals have over their own day-to-day security; about her personal life, particularly the painful breakup of a long-term romantic relationship; and about her slow personal journey to self-acceptance and moving beyond her early sense of the profound insecurity in her world.

Eve Ensler is an internationally renowned playwright whose best-known plays include The Vagina Monologues *(1996) and* The Good Body *(2004), both of which she starred in for their original productions. Ensler founded an international movement, V-Day, to raise money for and awareness of issues related to violence against women.*

There is, however, at least as much space in *Insecure at Last* given over to the lives and issues of other people as there is to the author's personal reflections and revelations. Since 1993, Ensler has traveled widely in her work as an activist, trying to raise global awareness of women's rights and improve the lot of battered and oppressed women in communities throughout the world. Among the women she writes about are young Bosnian women who endured internment in Serbian rape camps during the wars in the former Yugoslavia in the 1990's. (Some of Ensler's interviews with these women, in fact, also found their way into and helped to inspire *The Vagina Monologues*.) She also describes encounters with activists from the Revolutionary Association of the Women of Afghanistan, who fight, often from across the border, for the girls and women in their homeland to receive such basic rights as primary education and adequate medical care. She visits a safe house for women in Ciudad Juárez, Mexico, a town near the Texas border where hundreds of poor young women have been kidnapped, raped, and murdered in the past decade. She takes readers to a writing workshop she teaches at a women's prison in upstate New York, to Sri Lanka where she interviews refugees from the tsunami that overwhelmed their land in December, 2004, and to New Orleans, where she speaks with poor and displaced victims of Hurricane Katrina, which flooded and devastated their city in 2005.

Throughout the travels she recounts the heartfelt descriptions of the people she encounters, Ensler keeps circling back to the question of security: What does the word really mean? How can people achieve it? Why do they want it so badly? Should it be people's primary goal? Curiously, it is only through her interactions with individuals whose lives are profoundly insecure that she is able to address the idea of security. Her interest in these issues and individuals clearly springs from her own childhood traumas and the abuse she received from her father, though she takes care not to draw too close an analogy between their situations and her own or to forget that her own life is one of relative privilege when compared to many of these survivors.

The style of the book, like its content, is difficult to pin down and to categorize. Though Ensler clearly has a sociopolitical ax to grind, she makes no attempt at straightforward narrative or thesis-and-support style argument. Rather, she weaves together stories, reflections, and allusions to build, layer by layer, toward a conclusion about the elusive nature of security that is clearly heartfelt but never fully articulated. There are even several poems in the text, though these tend toward the literal and often lack subtlety—"She stamped thousands of coupons of products/ She would never afford" or "I no longer believe your lies/ About freedom and democracy." Readers will most likely find Ensler's loosely structured and moving prose more convincing, and indeed "poetic," than her versification.

The entire, rather diffuse, book spins out of the author's attempt to come to grips with and make concrete, for herself and her readers, a single abstract word, "security." It is a word that, as Ensler points out, became much more prominent in the discourse of the United States (and elsewhere) after the terrorist attacks on New York and Washington, D.C., on September 11, 2001. Indeed, the underlying political purpose of the book has surprisingly little to do with Bosnian rape victims, Mexican factory workers, or even the author's own life journey. Rather, the book is meant as an indictment of the administration of U.S. president George W. Bush, particularly in its response to the terrorist attacks, the subsequent wars in Afghanistan and Iraq, and the aftermath of Hurricane Katrina. It is Ensler's contention, though hardly one unique or original to her, that the Bush administration capitalized on fear and insecurity in the wake of the attacks to concentrate and solidify their own power base. She believes that the American people have been manipulated, that their natural desire to feel secure has been turned against them, made the most important motivating force in public life, and used in support of policies that actually make life less secure and comfortable for the poorest and most vulnerable citizens of the country and the entire world.

Those readers who agree with Ensler's underlying political assumptions will find much to appreciate in *Insecure at Last*. They will find deep passion, moving examples from the lives of many individuals, and passages of lyrical, quotable prose. When she writes of the dust in the air of Manhattan after the terrorist attacks as the same dust she has encountered in war zones around the world and asserts that "the economic policies and military actions of the U.S. have been responsible for spreading this dust in Chile, Nicaragua, Somalia, Grenada, Afghanistan, Iraq, El Salvador," many readers will find themselves nodding in agreement. Those readers, however, who do not share the author's politics before they begin reading are unlikely to be much moved or to have their opinions shaken. One of the faults of the book is that the key central term "security" remains undefined, with Ensler's usage slipping casually between personal, physical, emotional, and national security. While this is clearly intentional—part of the point is that these various meanings of security are difficult or impossible to disentangle and are sometimes at odds with one another—it makes the book's central argument fairly easy to refute or dismiss on grounds of logical inconsistency.

Strict adherence to logic, though, is not here or in her other works Ensler's primary concern. Her role as cultural critic is closer to that of prophet crying in the wilderness than that of social scientist or historian. Her appeal—built on allusions, personal vignettes, and symbolic language—is calculated to work more on the readers' emotions than on their intellects, as attested by the book's cover image of the author in a full-throated scream. What the whole of *Insecure at Last* lacks in focus and clarity, then, it makes up for in passion. The book will certainly be of interest to Ensler's many fans and to others as a documentation of a particular cultural moment and one fervent response to that moment.

Janet E. Gardner

Review Sources

Booklist 103, no. 2 (September 15, 2006): 4.
The Boston Globe, October 4, 2006, p. F3.
Glamour 104, no. 10 (October, 2006): 225.
Library Journal 131, no. 15 (September 15, 2006): 77.
O: The Oprah Magazine 7, no. 10 (October, 2006): 240.
Publishers Weekly 253, no. 32 (August 14, 2006): 195.

INTERROGATION PALACE
New and Selected Poems, 1982-2004

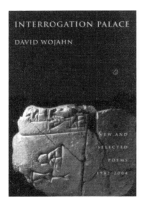

Author: David Wojahn (1953-   )
Publisher: University of Pittsburgh Press (Pittsburgh).
   216 pp. Paperback $14.00
Type of work: Poetry

> *This collection of selected and new poems provides a solid introduction to one of America's most brilliant contemporary poets*

David Wojahn's 1982 collection, *Icehouse Lights*, was selected by the highly acclaimed American poet Richard Hugo as the winner of the Yale Series of Younger Poets. The volume also won the 1983 Poetry Society of America's William Carlos Williams Book Award. This was high praise for a first collection, and Wojahn has continued to grow as a poet, establishing himself as one of America's most distinguished contemporary poets. Since 1982, Wojahn has produced five extraordinary collections, including *Glassworks* (1987), *Mystery Train* (1990), *Late Empire* (1994), *The Falling Hour* (1997), and *Spirit Cabinet* (2002). In addition to poetry, Wojahn wrote the fascinating collection of essays *Strange Good Fortune: Essays on Contemporary Poetry* (2000) and edited the posthumous poetry collection of his late wife Lynda Hull, *The Only World* (1995). In 2006, he edited the *Collected Poems* of Hull. Wojahn, however, is first and foremost a poet. He probes the human condition and strives to wed the personal with public events and cultural icons that are familiar to Americans.

Although Wojahn's first collection shows a youthful poet in the throes of finding his own voice, there are subjects that he raised in this somewhat derivative volume that he has revisited in subsequent collections. Wojahn believes in the power of memory and in the tricks that it can play on an individual's life. The importance of family history is one of the recurring themes of Wojahn's poetry. How people remember episodes in their lives and in the life of the country are prominent topics in all of his collections. How one grows up, deals with tragedies, confronts mortality, and finds meaning while continuing to move forward are issues that are close to Wojahn's heart. The poet is clearly influenced by such eminent poets as Robert Lowell, John Berryman, Louis Simpson, Frank O'Hara, and James Wright: He admires the poets of the past who aimed for greatness. In recent years, Wojahn has been saddened by what he considers the "Era of Downsize." He admires Lowell for his boldness and considers Lowell's poem "For the Union Dead" the "most enduring American political poem of the last half-century." Wojahn speaks of Lowell as being the last American poet who aspired to "Greatness in the old fashioned, capital-G sense." It is important to understand that Wojahn believes in the need for the poet to be driven, to reach for the stars. He clearly attempts to write large, to write with passion about issues that hit home for everyone. He continues to believe that poets can make a difference, whether on the page or in the classroom.

For Wojahn, the personal saga must rise to the surface, must be confronted. He has stated that he looked at his first collection as a "book which attempts a kind of self-discovery through the use of my models." He viewed his second collection as one in which he looked for "self-acceptance, and the struggle to cre-

~

David Wojahn, an award-winning American poet, has published several highly acclaimed collections. He also is the author of the collection of essays Strange Good Fortune: Essays on Contemporary Poetry *(2000) and the editor of posthumous volumes of his late wife Lynda Hull's poetry.*

~

ate a voice that's more individual." It is not unusual for a poet to grow into his or her own voice over a number of poetry volumes, nor is it always easy to shake the influences that inspired the poet in the first place.

Wojahn strives to give the attentive reader new and intriguing perspectives on American history. There is an ambition in the poet's work to enlighten, educate, engage, and amuse. It is no easy task, and it is possible for any poet to incorporate too many things, to "juggle too many balls" at once. Wojahn has stated that "poetry is the most conservative of the arts." Poetry has "its roots . . . deeply embedded in early literate culture." Wojahn sees contemporary American society as having no regard for the "inner life of the individual," thus "there is something subversive about the writing of poetry," precisely because "poetry insists that our feelings, both about society at large and ourselves as participants in that society, have some value—some individual and specific worth."

Wojahn believes that writing poetry must be perceived as a political act. He sees a "political connection . . . within poems through an assertion of self-awareness." A poet must believe in individual expression, must believe in the value of the individual in relationship to society. With *Interrogation Palace*, the reader can see how the poet has developed over more than twenty years. With each new collection, Wojahn has become more and more willing to tackle the urgent concerns of the United States. *Interrogation Palace*, which includes poems from Wojahn's previous six collections, opens with nine new poems that show how Wojahn has stayed current, stayed aware of the "political climate" in the United States. One of the most openly political poems of Wojahn's career is "Dithyramb and Lamentation." The poem is divided into six sections. The poet makes his disgust for President George W. Bush and his war in Iraq more than evident by naming section 5 "George W. Bush in Hell." Based on Dante's Canto XXVI from the *Inferno* (1308-1321), these powerfully bitter lines have President Bush brashly speaking his mind: "Truth was my toy. No counsel could dissuade/ My certainty, nor satisfy my cronies' greed./ For to exercise my zealotry I gave them leave/ To pillage & bring havoc. Their coffers overflowed/ With booty."

For his second collection, *Glassworks*, Wojahn focused on a series of poems about family and friends. One of the three poems from *Glassworks* that is included in *Interrogation Palace*, "Satin Doll," speaks of the failure of an aunt's marriage back when big band music was popular. He views a photograph of her that was taken years before he was born and remembers the details of her life in such lines as

> It's probably the year her marriage
> fails, though the photo, blackened now
> on the edges of its sepia, doesn't say:
> my aunt on the hood of the blue Chevy coupe,
>
> straw hat and summer dress. It's the year
> she carries the novels and notebooks
> into the backyard to burn them, and when she finishes
> her dress and apron are covered with ashes, rising
>
> in what she wants to call a pillar of fire
> but it is only smoke on a damp day.

In the poem, Wojahn invites the reader to see a woman who finds strength in the face of adversity.

For his 1990 collection *Mystery Train*, Wojahn includes a daring sequence of sonnets that concern the power and absurdity of popular culture. Within the intricate craftsmanship of the sonnet form, Wojahn shows readers the wild and chaotic world of rock and roll. There is "James Brown Quaking the Apollo" in sequence 1, Buddy Holly watching the film *Rebel Without a Cause* (1955) in sequence 2, and the Beatles on tour in Hamburg, Germany, in sequence 8. Another several legendary icons appear in subsequent sequences. Wojahn presents the fierce rebellion of the music as well as the sadness and the self-destructive elements that went hand-and-glove with the excitement. It is an astounding poetic accomplishment and shows how Wojahn rapidly was establishing himself as a major voice of contemporary poetry. In one of the new poems in *Interrogation Palace*—"Homage to Blind Willie Johnson"—the poet tenderly pays tribute to one of America's great blues singers.

In 1994, Wojahn published what has to be considered his most raw and dark volume with *Late Empire*. Many of the poems found in the collection are about miseries of a psychic nature. The merging of the political and personal serve to heighten the gloom that pervades the collection. Of the six poems from *Late Empire* included in *Interrogation Palace*, one of the most touching is "Tomis." In this poem, Wojahn tells the story of a woman's daughter who disappears in Latin America. The daughter's bones eventually are identified, and what is left "could fit in a shoebox, a hatbox, a larger purse." 1994 was a tragic year personally for Wojahn, as his wife, Lynda Hull, was killed in an automobile accident. Poems that touch on this tragedy are included in his 1997 collection *The Falling Hour*. He dedicated the volume to Hull and his sense of loss is palpable, the grief never far below the surface.

Wojahn does not wallow in his tragedy though. While a thread of grief runs through much of Wojahn's work, he has not given up on life or the power of poetry. He truly believes in the resiliency of life and that poetry can serve as a positive force. His 2002 collection *Spirit Cabinet* is inhabited by the dead. The dead seem to live on in history, in memories. It is up to the living to find a way to go on without the undue influence of all the ghosts. While the living can become trapped by the past, by demons both real and imagined, the poet remains a strong proponent of survival, of learning the hard lessons of life and not giving up.

Over the years, critics have praised Wojahn for his range. He has proven himself to be adept at both formal and free verse. He also is at home writing about personal and public subject matter. He is a master at dissecting the public and private lives of the famous and of the common man, and this is fully on display in the truly wonderful collection *Interrogation Palace*.

Jeffry Jensen

Review Sources

The Hudson Review 59 (Summer, 2006): 317.
Library Journal 131, no. 2 (February 1, 2006): 82.
Poetry 189, no. 4 (January, 2007).
Publishers Weekly 252, no. 48 (December 5, 2005): 33.

INTUITION

Author: Allegra Goodman (1967-   )
Publisher: Dial Press (New York). 344 pp. $25.00
Type of work: Novel
Time: The 1980's
Locale: Cambridge, Massachusetts

A research biologist's romantic involvement with a col-
league dissolves when that colleague goes public with her
suspicions that the discovery of a possible cancer-curing
virus may be based on falsified data

Principal characters:
> CLIFF BANNAKER, a young research biolo-
> gist doing postdoctoral work at a presti-
> gious institute
> ROBIN DECKER, a research biologist and Cliff's colleague, with whom he
> is romantically linked
> SANDY GLASS, an ambitious, dynamic oncologist who heads the labora-
> tory
> MARION MENDELSSOHN, Sandy's brilliant but more cautious partner
> XIANG FENG, a Chinese biologist who works with Cliff on his research
> project
> KATE GLASS, Sandy's teenage daughter
> JACOB MENDELSSOHN, Marion's husband, a professor of microbiology

Although *Intuition*'s subject is scientific fraud, this topical issue is also the occasion for a series of character studies of various scientists whose work is inevitably shaped by the nature of their personalities. Of particular interest is the character of Cliff Bannaker, whose lucky discovery of a possible cancer-curing virus sets the plot in motion.

Cliff is about to lose his position at the Philpott Institute in Cambridge, Massachusetts, because his work has come to nothing. Bitter and at the end of his rope, he gains a sudden reprieve when "his" virus, R-7, begins suddenly to arrest the growth of tumors in his mice. The laboratory, which had been concerned about its future federal funding, revels in the discovery. Its future and Cliff's seem assured when his paper, coauthored with the laboratory heads, appears in the prestigious scientific journal *Nature*. This results in new funding and leads *People* magazine to trumpet the possibility of a giant step in the treatment of breast cancer.

The two codirectors of the laboratory, Sandy Glass and Marion Mendelssohn, eagerly embrace Cliff's findings. Sandy, an ebullient oncologist, likes to live well and think big, and he is certain Cliff's findings represent a tremendous breakthrough that will both make a genuine contribution to the field of medicine and bring success to all concerned. His shyer partner, Marion, on the other hand, suggests restraint and emphasizes the importance of careful, methodical research. While the flashy, freewheel-

ing Sandy arranges to have Cliff's prelimi-
nary findings published and encourages the
popular press to take an interest, Marion begins to feel that she has been asked to believe
in Sandy and in Cliff in the teeth of the actual
evidence. She wonders whether her high standards will be compromised by Sandy's educated guess that Cliff's findings are sound. It
is over this issue that the successful workplace collaboration of Marion and Sandy begins to fall apart.

> ~
>
> *Allegra Goodman was born in
> Brooklyn, New York, but grew up in
> Hawaii, where her parents were
> university professors. She attended
> Harvard and received a Ph.D. in
> English from Stanford. Named by* The
> New Yorker *as one of the twenty best
> writers under forty, she is also the
> recipient of a Whiting Award.*
>
> ~

To further complicate matters, Marion and
Sandy do not share the same religious perspective. Sandy, whose original name was
Sam Glazeroff, is a Jew who has married an upper-class Episcopalian; the only holiday
he is seen celebrating is in the context of his hosting a splashy Christmas party that is far
more social than it is spiritual. Marion's religious life, on the other hand, is demonstrated by her celebration of a traditional Passover with her family and coworkers.

Marion and Sandy ask Cliff's girlfriend, Robin, whose research is not going well,
to abandon her own project and work on replicating Cliff's results, even though she
officially outranks Cliff. Feeling both envious of Cliff's new status and unable to con-
firm his results, Robin is beset by a sense of failure. In her role as mother hen, Marion
attempts to cheer Robin up by offering her a position as a teaching assistant to
Marion's husband, Jacob. Jacob, who has always felt that his brilliant wife has been
required to play second fiddle to the charismatic Sandy, stirs things up by having a
quiet word with Robin about the possibility that Cliff's results are fraudulent. Jacob's
sly conversation encourages Robin to bring her suspicions to Sandy and Marion.
When the two directors choose to side with Cliff, Robin has no choice but to leave the
institute. She also breaks up with Cliff, who is hurt that Robin has no faith in him or
his work. He refuses to entertain the idea that his findings may be the result of sloppy
work, and he denies any deliberate fabrication. Robin herself wonders if her scrutiny
is simply schoolmarmish and whether it has led to the inhibition of a gifted scientist's
natural creative processes.

Thoroughly alienated from the institute and from Cliff, Robin cannot leave the issue alone. She takes her suspicions to a watchdog organization, the crusading but
questionable Office for Research Integrity in Science. Soon a windy local congressman holds public hearings on the issue in order to fuel his political agenda. As a result,
the entire institute is made suspect, and Robin finds herself responsible for a ridiculous public interrogation not simply of bad science but also of the legitimacy of science itself. Because Robin's actions have resulted in a full-fledged scandal, Cliff's
partner Xiang Feng, who had been made into a star by *People* magazine's article on
Cliff's experiments, is suddenly facing deportation back to China. As the scientists at
the institute are subjected to political machinations as well as a media circus, the entire issue is blown out of proportion.

Nevertheless, even though she is not truly sure whether her motives are too much poisoned by a measure of jealousy or vindictiveness, Robin does not cease to debunk Cliff's project. Amid the questioning of his professional character, evidence surfaces that seems to revise the dynamics of his and Robin's affair. Encouraged by her zealous lawyer, Robin forms a new perspective on her relationship with Cliff that hints that he may have subjected her to some sexual coercion. In the end, Robin begins to feel that everything about Cliff, both professionally and personally, has been something of an illusion.

The congressional committee rules that Cliff has fabricated his evidence—but an appeal overturns this decision, suggesting that the committee was politically motivated and anti-Semitic. By this time, however, the events set in motion by Cliff's discovery and Robin's doubts are precipitating the breakup of Sandy and Marion's partnership. Marion realizes that she may have put too much faith in Sandy and not enough in herself. Sandy leaves the institute for a visible job that will involve more fund-raising than research, while Marion continues quietly to work on the cure for breast cancer on her own. Cliff and Robin also go their separate ways, and there is no clear answer to the issue of whether or not Robin's suspicions about Cliff were well founded.

Some insights into Cliff's psychological life are revealed, however, when he is sent a copy of Oscar Wilde's novel *The Picture of Dorian Gray* (1891) by Kate Glass, Sandy's teenage daughter with whom Cliff has struck up a semi-flirtatious friendship. Wilde's spiritually inflected novel about a man whose devil's bargain permits a split personality that allows him to be less than accountable for his actions suggests that Cliff, as well, has compartmentalized his personality in a similar manner. He may be fudging or blurring inconvenient facts in a way that is not clear even to him, much less to others. Although not a major presence, Kate is an important one in that she is one of the few characters who represents the humanities in this novel, and her bringing Wilde's novel to Cliff's attention echoes her earlier introducing him to the poetry of John Donne.

One of the reasons for the inclusion of Kate's perspective is that it affirms the value of literature as a tool for understanding human nature. Goodman is clearly suggesting that reading serious literature could help Cliff develop a moral compass which would be invaluable for him as a scientist. Additionally, the literary works Kate recommends to Cliff emphasize the importance of understanding the moral imperfection inherent in human nature, an awareness that would be a counterpoise to the insouciance of scientists such as Sandy and Cliff.

Although Cliff's personality is a creative, intuitive one, Goodman suggests that his intuition may be a form of self-serving wishful thinking. As a result, he could be a potentially dangerous risk-taker, who, like Sandy, can lose touch with reality without being aware of it. Sandy and Cliff can be said to be guilty of spreading false hope, even of setting themselves up as false messiahs. Like Cliff the dreamer, the more realistic Robin also uses intuition in her investigation into the veracity of Cliff's findings. Although her use of intuition is neither expansive nor euphoric, the reader is led to believe Robin's suspicions were more correct than the empty promises of Cliff's slapdash data.

In the end, it is Robin who turns up at Marion's presentation of sound and meticulous research that may truly represent some advance in the battle against breast cancer. Despite the previous acrimony between them, the ever-vigilant and questioning Robin is on the verge of once again accepting Marion as a mentor. In a slow and steady way, Marion is making real progress in her research. Ultimately, it is Marion who earns Robin's rapt attention and who gives the waiting Robin her attention in return. No longer subject to the big-deal expectations of Sandy and Cliff, Robin and Marion have weathered the irrational exuberance and speculative frenzy that seemed to develop in the wake of Cliff's dubious discovery. Both have sustained their faith in science, no longer distracted by the magic wishes and cut corners associated with Sandy and Cliff. Although hopes for a big scientific breakthrough have been dashed, and although the little family of Philpott's scientists has been disbanded, Marion and Robin's new understanding, at the end, also suggests a mother-daughter relationship free of dysfunction.

Goodman has set her novel in the mid-1980's, before the volley of scandals involving deceptive or erroneous scientific data. In that decade, there was far less awareness of the degree to which scientific ambition could foster scientific fraud. That there was little known history of scientific fraud permitted Cliff and Sandy to opt for immediate action over analysis and introspection and made Robin's suspicions seem less immediately persuasive. Although set in the 1980's, Goodman's book very much addresses the problems inherent in a continuing cultural system that puts excessive pressure to perform on young researchers, and in which economic considerations may subvert the pursuit of scientific truth.

Goodman's canny choice of the 1980's time frame also creates a distance that allows her to suggest her realistic story can work as a fable applicable to issues beyond those of science. Even as the family and spiritual issues Goodman had considered in her earlier novels translate surprisingly well to the venue of the scientific community, so does her study of bad science speak to issues beyond the biology laboratory. Her careful introduction of the concept of sin through a minor character's enthusiasm for the poetry of John Donne is simply one of the ways in which she raises moral and spiritual questions that act as a correction or counterpoise to her depiction of a society shaped by utopian fantasies and an ethos of personal enrichment and narcissistic entitlements. Although her exploration of the world of scientific research is accurate and astute, what is most impressive is her deft depiction of a family in which parental pressure to perform and succeed may result in the deformation and corruption of the core values of the children. That this is a workplace family does not alter Goodman's conviction that character matters, and that at length the truth will out.

Margaret Boe Birns

Review Sources

The Atlanta Journal and Constitution, April 23, 2006, p. K7.
Booklist 102, no. 8 (December 15, 2005): 5.
Entertainment Weekly, no. 866 (March 3, 2006): 104.

Kirkus Reviews 73, no. 23 (December 1, 2005): 1246-1249.
Los Angeles Times, March 5, 2006, p. R2.
Nature 440 (April 20, 2006): 996-997.
The New York Times 155 (March 21, 2006): F3.
The New York Times Book Review 155 (March 5, 2006): 5.
Science 312 (May 5, 2006): 698-699.
The Wall Street Journal 247, no. 58 (March 11, 2006): P11.
The Washington Post, February 26, 2006, p. BW03.

JAMES TIPTREE, JR.
The Double Life of Alice B. Sheldon

Author: Julie Phillips
Publisher: St. Martin's Press (New York). 480 pp.
 $27.95
Type of work: Literary biography
Time: 1915-1987
Locale: The United States

Phillips presents an account of the life of Alice Bradley Sheldon, artist, psychologist, and writer, who concealed her identity as a writer behind the pseudonym of James Tiptree, Jr., and fooled many people into believing that she was a man

Principal personages:
ALICE BRADLEY SHELDON, a writer
WILLIAM DAVEY, her first husband, also a writer
HUNTINGDON SHELDON, her second husband
MARY HASTINGS BRADLEY, her mother

In the biography *James Tiptree, Jr.: The Double Life of Alice B. Sheldon* Julie Phillips describes how, in late 1976, it was discovered that science-fiction writer James Tiptree, Jr., who was also well known for his correspondence with his readers, was actually a woman named Alice Bradley Sheldon. Born Alice Bradley, she described herself as "nothing but an old lady from Virginia." After her identity was discovered, she continued to write and to publish, but somehow her work had lost its edge. Nonetheless, the science-fiction world was electrified all over again nine years later, when it was announced that Alice Sheldon had killed her husband and then turned the gun on herself, in what was believed to be a suicide pact.

Although Tiptree was reticent about his life, Alice Sheldon's early life was documented in extraordinary detail. Her mother, Mary Hastings Bradley, was a society beauty, a novelist, and an adventurer who traveled extensively in Africa with her husband and Alice. Indeed, Alice's adventures in Africa became the stuff of two of Bradley's books for children. Alice was with her parents when they traveled with Carl Akeley on an expedition intended to collect gorilla specimens for the American Museum of Natural History but also to discourage further hunting of gorillas by having Bradley shoot one. The intended message was that if a woman could kill one, why would a man want to do so? Alice hoped she would have a gun of her own, just like her mother's, but this was not permitted.

Mary Bradley's position on the expedition was complex. Bradley had been criticized for leading such an adventurous life. She worked hard to show that she could lead the life she chose and still be a good mother to her daughter. Alice's role was to be the perfect daughter, willing to be carried across Africa like a parcel, always neatly

∽

*Julie Phillips is a journalist who has
written on books, film, feminism, and
cultural politics for publications
including* Newsday *and* Interview. *Her
biography of Alice B. Sheldon arose
from articles about feminist science
fiction and James Tiptree, Jr., which
appeared in* Ms. *and the* Voice Literary
Supplement, *respectively.*

∽

dressed and well behaved, a credit to her mother. Alice Bradley learned early on that everything must be subordinated to her mother's needs, that all must appear conventional, yet beneath the perfect appearance there was the heart of a rebel, an element of Alice's character that came to the fore as she grew older. She was a bright child and a good scholar, but she had few if any friends and found it difficult to fit in. Her entire life was be characterized by a search for self.

As she grew older, it was not clear what Alice would do with her life, although there was some vague thought she might be an artist, for she had talent. However, the messages she received from her mother were contradictory. On one hand, Mary Hastings Bradley wanted her daughter to have a career, as she had had, although what form this career might take was uncertain; on the other hand, she wanted her daughter to find a good man and make a decent marriage. She was determined her daughter would make her debut into society, which she duly did, only to elope a few days later with the first man to propose to her, a charming and wealthy young man named William (Bill) Davey, who wanted to be a writer. The couple moved to Berkeley, California, where both attended university classes. Bill encouraged Alice to paint. The marriage was not a success. Davey was a drunkard, hopeless with money, while Alice had no interest in keeping house for him. Instead, she worked at her art and learned to shoot. The marriage was physically violent and came to an end in 1940. Divorced, Alice looked around for something else to do with her life. She decided to join the Women's Army Auxiliary Corps. Her organizational skills found an outlet in working as a supply officer, something at which she proved to be successful, though others resented her abilities. Alice then transferred to Washington, to the Pentagon, and found herself working in the new discipline of photointelligence, examining and interpreting aerial reconnaissance photos. This work took her to Europe, where her new commanding officer, Colonel Huntingdon Sheldon, generally known as Ting, fell in love with her.

The child of kind but emotionally distant parents, sent to boarding school, and uncertain of what he would do with his life, Ting had much in common with Alice, and the relationship flourished. Whether Alice loved Ting as a husband or more as a friend is open to debate. Throughout her life, Alice was attracted to women as well as to men, although her attempts to establish relationships with other women were invariably unrequited. She also chafed against the obligations that she felt society placed upon women, the very restrictions her mother had sought to push aside in her own life but that she had inevitably placed upon her own daughter.

Nonetheless, Ting and Alice were married and set out on a new adventure, running a chicken farm in New Jersey. The idea was that for four or five months of the year they would work intensely, while the rest of the time would be available for other enterprises. Alice, having abandoned her painting, had turned instead to writing, something else she had done throughout her life. The chicken farm experiment, while not disastrous, was not a success; when Alice reemerged, it was to pursue a degree in psychology, eventually earning herself a doctorate. Even in her chosen academic career, however, Alice could not find a place for herself. As her academic career ended, she turned again to writing and to science fiction.

It was not uncommon for female science-fiction writers to disguise their gender by using a pseudonym or their initials rather than their full names. More than one editor refused to believe that women could write science fiction. Thus, "James Tiptree, Jr.," a pseudonym concocted as a joke by Alice and Ting, was to become an important escape for Alice Sheldon. Through Tiptree's persona, she was at last able to engage fully with the world and give free rein to those parts of her character that an "old lady from Virginia" perhaps should not have, especially not while her mother was still alive. Tiptree was everything Alice longed to be and felt she could not be: cheerful, boisterous, witty, competent, mysterious, and gregarious.

As Tiptree's stories became known, she began to receive and respond to fan mail, and she became as well known for her correspondence as for her stories. The stories reflected the darker side of Alice's personality and her growing concern with the state of the world, whereas Tiptree's personality was easygoing. The apparent disparity between the man who wrote with such understanding about women and the bon vivant of correspondence was much discussed. How did he achieve such understanding of the female psyche? When Tiptree's real identity was revealed, many claimed to have known all along, but the general response to the news suggests that few people guessed. Certainly, no one had realized that fiction writer Raccoona Sheldon, a second identity that Alice Sheldon created, was in any way connected with Tiptree.

Once everyone knew, Tiptree fell silent. Alice continued to write but had lost the freedom that Tiptree gave her. The stories dwindled away. All of her life, Alice had suffered from depression, and by 1987 she had convinced herself that Ting, thirteen years older and with failing eyesight, was in very poor health. She had talked about suicide before, and she and Ting seemed to have agreed on a suicide pact. However, evidence suggests that even at eighty-four, Ting was not ready to die. On the night of May 18, 1987, as Ting lay sleeping, Alice Sheldon shot him in the head. Then, after calling her lawyer and her stepson, she turned the gun on herself.

While she struggled throughout life to find a place where she felt comfortable, in death Alice Sheldon has proved an inspiration to women and men alike. She often wondered whether she had been cowardly in publishing under a man's name; a proper feminist would have published under her own name. In 1991, the writers Pat Murphy and Karen Joy Fowler established an award to promote science fiction that reenvisions gender roles, an award that is supported and funded by an extraordinary grassroots movement within the science-fiction fan community and that has proved hugely successful in expanding perceptions of science fiction.

Whether Tiptree or Sheldon would have appreciated the existence of a biography is debatable, but their many admirers are in agreement that Phillips has produced an exemplary account of their strangely intertwined lives.

Maureen Kincaid Speller

Review Sources

Booklist 102, nos. 19/20 (June 1-15, 2006): 29.
Entertainment Weekly, nos. 891/892 (August 18, 2006): 142.
Fantasy & Science Fiction 111, nos. 4/5 (October/November, 2006): 40-50.
Kirkus Reviews 74, no. 10 (May 15, 2006): 510.
The New York Times 155 (August 3, 2006): E6.
The New York Times Book Review 155 (August 20, 2006): 1-8.
Publishers Weekly 253, no. 12 (March 20, 2006): 44.
The Times Literary Supplement, October 13, 2006, p. 27.

THE JUDGMENT OF PARIS
The Revolutionary Decade That Gave the World Impressionism

Author: Ross King (1962-   )
Publisher: Walker & Company (New York). 464 pp.
   $28.00
Type of work: History and fine arts
Time: 1863-1874
Locale: Paris

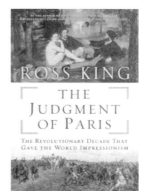

A history of some of the Paris art movements in the nine-teenth century, set within their political and cultural con-texts

   Principal personages:
      JEAN-LOUIS-ERNEST MEISSONIER (1815-
         1891), a French painter of Napoleonic
         history scenes
      EDOUARD MANET (1832-1883), a French painter of a realist style
      NAPOLEON III (LOUIS-NAPOLEON BONAPARTE, 1808-1873), emperor of
         France in the Second Empire
      ALFRED-EMILIEN O'HARA, the comte de Nieuwerkerke (1811-1892),
         director-general of museums of France
      GUSTAVE COURBET, (1819-1877) a French realist painter
      CLAUDE MONET, (1840-1926), a French Impressionist painter
      ÉMILE ZOLA, (1840-1902), a French writer and champion of Manet

From the perspective of almost 150 years, the talented painters who successfully created important new directions in art in mid-nineteenth century Paris are valued not only for the prices that their works command at art sales and auctions but also for their historical position as the initiators of modern art. At the time that these artists, such as Edouard Manet, Gustave Courbet, and Claude Monet, among others, were painting, their works were often reviled and misunderstood. Most of the respectable art critics in the press, the artistic establishment represented by the École des Beaux-Arts, and the public at large, found these new paintings either horrifying or laughable. *The Judgment of Paris* examines in rich detail the critical decade between about 1863 and 1874 to see how these innovative artists, rebelling against the confining artistic conventions of their era, gained greater acceptance as vanguards of the new artistic directions of the future.

   The author of this book, Ross King, uses two of the key participants in this artistic struggle to depict the changing fortunes and shifts in attitude about art in Paris in this crucial time during the third quarter of the nineteenth century. Jean-Louis-Ernest Meissonier represents the older, traditional artistic values, while King uses the career of Edouard Manet to reveal in its sophistication and complexity the far-reaching rebellion against artistic convention and authority. At the time, the popular Meissonier,

Ross King, who lives in England, has written two novels and the popular art history books Brunelleschi's Dome *(2000) and* Michelangelo and the Pope's Ceiling *(2002).*

a meticulous painter of genre scenes, was especially famed for historical canvases depicting key triumphant moments in the campaigns of Napoleon Bonaparte. He was not only a highly respected painter within the Parisian École des Beaux-Arts and the Paris Salon; he was also one of the wealthiest painters of the day, producing works that brought the most exorbitant prices in the art market.

Manet painted shocking works that challenged traditional art in subject matter and style of painting. He struggled to have his works accepted for the Paris Salon, an annual juried exhibition of French painting with medals awarded for excellence, and found no buyers for his art until very late in his career. Struggling to make his way in the competitive art world of that time, he managed financially only thanks to timely support from his mother's coffers.

As a measure of the change in reputation of these two artists over the following 130 years, Manet's paintings currently occupy honored places in the great museums and collections of the world. They are keystones of art historical studies of this period. When Manet's paintings appear for auction, they command high prices from prestigious institutions and wealthy collectors. In contrast, Meissonier's paintings languish in inconspicuous corners and storage vaults of museums. As a result, few people outside the ranks of art historians specializing in French nineteenth century painting have ever heard of him.

In his unfolding narrative of this crucial artistic decade, King follows these very different trajectories of artistic fame. His work traces in well-documented anecdotes the careers of Manet and Meissonier in tandem. While Meissonier was at the height of his fame, Manet was shocking the art world with his now famous paintings such as *Le Dejeuner sur l'herbe*. That work depicted a picnic in the woods attended by two young men in contemporary dress finery alongside a provocatively posed woman in the nude. Another equally famous work, *Olympia*, provided another twist on the classical nude form of the reclining Venus, with Manet's nude woman on a chaise looking more like a Parisian courtesan. Manet's painting style and technique, with strong highlights, scant modeling, and broad planes of thickly applied color, also defied the carefully detailed, refined, and precisely layered painting technique favored by the École des Beaux-Arts.

While Manet was challenging reigning artistic taste and decorum from his studio in the midst of a bohemian quarter of Paris and mingling with fellow artistic and literary rebels in Parisian cafés, Meissonier was trying to secure his reputation as a great painter for the present and the future by painting historical battle scenes from the glories of the Napoleonic campaigns. Manet dashed off his paintings rather quickly, compared to the precise and meticulous Meissonier, who labored over every tiny detail with sketches, models, and authentic artifacts. He expended much care to be accurate in his depiction of military uniforms, the movement and gait of horses, and the physical setting in which a battle took place. He lived and worked in a grand country mansion and studio at Poissy, near Paris, as befitted a painter of his stature.

Although Manet and Meissonier knew of each other, they did not interact on a personal level. When Manet managed to get some of his works accepted for the Paris Salon, his surname brought his works into juxtaposition with Meissonier's in the alphabetically arranged display chamber of the salon, Room M. There the differences between style and subject matter of these two artists were clearly on display to the Paris audience. Contemporary opinion was admiring of Meissonier and dismissive of the more ambitious work of Manet. Manet's paintings were often rejected by the conservative juries; these panels stamped his works of art on the back with a red R for *refuse*. It was a harsh verdict for the artists to be so derided in public. In 1864, the number of artists whose works were rejected by the jury was so large that the famous *Salon des Refuses* was organized to show these works separately. Manet's paintings, including *Le Dejeuner sur l'herbe*, were viewed among the *refuses*.

Although this book focuses on the contrasting styles and approaches of Manet and Meissonier, King also includes discussions of other artists. He examines the work of Alexandre Cabanel as an example of a traditional academic painter whose somewhat erotic paintings of mythological subjects garnered prizes at the salons. Among the *refuses* were many artists who, like Manet, were experimenting with different forms of painting and subject matter that included scenes of contemporary life. Gustave Courbet was a realist painter whose works often depicted the simple dignity of the peasant. Several painters such as Claude Monet and Pierre-Auguste Renoir favored *plein air* landscapes and experimented with ways to achieve the "impression" of light in the open-air landscape. Edgar Degas, likewise, used color and perspective in new ways in his depictions of scenes from the theater and ballet. Paul Cezanne's paintings, with their dense planes of color, went even further away from conventional styles.

This group of "revolutionary" French painters lived in a Paris that was rife with political turmoil. Throughout the book, King interweaves discussion of the political situation with the artistic ferment. Until 1870, Napoleon III (Louis-Napoleon Bonaparte) managed to placate the masses in various ways, while maintaining control of the Second Empire. The arts came under political control through the comte de Nieuwerkerke, the director general of museums and head of the salon and its jury. The *Salon des Refuses* was a political ploy to keep unrest in check. The Second Empire collapsed in 1870-1871 with the French defeat in the Franco-Prussian war. The revolutionary social agitation that had been simmering exploded with the Commune and its ruthless suppression during Bloody Week in 1871, ushering in the Third Republic.

The Judgment of Paris presents the revolution that was occurring in French painting within this grand sweep of French cultural and political history. This integration of artistic, political, and cultural forces is one strength of the book. The art is seen as part of a larger whole.

The author is especially good at bringing this broader historical canvas to life by developing telling details that illuminate what life was like for the painters living and working in Paris. King is adept at describing the environment of the salon, which took place at the Palais des Champs-Elysees, a large, 250-yard-long exhibition hall that hosted equine shows, displays of pigs, and cheese shows, as well as "high" art at various times. He paints a vivid picture of the artists bringing their work for display before the jury in handcarts and wheelbarrows. He says that as the deadline for submission approached, the avenues and bridges leading to the Palais des Champs-Elysees "grew thick with swaying trolleys and wobbling carts." He also describes the crowd scenes as the public poured into the salon and their reactions to the most notorious paintings.

However, despite its strengths, this book seems to struggle against itself. For one thing, the connection between political and artistic revolution in that decade is a tenuous one. Although the artists, like all citizens of Paris—and France—were affected by the political turmoil in the wake of the Franco-Prussian war, the artists themselves, with the exception of Courbet, who was a leader in the Commune, distanced themselves from political involvement. Most of these "revolutionary" painters, including Manet, fled from Paris to the south or north of France during these uprisings.

Another problem is that the two protagonists, Manet and Meissonier, chosen by King to highlight the artistic struggle between tradition and innovation, were not leaders of any artistic movement or group. In fact, both were somewhat atypical. Meissonier craved acceptance by the academic artistic establishment, but he never really produced grand works in that tradition. Instead, he concentrated on small-scale battle scenes from the recent Napoleonic campaigns and his popular *gentilhommes*. In addition, he excelled at *plein air* landscapes.

Manet also sought acceptance in the salons and among the art critics. He rarely worked outdoors; instead, he worked primarily in his studio, painting new ways of looking at traditional paintings that he had viewed in Italy, Spain, and in the Louvre collection. He refused to show his paintings in the first organized exhibit of Impressionist paintings. Although in later life he associated and painted with some of the Impressionists such as Monet and Renoir, his body of work was not, strictly speaking, Impressionist. If the decade that is the subject of King's book "gave the world Impressionism," as the subtitle indicates, Manet was not a formative leader of this artistic movement.

When King discusses the critical reception of Meissonier's long-awaited masterpiece, *Friedland*, a painting of a famous Napoleonic battle that was a decade in the making, he says some of the critics pointed out that "the whole of *Friedland* was something less than the sum of its parts." The same criticism applies to this book. It is enlivened with a wealth of anecdotal detail about the artists and their living and working environments. The political background is developed well. However, the real story is the art itself. The visual works remain so embedded in the surrounding details and political background that the art never comes to the foreground to speak for itself.

Karen Gould

Review Sources

Booklist 102, no. 6 (November 15, 2005): 4.
The Boston Globe, February 5, 2006, p. E7.
Houston Chronicle, February 19, 2006, p. 16.
Kirkus Reviews 73, no. 24 (December 15, 2005): 1312.
Library Journal 131, no. 2 (February 1, 2006): 76.
Los Angeles Times Book Review, February 26, 2006, p. 4.
Maclean's 119, no. 7 (February 13, 2006): 50.
The New York Times 155 (February 10, 2006): E42.
The New York Times Book Review 155 (March 26, 2006): 14.
Publishers Weekly 252, no. 50 (December 19, 2005): 56.
The Washington Post Book World, March 12, 2006, p. BW08.

KATE
The Woman Who Was Hepburn

Author: William J. Mann (1963-   )
Publisher: Henry Holt (New York). Illustrated. 621 pp.
   $30.00
Type of work: Biography
Time: 1907-2003
Locale: New England, California, New York City, En-
   gland, Europe, Africa, and Australia

*Mann presents the private and public life of Katharine
Hepburn, with special emphasis on an in-depth understanding of her personality as formed by her childhood in a
family with a fiery father and a free-thinking mother who
nevertheless submitted to the dominance of her husband*

Principal personages:
   KATHARINE HEPBURN, a Hollywood star
   KIT HEPBURN, her mother
   DR. THOMAS HEPBURN, her father
   GEORGE CUKOR, a Hollywood director
   HOWARD HUGHES, a wealthy aviator who was romantically involved
      with Katharine
   LAURA HARDING, Katharine's friend and possibly romantic partner
   LELAND HAYWARD, Katharine's acting agent
   H. PHELPS PUTMAN, a poet who was romantically involved with Katharine
   LUDLOW OGDEN SMITH, Katharine's husband
   SPENCER TRACY, an actor who was romantically involved with Katharine
   PHYLLIS WILBOURN, Katharine's secretary

Following in the footsteps of several biographers, including A. Scott Berg, Garson
Kanin, Barbara Leaming, and even Katharine Hepburn herself in *Me: Stories of My
Life* (1991), William Mann produces a well-researched and carefully documented
work that is a sensitive and thorough examination of the extremely complex personality of one of America's most glamorous and talented film and stage stars. In *Kate: The
Woman Who Was Hepburn*, Mann takes readers through the ninety-six years of Hepburn's life with great attention to the details not only of her public personality but also
of the private person who so assiduously created and nurtured that public image.

Born in New England to a family with social aspirations, Katharine had to share
the attention of her parents with five brothers and sisters. She was especially competitive with her older brother, Tom, who claimed the attention of her father, a physician
specializing in venereal disease. Katharine might have turned to her mother, Kit, for
attention had not Mrs. Hepburn been frequently away from home campaigning first
for women's suffrage and later for their right to birth control. Mann's perspicuity in

understanding the private aspect of Hepburn's life is nowhere better demonstrated than in his emphasizing the importance of her experience as a young girl trying to gain her father's attention and praise.

William J. Mann is the author of several novels and four film-related books. He has written for The Boston Globe, *the* Los Angeles Times, The Hartford Courant, *the online magazine* Salon, *and other publications.*

Her lifelong participation in demanding sports actually began when she competed in physical activity with her older and athletic brother. Finally, she threw off her girlhood altogether and took on the dress and persona of a boy, wearing boys' clothes and short pants and calling herself "Jimmy." As Mann so aptly observes, "Jimmy" remained the central part of her private character for the rest of her life, which helps explain her preference for slacks and pantsuits over the elaborate dresses more common to the women of her era and social status. It was the persistence of "Jimmy" in her personality that moves Mann to point out that while Hepburn emulated her mother as an independent woman, she would rather have been a man much like her father.

Hepburn left her family for Bryn Mawr College, where she had academic problems for her first two years but in her final years was able to pull herself together, perhaps because she began to appear in plays and to attend plays in New York with campus friends. Somewhere the urge to be an actress was ignited, in no small measure by her constant need to be the center of attention, a need never really satisfied at home. What may also have attracted her to acting was that the theater and its practitioners have always exhibited a liberal attitude toward complex sexual makeup. Indeed, one of the major themes of Mann's book is the sexual ambiguity exhibited by Hepburn. As she was completing her work at Bryn Mawr, whatever her sexual ambiguities in her mature years, she fell in love with the rising poet H. Phelps Putman.

Immediately upon graduating Kate took a role in *The Czarina* with the Auditorium Players in Baltimore and performed in two other productions before the company went out of business. Moving to New York she lived with Phelps Putman in a relationship that was apparently platonic. At this time she met the man who would ultimately become her husband, Ludlow Ogden Smith, known to her as "Luddy." Kate was not in love with Luddy, but, trying to recover from the demise of a Broadway show in which she had had a significant role, she married the man whom she often characterized as the best friend she ever had. Indeed, there never seemed to have been much sexual activity between the two, and just as Kate seemed to have bisexual tendencies, so did Luddy. It was in 1930 that Kate met Laura Harding, the woman who would in one way or another share her life for many years. It was also in 1930 that Hepburn played a major role in *Art and Mrs. Bottle*, a show that became a Broadway hit. There followed two successful theatrical years and, most important, her contact in 1932 with the agent Leland Hayward who would arrange for her first Hollywood film roles. Once in Hollywood, the woman whom audiences knew as Katharine Hepburn began to emerge, even as the more private Kate remained intact as she manipulated the external image of a movie star.

Hepburn's first motion picture, *Bill of Divorcement* (1932), directed by George Cukor, was a smash hit, and overnight she became a movie star of tremendous significance. She was compared with Greta Garbo and characterized as the most exciting new face since Marlene Dietrich. Kate now had the worldwide fame and attention she had been seeking all of her life. Important also was that Hepburn had begun an artistic partnership with Cukor, who would remain her great friend and director throughout her life. Hepburn loved living in Los Angeles where she could take long walks in the fields and swim nude in the ocean. She rarely went back east to visit her husband, and in 1933 Luddy's hopes for children were crushed by a dangerous and complicated surgery performed on Hepburn by her father, a procedure that suggests uterine cancer.

Hepburn was having little to do with her husband anyway. She was spending most of her time with her friend Laura Harding at the soirees given at Cukor's house, and Mann makes the unqualified point that Cukor's circle was openly homosexual. The relationship between Kate and Cukor was close. He led her through all of her early triumphs in film. He was, as Mann so aptly observes, the father Kate had longed for all of her life, and it was in *Little Women* (1933), directed by Cukor, that Hepburn became the unquestioned reigning queen of international film actresses, critic after critic praising her work and calling the film triumphant.

Her new stardom, however, would soon be tarnished. In 1934 Hepburn suffered two artistic setbacks, first in a poorly received film and then in *The Lake*, a Broadway production that failed miserably, characterized by Dorothy Parker's famous remark that in the play Hepburn had run the gamut of emotions from A to B. Nevertheless, Hepburn would become a fine actress, and under the guidance of George Stevens she once again triumphed in the 1935 film *Alice Adams*. By this time she was a fixture in the Hollywood heavens. She had divorced Luddy and seemed to be attracted to several strong men, perhaps the most famous of whom was the aviator Howard Hughes, whose relationship with Hepburn would be revisited in the 2004 film *The Aviator*.

Mann notes readers that Hepburn continued to have close relationships with women and, like most of the men in Hepburn's love life, that Hughes was rumored to be bisexual. Nevertheless Kate was about to toss aside the tomboy image that permeated her early work. In the 1940 film *The Philadelphia Story*, she appears as mature, beautiful, glamorous, and sensitive. Moreover, the times were catching up with her offscreen image of a woman in slacks. The war was forcing women to be more assertive. Rosie the Riveter had arrived and many women were now "in pants." Hepburn was also to become her most feminine in the 1942 hit *Woman of the Year*. It was her first film for MGM, but even more important, it was her first film with the man with whom she would be associated for the remainder of her life: Spencer Tracy.

In the several hit films they made together, Hepburn is always the brittle, sharp beauty who is brought into submission by Tracy's character: a man of dominance and strength. Mann points out that the relationship depicted is exactly that of Hepburn's parents. Moreover, although Tracy was married, he and Hepburn apparently lived together for several years in much the same relationship as that depicted in their films. Hepburn was a star in the film heavens, made all the brighter by her famous costar. Mann questions whether the relationship was ever sexual though. He does not doubt that the two shared a deep and abiding love, but he observes that Hepburn continued close relationships with her female friends, especially Laura Harding. He also indicates that Tracy had sexual interests in males. Whatever the case, the two continued together both on screen and off screen for a lifetime.

Although she now had her perfect image partner in Tracy, Hepburn suddenly had other image problems. In the late 1940's she was suspected of being a communist by the House Committee on Un-American Activities. Always one to polish her public image, she starred with Tracy in *Adam's Rib*, a film about the ideal American couple, which became the biggest box office attraction of 1949-1950. Then she portrayed herself as a woman who sacrifices her life for her country in *The African Queen* (1951), another of her great successes, this time appearing not as a brittle beauty but as a middle-aged woman bent on serving her country. When she returned from filming in Africa, she found Tracy living in a rented cottage on Cukor's estate, drinking heavily and gaining weight. Moving into a nearby cottage, she now began her long ordeal as Tracy's nursemaid. She also entered the final phase of her public life in which she would become not simply a movie star but a genuine actress and theater artist.

The story of Hepburn as a truly fine dramatic actress occupies the latter third of Mann's book. Tracy had died in 1967, and, while she still had Laura, Hepburn began to lean all the more heavily on her secretary, Phyllis Wilbourn. Hepburn's persona of artist—not star—began with *Guess Who's Coming to Dinner* (1967), a film about interracial marriage for which she received an Oscar, one of four such awards, the last of which would be for *On Golden Pond* (1981). There was also a 1962 film version of Eugene O'Neill's play *Long Day's Journey into Night* (pr, pb. 1956) and many years of work in classics by William Shakespeare, George Bernard Shaw, and even the ancient Greeks. In all, at her death at ninety-six Hepburn had ventured bravely and had climbed to the pinnacle of her profession to be venerated internationally as a true artistic treasure.

William Mann's story is indeed long, but such an exceptional subject requires more than simply adequate attention. He is further to be complimented in his perceptive examination of Hepburn's complicated psychology as well as that of her close associates. While he delves into both heterosexual and homosexual arrangements, he does so without lasciviousness. In all, this is a book of interest not only to those who grew up in the last century but to anyone interested in the complex psychology of public figures.

August W. Staub

Review Sources

Booklist 102, no. 22 (August 1, 2006): 4.
Kirkus Reviews 74, no. 16 (August 15, 2006): 826.
Library Journal 131, no. 15 (September 15, 2006): 62.
The New York Times 156 (October 2, 2006): B1-B2.
Publishers Weekly 253, no. 32 (August 14, 2006): 190-191.
The Spectator 302 (November 11, 2006): 57.
Variety 404, no. 10 (October 23, 2006): 39.

THE KEEP

Author: Jennifer Egan (1962-   )
Publisher: Alfred A. Knopf (New York). 240 pp. $23.95
Type of work: Novel
Time: The present day
Locale: A castle somewhere in Eastern Europe and a
prison in the United States

*Danny accepts his cousin Howard's invitation to the
European castle he has purchased although they have not
spoken in years. That story takes place inside a story of a
writing class held in a prison*

Principal characters:
    DANNY, a New York City hustler on the run
        from a deal gone sour
    HOWIE (HOWARD), Danny's cousin, whom he abandoned in a cave when
        they were children
    MICK, Howie's second-in-command, a capable but somewhat dangerous
        man
    BARONESS VON AUSBLINKER, hereditary heir to the castle, who has
        locked herself in the keep to foil Howie's renovation plans
    RAY, the convict who is writing *The Keep* for his prison writing class
        assignment
    HOLLY, Ray's writing teacher, vulnerable but hiding some secret of her
        own

Jennifer Egan became known for taking gutsy chances with her last book, *Look at
Me* (2001), about a supermodel who ruins her face in a car accident. In *The Keep*, Egan
also juggles characters and plotlines, but the initial effect seems more annoying than
gratifying. The intrusive narrator's voice is just a little too clever, while the "writing" he
supposedly does is hardly first class, despite an occasional brilliant image.

At the end of the novel, when the focus shifts from the alternating personas of
third-person Danny, the character, and first-person Ray, the narrator, to the first-
person narrator of Holly, the writing teacher, one wants to forgive Egan for any previous annoyance. The discovery of which of *The Keep*'s characters was Ray, though not
stunning, leads to a retroactive appraisal of the work as a whole.

Not many of the characters are likable. Danny is twitchy and absorbed with placing himself in relation to the world around him, the hipster with the velvet coat and
special boots who is haunted by the past. As he waits in the darkness at the locked castle gate for someone to let him in, he relives with apprehension the prank he and an
older cousin played on the adolescent Howie. Danny senses that somehow that act
changed him from the golden boy who should have been a success in the world to the
hustler he had become. Now that readers know this awful secret that the grown-up rel-

∽

Jennifer Egan was a finalist for the National Book Award for her novel, Look at Me *(2001). Her other books include* The Invisible Circus *(1995), which was made into a film in 2001, and a short-story collection called* Emerald City *(1996). She writes nonfiction for* The New York Times Magazine.

∽

atives never knew, they share Danny's apprehension about why Howie has invited him.

When Howie finally enters the stage, he is nothing like Danny's memories of his young cousin. Instead of a fat, fish-belly white, nerdy kid, Howie is fit, tanned, and oozing power. Danny has monitored Howie's rising fortunes through the family grapevine, but this vision is so radically different from the truth that he is unnerved. Howie displays no trace of emotional reserve or threat toward Danny. He has purchased this castle for the express purpose of turning it into a New Age hotel where people leave their cell phones and laptops at the door and seek to experience their own imagination. Howie is a bit of a cipher as well. Beyond his enthusiasm about this project, he does not share what is inside him.

Throughout this first chapter, as readers meet Danny and learn where he is and why he has come (at least as far as he knows himself), the narrator of the story intrudes more and more. The intrusion begins as a casual complaint about how hard the mechanics are of switching the character Danny from memory to memory and progresses to outrightly addressing the reader. The narrator, who identifies himself as Ray, a convict working on an assignment for a writing class, actually anticipates the thoughts an annoyed reader might have.

The chapter ends with a transition that places Ray in his prison classroom. In the following chapter, Egan returns to the castle and to the characters that Ray is supposedly creating. The story remains focused on the castle for several chapters before returning to the prison classroom. Another setup by the author occurs when one of Ray's classmates demands to know which character represents Ray. Now the reader is left to wonder whether the story is based on true events and, if so, whether Ray took part in them.

The characters Egan creates for the prison sequences are more fully developed and realistic than the characters in the castle story. This seems to be an attempt on the author's part to differentiate the two stories by the writing skills of the supposed creator. Egan has achieved this perhaps too well; the castle story often becomes mired in cliché and awkward constructions. There are even many extraneous scenes.

The novel contains little in the way of humor. One of the few darkly hilarious scenes involves Danny's meeting with the Baroness von Ausblinker. From his first distant view of the baroness through a window of the ancient keep, Danny has romanticized her. The beautiful young blonde woman he imagined turns out to be a caustic woman in her nineties. She has locked herself within the keep, refusing to relinquish the ancient family seat to Howie's renovation plans. Despite her age and decrepitude, Danny falls under her spell when she allows him into the keep, and in a somewhat hallucinatory experience, he appears to have slept with her. Neither Danny nor the reader is actually sure until the baroness alludes to it through a locked door.

The Keep explores such issues as betrayal, survival, and new beginnings in both stories. Many of the major characters possess an ability to reinvent themselves despite horrific past experience. Howie, the boy who was abandoned underground for three days, descends into a criminal life that lands him in a reform school; yet he earns "insane wealth" as a bond trader in Chicago and retires at age thirty-four. Danny, the former golden boy, fails to live up to his promise and yet learns to understand and survive in the shady world of New York. Holly, the creative writing teacher, rises above her former drug addiction to teach a different sort of freedom to the prison inmates.

As the lives of the characters in the castle story become more intertwined, Ray imagines that he can establish a relationship with Holly. The reader does not see, in what he relates of their contact, any reason to believe this is anything more than sympathy and encouragement. However, when Ray is injured by another prisoner and nearly dies, Holly visits him and reveals that she has deeper feelings for him.

Ray survives, as Howie survived, as Holly survived, and as Danny has managed to survive after the loss of his satellite dish cut him off from the world. Imagination is the key. Those who can imagine something better coming after tragedy can survive and continue. Howie's vivid imagination, described earlier in the wild game, Terminal Zeus, which he and Danny played when they were younger, sustained him when he was alone and in the dark. Ray joined the writing class to escape his crazy cellmate and found escape both in writing down the castle story and in imagining he is developing a relationship with Holly. Danny's imagination leads him into odd situations, such as his liaison with the baroness, but it also provides him with visions that replace his restless need to manipulate something, to be in charge by being next to the guy with the power.

Finally, the castle story comes full circle when Danny buys a map in the nearby town that appears to be an old, detailed map of the castle, including the underground tunnels mentioned by the baroness. Howie's excitement is boundless. Though it is dark, he exerts his control by insisting that everyone go, even the baby, snuggled into a carrier against his wife's chest. Danny goes underground again with his cousin.

Only this time, they are all trapped. The entrance to these tunnels is accessed through the keep itself, and although the windows are dark, the baroness notices their movements. While they examine the wine cellar in one room and the medieval torture devices in the next, the baroness shuts the trapdoor behind them and securely bolts it shut. She mocks Danny's entreaties, claiming not to care what happens to them: "You don't believe me. You can't believe I won't do what you want me to do. You're children, you Americans, every one of you. And the world is very, very old."

When Howie finds out they are trapped, he completely breaks down into hysterics, apparently reliving the experience of his childhood when Danny left him behind in the cave. However, this time, Danny has a chance at redemption, and he comes through. He gets them moving without any real idea where to go, but finds a stairwell that he climbs to the surface. He needs Mick to help kick out the door, and together they succeed.

After their escape, both Danny and Mick sense the dynamic has changed. Mick has lost his place, and Danny has taken it, along with Howie's power. Without the opportunity Howie gave him, without the role Howie assigned him, he has nothing. While

Danny finally admits his guilt to Howie, who will not really accept it, they make peace and plan to work together. Suddenly, Danny notices Mick, and in the violence that takes place, the point of view shifts from one paragraph to the next, from third-person Mick to first-person narrator Ray, who is also Mick, and now the whole story makes sense.

As Danny dies, sinking down into the circular pool, he finds a door that becomes a window through which he sees Mick/Ray. Thus he survives, in the memory of his killer's imagination.

This is the point at which Egan's efforts seem rewarding. The next chapter's narrator is Holly. Ray has sent her his completed manuscript along with forty pages of diary entries. She reads it all and cries and then readers learn how she has held it back after Ray's escape from prison. She is taken in and questioned, but she does not betray his trust. One learns, finally, what Holly's secret sorrow is about. Then, incredibly, she discovers that there is a hotel called The Keep, described just as Howie's vision was laid out in the manuscript.

The resolution of the novel is incomplete and yet still satisfying. Holly does not find Ray when she travels to this luxurious hotel, but we know all that happened at last, and the reality of all that was imagination sustains us.

Patricia Masserman

Review Sources

Booklist 102, no. 17 (May 1, 2006): 5.
Entertainment Weekly, no. 889 (August 4, 2006): 71.
The New York Times 155 (July 20, 2006): E10.
The New York Times Book Review 155 (July 30, 2006): 1-7.
The New Yorker 82, no. 25 (August 21, 2006): 82.
Publishers Weekly 253, no. 14 (April 3, 2006): 34.
Seattle Post-Intelligencer, September 15, 2006, p. 36.
The Village Voice 51, no. 31 (August 2, 2006): 59.
The Washington Post, August 9, 2006. p. C5.